Drama and the World of Richard Wagner

Drama and the World of Richard Wagner

· *DIETER BORCHMEYER* ·

Translated by Daphne Ellis

PRINCETON UNIVERSITY PRESS
PRINCETON AND OXFORD

First published in German under the title *Richard Wagner:*
Ahasvers Wandlungen © Insel Verlag Frankfurt am Main 2002.
English translation © 2003 by Princeton University Press
Published by Princeton University Press, 41 William Street, Princeton, New Jersey 08540
In the United Kingdom: Princeton University Press, 3 Market Place, Woodstock,
Oxfordshire OX20 1SY

Library of Congress Cataloging-in-Publication Data

Borchmeyer, Dieter.
[Richard Wagner. English]
Drama and the world of Richard Wagner / Dieter Borchmeyer ; translated by Daphne Ellis.
p. cm.
Translation of: Richard Wagner : Ahasvers Wandlungen.
Includes bibliographical references (p.) and index.
ISBN 0-691-11497-8 (alk. paper)
1. Wagner, Richard, 1813–1883—Criticism and interpretation.   2. Wandering Jew.
I. Title.
ML410.W19B7513 2003
782.1'092—dc21   2003043394

British Library Cataloging-in-Publication Data is available

This book has been composed in Times Roman

Printed on acid-free paper. ∞

www.pupress.princeton.edu

Printed in the United States of America

1 3 5 7 9 10 8 6 4 2

• C O N T E N T S •

WAGNER is the most controversial artist in the entire history of culture. In his notes for "Mind and Art," Thomas Mann—then undergoing the first great Wagner crisis of his career—described the composer's works as "the most problematic in the history of art, open to criticism to the highest degree, yet ultimately impossible to criticize inasmuch as they are a European phenomenon of the most tremendous kind."[1]

For more than a century, Wagner's works have dominated the stages of all the world's leading opera houses alongside those of Mozart and Verdi, yet his hegemony is far from unchallenged. Whereas there are those who, like Thomas Mann in a 1927 essay, regard him as "virtually without precedent as an artistic force, probably the greatest talent in the whole history of art,"[2] others question his supreme status as an artist or at least as a musician, arguing that his primary aim was not art and seeing in his works the expression of a dubious ideology.

Such widely differing opinions may be not untypical of responses to even the greatest artists while they are still alive, but this polarization of views is altogether unique in the case of an artist whose vast and unabated influence over one hundred and fifty years cannot simply be explained away in terms of passing fashions. There are neither Shakespeareans nor Mozartians, but there are Wagnerians of all shades of opinion, Wagnerians young and old, Wagnerians who cast their nets over even the most recent writings on the subject. And, although there are no anti-Shakespeareans or anti-Mozartians, there is a party of anti-Wagnerians that is even more militant than in Wagner's day.

As a rule, artists who were violently controversial in their own day sooner or later achieve classic status, no longer sparking dissent in literature and public opinion; a good example of this in Germany is Bertolt Brecht. But the case of Wagner is unique in the history of culture: in spite of the political, social, ideological, and aesthetic upheavals of the last one hundred years, Wagner's works, together with his artistic personality, continue to provoke disagreement and militate against their becoming classics.

Even the most serious writers on Wagner—mainly in Germany but increasingly in the Anglo-Saxon world—seem incapable of treating the object of their attentions with the same degree of calmness and composure that other writers bring to bear on comparable subjects. Few who write on Mozart or Beethoven, Goethe or Thomas Mann, feel obliged to begin by apologizing or announcing a polemical intent. With Wagner, by contrast, this is almost always the case. Writers who grapple with the subject feel that they have to take a particular line, defending or attacking Wagner, apologizing for adopting a positive stance, or engaging in breast-beating polemics in an attempt to demonstrate to the world their moral and intellectual integrity.

The merest glance at writings on Wagner, including the most recent ones on the composer's life and works, is enough to convince the most casual reader that he or she has wandered into a madhouse. Even serious scholars take leave of their senses when writing on Wagner and start to rant. There are transcendental Wagnerians with their heads in the clouds, phallo-Wagnerians whose sights are set somewhat lower, meekly feminist *Wagnériennes*, and brashly political *Wagnerianer*—and in every case there are their polemical opposite numbers, busily condemning and unmasking Wagner in the name of the very same values and on the strength of the very same evidence, their desire to unmask Wagner driving them to the very brink of scientific and psychological flagellantism and persuading them to see a causal link between *Parsifal* and Auschwitz.

I have no wish to join in this tiresome chorus of voices raised for and against the composer. Instead, the first half of this book (chapters 1–9) presents an overview of all of Wagner's stage works, including the "outlawed"[3] early operas, the unfinished works, and the ones that Wagner never set to music.[4] These works are examined, diachronically and synchronically, from a literary point of view. The second— shorter—half (chapters 10–14) deals with a number of contemporary and later figures whose influence on Wagner, and vice versa, is of paradigmatic importance for our understanding of the composer and his impact on others.

This second section is shorter than its counterpart in the German original: chapters on Wagner's response to Goethe and Schiller and on his relations with two literary contemporaries, Heine and Grillparzer, have been cut, as has a chapter on Franz Werfel's novel about Wagner's great musical and dramatic antithesis, Giuseppe Verdi. In each case, my American publisher felt that these chapters were geared toward a German audience and that they presuppose a background knowledge that cannot be taken for granted in the case of English-speaking readers.

I do not deny that this book is fueled by a real passion, but in Thomas Mann's opinion, passion also embraces criticism. In fact, Mann might be described as this book's *spiritus rector*, a guiding light in this exploration of the fields that Wagner tilled and whose fruits were then garnered by others. Alongside Mann, Nietzsche's appeal to "philology" is one of the most important sources of inspiration in these attempts to grapple with Wagner's works. "People think that philology has had its day," Nietzsche wrote in an unpublished jotting in 1875, "but I think that it hasn't yet begun." He went on to justify this as follows: "The greatest events to affect philology are the appearance of Goethe, Schopenhauer, and Wagner: they open up a perspective that takes us far beyond them."[5]

This comment dates from a period when Nietzsche had already begun to move away from Wagner. But this does not alter the fact that, for him, Wagner was first and foremost a philological phenomenon, as, indeed, he remained to the very end. A failure to recognize this constituted a cardinal failing on the part of scholars in general: "How things stand with philologists is shown by their indifference to Wagner as a phenomenon. They could have learned more from him than from Goethe—they haven't even looked at him. This shows that they are led by no great need to do so, otherwise they would sense where their sustenance is to be found."[6] This "indifference" on the part of scholars toward one of the central figures in the history of German culture is largely a German phenomenon, whereas English, American, and French scholars have been far less guilty of losing sight of Wagner, a state of affairs that is hardly surprising when we consider the remarkable impact of Wagner on European literature in general from the end of the nineteenth century.[7]

In his book *Der traurige Gott* (The grieving god), first published in 1978 and revised in 2001, Peter Wapnewski explicitly lays claim to "the philologist's right to Wagner," as the composer "cannot be grasped or understood with the resources of only a single discipline or from only a single perspective, for only academic disciplines in their totality can hope to come to terms with this multifaceted material through a constant exchange of views." It is this, Wapnewski concludes, that constitutes "the unique position of this man in the history of art and the arts."[8] The fact that, at least in Germany, the most successful books on Wagner in recent decades have been written for the most part by nonmusicologists whose main concern has been the literary aspect of his works seems no accident. And the fact that there has long been no genuinely comprehensive study of Wagner from a musicological angle—none that could stand comparison with works on other great musicians from this period—suggests that, as a phenomenon, Wagner's ability to straddle a multiplicity of disciplines means that musicologists are repeatedly stretched to the very limits of their specialist field of competence.

Wagner's claim to be treated as a totality means, in turn, that he has been claimed by countless different disciplines, and this has naturally led to dilettantism—the very dilettantism of which Wagner himself and his allegedly "total work of art" stood accused from the very beginning. Just as he wanted to have his say on everything, so the whole world now demands to have its say in turn. Yet in their treatment of Wagner, writers display a lack of scholarly precision found with no other artist of his stature.[9] One of the great desiderata of Wagner scholarship is a specialist journal of its own. Whereas virtually all other leading composers have their own yearbooks and related publications, Wagner does not. Nor is there a specialized bibliography—particularly necessary in Wagner's case in order to provide an overview of writings in the numerous disciplines that he embraces.

Few other artists of such importance have generated such a wealth (perhaps not the *mot juste*) of self-opinionated writings, which, compromised by the authors' own tendentious ideas, run the full gamut of pointless inanity from gossip to nonsense, adopting so blatantly militant a stance both for and against the composer that any reaction would be improper. "Don't even ignore it" is a Viennese maxim that I have taken to heart as my motto. At the same time, the general reader will understand that the current state of research is barely touched on in the annotation to this volume, which is limited in the main to relevant writings from the last twenty years. Even more rarely are these questions discussed in the text itself.[10]

Twenty years ago I published my first major work on Wagner: *Das Theater Richard Wagners* (The theater of Richard Wagner) (Stuttgart, 1982). Coming five years after the publication of Cosima Wagner's diaries, this book was the first comprehensive attempt to interpret this unique source and, at the same time, the first systematic account of Wagner's aesthetic theory to have appeared in recent times. It was against this background that I examined Wagner's music dramas. *Drama and the World of Richard Wagner* adopts an alternative, less theoretical approach, with Wagner's works being interpreted rather more on their own terms and within the framework of their literary points of reference, even though Wagner's theoretical writings will always play an important role in any account of his music dramas.[11] In the case of a number of works—notably the *Ring*, but also the Romantic operas and *Parsifal*—my interpretive stance has changed substantially from the one that I adopted in 1982. This change was already clear from the English version of *Das Theater Richard Wagners*, which was published by Oxford University Press in 1991 under the title *Richard Wagner: Theory and Theatre* and for which a number of chapters were largely rewritten.

Many of the chapters here are based on preliminary works that have already been published in specialist journals and collections of essays,[12] as well as in the program books of the Bayreuth Festival. Without the inspiration of the Bayreuth Festival and the conferences held in Bayreuth during the 1990s, this book could scarcely have been written. Even greater is my debt to the conversations that I have had over the years with many Wagnerian friends and colleagues, foremost among whom are my two main correspondents in America, Walter Hinderer and Hans Rudolf Vaget. It is a pleasure to thank them here.

References to Wagner's collected writings are included in the main body of the text, with the volume number followed by the page number (for example, 5:26). Volumes 1–10 are quoted according to the *Gesammelte Schriften und Dichtungen*, 2d ed. (Leipzig, 1888) (henceforth GS), and volumes 11–16 according to the *Sämtliche Schriften und Dichtungen* (Leipzig, 1911–14) (henceforth SS). Wagner's original orthography has been retained throughout. Cosima Wagner's diaries are quoted from *Die Tagebücher, 1869–1883*, ed. Martin Gregor-Dellin and Dietrich Mack, 2 vols. (Munich, 1976–7), and are indicated by the letters CT followed by the date of the entry. Quotations from *My Life* (ML) are taken from Martin Gregor-Dellin's edition (Munich, 1976). The abbreviation WWV refers to *Wagner Werk-Verzeichnis: Verzeichnis der musikalischen Werke Richard Wagners und ihrer Quellen* (Wagner work catalog: Catalog of the musical works of Richard Wagner and their sources), ed. John Deathridge, Martin Geck, and Egon Voss (Mainz, 1986).

In general, the quotations from Wagner's music dramas are reproduced from the *Gesammelte Schriften und Dichtungen*, rather than from the various vocal scores. On this point, I accept the line taken by Egon Voss in the afterword to his edition of the libretto of *Tannhäuser* (Stuttgart, 2001): he argues that to reproduce the wording of the full score in a book such as this is questionable, as this wording makes sense only in conjunction with the music and, above all, in the context of the stage directions. A libretto, argues Voss,

> is *sui generis*, an independent form that has its own meaning as a poetic and literary genre. Wagner himself saw his librettos in this light and called them "poems," using particular verse forms and rhyme schemes for the sake of their poetic quality. A similar goal was served by his decision to set the text as short and long lines, which he insisted should be preserved when these texts appeared in print. That Wagner attached great importance to the words as such is clear from the fact that he published these texts independently. (97–98)

Drama and the World of Richard Wagner

Love's Madness, Fairy-Tale Enchantment, and a Sicilian Carnival

DIE HOCHZEIT, DIE FEEN, *AND* DAS LIEBESVERBOT

We must seize our chance and honestly seek to cultivate the

age's new forms, and he will be its master who writes in

neither an Italian nor a French—nor even in a German—style.

—Richard Wagner, "German Opera" (1834)

IN 1830 the seventeen-year-old Wagner first turned his hand to writing an opera,[1] but beyond the fact that he described it as a "pastoral opera" and that it was modeled on Goethe's pastoral play of 1768, *Die Laune des Verliebten* (The caprice of the infatuated lover), we know nothing about it, as he quickly abandoned the idea, and no text or music has survived. His next operatic venture (WWV 31) dates from the year of Goethe's death—1832—and on this occasion Wagner completed the libretto and made a start on the score. Three numbers were set, and these have survived,[2] but Wagner later destroyed the libretto on the grounds that his sister Rosalie hated it. (This is entirely plausible, as Rosalie was then working as an actress at the Royal Saxon Court Theater in Leipzig and was therefore in a position of some influence. Wagner evidently hoped for her support in this and other operatic ventures.) In his "Autobiographical Sketch" of 1843, he refers to it as an "operatic text of tragic import, although I no longer remember where I found the medieval subject" (GS 1:8). Later, in *My Life* (ML 75), he recounts the plot of the opera in some detail and states that he had first encountered it in Johann Gustav Gottlieb Büsching's *Ritterzeit und Ritterwesen* (The age of chivalry and nature of chivalry), a farrago of fact and fiction about the Middle Ages that had been published in Leipzig in 1823 and whose importance for Wagner cannot be overstated, for it was here that he found the seeds of ideas for all his operas based on medieval themes, up to and including *Parsifal*. (A copy of the volume also found its way into Wagner's library in Bayreuth.)

PRE-ECHOES OF *TRISTAN UND ISOLDE*

A frenzied lover climbs up to the bedroom window of the fiancée of a friend of his, where she is waiting for her lover; she struggles with the madman and hurls him down into the courtyard, where every bone in his body is broken. At his funeral, the fiancée utters a cry and sinks lifeless upon his corpse. (GS 1:8–9)

Wagner was so attracted to this tale that he even thought of turning it into a short story in the style of E.T.A. Hoffmann. It is based in turn on a medieval verse narrative by an anonymous late-thirteenth-century German poet. (Its title, *Frauentreue* [Women's fidelity], is not authentic but derives from an epilogue added by a later poet: "Das heizet vrouwen triuwe" [This is an example of women's fidelity].) The young Wagner knew this poem only at second hand, namely, from Büsching's retelling of it, but by the time that he came to dictate *My Life*, he had already forgotten it, so much so that he confused its plot with that of his own libretto. Only much later did he get to know the original in Friedrich Heinrich von der Hagen's 1850 three-volume anthology, *Gesammtabenteuer* (Compendium of adventures). "In the evening," we read in Cosima Wagner's diary for 1 May 1873, "R. reads me *Frauen Treue* [*sic*] by Konrad von Würzburg, the original of his *Hochzeit* [The wedding]." (Wagner was in error in attributing the poem to Konrad von Würzburg, who was in fact the author of the previous texts in Hagen's collection.)[3] It left a "wonderful impression" (CT, 1 May 1873). Wagner was clearly so fascinated by the poem that he read it again eight years later. "We are very moved by its great respectability," Cosima noted on 17 October 1881. "There is something almost petit-bourgeois about it, in spite of all its boldness." And she follows this up with a remark on the middle-class husband of the story, a comment that suddenly makes it clear what Wagner found so fascinating about this tale: "In the husband R. recognizes his King Marke" (CT, 17 October 1881).

Büsching's bombastically overwritten summary of the plot of the original thirteenth-century poem runs as follows:

> A worthy warrior and knight, overbold in both body and spirit, had set his mind—as many a God-fearing knight would do—on winning a woman's favors by dint of chivalry, which had cost him full many a gory wound. . . . In the course of his journeyings in search of adventure, this knight came to a town. He did not know the people here, with the exception of a single townsman whom he met here and who belonged to his circle of acquaintances. The knight approached him, addressed him as an acquaintance, and asked where he could find the most beautiful woman in the town.[4]

The townsman informs him that he will be able to see all the townswomen at the forthcoming service that is held each year to commemorate the consecration of the local church. And here the knight discovers a woman who robs him of his senses: "Si kam im zuo der selben stunt / mitten in sînes herzen grunt, / darûz si nimmer mêr geschiet, / biz der tôt ez verschriet" [All at once she entered the very depths of his heart, remaining there until death destroyed it].

The knight who arrives in town, becomes friendly with a member of the local burgher class, and falls in love with a middle-class woman at a church service—the reader is inevitably reminded of *Die Meistersinger*. In the case of *Die Hochzeit*, Wagner took up neither the motif of the meeting in church nor the social relationship between the knight and his lover, but instead described her as a "lady of noble birth" (ML 75). Neither she nor either of the two men is given a name: all are referred to merely by their social status. Büsching goes on to explain how the knight pointed out this lady to the townsman who was accompanying him, and the townsman recognized her as his own wife. With a smile, he asked the knight to stay with him as his guest, but the latter declined, so oppressed was his heart, and each day he wandered through the town, hoping for a glimpse of the woman he loved. He took lodgings close to her home, so that he could see her all the more often.[5]

It was not long before the woman noticed the lovesick knight and began to grow wary, "wan si ze nieman liebe truoc, / wan z'ir êlichen man" [as she had never loved anyone apart from her lawfully wedded husband]. At this point, Büsching interrupts his summary of the plot, returning to it later and completing it at a totally unexpected point in his narrative. Wagner must have read Büsching's work very carefully for him to have been able to make sense of the story and reconstruct the overall context.

The knight organizes a tournament for the sake of the woman he loves, appearing at it wearing only a silk shirt.[6] The point of an opponent's spear becomes embedded in his side, and he will allow only this one woman to remove it: "Mich sol nieman tuon gesunt, / wan durch der willen ich wart wunt, / læt mich diu sus verderben, / sô wil ich gerne sterben" [No one shall cure me except the one for whose sake I was wounded; if she leaves me thus to perish, I'll gladly die]. The idea of a knight being healed by the woman he loves is familiar, of course, from the exposition of *Tristan und Isolde*. Yet Büsching omits this very motif in his retelling of the plot of *Frauentreue*.[7]

The woman is fully aware of the erotic nature of the knight's request and so she initially refuses to draw the tip of the spear from his wound, and it is only in response to her husband's earnest entreaties that, almost dying of shame, she agrees to do so. At this point, Büsching picks up the story again, offering only the briefest account of its tragic outcome.[8] The knight has scarcely recovered when he enters the couple's bedroom at night and forces himself upon the wife. In keeping with medieval custom, she was sleeping naked but manages to slip on a silk nightshirt. So violent is their struggle that the knight's wound reopens, and, in a manner reminiscent of Wagner's Tristan, he bleeds to death. Secretly she carries his body back to his lodgings, finally conscious of the greatness of his love for her: "Alrest diu vrouwe gedâhte, / der grôzen liebe ahte, / die der ritter zuo ir hâte: / dô was ez leider nû ze spâte" [Only now did the woman bethink herself and heed the great love that the knight felt for her: alas, it was now too late]. He is laid out in his coffin in church, whither the woman comes to offer a funerary sacrifice. Only her maid knows the secret of her love. (Again there is a striking parallel with *Tristan und Isolde*, this time with Brangäne.) Standing before the altar, she removes one article of clothing after another—"si vergaz vor leide gar der scham" [in her grief she even forgot all sense of shame]—until she stands there in her shift, then sinks lifeless upon the knight's body in a kind of medieval *Liebestod*, or Love-death.[9]

The whole story is permeated with a series of subtle correspondences: at the beginning the townswomen are placed on show, whereas at the end it is the knight's corpse that is laid out on display; the first and last encounters between the knight and his lady take place in church; and there is the recurrent motif of the silk shirt or shift that the knight wears in fighting for his lover and that she in turn wears, first when defending herself in the bedroom and second when standing before his bier. Both here and in the tournament the silk shirt or shift serves to symbolize an amorous relationship that flouts social etiquette. Just as the knight sacrifices his personal safety in the tournament, so the woman sacrifices her honor, hitherto staunchly upheld, in an exhibitionist act that was even more provocative in the case of a middle-class woman than it would have been with a woman of noble birth and that is quite unprecedented in church. Thus she challenges the world, formally excluding herself from society with a finality that can end only with her death. A tale of such erotic eccentricity was conceivable only in the late Middle Ages. "Diu minne kan niht mâze hân" [Love cannot show moderation], we read in one of the poems of Konrad von Würzburg,[10] the thirteenth-century poet to whom Wagner attributed *Frauentreue*. Perhaps the most remarkable aspect of all this is that Wagner discovered this tale—it was virtually unknown in his own day but anticipates many of the relationships of his later music dramas—hidden away among the chaff of Büsching's rhapsodically rambling work.

The reader who is unfamiliar with the intricacies of medieval relationships and who assumes the existence of an unambiguous ethical order in which marriage is inviolate will be surprised by the glorification of a love that overrides the ties of middle-class marriage by demonstrating its allegiance to a higher code of ethics involving knightly *triuwe*, or fidelity. This emerges not only from the prologue to the poem, in which the anonymous poet praises the lovers' reciprocal *triuwe* and describes the woman as "diu guote,/diu reine, wolgemuote" [good, pure, and well disposed], but also, and more especially, from its ending, where even the husband sings his wife's praises when she dies for love of the knight: "ein wîp sô gar ân' valschen list" [a wife so pure and lacking in falsehood]. (Such praise is presumably possible, as the love between the knight and his lady stops short of actual adultery, a point on which it differs from that of Tristan and Isolde.) And the tale ends with the common burial of the two lovers: "Dâ legte man sie beide/mit jâmer und mit leide/in ein grap, die holden./Sus het si im ver-golden,/unt tet im ganze triuwe schîn" [Then with grief and anguish both were laid in a single grave, the lovers. Thus she had requited him and given him proof of her steadfast fidelity].

It comes as no surprise to find that the older Wagner was fascinated by the links between this tale of medieval love and his own *Tristan und Isolde*, even though he did not explore many of their motivic correspondences in *Die Hochzeit*—indeed, he was unable to exploit them, as Büsching had passed over them in silence. Instead, he introduced a number of new motifs that anticipate other themes in his later works. The marriage between Ada and Arindal, for example, resembles that between Isolde and King Marke in that both serve to bring peace and reconciliation to two warring families or nations. In other words, Ada, the main female character, has evidently agreed to marry Arindal on rational grounds, which in turn explains the undeclared erotic fascination that Cadolt exercises over her. Cadolt later enters her bedroom, and, as Wagner explains in *My Life*, "his somber glance strikes her to the heart" (ML 75).

In spite of the differences between *Die Hochzeit* on the one hand and *Frauentreue* and Büsching's résumé of its contents, on the other, there is no denying the similarity between the two subjects or their affinities with the relationship between the three main characters in *Tristan und Isolde*—arguably another reason why Wagner described the libretto in such detail in *My Life* and why he repeatedly returned to it in the final years of his life. The idea of a love that not only destroys an existing marriage but undermines social conventions; the refusal of one of the partners to acknowledge this love (in *Die Hochzeit*, it is Ada, whereas in *Tristan und Isolde*, it is Tristan); the "mysterious strength of these passionate but suppressed emotions" (ML 75) that then break out with all the greater force; and their fatal consequence in the form of a Liebestod and the death of the surviving partner: these are all unmistakable motivic parallels between *Die Hochzeit* and *Tristan und Isolde*. When we read in Wagner's "Autobiographical Sketch" that the bride "sinks lifelessly over the body" at the end (GS 1:9), we are bound to think of the end of *Tristan und Isolde*, where we likewise read in the stage directions that Isolde "sinks down on Tristan's body" (GS 7:81). As Bernd Zegowitz has explained in the context of *Die Hochzeit*, "This sinking upon the body indicates two things. It is both a symbol of Ada's unconsummated bridal night with Arindal and a substitute for their embrace in the bedroom, an embrace that she herself interrupted. Their actual wedding thus takes place in death."[11]

In *My Life*, Wagner describes *Die Hochzeit* as "an out-and-out night piece of the blackest hue," claiming that it was inspired by E.T.A. Hoffmann and by the "musical mysticism" of which he was then so fond. "I executed this plan in black on black, disdaining any ray of light and in particular any operatic embellishment, which would have been inappropriate here" (ML 75–76). Two ideas emerge from this statement, both of which were to be of immense importance for Wagner the later music dramatist: first, his Romantic affinity with night, an affinity that was to leave its mark not only on his adaptation of Hoffmann's *Die Bergwerke zu Falun* (The mines at Falun) ten years later but also on his great hymn to the night, *Tristan und Isolde*; and, second, his decision to dispense with elaborate operatic conventions.

Neither of these elements seems to have found favor with Wagner's family, especially his sister Rosalie, although their displeasure may also have been sparked by the relationship between the three characters, a relationship abhorrent to their sense of bourgeois morality. Wagner's next operatic project was his self-styled "Romantic opera in three acts," *Die Feen* (The fairies, WWV 32) of 1833–34, his first completed work for the operatic stage. Although it, too, inhabits a world of Romanticized medievalism, it could hardly be more different from *Die Hochzeit* in every other respect. The "ray of light" that Wagner had spurned in *Die Hochzeit* and the "operatic embellishments" that he had formerly avoided as "inappropriate" are now back in force, enjoying a theatrical revival that has encouraged Bernd Zegowitz to speak of an outright "repudiation of *Die Hochzeit*"[12] and of its supersession by bourgeois morality. The irreconcilability of marriage and physical love that Wagner had treated in *Die Hochzeit* is countered for the first and last time in his works by the glorification of the family, a shift intended to please and pacify his sister Rosalie. The fact that he again named his two main characters Ada and Arindal merely highlights the contrast between the two works; as Egon Voss has suggested, Wagner seems to have taken over the names unchanged "in order to rehabilitate the institution of marriage, which had come off so badly in *Die Hochzeit*."[13]

Ada and Arindal have been married for eight years, and their marriage has been blessed with children. No other opera by Wagner was to adopt such an inviolate view of family life.[14] In all his later works, children appear only as adolescent orphans lacking one or both parents or they are the result of illicit unions. Mothers are either dead or passed over in silence (the only exceptions are Erda, who appears as Brünnhilde's mother in the *Ring* but has no contact with her daughter, and the mother of Isolde, who never appears onstage), whereas fathers are always widowers, and marriages, invariably childless, are always unhappy or at least beset by trouble and doomed to failure from the outset, assuming that they were contracted in the first place. In short, *Die Feen* is the last of Wagner's operas to present a wholesome picture of family life. In the words in *Opera and Drama* (GS 4:56), love is always seen as a "disruptive force," undermining social institutions and conventions. Only in *Die Meistersinger* is a fragile link forged between love and social conventions.

As a paean to marriage, *Die Feen* is therefore a remarkable exception in Wagner's works—Egon Voss calls it "an opera for Wagner's family,"[15] and the note of irony is unmistakable. There is a hidden reference to this in the second-act finale of the opera, at Ada's words "O Himmel, schütz' ihn, schütz' ihn vor Verdacht" [O heaven, protect him, protect him from suspicion] in bars 285–89, which quote from Wagner's melodrama "Ach neige, du Schmerzenreiche" [Ah, look down, thou rich in sorrow's crown], one of his *Sieben Kompositionen zu Goethes Faust* (Seven compositions for Goethe's *Faust*, WWV 15) from 1831. This last-named work was evidently written for Rosalie, who at this time was playing Gretchen in Goethe's play at the Leipzig Stadttheater.[16] Wagner's emphatic repudiation of *Die Feen* in later life—and from none of his early stage works did he distance himself so radically[17]—is no doubt bound up with his feeling of unease that in an attempt to curry favor with his family, he had denied an essential part of his true nature as an artist and paid tribute to convention both formally and thematically, the very convention that he had mercilessly pilloried in *Die Hochzeit*.

In Search of Gozzi

In *My Life*, Wagner claims to have "written *Die Hochzeit* without operatic embellishments and to have treated the subject in the blackest possible vein," whereas *Die Feen* is said to have been "decked out with a diversity that bordered on the intolerable."

> As for the poetic diction and the verses themselves, I was almost intentionally careless, as I was no longer entertaining my earlier hopes of making a name for myself as a poet.

> I had become a "musician" and a "composer" and wanted to write a suitable "libretto,"
> as I now realized that no one else could do this for me, as a libretto is something unique
> and, as such, simply cannot be brought off by a poet or a man of letters. (ML 81)

The words that appear in quotation marks are evidently used ironically here; after
all, it was a fundamental principle of Wagner's later reforms that the dualism of
words and music in opera should be overcome and that the text should no longer
be merely a means to an end, and the "composer," for his part, would become a
dramatist. In the "artwork of the future," poetry and music were to be equally
committed to fulfilling the "aim" of the drama. In Wagner's eyes, *Die Feen* still
fell far short of this goal.

Here, too, the writings of E.T.A. Hoffmann were influential. Wagner was familiar with Hoffmann's narrative "Der Dichter und der Komponist" (The poet and
the composer) from his *Serapionsbrüder* (Serapion brethren) cycle. In this story,
which takes the form of a dialogue between a poet and a composer, the imaginary
composer advances the idea of a "musical drama" or "Romantic opera" in which
"music emerges directly from the poem as a necessary product of it" and argues
that the ten fairy-tale plays, or *fiabe dramatiche*, of Carlo Gozzi (1720–1806)
would be ideal subjects for operas: "In his dramatic fairy tales he achieved everything that I demand of the operatic poet, and it is beyond belief that this rich vein
of excellent subjects has not been tapped more often than it has been."[18]

Wagner was to follow up this suggestion and launch his career as a music
dramatist with an adaptation of Gozzi's *La donna serpente* (The serpent woman),
which had received its first performance in Venice in 1762. In doing so, he ushered
in a long series of Gozzi operas that was to continue until well into the twentieth
century, with the *Turandot* operas of Busoni and Puccini, Prokofiev's *Love for
Three Oranges*, and Henze's *König Hirsch*. Even before Wagner, *La donna serpente* had already been adapted for the stage by Friedrich Heinrich Himmel,
whose *Zauberoper* (magic opera) *Die Sylphen* (The sylphs) was staged in Berlin
in 1806. In the twentieth century it provided the basis for Alfredo Casella's *La
donna serpente*, first heard in Rome in 1932. And Gozzi himself was the main
character in *Die Familie Gozzi* (The family Gozzi), an opera written in 1934 by
the pianist Wilhelm Kempff. Nor should we forget Hofmannsthal and Strauss's
Die Frau ohne Schatten (The woman without a shadow), which, although not directly based on Gozzi, takes over a number of motifs and names as well as the
general oriental atmosphere of the Italian playwright's fiabe dramatiche.

Gozzi has gone down in the history of the theater as an exponent of the Italian
improvised comedy, or *commedia dell'arte*, a genre that he both defended and reformed. By this date in its history, the commedia dell'arte had become ossified as a
result of the constant repetition of the same stock situations. Gozzi's hated archrival,
Carlo Goldoni, attempted to remedy this problem by turning the commedia dell'arte
into a more sophisticated form of comedy involving realistic characters and a fixed
text, whereas Gozzi himself sought to preserve its original spirit of improvisation
and to breathe new life into it by introducing fantastical, fairy-tale elements, drawing on themes and motifs from the *Arabian Nights* and from an anthology of fairy

tales by Giambattista Basile known as the *Cunto de li cunti* (1634–36). Although Gozzi's fiabe dramatiche generally rely on fixed texts, the scenes involving commedia dell'arte characters are merely sketched out in the manner of a scenario, leaving the actors greater or lesser scope for improvisation. These fairy-tale comedies were initially immensely successful, so much so, in fact, that Goldoni was driven from Venice and forced to settle in Paris. But in Italy, audiences soon tired of them, with the result that they eventually fell into neglect, whereas in Germany they flourished and proved hugely influential thanks to Schiller's adaptation of *Turandot* and, above all, to the enthusiastic response of the Romantics, who even compared Gozzi with Shakespeare. Presumably it was Wagner's scholarly uncle and mentor, Adolf Wagner, who drew his nephew's attention to Gozzi. Adolf had known both Hoffmann and Tieck personally, had corresponded with Jean Paul, and in his youth had even known Schiller. In 1804 he translated *Il corvo* as *Der Rabe* (The raven), and in his essay *Theater und Publikum* (Theater and public, 1823) he singled out Gozzi for special mention, praising him as a writer who had raised comedy from the depths into which it had sunk at the hands of the bourgeois realists of the Enlightenment and rescued it "from ordinariness and triviality" by restoring it "to the world of the lighthearted imagination."

It is clear from Cosima's diaries that Wagner never lost his enthusiasm for Gozzi. On 13 October 1872, for example, he explicitly aligned himself with Gozzi in the latter's rivalry with Goldoni, although he was wrong to claim that unlike Goldoni, Gozzi "felt the common people's instinctive hostility to dabbling in literature." Rather, the opposite was the case, with the aristocratic Gozzi regarding the rabble with unfeigned contempt, whereas Goldoni had sought to invest his lower-class characters with a greater degree of individuality.

In his "Letter to an Actor on Acting" (1872), Wagner commended Gozzi for rehabilitating improvisation in his fiabe dramatiche. In his adaptation of *La donna serpente*, of course, he had no choice but to cut the improvised scenes or write them out in full—no other alternative was possible in an opera. The masks of the commedia dell'arte tradition are replaced by other, more or less comic characters who, in keeping with Wagner's decision to transfer the action from Gozzi's semi-oriental, semi-Venetian fairy-tale world of masks to a Nordic realm, now sport such incongruous names as Gunther and Gernot, with the heroes of the *Nibelungenlied* reduced to the point where they have become comic servants. The name Arindal, which Wagner had already used for the male protagonist in *Die Hochzeit*, was taken over from Ossian—Wagner may have found it in Goethe's *Werther*, where it also occurs. The typically Gozzian tendency for the tragic and the sublime to be infiltrated by comic elements and the predominance of the grotesque that so fascinated the Romantics are two aspects of the original that are much reduced in Wagner's libretto, even though here, too, the alternation between tragic and comic scenes has been preserved in essence.

In general, Wagner has taken over intact the plot of Gozzi's tragicomedy, the main difference being the change of imagery surrounding Ada's transformation, a change of which Wagner was particularly proud, as he explained in *A Communication to My Friends* (1851): "A fairy who renounces her immortality in order to gain possession of the man she loves can win mortality only by meeting certain strict conditions. If she fails to meet them, her mortal lover is threatened with the harshest of fates" (GS 4:252–53). But the ordeal—I will return to the conditions bound up with it—proves too much for her lover. Whereas in Gozzi the fairy is now turned into a snake (only her lover's kiss can turn her back again), Wagner altered the ending in such a way that "the spell on the fairy, who has been turned to stone, can be broken only by her lover's impassioned singing" (GS 4:253).

The motif whereby a human being is turned to stone or becomes a statue has a long and venerable tradition in myth, recurring most recently in Christoph Ransmayr's Ovid-inspired novel *Die letzte Welt* (1988)—in 1990 an English translation appeared under the title *The Last World*—within the framework of a postmodern take on the *Metamorphoses* in which the character of Battus is quite literally petrified. The reader will also be reminded in this context of Lot's wife, who is turned to a pillar of salt in the Bible, and of the Greek Niobe, who turns to stone in her grief at her children's murder. The motif is found in myths and fairy tales throughout the world, as is its counterpart whereby the statue is restored to life. Unsurprisingly, it also occurs repeatedly in Gozzi, most notably in *Il corvo*, a piece of which Wagner thought very highly and whose contents are summarized in detail in Hoffmann's "Der Dichter und der Komponist" (The poet and the composer). And it is found, too, in Gozzi's *L'augelin belverde* (The green bird), in which one after another of the characters is turned into a statue and back again. In short, Wagner replaced one motif from Gozzi with another. But the way in which he interpreted it derives from elsewhere, for the idea of a statue coming back to life through music is strikingly reminiscent of the end of Shakespeare's *Winter's Tale*, which Wagner undoubtedly knew. Here the apparent statue of Leontes' wife, Hermione—it is, in fact, Hermione herself—is restored to her original human form to the sound of music. This idea of a statue coming to life is associated above all with the classical myth of Pygmalion, the sculptor who fell in love with the statue that he had made, so that Venus breathed life into it for him. By the eighteenth century this motif had come to symbolize the very existence of the artist who by dint of his creative fire breathes life into what was dead and artificial. Two strophes from Schiller's poem "Die Ideale" (1795) illustrate this idea:

> Wie einst mit flehendem Verlangen
> Pygmalion den Stein umschloß,
> Bis in des Marmors kalte Wangen
> Empfindung glühend sich ergoß,
> So schlang ich mich mit Liebesarmen
> Um die Natur, mit Jugendlust,
> Bis sie zu athmen, zu erwarmen
> Begann an meiner Dichterbrust,
>
> Und, theilend meine Flammentriebe,
> Die Stumme eine Sprache fand,
> Mir wiedergab den Kuß der Liebe
> Und meines Herzens Klang verstand;

Da lebte mir der Baum, die Rose,
Mir sang der Quellen Silberfall,
Es fühlte selbst das Seelenlose
Von meines Lebens Widerhall.

[As once Pygmalion, fondly yearning,
    Embrac'd the statue form'd by him,
Till the cold marble's cheeks were burning,
    And life diffus'd through ev'ry limb—
So I, with youthful passion fired,
    My longing arms round Nature threw,
Till, clinging to my breast inspired,
    She 'gan to breathe, to kindle, too.

And all my fiery ardour proving,
    Though mute, her tale she soon could tell,
Return'd each kiss I gave her loving,
    The throbbings of my heart read well.
Then living seem'd each tree, each flower,
    Then sweetly sang the waterfall,
And e'en the soulless in that hour
    Shar'd in the heav'nly bliss of all.

                   (Trans. Edgar Alfred Bowring)]

The ideas that Wagner found in Gozzi were combined with others drawn from *The Winter's Tale* and from the myths of Pygmalion and Orpheus, who not only tamed wild beasts with his singing but caused the very stones and trees to move, thus producing a potent mix of symbols in which Arindal becomes an artist who through the power of music breaks the spell on his lover, who has been turned into a stone statue. (Musically and dramatically, the model for this scene is Hades in Gluck's *Orfeo ed Euridice*, where Orpheus's singing and playing melt the hearts of the unfeeling Furies.)

Ja, ich besitze Götterkraft!
Ich kenne ja der holden Töne Macht,
Der Gottheit, die der Sterbliche besitzt!
Du, heiße Liebe, Sehnsucht und Verlangen,
Entzaubert denn in Tönen diesen Stein!

                   (SS 11:56–57)

[Yes, godly strength I own!
I know sweet music's power,
The godhead that the mortal owns!
O fiery love, desire and longing,
Uncharm this stone through music's tones!]

Two of the themes found here—the idea of a creature from the spirit world who yearns to become human and who is prepared to forgo his or her immortality for

the sake of human love, and the tragic clash between the spirit and human worlds—
are central to many Romantic operas of the first half of the nineteenth century, beginning in 1816 with Hoffmann's *Undine* and culminating in 1850 with Wagner's
Lohengrin. Heinrich Marschner's two operas *Der Vampyr* (1828) and *Hans Heiling* (1833) are part of the same tradition.

The idea of testing the love of a human being who enters into a relationship with
a figure from the spirit world and who is required to obey an almost impossible injunction is common to three of Wagner's Romantic operas, *Die Feen*, *Der fliegende
Holländer*, and *Lohengrin*. In *Die Feen* and *Lohengrin* the test involves not asking
a question: the human partner is not allowed to fathom the mystery surrounding the
otherworldly being who has entered his or her world. This, too, was a classical motif,
as Wagner was fully aware (GS 4:289); suffice it to mention Zeus and Semele, and
Amor and Psyche. The motif recurs, at least peripherally, in Wagner's unfinished
sketch for *Wieland der Schmied* (Wieland the Smith, 1849–50), where it is said that
the Prince of the Light Elves approached Schwanhilde's mother in the form of a
swan, much as Zeus approached Leda. They lived together for three years until "the
mother, in her foolish eagerness, desired to know who her husband was, a question
that she had been told not to ask. Then the Prince of the Elves swam away through
the waves in the form of a swan" (GS 3:182). Here motifs from the myths of Leda,
Semele, and Psyche have merged with others from *Lohengrin*.

In Gozzi's *La donna serpente*, Farruscad violates a similar injunction by searching his wife's boudoir, and in *Die Feen*, Arindal—anticipating Elsa in *Lohengrin*—
urges his lover "to tell him who she is and whence she comes" (SS 11:9). According
to *My Life*, Ada has to impose the harshest ordeals on her human lover (the ban on
questions is only one such test of his love), for "only by triumphing over them can
he free her from the fairies' immortal world and allow her, as a loving wife, to share
in the fate of all mortals" (ML 80). This motif is strikingly reminiscent not only of
Undine but also of a twentieth-century opera to which I have already referred, *Die
Frau ohne Schatten*.[19] Hofmannsthal is known to have studied Wagner's music
dramas in detail while working on his libretto, and there is no doubt that *Die Feen*
provided him with a number of ideas, even if the many parallels between the two
works—the fact that the Empress, whose father is from the spirit world, originally
assumes the form of an animal caught by the mortal huntsman who is later to become her husband; the idea of an ordeal; and the transformation into a statue—can
also be explained by reference to the fact that both librettists were drawing on
Gozzi. Strauss, too, was familiar with *Die Feen*, as he helped to prepare the work's
first performance in Munich in 1888. (To his annoyance, the premiere was entrusted instead to his superior, Franz Fischer.) The production remained in the
Munich repertory for many years, and in 1895 Strauss's wife, Pauline de Ahna,
took the part of Ada.

A comparison between *Die Feen* and Gozzi's *La donna serpente* reveals the
extent to which Wagner refashioned many of the situations that he found in his
source, aligning them with the spirit of the great poetic and musical impressions of
his youth. Shakespeare's influence is evident not only in the parallel with the final
scene of *The Winter's Tale* but also in a number of reminiscences of *A Midsummer*

Night's Dream, and Arindal's mad scene in act 2, for which there is no direct parallel in Gozzi, recalls *King Lear*, a work that had already inspired Wagner's first work for the theater, the tragedy *Leubald* WWV 1 (see also ML 32). Mad scenes were of course a regular feature of nineteenth-century operas, most notably Masaniello's in Auber's *La muette de Portici* (The mute girl of Portici), a work that played a paradigmatic role in the young Wagner's life. In much the same way, Weber's *Oberon* has left its mark on the action in many small ways, both musically and poetically, including the appearance of the King of the Fairies at the end. The ordeal scene in the final act, with its Chorus of Men of Bronze, and the earlier "purification" of the children of Ada and Arindal by what they think is death by fire (see SS 11:40–45) are clearly modeled on the penultimate trial undergone by Tamino and Pamina in *Die Zauberflöte* (The magic flute). The last-named work has left its mark on *Die Feen* in other ways, too, with the scene between Drolla and Gernot in act 2 evidently inspired by the duet between Papageno and Papagena; other aspects of the scene can be traced back to Pedrillo and Blonde in *Die Entführung aus dem Serail* (The abduction from the seraglio) and to Sherasmin and Fatima in *Oberon*. Even more important are the influences to which Wagner himself admitted: Beethoven (Ada's great *scena* and aria in act 2 is clearly based on Leonore's "Abscheulicher") and, above all, Weber and Marschner, whose Romantic operas inspired the words and music of *Die Feen*.[20]

PRE-ECHOES OF THE LATER WAGNER

For all that *Die Feen* contains many reminiscences of Wagner's musical models, it goes far beyond the mere imitation of well-tried devices, not least as a result of its dramatic intensity, an intensity that has persuaded one commentator to write of "an impassioned young man with the strength of a wild animal mobilizing all the resources of the Romantic music theater."[21] And, like Wagner's next opera, *Das Liebesverbot* (The ban on love), it also contains many presentiments, not to say pre-echoes, of his later works. The rising semiquaver figure in the introduction to the overture, for example, points the way ahead to what is arguably Wagner's most important purely instrumental work, his *Faust* Overture. And the unaccompanied *preghiera* (prayer) at the start of act 3 recalls the prayer before the single combat between Lohengrin and Telramund in act 1 of *Lohengrin* (in this case the model is almost certainly the unaccompanied *prière* in act 3 of *La muette de Portici*). Even Wagner's later use of the leitmotif for psychological ends is already adumbrated here, notably in the theme of Gernot's Romance about the witch Dilnovaz, which Gernot sings in an attempt to persuade Arindal to abandon Ada on the grounds that she, too, is no more than a sorceress. This theme returns in act 2 at the very moment when Arindal himself begins to doubt Ada as a result of the terrible trials that he thinks she has inflicted on him. Or take the braying horn calls at the beginning of Arindal's mad scene, a passage intended to imitate the sound of barking dogs and one that clearly anticipates Sieglinde's hallucinatory vision of a pack of snarling hounds in act 2 of *Die Walküre*.

According to Paul Bekker, "the youthful composer had suddenly struck down to the foundation of his own genius" in this scene.[22] And, as Werner Breig has pointed out, it is significant that Wagner's music gains in its "power of expression and originality in scenes where the border states of consciousness are characterized in musical terms."[23] Among these scenes are some that are almost Kleistian in their ability to merge dreams and reality, notably in Ada's first appearance before Arindal in act 1 (SS 11:19–20). Wagner's interest in "border states of consciousness" is already clear from *Leubald*, which he wrote when he was only fourteen and whose titular hero spends long periods in a state of mental confusion. Wagner claimed that it was in order to set *Leubald* that he learned how to write music (ML 38), although it seems unlikely that he had anything more in mind than incidental music in the style of Beethoven's music for Goethe's *Egmont*. "I am no composer," he told Cosima on 31 January 1870. "I wanted to learn enough only to compose *Leubald und Adelaide* [*sic*]; and that is how things have remained—only the subjects have changed."

Far more important than these occasional pre-echoes of the music of Wagner's later works are the ways in which themes and characters and their interrelationships are prefigured in *Die Feen*. No matter how much Wagner may have changed artistically and ideologically, certain prototypical scenes remain pivotal to his plots from his very first opera through to his last. A classic example of this is what we might call "the poetics of the glance"[24]—to borrow a term from Jean Starobinski's famous chapter on Racine.[25] In his mad scene, Arindal remembers pursuing the hind and how, struck down by his arrow, it had revealed itself as the fairy Ada.

> O seht, das Tier kann weinen!
> Die Träne glänzt in seinem Aug'!
> O, wie's gebrochen nach mir schaut!
>
> (SS 11:48)

> [Behold, the beast can weep!
> A teardrop glistens in its eye!
> Oh, how dulled it gazes up at me!]

This image of the animal's dying glance directed at the huntsman is bound to remind the reader of the moment when Gurnemanz directs Parsifal's gaze at the swan that he has killed: "Gebrochen das Aug', siehst du den Blick?" [Its eye is dulled, do you see its glance?] (GS 10:335) At this point Parsifal feels the first stirrings of pity and breaks his bow. (Not until later does he acquire the maturity and experience to fathom the full depths of human suffering through the agony that Amfortas feels.) Thus, in Wagner's mind the glance was associated with pity and compassion. Here it is worth mentioning an episode from Wagner's own life, an episode, moreover, that occurred while he was working on *Die Feen*. During his time in Würzburg, Wagner frequented a local beer garden known as Der letzte Hieb (the place still exists), and on one occasion he became involved in a fight with a fellow reveler to whom he had taken a dislike. Wagner struck his opponent roundly on the skull "and caught the bewildered look he gave me." The man's gaze traumatized him, leaving him with an abiding sense of guilt and a loathing of all forms of physical violence. In this context he describes how, even in his adolescence, he could already "empathize with the sufferings of others, especially with those of animals" (ML 83–84).

The hind's dying glance wakens Arindal's love of Ada. This too is a prototypical scene in Wagner's works. Think of the moment when Isolde recalls how she once stood before Tristan, sword in hand, and how he gazed up at her from his sickbed.

> Von seinem Bette
> blickt' er her,—
> nicht auf das Schwert,
> nicht auf die Hand,—
> er sah mir in die Augen.
>
> (GS 7:11)

> [From his bed
> he looked up,—
> not at the sword,
> not at my hand,—
> he looked into my eyes.]

The sense of compassion kindled by this glance prevents Isolde from exacting revenge. The glance of the victim stirs a glance of compassion that turns to an expression of love. That compassion and love are always synonymous in Wagner's works is clear from the look of suffering in the eyes of the portrait of the Flying Dutchman in Daland's house, a look that arouses Senta's compassion and love. "Kann meinem Blick Theilnahme ich verwehren?" she asks Erik [Can I prevent my gaze from feeling sympathy?] (GS 1:275). But Erik is right to suspect that Senta's gaze expresses more than mere sympathy.

Another typical motif that links *Die Feen* with *Der fliegende Holländer*, *Tannhäuser*, *Lohengrin*, and *Die Walküre* can be described, in Thomas Mann's words, as "sympathy with death," albeit not yet in the sense understood by the *décadents*. Like Lohengrin, Ada hails from a timeless world, a *"paradis artificiel,"* and, like Lohengrin, she is prepared to renounce this world and her immortality for the sake of love. As I have already noted, a condition is attached to this decision, in that Arindal and Elsa are famously banned from asking about the origins and nature of their otherworldly partner for a certain period of time. Neither has the strength to stick to this condition. Lohengrin, in Wagner's words, "admits to his divine origins and returns, annihilated, to his lonely state" (GS 4:296). Here, paradoxically, the character's return to a timeless state from one of temporality signifies "annihilation." Arindal, by contrast, is banished from the fairy-land paradise and transported to a "desolate rocky landscape" (SS 11:10). The speed with which this change takes place inevitably recalls the way in which Tannhäuser is suddenly transported from the Venusberg to the valley at the foot of the Wartburg. Although both the Venusberg and the fairy land are different worlds, there is a sense in which, being beyond time, they are also beyond space, which explains how the fairy world into which Arindal had stumbled while out hunting can penetrate the human world in the second half of act 1 as suddenly as the Venusberg erupts into the valley of the Wartburg in act 3 of *Tannhäuser*.

Like Lohengrin, Ada remains behind, annihilated, in her lonely paradise: "Zu traurig hartem Lose / wird mir Unsterblichkeit" [Immortality is now my grievous fate] (SS 11:19–20). And there is the same paradox as before: for Ada, immortality means "being dead forever" (SS 11:20). But Arindal is given a further chance to win back Ada by means of a new ordeal, an opportunity not found in *Lohengrin*. In act 2, the two fairies Zemina and Farzana offer Ada a choice between the timeless fairy realm and the world of human mortality: "Hier langer Tod und dort ein ewig Leben" [Here lengthy death and there eternal life] (SS 11:35). But for Ada, this set of values no longer applies; for her, immortality betokens a "lengthy death," whereas mortality is the equivalent of "eternal life."

> Ich könnte allem mich entzieh'n,
> steht mir's nicht frei? In ew'ger Schöne
> unsterblich, unverwelklich blüh'n!
> Es huldigt mir die Feenwelt,
> ich bin ihr Glanz und ihre Zier,
> es ehrt ein unvergänglich Reich
> mich, seine hohe Königin!
> Ich könnte allem mich entzieh'n,
> in Feenpracht unsterblich blüh'n!
> Betrogen, Unglücksel'ge!
> Was ist dir Unsterblichkeit?
> Ein grenzenloser, ew'ger Tod,
> doch jeder Tag bei ihm
> ein neues, ewiges Leben!

(SS 11:36)

> [I could withdraw from all of this,
> Am I not free to do so? In endless beauty
> I would bloom, immortal and unfading!
> To me the fairy realm pays tribute,
> I lend it sheen and luster,
> A realm, imperishable, honors
> Me, its high-born queen!
> I could withdraw from all of this
> And flourish in undying fairy splendor!
> Deceived, unhappy woman!
> Of what avail is immortality to you?
> A boundless, endless death,
> Yet every day with him
> Is new, eternal life.]

In much the same way, Tannhäuser yearns to escape from Venus's timeless realm and rediscover temporality and mortality.

Wenn stets ein Gott genießen kann,
bin ich dem Wechsel unterthan;
nicht Lust allein liegt mir am Herzen,
aus Freuden sehn' ich mich nach Schmerzen.

(GS 2:6)

[A god may know eternal joy,
But, human, I am bound to change;
My heart is set on more than mere delight:
For in the midst of joy I long for pain.]

"O, Göttin," he goes on, "woll' es fassen, / mich drängt es hin zum Tod!" [Oh, goddess, try to understand, it's death for which I crave!] (GS 2:11). It is not immortality that confers life on him, but mortality, with the result that he is alarmed when Venus threatens him with the same fate as Ahasuerus and the Flying Dutchman: "Wenn selbst der Tod dich meidet, / ein Grab dir selbst verwehrt" [When death itself avoids you, the grave is closed to you] (GS 2:11).

Siegmund, too, rejects Brünnhilde's offer of "eternal bliss," dismissing such joys as "hollow" (GS 6:53). Instead, he prefers a life of suffering at Sieglinde's side, and his decision leaves the Valkyrie so shaken that she ceases to be the "unfeeling maid" that Siegmund takes her to be (GS 6:53). Abandoning the world of timeless, painless divinity, Brünnhilde violates Wotan's decree out of her sense of solidarity with the suffering human couple before her and in that way becomes human and mortal in turn.

The fairies in Wagner's first opera are likewise "unfeeling maids," insensitive members of a world that knows neither mortality nor the experience of emotion and suffering bound up with it. Just as Brünnhilde abandons the Valkyries, so Ada, by becoming a sentient human being, leaves behind the unfeeling fairy band. Like the Nurse in *Die Frau ohne Schatten*, Zemina and Farzana embody the lack of compassion of the fairy world and stake everything on the belief that Arindal will fail the tests imposed on him and that Ada will in consequence return to their own immortal world. (The eponymous heroine of *Die Frau ohne Schatten* is in many ways related to Brünnhilde: she too is moved by her sense of solidarity with suffering humanity to abandon the shadowless, timeless, and emotionless spirit world that she had once inhabited.)

In the case of *Die Feen*, immortality has the last word, thereby asserting a priority that is puzzling and at odds with Wagner's "sympathy with death." As such, this highlights the change in Wagner's thinking since *Die Hochzeit*. Whereas Farruscad and Cherestani share a human fate in Gozzi's *La donna serpente*, Ada and Arindal are removed from this "earthly dust" (SS 11:58) and welcomed into a world of immortality. This change makes sense only against the background of the myth of the artist that derives from the Orpheus legend and transfigures the end of the opera: through his singing and playing, Arindal has broken the spell on the stone statue of Ada, an artistic feat by dint of which he becomes "more than a man—immortal" (SS 11:57). By being transported to the fairy world, he undergoes the sort of apotheosis that is typically associated with the artist.

FROM *DIE FEEN* TO *DAS LIEBESVERBOT*

Die Feen was the only one of Wagner's thirteen completed operas not to be performed during his lifetime. He had already finished the libretto by the time he took
up his first professional engagement as chorus master in Würzburg in January
1833. The post had been obtained for him by his brother Albert, who was already
working at the theater as a singer and stage manager. On his way to taking up his
new post, Wagner broke his journey in Bamberg and, according to his later account
in *My Life*, "recalled E.T.A. Hoffmann's stay in the town and the genesis of his
Fantasiestücke [Fantasy pieces]" (ML 81), a comment that indicates the extent to
which Wagner was still in thrall to Romantic poetry at this time. He worked on the
score of *Die Feen* throughout the twelve months that he spent in Würzburg, completing it on 6 January 1834 and possibly even arranging a concert performance
of excerpts from it.

Wagner returned to his native Leipzig in January 1834 and for a time hoped that
the local theater would stage his first completed opera, but the promised production
was repeatedly postponed, and finally it was abandoned altogether. During his negotiations with the theater, Wagner was persuaded to provide the work with spoken
dialogue in the style of an *opéra comique*,[26] although these passages of dialogue are
limited to the comic scenes, in other words, to the ones that were largely improvised
in Gozzi's original. Here Wagner followed his source far more closely than in the
sung recitatives, thereby giving much greater scope to low comedy and parody.

In the event, *Die Feen* reached the stage neither in this nor in any other form at
this time, a state of affairs that was due first and foremost to the fact that, according
to *My Life*, Wagner had already lost interest in the work soon after completing the
score: "The very act of starting on the composition of *Das Liebesverbot* put me in a
frame of mind in which I soon lost interest in the older work" (ML 104).[27] This new
frame of mind found unambiguous expression in Wagner's earliest writings from
1834, namely, in the essays "German Opera" and "Pasticcio by Canto Spianato."
Although the authorship of the second article admittedly remains contentious,
both attest to a sudden turning away from German Romantic opera or, as Wagner
would later express it, his lapse into the shallow world of French and Italian opera
of the most "frivolous" and "fashionable" kind (GS 4:256). Now he contemptuously dismisses his earlier model Weber, reserving his greatest scorn for the very
opera to which he had previously owed so much and on which he was later to
draw for inspiration: *Euryanthe*.

Wagner's aesthetic volte-face was closely connected with his conversion to the
Young German movement of the 1830s, a movement whose leading spokesman,
Heinrich Laube, had been a personal acquaintance of his for some time. Indeed, it
was in Laube's *Zeitung für die elegante Welt* (Journal for polite society) that
Wagner's first piece of journalism, "German Opera," was published on 10 June
1834. Wagner ends this article with the words "We must seize our chance and
honestly seek to cultivate the age's new forms" (SS 12:4), meaning that he was now
resolved to turn his back on the escapism and mysticism that he had glorified in

Die Feen, notably in the way in which Ada and Arindal are spirited away to fairyland at the end of the opera. This flight from the present was to be replaced by an active engagement with the here and now and, more especially, by a glorification of sensuality. In this spirit Wagner conceived *Das Liebesverbot* in 1834, completing its libretto later that year, only months after putting the finishing touches to the score of *Die Feen*. If readers were to compare the themes of his first two operas, Wagner wrote in 1851 in his *Communication to My Friends*, they would see that

> there existed within me the potential for developing in one or other of two fundamentally different directions: the utter seriousness of my basic nature was now contrasted with a mischievous propensity for wild and sensuous abandon and rebellious pleasure that seemed to be in the starkest possible contrast to it. This contrast becomes particularly clear when I compare the music of these two operas. . . . Anyone who was to compare the music of my later opera with that of *Die Feen* would find it hard to believe that so striking a change of direction could have taken place in so short a time. (GS 4:255–56)

Wagner was guilty of a certain exaggeration here; just as there are occasional traces in *Die Feen* of the influence of Italian opera, especially Rossini, so the composer of *Das Liebesverbot*—unlike the author of the dismissive article "German Opera"—was far from denying the influence of Weber or Beethoven in a number of scenes in the work. (In the case of Beethoven, there are even thematic parallels between *Das Liebesverbot* and *Fidelio*: the second acts of both operas begin with a dungeon scene, with the prisoner then rescued by a woman and the opera ending with a deus ex machina that brings to an end the tyrant's despotic rule.)[28] And there are also musical and literary links between *Das Liebesverbot* and *Tannhäuser*, the most striking of them being the Dresden Amen that is pre-echoed in the "Salve Regina" in act 1, scene 2 of *Das Liebesverbot*. I shall have more to say about the literary reminiscences in my chapter on *Tannhäuser*. Here it is sufficient to recall Isabella's exclamation in the opening act of *Das Liebesverbot*: "O, wie so öde das Leben bliebe, / gab er [Gott] nicht Liebe und Liebeslust" [Oh, how barren life would be if God had not given us love and love's pleasure] (SS 11:84). Her words are an almost literal anticipation of Venus's great cry in *Tannhäuser*:

> Ach! kehrtest du nicht wieder,
> dann träfe Fluch die Welt;
> für ewig läg' sie öde,
> aus der die Göttin schwand!

(GS 2:10)

> [Ah! if you were not to return,
> a curse would blight the world;
> forever it would then lie barren
> when forsaken by the goddess!]

But the most striking link between Wagner's first attempt at a German Romantic opera and its "frivolously Italianate" successor is the fact that both derive at least part of their inspiration from the commedia dell'arte tradition. In the case of *Das Liebesverbot*, this finds its most salient expression in the burlesque episodes such as the trial scene involving Brighella (whose very name recalls the commedia dell'arte style), Pontio, and Dorella in act 1, where the Italian tradition is far more palpable than in *Die Feen*.

Although Wagner later returned to the German Romantic tradition in *Der fliegende Holländer* and came to regard as an aberration his enthusiasm not only for French and Italian operas but also for the world of ideas associated with the Young German movement, he consistently refused—for the reasons suggested here—to agree to a production of *Die Feen* or even to the publication of the work during his lifetime. But although he excluded it from his collected writings, he regaled his friends with a reading of excerpts from it one year before his death.

Not until 1888, two years after the death of King Ludwig II, to whom Wagner had donated the full score of the opera in 1865, did *Die Feen* receive its first performance at the Court Theater in Munich, a performance that took place against the wishes of Cosima Wagner; but since she did not own the performing rights to her late husband's first two operas, her claim that Wagner had never wanted the work to be staged fell on deaf ears. The production was directed by Karl Brulliot, "with scenic arrangements, stage machinery, and lighting" by Karl Lautenschläger, and was a spectacular success, not least as a result of its unparalleled extravagance, remaining in the repertory until 1899. According to Theodor Helm's review of the first performance,

> the final apotheosis was the most beautiful and magical sight that we have ever seen in this genre, indeed, it is impossible to describe the enchanting effect of the sculptural groups rising up to dizzying heights, the fantastical calyxes, seashells, and gemstone crystals opening up on every side, and, finally, the electric lighting that was used on such a massive scale.[29]

A second production was mounted at the Prinzregententheater in 1910, conducted by Felix Mottl and performed as part of the Munich Festival, but on this occasion the work was a resounding failure. Of the handful of subsequent productions, it is sufficient to mention only the two most notable ones: in 1981, at the Wuppertal Opera, Friedrich Meyer-Oertel staged the work from an ironic perspective, seeing the Romantic fairy-tale world as an oneiric product of the nineteenth century, resonating with allusions to the real life of the times. As such, the opera was seen as the projection of a society that sought refuge from life's demands in a world of empty illusion.[30] In this way, the anti-Romantic stance that Wagner temporarily adopted under the influence of the Young German movement was projected back onto his first completed opera, with Romantic opera called into question by means of its own conventions. Meyer-Oertel restaged *Die Feen* at Munich's Theater am Gärtnerplatz in 1989, and on this occasion he adopted a different approach to the piece, turning it into what the German music critic Karl Schumann described as a "kind of delirium on the part of a Romantic *Zauberoper*."[31] The postmodern sets and costumes by Dieter Flimm and Maria Lucas combined fairy tale and reality,

history and myth, in a virtuoso and often puzzling game of associations in which
time and place were forever shifting. The fairy realm was a hermetically sealed
world of women that rejected the importunate Arindal. Certain elements evoked the
Romantic grotesquerie of E.T.A. Hoffmann, and others recalled a modern nightclub,
with choreography by Ursula Linke based on the style of modern Ausdruckstanz
(expressive dance). Arindal was part Orpheus and part Ludwig II, finally triumphing
over the celestially cold world of womenkind and finding himself transported to the
starry vault above. The opera, in short, was interpreted as an exploration of the ideology underpinning much of nineteenth-century art.

Bel Canto Opera as an Erotic Utopia

In "German Opera" (1834), his first theoretical essay, Wagner stressed the "infinite
advantage" that the Italians enjoyed over the Germans in bel canto opera—the
voice-dominated opera that in Wagner's view was then the only type of opera
worthy of the name. He was "heartily sick of the endlessly allegorizing orchestral
turmoil," a complaint that sounds very similar to the anti-Wagnerian attacks that
were later to be leveled at the symphonic use of the orchestra in the Wagnerian
music drama. Rather, he yearned for "simple, noble singing" and decried "this
wretched erudition—the source of every German ill" (SS 12:1–2). Dieter Rexroth
has suggested, with some plausibility, that the musical theme that Wagner uses to
symbolize Friedrich's ban on love in *Das Liebesverbot*—the theme represents the
governor's antisensualist morality and almost amounts to a leitmotif—is treated
as a textbook case of motivic fragmentation in the course of the opera in an attempt to parody this "German erudition."[32]

This preference for Italian bel canto opera and French opéra comique continued to leave its mark on Wagner's writings throughout the next four years. In
"Dramatic Singing" (1837), for example, we read: "Why should we Germans not
openly and freely admit that the Italian has the advantage over us in singing, the
Frenchman in terms of his lighter and livelier treatment of operatic music?" (SS
12:15). And in "Bellini: A Word in Season," Wagner demands "Song, song, and
once again song, you Germans!" Just how far he was capable of going in his enthusiasm for Bellini emerges from his remark that "in *Norma*, which is undoubtedly Bellini's most successful work, even the poem soars up to the tragic heights
of the ancient Greeks" (SS 12:20–21).

Wagner's enthusiasm for Bellini stemmed, as we know, from Wilhelmine
Schröder-Devrient's performance as Romeo in a production of *I Capuleti e i
Montecchi* in Leipzig during the early months of 1834. It was one of the seminal
experiences of his youth, and one to which he repeatedly returned even at the end
of his life. On 23 March 1878, for example, he told Cosima that he thought the
"rapture" of the second act of *Tristan und Isolde* was due entirely to Schröder-
Devrient's performance in 1834. Throughout the mid-thirties Wagner's imagination as a music dramatist was fired above all by Bellini and also, of course, by
Auber, especially the latter's *La muette de Portici*.

When Wagner superintended a collected edition of his writings toward the end of his life, he refused to include in it not only the texts of his pre-*Rienzi* operas but also the newspaper articles that he wrote before 1840. Yet it would be wrong to conclude from this that this refusal went hand in hand with a rejection of French and Italian opera. For French opera in particular—especially the works of Méhul, Boieldieu, Auber, and Halévy, whose grand opera *La juive* (The jewess) was, in his view, in the best tradition of French opera—he retained a remarkably high opinion that found expression in often surprising ways in his conversations with Cosima, so that Nietzsche's oft-repeated remark that Wagner's place was not really among the Germans but in Paris makes sense against the background of the abiding fascination French opera exerted on him.[33]

"We must seize our chance and honestly seek to cultivate the age's new forms, and he will be its master who writes in neither an Italian nor a French—nor even in a German—style" (SS 12:4). With these words Wagner concludes his essay "German Opera," repeating a demand that was typical of those made by the members of the anti-establishment Young German movement, most notably in Laube's novel *Das junge Europa* (Young Europe, 1833) and in various articles that appeared in Laube's *Zeitung für die elegante Welt*, in which Wagner too published some of his early articles. The Young Germans inveighed against obscurantism, reactionary church orthodoxy, ossified puritanical morality, and the recidivist policies of Germany's particularist states, at the same time championing the rebellions and revolutions of recent years, whether in the form of the Greek War of Independence, the July Revolution in Paris, or the Polish Uprising. They demanded that the artist play an active role in contemporary events and, rather than falling back on a mythical past, portray the realities of the present day. They praised a life of sensual beauty freed from the trammels of all conventions. And they espoused the Utopia of universal politics transcending all national boundaries. These were all ideas that Wagner, too, shared, just as he shared the general enthusiasm for Laube's literary model, Wilhelm Heinse's 1787 novel, *Ardinghello und die glückseeligen Inseln* (Ardinghello and the blessed isles). For the writers of the Young German movement, the eponymous hero of Heinse's novel embodied their ideal of hedonistic sensuality and free love. At the end of the novel, this ideal is finally realized on the Utopian Blessed Isles of the work's title, a propertyless state in the Aegean where each individual is allowed to express his or her individuality in whatever ways he or she chooses.

Wagner, too, read Heinse's novel, and, such was his enthusiasm, he retained a lively memory of it for the rest of his life, returning to it a week before his death in February 1883 in the context of ownership: "It's this that I liked so much about Heinse's 'Blessed Isles'—the people there owned no property, in order to avoid the many miseries bound up with it" (CT, 5 February 1883). One of the most striking aspects of Wagner's intellectual development is that, however much he may later have tried to deny them on ideological grounds, he was never entirely successful in breaking free from earlier enthusiasms, a characteristic that is palpably plain from virtually every page of Cosima Wagner's diaries.

Looking back on the 1830s from the vantage point of the 1860s, Wagner recalled the "exuberant Young German mood" of those years (ML 90), a mood to which he abandoned himself wholeheartedly and that found immediate artistic expression in his self-styled "grand comic opera" *Das Liebesverbot oder Die Novize von Palermo* (The ban on love, or The novice of Palermo, WWV 38).[34] The work was finished in March 1836 and given its first—and only—performance under Wagner's own direction in pitiful provincial circumstances at the end of that month. Wagner's graphic account of the performance in his autobiography makes particularly entertaining reading. In his article "Pasticcio," he had spoken of the need "to seize true warm life as it is" (SS 12:10–11); and this is the goal that he set himself in his "carnival opera," a free adaptation of Shakespeare's *Measure for Measure* "but with the difference"—Wagner explained in his "Autobiographical Sketch"—that "I eliminated its serious elements and in that way remodeled it in the true spirit of Young Europe: free and open sensuality triumphed over puritanical hypocrisy simply by being itself" (SS 1:10).[35]

The action was shifted from Shakespeare's unhistorical Vienna to Palermo, and the governor Friedrich, who takes over the affairs of state in the absence of the king (rather than the Duke in *Measure for Measure*), is turned into a priggish German who, with his fanatical hatred of sexual love, embodies all the typically German vices against which the Young Germans fulminated. Wagner would have had an even more compelling reason than Shakespeare to locate the action in Vienna, except that—as Egon Voss has pointed out—the work would then inevitably have been regarded as a "critique of the reactionary and repressive policies of Metternich's regime," with Friedrich identified with Metternich himself. Wagner's decision to transfer the action to Sicily was thus, in part, an attempt to sidestep the censor.[36]

The ban on love imposed by the Teutonic moralist is ultimately subverted by the Mediterranean sensuality of the Sicilian population. Indeed, "love's antipode," as he is described in the libretto (SS 11:97), falls under the spell of love, consumed as he is by his passionate feelings for Isabella. These feelings undermine his entire moral system: "Wretch! What has happened to the system that you so carefully arranged?" (SS 11:106). In Friedrich's self-accusation in act 2, we hear a remarkable pre-echo of the sufferings of another character who, hostile to love, suddenly falls victim to an erotic passion with catastrophic results; as a sign of his transgression, he is struck down by the same spear with which he had set out to destroy an infamous hotbed of passion—the magic garden created by yet another enemy of love, Klingsor, who had even gone so far as to castrate himself in an attempt to overcome sexual desire. In spite of—or precisely because of—the differences between the two situations, there is a striking parallel between Wagner's "youthful transgression" (as he described *Das Liebesverbot* when donating the score to Ludwig II at Christmas 1866) and *Parsifal* (which he famously called his "farewell to the world").

The first modern production of *Das Liebesverbot* since its disastrous premiere in 1836 took place at Munich's Nationaltheater on 24 March 1923, when the conductor was Robert Heger. "This early Wagner," wrote Alfred Einstein on that occasion, "seems to be a slap in the face for his later self; to judge by its aim, *Das Liebesverbot* is the very antithesis of *Parsifal*."[37] Yet there is also a remarkable dialectic link between these two antithetical works: the governor Friedrich is not only the hypocritical representative of a duplicitous morality, enjoying the very thing that he denies others, he experiences the power of sexual love as a demonic constraint that renders him unconscious of his actions ("I am not conscious of myself," he says at one point in the opera; SS 11:84), so that, almost like Kundry, he desires sexual congress as much as he longs for "salvation" (SS 11:106). Here desire is depicted as a form of perverse salvation, as "God and hell" in one (SS 11:107). As such, it already looks forward to the ultimate paradox of Parsifal's words to Kundry: "In höchsten Heiles heißer Sucht / nach der Verdammniß Quell zu schmachten" [To pine for the source of all damnation in ardent yearning for supreme salvation] (GS 10:361).

When Friedrich promises to spare the life of Isabella's brother, Claudio, in return for her love, while in reality giving orders for his execution to be brought forward, it is impossible not to be reminded of Scarpia and Tosca. Yet the superficial parallel cannot conceal a more deep-seated difference between the two relationships. "Claudio, you'll die—I'll follow you!" Friedrich decides (SS 11:107); the law may not yield to passion, so that he is prepared to sacrifice himself to it and condemn himself to death. "Death and lust await me" (SS 11:107). First he will couple with Isabella, then have himself put to death.

This view of erotic love as a compulsive force that dooms the lover to death already contains within it a number of aspects of the erotic longing familiar from Wagner's later works. In much the same way, the idea of a ban on love itself recurs in manifold variations, not only in *Die Bergwerke zu Falun* (WWV 67), where human love is banned in the name of art (symbolized by the paradis artificiel of the Mountain Queen), but also in *Tannhäuser*, where earthly love is proscribed in favor of its heavenly counterpart; in the *Ring*, where love is abjured in favor of power; in the unrealized project for *Die Sieger* (The victors, WWV 89); and in *Parsifal*, with its rejection of erotic love, which is seen as an expression of the "will" that causes pain and suffering.

The ban on love imposed by the governor of Sicily involves other elements that go far beyond questions of individual psychology, even though they remain closely associated with such questions. Friedrich is no "loyal servant of his master," to quote the title of Grillparzer's tragedy on a not dissimilar subject, but a man who out-Herods Herod. Although the populace accepts the absent king's reign as a matter of course, Friedrich turns it into a form of gloomy, misanthropic despotism. Needless to say, the populace sees straight through him and realizes that the ascetic lifestyle that he tries to impose on them is not God's but the Devil's, precisely because his interest in morality is not an end in itself but a means to the end of power. When he tells the townspeople that he intends to hand them over "to the king pure and undefiled," they mutter among themselves: "How unctuously the man speaks, the Devil must have got into him" (SS 11:81). The man who tries to create a world of pure virtue and yet refuses to accept that tares are bound to grow with the wheat will produce not heaven on earth but only hell. (In this context it is enough to recall the character of Robespierre in Büchner's *Dantons Tod*.)

Although Friedrich regards himself only as the king's temporary replacement and as subordinate to the inviolable law, he is nonetheless a self-seeking careerist just like Goethe's Clavigo, on whose career his own is evidently modeled. Just as Clavigo has abandoned his mistress, Marie Beaumarchais, so Friedrich repudiated his wife, Mariana, as soon as he began to climb the ladder of success.

> [D]och er, der arm und unbekannt
> Sizilien einst betrat,
> gewann des Königs Gunst, und stieg so hoch,
> daß er, von Ehrgeiz nur entflammt,
> der Liebe stilles Glück verschmäh'te,
> und mich, die Gattin, bald verließ!

(SS 11:68)

> [But he who once, unknown and poor,
> Set foot on Sicily
> Won his monarch's favor and rose so high that,
> Fired by ambition alone,
> He scorned love's silent happiness
> And soon forsook me, who was then his wife.]

Unlike Clavigo, Friedrich had never really loved his wife, as he himself admits: "I've never loved—Mariana learned this for herself when, cold and faithless, I abandoned her" (SS 11:106). In Friedrich, the instinctive desire for power overrides all other considerations, including even love.

It is no exaggeration to claim that here there is already a trace of the opposition between power and love that constitutes one of the main themes of the *Ring*, even if in *Das Liebesverbot* the contrast is still colored by the ideas of the Young German movement. Here the power of erotic desire implies freedom in a moral and political sense, whereas puritanism is equated with reactionary despotism. After all, it has always been in the interests of authoritarian regimes to maintain a sense of "morality," a point on which we are once again reminded of the *Ring*, in which love figures as a seditious force, rebelling against custom and ossified laws. (In *Opera and Drama*, Wagner describes it as an "agitator"; GS 4:56.) Such love is represented above all by the Wälsungs, and, significantly, it is decried by Fricka, who upholds moral "custom" and who regards the "despotic nature" of love (GS 4:56) as a disruptive force, undermining the social and moral order to which she clings unwaveringly and legalistically. "Stets Gewohntes / nur magst du versteh'n," Wotan complains in *Die Walküre* [You understand only what you've always been used to] (GS 6:31).

Friedrich, too, clings to the "law," using it to combat "passion" (SS 11:107), against which he discharges the law like some fatal arrow at the very moment when he himself falls prey to desire. His attempts to enhance his own power and advance his career are inextricably bound up with reactionary and despotic laws and a morality that is hostile to both life and love. Wagner is implacable in exposing his hypocrisy, tempting one to recall Nietzsche's ploy of opening his reader's eyes by exposing and laying bare "ascetic ideals," especially in *Parsifal*. ("What does it mean," he asks in *On the Genealogy of Morals*, "when an artist like Richard Wagner pays homage to chastity in old age?")[38]

Remarkably, then, Wagner's "youthful transgression" already anticipates the critical method that Nietzsche was to apply to the composer's own "farewell to the world." Yet Wagner was to rescind *Das Liebesverbot* in 1866—a year after his prose draft for *Parsifal*—and to do so, moreover, in the spirit of his final work. In the quatrain that he wrote for Ludwig II, when presenting him with the holograph score, he equated the earlier opera with Amfortas's transgression while hoping that he might be absolved by Parsifal/Ludwig:

> Ich irrte einst, und möcht' es nun verbüßen;
> Wie mach' ich mich der Jugendsünde frei?
> Ihr Werk leg' ich demüthig Dir zu Füßen,
> Daß Deine Gnade ihm Erlöser sei.[39]

> [I once transgressed and now would fain atone;
> But how can I cast off this youthful sin?
> I humbly lay its work before your feet,
> That it may find redemption through your grace.]

Turning his back on the Young Germans' glorification of erotic love, Wagner paid homage to chastity even here.

In *Das Lieberverbot*, the ban on love is directed not only at free love but at all forms of sybaritic pleasure, chief of which is its institutionalized manifestation in the form of the carnival: the anarchic expression of hedonistic pleasure is bound to be eyed with suspicion and regarded as dangerous by any despotic regime. Luzio's Carnival Song, especially its last two lines, at least toys with the idea of rebelling against family and moral values and, as such, with anarchy.

> Jetzt gibt's nicht Weib, noch Ehemann,
> tralalalalala!
> Es gibt nicht Vater und nicht Sohn,
> tralalalalala!
> Und wer das Glück ergreifen kann,
> la!
> Der trägt es im Triumph davon!
> La!—
> . . . . .
> Wer sich nicht freut im Karneval,
> dem stößt das Messer in die Brust!

(SS 11:111)

> [There are no longer wives or husbands,
> Tralalalalala!
> No longer fathers and sons,
> Tralalalalala!

> And he who can grasp good fortune,
> La!
> Will carry it off in triumph!
> La!—
> . . . . .
> If a man won't take pleasure in the carnival,
> You should thrust your knives deep in his breast!]

Curiously enough, this Carnival Song was the first piece of Wagner's operatic music to be published, appearing in 1837 as a supplement to the periodical *Europa*.[40]

Readers familiar with Goethe's writings will recall his description of the Roman carnival in 1788. The carnival, Goethe explains, derives from the Saturnalia, which was celebrated in ancient Rome as a reminder of the golden age of Saturn and for its duration accorded Rome's citizens the "privileges" of freedom and equality, which were believed to have existed in that mythical past: "The difference between high and low seems to be set aside for a moment; everyone draws closer to everyone else." Often the excitement threatens to descend into physical violence, and Goethe, with a certain horror, observed the narrow dividing line between violence and catastrophe in this "modern Saturnalia," which he describes as a "festival of universal license and unconstraint." His final remark that "freedom and equality can be enjoyed only in the frenzy of madness"[41] reminds us that the French Revolution was to break out only eighteen months later. (Franz Grillparzer's short story "Der arme Spielmann" [The poor minstrel] likewise describes a Saturnalian celebration whose outward trappings remind the author of a revolutionary uprising.)

And it is as an uprising—a kind of love-driven revolution—that the carnival is meant to be seen at the end of *Das Liebesverbot*. Here Wagner offers an impressive display of the art of ensemble writing, an art that he had acquired from his knowledge of opéra comique. When Jean-Pierre Ponnelle staged this scene in his 1983 production for the Munich Nationaltheater, he drew on his own intimate knowledge of French and Italian musical comedy and created such a virtuoso stage picture that one was left wondering why so highly effective a work is rarely seen in the opera house. As before, Wagner modeled his own account of the uprising on Auber's handling of crowd scenes in *La muette de Portici*. Claudio, who had been condemned to death, is freed by the crowd, and the governor's puritanical dictatorship is brought to an end. Friedrich, as we know, has privately decided to have himself executed, and he now calls on the populace to carry this out: "Sentence me by my own law!" But they refuse: "No, the law is abolished! / We mean to be more merciful than you!" (SS 11:123).

In short, the revolution does not destroy the despot but frees him from his own tyrannical law, and at the end he is even invited to lead the procession of masks that sets off to meet the king on his return to Palermo. In *A Communication to My Friends*, Wagner described this moment as follows: "Shakespeare resolved the resultant conflicts by means of the public return of the Duke, who had secretly observed events: his decision is a serious one, based as it is on the judge's 'measure for measure.' I, on the other hand, brought about the denouement by means of a revolution" (GS 4:254). Here the populace genuinely triumphs, and the carnival becomes a celebration of a free community ruled by sexual desire. "Let's hold a threefold carnival," the opera concludes, "and may its pleasures never cease!" (SS 11:124).

Even so, Wagner's comment that he "brought about the denouement by means of a revolution" is not to be taken entirely literally, as this is no real revolution. Not even the tyrannical Friedrich has a "knife thrust deep in his breast," for all that he "takes no pleasure in the carnival" (SS 11:111). A general wish to get married replaces the desire for political change. No Bastille is stormed. Instead the revelers announce their decision to tear down all the "houses of mourning," and the king, who had after all appointed Friedrich as his governor, is welcomed home, for, as Luzio explains to Friedrich, "he prefers lively jests to your own sad laws" (SS 11:124). At the end of the opera, the unpopular governor is unmasked, only for him to don another mask in the republican spirit of the carnival, whereupon a procession forms, with the reunited couple Friedrich and Mariana at its head. As it sets off to meet the king to the sound of cannon shots, pealing bells, and a military march, the revolution gives way to a legally recognized monarchy enlivened by a spot of saturnalian revelry. The final stage direction in the libretto reads, significantly: "At the end a salvo of rifles" (SS 11:124).

There is no doubt that if Wagner sought to take the sting out of the idea of a popular uprising, it was not least because of the censor. Yet it would be wrong to lose sight of the fact that for all his revolutionary views, the older Wagner was never an antimonarchist. (The same is true of many leaders of the earliest phase of the French Revolution.) In his address to the Dresden Vaterlandsverein, "How Do Republican Aspirations Stand in Relation to the Monarchy?" (1848), he was to demand that "the king should be the first and truest republican" (SS 12:225). This is an idea to which many revolutionaries subscribed, not only in 1789 but in 1848 as well. Wagner never really abandoned the notion of a popular republican king,[42] and it continued to leave its mark on the hopes that he placed in Ludwig II and on his 1867–68 series of articles, "German Art and German Politics." Even the original version of *Siegfried's Tod* (Siegfried's death, 1848) is influenced by this idea of a republican ruler, an idea repudiated only a short time afterward, following Wagner's disenchantment with the conduct of the German princes during and after the revolution of 1848–49. "Allvater! Herrlicher du!/Freue dich des freiesten Helden!" [Father of the universe! Glorious god! Rejoice in the freest of heroes] (GS 2:227) is how Brünnhilde had originally ended her peroration.

Although at first sight *Die Feen* seems to be closer in spirit to Wagner's later "Romantic operas" than *Das Liebesverbot*, there are in fact more thematic pre-echoes of the great music dramas in this "youthful transgression," for all that they appear in unfamiliar surroundings. From a linguistic point of view, the text of *Das Liebesverbot* is—relatively speaking—the most carefully elaborated of Wagner's pre-1839 librettos, the commedia dell'arte scenes involving Brighella being some of the most inspired products of the composer's comic muse. As he noted in

A Communication to My Friends, *Die Feen* and *Das Liebesverbot* represented opposing "trends." The need to achieve a "balance" between them was his chief concern during his "subsequent development as an artist" (GS 4:256). In advancing this view, he was conceding that the "sensuality" of Italian bel canto opera and French opéra comique was to a certain extent "preserved"—in the sense of the Hegelian "aufgehoben"—in the music dramas of his maturity.

On the Uses and Disadvantages of History for the Music Drama—Grand Opera

DIE HOHE BRAUT, RIENZI, *AND THEIR CONSEQUENCES*

The basis of history is man's social nature: the whole

movement of history develops out of the individual's need to

combine with the essence of his species in order to ensure that

his own abilities achieve their highest potential in society.

—*Richard Wagner,* Opera and Drama

IN 1836, shortly after completing the score of *Das Liebesverbot*, Wagner drafted a "grand opera" for Paris that marks a change of direction toward dramatized history, albeit history of a different kind from the one we encounter in the distorting mirror of his first theatrical experiment. Wagner's dramatic career had begun in 1826 with *Leubald*, which, as his first known work, duly figures as WWV 1 in the *Wagner Werk-Verzeichnis*.[1] Completed in 1828, it had to wait another 160 years for its first publication.[2] Even its opening sentence—"Why, a pox on you, landlord, you keep a poor alehouse; you serve a poorer measure of wine than the dear Lord has given you villainy"—shows clearly what sort of a work this is and what kind of linguistic models have left their mark on it. Goethe's *Götz von Berlichingen* begins with a similar plea to pour out a generous helping of spirits: "Hänsel, another glass of brandy, and make it a Christian measure."[3]

Wagner's first drama follows the fashion for *Ritterdramen*—plays about knights and chivalry—that had been triggered by *Götz von Berlichingen* more than fifty years earlier and that was now already outdated. Goethe's play was the first historical drama in German literature, availing itself of a pseudohistorical language and late-medieval setting that set the tone for decades. In both these respects, Wagner follows his Goethean model closely, although all sense of history has been systematically removed from this monstrous figment of his dramatic and perfervid imagination, his neo-Shakespearean tale of robber barons and gothic horror containing no trace of the late-medieval legal background that Goethe had sought to depict with his lawyer's eye for meticulous historical detail.

DIE HOHE BRAUT: THE PLAN FOR A REVOLUTIONARY OPERA

When Wagner returned to history in 1836, it was under the influence of French grand opera. His five-act grand opera *Die hohe Braut oder Bianca und Giuseppe* (The high-born bride, or Bianca and Giuseppe, WWV 40) is set "in and around Nice in 1793" and occupied him intermittently from 1836 to 1842. In the event, he completed only the libretto, and it was Jan Bedřich Kittl, his friend in Prague, who finally set it to music, enjoying what appears to have been some success when it was unveiled in the Czech capital in 1848 under the title *Bianca und Giuseppe, oder: Die Franzosen vor Nizza* (Bianca and Giuseppe, or The French at the gates of Nice).[4] Here we again find Wagner asserting his aesthetic allegiance to the Young German movement, which in 1835 had been denounced by the Federal Diet as a threat to the security of the state. Writing in his own *Zeitung für die elegante Welt* on 11 July 1833, Heinrich Laube, the movement's leading representative, had praised Heinrich Koenig's novel *Die hohe Braut* as a superb example of historical reporting,[5] and it was on Koenig's novel that Wagner based his latest libretto.

It is symptomatic of Wagner's limited understanding of grand opera that he believed that a subject so steeped in the antiestablishment liberal Zeitgeist might appeal to Eugène Scribe, the accredited librettist of the Académie Royale de Musique; evidently he did not yet see that the Paris Opéra was the home of political compromise. In August 1836, while he was still living in Königsberg, he prepared a French translation of the prose draft, which he had presumably drawn up only a short time earlier, and sent it to Scribe in the pitifully naive hope that the latter would work up the draft into a libretto for Wagner and obtain a commission for him to set the work to music.[6] Having had no reply from Scribe (it later turned out that the librettist had not received the original letter), Wagner appealed to Meyerbeer in 1837[7] and sent a further copy of the French version of the scenario to Scribe. Had he known the ways of the Paris Opéra, he could have spared himself the trouble, since commissions were awarded at best to established composers. Otherwise, young composers and librettists simply submitted completed works, whose fate was then decided by a special committee charged with adjudicating on such matters.

The obstinacy with which Wagner continued to beat at this closed door is clear from a letter that he wrote to August Lewald in November 1838, begging the latter to use his influence with Scribe and obtain for him a commission from the Académie Royale. The fact that Wagner prepared his own French translation of the draft while he was living in Paris—probably during the summer of 1840—suggests that even as late as this he had not abandoned the idea of seeing *Die hohe Braut* staged at the Paris Opéra. (At about this time he drew up the French prose draft of *Der fliegende Holländer*, which he also hoped Scribe would work up into a libretto, thereby enabling him to obtain a commission from the Opéra.)

Only when all these efforts had proved fruitless did Wagner lose interest in setting the subject to music, although in 1842, assuming the mantle of Scribe, he worked up the draft into a libretto and offered it—in vain—to a whole series of other composers, including his colleague in Dresden, the Kapellmeister Carl Gottlieb Reißiger. In the end, it was Kittl who set it, introducing various changes and, in an attempt to circumvent the local censor, toning down its revolutionary message; as Wagner commented wryly in *A Communication to My Friends*, the original libretto—unfortunately no longer extant—was performed in Prague "with various imperial and royal Austrian modifications" (GS 4:273). This is particularly true of the ending, which was almost certainly not by Wagner. In other words, the version of the libretto that was published in 1911 in volume 11 of Wagner's collected works is not authentic, in spite of the restitution of the original title, so that we need to turn to the prose draft to gain a clearer idea of Wagner's intentions.[8]

The action, as I have already noted, takes place in and around Nice in 1793, the year in which the town was annexed by the French. Political and private actions are interwoven in the kind of dialectic counterpoint that had characterized Scribe's librettos from the time of *La muette de Portici*—a work that Wagner admired throughout his life. There is ample provision not only for rabble-rousing crowd scenes, a legacy of the French Revolution both in the theater and in real life, but also for the public festivals that in Scribe's case were influenced by the Théâtre de la Foire and by the vaudeville, as well as by actual revolutionary celebrations.[9] Indeed, there is even a church scene replete with an organ of a kind that had been a regular part of grand opera since Scribe first collaborated with Meyerbeer on *Robert le diable* (Robert the Devil) in 1831. (In Wagner's draft, as in *La muette de Portici*, the scene in question involves a wedding ceremony in keeping with grand opera's predilection for striking dramatic contrasts.)

It certainly looks as though Wagner did everything in his power to make his prose draft as palatable to Scribe as he could. Yet Scribe ignored the draft, evincing a lack of interest that is hardly surprising when we recall that he had just reached the pinnacle of his fame with *Les Huguenots* (1836); as the most famous librettist of his day, he can have felt little inclination to provide a libretto and a commission for an unknown composer from Königsberg. But there is more to it than that. However well Wagner appears to have assimilated the dramaturgical ideas of Scribe and grand opera, there was one essential point on which his plan no longer chimed with the spirit of the times. The revolutionary verve of *La muette de Portici* (1828) had been celebrated by audiences in its own day and had even sparked the popular uprising in Belgium in 1830, when the work was first performed in Brussels—in spite of the fact that the end of the opera is by no means prorevolutionary. But since the establishment of the July Monarchy in France, such enthusiasm had long since given way to pessimism, a mood that finds trenchant expression in both *Robert le diable* and *Les Huguenots*.

In his waspish account of the "political significance" of *Robert le diable*, Heinrich Heine had located the work in a political wasteland between the Revolution and the ancien régime, with its hero "hovering between these two principles as the *juste milieu*."[10] Whether or not we agree with Heine, there is no doubt that the revolutionary thrust of Wagner's *Die hohe Braut* and especially its final tableau, with a military band and the Marseillaise, would have been wholly unthinkable on the stage of the Académie Royale de Musique in the late 1830s.[11] Nothing could have been further from Scribe's mind than to prepare a libretto based on such a draft. At the very time that Wagner was writing to him with his own operatic plans, Scribe was working on a play—*Bertrand et Raton ou L'art de conspirer* (1837)— which, much to the delight of its bourgeois audiences, made fun of all revolutionary enthusiasms and did so, moreover, on the very eve of the workers' uprisings in Paris and Lyons.

During his years in Paris between 1839 and 1842, Wagner must have realized that his revolutionary opera would never succeed at the Académie Royale de Musique. Writing in 1871 in his "Reminiscences of Auber," he cites *La muette de Portici* as an example of the change in public attitudes.

> In the eyes of the nations of Europe, the July Revolution in Paris looked every bit as likely to excite their sympathies as *La muette de Portici* had previously done in the theater; both spread the same sense of terror among the supporters of the various legitimacies. Performances of the opera even caused riots to break out, with the work being recognized as the obvious theatrical precursor of the July Revolution. Rarely has an artistic phenomenon been so closely associated with an event of such universal importance. (GS 9:58)

La muette de Portici, Wagner argued, had constituted "an excess on the part of its author," who, in perpetrating it, had transgressed the boundaries of his normal artistic sphere, which was that of opéra comique.

> In much the same way, the July Revolution was very soon regarded by French politicians or, to be exact, by the whole of the population as an excess on the part of the popular spirit in Paris. When I arrived in Paris at the end of the thirties, people no longer gave the July Revolution a moment's thought. Indeed, the mere memory of it appalled them. If *La muette de Portici* was still performed, it was simply as a stopgap, and in so tired a production that I was advised against attending it. (GS 9:58)

Here *La muette de Portici* is seen as a "theatrical precursor" and counterpart of the Revolution, which it is even said to have triggered, only to become as "neglected" as the latter. Wagner was not alone in advancing this view of the famous opera.[12] That it rests on a creative misunderstanding is evident. *La muette de Portici* is wholly antirevolutionary in its aim[13]—the press laws of 17 March 1822 would in any case have made it unthinkable for a revolution to be depicted onstage in a positive light. And yet, as a result of the dynamics of the events that it depicts and the suggestive impact of an uprising visualized in such dramatic terms, the opera could later be interpreted as revolutionary and even be said to be capable of "causing riots to break out." How can we explain this discrepancy between the work's underlying aim and the response that it later elicited?

La muette de Portici had surprised its audiences because it was "completely new," Wagner wrote in his "Reminiscences of Auber": "Never before had there been an operatic subject so full of life." It was no longer the individual numbers that counted but "always an entire act, taken as a whole, that caught the audience's interest and held it in thrall." In other words, Wagner is clearly applying to Auber's opera the standards that he himself demanded of the music drama, where whole acts were assembled, like the movements of a symphony, to create a single "entity" (see GS 10:185).

> For what was new about this music for *La muette* was its unusual concision and drastic compression: the recitatives rent the air like lightning flashes; from them we passed to the choral ensembles as though we were caught up in a tempest; and in the midst of this chaos of fury came energetic requests for calm reflection or renewed calls to arms; then wild exuberation once again, murderous turmoil, interrupted in turn by moving imprecations born of anxiety or by an entire nation murmuring its prayers in unison. (GS 9:45)

Clearly it was the novel dramaturgy of the crowd scenes that fascinated contemporaries—a crowd that no longer maintained a statuesque stillness but was goaded by its emotions into joining in the action.[14] According to Wagner, one of Auber's "most influential innovations" was his "vivid grouping of the choral ensembles, where, almost for the first time, he persuaded the chorus to act as a crowd that was genuinely involved in the action and that was of serious interest to us all" (GS 9:48).

It was not just the rebellious ambitions of the crowd—violently affected and therefore violently affecting—but also their very real theatrical presence that clearly had revolutionary implications for both Wagner and his contemporaries. Yet of equal, if not greater, importance was the work's emotive impact, an impact that, independent of its underlying aim, exercised an appeal whose dynamic (and inflammatory) thrust passed over the footlights and into the audience—and beyond the control of its creators. It was precisely this onstage presence of the crowd that, independent of its role within the action, had so stirring an impact as to "cause riots to break out." And not only its onstage presence. According to the German musicologist Ludwig Finscher, the crowd scenes in *La muette de Portici* owe much of their impact to Auber's reminiscences of the music associated with the Revolution of 1789.[15] Of particular interest here is the duet for Masaniello and Pietro, a number famous in its own day and of undoubted political effectiveness, not least because it contains, in the words "Amour sacré de la patrie [Sacred love of the homeland]," not only a quotation from the Marseillaise (still banned at the time that the opera was written) but unmistakable rhythmic reminiscences of it. (It is tempting to speak here of a subtext in the music.) Also worth recalling is the chorus at the end of act 3: "Marchons! des armes! des flambeaux! / Courons à la vengeance!" [Forward march! To arms! Torches! / Let's hasten to vengeance!] The final lines of the first stanza of the Marseillaise run "Aux armes, citoyens! formez vos battaillons! Marchons! qu'un sang impur abreuve nos sillons!" [To arms, citizens! Draw up your battalions! / Forward march! May an impure blood imbrue our fields!].

The mass demonstrations that followed in the wake of the Storming of the Bastille led to a wholly new, republican perception of the public at large that also found expression in plays and operas.[16] In particular, this perception was reflected in what might be termed the aesthetic mobilization of the populace, which was employed as a massed choir at popular celebrations. At the Feast of the Supreme

Being on 8 June 1794, for example, the choir comprised some 2,400 citizens. The revolutionary composer Étienne-Nicolas Méhul even planned a "national festival opera" in which all the inhabitants of Paris would have taken part. Understandably, the plan came to nothing. Equally understandable is the fact that following the Bourbon Restoration of 1815–30, when republicanism again became a dirty word, the onstage presentation of a seditious crowd, especially in forms clearly derived from the older revolutionary tradition, should exercise so immensely powerful an impact on a public that was again ready for revolutionary change. As Ludwig Finscher has shown with reference to productions of *La muette de Portici* in Frankfurt in around 1830 and again around 1848, this impact was by no means limited to France. In 1831, for example, frequent riots erupted in the auditorium, and the revolutionary duet for Masaniello and Pietro evidently had to be repeated at every performance. (The German translation used at these early performances included the words "Der Unterdrückung mächt'ge Schranke/drängt siegreich fester Muth zurück,/O Land, dem ich das Leben danke,/bald dankst du mit der Freiheit Glück" [Oppression's mighty barrier/is driven victoriously back by stern resolve;/O land to which I owe my life,/you will soon thank me with liberty's good fortune].) Fistfights are said to have broken out among the performers, with the chorus of Neapolitan townsfolk ranged against the local militia, who had been drafted in as extras to play the part of Spanish soldiers.[17] In a conversation with Johann Peter Eckermann on 14 March 1831, Goethe had referred to the political impact of the opera, regarding it not as a revolutionary work but as a "satire on the common people" and relating its appeal to the fact that "it contains no visible justification for a revolution, but this pleases people because it allows them to read into those passages that have been left blank whatever they find objectionable in their own town or country."

Nonetheless, there is no getting away from the fact that the characterization of both the rabble-rousing hero Masaniello and of the mob is dominated by nonrevolutionary features that were to become increasingly typical of the later development of French grand opera in general. Chief of these elements are the problematic nature of the hero and the transformation of the mutinous crowd into a bloodthirsty rabble. The fourth act opens with a solo scene for Masaniello in which he questions his role as the people's liberator, and indeed it emerges from the subsequent scenes with the insurgents that the people have degenerated from slaves into tyrants. When Masaniello revolts against "blind fury," the rebels accuse him of treachery. The conflict stems from the fact that Masaniello allows Alphonse, the representative of Spanish foreign rule, to stay in his house with his fiancée, Elvire. It is symptomatic of the opera's ability to enlist our sympathies in an entirely nonrevolutionary manner that Alphonse and, above all, Elvire are portrayed in a wholly positive light. Alphonse appears from the outset as a basically magnanimous prince who is wracked by pangs of conscience because of his indiscretion in seducing the fisherman's daughter, Fenella—the "mute girl" of the opera's title. Blame for the terrible tyranny of the Spanish oppressors is laid squarely at the door of Alphonse's father, the viceroy of Naples, who, significantly, never appears in the opera.

The fourth act ends with what Gerhart von Graevenitz has described as the "ruler's traditional advent,"[18] in which, to quote the stage directions, Masaniello receives "the golden keys of the city [that is, Naples], a chain of honor, sword, ermine cloak, and crown." Taken with the culminating *trionfo*, this scene shows Masaniello at the very pinnacle of his fame, at least on an outward level. Yet he is now at odds with the world, and the somber threats of the conspirators, contrasting with the cheering of the populace, already foreshadow the work's tragic ending. The fourth act also shows the crowd increasingly dominating the action, so that the individual actors in the drama become more and more powerless in the face of collective forces—even where the heroic individual appears to triumph, as in the ruler's traditional arrival in the finale of this act. After all, it is the crowd that has forced Masaniello to assume the traditional role of the triumphant hero, that same crowd whose excesses he execrates at the beginning of the act and whose victim he will become in the fifth and final act. He was their "idol," says Borella—their "victim," Alphonse retorts. (Masaniello has once again saved Elvire's life, and Alphonse in turn seeks to save Masaniello's: our sympathies are swayed in a decidedly counterrevolutionary direction.)

The opera ends with the death of Masaniello, who is not only poisoned by Pietro but lynched by a mob of rebellious fishermen. The old tyrannical rulers are reinstated following the ignominious flight of the "rebellious hordes" (to quote Alphonse); and the eponymous heroine kills herself in spectacular fashion by hurling herself into the lava streaming from the erupting Vesuvius. In consequence, the uprising is completely disavowed. The volcanic eruption at the end is seen as a symbol of divine anger, inspiring the townspeople to sink to their knees in guilt-stricken prayer ("Grâce pour notre crime! / Grand Dieu, protège-nous!" [Pity us our crime! / O Lord, protect us!]), thereby giving unequivocal expression to the opera's antirevolutionary thrust.

Revolt became one of the principal themes of French grand opera from the time of *La muette de Portici* onward, but so, too, did its failure, both material and moral. There seems little doubt that this failure reflects the trauma induced in the bourgeoisie by the Reign of Terror of 1793–94. Significantly, all Scribe's opera librettos revolve around this sense of trauma, with which audiences had evidently not yet come to terms. In this context, Gerhart von Graevenitz has drawn attention to Scribe's "literally programmatical play on the first revolution," *Avant, pendant et après* (Before, during, and after). What Scribe shows here, according to Graevenitz, is

> the way in which the Terror stems from the arbitrary rule of privilege and the ancien régime, delivering liberty straight back into the hands of chaos: only after the Revolution, when insurrection and Terror had died down, was it possible to imagine a future world ruled by order, when obligations would be met and the classes reconciled.[19]

Here, then, is a quintessential expression of the ideology of the *juste milieu*, in which the bourgeoisie saw itself as the well-tempered middle ground between the aristocratic Restoration imposed from above and the Reign of Terror inflicted from below.

Liberal-conservative audiences were fully in sympathy with the struggle for freedom from tyranny that they saw acted out on the operatic stage, at the same time living in far too great a fear of losing all that they had already achieved for them ever to see themselves as revolutionaries.[20] By playing off private and political actions in contrapuntal symmetry, Meyerbeer in particular achieved an ingenious hold on his audiences' sympathies, allowing them to identify with the insurgent while giving them the satisfaction of seeing insurrection put down. Those features of the private individual that elicit the audience's sympathy achieve what Christhard Frese, writing in the context of *Le prophète* (1849), has termed an "apotheosis in death,"[21] while the revolt itself is called into question. With the exception of Rossini's *Guillaume Tell*, which received its first performance in Paris in 1829 on the very eve of the July Revolution, all those examples of French grand opera from *La muette de Portici* to *Le prophète* that involve an uprising end with the death of their "sympathetic" hero. And, significantly, this ending always takes the form of a spectacular natural disaster involving a whole array of stage effects, from the volcanic eruption that ends *La muette de Portici* to the collapse of the palace at Münster that buries all the characters in *Le prophète*.

Where does Wagner's draft for *Die hohe Braut* stand in all this? As I have mentioned, the action takes place in 1793, a traumatic year in the history of the French Revolution, when the French revolutionary armies were on the point of capturing Nice. (This was a favorite theme in the post-1789 revolutionary theater: following the ending of feudal theatrical privileges, theaters sprang up all over Paris, and plays with titles such as *La prise de Toulon par les Français* [The capture of Toulon by the French] were very much the order of the day.) The male protagonist is Giuseppe, the son of a magistrate on the estates of the Marchese Malvi outside Nice. The Marchese himself is a representative of the old House of Savoy. Giuseppe loves Malvi's daughter Bianka [*sic*], but her father has decreed that she shall marry Count Rivoli, who comes from the same social background as the Malvis. Bianka, however, loves the magistrate's son, who is also her foster brother. This conflict, redolent of eighteenth-century bourgeois tragedies, is inextricably bound up with the precarious political situation that obtains in Nice.

The opening act begins with preparations for celebrations that Malvi has promised to hold for his subjects following his return from Turin, where he has been visiting the king of Savoy. But the carefree atmosphere is marred by the beggar Cola.

> Cola humorously mocks the townspeople's mild-mannered devotion to their masters. Once the French have crossed the Var, there will no doubt be many changes & it may well be asked whether their noble lords will dance to the townspeople's tune in order to keep them amused. Laughter. *Cola*: There's nothing to laugh at, they need only to look toward France to see freedom & equality; marcheses are there a thing of the past & the beggar is the true-born man. Don't they want the same thing here?

Cola is put in his place by Bonatti, a corporal garrisoned at Fort Saorgio outside the town: "No doubt Cola is one of those night birds from the mountainous frontier region who are in the pay of the French?"

At this point it is worth glancing briefly at the libretto of Kittl's opera, even though we cannot of course be certain which parts were written by Wagner and which are the work of another hand. Nonetheless, it can be said at the outset that Kittl's libretto is a sorry effort that retains little trace of the draft's explosive political force. Wagner certainly had good reason to ask that his name not appear in the libretto when it was published in 1848.[22] From the very first scene of the opera, it is clear that Kittl's main concern was to depoliticize the subject as far as he could, although it is conceivable that self-censorship on Wagner's part in his 1840 French prose draft had already set a precedent here.[23] There is no longer any mention, for example, of the Marchese's journey to Turin, which was evidently politically motivated, bound up as it was with the threatened French invasion. Cola is merely a melancholy beggar who on seeing the dancing peasants and townsfolk laments his lost youth, so that it makes absolutely no sense for the soldiers to lay into him with such fury on the orders of their corporal.

But let us return to Wagner's draft and to the second scene, in which Giuseppe takes Bianka to task for agreeing to her betrothal with Rivoli. When he asks her whether she intends to "bow to her father's wishes," she replies that

> she has to do so, otherwise he, too, will be lost. Her father knows of her love & harbors the darkest suspicions regarding Giuseppe, who he knows is in league with the radicals who are hidden in the mountain passes and who have joined forces with the French. She has to obey—or at least to renounce him, since they are separated by social station & birth.

This sounds very much like Luise Miller's message of renunciation in Schiller's *Kabale und Liebe*, except that in Wagner's case the social standing of the two characters is reversed. Giuseppe, like some latter-day Ferdinand, refuses to submit to his fate and seeks to overturn the existing social order and reassert the sway of natural law.

> Giuseppe: "Does nature divide us? Did we not suck at one and the same breast, drinking in the mother's milk of universal brotherhood? Shall we be parted by the lamentable state of our wretched institutions, which fly in the face of nature?—I intend to destroy them & make you like myself!" . . . Giuseppe swears that he will destroy all the bonds that order the world and that he will place the Marchese's daughter on an equal footing with the magistrate's son.

In the libretto to Kittl's opera, this passage sounds substantially more innocuous. True, Giuseppe asks: "What are laws, what are rights beside this bond of nature?" (SS 11:142), but the inflammatory lines "The brazen bonds that part us I'll shatter with my mighty hand" (SS 11:143) are totally overshadowed by the frenzied despair of his threat to murder his rival. Giuseppe's role is reduced to little more than that of a jealous lover, while Bianca [*sic*] not only accepts the existing order with a sigh of resignation, she embraces it as an institution that, however problematic, is nonetheless both meaningful and necessary.

Wie wollte ich den Banden widerstreben,
die gütig uns vereint zu Leid und Lust,
als wir beim ersten Eintritt in dies Leben
Verwandtschaft tranken an derselben Brust?
　Doch ach! Gesetze, Vaterrechte,
　und trotzten sie auch der Natur,
　sind unbesiegbar strenge Mächte,
　wer sie bekämpft, verdirbt sich nur.

(SS 11:142)

[How could I e'er oppose those ties that bound
Us both, when we, with joy and sorrow blest,
Upon our entry into life's dear round
Drank loving kinship at one mother's breast.
　But ah, men's laws, paternal dues,
　Though nature's law be scorned withal,
　Are forces so invincible
　That to resist them's death to all.]

According to Wagner's prose draft, the peasants reassemble for the first-act finale, when the Marchese appears with Rivoli and reports that

> he has just returned from Turin, where the court is rife with rumors that a pernicious spirit of innovation & insurrection is infecting Nice & the area covered by his estates; French troops are massing on the banks of the River Var that forms the frontier with France & are threatening to invade Nice, an attack that will lead to the violent overthrow of the existing order;—they should resist the blandishments of this degenerate rabble & unite in opposing their plans with all possible resolve. He has stood surety with the king for his subjects' loyal disposition & so he is now asking them not to show themselves unworthy of that trust.

This speech, too, is considerably reduced in length and toned down in the libretto, where there is now only a general reference to the fact that the "enemy" is close at hand and that a firm stand will have to be taken against them (SS 11:144). There is no longer any talk of the desire for "innovation & insurrection" within the country's borders or of the threatened "overthrow of the existing order."

The mood of celebration is interrupted by the arrival of the harpist Brigitta, in whom Rivoli recognizes his own sister. She had, he says, "dishonored the family name by falling in love with a commoner" (in the libretto this becomes "a base individual"; SS 11:146), as a result of which she has been "repudiated." Rivoli "tramples her underfoot." (In the libretto he "thrusts her from him, so that she sinks to the ground"; SS 11:145.) This barbarous behavior places the representative of the existing social system in an altogether negative light, on which point Wagner differs fundamentally from Auber, who had ensured that the representatives of the old order always enjoyed a certain measure of sympathy.

In the prose draft, Malvi assumes from a comment by Bianka that Giuseppe is in league with the "radicals." That his suspicions are unjustified is shown by the fact that Giuseppe, having heard that the radicals are planning an attack on the Marchese's life, had hurried off to warn him while he was still on his way back from Turin. This is the same motif of the rebel who spares his enemy's life which we know from *La muette de Portici*. So grateful is Malvi for Giuseppe's warning that he agrees to Giuseppe's having the dance of honor with Bianka at the forthcoming festivities, but when Giuseppe deliberately provokes Rivoli in his attempt to coerce the Marchese into making good his promise, the latter takes back his word, thus prompting Giuseppe to retort, "Breach of promise & perjury! That's the sort of person you are!" He seizes Bianka and dances with her, whereupon guards are summoned and Giuseppe is on the point of being captured and led away in spite of his violent resistance when Sormano, one of the radicals, emerges from the crowd and, brandishing his dagger, draws Giuseppe after him. In Kittl's libretto, there is—significantly—no trace of Giuseppe's warning that the Marchese's life is threatened by supporters of the Revolution, nor, consequently, does Malvi agree to Giuseppe's dancing with Bianka. Nonetheless, Giuseppe still insists—for no obvious reason—that as the son of a magistrate he has a "right" to this dance. On being denied that right, he exclaims, "Ha! Perjury! Deception and outrage!" (SS 11:148), although it is far from clear who is supposed to have committed this act of perjury. The depoliticization of the action thus robs this scene of much of its meaning.

The second act transports us to the "Alpes Maritimes on the border between Nice & France." Sormano tells Giuseppe that he is Brigitta's husband and that because of his secret marriage to her, he had once been shamefully mistreated and driven into exile on Rivoli's orders. He now refuses to appear in Brigitta's sight until he has avenged both her and himself. His vengeance will take the form of a revolution in the territories held by Savoy. He seeks to win over Giuseppe to his cause, arguing that they arc both in the same position: "We are united by the selfsame hatred. Rivoli is your enemy because he is betrothed to your lover; he is my enemy because he is the brother of my wife, whom yesterday you saw shamefully trampled underfoot."

Revolutionary activity is thus privately motivated, just as it is in *La muette de Portici*, where Masaniello places himself at the head of the fishermen's uprising in order to avenge his sister, Fenella. Private concerns are also, of course, a political issue, since the oppression of the populace by their superiors assumes the form of a personal insult in both operas. "It is no doubt clear from all this," Sormano tells Giuseppe, "why I feel such bitter hatred for the aristocracy & their arrogant ways." Hence his links with the French revolutionary army. "They should follow the example set by the French & with their help introduce the new equality into Nice, Savoy, & Piedmont too." Giuseppe should "join forces with them, for once he has helped to place the aristocrat on an equal footing with the bourgeois, the Marchese's daughter will be his." This *scena* and duet end with a stretta: "He inflames Giuseppe's feelings until they are white-hot. . . . Together they vow to avenge their shame & to shed their life's blood in return for their country's freedom."

The underlying thrust of this scene is turned on its head in Kittl's libretto, where Sormano has been transformed from the wholly positive figure of the prose draft into an almost entirely negative one. Only reluctantly does Giuseppe follow his rescuer into the mountains, adopting an emphatically hostile stance toward Sormano's conspiracy: "Betrayal of our fatherland! O heinous crime!" (SS 11:152). Sormano accuses Giuseppe of cowardice and attempts to detain him by every means at his disposal, but in vain. As Giuseppe finally turns to leave, Sormano fires his pistol into the air, which is the prearranged signal for his fellow conspirators to emerge from their hiding places at the back of the stage: "At Sormano's shot, all of them break cover, surrounding Giuseppe and forcing him downstage." He is forcibly prevented from leaving, although he refuses to throw in his hand with Sormano's band of conspirators, and continues to cry out: "Treachery! Betrayal of our fatherland!" (SS 11:154). Those actions which, in the prose draft, are carried out in the interests of a fatherland for whose freedom the characters are prepared to shed their life's blood are depicted in the libretto as tantamount to treason. That the conspirators—who resemble nothing so much as a band of robbers—deprive Giuseppe of his freedom (they urgently need his help, as he knows his way around the mountains far better than they do), only to emerge as nature lovers who worship the setting sun and even kneel down in "silent prayer" at the sight of this "glorious spectacle," stretches our credulity to breaking point.

The motif of the setting sun occurs in a completely different context in the prose draft. Here, too, "the ravines fill with conspirators" in the final scene of act 2, but on this occasion they have no reason to surround Giuseppe and to detain him by force. Instead, they can rejoice in the fact that they have "won him over." And now they all celebrate the sunrise.

> Morning has gradually broken. The sun disperses the mists, the ice-capped peaks glow in its crimson light. At the back an open vista stretches out beyond the jagged mountain peaks from where Sormano and the other conspirators can look down on the French camp.—All fall to their knees in prayer & greet the young sun that is to bring them their new freedom.—From far below comes the sound of the reveille played by the French military band, a moment later the freedom songs of the French army can be heard, rising up from the valley.—Roused by these strains, Sormano, Giuseppe, & the conspirators prepare to set out. The music rising up from below forms an accompaniment to the impassioned singing of the conspirators on stage.

This is a typical revolutionary tableau in which Wagner significantly avails himself of the emotive appeal of the French revolutionary hymn.

The rising sun was a favorite symbol of the French Revolution, with Hegel, for example, famously describing its outbreak as a "glorious sunrise: all thinking people have helped to celebrate this epoch."[24] And in the sixth canto of Goethe's *Hermann und Dorothea*, the Judge sums up the general mood during the early years of the Revolution:

> Denn wer leugnetes wohl, daß hoch sich das Herz ihm erhoben,
> Ihm die freiere Brust mit reineren Pulsen geschlagen,
> Als sich der Glanz der neuen Sonne heranhob,
> Als man hörte vom Rechte des Menschen, das allen gemein sei,
> Von der begeisternden Freiheit und von der löblichen Gleichheit.

[For who will deny that his heart did not race at the thought,
That his pulse did not quicken, his breast beat more freely,
When the glorious light of the new-risen sun was first seen
And we heard of those rights—rights of man—that were common to all,
Of freedom's sweet breath and commendable equality?]

The scene with the conspirators, including the final tableau, is inspired, of course, by the scene on the Rütli in Schiller's—and Rossini's—*William Tell*. (The Tell legend was one of the most popular subjects during the French Revolution, both in the theater and elsewhere.[25] And Schiller's final play turned it into a kind of parable of the Revolution. With Rossini's final opera, indebted as it is to the tradition of French revolutionary opera à la Grétry, Méhul, Cherubini, and Paer, this parable comes full circle, so to speak, returning in 1829 to the scene of its historical origins, namely, the stage of the Paris Opéra, where it foreshadowed the revolution of July 1830.) In Schiller's Rütli scene, too, a mountainous ice-capped massif cuts off the back of the stage, and the scene ends, like Wagner's, with the confederates worshiping a rising sun that clearly has revolutionary overtones: "All have spontaneously removed their hats and observe the dawn in reverent silence." In Schiller's play the scene culminates in the lines

Bei diesem Licht, das uns zuerst begrüßt
Von allen Völkern, die tief unter uns
Schwer athmend wohnen in dem Qualm der Städte,
Laßt uns den Eid des neuen Bundes schwören.

(II.1443–46)

[By this first light of dawn that greeted us
Before those other nations that repine
Beneath us in the city's choking air,
We'll swear an oath to our new federation.]

Like the corresponding scenes in Rossini's *Guillaume Tell* and Wagner's prose draft for *Die hohe Braut*, this tableau ends the second act. "As they go off," reads Schiller's stage direction, "the orchestra enters with splendid verve, and the curtain remains up on the empty stage for a while, showing the spectacle of the sun rising over the ice-capped mountains." This is already a scene from the sort of grand opera in which sunrises and sunsets were among the most popular of all stage spectacles, the most famous example being Meyerbeer's *Le prophète* (1849).

In Kittl's opera the sunrise has been reduced to a mere stage effect and robbed of its political symbolism. Nor does it form the end of the second act, as it did in Wagner's draft, but has been conflated with the third act, an arrangement for which Wagner himself was almost certainly responsible.[26] Giuseppe has not joined in the morning prayers of the conspirators; clearly he has no time for the glorious sunrise but stands "alone at the front of the stage," gazing down "dreamily into the brightly lit depths" from which his "beloved's homeland" smiles back at him (SS 11:155). A chorus of pilgrims straight out of *Tannhäuser* approaches, bearing Brigitta's body. She has killed herself after being cruelly mistreated by Rivoli. Sormano collapses in despair. At precisely this moment the strains of wedding music are heard from the other side of the stage, a use of dramatic contrast typical of grand opera. The music heralds the wedding of Rivoli and Bianca. And now it is Giuseppe's turn to call on Sormano, insensate with grief, to wreak vengeance on their enemies. They add their voices to the chorus of conspirators in an expression of their bloodthirsty desire for revenge. (The draft and finished libretto are largely identical here.)

Kittl's libretto omits the failed assault on the fort at Saorgio which forms the third-act finale in Wagner's prose draft, so that we discover only its repercussions, namely, that Giuseppe and Sormano have been taken prisoner and sentenced to death. The fourth act in Wagner's prose draft and the corresponding third act in Kittl's opera deal with Clara's successful—and lavishly theatrical—attempt to save the two prisoners. Her unrequited love for Giuseppe constitutes a subplot that we may conveniently pass over here in order to move quickly to the final act, set outside the cathedral in Nice, where the wedding between Rivoli and Bianka is on the point of being solemnized. The ceremony ends with the death of both of them when Rivoli is murdered by Sormano, and Bianka, who prior to the service had taken poison, dies in Giuseppe's arms. In the meantime the French have marched victoriously into the city.

Up to this point the action of the final act has been more or less the same in both prose draft and libretto. In the final scene of all, however, the two once again diverge fundamentally. In Kittl's opera Bianca dies, imploring Giuseppe: "Go, fight for your country and die with honor," which he duly does.

> Zu meines Königs Fahnen
> kehr' reuig ich zurück,
> und such' auf blut'gen Bahnen
> den Tod, mein einzig Glück.
>
> (SS 11:176–77)
>
> [My liege's flag once more
> I ruefully enclasp
> And seek, imbrued with gore,
> The welcome of death's grasp.]

The chorus repeats these lines, changing the first person into the third. Remarkably, Kittl's opera bypasses Wagner's draft at this point and goes back, at least in part, to Koenig's novel, in which Giuseppe again becomes a royalist, even bringing home his "high-born" bride, who, in this version, has thoughtfully refrained from taking poison. Of course, this happy ending—which is at odds with the novel's underlying liberalism—is not taken over by the libretto, where Giuseppe, brandishing his sword, rushes toward the French soldiers as they surge onto the stage and is struck down by a single bullet. The ending of the prose draft, following Bianka's death, is strikingly different:

As Clara runs in, Giuseppe sinks into her arms with a terrible cry. At the same time a cannon shot is heard from the citadel,—the cry quickly goes up: "The French!

The French!"—To the sound of military music & the singing of the Marseillaise, the French army enters with flags waving, while the tricolor can be seen fluttering in the distance on the fortress at Saorgio.—Tableaux.

The action ends with the private tragedy of the revolutionaries, but the Revolution is not affected by it, as was the case with Auber's *La muette de Portici*. Rather, the Revolution triumphs unequivocally, a triumph compellingly embodied in the singing of the Marseillaise, even if the protagonists are trampled underfoot in the process. The symbolic value and appeal of the Marseillaise was still so great in the early nineteenth century that—as Wagner no doubt reckoned—it was impossible for audiences to distance themselves from it. A scene in which the whole cast joined collectively in the Marseillaise could elicit only a positive response. (During the revolutionary era, the Marseillaise was regularly sung by Parisian audiences not only before performances in the city's theaters but also during the intervals and even at particularly patriotic moments in the action. This custom even caught on for a time in Germany: as late as 1848 opera audiences in Frankfurt insisted on singing the Marseillaise at the end of a performance of *La muette de Portici*. As the *Allgemeine musikalische Zeitung* reported, "The orchestra duly obliged, and the chorus of Neapolitans struck up enthusiastically with 'Allons enfants!' ")[27]

In the grand operas of the period, the death of the mutinous hero was regularly associated with some disaster, natural or otherwise, but, as we have seen, this is not the case with *Die hohe Braut*. Instead of a volcanic eruption or a palace collapsing in ruins, we have a revolutionary tableau that would have been unthinkable on the boards of the Paris Opéra. The fine balance between the work's revolutionary contents and a pessimistic interpretation of those contents such as we find in Meyerbeer's mature operas is one that we look for in vain in Wagner's draft. In contrast to those works that set the tone of French grand opera, the rebel's tragic end does not in any way reflect the failure of the (revolutionary) cause that he espouses. Rather, this cause emerges victorious, in trenchant contrast to its hero's private fate. The dialectic relationship between private and political actions that has been taken over from grand opera ultimately falls apart here.

This is also true, *mutatis mutandis*, of Kittl's opera. Whereas the Revolution is warmly embraced in Wagner's prose draft, the defeat of the royalist Savoyard army is viewed in the opera as an altogether terrifying event, with the French invasion being seen as a very real disaster, and although a new order, with all its unknown terrors, triumphs over the old one, there is no sense in which the hero's downfall implies any criticism of the new order. In this, the ending of Kittl's opera differs from the final scenes of the grand operas mentioned earlier.

In Kittl's opera, the emphatically revolutionary thrust of Wagner's prose draft, already toned down in its French version of 1840, has been replaced by an emphatically reactionary one. What was Wagner's reaction to this? In a letter to Kittl of 4 January 1848, he writes as follows, evidently in full knowledge of his friend's reworked libretto.

What distresses me most is the alteration that has been made to the ending. Do you know what the ending of an opera is?—*Everything*! I had very much reckoned on the ending being violently stirring and tempestuously fast-moving; the terrible catastrophe that overtakes the characters as they are leaving the church should not be mitigated in any way,—all that we should be left with is the terrible sense of sublimity inspired by the workings of the world's great destiny, here personified in the French revolutionary army, which marches in, in dreadful splendor, over the ruins of old (family) relationships. In my view this allusion should in no way be toned down if the ending is to remain, as I conceived it to be, the most sublime moment of the whole work; if it is retained in the form in which I conceived it, the great sense of reconciliation inspired by the appearance of the French will lie in the fact that what we see entering here before our very eyes is a new world order whose birth pangs were the sufferings that up to this point had invested the drama with its forward momentum.[28]

In other words, Wagner reasserts his faith in the revolutionary final scene that he had drafted a good ten years earlier. Nor is it surprising that he should do so. After all, these lines to Kittl were written in 1848. Only a few months later Wagner was to write his *Greeting from Saxony to the Viennese* in which he celebrates Vienna's March Revolution in highly rhapsodic terms:

> Aus Frankreich scholl der Freiheitsruf:
> wir haben ihn nachgesprochen;
> die Bande, die uns Knechtschaft schuf,
> sie werd' von uns zerbrochen.
> . . . .
>
> Das war im Anfang Lobes wert;
> uns trieb die Tat des Franken,
> in unsrer Hand das Freiheitsschwert,
> ihm hatten wir's zu danken.[29]

(SS 12:358)

> [In France the cry of liberty rang out
> And back again its echo thundered;
> Bonds that hateful slavery had wrought
> Must needs by each of us be sundered.
> . . . .
>
> At first this earned our praise, when we,
> Encouraged by the doughty Frank,
> The sword of freedom held aloft
> And knew 'twas him we had to thank.]

At about the same time as this, Wagner addressed a petition to Franz Jacob Wigard, a member of the Frankfurt National Assembly, in which he made a number of demands, including "arming the populace" and a "defensive and offensive alliance" with France. Refractory princes should be "indicted," he wrote.[30] The following year, Wagner himself mounted the barricades in Dresden.

The revolution of 1848–89 is already foreshadowed in Wagner's letter to Kittl, in which he draws on the high-flown language of revolutionary rhetoric and speaks of the "workings of the world's great destiny" sweeping away the "old order" in its "dreadful splendor" and creating a "new order." Similar sentiments occur in a paean to the revolution that appeared in August Röckel's *Volksblätter* on 8 April 1849 and that was probably penned by Wagner himself.

> Yes, we see that the old world is crumbling away and that a *new* one will arise from it, for the sublime goddess Revolution comes surging along on the wings of the storm ..., the eternally rejuvenating mother of all mankind..., and wherever her mighty foot comes to rest, all that an idle whim had built for eons falls in ruins, and the hem of her garment sweeps its last remnants away! (SS 12:245–46)

The note struck by Wagner in his letter to Kittl seems merely to have alarmed his correspondent, who clearly had half an eye cast anxiously in the direction of the censor's office, with the result that he ignored all of Wagner's suggestions for revising the opera's finale. Evidently Kittl found the act of "treason" committed by a hero called Giuseppe who hails from Savoy so despicable that he wanted to see him somehow purged of it, whereas for Wagner it was "altogether unimportant, so affecting is this ending."

> But if you insist on this point [that is, that "Giuseppe should not be dismissed with the reproach of high treason hanging over him"], at least let it be sorted out as quickly as possible:—let him pick himself up with the cry: "Close the gates! The French!" and, with the expression of a man who, seized by insane despair, is determined to die at all costs, let him shout out to the people, "Follow me, if you love your king!"

It is a suggestion remarkably reminiscent of the end of Büchner's *Dantons Tod*, where Lucile, following the death of her husband, Camille, provokes her own arrest by calling out "Long live the king!" In both cases we are dealing with a desperate act that has nothing to do, of course, with the sort of rueful return to the king's colors with which Kittl rounds off his opera.

> But for heaven's sake, let's have no *longueurs* here, nothing tender or soulful; from the moment we hear the cry of terror already described, there should be no further interruptions of any length; from now on the final torrent has been unleashed, which nothing can hold back if its touching impact is not to go completely cold.[31]

This, then, was Wagner's advice to Kittl, advice that, as we know, went unheeded. Instead of the above, Kittl offers an extended choral finale with what—in view of the impending arrival of the French troops—is bound to appear an absurdly implausible hymn in praise of the "rueful" Giuseppe. Above all, Kittl must have been alarmed by Wagner's insistence that the work should end with the Marseillaise. "If the censor refuses to let you use the Marseillaise, you must extemporize something else like it.—I implore you to heed my well-meaning advice!"[32] Of course, Wagner was wasting his breath, and his plans for a revolutionary opera were stranded on the shoals of reaction.

In the case of *Die hohe Braut*, Wagner got no further than completing the libretto of a planned grand opera, whereas his next operatic project also drew on his skills as a composer. This was the comic opera *Männerlist größer als Frauenlist oder: Die glückliche Bärenfamilie* (Men's cunning greater than women's cunning, or The happy family of bears, WWV 49). Dating from 1838, it was intended as a comic counterpart to the tragic *Die hohe Braut*, its reminiscences of the ancien régime in stark contrast to the revolutionary thrust of the earlier work. Its libretto represents Wagner's only attempt to explore the world of the number opera with spoken dialogue in the style of the French opéra comique and German *Spieloper* of the Biedermeier period.[33] Its source is one of the tales that make up the *Arabian Nights*, although, to quote Wagner's autobiography, the action was transferred from Baghdad and relocated "in our own time and in modern costume" (ML 145). What attracted him to the subject was once again the possibility of lampooning the aristocracy in the spirit of the Young German movement. In *My Life*, he notes that he had imagined a degenerate aristocratic society "made up of the elite of the most stuck-up French émigrés from the time of the Revolution" (ML 145). Although he completed the libretto (it is the only one of his unfinished operas to survive in an authentic form), he abandoned the music after sketching the first three numbers, a decision that in his 1843 "Autobiographical Sketch" he attributed to his "horrified" discovery that he was "once again on the way to composing music à la Auber." When he revised this essay in 1871 for republication within the framework of the collected edition of his works, he changed Auber's name to Adolphe Adam (GS 1:12), presumably because in the meantime he had come to think more highly of Auber's music. Not until 1994 did the composition sketch of the first three numbers come to light. The introduction is a strictly symmetrical number with an orchestral prelude and postlude framing a section for chorus and soloists; the other two numbers are a duet and a fragmentary trio. All three numbers are influenced less by the French comic operas of the period than by Rossini, whose *Barbiere di Siviglia* (Barber of Seville) is quoted almost literally in the trio's descending triplets.[34]

From Cola di Rienzo to Rienzi

Wagner's third complete stage work was written between 1837 and 1840 and is coeval, therefore, with *Die hohe Braut* and the satyr play *Die glückliche Bärenfamilie* (The happy family of bears). Described by Wagner himself as a "grand tragic opera in five acts," *Rienzi, der Letzte der Tribunen* WWV 49 (Rienzi, the last of the tribunes) was again based on a historical novel, this time Edward Bulwer-Lytton's *Rienzi: The Last of the Roman Tribunes* (1835), which Wagner read in 1837 in one of two German translations that had appeared the previous year. The first prose sketch was drafted immediately afterward and was followed in 1838 by a detailed prose draft and the libretto. In the case of *Die hohe Braut*, Wagner evidently preferred not to start work on the score until he had received a commission from the Académie Royale de Musique, but it is clear from the musical sketches in the first draft of the libretto that he envisaged his own musical setting of *Rienzi* from the very beginning. He started work on the score on the day after he finished the libretto, completing it in Paris in November 1840.[35]

Rienzi opens with a near riot. The curtain rises on a street close to the basilica of the Lateran. It is night. Orsini and several of the *nobili* are in the process of abducting Irene, the sister of the papal notary Cola Rienzi, but they are surprised by Steffano and Adriano Colonna. The Orsinis and the Colonnas are long-standing enemies, and their representatives, together with all the other nobili whom they have in tow, draw their swords on each other. The townspeople gather around the combatants and, fired by their own private hatreds, attack both parties in turn, ignoring the papal legate and his attempts to restore calm. At this point Rienzi enters, and the fighting stops at once, with even the nobili rooted to the spot by the notary's "commanding presence," in spite of their contempt for the "plebeian" (GS 1:33) whose sister they are in the process of abducting.[36] In an impassioned address, Rienzi blames the nobili for Rome's ruin, earning only their scorn for his—historically attested—oratory.

> Das alte Rom, die Königin der Welt,
> Macht ihr zur Räuberhöhle, schändet selbst
> Die Kirche; Petri Stuhl muß flüchten
> Zum fernen Avignon;—kein Pilger wagt's,
> Nach Rom zu zieh'n, zum hohen Völkerfeste,
> Denn ihr belagert, Räubern gleich, die Wege;—
> Verödet, arm—versiegt das stolze Rom,
> Und was dem Ärmsten blieb, das raubt ihr ihm,
> Brecht Dieben gleich, in seine Läden ein,
> Entehrt die Weiber, erschlagt die Männer:—
> Blickt um euch denn, und *seht*, wo ihr dieß treibt!
> Seht, jene Tempel, jene Säulen sagen euch:
> Es ist das alte, freie, große Rom,
> Das einst die Welt beherrschte, dessen Bürger
> Könige der Könige sich nannten!—
> Banditen, ha! sagt mir, giebt es noch Römer?
>
> (GS 1:36)

> [Our ancient Rome, the queen of all the world,
> You've turned into a robbers' cave, the church
> You desecrate, and force the Holy See
> To distant Avignon; no pilgrim dares
> To come to Rome's high festivals, for you,
> Like highwaymen, besiege the paths they'd take.
> Deserted, poor—the once-proud city dies.
> The pauper's last remaining crumbs you steal
> From him and, thieflike, break into his shops.
> You violate our women, kill our men.
> Now look around and see the harm you've caused!
> The temples and the columns plainly state
> That here you see the free and ancient Rome
> That once subdued the world. Her citizens
> Could call themselves the kings of kings!
> Ha! Bandits! Say if Romans still exist.]

This introductory scene, with Irene's attempted abduction, is neither historically authenticated nor part of Wagner's main source, Bulwer-Lytton's novel, where we find, rather, a related episode: here the Orsini plan to violate Rienzi's sister but are prevented from doing so by Adriano. Rienzi does not appear in this scene. Nonetheless, this turbulent opening captures to perfection the conditions that obtained in Rome in the early fourteenth century; contemporary sources paint a somber portrait of a city abandoned by its papal rulers and sinking into a state of chaos and anarchy at the hands of the predatory, pillaging, and fractious robber barons.

At the same time, the Roman citizens had lost none of their ancient faith in "Roma aeterna," so firmly convinced were they that of all the great cities in history, Rome alone had the power to keep on renewing itself and to rise up again like a phoenix from the ashes.[37] The municipal pride of the citizens found expression in the Senate, which was revived in 1144 as the *sacer senatus*, when it claimed for itself the right to choose its own king. As a result of this King Heinrich VII of Germany was invited to Rome by the local citizenry in 1312 and crowned in the Lateran in the face of fierce opposition from the cardinals who represented the pope. (The Lateran was used because the Vatican was occupied by the Guelphs.) An even more powerful demonstration of municipal sovereignty came in 1328 with the coronation of Heinrich's successor, King Ludwig of Bavaria, who had been excommunicated by the pope fulminating from his retreat in Avignon. Neither here nor in the case of the historical Cola di Rienzo was the papal ban the terrible magic weapon that it appeared to be in the eyes of both Wagner and the writer and dramatist Julius Mosen, whose tragedy on the same theme we shall consider in a moment; when the ban of excommunication is proclaimed by the papal legate at the end of act 4, the populace flees in horror from the tribune that it had once worshiped. By the following act they are hurling stones and burning torches at their "curse-laden" leader (GS 1:87). In fact, the Roman people's repudiation of the historical Cola di Rienzo and his subsequent murder were unrelated to the ban of excommunication (which was in any case later rescinded) but were mainly the result of the high level of taxes that he tried to levy on them. Squeezing the taxpayer is not, however, the sort of motif that would cut much ice in a historical opera.[38]

Legend has it that following his coronation in the Lateran in 1312, Heinrich VII wanted to visit Saint Peter's, where the ceremony should by rights have taken place but which was occupied by the opposing Guelphs. In the event, he was betrayed and forced to flee to a tavern, where he enjoyed the wine and other pleasures afforded by the landlord's wife, the landlord himself being conveniently absent. The following year saw not only the death of Heinrich VII but also the birth—in the same tavern—of a man who for more than five centuries was to be a symbol of Roman pride and the idea of national unity: Cola di Rienzo. The son of an innkeeper and a washerwoman, he owed his charismatic reputation to the rumor that he was of imperial birth. He himself was convinced that the rumor was true and was able to persuade the rest of the world, including even King Charles IV, that this was so, adducing it as an argument in his long-running battle with the

Roman aristocracy, who repeatedly sought to humiliate him with their references to his low birth.

At the age of twenty, Rienzo witnessed for himself the anarchy that prevailed in Rome at this time, when his favorite brother was murdered, sowing the seeds of the hatred that he bore the Colonnas, who, following the murder, refused to accord him justice. This hatred culminated in 1354 in his own murder and the despoliation of his body. Wagner's Rienzi alludes to this in his first scene: "You murder our own brothers—tender boys—/ and long to violate our sisters too!" (GS 1:36).

Three factors determined the course of Rienzo's life: his own prophetic belief in his political mission (a belief grounded in his conviction that he was of imperial extraction); his indignation at social conditions in Rome as a result of the misrule of the nobili; and his enthusiasm for Roman antiquity. Rienzo studied rhetoric and jurisprudence, acquiring in the process a lasting reputation as an important Humanist scholar with a particular interest in inscriptions. His historical and antiquarian studies were all aimed at reviving ancient Roman ideals. Remarkably, he succeeded in investing antiquarian scholarship with a popular appeal by treating it as the subject of, and inspiration behind, his brilliant public speeches. With his impassioned appeal to the monuments of classical antiquity that were increasingly falling into ruin, overgrown with grass and weeds and overrun with goats, and by explaining Latin inscriptions and interpreting works of sculpture, he filled his fellow Romans with a very real enthusiasm for past glories, recalling their lost rights and freedoms and opening the prospect of a future free from oppression and suffering.

In act 2 of Wagner's opera, Rienzi stages a great pantomime depicting the rape of Lucretia and Tarquinius's expulsion from Rome. In much the same way, the historical Rienzo would prepare the largely illiterate Roman people for the city's rebirth by showing them scenes from its republican past. Here Wagner was little less than inspired in his ability to combine three historical phenomena: first, there is Rienzo's method of teaching by example, whereby he sought to introduce his ideas to the as yet illiterate populace by representational means; second, this method was revived at the time of the French Revolution, which typically saw itself in terms of Republican Rome, with its leaders attempting to appeal to their again largely illiterate audience by means of highly effective and visually striking images; and third, we have the subculture of the French boulevard pantomime, which Wagner may be said to have ennobled by introducing it into a grand opera, a point brilliantly illustrated by Hans Lietzau in his 1983 Munich production of the opera. (Here, too, one suspects the formal influence of *La muette de Portici*, whose heroine participates in the action only through mime. Auber's work was in fact originally intended as a comic opera, a genre not too far removed from the boulevard pantomime in terms of the social hierarchy of the theater, whereas the marriage of grand opera and mime was a misalliance from the outset.)

It is significant that in choosing Lucretia and Brutus as the theme of his pantomime, Wagner was harking back to one of the most popular Roman subjects of the revolutionary period. When Brutus raises his sword aloft "with a heroic gesture" and vows to end the tyrant's reign, a vow that is then repeated by his fellow conspirators (GS 1:57), it is impossible not to recall the oaths that were sworn either in real life or in representational form at the time of the French Revolution, from the Tennis Court Oath of 20 June 1789 to Jacques-Louis David's *Oath of the Horatii* of 1784. (Also of relevance here is the oath on the Rütli in Schiller's and Rossini's *William Tell*, a scene likewise indebted to the formal oaths of the French Revolution.) As we know, the dumb show in Wagner's *Rienzi* outstripped the resources of the contemporary theater and had to be replaced by the usual ballet. Indeed, it is clear not only from this particular incident but, more especially, from the Venusberg scene in *Tannhäuser* that however much Wagner may have been fascinated by the genre, he had no luck with these mimed scenes within the theater of his own day. (Similar, if briefer, scenes include the dumb show between Siegmund and Sieglinde in act 1 of *Die Walküre*, Brünnhilde's awakening in *Siegfried*, and Beckmesser's arrival in Sachs's workshop in act 3 of *Die Meistersinger*.)

But let us return to the historical Rienzo. In 1342 he visited Clement VI in Avignon as an emissary of the people's party and impressed the pope with his princely manners and infectious oratory. The following year he was appointed papal notary in Rome, an appointment that he used systematically to turn the populace against the *barone*, as the aristocrats were called. As part of his plan, he lulled the leading aristocratic families into a false sense of security, even playing the part of the court fool at their tables. This aspect of his personality is similarly mentioned in the opera: "Ha ha! The fool! Laugh him out of court!" exclaim the nobili on his first appearance (GS 1:37). And after Rienzi has seized power, Steffano Colonna complains about "the plebeian whom I once kept at table for my sport" (GS 1:51). Rienzo staged his bloodless coup d'état in 1347, a highly opportune moment in terms of both foreign and domestic policy, as the leading aristocratic families were not in Rome at the time. With the agreement of the papal legate, he occupied the Capitol and invited the citizenry to attend a parliamentary assembly the following Whitsunday, the choice of date again dictated by his keen sense of the symbolic significance of particular times, signs, and places.

This is the historical background of the final scene in Wagner's opening act, a scene introduced by the famous sustained a' on the onstage trumpet (GS 1:46). Here, too, Rienzi's putsch is made easier for him by the absence of the leading aristocratic families, even if the reasons for that absence are operatically inauthentic: the Orsinis and Colonnas are still arguing over the abortive abduction of Irene and have now resorted to an armed struggle outside the gates of the city. In the following scene, Wagner has condensed the events of several months into a single day. Here Rienzi refuses to accept the title of king, justifying his refusal as follows:

> Nicht also! Frei wollt' ich euch haben!—
> Die heil'ge Kirche herrsche hier,[39]
> Gesetze gebe ein Senat.
> Doch wählet ihr zum Schützer mich

> Der Rechte, die dem Volk erkannt,
> So blickt auf eure Ahnen hin,
> Und nennt mich euren Volkstribun.
>
> (GS 1:48)

> [Not so! I wished you to be free!—
> The Holy Church alone shall reign,
> The Senate shall ordain your laws.
> But if you want me to protect
> The rights that you, the folk, espouse,
> Then take your forebears as your guide:
> Appoint me tribune of the people!]

Rienzi regards himself as a mere servant of the law to which every citizen should be "subservient" (GS 1:47). But the first rule is the freedom of all Romans. In consequence, he rejects the cult of his own person, a rejection uncharacteristic of his historical prototype, who, given the fourteenth-century background, could conceive of Rome only as an imperial state. Wagner's Rienzi insists: "The greatness of both peace and of the law / You should acknowledge, not my own" (GS 1:51).

Rienzo's first period in power lasted a mere seven months, but during this time he succeeded in restoring peace to the city, a peace that generations of popes and emperors had sought but failed to achieve. His great program of municipal reform, especially his reorganization of the army and his thoroughgoing changes to the judiciary and to the city's financial system, had far-reaching consequences in spite of Rienzo's own failure. Indeed, he was even successful in integrating the most powerful aristocratic families into his new and more peaceful order. Nor was he content merely to regenerate the city; he also wanted to restore it to its former glory as *caput mundi* (head of the world) and to found a *universa sacra Italia* (sacred universal Italy) with Rome as its head. He pursued this aim by sending messengers of peace to the various city-states in Italy that were keen to enter into an allegiance with Rome and that wanted diplomatic and military support. The result of these efforts is seen in the opening scene of act 2 of *Rienzi*, which depicts the messengers' return. Petrarch was friendly with Rienzo and in a series of open letters lent his impassioned support to the idea of an "Italia una" (united Italy). In these letters he celebrated Rienzo's achievements in stirring lethargic Rome from her deathly slumbers and, apostrophizing him with the heroic names of Rome's glorious past—Romulus, Brutus, and Camillus—hailed him as a savior who had restored liberty and peace to Rome.

Yet within only a few months, Rienzo's star had begun to set. The main reason seems to have been the haste with which he sought to implement his far-reaching political goals. Appealing to the Roman citizens' unique right to elect their own emperor, he invited the German princes to Rome to set forth their claims. (There is a reference to this in the opening scene of act 4, where Cecco complains, "We owe this to the arrogance with which Rienzi denied the German princes the right to elect the Roman emperor"; GS 1:76).

Although, as we shall see, Rienzo never denied the rights of the Holy See, Pope Clement VI saw his own claims to power threatened by Rienzo's imperious manner, to say nothing of his declaration of independence (taking all of Italy with him) and his strict exercise of power. He also denounced Rienzo's reintroduction of the triumphal rites and gestures of the past and the lavish and symbolic show of power, dismissing them as a revival of heathen practices. Certainly, Rienzo was misled by his knowledge of antiquity into interpreting his role and each of his political acts as inspired in part by Roman antiquity and in part by biblical ideas. To this frame of typological reference he was able to give striking visual and rhetorical expression by means of words, images, and ceremonial rituals. Nothing lacked symbolic significance, with each of his official actions revealing a Roman or Judeo-Christian prototype. In his attempts to invest his rule with symbolic resonance, he risked provoking even his staunchest supporters, most notably when he bathed in the font of the emperor Constantine, prevailed on the Roman people to dub him Knight of the Holy Ghost, or had himself crowned Tribunus Augustus. Although Wagner played down these historically authenticated aspects of his hero's behavior in order to portray him as a selfless champion of Roman idealism and as a mere servant of the law opposed to the cult of his own personality, he did not entirely eliminate the tribune's love of imperious pomp from his picture of Rienzi as a person. At the beginning of act 2, for example, Rienzi appears "as tribune, dressed in fantastical and luxurious clothes" (GS 1:49), and at the end of act 3, he mounts a "triumphal car and is led away by the people" (GS 1:75).

A series of serious political misjudgments increasingly undermined Rienzo's position. He forfeited the goodwill of the patrician families by his undiplomatic actions and by arbitrarily arresting a number of their leading members, whom he falsely suspected of harboring murderous designs against him and whom he was forced to pardon at the last minute. If Rienzi's actions seem magnanimous at the end of act 2, when he pardons the nobili in response to pleas for clemency on the part of Adriano and Irene, the same cannot be said of his historical counterpart, whose actions were prompted by his desire to avoid an act of judicial murder. The Roman barons were so angered by Rienzo's arbitrary actions that led by Colonna, they raised an army and, encouraged by the fact that the pope had turned against his erstwhile representative in Rome, confronted Rienzo's Militia of the Holy Ghost at Porta San Lorenzo on 20 November 1347, only to see themselves comprehensively routed, with the Colonnas especially suffering the most annihilating defeat. (These events form the background of Wagner's third act.) In the eyes of many historians this battle marked the first victory of the idea of an Italian state over the feudal power of the Roman barons, who, in spite of Rienzo's subsequent downfall, were unable to win back their power.

In Wagner's opera, Rienzi addresses the dependents of those who have been killed in battle.

> Jungfrauen, weinet! Ihr Weiber, klaget!
> Wehrt nicht der Tränen heiligem Strom!
> Doch euren Herzen tröstend auch saget!
> Die wir[40] verloren, fielen für Rom!

(GS 1:73)

[You virgins, weep! You wives, lament!
Don't stanch the holy flood of tears!
But let your hearts be comforted:
The men we've lost all fell for Rome!]

The historical Rienzo was far less magnanimous than this and paid no heed whatsoever to the "holy flood of tears," refusing even to allow the bodies of the slain to be buried in the Colonnas' family vault at Ara Coeli and driving away their grieving widows. A few days later he summoned his Sacra Militia and, to the blare of trumpets, returned to the scene of the battle. There, according to the fourteenth-century *Vita di Cola di Rienzo*, he bade his son dismount and, taking some ditch water mixed with the blood of the dead Colonna, asperged his son with it and thus dubbed him a Knight of Victory. The author of the *Vita* tells this story with palpable disgust and reports that the Roman people likewise balked at this gruesome ritual.

But this brilliant victory could not stop Rienzo's star from continuing its downward trajectory, as his position became increasingly untenable as a result of problems both at home and abroad: the death of the emperor Ludwig of Bavaria; the failure of his attempts to unite the country as a result of conflicting interests among the Italian cities; the opposition of the pope; conflicts with his own supporters; and, not least, the complaints of the Roman townspeople about his ostentation and their crippling burden of taxes. All these factors conspired to force Rienzo to abdicate and to flee from Rome on 15 December 1347, less than a month after his victory over the Colonnas.

For the next two years Rienzo avoided his papal pursuers by living as a hermit in the Abruzzi and, like Joachim of Floris, hoping for the dawn of a new age of the spirit. In this context, it is worth reminding ourselves of Konrad Burdach's comments in his monumental documentary study of Rienzo.

> Rienzo is the contemporary of the spiritualists and flagellants, and of the apocalyptic prophets of both sexes. The Rome that acclaimed him and tore him apart was also the home of Saint Bridget and Saint Catherine of Siena, both of whom preached the gospel of religious politics. He was a visionary, and in that respect he resembled both these women.[41]

The chiliastic visions of this period contain frequent references to the return of the Hohenstaufen emperor Friedrich II, a third Friedrich, who, like his historical predecessor, would be a Divus Augustus and Caesar Augustus and would restore Rome to its former greatness, making it the capital and center of a new Roman empire. Rienzo, too, hoped that the emperor would usher in a new age. In 1350 he traveled to Prague to enlist the support of the emperor Charles IV in his campaign against Rome. But unlike his predecessors, the new king hoped to acquire the crown not through the people of Rome but through the pope. "The new emperor gets on with the pope," Baroncelli comments in act 4 of Wagner's *Rienzi*, where the king is already described as the emperor (GS 1:76). Charles IV detained Rienzo in Prague, keeping him under a kind of house arrest that allowed him to maintain contact with German Humanists, notably Johannes von Neumarkt, and to continue his prolific correspondence. It is clear, not least from Burdach's researches, that through his speeches, letters, and personal influence, Rienzo played an important role in the early history of Humanism in Germany.

In 1352 Rienzo was handed over to Pope Clement VI and, following a spectacular journey through Germany, delivered to the Curia in Avignon. Rienzo was a thorn in Clement's side, not least because he wanted the latter to combat the growing secularization of the church and to return to Rome, a city that, in the circumstances, could hardly have been more unwelcoming. As a result, Clement was in no hurry to institute proceedings against Rome's dethroned liberator. But Clement's successor, Innocent VI, who was pope from 18 December 1352 to 12 September 1362 and who immediately set himself the task of combating the secularization of the church as the *ecclesia carnalis*, fully rehabilitated the former tribune with whose views he was in sympathy, even confirming him in his title of Knight of the Holy Ghost and sending him back to Rome as papal senator.

Throughout his arrest, Rienzo had repeatedly described himself as "dormiens in sepulcro" (sleeping in his tomb),[42] the "sepulcrum" being his life as a hermit in the Abruzzi and his imprisonment in Prague. But he was convinced that, like Christ, he would rise from the dead and emerge from his tomb. Behind the image of the man sleeping in his tomb is the belief that God reveals himself to the elect in caves hidden away in wild mountain fastnesses, just as he once did to Elijah and to Saint Francis in the *carceri* of the Monte Subasio near Assisi.

And Rienzo's prophetic announcement of his resurrection now came true in the form of his return to Rome and resumption of the reins of power. On 1 August 1354, seven years to the day since he had proclaimed the sovereignty of the Roman people, Rienzo returned to Rome as a papal senator, acclaimed by scenes of unprecedented jubilation and passing through triumphal arches and a veritable sea of olive branches. But in the meantime the former favorite of the people had grown fat, and illness had driven him to drink; arbitrary legal decisions, unscrupulous financial measures, and burdensome taxes very soon proved his downfall. The Colonnas were still brooding on ways of avenging their defeat at the Porta San Lorenzo, and on 3 October 1354 they succeeded in fomenting a popular uprising against Rienzo. Fleeing from the burning Capitol, he was recognized by his gold bracelets and murdered. Covered only with the remnants of his once magnificent costume and lacerated by the blows of a thousand swords and daggers, his body was dragged through the city, with his feet tied together, after which his head was torn off and his brain spattered over the street. For two days his mutilated body hung in the Piazza San Marcello like that of a slaughtered animal, a target for the stones of passing street urchins. Contemporary accounts go on to report that in an act of gruesome symbolism, the leaders of the Colonna family then ordered the decaying body of the Tribunus Augustus to be taken to the Campo dell'Austa, or Augustus Square, a place that had symbolized Rienzo's dream of Italy's rebirth and of a new Augustan age of universal peace. Here the barbarically desecrated remains of the man who in the eyes of the civilized world had long been a credit to the human race were handed over to the Jews, who burned him on a pile of dry thistles and scattered his ashes to the four winds. His humiliation was complete.

No one suffered more than Petrarch at the shameful end of so dear a friend. He had celebrated Rienzo's years in power with a whole series of enthusiastic open letters and poetic epistles, only latterly striking a more dubious and critical note. When Rienzo was forced to abdicate, he continued to represent his case at the Curia in Avignon while reproaching him for his weakness and for abandoning his earlier program of reforms. Rienzo's repeated flight from Rome did not square with the heroic picture that he had devised for him. The hero's death in the burning Capitol, with which Wagner's opera ends, would undoubtedly have suited his Humanistic taste somewhat better.

The nobles and the rabble had, between them, brought about Rienzo's fall from power, but the memory of his brilliant rule was kept alive among Rome's middle classes. The twentieth of May—the date on which he came to power—was declared a public holiday under the municipal laws of 1363, laws for which Rienzo had helped to pave the way. At the same time, however, historians took little interest in him as a figure, and not until 1624 was the *Vita di Cola di Rienzo* unearthed and printed. A life by the French Jesuit Jacques Androuet dit du Cerceau invested Rienzo with the negative features of charlatanism, megalomania, morbid ambition, and even madness, also found in Schiller's 1788 *Geschichte der merkwürdigsten Rebellionen und Verschwörungen* (History of the most remarkable rebellions and conspiracies); they remain indissolubly associated with him even today, in spite of the researches of Zefino Re (1828), Felix Papencordt (1841), and, in particular, Konrad Burdach and Paul Piur. Burdach and Piur's edition of Rienzo's correspondence (1912–29) includes not only a wealth of contemporary documentation but also Burdach's own comprehensive account of Rienzo's life and times, an account that ought to have rendered untenable the anachronistic blackening of Rienzo's character that is still occasionally found.

The literary rediscovery of Rienzo coincided—significantly—with the French Revolution, whose cult of Republican Rome made it particularly susceptible to Rienzo's idealized vision of Rome, and his struggle with the nobili inevitably seemed to reflect its own ideals. The first drama on the subject of Rienzo is the work of the Jacobin François Laignelot and dates from 1791, and the earliest English adaptation is Mary Russell Mitford's 1825 tragedy *Rienzi*. Mitford's play was familiar to Edward Bulwer-Lytton, whose novelistic account of Rienzo's life, the three-volume *Rienzi: The Last of the Roman Tribunes* (1835), proved hugely successful not only in the English-speaking world but also in Europe and unleashed a veritable flood tide of dramatizations in Italy, France and especially Germany. The two most important versions in German are Wagner's five-act opera, in which Rienzo's two periods in power, in 1347 and 1354, are telescoped together, and Julius Mosen's tragedy *Cola Rienzi*, which was written independently of Wagner's, although it received its first performance in the same year (1842). Wagner, by his own admission, thought "very highly" of Mosen's work (ML 234), and there is no doubt that *Cola Rienzi* is an estimable piece. Finally, in 1974, the world of literary scholarship was surprised to learn of the existence of an operatic fragment, liberally annotated with drawings, that the young Friedrich Engels had written in 1841.[43] This, too, was clearly inspired by Bulwer-Lytton's novel, to which I shall return in a moment.

In *My Life*, Wagner claims that his Dresden rival Julius Mosen was unable to accept the spectacular success of his own opera on the same subject and that consumed by bile and envy, he made disparaging comments about the literary qualities of the libretto, even though Wagner himself had acknowledged that Mosen had "treated the material in a way that was in part new and, I thought, most affecting. And so I asked him to pay no attention to my own libretto, since, as a poem, it could not possibly be compared to his; he did not have much difficulty acceding to this request," Wagner adds with scarcely suppressed irony. Mosen had been associated with the Young German movement, and the aggressively anticlerical thrust of his play, with its tendentiously simplistic and even antihistorical approach to its subject, meant that he had considerable difficulties with the Dresden censor. According to Wagner, Mosen was particularly resentful of the fact that the censor had raised no objections to his opera, because in an opera "no one pays any attention to the words" (ML 247).

The source of all these dramatizations was Bulwer's *Rienzi*, a historical novel in the Romantic tradition of Sir Walter Scott. Although Bulwer idealizes his hero in a number of ways, he is careful not to gloss over his negative characteristics. His account of the historical background rests on a close study of the sources and strives for the greatest possible authenticity, even though he introduces a number of fictional episodes. In his quest for historical objectivity, he also attempts to be fair to Rienzi's enemies, even to Fra Monreale, the feared leader of the bandits and mercenaries, whom Rienzi executes during his second period in office. (The scene in which he condemns him to death forms the gripping climax of Mosen's virtuoso tragedy.)

Monreale is also one of the main characters in Engels's unfinished drama, where he is romanticized in much the same way as he is in Bulwer's novel. Just as in Wagner's *Rienzi*, the motivating force behind the drama is Adriano Colonna's desire for revenge, so Engels's tragedy revolves around the character of Monreale's lover, Camilla Colonna, and her attempts to avenge his death. This love affair between an aristocrat and the leader of a band of brigands frequently risks upstaging the actual hero and encourages the spectator to sympathize with Camilla and Monreale even though they are guilty of betraying Rienzi. Here Engels follows directly in Bulwer's footsteps, even though Rienzi himself remains the figure with whom Engels most closely identifies. At least to the extent that we can draw any conclusions from the fragmentary nature of the draft, Rienzi is the victim of revenge, betrayal, and hostility on the part of the common people, who are stirred up against him by the calumnies of the aristocracy. The second scene in act 2 begins with the following monologue:

> Fluch über die Verräther! Mir das Volk
> Abwendig zu machen, mich zu verläumden,
> Als wollt ich prassen von des Armen Schweiß!
> Fluch über sie! Bleibt mir das Volk nur treu
> So soll die Zukunft mich glänzend rechtfertigen.
> Mein Volk, für das ich gern gelitten,

Verwünschung, Kerker, Bann u. Fluch,
Für das in der Tyrannen Mitten
Ich trat und muthig rief: Genug!
Mein Volk, Du sollst nicht untergehen
Zu Schimpf und Schande, feig u. schlecht,
Du sollst mir herrlich auferstehen,
Ein stolzes, siegendes Geschlecht![44]

[A curse on all these traitors! Ah, they seek
To turn the folk against me and to claim
I want to feast upon the pauper's sweat!
A curse on them! But if the folk stays true
To me, posterity will prove me right.
My folk, for which I've suffered curses and
Imprisonment, been driven from the church,
And stepped into the tyrants' lair and called
On them to end their wilful ways: Enough!
My people, you'll not perish shamefully
Through cowardice and meanness. Rather, you
Shall rise again in glory and renown,
A proud and all-triumphant race of men!]

Rienzi adopts a similar stance when confronting the people in the final scene that Engels completed.

Ihr Bürger Roms! Warum schaart Ihr Euch
In dichten Haufen, mit Schwert und Speer
Hier vor dem Capitol?
Vertraut Ihr mir nicht mehr, den Ihr selbst erwählt,
Dem Ihr selbst diesen Purpur gelegt um die
Schultern? Was hab ich wider Euch gethan?
Laßt mich vollenden mein Werk,
Laßt mich die alte Herrlichkeit erneun,
Zu Herrn der Welt Euch machen,
Frei in selbstgegebnen Gesetzen
Und hört, nicht der Verläumdung Stimme,
Und richtet mich nach meinem Thun![45]

[You citizens of Rome! Why gather here
Outside the Capitol in close-knit groups
With swords and spears? Why is it that you've lost
Your trust in me—in me whom you yourselves
Elected when you placed this scarlet cloak
Around my shoulders? Tell me what I've done!
No, let me finish off the task I set
Myself, revive your ancient majesty,
And make you masters of this world of ours.

Be free within your self-appointed laws
And do not heed base slander's brazen voice,
But judge me by my actions and my deeds!]

Engels was clearly anxious to exonerate the common people and absolve them from all blame for Rienzi's downfall. Even more than Wagner, he attributes the mass rebellion against Rienzi to intrigue on the part of the powerful nobili. In this, he departs significantly from Bulwer's novel by introducing a democratic note. Bulwer is in fact critical of the populace, whom he depicts, like Shakespeare in *Julius Caesar*, as a fickle mass, blindly following the dictates of the moment, hailing its leaders one day, only to crucify them the next, and finally degenerating into a multiheaded, snarling beast. It is they, in Bulwer's view, who are ultimately to blame for the tribune's downfall. Here we already see signs of the change of political allegiance that was a notable feature of Bulwer's own life as a parliamentarian: until 1841 he was a member of the liberal Whig party, but in 1852 he reentered the House of Commons as a Tory.

For both Engels and Wagner, Rienzi was a modern republican folk hero concerned not with his own advancement but with making the common people the masters of the world, subservient to no laws except those that are "self-appointed."[46]

So schwör ich vor Gottes Angesicht,
Mein Leben zu weihn Eurer Freiheit,
Daß groß und frei die alte Roma
Wieder ersteh aus ihren Trümmern!
Ich will nicht ruhn, nicht rasten will ich,
Bis Rom in altem Glanz ersteht,
Und voll der vergangnen Herrlichkeit
Leuchtet vor allen Völkern der Welt!
Dem Phönix gleich, der stolzer und prächtiger
Aus seiner Asche sich wiederum schwingt empor,
So möge unvergänglich u. neu erstehn
Die alte Zeit, die Weltenbezwingerin![47]

[And so, within the sight of God, I swear
To dedicate my life to you and make
You free again. From ruins, ancient Rome
Shall rise both great and free in turn. I shall
Not sleep, I shall not know a moment's rest,
Till Rome arises in her ancient pride
And, filled with all her erstwhile majesty,
Illumines all the nations of the world.
She shall be like the phoenix as it soars
Aloft again, yet prouder than before.
Thus shall that golden age return anew
And, ageless, conquer all the world once more.]

Here Engels uses the image of the phoenix, an image that as we have already seen, was one of the topoi associated with the cult of Rome. In particular, it was applied to Rienzo by Petrarch.

It is impossible not to be reminded of Wagner's Rienzi at this point. In both cases, the last of the Roman tribunes is purged of all his negative attributes and turned into a selfless political idealist. Mosen's Rienzi, conversely, creates a substantially deeper impression: only during his initial period of rule is he the idealist who transcends his materialist surroundings and rises above his fellow conspirators. But his mood darkens in the wake of his first fall from favor, and it is as a different person that he returns to Rome. He regards his allegiance with Monreale (here called Montreale) as a pact with the devil: "Here, Devil, take it! Take my soul! (They shake hands.)" Now "evil spirits throng our midst and bring / With them deep hatred, blood lust, and excess,"[48] robbing his ideals of their pristine purity. "Ah, who has robbed you of your goodly heart?" Enrico asks him in the final act, prompting the following reply:

> Still! Still davon! Ich war ein frommer Narr;
> Ich suchte die Gerechtigkeit hienieden!
> Ich war ein Tor, es gilt nur die Gewalt!
> Und mit Gewalt will dieses Volk ich peitschen
> Aus seinem Sumpfe der Verworfenheit;
> So lang will ich es schütteln in dem Sieb,
> Bis nur noch ächte Römer übrig sind.
> Mit Schrecken und Entsetzen zwing ich sie.
> Um jung zu machen ein verdorbnes Volk,
> Kennt nur der Arzt zwei Mittel: Stahl und Feuer.[49]

> [Be silent! Hush! I was a holy fool!
> I looked for justice here on earth, but was
> A fool to do so. Force is all that counts!
> And I'll use force to goad the common folk
> And raise them from depravity's morass
> And shake them in my riddle till I'm left
> With only true-born Romans. I'll carry out
> My plans by filling them with terror and
> Dismay. To cure degeneracy's ills
> The doctor's only means are steel and flame.]

Rienzi has become a kind of Robespierre, resolved to restore Roman virtue by means of terror.

Bulwer's novel spawned a whole series of dramas and novels on the subject of Rienzi, but even after its influence had waned, the figure of the Roman tribune continued to exercise the imagination of writers well into the twentieth century, enjoying a particular boom at the time of the Risorgimento, whose hero Garibaldi was hailed as "Rienzo redivivus." It is worth recalling in this context that Wagner was an ardent admirer of this latter-day Rienzi and did everything in his power to see him in person, finally achieving that aim in Acireale on 27 March 1882, a few months before Garibaldi's death, when Cosima noted in her diary that Wagner had been deeply moved by the sight of Italy's national hero. On hearing of his death, he told Cosima that he was "a classical figure who belonged to the time of Timoleon" (CT, 3 June 1882). Wagner's *Rienzi* was first performed in Italy at the Teatro La Fenice in Venice in 1874 in the wake of the spirit of national enthusiasm that followed Italian reunification. The translator was Arrigo Boito, who, when revising the libretto of *Simon Boccanegra* in 1881, introduced a reminiscence of Rienzi into the finale of act 1, a reference undoubtedly inspired at least in part by Wagner's opera.

In *A Communication to My Friends*, Wagner explained his enthusiasm for Rienzi as follows:

> From the misery of modern private life, where I was unable to find even the least subject worthy of artistic treatment, I was carried away by the idea of a great historico-political event, in the enjoyment of which I was bound to find an edifying distraction from cares and conditions that struck me as utterly fatal to art. (GS 4:257)

Wagner regarded the pitiful state of the private modern world as inimical to art in general; only public life, only great historical and political events, had the emotional resonance that seemed to him worthy of true art. In Rienzi's case, he stripped the character of all private concerns. The hero's only close relationship is with his sister, but even this is no tender loving relationship between siblings but a bond that stems from their joint renunciation of all private human relationships and that revolves entirely around Rome: "Rome alone is living at this hour" (GS 1:85).

As a result, Wagner's Rienzi is unmarried. In this he differs not only from Bulwer's hero but also from his historical prototype. His only bride, he insists, is Rome. For both Bulwer and Engels, Rienzi's marriage plays a central role, with Engels in particular hymning marital love in a manner that harks back to Beethoven's *Fidelio*. In Mosen's case, Rienzi's wife is a pallid figure, a sexless embodiment of Roman heroism, whereas in Wagner's opera, the historical Rienzo's wife is replaced by his "heroic sister" (GS 1:83), whose stature far transcends that found in Bulwer's novel. Irene has renounced her love of Adriano out of her loyalty to her brother. In the second scene of act 5, she asks Rienzi if he knows what it means to renounce love because, she says, he has "never known love," to which he replies:

> Wohl liebt' auch ich!—O Irene,
> Kennst du nicht mehr meine Liebe?
> Ich liebte glühend meine hohe Braut,
> Seit ich zum Denken, Fühlen bin erwacht,
> Seit mir, was einstens ihre Größe war,
> Erzählte der alten Ruinen Pracht.
> Ich liebte schmerzlich meine hohe Braut,
> Da ich sie tief erniedrigt sah,

Schmählich mishandelt, grau'nvoll entstellt,
Geschmäht, entehrt, geschändet und verhöhnt!
. . . .

Mein Leben weihte ich einzig nur ihr,
Ihr meine Jugend, meine Manneskraft;
Ja, sehen wollt' ich sie, die hohe Braut,
Gekrönt als Königin der Welt:—
Denn wisse, *Roma* heißt meine Braut.

(GS 1:83–84)

[I once knew love! Irene, oh! can you
No longer call to mind that love of mine?
How ardently I loved my high-born bride!
As soon as I could think and feel, I knew
The greatness that had long ago been hers:
The ancient ruins' splendor told me so.
The love I bore my high-born bride now pained
Me, when I saw how much she'd been abased,
So shamefully disfigured and defamed,
Maligned, dishonored, raped, and mocked!
. . . .

I sacrificed my life to her alone,
To her I gave my youth and manhood's pride,
My only wish to see my high-born bride
Crowned queen of all the world: for you must know
My bride was known to all the world as Rome!]

The mystical aura of the high-born bride was clearly inspired by the biblical Song of Songs and played a central role in the thinking of the historical Rienzo, albeit in a fundamentally different sense from the one found in the lines quoted here.[50] One of Rienzo's—and Petrarch's—favorite images was borrowed from Dante, who, like them, saw Rome as the legitimate bride of both emperor and pope. The "marriage" between Rome, the emperor, and the pope constituted an indissoluble sacrament that was equally binding on all parties, a belief that was of signal importance in terms of constitutional law: only through his association with Rome did the emperor become the legitimate representative of the universal principality that the city embodied. This is why the historical Rienzo refused to allow the German princes to elect their own emperor. However, the Roman people could elect only the German king as their emperor. At no time did Rienzo deny the principle that the pope and emperor had a sacred right to Rome, so that in 1343 he invited Clement VI to return to the city from Avignon and assume his rightful place beside his abandoned "sponsa" Rome. In exactly the same spirit, he wrote to King Charles IV only a few days before his death, appealing to him to marry his bride, Rome. Rienzo saw it as his political goal to reconcile Rome's two "sponsi," to overcome the enmity between the Guelphs and Ghibellines and to revive the Augustan empire within the spirit of Christianity.

The historical Rienzo was neither the usurper nor the dictator that he is anachronistically claimed to be and would never have dared to describe Rome as his bride. True, he referred to the legend of his imperial descent and described himself as Rome's illegitimate "sponsus," but, following his dethronement, he wrote to the archbishop of Prague to say that he had had to abdicate because he was only the illegitimate scion of the emperor Heinrich VII, who had not been crowned in the rightful place. As a result, he had not been able to prove his worth as Rome's true "sponsus." Charles IV was her lawful bridegroom and should now take her as his wife.

> I do not want this emperor [Charles IV] to enter the bridal chamber of my mother, Rome, in secret and as an adulterer, as was the case with his predecessor, his grandfather [Heinrich VII]. He should come as the rightful bridegroom with a public display of delight, not like his forebear, who, accompanied only by a handful of companions, stole into the city along treacherous pathways. No, he should be surrounded by the jubilant populace and greet his bride, our mother, not as a barmaid, but as a queen.[51]

Here autobiographical details are imaginatively combined with potent symbols and biblical typology to produce a heady rhetorical brew. Note in particular the ambiguity of the word "mother" and, in the contrast between the queen and the barmaid, an allusion to Saint Paul's Letter to the Galatians (4:22–31), in which a contrast is drawn between Abraham's two wives, the bondmaid and the freewoman. Just as it was prophesied that the Messiah would be preceded by a forerunner, so Rienzo imagined himself as the forerunner of the emperor, who would restore Augustan rule in all its former glory.

When Wagner's Rienzi refers to his "high-born bride," he is no longer thinking of the symbol in the way that the historical Rienzo did but has invested it with an entirely new meaning: Rienzi is completely devoted to his idealized vision of Rome, demonstrating a commitment to that vision that excludes all divided loyalties and precludes all private cares and passions. Ultimately, he alone is capable of embodying so idealized a picture of Rome, hence his description of himself as "the last Roman" (GS 1:88). For the radical political idealist, it is all or nothing. Since the real-life Rome can no longer be reconciled with the ideal Rome, it must cease to exist.

> Furchtbarer Hohn! Wie! Ist dieß Rom?
> Elende! unwerth eures Namens!
> Der letzte Römer fluchet euch!
> Verflucht, vertilgt sei diese Stadt!
> Vermod're und verdorre, Rom!
> So will es dein entartet Volk!

(GS 1:88)

> [Most terrible contempt! What! Is this Rome?
> You wretches! How unworthy of your name!
> The last remaining Roman curses you!
> Accurs'd, annihilated let Rome be!

> Now molder into dust and perish! See,
> Your folk, degenerate, would have it so!]

The reproach that the historical Rienzo leveled at the Roman people—that they were dull witted, lazy, and senescent—is used here to deny the myth of the Eternal City, an exaggerated claim that has no basis either in history or in Bulwer's novel. The bleak pessimism of these lines was heightened by the opera's final scene, in which the nobili returned to attack the common people. In 1847 Wagner rewrote this speech, and it is this later version to which Cosima Wagner gave canonical validity through the highly questionable version of the work that she helped to prepare after Wagner's death. Here the curse on Rome is replaced by a renewed appeal to the idea of "Roma aeterna."

> Wahnsinnig Volk! Wen greift ihr an?
> Wie glaubet ihr mich zu vernichten?
> So hört von mir das letzte Wort!
> So lang die sieben Hügel Romas stehn,
> So lang die ewge Stadt nicht soll vergehn,
> Sollt ihr Rienzi wiederkehren sehn![52]

> [O nation crazed by fear! Whom is it you
> Attack? You think you can destroy me? No!
> I'll have the final word! The seven hills
> Of Rome shall sooner cease to rise above
> You all, Eternal Rome shall perish ere
> I die: you'll see Rienzi come again!]

Here the belief that Emperor Friedrich will one day return is transferred to Rienzi, whose historical prototype had seen himself only as the precursor of the third Friedrich, as someone who merely paved the way for the new Age of the Spirit, when Eternal Rome would achieve its true historical significance.

Another historical figure who saw himself as a latter-day Rienzi was Adolf Hitler. According to Hitler's childhood friend August Kubizek, in 1906 Hitler attended a performance of Wagner's opera in Linz and afterward described his feelings to him: "Like flood waters breaking their dykes, his words burst forth from him. He conjured up in grandiose, inspiring pictures his own future and that of his people." As late as 1939, Hitler told Kubizek: "In that hour it began."[53] And, according to Albert Speer, it was no accident that his party rallies began with the *Rienzi* Overture.[54] (Nor is it any accident that this overture, with its festive and heroic strains, was also played to mark the tenth anniversary of the founding of the Soviet Republic. The choice was clearly a conscious one: after all, Rienzi had risen from the ranks of the proletariat to free his country, and at least in Wagner's version could easily be reinterpreted as a precursor of the socialist revolution.)

According to Hitler, the innkeeper's son Rienzi had ousted the corrupt Senate and restored the empire to its former greatness: "Listening to this blessed music as a young man in the theater at Linz, I had the vision that I too must someday succeed in uniting the German Empire and making it great once more."[55] It scarcely needs to be pointed out that apart from a handful of superficial similarities, Hitler had nothing in common with the historical Rienzo or with his concept of an empire embodied in the emperor and pope, a concept in which the spirit of the Middle Ages was merged with that of the Humanist Renaissance. Only by adopting an antihistorical approach to the subject is it possible to see any connection between Wagner's hero and the leadership myth of the National Socialists.[56] Udo Bermbach has proposed a far more convincing interpretation of Rienzi as a typical example of the "charismatic leader" as defined by Max Weber, a "conservative revolutionary" who "would like to restore lost traditions."[57]

Rienzi places himself entirely in the service of freedom, peace, and the laws to which he, too, is subservient. He wants nothing for himself but seeks only to uphold the idea of Rome. He rejects the offer of kingship and, as upholder of the rights of the common people, accepts the title "people's tribune" (GS 1:48). He is concerned not with his own "greatness" but with that of "peace and of the law" (GS 1:51). For the sake of peace, and at the price of his own safety, he spares his enemies after their underhand attempt on his life. And in his ardent prayer at the start of act 5, he prostrates himself before the Almighty (GS 1:82). With the exception of a mere handful of details wrenched from their context, the opera affords examples of only the crassest contrasts between Rienzi and Hitler. Certainly Hitler chose not to see the tribune's failure and the victory of reactionary forces implied by the ending of the opera. (Historically speaking, Rienzo's achievements were by no means as inconsequential as Wagner suggests.) Other propagandists of the Third Reich, including Hermann Johannes Müller, were more consistent when they suggested that only the first three acts should be staged as a festival opera celebrating the new state and that it should be given under the title *Rienzi's Greatness*. If comparisons are to be drawn between Rienzi and Hitler, it would be more sensible to draw them between Hitler and the hero of Mosen's tragedy, who starts out as an artist but who, early in the work, casts aside his zither as a symbol of poetry and exchanges art for politics, dreaming of "world domination" and, disenchanted by Rome's betrayal of him, enters into a pact with evil, finally degenerating to the point where he is no more than a cruel tyrant.

RIENZI AND GRAND OPERA

For Wagner, *Rienzi* was an experiment in grand opera, a genre whose "theatrical and musical splendor" and "musically inflated passions, with their hankering after effect," he sought to "surpass with reckless extravagance," thereby "outdoing all previous examples of the genre." This passage comes from Wagner's much later account in his *Communication to My Friends* (GS 4:258), where his wish to outdo his predecessors is equated with a desire to transcend the genre of grand opera. According to Gerhart von Graevenitz, Wagner produced the perfect imitation of a libretto by Scribe in writing *Rienzi*, a work famously, if inaccurately, described as "Meyerbeer's best opera." "He squeezed the subject matter of Bulwer-Lytton's novel into the straitjacket of the plot of *La muette de Portici*, while combining it with the political message of *Les Huguenots*, with its skepticism toward the revolution."[58] Yet, however close Rienzi may be to a grand opera in style, Graevenitz's thesis undoubtedly goes too far. Indeed, as Egon Voss has pointed out, it seems highly unlikely that Wagner was even familiar with *Les Huguenots* at the time that he wrote his libretto.[59] And, as we shall see, Meyerbeer's "skepticism toward the revolution" has little in common with the underlying thrust of *Rienzi*, quite apart from the fact that the specific features of Scribe's work as a librettist—his habit of dividing the exposition over two acts and the dialectics of political and private actions—are conspicuous only by their absence in Wagner's libretto. Dramaturgically speaking, the main idea in *Rienzi* is the contrast between the great individual and the masses who are not his equal, and the opera owes this rather to Spontini's *Fernand Cortez*. Originally staged in 1809 but frequently revised, most notably for the Berlin production of 1832, this is a work that Wagner himself acknowledged as one of his early models. Certainly, a comparison between *Rienzi* and *La muette de Portici* reveals far greater and more substantial differences than similarities in terms of their actual contents.

This is clear from the very first scene, in which three choral groups—the two opposing aristocratic parties and the common people—confront each other onstage (a confrontation that anticipates the dynamics of the ensemble finales in Meyerbeer's opera). Auber, by contrast, tends to avoid such dramatic confrontations between choral groups, preferring to locate them offstage. (Remarkably, perhaps, this type of confrontation also characterizes the opening scene of Engels's unfinished libretto.) The nobili's assault on the virtue of the tribune's sister may seem to suggest a link between *Rienzi* and *La muette de Portici*, yet the role that the motif plays in both works is in fact fundamentally different.

Masaniello becomes a rebel out of his sense of outrage at his sister's abduction. In much the same way, Giuseppe and Sormano in Wagner's *Die hohe Braut* join the revolution as the private victims of tyranny. (To a certain extent it was Schiller—in many ways the forerunner of nineteenth-century opera—who in William Tell created the prototype of the figure who becomes a political hero because of some private injury.) But there is nothing in Rienzi's relationship with his sister to provide him with any private motive to rebel. For Rienzi, the attempted abduction of his sister—which is prevented not by Rienzi but by Adriano—is merely a further link in the chain of the acts of brutality perpetrated by the nobili. Whereas Masaniello is motivated by a desire to avenge his sister's violated honor, this is not the case with Rienzi, a point that Wagner stressed in a letter that he wrote to the tenor Albert Niemann on 25 January 1859. The "original motive of vendetta" for his brother's murder was increasingly replaced in the character's mind by a sense of patriotism, as was already clear from the opening scene.

When R[ienzi] first appears among the people, it is, as it were, simply as a peacemaker, in all his deeply self-conscious dignity. He then sees the ladder at the window of his house; a glance at Irene and the nobili tells him everything. "And so yet another assault on my family, then it was murder, today an attempted abduction!" Carried away by deadly hatred and seething with fury, he acts overly-precipitately as he launches into his recitative against the nobili. Entirely spontaneously, however, his injured personal interests quickly expand to embrace his violated fatherland; he grows in stature and becomes ever greater, and with the words "Are you yet Romans?" he stands before the degenerate assembly like the god of vengeance himself. From now on he regains all his sublime calm and dignity.[60]

Initially, therefore, it was vengeance that motivated Rienzi's political actions: he too had "kindred blood to avenge" (GS 1:42). But ultimately he is concerned only with symbolic revenge for his brother's murder, a crime for which he "appealed in vain for justice" (GS 1:42). (The futility of this appeal is historically authenticated.) This desire for vengeance grows increasingly remote from the emotion that sparked it, as Rienzi aims to fight for freedom in a state of "calm" (GS 1:36), "without madness" (GS 1:39), and with none of the "rage" (GS 1:41) to which his brother once fell victim. He now intends to ensure that his revenge contains no element of a private vendetta, no sense of subjective emotion; he is resolved to be Rome's champion alone. In his letter to Niemann, Wagner explained this to impressive effect.

> *Nothing* affected Rienzi so deeply in his youth as the brutal killing of his little brother by the soldiers of the nobili, against whom he was unable to obtain justice. Starting out from a desire for vengeance, but failing to find satisfaction anywhere, he began to ponder the matter and learned to see its causes in the *general* misery of his age and, more especially, of his own fatherland. In order to account for this, he familiarized himself with his country's history; going back from one source to another, he finally reached Roman antiquity and immersed himself enthusiastically in contemplation of the grandeur and greatness of ancient Rome, and, on turning back to the present, became conscious of a tremendous decline, so that where he had previously brooded only on the reasons for his own unsatisfied vengeance, he now saw the general decay of the entire world, a decay from which he resolved to free it. And so the original motive of "vendetta" became a purified patriotism of visionary sublimity, which, once he had suppressed all memory of the injury he himself had suffered, gave him the wonderful power which, for a time, he exercised over his people.

For this reason, Rienzi repudiates his earlier vow to be avenged on the Colonnas the moment he realizes that there is a chance of winning over one of the Colonnas—Adriano—to the cause of liberating Rome. At this moment his subjective need for revenge disappears, destroyed by the vision of Rome that takes over Rienzi's whole being and extinguishes all subjective and private emotions: "Be mine, Adriano! Be a Roman!" (GS 1:42). At the critical moment, the desire for vengeance even turns into its exact opposite, for, as Rienzi explains to Adriano in the opening act of the opera, "Woe betide the man who must avenge kindred blood" (GS 1:42). Adriano refers back to these words in act 2, when Rienzi is on the point of having Colonna executed for the attempt on his life: "How dare you, freedom's blood-stained slave! Give me a kinsman's blood on which to wreak my vengeance!" Rienzi reacts with the words: "Unhappy man! Of what have you reminded me?" (GS 1:60). Evidently he has remembered his murdered brother, so that he suddenly sees Adriano in the same situation as himself and in consequence pardons his would-be assassins "in order"—to quote Wagner's letter to Niemann—"to destroy the last remaining seeds of his feeling of personal vengeance. . . . Now his thoughts are completely pure." *La clemenza di Rienzi!*

The obligation to seek revenge is a regular part of any system of feudal values. Here it is enough to recall such a typical study of feudal honor as Verdi's *La forza del destino* (The force of destiny) and the Spanish play on which it is based, Angel de Saavedra's *Don Alvaro*: the honor bound up with social rank and the resultant obligation to avenge any slight to that honor override all other considerations, whether of a private or nonpersonal nature. But Rienzi's "revenge" transcends all personal considerations, including those of family and social standing, being concerned only with the suprapersonal interests of Rome. At the same time, it becomes clear from the unfolding action that Adriano is not really capable of rising above himself and achieving the nonpersonal standpoint of the Roman citizen. Instead, he becomes increasingly enmeshed in the toils of his own feudal background, with its concerns for social status, family, and subjective emotions. As Wagner himself explained to Niemann in his letter of 25 January 1859,

> As for Adriano, it is his enthusiasm that is the starting point for his actions, an enthusiasm that Rienzi is able to inspire in him on the strength of the young man's love of Irene. But instead of maintaining this enthusiasm, which in Rienzi finally overrides all natural and personal relationships, Adriano sinks back to the level from which Rienzi had set out in order to rise to his present greatness. "Blood" comes between them, and Adriano cannot rise above the feeling of "vendetta"; he remains ensnared in the trammels of mere family ties, whereas Rienzi has only the state as a whole in mind, with the result that, fired by his passionate thirst for vengeance and scarcely restrained by his love, Adriano perishes powerless and demented, while Rienzi, launching into the Battle Hymn, allows himself and the Capitol to be destroyed by an ungrateful and misguided populace.

Rienzi's attitude is entirely antifeudal. This is clear not only from his political views but also from his emotional control. From the very outset he is revealed as a man who upholds the rule of law and abhors all arbitrary force, whether on the part of the nobili or on that of the people: "Calm down! (*To the populace*) And you, have you forgotten what you swore to me?" (GS 1:36). Evidently the people had sworn that they would not use force, and Rienzi insists on this oath of theirs: "Get back! Recall your oath!" (GS 1:37). He execrates physical violence and the emotions that precede it, namely, hatred and mass hysteria. (Masaniello's purely private horror at the excesses of the mob becomes sound political judgment in the case of Rienzi.)

> Freiheit verkünd' ich Romas Söhnen!
> Doch würdig, ohne Raserei,
> Zeig' jeder, daß er Römer sei!

(GS 1:39)

[You sons of Rome shall all be free!
But worthy, free from frenzied rage,
May each of you a Roman be!]

It was, after all, the blind emotions sparked by anarchy that had proved Rome's downfall, with the result that only calm and strict emotional self-control could restore a state of new social and legal order. In adopting this attitude, Rienzi resembles the rebellious hero of Lessing's unfinished tragedy, *Samuel Henzi* (1749), who remains within the law while resisting Bern's corrupt aristocratic rulers. He "does nothing for himself and everything for the state," distancing himself from his fellow conspirators, who are driven by "blood lust," "anger," and other blind emotions and who, like Baroncelli and Cecco in *Rienzi*, accuse their leader of a lack of resolve.[61] In this respect, Rienzi harks back to a type of hero who was widespread in eighteenth-century plays and operas and who, by suppressing all human emotions, stands apart not only from the heroic emotions of the feudal aristocrat, with his anachronistic features, but also from the excesses of the rabble. (The best example of this type of character is Mozart's Emperor Titus.)

With his demand that his fellow citizens act unemotionally within the framework of the law, Rienzi likewise finds himself caught between two factions, the common people and the nobili, both of whom are characterized by blind emotion. During their very first encounter in the opera, Adriano predicts that Rienzi's attempts to establish peace will fail.

Doch an das Ziel der stolzen Wünsche
Gelangst du nur durch blut'ge Bahn,
Durch eines feigen Pöbels Wuth,
Durch meiner Brüder, meines Vaters Blut!

(GS 1:41)

[But if you'd reach your proud and lofty goal,
You'll do so only steeped in Roman blood,
You'll rouse the craven rabble's rage and shed
My brothers' and my father's noble blood.]

Adriano thinks only in terms of emotions. Although his prophecy comes true, it does so in a way that he himself would not be prepared to admit, as Rienzi is forced to steep his hands in blood only as a result of the nobili's repeated acts of treason. Meanwhile, the fury of the common people is unleashed by the church's betrayal of Rienzi and by the false report of his own high treason, a report spread by his former fellow conspirators and duplicitously confirmed by Adriano, who is motivated by his desire to avenge his father's entirely justified death.

The mob is led astray by the powers that be, and it is the latter who, in their unbridled passion, are the guilty party. Adriano is so caught up in his system of emotional values, with its anachronistic view of "chivalry" (GS 1:67) and family honor, that as soon as "kindred blood" is involved, he loses all sense of right and justice, all capacity for judging things objectively. The anachronistic nature of his moral concepts is reflected in the fact that the role is a breeches part of the kind that had likewise long been an anachronism in opera. Here the reader is involuntarily reminded of Mozart's Sextus: like Adriano, Sextus too is torn between two systems of values. Neither character, moreover, is developed as a psychological portrait, being influenced, rather, by a dialectic that was derived solely from operatic convention and that was already something of an anachronism even in Mozart's day.

Adriano's thinking, then, is feudally oriented, with its particularist obsessions with status, family, honor, and, above all, revenge. As such, it contrasts with Rienzi's thinking, which is that of a modern, unitarian statesman, who uses reason to control emotion and abhors physical violence, subjecting to strict control the emotions that lead to such violence.[62] In his letter to Niemann, Wagner underlines this contrast, pointing out that "while Adriano increasingly forgets Rome, his fatherland, and freedom and sees only his murdered father, Rienzi now puts all thought of fraternal vengeance behind him and is fully conscious in himself of representing only Rome, his fatherland, and freedom." Mosen's summarization of the basic idea behind his own tragedy on the subject is even more true of Wagner's opera: "In Cola Rienzi the ancient Roman idea of the state attempts to realize itself as a modern state by rebelling against the Middle Ages, so that the hero of the tragedy may be seen as a precursor of the struggle that is still being fought today."[63]

To a certain extent Rienzi is a modern variant of the hero of classical myth, a latter-day Theseus, who rids the land of robbers and restores peace.

> Bestraft sei streng Gewalt und Raub,
> Und jeder Räuber Roma's Feind.
> Verschlossen sei, wie jetzt es ist,
> Den Übermüth'gen Roma's Thor;
> Willkommen sei, wer Frieden bringt,
> Wer dem Gesetz Gehorsam schwört.

> (GS 1:47)

> [All robbery and force shall be condemned,
> And robbers all shall be the foes of Rome.
> And may our city's gates forevermore
> Be closed to overweening arrogance.
> Be welcome those who come to us in peace
> And swear obedience to our Roman law.]

Rienzi's concept of peace is coterminous with his desire to set aside all particularist interests in favor of the unity not only of Rome but of all Italy ("May all of Italy be free! Hail to the Italian confederation!" [GS 1:55]). This also explains why he is willing to pardon his attackers in act 2: "Keep the peace! Avoid all bloodshed! . . . O let the heavenly light of mercy shine into your hearts once more!" (GS 1:62). In spite of Graevenitz's claims to the contrary, here we are not dealing with "arbitrary clemency" of the kind found in *La muette de Portici*, still less with a "treacherous act of mercy toward the old oppressors."[64] To conceal an enemy in one's cottage, as

Masaniello does, is by no means the same as a public act of mercy, which has a long and venerable tradition as an example of wise statesmanship dating from Augustus's act of forgiving Cinna for his planned assassination attempt. In his treatise *De clementia* (On clemency), addressed to the emperor Nero, Seneca singles out this act as an example of politically expedient clemency designed solely to guarantee the ruler's safety. In turn, Corneille used it as the basis of his drama *Cinna, ou La clémence d'Auguste* (Cinna, or The clemency of Augustus, 1641), a play that subsequently left its mark on Metastasio's epoch-making libretto for *La clemenza di Tito*, a text that inspired settings by some forty different composers, including Gluck and Mozart. In each case, the ruler's clemency is based not on human weakness but on careful political and legal calculation.[65] The ruler weighs the relative merits of strictness and clemency in the light of the public good, and if Corneille's Augustus and Metastasio's Titus decide in favor of clemency, it is purely and simply because they are convinced that the political advantages of their clemency outweigh the advantages of insisting on the letter of the law.

In spite of the skeptics who were afraid that clemency would result in renewed rebellion, Augustus and Titus were proved right, whereas Rienzi's act of clemency turns out to be a miscalculation, with the populace, including Baroncelli and Cecco, reproaching him: "You've done us wrong by placing mercy before justice!" (GS 1:65). In spite of their oath, the old oppressors do not feel morally bound by Rienzi's act of forgiveness and rearm themselves in order to rise up once more against the new order. Here in fact we find a superficial parallel with the plot of *La muette de Portici*, but the clemency shown by Masaniello, who by now has lost all faith in the idea of rebellion, fails to impress Alphonse, who feels no moral obligation to support the fishermen's uprising. Nor do we hear anything of an oath similar to the one sworn in *Rienzi*. Moreover, whereas Masaniello is regarded— with some justification—as a traitor by Pietro and the fishermen for sparing the life of his enemy, the only treasonable action in *Rienzi* is the malicious rumor put about by Baroncelli and Cecco in act 4: "Do you think it was Rienzi's clemency that moved him to be merciful? I see quite clearly it was treachery" (GS 1:76).

Misled by this rumor, the common people abandon Rienzi. At the end of *La muette de Portici*, Borella and Alphonse sum up the abrupt change of heart on the part of the lower orders in the words "Il en était l'idole—Il en est la victime [He was their idol—He is their victim]," words that could equally well be applied to Rienzi and the Roman populace. Yet the endings of the two operas could hardly be more different. In *La muette de Portici* the fanatical mob kills its erstwhile idol in the belief that he has betrayed the revolution, whereas it kills Rienzi because the church has excommunicated him: "Come on and honor the church's supreme command!" (GS 1:87 and 89). The real reactionaries are the common people; it is they, not Rienzi, who betray the revolution—and they are not even thanked for doing so, as it emerges from the final stage direction that the nobili "lay into the common people" (GS 1:89).

Whereas Masaniello loses his faith in the revolution and is inwardly torn apart, his mind sicklied o'er with the pale cast of thought,[66] Rienzi remains true to his republican ideals right up to the end. The common people betray their "Roman pride" and break their "Roman vow," and so the "last remaining Roman" curses the "degenerate folk" (GS 1:88). The Capitol goes up in flames and collapses in a grand operatic gesture that draws on all the stage resources of the period and is typical of the cataclysmic disasters with which this sort of opera tended to end. Yet its underlying meaning is fundamentally different, not so much looking back to grand opera as forward to the catastrophe that ends *Götterdämmerung*, a catastrophe that the protagonists bring down on themselves. Rienzi's and Irene's apotheosis is not qualified, as it would be in a grand opera, by the Nemesis-like character of the final catastrophe that allows the spectator to feel a certain private human sympathy with the insurrectionist while condemning the insurrection itself. (*Rienzi* lacks the contrapuntal interplay between private and political actions that would make it possible to draw a distinction between rebel and rebellion, so that it is impossible, therefore, for our sympathies to be divided.) At best, the destruction of the Capitol represents the workings of Nemesis for Adriano, who perishes in its ruins.

The ultimate downfall of Rienzi and Irene, by contrast, marks the tragic end of two characters who, like Siegfried and Brünnhilde, triumph in a notional sense and who embody the principle of hope. The pessimistic ending of the original version of the opera may cast a shadow over this principle, but the 1847 revisions, by recalling the myth of the Eternal City, help to underline it. Yet in neither case do we find any trace of the sort of revolutionary pessimism that was typical of Meyerbeer's Paris operas. Wagner's pessimism is directed not at the idea of revolution as such but at the common people, who are not equal to this idea. In his letter to Niemann of 25 January 1859, Wagner offers a superb account of the tragic difference between Rienzi and "his" people. (The importance of this letter, from which I have already had frequent occasion to quote, stems from the fact that Wagner is able to distance himself from a work that he had long since outgrown, so that he had no need to adopt his usual practice of foisting a new meaning on it after the event.) Here Wagner makes it clear that Rienzi has grown remote from the people because his character has been depersonalized, ultimately becoming an "idea" that the world fails to understand and that has acquired a monumental fixity.

> But Rome, the fatherland, & freedom now exist in him, & in him alone. The populace itself knows none of this; only half aware of what is going on, they side with Adriano, for they too can see only their own brothers and sons who have fallen in battle and for whose deaths they now blame Rienzi. . . . Scarcely has he won over the conspirators outside the church with his all-powerful grandeur & enthusiasm when everyone recoils before him, aghast at his excommunication. For he now sees that only his idea was real, not the common people. He remains great and noble, but as rigid as a statue, his gaze fixed firmly in front of him in sublime and rapt contemplation, just like his idea, which has likewise turned to stone like some monument and which the world is unable to grasp. . . . His final scene with Irene allows him to savor the joy and anguish of this idea one last time. . . . She has renounced her love and thus, like her brother, has enabled the idea to triumph over passion.

Rienzi is the tragedy of the political idealist, of the revolutionary with no people to lead.

From History to Myth

Wagner's interest in history was by no means exhausted with *Rienzi*. Although history is overshadowed by myth in *Der fliegende Holländer*, three of his later projects were for large-scale historical dramas: *Die Sarazenin* (WWV 66), *Friedrich I.* (WWV 76), and *Jesus von Nazareth* (WWV 80). The first of these projects—an opera about Manfred, the son of the Hohenstaufen emperor Friedrich II—dates from the end of 1841, when Wagner was still living in Paris and had just completed *Der fliegende Holländer*. The detailed draft that has come down to us was prepared in Dresden in 1843. Writing in *My Life* more than twenty years later, Wagner attributed his interest in the project to his rekindled enthusiasm for German history; in particular, his reading of the revised edition of Friedrich von Raumer's six-volume *Geschichte der Hohenstaufen und ihrer Zeit* (History of the Hohenstaufens and their age, 1840–41) had given him the idea of using the figure of Manfred to conjure up a picture of the "brilliant emperor Friedrich II, whose fortunes aroused my liveliest interest" (ML 221) and who struck him as important in terms of our understanding of the role of the historical Cola di Rienzo. According to Wagner, Manfred's life had much in common with Rienzo's, even though Manfred did not have the same idealistic strength of character but needed the prophetlike figure of the Saracen Fatima to lead him "from victory to victory and ultimately to the throne" (GS 4:270). (There is a striking parallel here with Schiller's Maid of Orleans, a character who almost literally haunts the majority of Wagner's music dramas.) Fatima is the natural daughter of Friedrich II and therefore his half sister. Manfred is passionately in love with her.

On this basis, I drafted the outline of a fairly substantial five-act dramatic poem that was intended to be ideally suited to a musical setting. The principal female character, who was to be of supreme romantic importance, was my own invention and was inspired by the historical fact that during his flight through Apulia and the Abruzzi, the young Manfred—betrayed at every turn, excommunicated by the church, and abandoned by all his followers—was enthusiastically received in Luceria by the Saracens, who supported him and accompanied him from victory to victory, up to and including his final triumph. Even at that date I was pleased to discover in the German mind the capacity to transcend the narrower barriers of nationalism and appreciate purely human qualities in whatever foreign guise they might appear, a capacity that struck me as reminiscent of the Greeks. In Friedrich II, this quality achieved its supreme expression; the fair-haired German of ancient Swabian stock, heir to the Norman kingdom of Sicily and Naples, in whom the Italian language found its first independent expression, laying the foundations for the development of science and the arts where only religious fanaticism and uncouth feudalism had previously contested the palm, assembling at his court the poets and sages of the East and surrounding himself with the most graceful examples of Arabian and Persian life and thought—he whom the Roman clergy had betrayed to the infidel while on a crusade, a crusade which, to the clergy's annoyance, he ended by signing a peace treaty with the sultan, who accorded the Christians more generous terms in Palestine than the bloodiest war could have brought—this wonderful emperor, excommunicated by the same church and finally embroiled in a hopelessly futile struggle with his century's rampant narrow-mindedness, now struck me as the supreme expression of the German ideal. (ML 221–22)

Here the cosmopolitan ideal is synonymous with the German ideal, a belief derived from the "universal Germanness" of Weimar Classicism—the formulation is that of Thomas Mann in his 1955 "Essay on Schiller." Goethe had expressed the same idea in his concept of world literature, giving it a poetical voice in his *West-östlicher Divan* (West-eastern divan), which adapts Arabian and Persian poetry for Western audiences in much the same way that Friedrich II did at his cosmopolitan court, in which world literature flourished as in some medieval Weimar. Or so Wagner would have us believe. That this court helped to establish an empire of peace in which the religions of East and West coexisted in mutual tolerance is an idea that recalls Lessing's *Nathan der Weise* (Nathan the wise), a play further linked to *Die Sarazenin* by the motif of thwarted incest—in the latter case, between Manfred and Fatima. But Young German ideas have also left their mark on the work. Under Friedrich II, the country is a medieval precursor of Laube's Utopian, universal republic transcending all existing national barriers. And Wagner's attack on "religious fanaticism and uncouth feudalism" looks back beyond *Rienzi* to the political writings of the Young Germans.

In *A Communication to My Friends*, Wagner notes that he saw the events of *Die Sarazenin* "in the fading light of a historical sunset" (GS 4:271), and in his essay *The Wibelungs*, published in 1850, he compares the medieval empire with the life cycle of a plant. In Friedrich I, this plant

> unfolded its fairest flower, but with him the flower faded; in his grandson Friedrich II, the most intelligent of all the emperors, the wondrous perfume of the dying bloom spread like a heady, fairy-tale-like intoxication through all the lands of East and West until, with the grandson of this last-named emperor, the youthful Konrad, the leafless, withered stem was torn from the ground, with all its roots and fibers, and trampled underfoot. (GS 2:152)

But Wagner later came to believe that the "fading light of a historical sunset" also cast its dying rays over historical opera as a genre, justifying his decision to abandon work on *Die Sarazenin* by arguing that political history was an unsuitable subject for the true music drama and that myth alone could fill this gap. Accordingly, it was to myth that he returned in *Tannhäuser*. The primacy of myth is central to Wagner's reform essays of the late 1840s and early 1850s, yet whether this was the main reason for his abandoning *Die Sarazenin* seems dubious in the extreme, and his explanation in *A Communication to My Friends* reads more like a post hoc justification:

> With *Die Sarazenin* I had been on the point of returning in more or less the same direction as my *Rienzi* in order to complete a grand, five-act "historical" opera; only the overwhelming idea of *Tannhäuser*, which lay far more powerful a hold of my individual being, forced me to continue in the new direction in which necessity had bade me strike out. (GS 4:272)

Certainly, there is no denying the grand operatic design of *Die Sarazenin*, with its dramatic use of contrast, its dialectic counterpoint between private and public actions (love and politics), and the opulence of its setting.[67] But nor can it be denied that even after this, Wagner returned to historical drama, and that even as late as at the end of 1845—the date of his completion of the libretto of *Lohengrin*—he still believed that myth and history could be combined in a single drama. In *Lohengrin* myth grows out of history, the authenticity of which Wagner was at pains to establish not least through his reliance on Jacob Grimm's *Deutsche Rechtsalterthümer* (German legal antiquities). His historicist approach is also clear from the clash between two mythical spheres, namely, the newer Christianity and the older paganism, white magic versus black magic, Lohengrin versus Ortrud, with the Christian element undoubtedly representing a more advanced state of human evolution. In his letter to Franz Liszt of 30 January 1852, Wagner discusses Ortrud's appeal to her "old, long-vanished gods" in act 2 ("Wodan! Dich Starken rufe ich! / Freia! Erhab'ne, höre mich!" [Wodan! I call on you, mighty god! / Freia! Sublime goddess, hear me!] GS 2:87) and, adopting the political vocabulary that he had made his own since the revolution of 1848–49, explains that "she is a reactionary, a woman concerned only with what is outdated and therefore hostile to all that is new . . . : she would like to eradicate the world and nature, simply in order to breathe new life into her decaying gods."[68]

Lohengrin represents a kind of synthesis of the young Wagner's dramatic aims, a compromise between grand historical opera and its Romantic myth-based counterpart. The possibility of treating history as myth is one that Wagner later ruled out. Of importance in this context are his remarks on the subject in *Opera and Drama* and especially his comments in *A Communication to My Friends* on his plans for a drama on the life of Frederick Barbarossa. This last-named scenario was first sketched in 1846 before being set aside, only to be taken up again and expanded in the winter of 1848–49. As such, it is closely associated with Wagner's contemporary dramatization of the Nibelung legend. In his discursive and speculative treatise *The Wibelungs: World History from Legend* from the same winter, Wagner examines the links between the legend of Barbarossa and that of the Nibelungs and adopts a mythological interpretation of the red-bearded emperor, whom he apostrophizes in *A Communication to My Friends* as "a reincarnation of the ancient heathen Siegfried" (GS 4:313).

Wagner's thinking was conditioned by his belief in mythical structures, so that history, too, struck him as made up of the cyclical repetition of archetypal patterns and, as such, as diametrically opposed to the linear method of observing history.[69] It is significant that even Wagner's "historical" operatic projects (excepting *Die hohe Braut*, which he wrote in an attempt to advance his career) involve subjects that are strongly influenced by quasi-mythical iterative structures. This was certainly true of Rienzi, whose titular hero, like his historical model, was wholly consumed by the idea of Rome as the Eternal City and who regarded himself as the man in whom Roman history would repeat itself. From this point of view, Wagner's rejection of history in favor of myth was a perfectly logical step.

There is little point in following Graevenitz and seeing in Wagner a late representative of the school of French grand opera, "endlessly repeating the same heroic image," a view that allows Graevenitz to conclude that Wagner merely "extended grand opera's political and ideological allegory into the world of myth" and even to claim that Siegfried remains "a typically grand operatic hero."[70] However much *Rienzi* may have been inspired by grand opera, its distinguishing features are undeniable. The recursive elements of grand opera are not simply present in Wagner's case but are expressly developed as themes in their own right, so that the whole idea of repetition has a positively programmatic force to it.

Wagner's decision to abandon dramatized history and turn to dramatic myth was based in essence on his conviction that history was to a certain extent a derivative of myth and that its essential manifestations could be subsumed within the prototypes of myth. This, at least, is how we must interpret his remark in *My Life* to the effect that his interest in Barbarossa waned as a result of the "greater appeal of a mythical treatment of the Nibelung and Siegfried legends, whose subject matter struck me as very similar to that of my earlier project" (ML 390).

In *A Communication to My Friends*, Wagner describes the time when he was simultaneously occupied with both Siegfried and Barbarossa: "Once again, and for the last time, myth and history confronted me, forcing me on this occasion to decide whether I should write a musical drama or a spoken play" (GS 4:311). As we know, he decided in favor of a musical drama. This account of the decision-making process has been disputed by the editors of the *Wagner Werk-Verzeichnis*,[71] who point out that Wagner noted down a fragmentary prose draft of *Friedrich I.* (Text II b) only after he had completed the libretto of *Siegfried's Tod*. This is true. Yet Wagner's claim that with *Friedrich I.* he intended to write a "spoken play" cannot be dismissed out of hand; his drafts for the first and second acts (reproduced in SS 11:270–72) contain so few specifically musicodramatic features and are so weighed down with historical details and other discursive elements wholly alien to the operatic tradition that there is no reason to question Wagner's version of events in *My Life*, according to which "this drama was to be in popular rhyming verse in the style of our Middle High German epic poets, with Lambert's *Alexanderlied* serving as my model" (ML 390).

It is clear from this final quotation that Wagner was fully conscious of the fact that a historical subject could be treated only in epic forms, forms that according to the theory advanced in *Opera and Drama* were bound to lead to the breakdown of form in the case of drama; for the theorist of *Opera and Drama*, only drama was a suitable vehicle for myth. This conviction—and ultimately also the fact that Wagner simply felt a greater need to write a music drama than to produce a purely literary work—explains why he abandoned his plan for a Barbarossa drama. Although his claim that Barbarossa and Siegfried were polar opposites smacks of a post hoc rationalization of the facts surrounding the genesis of these two projects, it nonetheless reflects his epistemological standpoint at least at the time that *The Wibelungs* went into print in 1850.

In *A Communication to My Friends*, Wagner explains that in his attempt to come to terms with the Barbarossa theme as the subject for a drama, he already felt impelled to adopt "the mythical mode" so that his hero might emerge with three-dimensional clarity from the "tremendous mass of historical episodes and relationships." According to Wagner, this approach meant compressing and condensing the diffuse mass of historical material until it could be grasped as a coherent entity, but, as he was all too well aware, it would also have meant "abandoning history," as history is conditioned, after all, by complex, suprapersonal "relationships," whereas myth is governed by the workings of "purely human individuality."

If Wagner had wanted to depict history *qua* history in his stage play (in other words, the "tremendous mass of historical episodes and relationships from which not a single link could be omitted"), the result would have been an "unmanageable conglomerate of incidents acted out onstage" and, as such, no longer a drama. If, conversely, he had adopted a mythical approach and reduced the complex historical framework to the purely human actions of his hero, the result would not have been a historical drama. He would have ended up with the "pure myth" that he had already found "in full perfection in Siegfried." According to Wagner's own account of the matter, his conviction that "pure history" was "unsuited" to drama as an art form persuaded him to abandon his plan for a play on the subject of Frederick Barbarossa and to turn to the subject that in any case constituted the secret semantic nucleus of that plan (GS 4:313–15).

Here we find Wagner arguing his case entirely within the spirit of the theory of myth that he advances in *Opera and Drama*. Myth, he insists, is the "concentrated image of the world's phenomena" (GS 4:31). "In myth, the creative urge of the common people aims to visualize the broadest grouping of the most manifold phenomena in the most succinct of all possible forms" and to "present them to us in three-dimensional guise" (GS 4:32). This process of concentration is already inherent in myth and finds its consummate expression in drama, an art form whose paradigmatic manifestation, in Wagner's view, was Greek tragedy: "Tragedy is nothing more nor less than the most perfect artistic expression of myth itself" (GS 4:34).

Just as myth is contrasted with history, so drama is contrasted with the novel as a formal type. Whereas drama—in Wagner's view—is committed to unity, the novel is concerned with variety. And whereas the perfect form of the drama, as developed by the Greeks, reflects a mythical view of the world, the structure of the novel is a reflection of the modern, godless, and prosaic world, a world dominated by science, politics, and history, which is incapable of being reduced, in its abstract, anonymous, and complex nature, to a three-dimensional form. "Just as drama reveals humankind as a living organism by treating the individual as the essence of the species," so the novel represents "the mechanism of history, according to which the species is made the essence of individuality" (GS 4:48).

Although Wagner turned his back on historical opera (and it is significant that, as we have seen from *Die hohe Braut* and *Rienzi*, he owed his inspiration mainly to the novel) and espoused the cause of musical drama and myth, history and the novel were by no means excluded from his artistic universe. As a "concentrated" form of real life, myth is bound to include history, just as drama embraces the novel. Wagner demonstrates this in detail in *Opera and Drama*.[72] The musical drama—the "drama of the future"—is to be the dominant form of the new age, using the imagery of myth to absorb the historical experiences of modern humanity, experiences reflected above all in the novel. When Wagner writes that myth is "the beginning and end of history," what he means is that "the course of this development does not mark a step backward but is rather a step forward in the direction of the attainment of the highest human ability." It is in myth as "justified by history" and in the musical drama that is "justified" by the novel that we shall find "a genuinely intelligible picture of life" (GS 4:91).

Although the myth-based music drama sees itself as the very opposite of the novel and grand opera, both of which opt for history as their subject matter, it remains dialectically related to these genres in terms of both form and content. On an institutional level, too, Wagner sought to contrast them with the "drama of the future" and to that end pursued a threefold stratagem. First, he envisaged a theater for his Nibelung tetralogy which, from the outset, would be far removed from the commercial world of metropolitan culture; second, this theater would be open only for festival performances; and, third, it would ignore all commercial considerations. In short, Wagner rejected out of hand the three most important institutional preconditions of grand opera.

The first production of *La muette de Portici* in 1828 and the July Revolution of two years later marked a new chapter in French operatic history not only aesthetically but institutionally, too. As soon as the administration of the Académie Royale de Musique was handed over to a private impresario by the name of Louis Véron, the Opéra ceased to be dependent on the king alone and, in keeping with its name, to serve as a vehicle for displays of royal ostentation. Instead, it became a symbol of the middle class's newfound prestige, a bourgeois Versailles, as Véron describes it in his *Mémoires d'un bourgeois*.[73] As the Opéra sank increasingly into debt and suffered from declining audiences under the Restoration, the only basis for its justification was success pure and simple—success in terms of mass appeal and economic viability. The enormous profits chalked up by the team of Scribe and Meyerbeer serve merely to confirm the extent to which under the July Monarchy the Opéra had turned into what Théophile Gautier termed "the chic cathedral of civilization."[74] It was this that Wagner sought to combat—and yet the outlines of grand opera can still be glimpsed through the structures of his musical dramas. "All of them entirely modern, entirely metropolitan problems," Nietzsche rightly observed in *The Case of Wagner*,[75] repeatedly emphasizing his conviction that Wagner belonged not in Germany, with all its small towns, but in Paris. Although Bernard Shaw approached the problem from a different point of view in his *The Perfect Wagnerite*, he too saw in Wagner's myth a portrait of modern society.

Writers have pointed out, not without justification, that Shaw basically adopted the exegetical method that Heinrich Heine had first applied to Meyerbeer's operas.[76] Together with Balzac, George Sand, Gautier, and Berlioz, Heine was one of those critics who, far from being dependent on reviewing as a source of income, could choose as and when they wrote and who, in the wake of the writings of the Saint-Simonians, imputed the "aesthetics of the social theater" to Meyerbeer's operas.[77] That such an aesthetic also left its not inconsiderable mark on Wagner's *Ring* is undeniable, yet there remains an essential difference: according to *A*

Communication to My Friends, Wagner could be persuaded to "take a sympathetic interest only in the purely human, only in subjects divorced from formal historical concerns" (GS 4:318), leading him to project modern experiences onto myth, which for him contained within it the archetypes of all important historical developments.

Myth, for Wagner, was not the (allegorical) image of a particular historical reality. Rather, reality was made up of recurring patterns mapped out by myth. This transhistorical line of thinking is reflected in an art form that goes back beyond those institutions that are a part of present-day historical and social reality. Instead, it seeks to establish a festival inspired by the Dionysia of Attic Greece. Thus tragic myth is relocated in the festival theater that reestablishes myth as the essential object of art.

The Transformations of Ahasuerus

THE FLYING DUTCHMAN AND HIS METAMORPHOSES

I must be wary of developing a passion for horses, as I might
learn something that I would then have to forgo. There is so
much that I've already had to renounce, and the Wandering
Jew can't be allowed to take a horse with him on his travels.

—*Richard Wagner to Mathilde Wesendonck, 21 June 1859*

IN WRITING *Das Liebesverbot*, Wagner had brusquely turned his back on the world
of German Romantic opera. Both *Das Liebesverbot* and its three successors, the
unfinished *Die hohe Braut* and *Männerlist größer als Frauenlist* and the completed *Rienzi*, attest to Wagner's predilection for Italian and French opera. Not
until 1840–41, with *Der fliegende Holländer*, did he return to German Romantic
opera and exchange history for myth, although even then he continued to waver,
as is clear from his plans for *Die Sarazenin*. As with *Die Hochzeit*, he again dis-
pensed with "all the operatic embellishments" with which he had "festooned" his
operas from *Die Feen* to *Rienzi* (ML 81). "*Dutchman* disappointed many who
awaited another *Rienzi*," writes Robert Gutman. "Their objections were similar to
those of the wealthy host in Strauss's *Ariadne auf Naxos*, displeased that his mag-
nificently appointed mansion be the scene of an opera set on a desert island."[1]

A FAUST OF THE OCEAN

Although he later attempted to conceal the fact, Wagner was inspired to write *Der
fliegende Holländer* by Heinrich Heine's *Aus den Memoiren des Herren von
Schnabelewopski* (From the memoirs of Herr von Schnabelewopski, 1834), with
its parodic description of a stage play about the Flying Dutchman.[2] (This play is,
of course, an invention of Heine's, although he may have been thinking of Edward
Fitzball's *The Flying Dutchman; or, The Phantom Ship*, which Heine could have
seen in London in 1827. Described by Ulrich Weisstein as a "subliterary grusi-
cal,"[3] Fitzball's "nautical drama" was an example of the sort of melodramas that
were popular in the English theater of the nineteenth century. If he did see it,
Heine would have picked up only a handful of motifs from the play.)

Wagner probably read Heine's short story in Riga in 1837–38, and from that date onward he was haunted by the legend of the Flying Dutchman. Writing to his Dresden colleague Ferdinand Heine in 1843, he insists that "the subject matter—long familiar to me from your namesake's writings—took on a quite special color and character among the skerries off the Norwegian coast, through which I sailed in the course of my famous sea voyage [that is, following his flight from Riga in 1839]."[4] He strikes a similar note in his "Autobiographical Sketch": "Sailing between the Norwegian skerries made a striking impression on my imagination; the legend of the Flying Dutchman, as confirmed by the sailors, took on a very definite and individual coloring in my mind such as only my adventures at sea could inspire" (GS 1:13–14). First, then, came the literary inspiration that Wagner owed to Heinrich Heine, followed by the "individual coloring" provided by his sea crossing to England.

In *My Life*, by contrast, Wagner says nothing about Heine's contribution to *Der fliegende Holländer*, a silence all the more puzzling when we examine the two different versions of the composer's "Autobiographical Sketch."[5] This "Sketch" was first published in Heinrich Laube's *Zeitung für die elegante Welt* in February 1843 (coincidentally, it appeared in the same issues as a serialized publication of Heine's *Atta Troll*). Here we read: "In particular, the authentically dramatic treatment of the redemption of this Ahasuerus of the oceans—something that Heine himself had invented—gave me all I needed to adapt the legend and use it as an operatic subject."[6] By the time that Wagner included this "Sketch" in the first volume of his collected writings in 1871, he was unwilling to concede that Heine had made any contribution at all to the scenario and rewrote the sentence as follows: "In particular, Heine's treatment of the redemption of this Ahasuerus of the oceans, which he took from a Dutch play of the same title, gave me all that I needed to adapt the legend and use it as an operatic subject" (GS 1:17). Even Wagner must have realized that this play was an invention of Heine's, but the latter was no longer allowed any credit for it. In *My Life*, as we have already noted, Heine's name is no longer mentioned at all in the context of the opera's genesis.

That Wagner was in fact fully conscious of Heine's contribution to the specific form of the legend that we find in the *Memoiren des Herren von Schnabelewopski* is clear from his remark in his "Autobiographical Sketch" that, while in Paris, he "came to an arrangement with Heine" over his plan to "use this legend as an operatic subject" (GS 1:17). As we know, he then wrote a French prose draft that he sold to the Paris Opéra for five hundred francs, although, as it turns out, this draft was almost certainly not used by the two French librettists, Paul Foucher and Bénédict-Henry Révoil, who produced the libretto set by Pierre-Louis Dietsch and staged at the Académie Royale de Musique in November 1842 under the title *Le vaisseau fantôme* (The phantom ship). In the event, this title was the most successful part of this last-named enterprise, and Dietsch's lackluster work survived for only eleven performances. Heine reviewed it anonymously for the *Augsburger Allgemeine Zeitung* on 26 March 1843, and his review makes it clear that he was fully conscious of his own creative contribution to the tale: "It was with repugnance that I saw the beautiful story, which a well-known German writer had devised and conceived in a manner already well suited to the stage, murdered in its French text."[7]

There is no doubt that in *Der fliegende Holländer*, Wagner gratefully seized on the "beautiful story" that Heine had invented and which, as the latter himself expresses it, already lent itself to the stage, even if he failed to show his gratitude to Heine in person. (Whether Heine knew Wagner's opera has unfortunately never been established.) Wagner's suppression of Heine's name not only is due to his increasingly idiosyncratic attitude toward Jews but was also connected with his aesthetic conviction that the musical drama as a genre sprang from "the spirit of the people." In other words, it derived from the folk's mythopoeic imagination. As a result, he was unwilling to admit that he had found virtually all the "folklike" subjects of his operas in modern adaptations. We shall have to confront this problem again when we examine *Tannhäuser*.

The tale of the Flying Dutchman is a typical modern legend that did not acquire its definitive form until the nineteenth century.[8] Various accounts of captains ensnared by the Devil in consequence of their foolhardy hubris—the pact motif familiar from *Faust*—or condemned to sail the seas for all eternity, bringing misfortune to every ship they encounter, are found among seafaring nations from the seventeenth century onward. Superstitious imaginations were fired especially by floating wrecks, which sailors beset by the perils of the sea believed were phantom ships presaging disaster. Wagner himself saw evidence of this superstition in 1839 during his hazardous voyage from Pillau to London.

This motif was regularly associated with the historical background of trade with the Dutch East Indies and with the geographic setting of the Cape of Good Hope, which was discovered in 1497, thus providing students of the legend's history with a *terminus a quo*. The vow sworn by Captain van der Decken (one of the Dutchman's names) to sail around the Cape at any cost was transformed by popular tradition into a symbol of the hubristic spirit of discovery that transgressed the boundaries of knowledge and experience laid down by the Bible and the church. The Dutchman is thus the maritime equivalent of Faust. It is impossible not to be reminded here of the prologue to Marlowe's *Tragicall History of D. Faustus*, first published in 1604, in which the Chorus comments on Faust's presumptuous quest for knowledge: "His waxen wings did mount above his reach,/And melting, heavens conspir'd his over-throw." And after Faustus has fallen into the Devil's clutches, the Chorus, in the final lines of the drama, exhorts the wise "Onely to wonder at unlawfull things,/Whose deepnesse doth intice such forward wits,/To practise more then heavenly power permits." These lines are as true of the Flying Dutchman as they are of Marlowe's hero. Even by the middle of the sixteenth century, Vasco da Gama's rounding of the Cape of Good Hope in 1497 was being demonized and mythologized by historians such as Gaspar Correia and, more particularly, by Luis de Camoens, whose *Os Luciades* (The Lusiads), written in 1572, portrays the Spirit of the Cape threatening to wreak vengeance on its discoverer for wresting its secret from it.

Literary adaptations of the legends dealing with the Flying Dutchman and his phantom ship are not found until the end of the eighteenth century, and by and large they ignore what were originally the religious implications of the captain's act of titanic defiance. The best-known poetic reworkings of the material are Coleridge's ballad "The Rime of the Ancient Mariner," first published in 1798; Wilhelm Hauff's "Geschichte von dem Gespensterschiff" (Story of the ghost ship) from his cycle of oriental fairy tales *Die Karawane* (The caravan, 1826); and the same author's "Die Höhle von Steenfoll" (The cave at Steenfoll) from his cycle *Das Wirtshaus im Spessart* (The tavern in the Spessart, 1828), together with Frederick Marryat's *The Phantom Ship* of 1839; and, finally, the parodic variant of the Dutchman theme in Heine's short story, mentioned earlier.

Wagner's opera dealt so comprehensively with the subject that it left room for very few later adaptations of any significance. Perhaps one of the most curious is the American feature film *Pandora and the Flying Dutchman*, starring Ava Gardner and James Mason (1950). Written and directed by Albert Lewin, it combines the legends of the Flying Dutchman and the Greek myth of Pandora to produce a romantic melodrama set on the Spanish coast, with local color provided by national costumes and flamenco rhythms. Hendrik van der Zee is condemned to sail the seven seas in his ghost ship as a punishment for murdering his guiltless wife in a fit of jealousy, until he finally discovers in Pandora Reynolds a woman who, by reminding him of his dead wife, allows him to find redemption.

ROMANTIC OPERA AND THE THEME OF *WELTSCHMERZ*

Long condemned to an oral existence, the legend suddenly entered literary life during the *Vormärz*, the period in German history between the Vienna Congress of 1815 and the March Revolution of 1848. Evidently, the theme struck a topical note. Yet the most typical feature of these literary reworkings is their affinity with the legend of Ahasuerus,[9] one of the great symbolic subjects of the age.[10] Like Hamlet, Faust, and Don Juan, Ahasuerus—the Wandering Jew—is one of those recurrent representatives of the mood of *Weltschmerz*, or world weariness, that could be described as the underlying mood of the age and that is comparable with the *Empfindsamkeit*, or *sensibilité*, of the second half of the eighteenth century. In his novel *Die Epigonen* (The epigones), first published in 1836, Karl Leberecht Immermann places the following words in Wilhelmi's mouth: "Men of all ages have known misfortune in plenty, but it is the curse of the present generation to feel wretched as a result of no particular suffering."[11] Johann Nestroy's farce *Das Haus der Temperamente* (The house of the temperaments, 1837) contains a scene between the melancholy Trüb and his no less melancholy, chronically depressed daughter Irene. When Trüb asks her, "Is there a particular reason for your pain today?" she replies, "Isn't the pain for which there is no reason the deepest of all?"[12]

Existence as such becomes our misfortune. In consequence, the yearning or unconscious illusion, felt by almost every individual, that we can somehow circumvent death is perverted to the point where it becomes the most terrifying of thoughts, namely, that we, like Ahasuerus or the Flying Dutchman, are condemned to eternal life, the "Wandering Jew of the ocean," to quote Heinrich Heine.[13] In Pierre-Jean de

Béranger's 1831 poem *Le juif errant* (The Wandering Jew, translated into German by Adelbert von Chamisso in 1838), the curse of a life that will not end is strikingly symbolized by a refrain that by dint of its constant repetition reinforces the idea of a perpetual existence. Chamisso's very free translation contains the following lines:

> Mich schlägt die Zeit mit ihrem Flügel,
> Doch altern?—weiß nicht, was es sei:
> Ich träume von dem jüngsten Tage,
> Ich ruf ihn ungehört herbei.

> [The rushing wings of time beat down on me,
> Yet "aging" has no meaning as a word.
> The Day of Judgment fills my thoughts and dreams,
> And yet my anguished calls remain unheard.]

His words inevitably recall those of the Flying Dutchman's entrance monologue. Béranger's refrain runs as follows:

> Noch drehet immer, immer, immer
> Die Erde sich in ihrem Lauf,
> Noch gehet immer, immer, immer,
> Die Sonne morgens wieder auf.[14]

> [Ever, ever, ever, ever:
> Endless is the earth's refrain.
> Ever, ever, ever, ever
> Dawns the morning sun again!]

Weltschmerz is a form of unhappiness that does not need to have a specific cause but has a metaphysical basis. This is the "breach in the world"—the German *Weltriß* was one of the most potent neologisms of the age[15]—signifying the grievous breach in the very essence of creation. Individual pain is an expression of the pain inherent in the world, individual inner conflict a reflection of what Georg Büchner (who was born in the same year as Wagner) refers to as the "breach in creation." By equating existence with suffering, Camille Desmoulins—one of the characters in Büchner's *Dantons Tod* (1835)—is able to conclude that simply because it exists, the world is like the Wandering Jew, longing to die and to be engulfed in the peace of oblivion: "The world is the Wandering Jew, oblivion is death, but death is impossible. Oh, not to be able to die, not to be able to die, as it says in the song." But, as Danton explains, annihilation is an ontological impossibility.

> The accursed argument that nothing that exists can cease to exist, something cannot become nothing! And I am something, more's the pity! Creation has spread itself so wide there is nowhere left that's empty, everywhere's teeming with life. The void has murdered itself, creation is its wound, we are its drops of blood, the world is the grave in which it rots." (The Conciergerie, Act Three)[16]

Here we have a metaphysic of Weltschmerz illustrated by means of a nihilistic countermythology. The void—oblivion—bears the scars of existence: all that exists is pain and suffering. "The stars prick the night like tears," says Danton on the eve of his death. "There must be great grief in the eye that shed them."[17] It is scarcely possible to say any longer whether it is the eye of God or the eye of oblivion that is meant here; God and oblivion have become one, united in the pain of existence. The more we suffer pain, the sooner we will merge in mystic union with the God who is oblivion. "We do not have too much suffering, we have too little, for it is through suffering that we attain God," Büchner is believed to have said on his deathbed.[18]

For all its ontological impossibility, oblivion remains a consummation devoutly to be wished; the goal of such yearning was absolute rest or peace. Danton (like Büchner) is a voluntaristic nihilist, not an ontological one, and on this point he is closely related to Arthur Schopenhauer, that quintessential philosopher of Weltschmerz, whose chief work, *Die Welt als Wille und Vorstellung* (The world as will and representation, 1819), ends with the word "nothing." This state of nothingness is Nirvana, a state of peace that marks the end of all desire and the restless workings of the will. It has often been asked, especially in recent years, whether Büchner had read Schopenhauer. In fact, Büchner is no more likely to have done so than the young Wagner, yet both of them were familiar with elements of his philosophy either through the unconscious and indirect assimilation of his ideas or simply on the strength of their elective affinities. Indeed, Wagner himself admitted as much following his reading of Schopenhauer in the autumn of 1854.

Peace as the goal of voluntaristic nihilism is a concept as familiar to Wagner as it was to Schopenhauer and Büchner. The Flying Dutchman longs to find this peace in love. Difficult though it is to imagine such an equation, the identification of love, death, and peace in oblivion is a further theme that links *Der fliegende Holländer* and *Dantons Tod*, a work that at first sight must seem as far removed as is conceivably possible from Wagner's Romantic opera. "I love you like the grave," Danton tells Julie in the opening scene of the play. When she turns away in dismay, he explains: "No, listen! It's said that peace and the grave are as one. So, if I lie in your lap, I'm already underground. My sweet grave, your lips are my passing bells, your voice my death knell, your breast my mound of earth, your heart my coffin."[19]

Only one thing can lift the curse that weighs on the Dutchman and condemns him to eternal life: a woman's pledge to be faithful unto death. It seems to be a condition that cannot be met. "To hope is futile! Vain to dream of death!" (GS 1:261). The only hope left to the Dutchman is the end of the world, the Day of Judgment itself:

> Wann alle Todten aufersteh'n,
> dann werde *ich* in Nichts vergeh'n.
> Ihr Welten, endet euren Lauf!
> Ew'ge Vernichtung, nimm mich auf!
>
> (GS 1:261)

> [When all the dead are raised again,
> Oblivion I shall then attain!
> You planets, you have run your course!
> Endless oblivion, I am yours!]

Not "redemption"—either through love or, at the end of time, when all the dead rise up again—but "annihilation" seems to be the Dutchman's fate, or so he thinks in a moment of utter despair. He believes himself excluded from both salvation and damnation: he, alone of all men, will sink into "oblivion." His "damnation" cannot be deferred to the "Day of Judgment" but is something he must suffer even now, inasmuch as he is denied the salvation of death. What were originally religious ideas concerning death (as a punishment for original sin), salvation (awakening to eternal life), and damnation (whether in the form of eternal death or the torments of hell after life on earth) are all turned on their head here.

In his opening monologue, the Dutchman tells of the countless vain attempts he has made to end his life by force:

> —Wie oft in Meeres tiefsten Schlund
> stürzt' ich voll Sehnsucht mich hinab:—
> doch ach! den Tod, ich fand ihn nicht!
> Da, wo der Schiffe furchtbar Grab,
> trieb *mein* Schiff ich zum Klippengrund:—
> doch ach! mein Grab, es schloß sich nicht!—
> Verhöhnend droht' ich dem Piraten,
> im wildem Kampfe hofft' ich Tod:
> . . . .
> Doch ach! des Meer's barbar'scher Sohn
> schlägt bang' das Kreuz und flieht davon.—
> Nirgends ein Grab! Niemals der Tod!
>
> (GS 1:260–61)

> [Engulf'd in ocean's deepest wave,
> Oft have I long'd to find a grave;
> But ah! a grave, I found it not!
> I oft have blindly rush'd along,
> To find my death sharp rocks among;
> But ah! my death, I found it not.
> And oft, the pirate boldly daring,
> My death I've courted from the sword;
> . . . .
> Alas! the sea's rapacious son
> But sign'd the cross and straight was gone!
> Nowhere a grave! No way of death!]

The same theme of repeated but futile attempts to put an end to life recurs in two ballads by Nikolaus Lenau, the Weltschmerz poet par excellence. In one of them, *Ahasver, der ewige Jude* (Ahasuerus, the Wandering Jew), written in 1833, the Wandering Jew laments:

> Ich stand, ein Bettler, weinend vor der Thüre
> Der Elemente, flehte um den Tod;
> Doch, ob ich auch den Hals mit Stricken schnüre,

Mein fester Leib erträgt des Odems Noth.
Das Feuer und die Flut, die todesreichen,
Versagten das ersehnte Todesglück;
Ich sah die scheue Flamme rückwärts weichen,
Mit Ekel spie die Welle mich zurück.
War ich geklettert auf die Felsenmauer,
Wo nichts gedeiht, als süßer Todesschauer,
Und rief ich weinend, wüthend abgrundwärts:
"O Mutter Erde, dein verlorner Sohn!
Reiß mich zerschmetternd an dein steinern Herz!"
Der Zug der Erdentiefe sprach mir Hohn,
Sanft senkten mich die fluchgestärkten Lüfte,
Und lebend, rasend, irrt' ich durch die Klüfte.
"Tod!" rief ich, "Tod!" mich in die Erde krallend,
"Tod!" höhnte Klipp' an Klippe widerhallend.
Zu Bette stieg ich lüstern mit der Pest;
Ich habe sie umsonst ans Herz gepreßt.
Der Tod, der in des Tigers Rachen glüht,
Der zierlich in der gift'gen Pflanze blüht,
Der schlängelnd auf dem Waldespfade kriecht,
Den Wandrer lauernd in die Ferse sticht,
       Mich nahm er nicht!

[I stood, a beggar, weeping at that gate
Where elemental forces harbor death:
I tried to hang myself—defy my fate—
But sturdy limbs scarce felt the want of breath.
Both fire and flood, which often bring release,
Denied that happiness I sought in vain.
The flames recoiled but left no sense of peace,
The flood tide spewed me out with grim disdain.
Though I might climb on beetling crag where naught
But death's sweet ecstasy were to be sought
And though I cried out, weeping at the smart,
"O mother earth, behold the prodigal!
Draw me, I beg you, to your stony heart!"
The earth made mock of me and caught my fall.
Curse-laden breezes, wafting me to earth,
Abandoned me to roam through barren lands.
"Death!" I cried and tore the earth with bloodied hands;
"Death," screamed the echo, mocking in its mirth,
I clasped the harlot death between my thighs—
The pox-infected whore ignored my sighs.
Death, which lurks in tiger's flashing maw, no less
Than belladonna's fatal loveliness,
Which worms its sinuous way through woodland glade

And lies in wait to bite th' unwary, paid
No heed to me.]

Elsewhere in the same poem we find Ahasuerus standing beside the bier of a friend who has died prematurely and whose final resting place he longs to share.

O süßer Schlaf! o süßer Todesschlaf!
Könnt' ich mich rastend in die Grube schmiegen!
Könnt' ich, wie *der* in deinen Armen liegen,
Den schon so früh dein milder Segen traf!
Den Staub nicht schütteln mehr vom müden Fuße!
Wie tiefbehaglich ist die Todesmuße!
Das Auge festverschlossen, ohne Thränen;
Die Brust so still, so flach und ohne Sehnen;
Die Lippen bleich, versunken, ohne Klage,
Verschwunden von der Stirn die bange Frage.

[O gentle sleep, O gentle sleep of ages!
Could I find rest within that winding sheet,
Could I but nestle in your arms, find sweet
Release like him whom early death assuages.
No longer shaking dust from weary limbs,
No longer subject to life's tedious whims,
His eye now firmly closed, washed free of tears,
His breast quite stilled, bereft of hopes and fears,
His uncomplaining lips are sunken now,
No anxious question clouds his tranquil brow.]

The Ahasuerus myth was popular throughout Europe during the years when Weltschmerz was in vogue, and even grand opera, from which Wagner had broken free with his own adaptation of the legend, availed itself of the theme, most notably in the person of grand opera's chief librettist, Eugène Scribe, who in 1852 prepared a libretto for Fromental Halévy inspired by Eugène Sue's hugely successful 1844–45 novel *Le juif errant*. In drawing attention to the existence of this work, Gerhart von Graevenitz has even suggested that Scribe was influenced by Wagner's dramatic ballad.[20] Certainly, Wagner was in personal contact with Scribe, having tried to interest him in his draft for *Die hohe Braut* in 1836 and later expressing the hope that Scribe would prepare a libretto for him based on his French prose draft of *Der fliegende Holländer*, to which he had given the title *Le Hollandais volant—(nom d'un fantôme de mer)* (The Flying Dutchman—[name of a sea phantom]).[21] Scribe no doubt read Wagner's draft and probably saw Dietsch's opera on the same subject when it was briefly washed ashore at the Paris Opéra during the winter of 1842–43. The Day of Judgment that Wagner's Dutchman conjures up in his opening monologue (GS 1:261) becomes an apocalyptic, all-consuming fire in Scribe and Halévy's opera, its aim again being to redeem Ahasuerus from the curse of eternal rebirth. The Dutchman's vision becomes a dream in *Le juif errant*, a dream from which Ahasuerus wakes only to face new and endless wanderings: "Marche! marche! marche toujours! Toujours!!! [Walk! walk! keep walking! Keep on!!!]"[22]

Like every subject typical of its time, the Ahasuerus myth was also adapted by writers of satire and parody bent on exposing the modish, posturing stance that such an attitude implied. Suffice it to mention the "Conversations between Satan and the Wandering Jew in Berlin" from Wilhelm Hauff's *Memoiren des Satan* (Memoirs of Satan, 1826). The Devil meets the Wandering Jew in Berlin's Tiergarten. The Wandering Jew's world-weary protestations are remarkably reminiscent of the Flying Dutchman's monologue, quoted earlier: "O midnight! When, oh when, will your cooling shadows sink upon these burning eyes? When will the hour approach when the graves will open and space may be found for one who may then be granted rest?" It is not long before he gets on the Devil's nerves.

> "To hell with you, you old grumbler," I finally expostulated, annoyed at the eternal wanderer's lachrymose manner. "How dare you strike up such a poetic jeremiad? Believe me, you should count yourself lucky that you're so special. There's many a cheerful soul who's far worse off in a certain place than you are here on earth."[23]

In order to bring a little variety into the Wandering Jew's monotonous existence, Satan invites him to an "aesthetic tea party" at the home of an aging spinster. Wracked by a sense of world-weariness, the spinster "has the air of those melancholically sanctimonious nuns who, having bidden farewell to the world with a broken heart, spend the rest of their lives consumed by an anguish both grand and vaguely interesting."[24] (The extent to which Cosima Wagner had appropriated this attitude is clear from her published diaries: for her, suffering had become a point of principle sustained by Schopenhauerian metaphysics.)

The suicide attempts by Lenau's Ahasuerus and Wagner's Flying Dutchman are motivated by a sense of existential suffering and, as such, reflect the constant readiness of this world-weary age to shuffle off its mortal coil. Here, too, there are parallels with the age of *Empfindsamkeit* and with the suicide epidemic that followed in the wake of Goethe's *Die Leiden des jungen Werther* (The sorrows of young Werther). In 1839, in his book *Deutschlands jüngste Literatur- und Kulturepoche* (Germany's most recent period in literature and culture), Hermann Marggraff described the contemporary craze for suicide in particularly graphic terms.

> For a time it was the pistol that was the order of the day with us, but now we have become more sophisticated and are no longer satisfied with shooting, hanging, drowning, and poisoning: more exquisite forms of death have been devised. . . . A number of mystics have crucified themselves; unrequited lovers and young poets whose melodramas were unsuccessful have, in this age of steam, choked themselves to death by inhaling coal fumes; Napoleonists have leaped to their deaths from the top of the column in the Place Vendôme; one girl swallowed several needles stuffed inside honey cakes until her innards became a mass of incurable ulcers; a man from Birmingham crawled inside a red-hot oven and burned himself to a cinder; others chewed and swallowed glass; one ingenious suicide threw himself under the bone-crushing wheels of a heavily laden vehicle, a novel idea that was soon taken up by others; and

an Englishman hanged himself by decorating himself with candles and acting as a chandelier for the company he had invited to supper.[25]

That this satirical account was no exaggeration is clear from the authentic reports of various suicide attempts made at this time, attempts as remarkable for their motivation as for the manner of their execution. It is against this background that we must see the death wish of Senta and the Flying Dutchman. Throughout the period from 1815 to 1848, there were many Sentas who, in literature and real life, hoped to "redeem" the men they loved by killing themselves. Perhaps the most famous case was Charlotte Stieglitz, who hoped that the shattering experience of her death would free her weak and sickly poet-husband from the writer's block from which he was suffering.[26] (Her hopes proved ill founded.) Theodor Mundt wrote a literary tribute to her in 1835, and the leading classical philologist August Boeckh compared her suicide with the myth of Alcestis, who went to her death so that her husband, Admetus, might live. The emotional egoism that not only Charlotte Stieglitz but society in general presupposed on the part of the husband is so typical of the age that we must beware of interpreting Senta's readiness to die as symptomatic of Wagner's own exploitative egoism as man and artist. (The tendency to interpret Wagner's music dramas in terms of his own personality is as deplorable as it is apparently ineradicable, for all that the myth has long since been exploded by Wagnerian scholars.) And Senta's tendency to hallucinate and fall prey to somnambulistic trances, which today strikes us as merely "operatic" and scarcely plausible from a psychological point of view (unless one interprets the whole opera as a psychopathological case, as Harry Kupfer did in his Bayreuth production of 1978–85, with the entire action seen as a figment of Senta's crazed imagination), is entirely typical of its time as a literary and historical phenomenon. Whereas the German Romantics had played with the "wondrous" in an entirely conscious way, turning it into an object of artistic experiment, the same element struck the period of restoration that followed as an expression of hallucinatory fantasies. In other words, the materialization of the "wondrous" was at odds with the views of the true Romantics, who were much closer to the Enlightenment than was long believed. From a historical point of view, *Der fliegende Holländer* is not so much a Romantic opera as an opera of the Vormärz.

AHASUERUS, HERODIAS, AND KUNDRY

Heine and Wagner were not the only writers to interpret the legend of the Flying Dutchman as a variant of the Ahasuerus myth. In Levin Schücking's 1851 short story "Die drei Freier," the three suitors of the title are Ahasuerus, the Flying Dutchman, and the Wild Huntsman (another mythical figure denied the peace of the grave).[27] The object of their courtship is an emancipated woman who owes her independence of mind to her Young German ideals and whom her suitors attempt to convert to true womanhood. The Wild Hunt is also mentioned in Heine's *Atta Troll*, where Heine dwells at some length on Ahasuerus's female counterpart, Herodias, who, as we know, was to be reincarnated as Kundry in *Parsifal*: "Herodias were you" (GS 10:346).[28] And on her first appearance in act 1 of the work, she is described by the Esquires as a kind of female equivalent of the Wild Huntsman: "But look, who's riding wildly there!/Hey! The mane of the devil's mare is streaming!... Flew she through the air?/And now the wild woman dismounts" (GS 10:326).

It is not generally known that the Wandering Jewess, Kundry—cursed to wander "endlessly through life" (GS 10:360)—is by no means an invention of Wagner's; the idea that Herodias was condemned to a life of restless wandering was already familiar in the Middle Ages.[29] (Ahasuerus and Herodias are both foils of Jesus' favorite disciple, John, who according to early Christian belief and legend would not die until Christ returned to earth.) This myth was taken up by Eugène Sue in his novel *Le juif errant*, which was published in France in 1844–45 and immediately translated into German. There is no doubt that Wagner was familiar with Sue's version. Here Herodias accompanies Ahasuerus on his restless wanderings through history, until, like Wagner's Kundry, she finally finds release. Yet another writer who breathed new life into the medieval motif was Karl Gutzkow, whose novel *Die ewige Jüdin* (The Wandering Jewess) was first published in 1869.

In his conception of the character of Kundry, Wagner may well have been influenced by Heine's *Atta Troll,* which, as we have seen, appeared in the same issues of the *Zeitung für die elegante Welt* as Wagner's "Autobiographical Sketch." Alternatively, both writers may have drawn their inspiration from the same source, Jacob Grimm's *Deutsche Mythologie*. It is worth adding here that throughout the nineteenth century, Herodias was often conflated with the figure of her daughter, Salome—here one thinks not only of Heine, who, as we shall see, clearly based his account on Grimm, but also of Stéphane Mallarmé.[30] Similarly, Wagner's Kundry is a reincarnation of both Herodias and Salome. The "she-devil" Herodias—Kundry is described as an "arch-she-devil" in *Parsifal* (GS 10:345)—is the subject of the following strophes in *Atta Troll*:

> Auf dem glutenkranken Antlitz
> Lag des Morgenlandes Zauber,
> Auch die Kleider mahnten kostbar
> An Scheherezadens Märchen.
>
> Sanfte Lippen, wie Grenaten,
> Ein gebognes Liljennäschen,
> Und die Glieder schlank und kühlig
> Wie die Palme der Oase.
> . . . .
> Wirklich eine Fürstin war sie,
> War Judäas Königin,
> Des Herodes schönes Weib,
> Die des Täufers Haupt begehrt hat.
>
> Dieser Blutschuld halber ward sie
> Auch vermaledeit; als Nachtspuk

Muß sie bis zum jüngsten Tage
Reiten mit der wilden Jagd.

In den Händen trägt sie immer
Jene Schüssel mit dem Haupte
Des Johannes, und sie küßt es;
Ja, sie küßt das Haupt mit Inbrunst.

Denn sie liebte einst Johannem—
In der Bibel steht es nicht,
Doch im Volke lebt die Sage
Von Herodias' blutger Liebe—

Anders wär' ja unerklärlich
Das Gelüste jener Dame—
Wird ein Weib das Haupt begehren
Eines Mannes, den sie nicht liebt?[31]

[On her glowing sickly features
Lay an oriental charm,
And her costly robes reminded
Of Scheherezade's sweet stories.

Soft her lips, just like pomegranates,
And her nose a bending lily,
And her members cool and slender
As the palms in the oasis.
. . . .

And in truth she was a princess,
Was the queen of far Judæa,
Was the lovely wife of Herod,
Who the Baptist's head demanded.

For this deed of blood she also
Was accurs'd, and as a spectre
With the wild hunt must keep riding,
Even to the day of judgement.

In her hands she evermore
Bears the charger with the Baptist's
Head upon it, which she kisses,—
Yes, the head she kisses wildly.

For she once loved John the Baptist;
In the Bible 'tis not written,
Yet in popular tradition
Lives Herodias' bloody love.

Otherwise there's no explaining
That strange fancy of the lady,—

Would a woman ever ask for
That man's head for whom she cared not?

(Trans. Edgar Alfred Bowring)]

Heine's source was undoubtedly the *Deutsche Mythologie* of Jacob Grimm, who cites numerous texts from the early Middle Ages, all of which tell how "Herodias (the daughter) was cursed on account of her blood guilt and condemned to wander the earth in the company of evil, devilish spirits. She is placed at the head of the Wild Hunt, either alongside Diana [in whose retinue she also appears in Heine's account of the tale] or in her stead." In short, the "Christian myth of Herodias" was "already combined with indigenous pagan tales even during the early Middle Ages." Quoting various sources, Grimm notes that "she was inflamed with love of John the Baptist, a love that he did not return."[32]

Modern readers will be reminded of Oscar Wilde's *Salome*, first published in French in 1893; but Wilde's play was by no means the only version of the tale after Heine to suggest an erotic motive behind the relationship between Herodias/Salome and John the Baptist. This theme was extraordinarily popular, especially in France, during the second half of the nineteenth century, so much so that only the most important adaptations in literature and the visual arts can be mentioned here.[33] (The popularity of the theme is further attested by Jules Laforgue's *Salomé*, a cynical parody of Flaubert's "Hérodias," published posthumously in his 1887 *Moralités légendaires*.) One or more of these versions undoubtedly left its mark on the Kundry scenes in *Parsifal*, just as the latter were in turn to influence the poems about Herodias and Salome by such fin-de-siècle writers as Wilde and Villiers de l'Isle-Adam.[34]

"Arch-she-devil, rose of hell! / Herodias were you, and what else?" Klingsor demands of Kundry (GS 10:345–46). The rose imagery is generally attributed to the influence of Baudelaire's *Les fleurs du mal* (The flowers of evil), yet, surprisingly perhaps, it is also found in two of Mallarmé's works, the fragmentary dramatic poem, *Hérodiade* (1876–87), and *Les fleurs* (The flowers, 1864), where it has an important symbolic function, more especially in connection with the figure of Herodias.

L'hyacinthe, le myrte à l'adorable éclair
Et, pareille à la chair de la femme, la rose
Cruelle, Hérodiade en fleur du jardin clair,
Celle qu'un sang farouche et radieux arrose![35]

[The hyacinth, the myrtle with her flash of white
And, like as any woman's flesh, the cruel rose,
Herodias, the garden's blossoming delight,
She in whose veins a wild candescent lifeblood flows!]

It is the curse of Kundry/Herodias, as it is of Ahasuerus, to keep committing the sin for which she was originally cursed. In Lenau's *Der ewige Jude* (1839), we read:

Weh mir, ich kann des Bilds mich nicht entschlagen,
Wie er um kurze Rast so flehend blickte,
Der Todesmüde, Schmach- und Schmerzgeknickte,
Muß ewig ihn von meiner Hütte jagen.

[Alas, that I might banish from my mind the sight
Of one who begged to rest awhile and catch his breath,
One whom, bowed down with shame and weary unto death,
I must condemn forevermore to endless flight.]

Just as Ahasuerus prevented Jesus from resting on his *via dolorosa* and struck him in order to hurry him on his way, so Kundry laughed at her Savior as he bore his cross. (This represents a radical reversal of the message that forms the metaphysical and ethical core of *Parsifal*, namely, elemental compassion for those in pain; Parsifal's failure to show compassion constitues his tragic guilt.) This is why Kundry is condemned to repeat her "accursed laughter" with compulsive regularity and to keep on embodying the depravity of Herodias/Salome in ever new reincarnations. The wild erotic desire that Parsifal's asceticism arouses in her is analogous to the frenzy she felt when, as Herodias, she had demanded the head of John the Baptist. And it is just as futile now as it was then.

"Ahasuerus, the wandering Jew, is nothing but the personification of the whole Jewish race," Schopenhauer had written in his *Parerga und Paralipomena*. It was the curse of this "gens extorris," this "John Lackland among the nations," to wander nomadically through history.[36] In the nineteenth century a parallel was often drawn between the Ahasuerus myth and the homelessness of the Jewish nation, especially with reference to the situation of Jewish writers. Both they and their contemporaries felt that they were destined to suffer from Weltschmerz. Just as the Jew represented the quintessential *homo melancholicus* in the tradition of Western melancholia, so inner conflict became a distinguishing feature after 1815, resulting in a special affinity between the Jew and the artist, who, more than anyone else, felt the Wandering Jew's rootlessness and the "breach in creation" referred to earlier. All "artists" and "men of genius," Nietzsche later wrote in *The Case of Wagner*, were "Wandering Jews."[37] Accordingly, Wagner was able to relate the Ahasuerus myth as much to himself as to Jews. His "anti-Semitism" is scarcely understandable without his sense of this affinity between the artist and the Jew. On 21 June 1859 he wrote to Mathilde Wesendonck to tell her that he would have to beware of developing a passion for horses, since "no horse was assigned to the Wandering Jew to accompany him on his travels."[38] And, just as he saw himself reflected in the figure of Ahasuerus, so he undoubtedly saw himself in the Flying Dutchman and the Wanderer, who, he told Cosima on 23 January 1879, was "a kind of Flying Dutchman."

THE WANDERING JEW'S LONGING FOR A HOMELAND

In his autobiographical apologia of 1851, Wagner described the Flying Dutchman as a synthesis of Odysseus, Ahasuerus (whom he interprets in a way wholly devoid of anti-Semitic features), and Columbus.

The figure of the "Flying Dutchman" is the mythical invention of the folk: an ancient aspect of man's essential nature expresses itself here with heart-enthralling power.

This feature, in its most universal significance, is the longing for peace from life's storms. In the bright Hellenic world we meet it in the wanderings of Odysseus and in the latter's longing for a homeland, house, and hearth, but also for his wife, who, for this civically minded son of ancient Hellas, was truly attainable and finally attained. Having no earthly home, Christianity embodied this feature in the figure of the "Wandering Jew": there was no earthly deliverance for such a wanderer as he, damned forever and for eternity to the living death of a life devoid of purpose and joy; the only goal left to him was the longing for death, his only hope the prospect of no longer existing. As the Middle Ages came to an end, a new and active impulse drew all nations back toward *life*, an impulse which, within the context of world history, found its most successful expression in the urge for discovery. The sea now became the terrain of life, no longer the tiny land-locked sea of the Hellenic world but the earth-encircling ocean. This marked a break with the ancient world: Odysseus's longing to return to his homeland, hearth, and wife, nurtured on the sufferings of the Wandering Jew, had become a yearning for death; it was now intensified in turn to become a desire for something new and unknown, something not yet visible but already dimly felt. This all but universal feature we find in the myth of the Flying Dutchman, this poem of a seafaring nation from the period in world history associated with the great voyages of discovery. What we encounter here is a remarkable mixture, produced by the spirit of the people, of the character of the Wandering Jew with that of Odysseus. As a punishment for his temerity, the Dutchman is condemned by the Devil—a clear symbol of the element of floodwater and storms—to roam the seas for all eternity. As an end to his anguish, he longs, like Ahasuerus, for death; this form of release, denied to the Wandering Jew, may be vouchsafed to the Dutchman through *a woman* who sacrifices herself to him out of love; the yearning for death thus drives the Dutchman to seek out this woman; this woman, however, is no longer the Penelope of Odysseus, wooed by him in ages past and caring for him at home; it is, rather, . . . *the woman of the future.* (GS 4:265–66)

Within this bold mythological synthesis, Wagner harnessed together classical antiquity (the longing for a homeland), the Middle Ages (the longing for death), and the modern age (the longing for the new) to create a Utopian myth. By taking to its absurd extreme the idea of being "in transit," the modern urge to discover new lands is transformed into a longing for oblivion. But what does Wagner mean by "the woman of the future,"[39] the woman whose fate it is to redeem the wanderer from the absurdity of his sempiternal odyssey?

In 1851, in *A Communication to My Friends*, Wagner saw the homelessness of the Flying Dutchman as a symbolic projection of his own situation during his years in Paris from 1839 to 1842. "An ardent, yearning patriotism awoke within me, such as I had never before suspected." Unlike the "civically minded" Odysseus, however, Wagner did not really yearn to return to his homeland. Germany was certainly no political ideal for him,

> for I was already alive to the fact that political Germany did not have the slightest attraction to offer me as compared, say, with political France. It was the feeling of homelessness in Paris that aroused in me this yearning for my German homeland; yet

this longing was directed not at old familiar haunts needing only to be rediscovered, but rather at a country pictured in my dreams, an unknown haven that was yet to be discovered. . . . It was the Flying Dutchman's longing for *womankind*, not, as I have said, for the wife who waited for Odysseus, but for the woman who would redeem me, the woman whose features had never before presented themselves to me in any clear-cut form but who hovered before my mind's eye as the expression of woman-hood itself; and this element now found expression in the idea of *a homeland*, the idea of being enfolded by an intimately close community, a community, be it added, which I learned to long for only when I realized what the idea of a "homeland" meant. (GS 4:268)

The same idea recurs in the closing sentence of Ernst Bloch's *Das Prinzip Hoffnung*, where "homeland" is defined as "something which shines into the childhood of all and in which no one has yet been."[40] For Wagner, this homeland, or *terra utopica*, was encapsulated in the image of the woman who could never be found. But in *Der fliegende Holländer*, of course, the woman who could never be found *is* found, and the "not yet" becomes the "now" in the moment of Utopian happi-ness that is the duet between Senta and the Dutchman in act 2.

> Wie aus der Ferne längst vergang'ner Zeiten
> spricht dieses Mädchens Bild zu mir:
> wie ich's geträumt seit bangen Ewigkeiten,
> vor meinen Augen seh' ich's hier.
>
> (GS 1:279)

> [Out of the mists of ages unremembered
> Her gentle image speaks to me:
> For in my dreams of yearning long unnumbered
> This was the face that I could see.]

It would undoubtedly be a trivialization of the work to see the Flying Dutchman's homeless, dispossessed state as a mere reflection of Wagner's years of deprivation in Paris. Rather, this homeless state is the stigma of the modern "absolute artist" in general. This idea, too, finds expression in *A Communication to My Friends*, where Wagner describes his Romantic operas (all of which, in Hans Mayer's view, are "coded dramas about the life of the artist")[41] as disquisitions on the lone-liness of the "pure" artist, a loneliness from which he seeks release through love. *Lohengrin*, in particular, is interpreted by Wagner as the tragedy of the "absolute artist" who longs in vain for a "homeland." In contrast to Lohengrin, who "returns, annihilated, to his loneliness" (GS 4:296), the Flying Dutchman achieves re-demption, but only when Senta joins him in his loneliness, a loneliness embodied in the sea into which she hurls herself in the closing moments of the opera. Time and again in his prose writings—but principally in *The Artwork of the Future*—Wagner described the sea as an image of the "essence of music." The image is fre-quently associated with a state of boundless isolation "between sea and sky" and with the yearning to set foot on land, "a homeland that constantly hovers before the mind's eye but is never reached" (GS 3:84). In this way, the seafarer becomes a symbol of the modern artist in general, and as such he is depicted by Poe, Swinburne, Baudelaire, and others.[42]

Two symbols come together, then, in the figure of the Flying Dutchman. First, he is the mythical reflection of the modern human being, for whom the urge to discover new lands has become an aimless journey into the infinite void. (Not only does this transform the modern optimistic belief in progress into a pessimistic view of history and a sense of world-weariness, it also means that the Flying Dutchman himself is engaged in a constant quest for a *terra utopica* that can become his home.) And, second, he is an existential symbol of the modern absolute artist in his alienation from life.

AHASUERUS AS A CONTEMPORARY

One of the most striking aspects of Wagnerian music theater is its ability to provoke parody and travesty, caricature and satire.[43] Uwe Hoppe's parodies, beginning with *Paxiphall und Lohengrün*, have become something of an institution in Bayreuth, where they have been performed every summer since the mid-1980s. Clearly, Wagner's music dramas lend themselves to parody on account of the latent comedy implicit in the clash between the naïveté of their mythological subject matter and the modern, "sentimental" manner in which that subject matter is presented. Time and again the juxtaposition of extreme naïveté and sensibility, of the brutally physical and the subtly psychological, has tempted writers to parody these works by transporting them from the world of heroic legend into a contemporary bourgeois setting. Even Nietzsche, in *The Case of Wagner*, permitted himself a joke at Wagner's expense, suggesting that the contents of his music dramas should be "translated into reality, into the modern—let us be even crueler—into the bourgeois."

> What becomes of Wagner then?—Among ourselves, I have tried it. Nothing is more entertaining, nothing to be recommended more highly for walks, than retelling Wagner in a more *up-to-date* style: for example, Parsifal as a candidate for a theological degree, with a secondary school education (the latter being indispensable for *pure foolishness*).What surprises we encounter in the process! Would you believe it? All of Wagner's heroines, without exception, as soon as they are stripped of their heroic skin, become almost indistinguishable from Madame Bovary![44]

The ease with which mythic themes can be translated into a modern idiom (an ease well illustrated by one of the basic tendencies of modern Wagner productions) is bound up with Wagner's repeated use of thematic material that had already been parodied even before he adapted it for his own dramatic ends. *Der fliegende Holländer* and *Tannhäuser* were both directly inspired by Heine's parodies. Indeed, all of Wagner's Romantic operas might be described as parodied parodies, with two minuses producing a plus. The subject has reacquired its former tragic seriousness, having lived through the experience of its own comic negation, or, to use Schiller's terminology, it is no longer a naive and unrefracted seriousness but a sentimental seriousness born of reflection and fully conscious of its own fragility—which explains why, in turn, Wagner's music dramas have repeatedly invited writers to parody them.

That it is but a single step from the sublime to the ridiculous is very much a precondition of the music drama that conjures up myth not as something past but as something present. Parody and travesty are the touchstone by which we judge the modernity of the mythicomusical drama. A glance at Cosima's diaries shows that Wagner was an obsessive parodist. Not only other people's works but his own, too, served as the constant butts of his parodic wit.[45] "One must be able to joke about the sublimest of things," he said on one such occasion (CT, 24 December 1877). As early as 1840 he had written French parodies of Senta's Ballad and the Sailors' Chorus, showing how tragic themes immediately evoked parodic associations in his imagination.[46] "Oh, that is my salvation, this ability to convert the most serious things into nonsense in a flash—it has always kept me from going over the brink," he told Cosima on 6 August 1878.

In the case of *Der fliegende Holländer*, there exists a travesty that might be said to restore Wagner's opera to the comic level of its parodic source, namely, Heine's *Memoiren des Herren von Schnabelewopski*. One of three "grotesque comedies" by Friedrich Huch, all of which date from 1911 (the other two are *Lohengrin* and *Tristan und Isolde*),[47] it features the "Ahasuerus of the ocean" as a world-weary *décadent*. He is bored not only by his interminable existence but also by the constant retelling of his life by men of letters. "My fate is like a bad penny, forever passed from hand to hand."[48] Like Helen of Troy in Goethe's *Faust*, he sees himself as a literary figure and, to his annoyance, feels that nothing ever happens to him that he has not already experienced as his own fictional doppelgänger. He is "a has-been, sung about in ballads. . . . It's an odd, almost eerie sensation, feeling everything twice over. For some time I've been obsessed with the idea that my whole fate is unfolding onstage and that I've been performing my own Passion play every seven years."[49] He wonders whether the picture of himself contained in Wagner's opera is a true reflection of his character: "Am I really as unsympathetic as I unfortunately appear to be there? So passively demanding? So vampirically egotistical?"[50] And he has to concede that "a man who has nothing else to think about in the world except his own redemption is bound to grow egotistical."[51] This is one of the passages in which a comic reversal of the tragic myth is transformed into an open criticism of Wagner's ideology of redemption, an ideology that Huch holds up to ridicule by exposing his hero as a monster of artistic egoism.

As in Wagner's opera, Senta falls in love with the Flying Dutchman, but her playing of the "Ballad from the *Flying Dutchman*," which she keeps picking out on the piano, finally gets on the Dutchman's nerves; there is nothing he likes less, he says, than music that is "badly performed."[52] He also feels uncomfortable at finding himself drawn into exactly the same situations as those he has seen on the operatic stage. Once again his rival is Erik, a "sentimental lyric tenor"[53] who has, of course, given up his uncertain existence as a huntsman, since Daland has said he can marry

Senta only if he gets a steady job. He now works in the local post office, a prosaic profession that Senta, eager for adventure, finds tedious in the extreme:

ERIK: Would you against love's simple pleasures rail?
SENTA: Away with you! Be gone! You smell of mail![54]

Huch's witty travesty was not intended to expose Wagner's Romantic opera to ridicule or to satirize it. Rather, it turns the tragic myth on its head, transferring it to a fin-de-siècle milieu and treating it as a subject for comedy. The result is a satyr play performed, as it were, as an intermezzo between the age of Weltschmerz and that of *décadence*.

Fritz Mauthner had a totally different aim in mind when writing his waspish parody, *Der unbewußte Ahasverus* (The unconscious Ahasuerus, 1878), a work that does not so much pillory a particular music drama as examine the role of the Ahasuerus motif in Wagner's works in general. Unlike Huch, Mauthner attacks Wagner and his followers head-on, mercilessly, and with caustic wit. The music, however, is spared: "If notes were all that you'd composed / To less contempt you'd be exposed"—thus the motto of the piece.[55]

Born in Bohemia in 1849, Mauthner was a journalist and writer on linguistics who published a whole series of parodies under the title *Nach berühmten Mustern* (After famous models, 1878–80) and whose novel *Der neue Ahasver* (The new Ahasuerus, 1882) uses the figure of the Wandering Jew to examine the problem of Jewish identity in the modern world. Here and elsewhere he satirizes many aspects of Wagner's works, including what he regarded as the turgid language of Wagner's prose writings, the composer's sense of a mission, his ideas concerning the "total work of art," alliteration and Wagner's related etymological and semantic speculations, the philosophical ballast that weighs down his theories on music (here one thinks of the second part of his main title, "The Thing-in-Itself as Will and Representation," and also of the fact that the action takes place in 1781, "the year of birth of the critique of pure reason"),[56] the bombastic and uncritical writings of disciples such as Heinrich Porges and Hans von Wolzogen, and, finally, the anti-Semitism of both Wagner and the Wagnerians, an anti-Semitism whose potential repercussions are evoked with terrifying clarity in Ahasuerus's closing lines.

> Erlöst durch die Länge des laubgrünen Liedes
> Wall' ich nach Walhall, wenn die Würgengel Wagners
> Den Hebräer Ahasver nicht hinterrücks hecheln.[57]
>
> [Redeemed by the length of the leafy-green lay,
> I'll hie me to Valhall, if Wagner's grim Vandals
> Don't heckle and hound Ahasuerus the Hebrew.]

The subtitle, "Bühnen-Weh-Festspiel" (Stage woe festival),[58] is intended, of course, to recall Wagner's *Bühnenweihfestspiel* (Stage consecration festival), the poem of which had appeared in print in 1877. But, otherwise, Mauthner's satire has little in common with *Parsifal*, unless we are to assume that Ahasuerus's redemption is in some way an allusion to the "Wandering Jewess" Kundry and her redemption in death. But Mauthner makes no attempt to parody the language of *Parsifal*, preferring to direct his barbs at the alliterative meter of the *Ring* and at the style of Wagner's theoretical writings. In terms of both form and content, *Der unbewußte Ahasverus* has more to say about the excesses of Wagnerism than about Wagner himself. But this kind of intentional distortion of the ideas of the author who is being parodied, together with a readiness to equate those ideas with current views about him, however much those views may be grounded in prejudice, has always been both legitimate and, indeed, crucial to parody as a genre. Parody can succeed and will be understood as such only if the audience recognizes its own prejudices and preconceptions in the work—and if it does so, moreover, with the laughter of recognition.

On one point, at least, Mauthner understood exactly what Wagner was trying to say, namely, the extent to which the Wandering Jew Ahasuerus was Wagner's constant companion in life. That this theme also had serious ideological implications for Wagner within the context of his rejection of "Jewishness" is clear from the ending of his infamous essay, "Jews in Music," where "the redemption of Ahasuerus—destruction" (GS 5:85)—is held out as the only course of salvation open to the Jews. The German word *Untergang* that Wagner uses here is notoriously difficult to pin down in English; it can mean anything from the setting of the sun to the sinking of the *Titanic* and is also found in the title of Oswald Spengler's *The Decline of the West*, in addition to being used to refer to the end of the world, the downfall of individuals, the doom of prophets, and in the colloquial expression "Du bist noch mal mein Untergang!" (You'll be the death of me). What Wagner appears to have meant was an end to the Jews' "special status," whereby they, and the modern human being in general, will be "redeemed as true human beings." At the end of this process of redemption, "we" shall be "united" with, and "indivisible" from, the Jews (GS 5:85). Mauthner's parody undoubtedly alludes to this final paragraph of Wagner's essay.

The action of *Der unbewußte Ahasverus* (which, its author claims, is the text of a Wagnerian music drama published, like *Parsifal*, in advance of its musical setting) is based on the conceit that Ahasuerus, the embodiment of the "antimusical" principle of Judaism (a further reference to "Jews in Music"), will be granted redemption only "when something exists that lasts somewhat longer / Than my lugubrious life,"[59] and this "something" is Wagner's famous "unending melody." "It is so unending that the Wandering Jew reverts to childhood." To this, Mauthner adds a footnote, which he attributes to Heinrich Porges (ironically, a Jew, although Mauthner seems not to have known this) and Hans von Wolzogen, whom he treats as typical representatives of the hagiographic school of Wagnerian "scholarship": "The Wandering Jew is redeemed by the Master's unending melody"; in other words, he may die. "Divine! And his wretched coreligionists do not even show themselves grateful. The Master is too good for them."[60] Thus Mauthner maliciously seeks to expose Wagner's presumption in proferring redemption to the Jews in the form of an offer that gives them only the chance of self-annihilation.

"Join unreservedly in this self-annihilatory and regenerative act of redemption, and we shall be united and indivisible" (GS 5:85). Thus Wagner ends his essay on "Jews in Music." He speaks not only of "self-annihilation" and "destruction" but also of "regeneration" and redemption through annihilation. The Jew shall rise from the ashes like a phoenix, no longer a Jew but a true human being. This idea recalls Karl Marx's 1843 essay *Zur Judenfrage* (On the Jewish Question), a work no less infamous than Wagner's, which sets out from the premise that assimilation is no answer to the Jewish question, since the Jew would simply be conforming to a lifestyle that was depraved and would be adopting, as it were, a corrupt identity. (Wagner, too, shared this conviction.) Assimilation would be achieved, Marx believed, only if the Jews ceased to exist as Jews as part of a process affecting the whole of a society that in Marx's view was alienated from its true self. What Marx describes as "supersession" (the Hegelian term *Aufhebung* can also imply preservation and assimilation) becomes a metaphysics of destruction and redemption for Wagner, an outlook explicable only in terms of the mood of Weltschmerz that characterized his age.[61]

The Ahasuerus myth is a myth about Wagner's life as an artist. The fact that he includes Jews in this myth suggests that the anti-Semitic use to which it was increasingly put in the second half of the nineteenth century and later (most notably in Franz Hippler's 1940 National Socialist propaganda film *Der ewige Jude*) did not yet apply to Wagner. For him, the legend of the Wandering Jew was still a modern Christian myth of general human significance, the myth of a man who doubts in his own redemption but who is nonetheless redeemed from the depths of utter despair.

Venus in Exile

TANNHÄUSER *BETWEEN ROMANTICISM AND YOUNG GERMANY*

Go to the frigid world of men,

From whose insipid, gloomy dreams

We gods of pleasure long since fled,

Deep in the earth's warm sheltering womb.

—*Richard Wagner,* Tannhäuser

WAGNER'S various autobiographical writings contain assorted accounts of the way in which he was "inspired" to write his operas and music dramas, many of these accounts being embroidered with corroborative detail intended to give artistic verisimilitude to a bald and otherwise unconvincing narrative. Time and again it has become clear to writers on Wagner that these "inspirational myths" deserve our deep distrust. One of the principal dogmas of Wagner's aesthetic ideology was his belief that the musical drama was born out of the spirit of the *Volk* and that its creator drew directly on the figures of the mythopoeic popular imagination. This helps to explain why, from *Der fliegende Holländer* onward, Wagner claimed that the basic idea behind each of his works came from popular tradition, so that, in looking back on the genesis of each piece, he either passed over in silence or else disparaged the modern versions of the tales that he himself had adapted. His later attempts to trivialize the influence of Heine's parodic account of the Dutchman legend is a classic example of his whole approach to his sources, as is his rewriting of the genesis of *Tannhäuser*. The fact remains that it was in modern adaptations that Wagner became familiar with the "popular" subject matter of all his Romantic operas, adaptations that were refracted, as it were, through a lens that was partly scholarly, partly poetic.[1]

What is true on a literary level is also true of the music, as Thomas Mann once pointed out. Writing in his *Reflections of a Nonpolitical Man*, Mann noted that German folk music plays a relatively insignificant role in Wagner's works, and he went on to quote the Swedish writer on music Wilhelm Peterson-Berger, who had claimed that Wagner "could strike a popular German note for the purposes of characterization, as he did in *Die Meistersinger* and *Siegfried*, but this was never the basis and starting point of his tone poem and is never the wellspring from which it bursts forth spontaneously, as it does with Schumann, Schubert, and Brahms." Mann concluded from this that "however authentic and potent it may have been, Wagner's Germanness was refracted and fragmented in a modern way; it was decorative, analytical, and intellectual, hence his fascination, his innate ability to make a cosmopolitan, planetary impact."[2]

THE GODS IN EXILE: WAGNER AND HEINE'S "ELEMENTARGEISTER"

In the case of both *Der fliegende Holländer* and *Tannhäuser*, the lens referred to here was that of Heinrich Heine, whose essay "Elementargeister" (Elemental spirits) appeared in 1837 in the third volume of *Der Salon*. (The first part of it had already appeared in French in 1835, in Heine's *De l'Allemagne*.) It is unlikely, to say the least, that Wagner, who not only knew Heine's writings at firsthand but who, as we know from his Paris feuilletons, could imitate Heine's style to perfection, was unfamiliar with this essay. The fact that he does not mention it in either *A Communication to My Friends* or *My Life* is no proof that he did not know it, as his silence on the subject is part and parcel of his tendency, from the 1840s onward, to suppress all knowledge of Heine.

In his essay, Heine develops an idea to which he was to return in 1853 in "Die Götter im Exil" (The gods in exile) and that was a recurrent theme in its author's life. Some of the elemental spirits of the essay's title, Heine believed, owed their existence to a "transformation of the old pagan gods" who, following Christ's victory over them, had gone into exile, "dwelling in subterranean seclusion" and "going about their demonic business with the other elemental spirits." There follows Heine's account of the Tannhäuser legend.

> Of all the tales told by the German folk, the strangest is the romantic legend of the goddess Venus, who, when her temples were torn down, fled to a secret mountain where she now leads the most fantastic life of pleasure in the company of the most carefree spirits of the air, together with fair nymphs of woodland and water, and many a famous hero who had suddenly vanished from the face of the earth. As you draw near the mountain, you can hear, even from a distance, the sounds of merry laughter and the sweet strains of a harp stealing into your heart like an invisible chain that draws you into the mountain. But you are lucky, for close to the entrance an old knight keeps watch, known to all as Faithful Eckart; he stands like a statue, resting on his great broadsword, but his honest and hoary head nods unceasingly, and sadly he warns you of the tender dangers that await you within the mountain. Many have been frightened away in good time, but others have failed to heed the old man's bleating voice and hurtled blindly into the pit of accursed desire.[3]

Heine was no doubt thinking of Ludwig Tieck's 1799 short story *Der getreue Eckart und der Tannenhäuser* (Faithful Eckart and Tannenhäuser), a tale that was also familiar to Wagner. Here, too, we encounter the idea of the gods of classical antiquity living in medieval exile. Before he takes up his position outside the Venusberg, where he warns others of the dangers that lurk within it, Eckart is told that "when sacred Christianity, newly emergent, had cast out pagan idols, devils fled into the mountain and sought refuge at the desolate center of the earth. Here, it is said,

Frau Venus holds court, gathering around her her hellish host of worldly desires and illicit wishes."[4] Tannenhäuser reports in a similar vein: "Thus the throng of smiling pagan gods approached me, Frau Venus at their head, and all of them bade me welcome; they were banished there by the power of the Almighty and are no longer worshiped on earth, but they continue to exert their secret sway from inside there."[5]

It is as an exiled goddess that Venus describes herself in Wagner's opera, when, "in an outburst of the most violent anger," she gives Tannhäuser permission to leave.

> Hin zu den kalten Menschen flieh',
> vor deren blödem, trübem Wahn
> der Freude Götter wir entfloh'n
> tief in der Erde wärmenden Schoos.
>
> (GS 2:9)

> [Go to the frigid world of men,
> From whose insipid, gloomy dreams
> We gods of pleasure long since fled,
> Deep in the earth's warm sheltering womb.]

The "insipid, gloomy dreams," or "illusions," to which Venus refers are an allusion to Christian morality, with its hostility to sensuality. For its part, Christianity dismissed the ancient gods not as "chimeras and monstrous products of deceit and error" (to quote Heine in "Die Götter im Exil") but as

> evil spirits plunged from their pinnacle of power by Christ's victory and now carrying on their lives on earth in the gloom of temple ruins and magic groves, luring to their ruin the weak-willed Christians who have lost their way and seducing them with their devilish wiles, with lust and beauty, and most of all with dancing and singing.[6]

This fraternization between pagan gods and the hellish fiends of Christianity—an association that, significantly, plays no part in Wagner's opera—finds expression in Tieck's short story in the motif of Satan guiding lost souls to the Venusberg.

In his 1861 essay on *Tannhäuser*, Baudelaire added a further variant to this idea of a link between Satan and the exiled Venus when he wrote that "*Tannhäuser* represents the struggle between the two principles that have chosen the human heart for their chief battlefield, in other words, the struggle between flesh and spirit, Heaven and Hell, Satan and God."[7]

> The radiant Venus of antiquity, the foam-born Aphrodite, has not passed unscathed through the dreadful shades of the Middle Ages. Her dwelling is no longer Olympus, nor the shores of a perfumed archipelago. She had retired into the depths of a cavern, magnificent, it is true, but illuminated by fires very different from those of benign Apollo. In going underground, Venus has moved a step towards Hell, and doubtless, on certain abominable feast days, she goes regularly to pay homage to the Archfiend, Prince of the Flesh and Sovereign of Sin.[8]

The notion that Christianity drove the classical gods into exile recurs repeatedly in the poetry of the late eighteenth and nineteenth centuries. Among the many poems that take as their theme the supplanting of natural deities by Christian monotheism is Schiller's *Die Götter Griechenlands* (The gods of Greece), first published in 1788, the opening strophe of which reads:

> Da ihr noch die schöne Welt regiertet,
> An der Freude leichtem Gängelband
> Glücklichere Menschenalter führtet,
> Schöne Wesen aus dem Fabelland!
> Ach! da euer Wonnedienst noch glänzte,
> Wie ganz anders, anders war es da!
> Da man deine Tempel noch bekränzte,
> Venus Amathusia!

> [Whilst the smiling Earth ye govern'd still,
>   And with Rapture's soft and guiding hand
> Let the happy Nations at your will,
>   Beauteous Beings from the Fable-land!
> Whilst your blissful worship smil'd around,
>   Ah! how diff'rent was it in that day!
> When the people still thy temples crown'd,
>   Venus Amathusia!

(Trans. Edgar Alfred Bowring)]

(Amathus was the site of a famous temple dedicated to Venus on the island of Cyprus.) In the second part of his *Wallenstein* trilogy, Schiller again takes up the theme of the gods in exile, placing the following words in the mouth of Max Piccolomini:

> Die alten Fabelwesen sind nicht mehr,
> Das reizende Geschlecht ist ausgewandert;
> Doch eine Sprache braucht das Herz, es bringt
> Der alte Trieb die alten Namen wieder,
> Und an dem Sternenhimmel gehn sie jetzt,
> Die sonst im Leben freundlich mitgewandelt,
> Dort winken sie dem Liebenden herab,
> Und jedes Große bringt uns *Jupiter*
> Noch diesen Tag, und *Venus* jedes Schöne.

(*Die Piccolomini*, act 2, scene 4)

> [The old and fabled beings have all fled,
> The lovely race is gone forevermore;
> And yet the heart must needs give tongue, old drives
> Bring back to mind old long-forgotten names,
> For in the starry firmament they dwell
> That once bestrode the earth with friendly mien,
> Yet smiling down on lovers' head, for still
> Today all greatness comes from *Jupiter*,
> All beauty, even now, is *Venus'* gift.]

Here we have a variant of the theme of the gods in exile, reinterpreted in the spirit of classical Humanism: the gods have migrated to the starry firmament, as projections of humankind. The neomedieval Romantic tradition, conversely, demonizes the gods and relocates their place of exile in the netherworld.

Both versions, however, presuppose the continuing existence of the classical gods, and this contrast between a "heavenly" Venus and a "demonic" Venus also plays a part in Wagner's *Tannhäuser*. Here it is Wolfram von Eschenbach who acts as a foil to the demonic underworld figure of Tannhäuser and who is characterized by his special affinity with the starry vault. Thus his eulogy to love in the second act begins:

> Da blick' ich auf zu *einem* nur der Sterne,
> der an dem Himmel, der mich blendet, steht:
> es sammelt sich mein Geist aus jeder Ferne,
> andächtig sinkt die Seele in Gebet.
>
> (GS 2:22)

> [But then I gaze on *one* bright star that shines
> Down from the dazzling heavens, passing fair:
> My thoughts, once straying far, are gathered,
> And fervently my soul sinks down in prayer.]

Who is meant by this one star? There is no doubt that it is Venus, the Star of Eve, the "loveliest of all the stars," that Wolfram famously apostrophizes in the third act. For him, the Star of Eve is the star of a "noble," renunciatory love, transcending erotic desire. It is Venus Urania, sacred or heavenly love, in contrast to Venus Cypria, the earthly or profane love that—as a force of the netherworld—Tannhäuser has tasted.

Writing in *A Communication to My Friends* in 1851, Wagner claimed that the decisive impetus behind *Tannhäuser* came not from any modern reworking of the legend but from "the *Volksbuch* and the simple Tannhäuser Ballad." Only here, he insisted, had he discovered in undistorted form the "simple, genuine folk poem that dealt with the figure of Tannhäuser" (GS 4:269). But where had Wagner found this "simple Tannhäuser Ballad"—by which he evidently meant the relevant poem from *Des Knaben Wunderhorn* (The boy's magic horn)? Certainly he had not encountered it in Arnim and Brentano's anthology, which he appears not to have known at this date. Still less will he have found it in their source, Heinrich Kornmann's *Mons Veneris: Fraw Veneris Berg* (1614). Quite simply, he must have read it in Heine's "Elementargeister," where it was printed in its entirety.

As for the *Volksbuch*, or chapbook, no such work exists. What Wagner must have meant is Ludwig Bechstein's collection of legends, *Die Sagen von Eisenach und der Wartburg, dem Hörseelberg und Reinhardsbrunn*, the first part of which appeared in 1835.[9] Not only did Wagner find an account of the Tannhäuser legend here, but the Venusberg, until then generally located in Italy, was transferred to Thuringia, whereas Tannhäuser was loosely associated with the Wartburg, "where he, too, was no doubt invited by the Landgrave." Bechstein's anthology also included, of course, an account of the Tournament of Song, which appears under the grammatically curious title of "Der Sängerkrieg auf Wartburg" (literally, The minstrels' contest on Wartburg), an ellipsis that recurs in the subtitle of Wagner's opera. Bechstein, it may be added, is also mentioned in Heine's "Elementargeister" as having sent the latter a copy of the older version of the Danheüser Ballad of 1515, a version to which I shall return in due course. ("The older version contains many variants and, to my mind, bears a much more poetical stamp," was Heine's assessment of the 1515 ballad.)[10]

But there was even more for Wagner to glean from Heine's essay, for it also contains references not only to Eichendorff's 1819 short story *Das Marmorbild* (The marble image) (a tale whose remarkable motivic parallels with *Tannhäuser* suggest, even if they cannot prove, that Wagner was familiar with this work, too) but also to Willibald Alexis's *Venus in Rom* (Venus in Rome, 1828), and, finally, to the common source of both these tales, Kornmann's aforementioned compilation, *Mons Veneris*, published in Frankfurt in 1614. In other words, Heine's "Elementargeister" contained virtually all that was worth knowing on the subject of Tannhäuser, including, not least, Heine's own parodic version of the legend.

VENUSBERG AND WARTBURG: TIECK, E.T.A. HOFFMANN, AND WAGNER

Wagner met Tieck—the "king of Romanticism," as Hebbel called him—in Berlin in 1847 and left a detailed account of his conversation with the seventy-four-year-old poet, who by then was the only surviving member of the first generation of German Romantic writers. Tieck knew the librettos of both *Tannhäuser*—which had, after all, been inspired to a considerable extent by his own *Der getreue Eckart und der Tannenhäuser* of half a century previously—and *Lohengrin*, and according to Wagner's report of their meeting, he was favorably impressed by them both (ML 360). It is clear from Cosima Wagner's diaries that Wagner continued to take a lively interest in Tieck's poetry and prose writings right up to the end of his life, and in *My Life*, he claims that his meeting was a valuable experience for him. Yet, only four years later, in 1851, when Tieck was still very much alive (he did not die until 1853), Wagner found it in him to be positively rude about the last surviving representative of classical Romanticism in his autobiographical self-defense, *A Communication to My Friends*. While not denying that he owed his first acquaintance with the Tannhäuser legend to Tieck's short story, rather than to the bogus German *Volksbuch* (in other words, Bechstein's account of the legend), he was forced by the constraints of his *völkisch* ideology to trivialize not only the debt that he owed to Tieck but also the influence of E.T.A. Hoffmann.

> In himself, of course, Tannhäuser was by no means unfamiliar to me: I had first made his acquaintance at an early age through Tieck's short story. At that time he had inspired me in a fancifully mystical way, much as Hoffmann's tales had left their mark on my youthful imagination; but at no point was any influence exerted on my artistic creativity from that particular quarter. (GS 4:269)

This is an altogether grotesque distortion of the truth, especially when we recall that Wagner's 1842 opera draft *Die Bergwerke zu Falun* (WWV 67) was based on

Hoffmann's homonymous tale and that it was to Hoffmann's "Der Kampf der Sänger" (The singers' contest) that Wagner owed not only his earliest knowledge of the legend of the Wartburg Tournament of Song but also (as we shall see) its specifically modern reworking. The passage just quoted continues: "I now reread Tieck's entirely modern poem and understood why its tendency to strike a note of mystical coquettishness and Catholic frivolity had failed to inspire any further interest in me" (GS 4:269). This interest, Wagner claimed, was the result of his reading the factitious *Volksbuch* and the Tannhäuser Ballad from *Des Knaben Wunderhorn.*

That Wagner should accuse Tieck, of all people, of "Catholic frivolity" is grossly unfair, given that Tieck was virtually the only Romantic who was not a convert to Catholicism and who was not even tempted to cast a wistful glance in the general direction of Rome. Indeed, it is difficult to avoid the suspicion that Wagner was attempting to foist upon Tieck the very criticism that had been leveled at his own adaptation of the legend. But there is also an echo here of the Young Germans' polemical dismissal of Tieck, an attitude that Heine shared. The fact that Heine fails to mention Tieck's tale in his "Elementargeister," even though he derived a number of important ideas from it, is no doubt due to sheer malice on his part. And in his own parody of the legend, with which he concludes his essay, Heine imagines Tannhäuser returning from Rome via Dresden, where Tieck was then living. The old poet, who was a severe critic of the Young German movement, is likened to a vicious but toothless dog.

> In Dresden sah ich einen Hund,
> Der einst sehr scharf gebissen,
> Doch fallen ihm die Zähne aus,
> Er kann nur bellen und pissen.[11]
>
> [In Dresden town I saw a dog
> Whose teeth are now all missing:
> It used to bite a lot, but now
> It barks when it's not pissing.]

Be that as it may, Tieck's "entirely modern poem" left a far more indelible mark on Wagner's interpretation of the legend than the putative popular tradition. His opera is a kind of compilation of Tieck's *Tannenhäuser* and Hoffmann's "Der Kampf der Sänger." Wagner found the beginnings of a link between these two tales not in Bechstein but in "Der Kampf der Sänger" itself, a story included in Hoffmann's *Serapionsbrüder* (Serapion brethren) cycle of 1819–21, where echoes of the Venusberg motif are already heard. Here the hellhound Nasias, in league with Heinrich von Ofterdingen's mentor Klingsohr, seizes the opportunity of a nocturnal visit to Wolfframb von Eschinbach to sing "a song about fair Helen and the rapturous joys of the Venusberg. In truth, the song was seductive, and it was as though the flames that Nasias belched forth turned to lustful desire and to vapors exhaling the pleasures of love, while dulcet strains surged back and forth like swaying cupids."[12]

All that was required now was the final philological impulse, and this was provided by a monograph brought to Wagner's attention by a friend in Paris, the philologist Samuel Lehrs. The book in question was C.T.L. Lucas's 1838 treatise *Ueber den Krieg von Wartburg* (On the war at Wartburg). (Here, as with Bechstein, the definite article is missing before "Wartburg.") Wagner was now able to fuse the two legends by replacing the legendary figure of Heinrich von Ofterdingen (a central character in all the accounts of the Wartburg Tournament of Song, ranging from the late-medieval *Wartburgkrieg* [Wartburg war], edited by Lucas, to Hoffmann's "Der Kampf der Sänger") with the figure of Heinrich (!) Tannhäuser, a historical poet who had himself become the subject of legend. It was an equation for which Wagner found spurious scholarly justification in Lucas's treatise.

> There is no doubt that Heinrich von Ofterdingen or Afterdingen was conceived as a minstrel knight who was famous in Wolfram von Eschenbach's day for the songs and perhaps also for the epic poems that he wrote. But if he appears as a mysterious figure even in our own poem about the Wartburg Tournament of Song—a poem which, like the legend based upon it, is our chief source of information concerning Ofterdingen—he becomes an even more mysterious, not to say mythical, figure through his original affinity or later association with the person of Tannhäuser. Although we may wish to distinguish between the poet Tannhäuser, who, under this name, is said to have sung songs of his own composition that have survived to this day, and the knight Tannhäuser, who betook himself to the Venusberg, it was inevitable that the two Tannhäusers should become merged together to form a single poetic figure, a confusion that makes it likely that Ofterdingen was related to both of them and that he became merged with them in the poetical view of the folk.[13]

Lucas seeks to prove his point with a wealth of speculative detail that no later scholar has seen fit to endorse, and his monograph would have been forgotten long ago had it not inspired Wagner to combine the figures of Ofterdingen and Tannhäuser. But, apart from this one idea, Wagner owed Lucas nothing. The latter's painstakingly annotated edition of the *Wartburgkrieg* left no discernible mark on Wagner's libretto, for the theme of the tournament, as in Bechstein's account of the legend, is not the nature of love but the praise of princes. Ofterdingen incurs the enmity of the other minstrels because he fails to praise the landgrave Hermann of Thuringia, at whose court the tournament takes place, but, to quote Lucas, "insists on praising the Duke of Austria."[14] His life is threatened, and he has no alternative but to seek refuge beneath the protective mantle of the unnamed landgravine: "Als er zuo der lantgrefin floch / under iren mantell er ir kroch" [And so he fled to the landgravine's side / And crept beneath her mantle, there to hide] (ll.138–39).

"Although I could use virtually none of this authentic version of the *Wartburgkrieg* for my own purposes," Wagner wrote in *My Life*, "it nonetheless showed me the German Middle Ages in a striking coloring of which I had until then had no idea" (ML 224). For all that, Wagner included very little of this "striking coloring" in his opera, preferring instead to borrow a number of important motifs from Hoffmann's

"Der Kampf der Sänger," and at the same time criticizing Hoffmann for having "seriously distorted the old legend" (ML 223). Whereas sexual love plays no part in the medieval *Wartburgkrieg*, the theme of love is central to Hoffmann's tale, where Wolfframb von Eschinbach and Heinrich von Ofterdingen are rivals for the hand of Countess Mathilde, a rivalry in which Wolfframb repeatedly proves himself a magnanimous friend. When open hostility breaks out among the minstrels, he is the only one to stand by Heinrich. This relationship was taken over into Wagner's opera with scarcely any shift of emphasis. It is strange, of course, that in Wagner's prose sketch (which remained unpublished until 1985),[15] there is barely a hint of any love between Wolfram and Elisabeth, whereas in the final libretto the reunion of Elisabeth and Tannhäuser ends with Wolfram's resigned acceptance: "So flieht für dieses Leben / mir jeder Hoffnung Schein" (GS 2:20) [And so all semblance of hope / Flees from me in this life]. In the prose draft, by contrast, Wolfram joins in the lovers' jubilant reunion.

The other important theme linking *Tannhäuser* with Hoffmann's "Der Kampf der Sänger" is the contrast between the demonic and dissonant artistry of Heinrich von Ofterdingen and Tannhäuser, an artistry associated with the subterranean forces of hell and the Venusberg, and the well-tempered conventional art of the other minstrels at the Wartburg court. Ofterdingen behaves in an altogether boorish manner during the Tournament of Song, displaying overweening arrogance in letting his fellow contestants see how little he thinks of their art: "While the others sang, he stared at the ceiling, shifting around in his chair, twiddling his thumbs, and yawning; in a word, he showed his displeasure and boredom in every possible way." His reaction to Wolfframb von Eschinbach's song—a song that leaves a deep impression on all its other listeners—is typical.

> Heinrich von Ofterdingen, however, frowned and, turning away from Wolfframb, took up his lute and struck a number of strange-sounding chords on it. He went and stood in the center of the circle and began a song whose melody was so unlike anything that the others had sung, so unheard-of, that all were seized by a sense of the greatest wonderment and finally of utter astonishment. It was as though the powerful sounds that he struck from his lute beat at the gloomy portals of some strange and fateful realm, conjuring up the secrets of whatever unknown force might dwell there. . . . Now the chords thundered out more powerfully than ever, red-hot vapors wafted in, and images of wanton rapture burned in this Eden of all delights that now gaped open before them.

But the reaction of Ofterdingen's audience is not general horror, as it is in Wagner's opera. Rather, they burst into tremendous applause, and Mathilde presses a laurel wreath on Ofterdingen's brow "as a prize for his singing." Only after some time has passed are the other minstrels struck by the "infamy of his songs," and, with the exception of Wolfframb, who "refused to pass judgment," they declare the tune with which Ofterdingen had praised Mathilde's beauty "a pagan abomination."[16] Here we come very close to the relationship between Tannhäuser and Elisabeth in Wagner's opera.

Hoffmann's reference to the "Eden of all delights" is an allusion to the Venusberg, which Nasias later apostrophizes in song. Of course, Ofterdingen himself has not been to the Venusberg. Instead, he projects all his erotic desires and ideas on Mathilde. Unlike Wagner's Elisabeth, Mathilde is not, therefore, the antithesis of Venus. The idea of the hero vacillating between sacred and profane love, embodied in two antithetical female types, plays only a peripheral role in Hoffmann's tale, although this is so widespread a theme elsewhere in Romantic poetry that it could almost be described as one of Romanticism's leading motifs.

Even before Hoffmann, Tieck had introduced the motif of "another woman" into the story line of *Der getreue Eckart*, a woman whom Tannenhäuser loves in vain. Thirty years before Wagner's opera, Tieck's short story had given Clemens Brentano the idea for an opera about Tannhäuser that he planned to write with Carl Maria von Weber.[17] Tieck knew about Brentano's plans, and one wonders whether he told Wagner about them when they met in 1847. In the event, of course, the idea was realized by two other, less important, figures; at almost the same time as Wagner was working on his opera, the poet Eduard Duller and the composer Carl Amand Mangold were writing their own *Tanhäuser* [*sic*], based on Tieck's novella and first performed in Darmstadt on 17 May 1846, when it proved initially more successful than Wagner's opera had been at its first performance in Dresden seven months earlier. Not only the music was preferred to Wagner's, so too was Duller's libretto. In this case, too, the hero's redemption by a woman's pure love is central to the action—although 'redemption' may not be the right word here, as the work has a happy ending, with the forces of darkness overcome and the lovers, Tanhäuser and Inniges, united in the here and now.[18]

Like Wagner, Mangold and Duller realized that the Tannhäuser legend was dramatically too lightweight to stand on its own, but whereas Wagner combined it, much more compellingly, with the legend of the Wartburg Tournament of Song, Duller—perhaps drawing on his knowledge of Lucas's *Ueber den Krieg von Wartburg*—linked it to the tale of the Pied Piper of Hamelin. Lucas had been the first to equate Ofterdingen/Tannhäuser with the Pied Piper in his 1838 treatise, an equation suggested by the fact that in the Venusberg legend the figure of the minstrel lures men into the mountain with the strains of his music. Tieck's Tannenhäuser reports that while still a child, he had heard of a minstrel who came from a "strange mountain" and that the minstrel's "wondrous sounds awoke such deep longing and such wild desires in the hearts of all his listeners that they had been drawn irresistibly along by the music, only to be lost inside the mountain. Hell then opened up its gates to these poor souls, welcoming them in to the sounds of the loveliest music."[19] (The reader may well be reminded here of the Strömkarl, the Nordic water sprite who figures in the scenario that Wagner drew up in 1860 for the ballet in his Paris *Tannhäuser* and who incites the company to orgiastic dancing.) Mangold's opera also includes the character of Faithful Eckart, who is replaced in Wagner's opera by Wolfram von Eschenbach: in the final scene of the opera, Wolfram clearly assumes the admonitory role of the old man on guard outside the Venusberg.

From Venus to the Virgin: A Romantic Conversion

The theme of two antithetical types of love embodied in two contrasting women is regularly associated in Romantic poetry with the myth of a demonized Venus, a myth that finds expression not only in the Venusberg legend but also, and more especially, in a medieval tale about a statue that comes to life, resulting in its betrothal to a passing knight.[20] Heine gives a delightful account of this tale, with all its manifold variants, in his "Elementargeister."

> The setting is generally Italy, and the hero . . . some German knight or other who, because of his youthful inexperience or willowy figure, is beguiled by beautiful she-devils with especially charming wiles. He is to be found on beautiful autumn days walking alone, lost in his solitary dreams, thinking perhaps of the forests of oaks at home or else of the flaxen-haired girl whom he left behind, the carefree dandy! But suddenly he finds himself standing in front of a marble statue, the very sight of which arrests him in his tracks. Perhaps it is the goddess of beauty herself, and he stands there face to face with her, and the young barbarian's heart is secretly ensnared by the age-old magic spell. What is it? Never before has he seen such slender limbs, and in this marble block he senses a life more intense than he ever found in the carmine cheeks and lips and in all the fleshly charms of any of his fellow countrywomen.[21]

The statue comes to life, and a dreamlike love scene ensues. Heine draws particular attention to Eichendorff's "beautiful tale" on the subject, *Das Marmorbild* (1819). In his own short story, "Florentinische Nächte" (Florentine nights), published in 1837 in the same volume of *Der Salon* as his "Elementargeister," Heine offers a variant on this theme, which he presents as a kind of summation of its various interpretations by the other German Romantics. The young Maximilian kisses the marble statue of a woman in an overgrown garden and in later life is repeatedly plagued by endless embodiments of the same artificial and fatal beauty. On one occasion, for example, he falls in love with the painting of a

> Madonna of breathtaking beauty. I then became a fervent churchgoer, and my thoughts were immersed in the mysticism of the Catholic faith. Like some Spanish knight, I should have been glad to fight each day to the death in defense of the Immaculate Conception of the Virgin Mary, Queen of all the Angels, the fairest woman in Heaven and earth![22]

These lines inevitably recall Wagner's famous letter to Ernst Benedikt Kietz of 6–10 September 1842, in which he describes a copy of Carlo Dolci's *Madonna Addolorata* in the church at Aussig (the painting was ascribed to Dolci in Wagner's own day but is now known to be a copy by Ismael Mengs): "It is a quite extraordinarily enchanting picture, & if Tannhäuser had seen it, I could readily understand how it was that he turned away from Venus to Mary, without being inspired to do so by any great sense of piety."[23] We are reminded, too, of Wagner's repeated comparison of Isolde with the figure of the Virgin in Titian's *Assunta*. As Cosima noted in her diary on 22 October 1882, Wagner denied "that the *Assunta* is the Mother of God, it is Isolde in the apotheosis of love."[24]

The idea of religious devotion as a form of secret lust recurs in Heine's "Florentinische Nächte," where Maximilian maintains that images of saints excite the Italian populace's erotic imagination: "And far from unprofitable is their reverence of those fair Madonnas, those lovely altarpieces that leave their mark on the mind of the bridegroom, while the bride herself thinks ardent thoughts of a handsome saint."[25] Heine himself recalled his own "Madonna period" in his *Geständnisse* (Confessions):

> I was always a poet, and so the poetry that blossoms and blazes in the symbolism of Catholic dogma and ritual was bound to reveal itself to me on a far deeper level than it does to others, and not infrequently during my youth I was overwhelmed by that poetry's infinite sweetness, its mysteriously blissful rapture, and its eerie longing for death. I too would sometimes swoon over the most blessed Queen of Heaven, I wrote elegant verses on the tales of her grace and goodness, and my first collection of poetry still contains signs of this wonderful Madonna period, signs that I later risibly took care to remove from all my subsequent collections.[26]

One of the poems that fell victim to Heine's self-censorship was his ballad *Die Weihe* (Consecration, 1816), in which the Madonna comes to life as an image of Venus. In a woodland chapel, a youth prays before the devotional image of the Virgin, whereupon the chapel suddenly vanishes and the Madonna is transformed into a "lovely maiden" who directs him toward the lands "where the myrtle blooms forever."[27] (The myrtle is sacred to Aphrodite.) "The Virgin Mary was, as it were, the fair *dame du comptoir* [barmaid] of the Catholic Church," Heine writes in *Die romantische Schule* (The Romantic School). "With her heavenly smile she lured its customers, especially the northern barbarians, and transfixed them to the spot. . . . The Catholic clergy invariably made some concessions to sensualism wherever the Virgin was concerned."[28] In much the same way, the interrelationship of Venus and the Virgin recurs with leitmotivic regularity in Heine's Italian *Reisebilder* (Travel pictures).[29]

This remarkable interplay between religious ardor and sinful lust and between images of Venus and the Virgin was a popular theme in Romantic poetry in general: the marble statues of the women in Brentano's 1801 novel *Godwi oder Das steinerne Bild der Mutter* (Godwi, or The stone image of the mother), for example, already hint at features of the Virgin Mary, and the identification becomes explicit in *Raphael und seine Nachbarinnen* (Raphael and his neighbors, 1824) by Brentano's friend, Achim von Arnim. Here the statue of Venus is identified with the hero's secret love, Benedetta. When Raphael is unfaithful to her and begins an affair with the demonic Ghita, he rediscovers the statue as a Madonna in a convent where Benedetta is living as a painter.

It may be added that the idea of Mariolatry as sublimated lust has a remarkable precedent in Schiller's *Maria Stuart*, first published in 1801. Here the religious zealot Mortimer confuses the images of Mary the Mother of Jesus and Mary Stuart, most notably in his final prayer, "Blessed Mary, pray for me" (1. 2819), a line that refers both to Mary Queen of Scots and to the Virgin Mary. And, following the disastrous encounter between Mary and Elizabeth, his ostensibly purely platonic regard for the former turns out to conceal an erotic passion in which religious and sexual fantasies are inextricably linked.

But no writer was more important in this Mariological nexus of erotic ideas than Clemens Brentano. Of all the Romantic writers, he was probably the least familiar to Wagner on the basis of his own reading yet arguably the most closely related in many different ways. Gabriele Brandstetter has described Brentano as a "poeta marianus," whose second name—Maria—provided him with a symbolic incentive to express his poetic self as a woman, using language that is sometimes erotic and sometimes mystical and religious.[30] Maria is even the pseudonym that Brentano used for some of his early poems, as well as being the name of the fictional author of *Godwi*. His poetry as a whole is notable for its mirror imagery involving eroticism and religion, with the result that his imagination is repeatedly fired by a typological and figural relationship between Eve and Mary, creating the paradoxical figure of a courtesan-virgin, a merging of Venus and the Virgin.

Centuries earlier, the Renaissance Platonists had paid tribute to a figure described by Edgar Wind as the "Venus-Virgo," embodied in the syncretistic figure of Venus disguised as a nymph of Diana, an idea based on a line (l. 315) in book 1 of Virgil's *Aeneid* in which Chastity and Love are merged through the mediation of Beauty.[31] On the basis of the goddess's dual nature, there developed the "semi-chaste, semi-voluptuous cult of Venus in which her double nature could be refined to the highest points of either reverence or frivolity or both."[32] This Venus-Virgo figure plays an important role in Edgar Wind's iconographic studies of Botticelli and bears more than a passing resemblance to Brentano's picture of the Virgin, an image centered around what Gabriele Brandstetter has called "the dual image of the Madonna conceived as a mysterious union of virginality and motherhood, chastity and love,"[33] with the Virgin's Immaculate Conception as a mystical prefiguration of Brentano's concept of poetic inspiration.

With Wagner, too, we find remarkable traces of a veneration of the Virgin. In his 1867–68 treatise "German Art and German Politics," Wagner the Protestant even defends "the dogma of the Immaculate Conception that has recently been granted canonical status" and that had caused indignation in the Protestant world when proclaimed by Pope Pius IX. Wagner, conversely, even presumes to claim, on the basis of "many a frivolous witticism" in the French and Italian press, that Catholic countries were incapable of understanding the doctrine. Rather, it had been left to the greatest poet of the Protestant world to explore the mystery of the Virgin in the final scene in part 2 of *Faust*, anticipating papal dogma by "ending his greatest poem with the beatific invocation of the Mater gloriosa as the loftiest ideal of spotless purity" (GS 8:101). For the older Wagner, there were two completely different ways of interpreting the Virgin: one was embodied in Raphael's *Madonna* in the Sistine Chapel and was "free of desire" (CT, 4 September 1879), and the other, represented by Titian's *Assunta*, signified sublimated desire and "the ecstasy of love" (CT, 8 December 1880). Here the Virgin is a transubstantiated variant of Venus.

This tendency to merge the myths of Venus and the Virgin is part of a long-standing tradition that extended at least as far as the early years of the twentieth century, one of its most significant manifestations being the "Madonna destroyer" in Heinrich Mann's *Die Göttinnen* (The goddesses, 1903).[34] In general, it is easy to understand why *Tannhäuser* should have proved so fascinating a work for the décadents, with Rudolf Kassner arguing that the English poets of the fin de siècle reacted "like pagans to images of the Virgin and like Christians to the Aphrodite of Melos." He goes on to note how "this brings them into close sympathy with Botticelli, who likewise had only one model for Venus and the Virgin Mary."[35] (This is by no means such an eccentric idea when we recall the figure of Venus-Virgo familiar to Botticelli.)

One of the most famous examples of the syncretic equation of Venus and the Virgin from this period comes from Thomas Mann's short story *Gladius Dei* (Sword of God, 1902). Here a latter-day Savonarola attempts to persuade a fine-arts dealer to remove an image of the Virgin from his display and to destroy it, claiming that it bears all the signs of pagan lust. "It was a Madonna, a piece of craftsmanship conceived in an entirely modern spirit and free of all conventionality. The figure of the Blessed Virgin was of bewitching femininity, undraped, and beautiful. Her large and languorous eyes were dark-rimmed, and her delicately, strangely smiling lips were half open."[36]

In 1896 Richard Dehmel published his poem *Venus Consolatrix*, in which Venus is wholly identified with Mary the Mother of Jesus and also with Mary Magdalene. (This, too, is a variant of the same theme, whereby a statue of Venus comes to life.) Its publication precipitated an obscenity trial in which Dehmel was accused of offending against religious and moral feelings, a charge against which he defended himself as follows:

> In this poem I have striven to achieve the highest ideal for which men have striven from time immemorial: the triumph of the spirit over the instincts. And I believe I may say that the struggle here is successful. It is not, of course, the victory achieved by the Christian spirit of the Middle Ages or by the pagan spirit of antiquity; it is the victory, rather, of a new humanitarianism.

The poem describes Lucifer—the "bringer of light" or morning star (the planet Venus in Roman mythology)—shining on a bracket in the poet's room and coming to life in the form of Venus and the Virgin Mary.

VENUS CONSOLATRIX

Da kam Stern Lucifer, und meine Nacht
erblaßte scheu vor seiner milden Pracht.
Er schien auf meine dunkle Zimmerwand,
und wie aus unerschöpflicher Phiole
durchflossen Silberadern die Console,
die schwarz, seit lange leer, im Winkel stand.

Auf einmal fing die Säule an zu leben
und eine Frau erhob sich aus dem Glanz;

die trug im schwarzen Haupthaar einen Kranz
von hellen Rosen zwischen grünen Reben.
Ihr Morgenkleid von weißem Sammet glänzte
so sanft wie meine Heimatflur im Schnee,
die Rüsche aber, die den Hals begrenzte,
so blutrot wie die Blüte Aloe;
und ihre Augen träumten braun ins Tiefe,
als ob da Sehnsucht nach dem Südmeer schliefe.
Sie breitete mir beide Arme zu,
ich sah erstaunt an ihren Handgelenken
die starken Pulse springen und sich senken,
da nickte sie und sagte zu mir: Du—
du bist mühselig und beladen, komm:
wer viel geliebt, dem wird auch viel verziehen.
Du brauchst das große Leben nicht zu fliehen,
durch das dein kleines lebt. O komm, sei fromm!

Und schweigend lüpfte sie die rote Rüsche
und nestelte an ihren seidnen Litzen
und öffnete das Kleid von weißem Plüsche
und zeigte mir mit ihren Fingerspitzen,
die zart das blanke Licht des Sternes küßte,
die braunen Knospen ihrer bleichen Brüste,
dann sprach sie weiter: Sieh! dies Fleisch und Blut,
das einst den kleinen Heiland selig machte,
bevor ich an sein großes Kreuz ihn brachte,
Maria, ich, die Nazarenerin—
o sieh, es ist des selben Fleisches Blut,
für das der große Heiland sich erregte,
bevor ich in sein kleines Grab ihn legte,
Maria, ich, die Magdalenerin—
komm, stehe auf, und sieh auch Meine Wunden,
und lerne dich erlösen und gesunden!

Und lächelnd ließ sie alle Kleider fallen
und dehnte sich in ihrer nackten Kraft;
wie heilige Runen standen auf der prallen
Bauchhaut die Narben ihrer Mutterschaft
in Linien, die verliefen wundersam
bis tief ins schwarze Schleierhaar der Scham.
Da sprach sie wieder und trat her zu mir:
Willst du mir nicht auch in die Augen sehn?!
Und meine Blicke badeten in ihr.
Und eine Sehnsucht: du mußt untergehn,
ließ mich umarmt durch tiefe Meere schweben,
mich selig tiefer, immer tiefer streben,

ich glaubte auf den Grund der Welt zu sehn—
weh schüttelt mich ein nie erlebtes Leben,
und ihren Kranz von Rosen und von Reben
umklammernd, während wir verbeben,
stamml' ich: o auf- auf- auferstehn.[37]

[Then came fair Lucifer, whereat my night
Grew palely shy before her gentle light.
She shone into my night-enshrouded room
And, poured as from an ever-brimming goblet,
Pale streaks of silver flowed across the bracket
Which, long since bare, now stood in starless gloom.

The statue all at once I thought was breathing,
A woman's form appeared before me there,
She wore a garland in her raven hair,
A wreath of roses, fronds of green enwreathing.
Her silken morning dress was white enough
To shame the fields bedecked with virgin snow,
And round her swanlike throat she wore a ruff
As red as blood or juice of bitter aloe.
Her nut-brown eyes were filled with dreams that yearned
For southern seas where sleepy sunlight burned.
She stood with arms outstretched above my bed,
I saw her wrists and saw, with awe o'erflood,
The firm pulsating rhythm of her blood.
And as she spoke, she nodded with her head:
"O ye that labor and are heavy laden,
And ye whose love is great, we can forgive.
You do not need to shun the life we live,
Of which yours is a part." Thus spoke the maiden.

And silently she raised her blood-red ruff
And fumbled gently with her samite dress
And opened up her collar wide enough
To trace with dainty fingertips' caress,
Kissed by her gentle Luciferian light,
The firm brown buds of her eburnean breasts.
Again she spoke: "This flesh and blood attests
To joys that did the infant child delight
Before I led him to be crucified,
I, Mary, I the chastened Nazarene—
Behold, it is the blood of that same flesh
That roused our Savior's longing ere he died
And ere I laid his body in the earth,
I, Mary, I the contrite Magdalene—
Arise, and look upon my wounds afresh
And learn to find redemption and rebirth!"

> And smiling she slipped off her dress and stood
> Erect in nakedness's potent form.
> Like sacred runes the scars of motherhood
> Stood proud upon her gently swelling warm
> And milky flesh: their lines did cicatrize
> The sable downy hair between her thighs.
> And stepping nearer me, she spoke once more:
> "Why do you flinch from looking in my eyes?!"
> And then my gaze was held as ne'er before:
> A deep-felt yearning would not let me rise
> But drew me down toward the ocean's bed
> Where ever deeper striving held me fast
> Until I thought I'd glimpsed the reason why
> This earth of ours exists. A life I'd never led
> Seized hold of me, whereat I clasped her by
> Her rosebud wreath; as quiv'ring limbs at last
> Grew calm, I stammered: "Rise up from the dead!"]

But let us return to Wagner. Within the terms of this thematic context, the work that is closest to *Tannhäuser* is undoubtedly Eichendorff's *Das Marmorbild*. Although we have no evidence that Wagner knew this tale, so many of the themes of Romantic literature in general—from Novalis's *Hymnen an die Nacht* (Hymns to night) to Tieck's *Der getreue Eckart* and Brentano's *Romanzen vom Rosenkranz* (Romances of the rosary)—come together here that motivic parallels between *Tannhäuser* and *Das Marmorbild* are not in the least surprising.

Like Wagner's Tannhäuser, the young poet Florio is torn between his pure love for the virginal Bianka and the demonic appeal of a marble statue of Venus that comes to life and seduces him. Whereas in Brentano's novel the two types of love embodied in Venus and the Virgin are no longer distinguishable, in the case of Eichendorff they are strictly segregated. Just as Florio is on the point of succumbing to the goddess's blandishments, he is brought to his senses by the distant strains of a song sung by Fortunato, his friend and guardian spirit. He utters a prayer and exorcizes the demonic spell. The story is set in Venus's garden, a setting significantly different, of course, from Wagner's Venusberg, tending, rather, to resemble Klingsor's magic garden in *Parsifal*. Indeed, even the Flower Maidens put in a brief appearance here: "As the strains of the lute and the rays of the evening sun glided over the flowery fields, beautiful girls rose up here and there from out of the flowers, as though waking from their midday slumbers."[38] The idea of Flower Maidens had in fact already been found even earlier, in Tieck's *Der getreue Eckart*. Like Parsifal, Tannenhäuser is surrounded by a throng of girls who beckon to him invitingly. "In the flowers there burned the charms of the girls and the lure of desire; in the women's bodies there blossomed the magic of the flowers; here colors spoke another language, sounds had new words to say, the world of the senses was held fast within a single bloom, and the spirits within it feted the infinite triumph of rampant desire."[39]

Eichendorff's tale culminates in a song sung by Fortunato, which appeared in the 1841 edition of his works under the title "Götterdämmerung" (Twilight of the gods). Not only the title causes readers to prick up their ears, but two of the poem's main themes return in Wagner's *Tannhäuser*. The first of them is the motif of Venus rising out of her subterranean realm each spring. (This motif is alluded to in the Shepherd's Song in act 1, "Frau Holda kam aus dem Berg hervor," where Frau Holda, according to Wagner's introduction to the first printed edition of the libretto, is the Germanic equivalent of Venus; see GS 16:186.) The second similarity between the two works is the appeal to the Virgin Mary, who is presented as the antithesis of the goddess of love.

> Wenn Frühlingslüfte wehen
> Hold überm grünen Plan,
> Ein leises Auferstehen
> Hebt in den Tälern an.
>
> Da will sich's unten rühren
> Im stillen Göttergrab,
> Der Mensch kann's schaudernd spüren
> Tief in die Brust hinab.
> . . . .
>
> Und unterm duft'gen Schleier,
> So oft der Lenz erwacht,
> Webt in geheimer Feier
> Die alte Zaubermacht.
>
> Frau Venus hört das Locken,
> Der Vögel heitern Chor,
> Und richtet froh erschrocken
> Aus Blumen sich empor.
>
> Sie sucht die alten Stellen,
> Das luft'ge Säulenhaus
> Schaut lächelnd in die Wellen
> Der Frühlingsluft hinaus.
>
> Doch öd sind nun die Stellen,
> Stumm liegt ihr Säulenhaus,
> Gras wächst da auf den Schwellen,
> Der Wind zieht ein und aus.
> . . . .
>
> Sie selbst muß sinnend stehen
> So bleich im Frühlingsschein,
> Die Augen untergehen,
> Der schöne Leib wird Stein.
>
> Denn über Land und Wogen
> Erscheint, so still und mild,
> Hoch auf dem Regenbogen
> Ein ander Frauenbild.

Ein Kindlein in den Armen
Die Wunderbare hält,
Und himmlisches Erbarmen
Durchdringt die ganze Welt.[40]

[When gentle springtime breezes
Waft o'er the verdant vale,
A sense of resurrection
Is felt in ev'ry dale.

Beneath the ground a stirring
Of gods long laid to rest
In silent tombs is welling
Within each human breast.
. . . .

And 'neath earth's scented mantle
At each awakening spring,
Of secret celebrations
The ancient forces sing.

Dame Venus hears them calling;
Birds carol all around;
She stirs in startled gladness
From out her grassy mound.

She seeks her former temples,
The airy columned fane,
And smiles to feel the breezes
Of springtime once again.

Forsaken are her temples,
Mute is the columned fane,
Grass grows upon a threshold
Exposed to wind and rain.
. . . .

And bathed in spring's pale sunbeams
She stands there all alone,
Her eyes cast down in sadness,
Her body turned to stone.

For over land and ocean
A rival form is seen,
A rainbow-colored vision
Both gentle and serene.

For lo, a newborn infant
The wondrous maiden holds,
And heavenly compassion
This world of ours enfolds.]

Tannhäuser as a Catechistic Morality Tale

In the version of the Tannhäuser Ballad printed in Nuremberg in 1515, the hero bids farewell to Venus in two lines that are missing from the later version of the ballad reproduced in *Des Knaben Wunderhorn* and in Heine's "Elementargeister": "Maria, mutter, reyne maydt, / nun hilff mir von den weyben!" [Mary, mother, purest maid, / Now help me flee from womankind!]. The 1515 version of the ballad was familiar to Wagner only from Bechstein, and it must have been from there that he took Tannhäuser's appeal to the Virgin Mary and his exorcism of Venus's magic spell. Yet the reasons that are given for Tannhäuser abandoning Venus are in fact completely different in the two versions. To understand why this is so, we need to examine the original meaning of the Tannhäuser legend, a meaning that Dietz-Rüdiger Moser has sought to elucidate in a recent book whose findings have not, however, been universally accepted.[41]

The Tannhäuser legend is part of a rich tapestry of popular Christian morality tales that grew out of the church's program of doctrinal teachings and that were therefore catechistic in character. In Moser's view, it was emphatically not their aim to denounce the pope as obdurate and self-righteous or to play off God's all-forgiving mercy against the church's evident lack of compassion, as was believed to be the case in the first half of the nineteenth century. The pope's rejection of the penitent sinner is merely a temporary measure that in reality conceals the promise of redemption. In the popular catechistic tales in question, motifs such as the miracle of the papal staff putting forth green shoots are found again and again. In one such tale, for example, the pope gives a particularly hardened sinner a black sheep, telling him that he will not find absolution until the sheep's black wool has turned white. The sinner thinks that he has been denied forgiveness (the pope conceals from him the fact that this is a temporary measure designed to prevent him from believing that his penance is too easy) and so he begins to weep uncontrollably. As each teardrop falls on the sheep's black coat, it leaves a white mark, until finally the fleece is as white as snow. Like the barren staff that bursts into leaf in the pope's hand, like the unseasonal blossoming of a tree, and like the countless other miraculous signs that comprise the topoi of Christian iconography, this miracle is the symbolic confirmation of a victory over nature as the result of an act of divine mercy, thereby indicating the end of penance and the remission of sin.[42]

But why does Tannhäuser seek out the pope in the first place? Carnal desire is such an everyday sin that the pope would have his hands full if he had to act as father confessor for every sinner guilty of that failing. There are, however, certain mortal sins that according to canon law so threaten the very fabric of the church that the power of absolution remains the sole preserve of the Apostolic see. This is still the case in canon law. Anyone familiar with its precepts will see at once that Tannhäuser undertakes his journey to Rome because he needs to consult the appropriate father confessor. But what is the precise nature of the mortal sin of which only the pope can absolve him? (This, after all, is a standard feature of all such legends dealing with penitent sinners.) Tannhäuser's stay in the Venusberg cannot, as such, be classed as a mortal sin, for any priest would have pardoned the sin of "evil desire" (Wagner calls it "böse Lust"; GS 2:36) without a moment's hesitation.

At this point we need to pause briefly to examine the history of the word *Venusberg* and its Latinized form *mons Veneris*. In his autobiography Wagner reports that Carl Friedrich Meser, the Dresden court music dealer, persuaded him to abandon the opera's original title, *Der Venusberg*, while the vocal score was already in production: "He claimed that I was not getting out and about enough and had failed to hear the most frightful jokes that he thought must emanate from the staff and students of the Dresden medical school, as they involved a degree of obscenity that was common currency only in such quarters" (ML 314). Here Wagner is guilty of appearing more naive than was the case, as it is clear from his letter to Robert Schumann of 13 June 1843 that he had altered the title soon after completing the libretto.[43] By this date at the very latest, Wagner must have realized that *mons Veneris* is a technical term used in medical science for the Mount of Venus and that, colloquially, it occurs as a sexual metaphor apparently predating attempts to identify the Venusberg as a geographic location. At all events, the German expressions "in Frau Venus Berg fahren" (to enter Lady Venus's mount) and "den Danhäuser spielen" (to play at Tannhäuser) are terms for sexual congress that were widespread in popular parlance.[44] When Wagner's Tannhäuser invites his fellow contestants to "enter the Mount of Venus" (GS 2:25), he is issuing an invitation that is unintentionally obscene.

But let us return to the question of Tannhäuser's mortal sin. Precisely what that sin entails emerges only in passing from the Tannhäuser Ballad in *Des Knaben Wunderhorn*, when Venus offers to give Tannhäuser one of her "playmates" as his "lawful wedded wife." Tannhäuser replies:

> Nehme ich dann ein ander Weib,
> Als ich hab in meinem Sinne,
> So muß ich in der Höllen-Gluth,
> Da ewiglich verbrennen.[45]

> [And if I took a different wife
> From her for whom I yearn,
> Then in hell's everlasting flames
> Eternally I'd burn.]

The identity of this other woman is made clear in the 1515 version of the ballad: it is Mary, Mother of God. It is she to whom Tannhäuser has sworn to be true. In short, his sojourn in the Venusberg represents a violation of his vow of celibacy, and only the pope can absolve this sin. Wagner was by no means the only writer to misinterpret Tannhäuser's journey to Rome as a penitential pilgrimage. Yet, in Moser's view, there can be no question of such a pilgrimage; rather, it is a visit to the appropriate confessor, as laid down in canon law, a visit, moreover, that cannot have been so burdensome when we recall that as a general rule, the Venusberg was located in Italy. The period of penance does not begin until after Tannhäuser has confessed to the pope, whose apparent refusal to absolve him amounts to no more than an expression of the fact that so far, Tannhäuser has completed only two of the three acts comprising the sacrament of penance. These three acts are repentance, confession, and atonement (penance in the narrower sense). But Tannhäuser still has to atone, which is why the time is not yet ripe for the remission of his sin. Such is the severity of his guilt that confession is not sufficient for absolution. Not until the end of the fifteenth century did the practice of absolving the sinner *before* he or she had completed the penance begin to gain acceptance. In the meantime, the pope promises Tannhäuser reconciliation even though he appears to present it as an impossibility by making it dependent on a miracle.

This point had been misunderstood even before the Reformation swept across Germany, with the hyperbolic "impossibility" of reconciliation seen as the sinner's definitive excommunication by an age no longer familiar with the rhetoric of the medieval church. But the pope would never have been justified in excommunicating Tannhäuser in this way. Indeed, had he done so, he would have been guilty of heresy, for it is one of the fundamental dogmas of the church that no sin is so great that it cannot be forgiven by virtue of Christ's act of redemption and the sacrament of atonement that he initiated. The author of the Tannhäuser Ballad of 1515 believed that the pope—Urban IV—had violated this elementary article of faith and that he was therefore condemned to eternal perdition: "Des must der vierte Babst Vrban / auch ewigklich sein verloren." [And so the pope, Urban the Fourth, / Must be lost forevermore.] These are the final lines of the ballad. The version reproduced in *Des Knaben Wunderhorn* is rather more moderate in tone.

> Das soll nimmer kein Priester thun,
> Dem Menschen Mistrost geben,
> Will er denn Buß und Reu empfahn,
> Die Sünde sey ihm vergeben.[46]

> [No priest should ever say such things,
> Nor leave a man unshriven,
> When offered penance and remorse,
> His sins should be forgiven.]

This represents the church's basic attitude, and one that has never been called into question, least of all by any pope.

This misunderstanding surrounding the original meaning of the Tannhäuser Ballad results in a hopeless contradiction in both versions of the poem known to Wagner. Of course, the miracle of the burgeoning staff duly takes place (as take place it must, given the basic outline of the catechistic tale of the penitent sinner), but it comes too late, for Tannhäuser has already made his way back to the Venusberg, overcome by despair at what he assumes to be the pope's sentence condemning him to eternal damnation. Such despair is an example of the unpardonable sin of *desperatio*—doubt in the possibility of mercy and, as such, an unforgivable transgression against the Holy Ghost. But this is absurd. According to the original catechistic meaning of the legend, Tannhäuser's return to the Venusberg signifies not a relapse on his part but simply the sinner's return to the place where he first committed his sin and where he must now atone: only there can he do penance by being constantly reminded of his sin. This, too, is an integral part of the well-established complex of motifs that make up the plots of all such penitential legends. Although only half understood, an awareness of this fact can still be glimpsed in both Tannhäuser Ballads, for in each of them Tannhäuser's reaction to the pope's pronouncement is entirely appropriate: he seems to interpret the pope's words correctly as the imposition of a stricter penance, for when the latter announces "Wann dieser Stecken Blätter trägt, / Sind dir deine Sünden verziehen" [But when this stick shall bear green leaves, / Your sins shall be forgiven], Tannhäuser replies:

> Sollt ich leben nicht mehr denn ein Jahr,
> Ein Jahr auf dieser Erden,
> So wollt ich Reu und Buß empfahn,
> Und Gottes Gnad erwerben.[47]

> [Yet should I live but one year more,
> A year ere I expire,
> I'd like to show remorse, atone,
> And so God's grace acquire.]

Tannhäuser even justifies his return to the Venusberg as a directive from God, which would be wholly nonsensical if it were not meant to be interpreted, in the sense outlined earlier, as a practical attempt to atone. But the ballad poet no longer understood this, and so he also failed to see that the miracle of the burgeoning staff signals the end of Tannhäuser's term of atonement in the Venusberg. Instead, the poet believed that Tannhäuser must remain there "forever and a day." Tannhäuser never discovers that God has forgiven his sins—in spite of the fact that in the meantime he has returned to this hotbed of iniquity out of a sense of utter despair. It should be clear by now that this ending makes theological nonsense.

It seems, therefore, that the 1515 ballad, together with its later revisions, as transmitted by Kornmann's *Mons Veneris*, Arnim and Brentano's *Des Knaben Wunderhorn*, and Heine's "Elementargeister," is the product of a layman's misunderstanding of the earlier legend of a penitent Tannhäuser or Danheüser, a legend already extant in a number of versions even before it found written expression. Indeed, exactly when the legend first came into being is a matter for speculation. Its historical protagonist, a minnesinger from the Austro-Bavarian family of the lords of Tannhausen, was active around the middle of the thirteenth century and is believed to have taken part in the Crusade of 1228. His dance poems, following the tradition of *nidere minne*,[48] delight in the detailed physical depiction of women's charms and may conceivably have inspired the legend of the Knight of Venus in the first place. A penitential hymn, or *Bußlied*, has also survived and has been attributed to him, although its authenticity has, not unnaturally, been called into question, so that it is impossible to say whether it was the hymn that inspired the legend or, conversely, whether the hymn is the reflection of an earlier legend.

HOHE LIEBE AND THE EMANCIPATION OF THE FLESH:
TANNHÄUSER BETWEEN ROMANTICISM AND YOUNG GERMANY

Popularized by Arnim and Brentano in their 1806 anthology, the Tannhäuser Ballad of 1515 enjoyed a peculiar upsurge of interest among the Young German writers of the 1830s, an interest evident not least from the publication of the complete text in Heine's *Der Salon*. Young German writers saw in it a reflection of their own theme of conflict; and in their polemical opposition to the mysticism of Rome, to rigid church orthodoxy, and to an old-fashioned morality inimical to sensuality, they could readily appeal to the ballad in support of their cause. That Wagner himself held Young German ideas is clear from his second opera, *Das Liebesverbot* (1836), and these concepts have also left their unmistakable imprint on *Tannhäuser*. The governor Friedrich, who is described as "love's antipode" (SS 11:97) in *Das Liebesverbot* and who abjures sexual love, is to a certain extent supplanted by the pope in *Tannhäuser*, with the ban on love and the threatened execution of those who infringe this ban replaced by the pope's apparent condemnation of Tannhäuser to eternal damnation for succumbing to "evil desire."

There are, in fact, many more parallels between *Tannhäuser* on the one hand and *Das Liebesverbot* and the Young German movement on the other. Tannhäuser flees from the Wartburg to escape from the constraints of social and poetic conventions that force him to repress his desires and seeks refuge in the boundless erotic freedom on offer in the Venusberg, fleeing, so to speak, from the Middle Ages into classical antiquity. The Wartburg poets, whose company he can no longer tolerate and who, following his return to the world, once more provoke him with their antierotic songs, glorify a desensualized type of *hôhe minne* that denies all possibility of sexual fulfillment and that is symbolized by the limpid reflection in a fountain's glassy surface. (The fountain of love has a long iconographic tradition, and there seems little doubt that Wagner knew Titian's *Love Sacred and Profane*, with its two allegorical female figures sitting beside a fountain whose surface is stirred by Cupid.)[49] "Und nimmer möcht' ich diesen Bronnen trüben, / berühren nicht den Quell mit frev'lem Muth" (GS 2:22) [The fountain's waters I would never ruffle / Or cloud its purity in wanton mood]: Thus Wolfram sings in praise of love. But for Tannhäuser, love is a single psychophysical entity whose very essence is destroyed the moment that mind and body are divorced. That is why he approaches the fountain not in a spirit of reverential contemplation but in order to drink from its waters.

> Des Durstes Brennen muß ich kühlen,
> getrost leg' ich die Lippen an.
> In vollen Zügen trink' ich Wonnen,
> in die kein Zagen je sich mischt.

> (GS 2:23)

> [For I must slake my raging thirst
> And, comforted, must place my lips
> To it. In heady draughts I drink
> Love's joys, undaunted by the deed.]

When Walther—who has as little in common with his historical prototype as he does with Walther von Stolzing's mentor in *Die Meistersinger* and who represents the insipid, conventional view of love at its most unadulterated—presumptuously reproaches Tannhäuser for his ignorance of love's true nature, the latter scornfully replies: "Wenn du in solchem Schmachten bangest, / versiegte wahrlich wohl die Welt" (GS 2:24) [While you were languishing so shyly, / The world would surely fade away]. In other words, humankind would perish if it were guided by a view of love that saw only "impious passion" (GS 2:23) in physical union. Worship befits only God and the world above.

> Doch was sich der Berührung beuget,
> euch Herz und Sinnen nahe liegt,
> was sich, aus gleichem Stoff erzeuget,
> in weicher Formung an auch schmiegt,—
> dem ziemt Genuß in freud'gem Triebe,
> und im Genuß nur kenn' ich Liebe.

(GS 2:24)

> [But all that craves your gentle touch
> And to your heart and senses speaks,
> And all that's made, like us, of flesh
> And blood, and nestles to your breasts—
> Let us enjoy with natural pleasure,
> For by enjoyment love I measure!]

This is Young German ideology at its most unadulterated. Provoked to the utmost by the arrogant impotence of the other court poets and by their mindless repetition of outdated clichés, Tannhäuser finally confesses to seeing in Venus his ideal form of love. His hymn to Venus puts a premature end to the contest, causing it to break up in "general disorder and horror" (GS 2:25). As such, it could hardly be more different from Wolfram's song, with which the tournament had begun. As we have already seen, this song, too, is addressed to Venus—not, of course, to Venus Cypria, the goddess of sensual pleasure, but to Venus Urania, the goddess of a spiritual and renunciatory love, which for Wolfram is embodied in the Evening Star. This is the Venus who alone inspires self-composure and devotion.

Tannhäuser's earlier flight from a world that had conceived of love as something superficial and conventional may be said to reflect his conversion from the sublimated view of love that was widespread during the High Middle Ages to the hedonism of classical antiquity, a hedonism that now leads an underground existence. The fact that even in exile the ancient gods still strive to interfere in our lives—indeed, that their putative influence protects the world from desolation—emerges from Venus's words to Tannhäuser, which, in the version of the libretto published in Wagner's collected writings, runs as follows:

> Ach! kehrtest du nicht wieder,
> dann träfe Fluch die Welt;

für ewig läg' sie öde,
aus der die Göttin schwand.

(GS 2:10)

[Ah! If you don't return,
The world shall know my curse!
Forever barren shall it be,
Abandoned by the goddess.]

This idea also occurs in the earliest version of the text, albeit less clearly formulated, and it is confirmed, almost paradoxically, by the Shepherd's Song at the beginning of the third scene of the opera: "Frau Holda kam aus dem Berg hervor, / zu ziehen durch Flur und Auen" (GS 2:11) [Dame Holda stepped forth from the mountain / To roam through field and meadows]. Even the Shepherd, embodying the *paradis vert* of lost innocence in contrast to the *paradis artificiel* of the Venusberg,[50] dreams a "lovely dream" (GS 2:12) about Holda/Venus. (Note the play on words between Holda and "manchen holden Traum" [many a sweet dream].) The first sounds that Tannhäuser hears on fleeing from the cave of lustful desire and entering a world that could hardly be more different from the Venusberg is a naive song in praise of the beneficent powers of the goddess of love. For Holda is one and the same as Venus, as Wagner expressly emphasized in his introduction to the first printed edition of the libretto. This passage is clearly inspired by Heine's "Elementargeister."

> The ancient Germanic goddess Holda, benign, gentle, and merciful, whose yearly progress through the countryside brought prosperity and fruitfulness to the fields, was forced, at the advent of Christianity, to suffer a fate similar to that of Wodan and all the other gods whose existence and miraculous powers, being so deeply rooted in popular faith, could not be wholly denied, but whose erstwhile beneficent influence was now seen as suspect and reinterpreted as something evil. Holda was banished to subterranean caverns and mountain interiors; her emergence into the world was thought to herald disaster, her retinue likened to that of the Wild Hunt. Later (while the common folk continued to believe unconsciously in her gentle influence animating nature [cf. the Shepherd's Song]), her name became merged with that of Venus, a name to which all ideas of an ill-starred magical being luring men to acts of evil desire effortlessly became associated. The interior of the Hörselberg near Eisenach was designated one of her principal seats in Thuringia; there Frau Venus held court in wantonness and lust. (GS 16:186)

Although condemned by Christianity as a den of iniquity, the Venusberg continued to exert a benign influence on the world of humankind, with Venus succeeding Persephone as the goddess of the classical underworld. Both were granted the right to return to earth each spring and awaken nature to new life. This, in essence, is the meaning of the Shepherd's Song: it too, then, is a secret hymn to Venus.[51]

The gods of classical antiquity embody the sensual desire proscribed and decried by Christianity but which, according to Heine, took possession of two of the performing arts while in its exiled state: dance and music. In turn, this idea recalls Søren Kierkegaard's examination of the Don Juan legend, first published in

Either/Or in 1843, in other words, while Wagner was working on *Tannhäuser*. Kierkegaard's main thesis is that Christianity "brought sensuality into the world" because "in the positing of something, the other that is excluded is indirectly posited." By adopting the standpoint of the "spirit," Christianity's denial of sensuality led to the emergence of that sensuality as a "positive principle."

> But when sensuality is viewed under the qualification of spirit, its significance is seen to be that it is to be excluded, but precisely because it is to be excluded it is defined as a principle, as a power, for that which spirit, which is itself a principle, is supposed to exclude must be something that manifests itself as a principle, even though it does not manifest itself as a principle until the moment when it is excluded.

According to Kierkegaard's dialectic line of argument, the indirect position that stems from the negation of an earlier position means that sensuality is always "viewed under the qualification of spirit." It came into the world in the form of a "principle," stigmatized by the spirit. Of course, it had existed even before this, otherwise it could not have been driven from the world, but at that stage in its history it had existed "in harmony and consonance" with the spirit, rather than being excluded and anathematized. This harmonious and "consonant" sensuality was represented by the "beautiful individuality" of the Greeks.

For the imaginary author of the disquisition on Don Juan, the proof that among the Greeks the erotic was merely an element, not a principle, was the figure of the god Eros, who did not represent or embody love and who did not, therefore, concentrate within himself the whole force of love. "Eros was the god of erotic love but was not himself in love." (This, of course, is not true, as is clear from the myth of Eros and Psyche.) Greek consciousness, according to Kierkegaard, "did not have the strength to concentrate all of it in a single individual." It was left to Christianity to achieve this. For Kierkegaard, it was Don Juan who embodied the sensuality concentrated in a single person.[52]

If we accept Kierkegaard's premises, we can also argue that only through Christianity's exclusion of sensuality did Greek myth find a representative figure that unlike the figure of Eros, possesses what it gives to others, concentrating and embodying within itself every aspect of sensuality, and that figure is Venus—not the classical goddess reigning on the heights of Mount Olympus, but the goddess exiled to the underworld by Christianity. The legend of the Venusberg also features in Kierkegaard's *Either/Or*, where it plays a role astonishingly reminiscent of Heine and Wagner. (The reader's sense of astonishment stems not least from the fact that Kierkegaard could not possibly have known that Wagner was working on *Tannhäuser* at this time.)

> As spirit disengages itself from the earth, the sensuous shows itself in all its power. . . . In the Middle Ages, much was told about a mountain that is not found on any map; it is called Mount Venus. There sensuousness has its home; there it has its wild pleasures, for it is a kingdom, a state. . . . There is heard only the elemental voice of passion, the play of desires, the wild noise of intoxication. There everything is only one giddy round of pleasure.

According to Kierkegaard, the "firstborn of this kingdom" is Don Juan.[53] Why is it not Tannhäuser? In this context, it is interesting to compare Kierkegaard's excursus on the Don Juan legend with Baudelaire's 1861 essay on *Tannhäuser*, an essay that Wagner knew well. Like Heine and Kierkegaard, Baudelaire traces the development of the legend whereby the Venus of classical antiquity was banished by Christianity. Here Baudelaire claims that the real subject of *Tannhäuser* was the "struggle between the two principles" of flesh and spirit—in other words, the theme found in Kierkegaard's Don Juan study (a text that Baudelaire is unlikely to have known).[54] For Kierkegaard, or at least for the imaginary author of the section on Don Juan, this would be an absurd idea, not least because in Wagner's case the spirit ultimately triumphs over sensuality. For him, music depicts the "sensuous-erotic in all its immediacy": this is its "absolute theme," however much its field of expression may extend to embrace other areas.[55] For Kierkegaard, then, Mozart's *Don Giovanni* is the "classic" work of music, for subject and form are in perfect alignment.[56] Although the titular hero of *Don Giovanni* embodies the principle of sensuality, the work does not constitute a reflection on this principle, for, in Kierkegaard's view, reflection requires language as its "absolute medium" and would therefore alienate the music from itself. (For this very reason Kierkegaard, or at least his alter ego, considered *Die Zauberflöte* a failure, as it relies too heavily on reflection.)

Had Kierkegaard known Wagner's *Tannhäuser*, no doubt he would have considered it a mistake that the composer used an opera rather than a philosophical treatise to explore the struggle between the spirit and sensuality; in his view, the work could have been continued only as a spoken drama following Tannhäuser's departure from the Venusberg. Baudelaire, for his part, does not draw such a clear distinction between sensuality and reflection as does Kierkegaard, with the result that for him the hero of sensuality is not Don Juan but Tannhäuser. He adopts a completely different approach from Kierkegaard's and from the latter's speculations on Leporello's Catalogue Aria and on Don Giovanni's 1003 victims in Spain, writing dismissively of the "wearisome crowd of victims, those endless Elviras," and playing off Tannhäuser against Don Juan.

> The pure idea, incarnate in the unique figure of Venus, speaks very much more clearly and eloquently. It is no ordinary rake, leaping from beauty to beauty, that we see here, but man, general, universal man, living morganatically with the absolute ideal of sensual love, the Queen of all she-devils, faunesses and satyresses which have been banished underground since the death of the great god Pan—in a word, with indestructible and irresistible Venus herself.[57]

In *Tannhäuser*, there is no strict opposition between the worlds of classical sensuality and Christian spirituality. Rather, the two are dialectically interrelated.[58] This is also true of the two women who embody this antithesis in the drama. Tannhäuser rebels against the dualism of spirit and sensuality, of sacred and profane love, and so it may be said that he initially sought out Venus because of Elisabeth. The latter was unattainable within the framework of *hôhe minne*, being an object of mere veneration, when Tannhäuser wanted to love her with both body and soul. In Venus, Tannhäuser was looking for Elisabeth, just as on his return to the Wartburg he looks for Venus in Elisabeth. For there can be no doubt that the hymn that Tannhäuser sings in praise of enjoyment in love is directed at none other than Elisabeth. It is not that he hesitates between the two women, for Venus is not a real person like Elisabeth, but that he thinks of Venus simply as an idea—the idea of a physically fulfilling love that he looks for solely in Elisabeth.

Wagner suggested as much in his 1852 essay *On Performing "Tannhäuser."* Following his return to the Wartburg, Tannhäuser's love for Elisabeth grips him like an "all-consuming fiery force." "With this fire, this ardor, he once enjoyed Venus's love and must now involuntarily fulfill the vow he freely swore on leaving her, 'henceforth to be her valiant champion against the entire world.' " During the Tournament of Song, "he is simply struggling to express his love of Elisabeth when he finally flaunts his colors openly as Venus's knight" (GS 5:153). Until that moment, Elisabeth lent her tacit support to Tannhäuser's message of love. Even before he left the Landgrave's court, she felt that Tannhäuser's songs were true to life and that, as such, they were in stark contrast to the love songs usually sung at court.

> Der Sänger klugen Weisen
> lauscht' ich sonst gern und viel;
> ihr Singen und ihr Preisen
> schien mir ein holdes Spiel.
> Doch welch' ein seltsam neues Leben
> rief euer Lied mir in die Brust!
> Bald wollt' es mich wie Schmerz durchbeben,
> bald drang's in mich wie jähe Lust:
> Gefühle, die ich nie empfunden!
> Verlangen, das ich nie gekannt!
> Was einst mir lieblich, war verschwunden
> vor Wonnen, die noch nie genannt.
>
> (2:18–19)

> [How often and how gladly I'd listen
> To the singers' skillful songs;
> Their singing and their praises
> Seemed a delightful game to me.
> But what a strange new world of feeling
> Your song awoke in my breast!
> At times I seemed to shake with pain,
> But then I'd feel a sudden joy:
> Emotions that I'd never felt!
> Desire I'd never known!
> What once seemed charming was displaced
> By joys for which I knew no name!]

Elisabeth's reaction to Tannhäuser's song is significant: she "makes a move to show her approval, but, as the rest of the audience maintains a solemn silence, she modestly restrains herself" (GS 2:23).

But if Tannhäuser does not see his departure from the Venusberg as a radical break with the type of love that Venus embodies, why does he leave the Venusburg at all? In the first of his three great hymns in praise of Venus (each of which starts enthusiastically enough, only to develop a more melancholy strain), he justifies his decision as follows:

> Nach Freude, ach! nach herrlichem Genießen
> verlangt' mein Herz, es dürstete mein Sinn:
> da, was nur Göttern einstens du erwiesen,
> gab deine Gunst mir Sterblichem dahin.—
> > Doch sterblich, ach! bin ich geblieben,
> > und übergroß ist mir dein Lieben;
> > wenn stets ein Gott genießen kann,
> > bin ich dem Wechsel unterthan;
> > nicht Lust allein liegt mir am Herzen,
> > aus Freuden sehn' ich mich nach Schmerzen:
> > aus deinem Reiche muß ich flieh'n,—
> > o, Königin, Göttin! Laß mich zieh'n.

(GS 2:6)

> [For pleasure, ah! for glorious enjoyment
> My heart cried out, my mind did thirst:
> And all you'd once revealed to gods alone
> Your favors now bestowed upon a mortal.—
> > But mortal, ah! I've yet remained,
> > Your love is far too great for me;
> > A god may know eternal joy,
> > But, human, I am bound to change;
> > My heart is set on more than mere delight,
> > For in the midst of joy I long for pain:
> > Your realm I now must flee,—
> > O queen, my goddess! Let me go!]

Tannhäuser yearns to escape from the eternity of a *paradis perverti* and return to the world of mortality, change, and pain, where time exists once more. (We have already encountered this typically Wagnerian motif in *Die Feen*.)

> Die Zeit, die hier ich weil', ich kann sie nicht
> ermessen:—Tage, Monde—giebt's für mich
> nicht mehr, denn nicht mehr sehe ich die Sonne,
> nicht mehr des Himmels freundliche Gestirne;—
> den Halm seh' ich nicht mehr, der frisch ergrünend
> den neuen Sommer bringt;—die Nachtigall

nicht hör' ich mehr, die mir den Lenz verkünde:—
hör' ich sie nie, seh' ich sie niemals mehr?

(GS 2:5–6)

[The time that I've been here no longer can I
Measure:—days and months for me exist
No longer, for I see the sun no longer,
And no longer see the heaven's smiling stars;—
No longer do I see the grass that, freshly green,
Proclaims another summer;—no longer do I hear
The nightingale that sings of spring's awakening.
Am I not to hear or see all these again?]

Tannhäuser has grown weary of eternal bliss. In much the same way, Tieck's Tannenhäuser had justified his decision to leave the Venusberg with the words "I longed to lead the sort of life that people lead in all unconsciousness, a life in which suffering alternates with joy; I was sated with so much brilliance and sought out my former home again."[59] And in his parody of the legend, Heine portrays his hero as "sick" of always being happy. "I pine for bitterness," he tells Venus.

Wir haben zu viel gescherzt und gelacht,
Ich sehne mich nach Tränen,
Und statt mit Rosen möcht ich mein Haupt
Mit spitzigen Dornen kronen.[60]

[Too much have we jested, too much have we laughed,
My heart for tears has long panted;
Each rose on my head I fain would see
By pointed thorns supplanted.]

This idea is elaborated in Heine's "Elementargeister" and, like the Ecce Homo reminiscence in the final line, clearly left a lasting mark on Wagner's thinking.[61]

If Tannhäuser attempts to escape from the Venusberg, it is not out of remorse or because he is conscious of having committed any sin (for only at the very last moment, just before he reaches the world aboveground, does he again apply Christian standards to himself and speak of repentance and salvation) but because he can no longer bear to be treated as a god—paradoxically, he suffers from a lack of suffering. His very first words are "Zu viel! Zu viel!" [Too much! Too much!] (GS 2:5), an overwhelming outburst with which he suddenly seems to heed the warning of the Seven Wise Men, "Ne quid nimis" [Nothing in excess], and to become intensely conscious of the human condition.

Tannhäuser is the opposite of the three classical sinners, Tantalus, Sisyphus, and Ixion. Whereas they were cast out of Olympus and sent to Tartarus for failing to take account of human limitations (and failing to do so, moreover, in an erotic context), Tannhäuser ascends from the underworld, where the Olympian gods now live in exile, and reenters the world aboveground precisely to rediscover the limitations of humankind and to feel human suffering again. At the same time he longs to leave the paradis artificiel of the Venusberg and return to the paradis vert of lost childhood innocence amid the "fresh green of the meadows" (GS 2:7) and the fields of his homeland. Above all, however, he feels threatened as an artist by enslavement and sterility—the very dangers that he had faced at the Landgrave's court amid the vacuous conventionality of the Wartburg poets, which he had sought to avoid by fleeing to the Venusberg.

Whereas he was denied enjoyment in the world of self-contained feelings of Thuringian society, enjoyment now prevents him from suffering. But both these emotions—suffering and enjoyment in their fullest intensity—form the substance of his poetry. Thus he argues with Venus:

> Bei dir kann ich nur Sklave werden;
> nach Freiheit doch verlange ich,
> nach Freiheit, Freiheit dürstet's mich;
> zu Kampf und Streite will ich stehen,
> sei's auch auf Tod und Untergehen!

(GS 2:9)

> [With you, I can be but a slave,
> And yet I yearn for freedom,
> For freedom, freedom I repine;
> I'm ready to fight and do battle,
> Though death and destruction be my reward!]

An idea that had been merely hinted at in the pre-Paris versions[62] emerges clearly from the 1861 revisions to the Venusberg scene: Tannhäuser is related spiritually to the Flying Dutchman. Both suffer from the endlessness of life and from their inability to die: "O Göttin, woll' es fassen,/mich drängt es hin zum Tod!" (GS 2:11) [O Goddess, understand me,/I feel drawn inexorably to death!] At this, Venus threatens him with the terrible fate of Ahasuerus: "Wenn selbst der Tod dich meidet,/ein Grab dir selbst verwehrt?" (GS 2:11) [If even death avoids you,/A grave's denied to you as well?]. At no point is it suggested that Wagner's Venusberg is a kind of hell, that the exiled gods are in league with Satan, or that this underground realm is a world of evil. The system of values associated with medieval Christianity has, so to speak, been suspended here. At this point Wagner comes astonishingly close to Kierkegaard, even though neither was aware of the other's work. That the Venusberg is "the kingdom of sin" is forgotten when it is actually present, "for it must be contained in the moment when it appears in aesthetic indifference. Only when reflection enters in does the kingdom manifest itself as the kingdom of sin." In Wagner's opera this is the moment when Tannhäuser, unexpectedly turning to Christianity, speaks of "atonement" and calls out: "My salvation lies with Mary!" But then, Kierkegaard continues, "Don Juan has been slain, then the music stops."[63] This sudden silence before reflection corresponds in Wagner's opera to the sudden collapse of the phantasmagorical Venusberg: "Terrible crash. Venus disappears" (GS 2:11). Up to this point, Venus's realm is a world of eroto-aesthetic beauty that maintains its apocryphal rights in the face of Christianity's prevailing values, rights that are also guaranteed to the exiled gods of classical antiquity in

Heine's "Die Götter Griechenlands," which is, as it were, a contrafactum of Schiller's similarly titled poem. This emerges with particular clarity from Wagner's 1860 sketch for the Venusberg ballet, a sketch that constitutes a kind of synoptic vision of erotic myths from ancient times, from Diana and Endymion to the Rape of Europa and the myth of Leda and the Swan. At the same time, this whole new scene is a remarkable anticipation of Nietzsche, with a Dionysian procession in which all the requisite properties and mythological characters irrupt with orgasmic frenzy into the Apollonian world of Venus's court. Christian values are completely overturned here, recalling *Heinrich Heine und die Abschaffung der Sünde*, the title of Dolf Sternberger's 1972 book on Heine and the "abolition of sin."

THE "DANCE OF THE FUTURE": HEINE'S AND WAGNER'S VENUSBERG BALLETS

In the Paris version of the Venusberg scene,[64] the Three Graces are discovered standing beside the couch of Venus and Tannhäuser. They embody moderation in this erotic cosmos. According to Wagner's detailed draft of this scene—dated 30 May 1860—they invite the lovers to "maintain a sense of grace and emotional propriety." The lascivious fauns are driven away by the "seriousness of their expressions." The dance that they initiate assumes "an increasingly calm and graceful character, in which desire finds only the gentlest and tenderest expression" (SS 11:416–17). The measured tone of this scene with the Three Graces is disrupted by the return of the fauns, who are bent on revenge, and by the army of wild bacchantes that slaughters a black ram. In his letter to Mathilde Wesendonck of 10 April 1860, Wagner wrote that he had originally thought of having "jubilant maenads carrying in the murdered Orpheus and tossing his head into the waterfall" (SS 11:415). Appalled, the Three Graces attempt in vain to restore order. In the fuller version of the draft, they are even abducted by the centaurs, whereas in the definitive version of the scene they finally approach Venus as victors, having "triumphed over the wild passions of the subjects of her realm. Venus glances at them in her gratitude" (GS 2:4).

Only in the definitive version of this scene is Venus depicted unequivocally as a goddess of moderation, a portrayal that may surprise many observers and that also contradicts her behavior toward Tannhäuser, yet it relates to a Neoplatonic idea in Botticelli's *Primavera* to which Edgar Wind has also drawn attention. Here Wind quotes Pico della Mirandola's belief that "the unity of Venus is unfolded in the trinity of the Graces."[65] Their dance is imbued with the spirit of Castitas, the third of the Graces, whose chastity is transferred to the other two. "In this she appears to have the sanction of Venus; for however recklessly Cupid may shoot his fire, Venus tempers the dance and keeps its movements within a melodious restraint." The Cupid who hovers over Venus, pointing his arrow at Castitas, embodies the impetuousness of love that is tamed by Venus. The "triadic dance" of the Graces is characterized by this tension between passion (Cupido) and moderation (Venus).[66]

In *Tannhäuser*, too, we find the image of Venus and her Graces united in a spirit of moderation, and Cupid becomes merely one of many such figures firing off their arrows. Here, of course, there is no hint of the transcendental dimension of

Botticelli's *Primavera*, an aspect encapsulated above all in the figure of Mercury, the leader of the Graces, who points toward the clouds and looks into the beyond, his gaze seeming to follow that of Castitas, who is inflamed by *amore divino* (divine love). In Wagner's case, the whole mythological apparatus is used only to conjure up a purely sensual and erotic world in contrast to the world of Christian spirituality. Here myth becomes mainly a backdrop.

Heine, too, wrote a Venusberg ballet that Wagner may have known. Drafted in Paris in 1846 and intended to "prevent the crows that are spying on me on all sides from proudly pluming themselves with a peacock's feathers,"[67] it forms the fourth tableau of his dance poem *Die Göttin Diana* (The goddess Diana), which he published in Hamburg in 1854 in the first volume of his *Vermischte Schriften* (Miscellaneous writings), where it is subtitled *Postscript to "Die Götter im Exil."* In his introduction, he states that the story was "essentially already contained in the third part of my *Salon*, from which many a Maestro Barthel has already drawn many a measure of fruit wine."[68] Here Heine was thinking of his essay "Elementargeister," and "Maestro Barthel" is almost certainly a dig at Wagner,[69] a supposition supported by the fact that the same volume of his *Vermischte Schriften* contains Heine's satirical poem "Jung-Katerverein für Poesie-Musik" (Young tomcats' society for poetry-music). Although this last-named work is nominally aimed at the "divine tomcat" Liszt, there seems little doubt that the second butt of Heine's satire was Wagner's poetically generated music.[70] It is certainly entertaining to think that in the case of *Die Göttin Diana*, too, Wagner may have again played the part of Maestro Barthel.

At all events, the parallels between the two "pantomimes" are certainly striking. Heine wrote his scenario at the suggestion of Benjamin Lumley, who was then director of Her Majesty's Theatre in London and who also commissioned his dance poem *Der Doktor Faust* in 1847. Indeed, the two commissions are closely related both formally and thematically. The fourth act of *Die Göttin Diana* was inspired by the Helen of Troy act in part 2 of Goethe's *Faust* and is set "on an island in the Greek archipelago."[71] It, too, is a "classico-romantic phantasmagoria" that tells of a fictitious meeting between medieval and classical man of a kind that Wagner was later to develop in *Tannhäuser*. For Heine, of course, pagan antiquity was synonymous with sensuality, and the Christian Middle Ages with spirituality. On this imaginary island, "nothing recalls a nebulous hereafter, mystical sensuality, and dread, or the otherworldly ecstasy of a spirit that is emancipated from the body; here everything breathes a sense of real and tangible bliss, with no feeling of wistful nostalgia, no foreboding or empty longing."[72]

In both *Die Göttin Diana* and Wagner's Paris Venusberg scene, the Apollonian reserve of the main group is suddenly caught up in the whirlwind of a bacchantic procession. "Helen's virgins take their cue from this expression of pleasure and tear the roses and myrtle from their hair, before winding vine leaves into their unkempt locks, and with streaming hair, rushing away as bacchants, brandishing their thyrsi."[73] As in Wagner's Paris *Tannhäuser*, Apollonian calm is restored in the end.

Unlike Kierkegaard, who saw in Faust the embodiment of "the demonic qualified as the spiritual" and, as such, a totally different character from Don Juan,[74]

Heine was convinced that "the real idea behind the Faust legend was a revolt against the spiritualist asceticism of the early Catholic Church on the part of a realistic, sensualist love of life."[75] In this sense, Wagner's Tannhäuser is a kind of Faust; like Faust, he is a seeker, a man who errs and rebels against medieval spiritualism in the name of classical sensualism. The same idea also underpins Heine's *Die Göttin Diana*, which represents a further variant on the theme of an encounter between the Middle Ages and antiquity embodied in the relationship between a "young German knight" and a character from Greek myth, in this case, the goddess Diana, who holds court with her retinue in a ruined temple. In Heine's hands, chaste Diana becomes a passionate lover. The reason for this metamorphosis may be found in Caput XIX of *Atta Troll*, where the exiled goddess appears at the head of the Wild Hunt, a new Diana who regrets her former chastity and looks back wistfully on a "bygone age when men were more beautiful."

> Spät zwar, aber desto stärker
> Ist in ihr erwacht die Wollust,
> Und es brennt in ihren Augen
> Wie ein wahrer Höllenbrand.[76]
>
> [Late, indeed, but all the stronger
> She to thoughts of lust awakens,
> And within her eyes 'tis burning,
> Like a very brand of hell.
>
> (Trans. Edgar Alfred Bowring)]

In Heine's dance poem, Diana tells her knight that "the old gods are not dead but merely hiding in mountain caves and ruined temples, where they visit each other at night and hold their celebrations."[77] One of these celebrations is taking place at the time that the poem is set, and again it is depicted as an agon between Apollonian and Dionysian forces, with the two gods even appearing in person: Apollo with the Muses, Bacchus with Silenus and satyrs.

> Apollo performs a song for the lovers, and his female companions perform a beautiful and measured dance around Diana and the knight. The music grows louder, and voluptuous melodies are heard from outside, with the sounds of cymbals and drums; and here is Bacchus, who enters blithely with his satyrs and bacchants. He is riding on a domesticated lion, and to his right is a pot-bellied Silenus astride a donkey. The satyrs and bacchants perform a series of wild and high-spirited dances, the bacchants have vine leaves or even snakes in their streaming hair, or else they are wearing gold crowns, waving their thyrsi, and adopting the exuberant, incredible, even impossible positions that we see on old vases and other bas-reliefs.[78]

In the end, Apollo and Bacchus dance together, their dance symbolizing the reconciliation of opposing principles. In this, they differ from their Wagnerian counterparts, where Bacchus's followers behave in a far more orgiastic and eccentric fashion than they do in Heine's Venusberg scenario.

Like Wagner's second act, Heine's second tableau is set in a "large hall in a Gothic castle" and involves a confrontation between what he describes as the "decorous" world of a medieval court and the world of the gods, which suddenly bursts upon it in the form of a bacchantic procession: "And we see a pas de deux in which the pagan pleasures of the Greek gods engage in single combat with the domestic virtues of Germanic spirituality."[79] In the third tableau, Diana and her knight approach the Venusberg, but Faithful Eckart bars their way and kills the knight in single combat. The fourth tableau, as we have already seen, takes place inside the Venusberg, which provides a home for "the famous men and women of the classical and medieval worlds" from Ovid to Goethe. "Popular belief" has located these men and women there "because of their sensualist reputation." (No doubt Heine secretly included himself among their number, alongside Goethe.) Here, too, the proceedings are dominated by dances performed by the contrasting groups associated with Apollo and Bacchus. The high point is the entrance of "Frau Venus with Tannhäuser, her *cavaliere servente*. Scantily clad, with garlands of roses on their heads, these two dance an intensely sensual pas de deux reminiscent of the most illicit dances of the modern period." (As we shall see in a moment, Heine was thinking above all of the cancan.) Apollo and Bacchus finally revive the dead knight, wakening him to new life.[80]

Whether or not Wagner was familiar with Heine's scenario, their two ballets are closely related: both are based on the idea of the gods in exile, an idea that is essentially Heine's. Not only that, in their aesthetic approach to dance as an art form, they are strikingly similar on one essential point. If Heine, in his scenario, recalls "old vases and bas-reliefs" and even takes as his model "the most illicit dances of the modern period," he goes far beyond the accepted limits of ballet at this period, just as Wagner did in his Paris Venusberg ballet. He, too, had representations of classical Greek dances before his mind's eye, representations that proved wholly unworkable in the theater of his own day.

"I demanded something unheard-of, something that departed radically from traditional choreographic practices," Wagner later wrote in *My Life* (ML 644). As he explained in his essay *On Conducting* in 1869, he spent many of the rehearsals for the Paris production trying to make the ballet master Lucien Petipa see "what a ludicrous contrast there was between my music and the wretched little tripping pas of his maenads and bacchants, and begging him to devise something answering to the Bacchanalian groups on famous classical reliefs, something bold and savagely sublime for his corps de ballet to perform." But Petita objected, saying that if he were to pass on to his dancers even a word of Wagner's instructions, the result would be "a cancan, and we should be lost" (GS 8:315). It is clear from his "Reminiscences of Auber" that Wagner mistakenly regarded the cancan as a national dance "in which the very act of procreation is symbolically consummated. How any element of artistry can make itself felt here is difficult to understand" (GS 9:53). Here Wagner is evidently thinking not of the cancan as danced onstage exclusively by women but of the dance that was performed with extremely lascivious poses in ballrooms from around 1830 onward, when its character began to change and it sank to new social and aesthetic depths.[81] It was this latter type that Heine, too, had in mind and that one commentator has referred to as the "langue verte de la chorégraphie" (vernacular of dance).[82] In fact, Heine had fewer reservations about the cancan than Wagner did, convinced, as he was, that he could see in its forms the "impossible positions" that he felt characterized bacchantic processions "on old vases and other bas-reliefs."[83] In his "Götter im Exil" he retells the tale of a "Bacchanale" celebrated by Dionysus "and the rest of his drunken company" in the midnight seclusion of a Tyrolean forest, where they "once again dance paganism's dance of joy, the cancan of the classical world, with no hypocritical disguises, and none of the usual interventions of the *sergeants de ville* [officers of the law] of some spiritualistic morality."[84] (These sergeants de ville used to arrest cancan dancers in the ballrooms of Paris.)

In Paris, Monsieur Chiccard (or Chicard) was hailed as the virtual inventor of the cancan, with Heine even congratulating him on the fact that the cancan bore "a great resemblance to the ancient dance of Silenus that was danced at the Dionysia and that acquired its name from Bacchus's worthy teacher, Silenus."[85] Unsurprisingly, Chiccard was flattered by so learned a reference to a dance decried as vulgar and compared to French slang.[86] If Heine had suggested *his* Venusberg scenario as a suitable ballet for the Paris Opéra, he would not have been in the least surprised by Petipa's fears that the corps de ballet would lapse into the madness of the cancan. "Exactly!" he would probably have replied. Certainly, Petipa would have been lost, as the Paris Opéra at this time was the home of classical ballet, a type of dance that Heine attacked and ridiculed with insistent regularity.

"There is nothing I detest more," writes Maximilian in the second of Heine's "Florentinische Nächte," "than the ballet at the Grand Opera in Paris, where the tradition of classical dance has been preserved in its purest form." He compares classical dance with *tragédie classique* (likewise dominated, in his view, by "affected unities and artificialities") and fulminates against this kind of poetics, with its "danced alexandrines, declamatory leaps, antithetical entrechats, and a noble passion that pirouettes so giddily on one leg that all you can see is sky and leotard, ideality and mendacity!"[87] Heine's satirical description of the ballet at the Paris Opéra makes it all too easy to imagine how Wagner's Venusberg must have been staged. In fact, one of the French critics who attended the first night of the 1861 production left a report whose ironies are no less barbed than Heine's:

> Twenty-four bacchantes walk from right to left, and raise their arms above their heads. . . . Then twenty-four fauns walk from left to right, raising their arms like the bacchantes. Sixteen nymphs follow the fauns, raising their arms in the same manner. Then sixteen youths, who were asleep on the rocks, wake up suddenly and raise their arms, as though stretching. Finally twelve Cupids, not to be different, raise their little arms in the air, without knowing why.[88]

In short, the Venusberg ballet degenerated into precisely the kind of absurd posturing that both Wagner and Heine mocked as typical of the ballet at the Paris Opéra. Wagner's ideas, like Heine's, could not be realized until the ground had been prepared by the revolution of *Ausdruckstanz*, or expressive dance.[89]

The narrator of the "Florentinische Nächte" likewise dreams of a "revolution in the art of dance," a revolution whose forms are suggested by his description of the ballerina Mademoiselle Laurence, who has no time for "the art of dance" in the sense of classical academic ballet technique, but, like many of the proponents of the later Ausdruckstanz, she

> danced as nature bids human beings dance; her whole nature was in harmony with her pas, not just her legs, her whole body danced, her features danced. . . . It was a dance that did not strive to entertain through outward forms of movement, rather the outward forms of movement seemed to be the words of a particular language that had something particular to say.[90]

On reading these lines, it is impossible not to be reminded of later definitions of Ausdruckstanz: dance as the body's natural "language." And again we find a reference to the orgiastic depictions of dance in classical times.

> Was it a national dance from southern France or Spain? These types of dance were certainly recalled by the impetuousness with which the dancer threw her little body this way and that, and by the wildness with which she sometimes tossed back her head in the wantonly bold manner of the bacchants whom we observe with astonishment on the reliefs on ancient vases.[91]

Mademoiselle Laurence resembles the cancan dancer Mademoiselle Pomaré (the stage name of Elise Sergent), to whom Heine paid tribute in the Pomare cycle of his *Romanzero* and with whom he seems to have been as infatuated as Herod was with Salome.

> Sie tanzt! Wie sie das Leibchen wiegt!
> Wie jedes Glied sich zierlich biegt!
> Das ist ein Flattern und ein Schwingen,
> Um wahrlich aus der Haut zu springen.
> . . . .
> Sie tanzt. Derselbe Tanz ist das,
> Den einst die Tochter Herodias'
> Getanzt vor dem Judenkönig Herodes.
> Ihr Auge sprüht wie Blitze des Todes.
>
> Sie tanzt mich rasend—ich werde toll—
> "Sprich, Weib, was ich dir schenken soll?
> Du lächelst? Heda! Trabanten! Läufer!
> Man schlage ab das Haupt dem Täufer!"[92]
>
> [She dances. How her figure sways!
> What grace her every limb displays!
> There's as much flitting, leaping, swinging,
> As if she from her skin were springing!
> . . . .
> She dances. 'Tis the very same
> That once Herodias' daughter came
> And danced to Herod. As she dances,
> Her eye casts round it deadly glances.

> She'll dance me frantic. Woman, say,
> What shall be thy reward to-day?
> Thou smil'st? Quick, herald! to the gateway!
> Decapitate the Baptist straightway!
>
> (Trans. Edgar Alfred Bowring)]

Significantly, it is Salome whom Heine equates with Mademoiselle Pomaré, as it was Salome who at the end of the century became the role most closely associated with the representatives of the New Dance movement, which broke away from classical ballet. Indeed, so numerous were the depictions of Salome in literature, the visual arts, and above all dance that the term "Salomania" was coined to describe this obsession.[93] Also worth recalling here is the figure of Herodias/Salome in Caput XIX of *Atta Troll*, a figure who was to leave an indelible mark on French artists of the fin de siècle. Here, Herodias/Salome passes before the poet's mind's eye with Diana's Wild Hunt, holding in her hand the head of John the Baptist and beguiling him with her gaze: "Wherefore didst thou gaze upon me / With such tenderness, Herodias?"[94]

Here Herodias is a ghost who seems to return in "Herodias II"—the original title of the poem, later renamed "Pomare." In much the same way, Heine's female dancers repeatedly remind us of "elemental spirits." Here one thinks first and foremost of Mademoiselle Laurence in "Florentinische Nächte": "She would sometimes turn pale, almost as pale as a ghost, her eyes would gape like those of a specter, around her lips trembled desire and anguish, and her black hair, framing her temples in sleek ovals, moved like the fluttering wings of a raven."[95] Among the more mystifying aspects of her dance is the way in which she occasionally bends down and places her ear to the ground, listening, "as though she could hear a voice speaking to her."[96] Not until many years later does the narrator learn Mademoiselle Laurence's life history and discover that her mother had been buried in a state of suspended animation and given birth to her in a grave, where she was discovered by chance by body snatchers. Since then she has been known as the "child of death" and reviled as a "ghost" and "vampire."[97] Only when she dances does she recall the earth: "I forgot myself and thought I was a completely different person."[98] She falls into a trancelike state that explains the "signature"[99] and curious form of her dance. This, too, is remarkably prescient of the free dance forms of the turn of the century: suffice it to recall the famous somnambulist dancer Madeleine Guipet, who was much admired by Georg Fuchs and other writers on dance and who, like Mademoiselle Laurence, had no formal training as a dancer. A "magnétiseur," or hypnotist, placed her in a trance before she could start dancing.[100]

It is significant that in his "Florentinische Nächte," Heine again recalls "the legend of the dead dancers known as willis: these women are young brides who died before their wedding day, but who retained in their hearts so overwhelmingly unsatisfied a desire to dance that every night they emerge from their graves, collect in groups on country roads, and, as midnight strikes, perform the wildest of dances there." These dances are an expression of unsatisfied sensuality and remind the narrator of the "madness of the Parisian women which is especially evident at balls."[101]

The furious dancing of the women of Paris—a nineteenth-century French source defines the cancan as "a sort of epileptic dance or *delirium tremens*"[102]—appears as a kind of revolt against the constraints of a spiritualist ideology on the part of suppressed sensuality, also finding expression in the legends of elemental spirits, in the midnight activities of the exiled pagan gods of pleasure, and in the willis who always express themselves through dance, which for Heine was the most sensual of all the arts.

The "Elementargeister" essay includes a more detailed account of the legend of the "dead bacchants."[103] This episode was the starting point for Théophile Gautier's scenario for Adolphe Adam's ballet *Giselle*, which was first staged at the Paris Opéra in 1841. Heine, who was friendly with Gautier, reports on the work in *Lutetia*, a review that contains a number of ironic, if amiable, comments on Adam's score, which is anything but bacchantic in tone. At the same time, his review constitutes one of his most important pronouncements on the aesthetics of dance as an art form. In particular he praises the prima ballerina Carlotta Grisi, who stood out from the conventional corps de ballet "like an orange among potatoes."

> Yes, she is just like one of those elemental spirits whom we always imagine to be dancing and whose powerful dance tunes are the subject of so many curious folktales. In the legend of the willis, this mysterious, frantic, even destructive desire to dance that is typical of all elemental spirits is transferred to dead brides; the exuberant desire on the part of nixies and elves to excite the early heathens is combined with the melancholically voluptuous thrills and the darkly exquisite terrors of the medieval belief in ghosts.

"Does the music reflect the ballet's fantastical subject matter?" Heine goes on to ask, and there follows a passage that is bound to make Wagnerians sit up and listen. Alluding to a "Nordic trip" undertaken by Adam, Heine notes that the extremely mild-mannered composer had not brought back with him any of the "powerful melodies" associated with the Nordic Strömkarl, melodies that "throw the whole of nature into turmoil."[104]

This Strömkarl is familiar to us from Wagner's sketches for the Paris Venusberg, where he appears with a misshapen fiddle, at the sounds of which the orgiastic dancing acquires a note of the wildest abandon, finally drawing into its sway "all manner of mythological beasts" (SS 11:418). Wagner undoubtedly owes his knowledge of this water sprite to his reading of Jacob Grimm's *Deutsche Mythologie*, where it is said that the Strömkarl can be lured out of hiding by throwing a black lamb or a white ram into a waterfall.[105] This is precisely what happens in Wagner's draft immediately before the Strömkarl appears, except that there the ram is black. Heine, too, clearly relies for his information on Grimm when he refers to a set of variations on the Strömkarl's melody, the eleventh of which must never be played, as it causes all the objects in the house to start to dance. Only the reference to the turmoil in nature is missing from Grimm's account. It is not inconceivable that Wagner owed the relevant motifs in his Venusberg ballet to this section from Heine's *Lutetia*.

For Heine, dance played the same role that music did for Kierkegaard, being the ultimate expression of the sensuality proscribed by Christianity.[106] It was, he argued, the only one of the arts that the church had refused to recognize, as it "all too clearly recalled the old temple worship of the pagans, whose gods were transformed into those elflike creatures to which popular belief ascribed a strange obsession with dancing." The "real patron saint of dance" was the Devil, "in whose impious company witches and warlocks dance their nightly rounds."[107] This, of course, is the theme of Heine's *Der Doktor Faust*, in which the Devil—Mephistopheles—is turned into a dancer—Mephistophela—in order to lure Faust to his ruin.

In *Lutetia* Heine informs his reader that according to a Breton folk song, dancing has been "cursed since the daughter of Herodias danced for the wicked king, who had John killed to please her." Classical ballet—which Heine again compares with *tragédie classique* and its allegedly Jansenist spirit—is an attempt to "Christianize this essentially pagan art." And he contrasts it with the sensuality of "so-called national dances." The same contrast is found, Heine believes, in the case of ballroom dancing, with the measured steps of the dances performed in polite society—dances "in name only"—compared with the genuine delight in dancing among the "lower orders," a delight that finds its most triumphant expression in the cancan. Heine follows this up with a detailed account of the way in which officers of the law are placed on duty in public ballrooms "to keep an eye on dancing morality with a darkly Catonian mien," immediately apprehending all who dare to dance the cancan and showing them the door.[108] There are further references to this practice in the passage from "Die Götter im Exil" quoted earlier and in two strophes suppressed from the published edition of the Pomare cycle, in which Heine describes the leaps of the cancan dancer's partner as "wild leaping, most obscene, with no grace or nobility," adding that "virtue's sergent de ville would be glad to take him to the police station."[109] Both here and in the passage from *Lutetia*, Heine—like Wagner—finds it difficult to conceal a certain aesthetic unease at the characteristic style of the cancan.

In Heine's view, the way in which the sergents de ville kept an eye on "popular pleasures" was indicative of "how far the French have gone in matters of liberty."[110] It is clear from the opening sentence of the forty-second section of *Lutetia* ("Here we are dancing on a volcano")[111] that the cancan was a symbol of a secret revolution among the "lower orders," bringing with it a radical reappraisal of existing values by calling into question not only "sexual relationships" but "bourgeois relationships, too, including every kind of enthusiasm, patriotism, loyalty, faith, family feelings, heroism, and divinity."[112] The cancan celebrated its wildest triumphs in the carnival celebrations at the Opéra-Comique, "where the masquerade invests the sense of demonic delight with an element of outrageousness that creates a satanic spectacle" and even a regular "Walpurgis Night."[113] Under the influence of Christian spiritualism, the Dionysia of classical antiquity were transformed into an infernal haunting.

Heine's aesthetics of dance looks forward to the dance movement of the late nineteenth century and at the same time is closely associated with a theme that occupied him throughout his life: the gods in exile. Although the same is not entirely true of Wagner, it is nonetheless remarkable that his Venusberg ballet is not only profoundly influenced by the same ideas as those found in Heine's writings of the period but that it, too, inspired leading figures of the Ausdruckstanz movement, which saw itself as a radical alternative to traditional ballet. Dance historians have repeatedly stressed that Wagner anticipated many of the new movement's main ideas with his demand—first formulated in *The Artwork of the Future* in 1849—that dance should be the basis of drama[114] and that following the classical model, it should be an elemental form of mimed expression diametrically opposed to the aesthetics of classical ballet.[115]

Although Cosima Wagner was generally resistant to new ideas in directing her late husband's works, she accepted that his vision of the Venusberg Bacchanal could be realized only by means of a new and superior form of dance. The Venusberg represents an alternative to the conventional world of the Wartburg and could not, therefore, be allowed to sink into conventionality in turn. In 1891 Cosima invited the internationally acclaimed ballerina Virginia Zucchi to choreograph the Venusberg scene in Bayreuth—the first time that *Tannhäuser* was to be staged in the Festspielhaus. Zucchi attempted to liberate the dancers' movements and free them from the conventions of classical ballet, but she does not seem to have succeeded in finding a convincing solution to the problems that this scene posed. In 1904 it was the turn of Isadora Duncan, one of the pioneers of the free dance movement, to tackle the scene, an engagement that shocked the devout, her unconventional lifestyle and fondness for dancing barefoot proving particularly unsettling.

The previous year, Isadora Duncan had published *Der Tanz der Zukunft* (The dance of the future), her statement of intent, the very title of which recalls Wagner's reform essay of 1849. Like Heine and Wagner before her, she sought inspiration in the figures on Greek vases and reliefs that she must have studied during an extended tour of Greece in 1903.[116] She must have been endlessly fascinated by Wagner's Venusberg ballet. Her ideas on how to choreograph it, which she wrote down for Cosima's benefit, and especially her realization of the Dionysian element that had so worried Petipa by suggesting affinities with the cancan were evidently formulated with Wagner's Venusberg scenario in mind.[117] Thus we find her referring to "masses rushing like whirlwinds in rhythms caught up by mad waves of this music, flowing with fantastic sensuality and ecstasy."[118] In a letter to Adolf von Hildebrandt of 17 April 1904, Cosima expressed her belief that Isadora Duncan "seems to me at her most significant in the bacchantic frenzy; but what she is striving to achieve and to emphasize is to bring to life and combine poses from classical reliefs." As Cosima must have known, this aim corresponded precisely with Wagner's own ideas, and in going back to those ideas, it simultaneously set an example for the way in which dance developed during the decade that followed. It is sufficient to recall Nijinsky's legendary choreography for *L'après-midi d'un faune* in 1912: Nijinsky's work was directly inspired by Isadora Duncan's idea of a rebirth of dance from the spirit of Greek vase paintings and reliefs and shocked contemporary audiences with its explicit sexuality.[119] Heine would no doubt have hailed Nijinsky's choreography as the ultimate realization of his dreams of a revolution in dance.

In the event, Isadora Duncan's choreography for *Tannhäuser* suffered from the dichotomy between her own approach to expressive dance and the conventional poses of the Bayreuth corps de ballet, whose members were unable to break free from the techniques of classical ballet, in whose forms they had been trained. Even so, the production marked a decisive step on the road to a more modern production style. A further step was taken in 1930 when Siegfried Wagner engaged Rudolf von Laban, another exponent of Ausdruckstanz, to choreograph the scene. Laban, who had first choreographed the Venusberg Bacchanal in Mannheim in 1921, was a passionate admirer of Wagner, whom he regarded as a pioneer of the modern dance movement, and, like Isadora Duncan, was profoundly influenced by the composer's own draft for this scene, but whereas Isadora Duncan's innovations had been limited in the main to her own solo contributions, Laban succeeded in combining the forms of expressive dance with the ability to direct large groups of dancers onstage—he referred to them as "movement choruses."[120]

A quarter of a century later, Wieland Wagner's 1954 Bayreuth production of *Tannhäuser* was choreographed by his wife, Gertrud Wagner, who was an exponent of Ausdruckstanz and a friend of Mary Wigman. In this way, the modern dance movement finally achieved its breakthrough in Bayreuth. Wagner's vision of an art form derived from Greek reliefs and vase paintings—a vision that he shared with Heine and that drew a clear dividing line between dance and traditional ballet—was no longer consigned to the future but was at last realized in the here and now.

THE "ABOLITION OF SIN" AND ITS RECANTATION: THE CONCEPTIONAL DILEMMA OF *TANNHÄUSER*

Wagner's scenario for his Paris Venusberg takes to its logical conclusion the sensualist thrust of the work, as described earlier. To a certain extent, the opera could be regarded as a Young German work: the artist flees from an illiberal society characterized by its hostility to sensuality and by its rigid conventionality, and he seeks the emancipation of the flesh in the classically inspired sensuality of the alternative world of the Venusberg. He then abandons the latter because the shallow erotic pleasures it has to offer cause him to sink into sloth, although it is never his intention to deny the experience of physical love that he has gained there. Following his return to society, he finds himself torn between his desire to praise a love that is physically fulfilling and the established forces of a society hostile to Eros. The conflict is irreconcilable, and the artist is driven from society.

This model does not, of course, exhaust the whole range of meanings contained in Wagner's opera. The Young German plot is harnessed together with a Romantic strand whose contrasting motivation results in a certain tension. When Tannhäuser leaves Venus, he does not disown her altogether. The principle of physical love that she embodies and the shadowless, timeless, and erotic pleasures that she offers cannot—by virtue of their total one-sidedness—provide Tannhäuser with a satisfactory basis for his life and art. He does not attempt to exclude this principle from his life but seeks to reincorporate it within the original framework of his existence, with permanence and change, pleasure and pain, spirit and sensuality, interrelated as polar opposites. That is why he can assure Venus:

> Nie war mein Lieben größer, niemals wahrer,
> als jetzt, da ich für ewig dich muß fliehen!
> . . . .
>
> Ja, gegen alle Welt will unverdrossen
> fortan ich nun dein kühner Streiter sein!
>
> (GS 2:8)

> [Never was my love greater, never truer
> Than now, when I must flee from you forever!
> . . . .
>
> Yes, against all the world, unflinching,
> Your valiant champion I shall henceforth be!]

This is a promise that Tannhäuser makes good during the Tournament of Song. But this explanation of his departure from the Venusberg is overshadowed by a second reason, which is suddenly introduced at the end of the scene without any previous warning, when Tannhäuser abruptly announces that "I shall find peace through atonement. . . . My salvation lies in Mary!" (GS 2:11). This, of course, prepares the way for an effective *coup de théâtre* in which the Venusberg suddenly vanishes from sight, but, from the standpoint of the previous scene and in the context of the dialogue contained there, this unexpected turn of events in the direction of Christian orthodoxy is altogether unjustified.

This superimposition of two unrelated motives leads to a basic contradiction in the conception of the Wartburg scene in act 2. In the libretto, Wagner has drawn a discreet veil over the reason why the Landgrave has organized the Tournament of Song at all. In the prose draft, it is the Landgrave (in the libretto, Wolfram) who informs Tannhäuser of Elisabeth's love and bluntly invites him to "sue for Elisabeth's hand."[121] Indeed, he even points out the best way of doing so ("Tannhäuser, let me show you the way to win this noble creature"):[122] Tannhäuser must win the Tournament of Song, and Elisabeth must hand him the coveted prize. She herself will be the prize. It is impossible to ignore the parallel with *Die Meistersinger* here, a work that, as we know, was originally intended to "follow on from my *Sängerkrieg auf Wartburg* as a richly allusive satyr play" (GS 4:282), in other words, as a bourgeois comedy that would form a pendant to the courtly tragedy of *Tannhäuser*. Even in the completed libretto there is no mistaking the reason for holding the contest: whoever sings most worthily of love, the Landgrave declares, will receive the prize from Elisabeth's hand: "Er ford're ihn so hoch und kühn er wolle, / ich sorge, daß sie ihm gewähren solle" (GS 2:21–22) [However high and bold be his demand, / I'll see she grants it]. It is impossible, then, to agree with Hans Mayer when he claims that there is a parallel between

Tannhäuser and Goethe's Tasso, both of whom are said to transgress the social limitations imposed on them, a transgression committed as a result of the love that each of them feels for his respective princess.[123] Elisabeth is the prize that persuades Tannhäuser to take part in the tournament.

Wagner had good reasons for drawing a veil over the motivation behind the tournament in the libretto (he was unable to remove it entirely), as it would have revealed all too clearly the fundamental contradiction at the root of the opera's conception. For how are we to explain the fact that following his homage to Venus, Tannhäuser suddenly falls in line with the values of Wartburg society and sets off, in a spirit of penance, for Rome—the selfsame man who, on leaving Venus, had sworn that he would face the world unflinchingly as Venus's "valiant champion"? Tannhäuser gives the following reason for his change of heart:

> Zum Heil den Sündigen zu führen,
> die Gott-Gesandte nahte mir:
> doch, ach! sie frevelnd zu berühren
> hob ich den Lästerblick zu ihr!
>
> (GS 2:28)

> [To guide the sinner to salvation,
> The God-sent woman came to me:
> But ah! to touch her impiously
> I raised my lustful gaze to her!]

At this moment Tannhäuser's love, with its yearning for physical fulfillment and Young German glorification of erotic love, suddenly assumes a sinful aspect. Elisabeth, who had been a tempting first prize in the tournament, is now expected to play a completely different role as divine intercessor. Tannhäuser's sin is not his sojourn in the Venusberg but the fact that he "shamefully failed to recognize heaven's mediator" (GS 2:28) and that he had projected on to her his erotic desires that is now to be seen as his sin. This is an interpretation on which Wagner himself insisted. These lines, he told Franz Liszt in his letter of 29 May 1852 (anticipating ideas that were expressed soon afterward in his essay *On Performing "Tannhäuser"*), encapsulate

> the whole meaning of Tannhäuser's catastrophe, nay, his whole essence. All his suffering, his bloody pilgrimage, everything stems from the idea contained in these lines: unless we hear them at this point, and precisely at this point, and unless we hear them as they must be heard, Tannhäuser as a whole remains incomprehensible, a wanton, vacillating—pitiful figure.[124]

Whenever Wagner goes out of his way to emphasize a point, we do well to mistrust him. And the same is true here. A glance at the prose draft reveals that the lines in question were not part of the work's original motivation. That they later grew in importance for Wagner is understandable. Without them—in other words, without the wholesale reevaluation of Tannhäuser's relationship with Elisabeth— his bloody pilgrimage to Rome, his outward appropriation of the code of values held dear by the other members of Thuringian society, would be insufficiently motivated. (If his "sin" had not been committed against Elisabeth, he could have set off for Rome immediately after leaving the Venusberg, as in the original legend.) The new motivation for his pilgrimage alters the course of the drama. Until then, Elisabeth had appeared to Tannhäuser not as an intercessor but as a lover who, like Tannhäuser, had yearned for the physical fulfillment of her love. Indeed, the Landgrave had even made a veiled promise of marriage to them both. Only after the scandal has broken over the Wartburg is Elisabeth transformed into an ascetic figure who in her prayer to the Virgin dismisses physical love as a "foolish illusion" and "sinful longing" (GS 2:32).

The ethos of renunciation that Wolfram proclaimed in the second act triumphs in the final act over the Young Germans' cult of Eros. The "abolition of sin" (to quote the title of Dolf Sternberger's book on Heine) is rescinded. Venus Urania scores a resounding victory over Venus Cypria, and the world of convention, in the shape of medieval Thuringian society and the church, is placed in the wrong. Divine mercy overrides their rigid norms, and the sinner is forgiven. *Tannhäuser* thus assumes a remarkable position midway between Wagner's second opera, *Das Liebesverbot*, and his final music drama, *Parsifal*: on the one hand, it looks back to the cult of Eros of *Das Liebesverbot*, and on the other, it anticipates the renunciatory ethos of the later work. In his letter to August Röckel of 23 August 1856, Wagner was to write of the "lofty tragedy of renunciation" of *Tannhäuser*, which he now saw, in a Schopenhauerian sense, as the "uniquely redeeming denial of the will."[125] The tale of the Young German artist who, transported back to the Middle Ages, set out to learn all about the emancipation of the flesh in the sensual world of antiquity is transformed at the end of the second act into a Romantic opera of renunciation and redemption.

Lohengrin

THE MYTHICAL PALIMPSEST OF WAGNER'S LAST ROMANTIC OPERA

> The symbolic meaning of the tale I can best sum up as
> follows: contact between a metaphysical phenomenon and
> human nature, and the impossibility that such contact will last.
> The moral would be: the good Lord would do better to spare
> us his revelations, since he is not permitted to annul the laws
> of nature: nature—in this case human nature—is bound to
> take her revenge and destroy the revelation.
>
> —*Richard Wagner to Hermann Franck, 30 May 1846*

WOLFGANG SCHADEWALDT, one of Germany's leading classical scholars, has described Wagner's music dramas as "mythic palimpsests" in which the underlying script of Greek myth is constantly visible beneath the surface layer of Germanic and Christian legend.[1] Wagner himself repeatedly stressed the importance of Greek myth and Attic tragedy in his choice of subject matter, and in *A Communication to My Friends*, his self-apologia of 1851, he even claimed to have derived the themes of his early operas from classical archetypes. If he also had recourse to subjects from the Christian Middle Ages, he wrote, it was because he was attracted by the constellations of classical myth that he could discern behind them.

> It is a fundamental error of our superficial way of looking at things to consider the specifically Christian outlook as somehow essentially creative in its manifestations. Not one of the most characteristic and affecting Christian myths is Christian in spirit: this spirit inherited them all from the purely human concepts of prehistory, merely remolding them to fit its own unique qualities. (GS 4:289)

Wagner then goes on to illustrate this by reference to *Der fliegende Holländer, Tannhäuser,* and *Lohengrin.*

> Just as the basic feature of the myth of the "Flying Dutchman" finds an earlier and still obvious embodiment in the Hellenic Odysseus; just as in tearing himself away from the arms of Calypso, in fleeing from Circe's blandishments, and in yearning for the earthly wife of his cherished homeland, this same Odysseus gave expression to the

fundamental features of a longing that, familiar to the Hellenic spirit, we rediscover, greatly intensified and immeasurably enriched, in the figure of Tannhäuser, so we encounter in Greek myth . . . the essential aspect of the Lohengrin myth. Who does not know the story of Zeus and Semele? (GS 4:289)

LOHENGRIN: JUPITER'S INCOGNITO

Brought up on a diet of Schiller, middle-class audiences in the nineteenth century were familiar with the story of Zeus and Semele, not least through Schiller's *Semele* (1782). Written while he was still at school, his second dramatic poem was described by Schiller as a "lyrical operetta," although it was never set to music. Its models were clearly the French operas lavishly staged at Duke Karl Eugen's court in Ludwigsburg and Stuttgart, many of which dealt with the amorous intrigues of the father of the gods. Indeed, Zeus's extramarital affairs with beautiful mortal women have always been a popular subject for operas, including Richard Strauss's *Die Liebe der Danae* (The love of Danae, 1944) and Giselher Klebe's *Alkmene* (1951), many of them based directly or indirectly on the Amphitryon plays of Molière and Kleist.

In his *Versuch über Schiller* (Essay on Schiller, 1955), Thomas Mann drew attention to the clear pre-echoes of *Lohengrin* in Schiller's *Semele*: "It was, after all, my first literary love, this 'operetta' about the creator's passion for the work that he has created—both as a poetic idea and even in terms of the language that he uses, Schiller clearly points to Kleist's *Amphitryon*." (In 1927 Mann had already devoted one of his finest essays to Kleist's play.)

Such literary and historical perspectives were unknown to me in my childish enthusiasm for the dramatic impact of lines such as

        "Then let me take you in my arms, as though

I were—"

           "Unhappy woman! Stop!"

"Saturnia—"

        "Be silent!"

         "Holds you fast!"

(Just as Juno persuades Semele to ask the forbidden question, so there is another pre-echo of Elsa's "Tell me your name!" and Lohengrin's "Stop!" and "Alas, our happiness is now all fled!") [Cf. GS 2:105–6][2]

Schiller's operetta involves an adulterous affair in a royal household. Juno (Saturnia) has discovered that her husband is having an affair with the Theban princess Semele and plots ways of ending their relationship. She assumes the guise of Semele's old nurse, Beroe, and insinuates herself into Semele's affections, much as Ortrud does with Elsa. Both women, moreover, use the same method, with Juno sowing the seeds of mistrust in Semele's heart, robbing her of the certainty that she has held a god in her arms, and leading her to fear that she has been taken in by a confidence trickster ("Men often come in gods' disguise / To catch a woman").[3] Juno urges Semele to put Zeus to the test: "He must reveal himself!"[4] But, as Juno knows, this will cause Semele's death, as no human being can bear the sight of the god's uncloaked divinity.

In the second scene of the operetta, Semele puts the fatal question in a way that bears striking similarities to act 3, scene 2 of *Lohengrin*, in which Elsa asks the Swan Knight about his origins—the very question that she has been told not to ask. As with Semele and Zeus, she obliges him to reveal his true identity and in that way to destroy her.

ELSA
Laß dein Geheimniß mich erschauen,
daß, wer du bist, ich offen seh'!

LOHENGRIN
Ach, schweige, Elsa!

ELSA
     Meiner Treue
enthülle deines Adels Werth!

Woher du kamst, sag' ohne Reue:—
durch mich sei Schweigens Kraft bewährt.

                      (GS 2:103)

[ELSA
Let me know your secret, so that I
May see quite clearly who you are!

LOHENGRIN
Ah, be silent, Elsa!

ELSA
     Confide in me,
Reveal that you're of noble birth!
Say, without remorse, from where you've come!
Through me the power of silence shall be proved!]

Lohengrin's attempts to set Elsa's mind at rest merely achieve the opposite, and his words

          Drum wolle stets den Zweifel meiden,
          dein Lieben sei mein stolz Gewähr;
          denn nicht komm' ich aus Nacht und Leiden,
          aus Glanz und Wonne komm' ich her

                      (GS 2:104)

          [So cast aside your doubts forever
          And let your love be my proud surety;
          I do not come from night and sorrow:
          From light and joy I journeyed here]

awaken in Elsa the same dread of the numinous that Kleist conjures up so impressively and oppressively in act 2, scene 5 of his own adaptation of the subject, when Alcmena begins to suspect that the man she believes to be her husband is in fact a god in disguise. The same dread inspires in Elsa an insane and self-destructive desire to know her husband's true identity, a desire that recalls the obsessive and insistent questioning in Sophocles' *Oedipus Tyrannus*. The three questions, "Tell me your name!" "Where have you come from?" and "What is your nature?" are like three hammer blows of fate that are sealed by Lohengrin with a gesture of ineffable sadness: "Alas! Our happiness is now all fled!" (GS 2:105–6). This must have been inspired by the stichomythia in the scene from Schiller's *Semele* that was quoted, in part, by Thomas Mann. Here is the same passage again, this time with Schiller's stage directions.

SEMELE
Then let me take you in my arms, as though
I were—

ZEUS (*crying out in his dismay*)
           Unhappy woman! Stop!

SEMELE
Saturnia—

ZEUS (*trying to shut her mouth*)
           Be silent!

SEMELE
           Holds you fast!

ZEUS (*turning away from her, pale*)
Too late! The sound's escaped! The Styx! It is your death
       You've begged for, Semele![5]

The parallel with *Lohengrin* is unmistakable. Baudelaire, moreover, noticed that this scene in *Lohengrin* bears a "striking similarity" to another classical myth, that of Amor and Psyche, "who in the same way was victim of a devilish curiosity, and, being unwilling to respect the secret of her divine spouse, sacrificed all her happiness by probing the mystery. Elsa hearkens to Ortrud, as Eve to the serpent. The eternal Eve falls into the eternal trap."[6] Here, then, is a remarkable affinity between Classical myth and Romantic opera.

Wagner's very first completed opera, *Die Feen* (1834), had been concerned with the same theme, a theme found in many of the works of this period, from E.T.A. Hoffmann to Carl Maria von Weber and Heinrich Marschner, namely, the tragic encounter between the spirit world and the world of humans. *Die Feen* even includes a forbidden question. "Above all," the fairy Ada enjoins her human lover, "you may not ask me for eight years who I am" (SS 11:9). Lohengrin is the male counterpart to Undine; like her, he longs to escape from the supernatural world and enjoy a loving relationship within the world of humankind. But his attempt to forge a link with the world of people ends as tragically as it does in Hoffmann's *Undine* (1816) and Marschner's *Hans Heiling* (1833).

In *A Communication to My Friends,* Wagner offers an impressive account of the way in which the mythic motif of the god who deigns to love a human being, whether Semele, Alcmena, Leda, or Danae, was transformed under Christian influence.

> The ethereal sphere from which the god yearns to descend to earth had expanded under the influence of Christian yearning to encompass the remotest corners of the universe. For the Hellene, it was still the cloud-locked realm of thunder and lightning from which shaggy-haired Zeus came down to earth to mix with men in expert likeness; for the Christian, the blue firmament dissolved into an infinite sea of yearning ecstasy in which the forms of all the gods were merged until finally only his own image as yearning man rose up toward him from the ocean of his own imagination. An ancient, oft-repeated feature recurs throughout the legends of those nations that dwell beside the sea or beside rivers that flow into the sea: upon the waves' blue mirror there draws near an unknown being of utmost grace and purest virtue who wins all hearts through the irresistible spell that he casts on them; he is the embodied wish of the man who dreams of happiness in that far-off land that he cannot know. The stranger vanishes again, disappearing across the ocean waves as soon as he is questioned about his true nature. (GS 4:291)

The myths that tell of Zeus's erotic adventures were transformed into the legends of the Grail and Lohengrin, with the Swan Knight becoming one of Jupiter's legendary aliases. The ethereal sphere of ecstatic yearning in which the gods of antiquity had merged with each other acquired a magical sound in the mystically otherworldly string textures of the prelude to the first act of *Lohengrin*.

The Christian transformation of the classical myth of the amorous affair between a god and a human found its most profound expression in Kleist's *Amphitryon*. Once again it was Thomas Mann who, in his *Versuch über Schiller*, drew attention to a hidden link between Schiller's "lyrical operetta," Kleist's "comedy after Molière," and Wagner's Romantic opera, quoting lines from Schiller's *Semele* in which Zeus expresses his loneliness and desire to descend to earth and be loved by one of his own creations.

> Lang schmachtet' ich, mein weltbelastet Haupt
> An deinem Busen zu begraben, meine Sinnen
> Vom wilden Sturm der Weltregierung eingelullt,
> Und Zügel, Steu'r und Wagen weggeträumt,
> Und im Genuß der Seligkeit vergangen!
> . . . .
> Sie naht—Sie kommt—O Perle meiner Werke.[7]
>
> [How long I yearned to lay upon your breast
> A head bowed down with worldly cares and let
> All thoughts of storm-tossed governance be lulled
> To sleep, relinquishing the reins of power
> And all its trappings, lost in blissful joy!
> . . . .
> But soft! She comes! O pearl of all creation!]

"Can it be true," Mann goes on, "that no one has yet heard in these lines a presentiment and pre-echo of the 'world-ordaining' Jupiter of Kleist's play, a god whose head is turned by desire and who, as the creator of the universe, addresses his lover as 'My darling creature' and 'My idol,' wistfully begging her:

> So viele Freude schüttet
> Er zwischen Erd' und Himmel endlos aus;
> Wärst du vom Schicksal nun bestimmt,
> So vieler Millionen Wesen Dank,
> Ihm seine ganze Fordrung an die Schöpfung
> In einem einz'gen Lächeln auszuzahlen,
> Würd'st du dich ihm wohl—ach![8]

> [Twixt earth and heaven he
> Pours forth such vast infinities of joys,
> If you were chosen now by fate
> To pay the gratitude of many millions
> Of creatures and to pay back all his claims
> Upon creation with a single smile,
> Would you, perhaps . . . Oh!]

Whether or not Wagner was familiar with Kleist's metaphysical comedy, there are astonishing similarities between *Amphitryon* and *Lohengrin*: not only do they share the theme of the god's loneliness and desire for human love, but both works are concerned on a covert level with the role of the artist, a theme treated openly in Schiller's *Semele*, which undoubtedly provided the inspiration for the two later works. Wagner's own exegesis of his opera certainly reads like an interpretation of Kleist's tragicomedy. Lohengrin, writes Wagner, sought the woman

> who would not ask who he was and whence he came, but who would love him as he was and because he was as he appeared to her. . . . In consequence, he had to conceal his higher nature, for only by not uncovering, by not revealing that higher—or, more correctly, *heightened*—nature could he be sure that he was not being merely admired or adored because of that nature or that he was not being humbly and reverentially worshiped as a being past all understanding, since he longed not for admiration and worship but for the only thing that could redeem him from his loneliness and assuage his longing—*love, to be loved* and *to be understood through love*. (GS 4:295–96)

This is a most touching, if highly speculative, interpretation of Lohengrin—but it might be even more valid as a close textual analysis of the character of Jupiter in Kleist's *Amphitryon*. Time and again, Jupiter, in the guise of Amphitryon, tries to tempt Alcmena into confessing that through the figure of her husband she loves him, the god.

> Du wolltest ihm, mein frommes Kind,
> Sein ungeheures Dasein nicht versüßen?
> Ihm Deine Brust verweigern, wenn sein Haupt,
> Das weltenordnende, sie sucht,
> Auf seinen Flammen auszuruhen? Ach Alkmene!

Auch der Olymp ist öde ohne Liebe.
Was gibt der Erdenvölker Anbetung
Gestürzt in Staub, der Brust, der lechzenden?
Er will geliebt sein, nicht ihr Wahn von ihm.
In ewge Schleier eingehüllt,
Möcht er sich selbst in einer Seele spiegeln,
Sich aus der Träne des Entzückens widerstrahlen.

[Ah, would you then, my worthy child,
Not sweeten his atrocious life for him?
Would you deny your breast when his head seeks it,
His head that orders all the worlds,
To rest upon its downy softness? Oh, Alcmena,
Olympus too is empty without love.
What good are nations prostrate in the dust
With adoration, to a heart athirst?
He wants their love, not their illusion of him.
Enshrouded in eternal veils,
He craves to mirror himself in a soul
And be reflected in a tear of rapture.]

To his dismay, however, Jupiter is forced to realize that Alcmena feels only reverence for the god and that her love is reserved for her husband ("Accursèd self-delusion lured me here!"). Yet in the process he acquires greater maturity as a creator who no longer lusts after his creatures but sees them with the artist's disinterested goodwill, thus allowing the play to end happily.

Mein süßes, angebetetes Geschöpf!
In dem so selig ich mich, selig preise!
So urgemäß dem göttlichen Gedanken,
In Form und Maß und Sait und Klang,
Wie's meiner Hand Äonen nicht entschlüpfte![9]

[O my sweet creature whom I so adore,
In whom I call myself so blessèd, blessèd!
One truer to the ultimate divine
Conception, both in form and mould,
Has not in eons gone forth from my hands!]

Lohengrin is not allowed to enjoy the happiness afforded by dispassionate observation. Like Jupiter in the works of both Kleist and Schiller, he wants to be "a *human being*, not a god, in other words, not an absolute artist."

Yet there still clings to him, ineluctably, the telltale halo of his heightened nature; he can appear only as a thing of wonder; the amazement of the common herd, the poisoned trail of envy cast their shadows even across the loving woman's heart; doubt and jealousy convince him that he has not been *understood* but only *worshiped*, and force from him an admission of his divinity, with which he returns, annihilated, to his lonely state. (GS 4:296)

There is a parallel not only with Kleist's reformed god but also with Schiller's Zeus, who explicitly professes to being an artist, suffering from his loneliness and poorer than his own loving creatures.

> Wie unbemerkt, verächtlich
> Verschwinden meine Welten, meine strahlenquillenden
> Gestirne, meine tanzenden Systeme,
> Mein ganzes großes Saitenspiel, wie es
> Die Weisen nennen, wie das alles tot
> Gegen eine Seele?[10]

> [How unobserved, derisively
> My worlds have disappeared, my radiant stars,
> My dancing planetary systems and
> My music of the spheres, as wise men have
> Been known to call it—but how dead this all
> Appears beside a living soul!]

Just as Pygmalion is tempted to kneel before the statue that he has created, so Zeus would like to kneel before Semele, "a man among men." "A word, and he will cast away his godhead, be flesh and blood, he'll die and will be loved."[11] But as a result of Juno's intrigue, he is not permitted to enjoy this boon and must remain an "absolute artist," as Wagner would have called him. Like Lohengrin, he returns, "annihilated, to his lonely state" following the revelation of his divine nature. Thus the god is prevented from being made human. In the last lines from Schiller's play quoted earlier, the allusion to the incarnation of the divine logos as Christ is unmistakable. Goethe took a similar approach in his conversation with Friedrich Wilhelm Riemer on 14 July 1807, when they discussed Kleist's *Amphitryon*. The play, Goethe opined, contained "nothing more nor less than a Christian interpretation of the story, with the overshadowing of Mary by the Holy Ghost."[12] The transfiguration of the myth of Zeus and Amphitryon and, indeed, of all the myths that tell of Jupiter's erotic adventures, allowing these myths to take on Christian resonances and express the mystery of Christ's incarnation, can be traced back to the early days of Christianity and has also left its mark on Wagner's *Lohengrin*.

THE END OF THE AGE OF MYTH

Like Schiller's *Semele* and Kleist's *Amphitryon*, *Lohengrin* can be interpreted as a work about an artist—this is certainly how Wagner interpreted it. At the same time, however, it addresses another theme, that of the world's disenchantment. In a diary entry of 11 November 1880, Cosima Wagner recorded a conversation about "the tragic element in *Lohengrin*, which offers no reconciliation." Wagner's last Romantic opera (and, indeed, his last official "opera"—no later work was to bear this designation) is the only one not to end on a note of redemption or transfiguration: all his later music dramas, including even *Götterdämmerung*, with its cataclysmic destruction of the world as we know it, allow at least the possibility of a new world order. In his parting speech, Lohengrin admittedly announces that the German Reich will prosper in the future, and Gottfried, turned back into a human being after having been Lohengrin's swan, seems to embody the Utopian vision of the child ruler, a figure of redemption with a long literary tradition extending from Virgil's Fourth Eclogue to the "child king" in the first version of Hugo von Hofmannsthal's tragedy *Der Turm* (The tower).

But this glimmer of hope on the horizon of Wagner's only outright tragedy brings no comfort to the work's tragic protagonists or to the populace, who, like the chorus in a Greek tragedy, break out in cries of woe at the end, lamenting the disappearance of the divine element from a world that has been profaned and secularized. Lohengrin withdraws from the world, disappearing "into the distance" (GS 2:114) in a way that mirrors his epiphany "in the distance" (GS 2:73) in act 1. Such an epiphany will never be repeated. The world is now abandoned to its own devices, with the sacred element withdrawing to a transcendental dimension.[13] As Wolf-Daniel Hartwich has written, "In the secularized modern world, Wagner can hold on to religion only by stressing its otherworldly character, a character that precludes secularization and that can find a medium of expression for itself only in absolute art."[14]

In *Lohengrin*, even Christianity results in the world's being robbed of its mystique and demythologized. In this respect, the work takes its place as part of a tradition involving an aesthetic critique of religion that stretches from Schiller's *Die Götter Griechenlands* to Heine's "Die Götter im Exil," albeit with a significant shift of emphasis. Here it is not the Greek gods but their Germanic equivalents who are driven into exile, and their apologist, Ortrud, is far from being a sympathetic representative of the age of myth. Indeed, in his letter to Liszt of 30 January 1852, Wagner called her a "reactionary," "a woman concerned only with what is outdated and for that reason hostile to all that is new." In her invocation of her "desecrated gods" in act 2 (GS 2:87), Ortrud seeks to "breathe new life into her decaying gods," gods who are "old and long-vanished."

These lines were written at the very time that Wagner was "breathing new life" into these gods in his libretto for the *Ring*, but there the context is completely different. Germanic myth provided Wagner with an aesthetically autonomous picture of what he called the "purely human" in its modern form, whereas Ortrud merely uses myth for her own ends. "Her nature is politics," he told Liszt. As such, she is motivated by "ancestral pride and by a hankering after the past" and after "departed generations," a feeling that is ultimately turned into "murderous fanaticism."[15] Here the reader is inevitably reminded of the political use of Germanic myth in the twentieth century.[16]

Ortrud is one of those "raving women"[17] from opera and drama of the eighteenth and nineteenth centuries who are survivors of an outdated world of power and emotions. (Among the characters who fall into this category are Mozart's Elettra, Vitellia, and Queen of Night and Weber's Eglantine, the last-named an immediate precursor of Ortrud in *Lohengrin*.) They engage in intrigue and "rage" in the hope of avenging the loss of their power, with Ortrud calling on spells and black magic in her attempt to achieve her egocentric and despotic ends, namely, a return to the pagan tribal society of her ancestors. She uses "evil spells" (GS 2:77) in a manipulative attempt to regain power, an approach at odds with the inviolable religious "wonder" (GS 2:73);[18] the pagan and Germanic tribal world that is conditioned by particularist ends is contrasted with the world of the Holy Roman Empire and its universalist and even republican aspirations. According to Wolf-Daniel Hartwich, "kingship and warrior status feature in the opera as the expressions of a consensus embracing the whole of society."[19]

Pagan magic is defeated at the end of the opera, when Gottfried, whom Ortrud has turned into a swan, reverts to his human form thanks to Lohengrin's white magic. On "seeing the spell lifted from Gottfried," Ortrud collapses with a cry (GS 2:114), as the lifting of this spell marks the end of her power. But at this point the numinous in a Christian sense also vanishes from the world. Two types of enchantment disappear: the age of the demonic and the age of the sacral. Somewhat remarkably, this finds expression in the ambivalent image of the swan, which belongs to both worlds, having passed from Ortrud's world of power politics into that of the Grail, which it expects to serve for a year before the spell on it is lifted. But this moment is brought forward as a result of Lohengrin's prayer, and the magic swan is replaced by the Grail dove that accompanies Lohengrin on his way home. The dove is a symbol of the sacral element that will henceforth exist only in a world of transcendence, having broken free not only from its earthly sphere but also from the world of myth to which the swan belonged.

The lifting of this spell inaugurates Gottfried's legitimate secular rule, a rule that must necessarily forgo all supernatural legitimation. In this, it differs from the purely charismatic rule of the "protector of Brabant"—Lohengrin refuses to be called Duke of Brabant (GS 2:90) or to be tied down institutionally. His rule is recalled by the three symbols of the horn, sword, and ring that he bequeaths to the future duke. Just as Goethe's Faust is left holding only Helen of Troy's dress and veil as a numinous reminder of her existence, so these three tokens of the vanished numen remain as a reminiscence of a state of the world in which the sacred and the profane had not yet been wrenched asunder.

Romantic opera had thus reached the end of the road. The lifting of the spell on the world made it impossible for myth to emerge directly any longer from historical reality. As a result, Wagner had to start all over again as a music dramatist with the *Ring*: here myth emerges into a world of art that is already divorced from history. The "wonder"—to quote from *Opera and Drama*—is divested of its "dogmatic" character and turned into a medium of artistic expression. Whereas the "dogmatic wonder" destroys the "natural connection between things" and adds only to our sense of mystification, the "poetic" wonder seeks to make things "intelligible to feeling" by compressing them. It is concerned not with "faith" but with "emotional understanding" (GS 4:81–83).[20] This is the way forward for the musical drama, now that the spell of enchantment has been lifted from reality. Needless to add, the myths that are reworked in the musical drama allow history's misunderstood mythic substance to resurface once again precisely because history and myth have now become separated.

Love and Objectification in the Music Drama

TRISTAN'S ISOLDE AND HER SISTERS

"The commandment says: Thou shalt not commit adultery!
But I say unto you: Ye shall not marry without love.
A marriage without love is broken as soon as entered into,
and whoso hath wooed without love, already hath broken
the marriage. If ye follow my commandment, how can ye
ever break it, since it bids you do what your own heart
and soul desire?"

—Richard Wagner, Jesus of Nazareth

NOWHERE IS Wagner's theory of the "wonder"—not the "dogmatic" miracle, but the "poetic" epiphany that "serves the poet's aim" of compressing "life's manifold phenomena in all their unending variety and imposing upon them a concise and clearly intelligible form" (GS 4:81–82)—more compellingly realized than in *Tristan und Isolde*, a work that may be described, with some justification, as a meta-Romantic opera. Or, to quote a diary entry of Richard Strauss dating from 1946, it "absorbed the whole of Romanticism, leading to its supreme culmination," at the same time "placing a divine copestone upon it with the most beautifully orchestrated B major chord in the whole history of music."[1]

TRISTAN UND ISOLDE OR THE KISS OF DEATH

In *Tristan und Isolde*, the "wonder" is the love potion, the drug prepared by Isolde's mother in her magic kitchen, the final enchantment of a disenchanted world in which the erstwhile magic powers of Isolde's family have lost their former potency.

> Entartet Geschlecht,
> unwerth der Ahnen!
> Wohin, Mutter,
> vergab'st du die Macht,
> über Meer und Sturm zu gebieten?

O zahme Kunst
der Zauberin,
die nur Balsamtränke noch brau't.

(GS 7:2–3)

[Degenerate race,
unworthy of your forebears!
On whom, Mother,
did you squander the power
to command the sea and storms?
O feeble art
of the sorceress,
who brews only healing draughts!]

The love potion symbolizes a metaphysical process of cognition in the sense understood by Schopenhauer and, at the same time, encapsulates a complex psychological state.[2] "Here, in the form of a poetic fiction," Wagner wrote in about 1850, "the vast chain linking together the most disparate phenomena is condensed to form a readily intelligible bond made up of only a handful of links, but these few links contain within them the strength and power of the whole chain: and this power is the wonder in art" (SS 12:279). These remarks on "the wonder in art" could have been written with *Tristan und Isolde* in mind.[3]

The love between Tristan and Isolde is not the result of the potion. Rather, the potion simply makes them conscious of their secret and suppressed passion. As Brangäne explains in the prose draft, it "revealed what had to be made manifest" (SS 11:334). They both think that they are taking poison—a poison that Isolde had asked Brangäne to produce from her mother's medicine chest—and as a result they are no longer kept apart by the barrier of illusory values and a defiant sense of self-preservation. Only in the belief that they are about to die can they confess to their love so uncompromisingly. There is no magic at work here, only a love beyond all magic, a love created by the magic of death. (Here one thinks involuntarily of the title of Calderón's play *El mayor encanto, amor* [The great enchantment, love].)

No other work in the whole history of music is so filled with what Thomas Mann called the "sympathy with death," and it seems no accident that the shadow of death—not just death in the theater, but in real life, too—has fallen across this death-fixated work three times during performances at the Nationaltheater in Munich, where it was first performed in 1865. Only a few weeks after its first performance, the tenor Ludwig Schnorr von Carolsfeld, who had created the part of Tristan, died suddenly. Half a century later, the conductor Felix Mottl collapsed during a performance and died a few days later on 2 July 1911. And on 20 July 1968, Joseph Keilberth suffered a fatal heart attack immediately after Isolde's words "ohn' Erwachen" [without awakening] in the love duet in act 2.[4]

The erotic attraction of death is at the heart of *Tristan und Isolde* and recurs in many literary guises in fin-de-siècle Europe, when the influence of Wagner was particularly profound among the décadent writers of the period, who repeatedly associated it with the composer's own death in Venice in 1883. Wagner had first visited Venice in 1858, when he had completed the second act of a work steeped in night and death, and he spent the final months of his life there. Among the writers for whom his death became one of the most potent myths of fin-de-siècle Europe[5] were Gabriele D'Annunzio, whose novel *Il fuoco* (The flame, 1900) describes in morbid and splendid detail Wagner's funeral cortege along the Grand Canal, Maurice Barrès's *La mort de Venise* (The death of Venice, 1902), and Thomas Mann's *Der Tod in Venedig* (Death in Venice, 1912), which contains a whole host of allusions to Wagner's life and art within the framework of the life story of a fictitious writer. And Wagner's music drama is, to a certain extent, the cause of death of the main characters in both *Buddenbrooks* (1901) and Mann's short story "Tristan" (1903): Hanno Buddenbrook's amateurish paraphrases of *Tristan* at the piano anticipate the death of a hypersensitive youth who has lost the will to live, and in "Tristan" the consumptive Gabriele Klöterjahn dies after the décadent writer Detlev Spinell prevails on her to play from the vocal score of the work, thereby inducing a fatal relapse.

An emotion that in Wagner's music drama involves the mystic union of love and death,[6] an experience in which the boundaries between Eros and Thanatos are blurred—and one whose traditions can be traced back via Schopenhauer, the German Romantics (especially Novalis's *Hymnen an die Nacht* [Hymns to night]), and Renaissance Platonism to pagan mysteries[7]—here becomes an act of aestheticist hubris and cruelty. As Schopenhauer had already noted, Greek and Roman sarcophagi include a strikingly large number of erotic motifs such as Leda and the Swan. In every case they depict the love of a god and a mortal: Bacchus and Ariadne, Zeus and Semele, and Ganymede or Diana and Endymion. According to Edgar Wind, "To die was to be loved by a god, and partake through him of eternal bliss."[8] The Renaissance Humanist Pierio Valeriano notes that

> those yearning for God and desiring to be conjoined with him (which cannot be achieved in this prison of the flesh) are carried away to heaven and freed from the body by a death which is the profoundest sleep; in this manner Paul desired to die when he said: I long to be dissolved and be with Christ. This kind of death was named the kiss by the symbolic theologians.[9]

The *mors osculi* or *morte di bacio* was the subject of countless observations by Renaissance philosophers. Wagner, too, came very close to this idea of a "death kiss," the "Eros funebre" that recalls the mystery of erotic images on classical graves, when on 15 August 1869 he told Cosima: "The kiss of love is the first intimation of death, the cessation of individuality, that is why people are so terrified by it." A similar idea is expressed by Friedrich Rückert in his poem "Nach Dschelaleddin Rumi."

> So schauert vor der Lieb ein Herz,
> Als wie vom Untergang bedroht.
> Denn wo die Lieb erwachet, stirbt
> Das Ich, der dunkele Despot.[10]

> [Thus hearts beset by love beat faster still
> As though destruction threatens them with ill.
> For when love wakens, then that self that I
> Abhor as despot of the dark must die.]

The union of Eros and Thanatos had been celebrated in German literature even before the Romantics, finding powerful poetic expression in the final scene of Goethe's dramatic fragment "Prometheus" (1773). Prometheus's Titanic assertion of his independence emerges as clearly from Goethe's famous hymn ("Bedecke deinen Himmel, Zeus") as it does from this fragment—"Tell them I don't want to," Prometheus informs the gods' messenger, Mercury, in the opening lines of the piece.[11] As such, this defiant Titan seems the very antithesis of Tristan and Isolde, who are no longer conscious of their own selves and long to be "no longer Tristan, no longer Isolde" (GS 7:50). Yet Goethe's fragment ends on a mystical note with the denial of the self. Dismayed, Pandora tells her father, Prometheus, about an incident that has left her puzzled, a love scene that she had not understood as such. The sinking down of the lovers, their kisses and tears, were a mystery to her, an unknown experience that she found deeply disturbing. "Say, what was all this that shook both them and me?" she asks her father, who replies simply that it was "Death."

PROMETHEUS
Da ist ein Augenblick, der alles erfüllt.
Alles, was wir gesehnt, geträumt, gehofft,
Gefürchtet, meine Beste. Das ist der Tod.

PANDORA
Der Tod?

PROMETHEUS
    Wenn aus dem innerst tiefsten Grunde
Du ganz erschüttert alles fühlst,
Was Freud und Schmerzen jemals dir ergossen,
Im Sturm dein Herz erschwillt,
In Tränen sich erleichtern will und seine Glut vermehrt,
Und alles klingt an dir und bebt und zittert,
Und all die Sinne dir vergehn
Und du dir zu vergehen scheinst
Und sinkst und alles um dich her
Versinkt in Nacht, und du in inner eigenem Gefühle
Umfassest eine Welt,
Dann stirbt der Mensch.

PANDORA (*ihn umhalsend*)
O Vater, laßt uns sterben![12]

[PROMETHEUS
It is a moment that is all-fulfilling.
Everything for which we've yearned, dreamed, hoped,
And feared, my darling. It is death.

PANDORA
Death?

PROMETHEUS

    When, in the deepest corner of your inmost heart,
You're shaken to the core and feel
Past joys and anguish once again,
Your heart tempestuously swells,
You seek heart's ease in tears, and yet
Your ardor grows, your body sings
And shakes, and all your senses fail,
You feel you're fainting, and you sink,
And all around you sinks in night,
And you, within your inmost thoughts,
Embrace a world in all its might,
Then humans die.

PANDORA (*throwing her arms round his neck*)
O father, let us die!]

Anyone reading these extraordinary lines by the twenty-four-year-old Goethe is bound to hear in them a pre-echo of *Tristan und Isolde*. The more independent and self-reliant that Prometheus encourages humankind to be, the greater the desire to remove the limitations on the self and to desire a selfless state in which death and love are one and the same.

 In discussing the kiss of death and the longing to be united with God (a longing projected on classical myths about the love between gods and mortals), Pierio Valeriano uses the image of the Assumption. Here, too, there is a link with Wagner, who on several occasions compared Isolde with the figure of the Virgin in Titian's *Assunta* in Venice, a work he greatly admired. On 22 October 1882, Wagner even denied that "the Assunta is the Mother of God; it is Isolde in the apotheosis of love." Wagner was intuitively aware that Titian's painting was somehow connected with the erotic view of death that we find in the writings of the Renaissance Platonists: the ascent of the mortal Virgin to heaven marks her ecstatic union with God, a veritable apotheosis of love.

 But Wagner no longer believed in the metaphysical basis of this apotheosis of love, which is why he relates it to Isolde and to an erotic view of death that ignores its former theological background. Love between gods and mortals is replaced by the experience of a purely human love that transcends all barriers, with the old religious ideas of Eros and Thanatos symbolically transferred to it. This is clear, not least, from Isolde's peroration, when she draws our attention to Tristan's prostrate form.

                    Immer lichter
                    wie er leuchtet,
                    Stern-umstrahlet
                    hoch sich hebt:
                    seht ihr, Freunde,
                    seht ihr's nicht?

                                        (GS 7:79–80)

[Ever brighter
how he's shining,
star-illumined
rising heavenward:
do you see it, friends?
Do you not see it?]

The wreath of stars is the Assunta's traditional attribute. And when Tristan and Isolde sing their hymn to love in act 2 with the words "Ohne Gleiche! / Überreiche!" [Past comparing! Rich beyond telling!] (GS 7:36), their lines recall Gretchen's prayer to the Virgin Mary toward the end of part 2 of *Faust*: "Du Ohnegleiche, / Du Strahlenreiche" [Thou who art past comparing / rich in rays of light] (ll.\12070–71).[13] Images from Marian mysticism are transferred to a love that however mystical is still very much of this world.

The fact that in Wagner's case this morte di bacio no longer involves an encounter between a god and a human and does not, therefore, imply entry into a state of eternal bliss is clear from a brief glance at the composer's other music dramas. With the exception of *Die Meistersinger*, which has a happy ending in keeping with its conception as a comedy, love is always associated with death and characterized by a total willingness to die. Ultimately, however, all the music dramas involve the merging of the lovers with each other, whether or not heaven gives its blessing to their redemption, as it does in *Tannhäuser*. At the end of *Der fliegende Holländer*, it is significant that it is not man who ascends to God but the man who, redeemed, ascends together with the woman who has brought him salvation and who shares in this *assumptio*: "In the far distance the Dutchman and Senta rise out of the water, both in transfigured form; he holds her in his arms" (GS 1:291)—here is a morte di bacio that has no transcendental dimension to it.

On the one occasion when a celestial being seeks to enter into a relationship with a human being, there is no sense of redemption: the gulf between Lohengrin and Elsa is so deep that they can only destroy each other. Although the story—by Wagner's own admission—is inspired by the myth of Zeus and Semele, Elsa dies without achieving the metaphysical transfiguration vouchsafed to her mythical forebear, and Lohengrin, having been forced into an "admission of his divinity, returns, annihilated, to his lonely state" (GS 4:296). Brünnhilde, I may add, is no longer one of the gods when she is woken by Siegfried, and there is an unbridgeable chasm between gods and people in *Die Walküre*. The kiss that Wotan implants on Brünnhilde's brow, so that she sinks into a kind of deathlike slumber, is no *bacio di morte* (kiss of death) raising her to a godlike status but quite the opposite, a kiss that robs her of her divinity and completes her transition to sentient humanity. Only a fellow human being can wake her from this sleep of death.

It is when we turn to *Tristan und Isolde* that we find a world wholly lacking in redemptive transcendence: this is Wagner's only work without God and without gods. In the vast synesthetic hymn with which the work ends, the lovers enter a state of mystical union with a pantheistically spiritualized universe.[14] Such is her sense of ecstasy at the approach of death that Isolde feels overwhelmed by sounds, breezes, waves, and perfumes. The particle "um" (literally, "around") is used repeatedly as a preposition and prefix to suggest an elemental medium that envelops the lovers on all sides and into which they finally merge,[15] a process expressed as "sweetly wafting away in perfumes," "drowning," and "sinking" into the "world breath's surging universe," with which the "sweet breath" on Tristan's lips is commingled (GS 7:80–81). In this way, Isolde enters into a mystical union with her dead lover and at the same time merges with the divine universe. "In Tristan, love should be interpreted not as Schopenhauerian but as Empedoclean," Nietzsche wrote in 1875 in one of his posthumously published fragments; love was "the sign and guarantee of an eternal unity."[16]

And we must admit that however pronounced the influence of Schopenhauer on *Tristan und Isolde*,[17] Wagner avoids the philosopher's pessimism, his affirmation of the world finding overwhelming expression in the closing moments of the work.[18] Isolde's love death has nothing in common with the extinction of all desire in nirvana, a state that according to Schopenhauer can be achieved only through renunciation. Indeed, Wagner specifically distanced himself from this aspect of Schopenhauerian thinking in his letter to Mathilde Wesendonck dated 1 December 1858 and in the surviving draft of a letter to Schopenhauer that he did not send. In both cases, he describes love as the "path to salvation" (SS 12:291), enabling the lover to raise him- or herself "above the individual impulse of the will."[19] It can be argued, therefore, that Wagner reinterprets Schopenhauer's "Metaphysics of Sexual Love" in the light of the latter's philosophy of death.[20]

The main philosophical source of *Tristan und Isolde* is Schopenhauer's treatise "On Death and Its Relation to the Indestructibility of Our Inner Nature" (1819)— the very text that Thomas Buddenbrook read when in search of metaphysical sustenance at a time when he had lost the will to live and was close to death. Here Schopenhauer expresses his belief that "dying is the moment of that liberation from the one-sidedness of an individuality which does not constitute the innermost kernel of our true being, but is rather to be thought of as a kind of aberration thereof. The true original freedom again enters at this moment, which . . . can be regarded as a *restitutio in integrum*."[21]

For Schopenhauer, however, this restitutio in integrum was the very opposite of sexual love: "self-preservation and maintenance are man's first aim," his principle "selfishness."[22] For Wagner, by contrast, sexual love is no longer tied to the utilitarian end of maintaining life but is identified with the longing for death, a state in which individual boundaries are transcended and the individual enters into a union with the universe: "selbst—dann / bin ich die Welt" [then I myself am the world] (GS 7:45). The identification of the love potion with the death potion—an identification absent from the earlier Tristan tradition[23]—is a profound and potent symbol of this.

Erotic love is related not only to death but also, in Wagner's view, to the type of love that Schopenhauer saw as diametrically opposed to erotic love: caritas, which is akin to compassion and sympathy. For Schopenhauer, caritas is "pure love," whereas erotic love is "selfish." Yet Schopenhauer concedes that "combinations of the two occur frequently."[24] And there is no doubt that the love between

Tristan and Isolde is essentially such a combination. "I pitied him in his anguish," Isolde says to justify her decision to spare her enemy Tristan, rather than avenging Morold's death by striking him down with his sword: "the sword—I let it fall" (GS 7:11). Is compassion the germ cell of her love or love the germ cell of her compassion?

In Schopenhauer's view, "death is the great opportunity no longer to be I."[25] But this is also the aim of the love that Tristan and Isolde feel, a love that can find fulfillment only in death. This explains why they exchange identity: "ISOLDE: 'You Isolde, Tristan I, no more Isolde!' / TRISTAN: 'You Tristan, Isolde I, no more Tristan!'" And it also explains why they long for an end to the "sweet little word 'and'" that separates their names and, as such, brings home to them the fact that they are not yet one but still "I" and "you" (GS 7:47 and 50).

They hope that through each other they will transcend their individual boundaries. It is not just death that is "the great opportunity no longer to be I"; this is also true of love, of death through love and of love in death. This is the message of *Tristan und Isolde*, a message conceived in the spirit of Schopenhauer but ultimately directed against him. And this message transfers to a world without transcendence an eroticism that—associated with death—derives ultimately from ancient mysteries but that was subsequently revived by the Neoplatonists of the Renaissance and by the early German Romantics.

WOMAN AS OBJECT OF VALUE: SENTA AND ISOLDE

Isolde's peroration may be said to pass through a series of concentric circles from the individual self to the immensity of space, a musical *assumptio* that transfigures the heroine, turning her into a saint of love who is virtually no longer of this world and who could hardly be in greater contrast to the picture of the humiliated and despised woman whom we encountered at the start of the work.[26] Among the specific features of Wagner's dramaturgy of sexual love is the tension resulting from the clash between its metaphysical potential and its social reality. This is revealed above all by the ambivalence of the principal female characters, whose love always threatens to founder on the dictates of a society hostile to love. Wagner's female characters are, on the one hand, saints of love, figures of redemption who bring salvation and, on the other hand, victims of a male-dominated world that is characterized by men's domineering attitudes and pride in ownership, a world that humiliates and exploits them and reduces them to the level where they are no more than pawns in men's quest for power.[27] And, once again, these figures of redemption, like Isolde, have to seek their salvation through humiliation and shame.

The motif of the bartered bride is found in no fewer than six of Wagner's thirteen operas and music dramas;[28] in *Der fliegende Holländer*, Daland is motivated by greed to pledge his daughter, Senta, to a seafaring Dutchman whose name he does not even know; in *Das Rheingold*, Wotan sells off his sister-in-law, Freia, to two giants but finally buys her back in order to ensure the survival of the world of the gods; in *Die Walküre*, Sieglinde recounts how she was abducted and handed over by "thieves" to Hunding as his wife (GS 6:14); in *Götterdämmerung*, Siegfried haggles with Gunther, obtaining Gutrune, the latter's sister, as his wife in return for his forcibly abducting Brünnhilde from the Valkyries' Rock; in *Tristan und Isolde*, Tristan brings home the defenseless Isolde as wife for his uncle King Marke, even though earlier he had hacked off her fiancé's head; and in *Die Meistersinger*, Veit Pogner offers his daughter Eva as first prize in a song contest.[29]

In patriarchal cultures, women have always been objects of barter and rapine both in myth and in history. Like Hebbel in his dramas from *Judith* to *Herodes und Mariamne*, which have women as their protagonists, Wagner uses these motifs to depict the objectification of women in modern civilization, a culture characterized by new forms of ownership fetishism as reflected in myth. His most detailed reflections on the relationship between marriage and ownership may be found in his prose draft for his planned drama *Jesus von Nazareth* (1849):

> If a woman was wooed by a man whom she did not love and he fulfilled the letter of the law of marriage with her, by that law she became his property: as a result, the woman's attempt to achieve her freedom through love became a sin—true satisfaction in love was something that she could attain only through adultery. (SS 11:289)

This is true of both Sieglinde and Isolde.

> Similarly, if children felt themselves blossoming out and wanted to give free expression to their love and if their parents did not exert their natural right over them in a spirit of love, then those children were bound to sin against the law in seeking to satisfy their love independently. But in the court of love, it was not they who sinned but the law that had done wrong by transferring the right of love to possession. (SS 11:289)

For Jesus of Nazareth, marriage became a "sin" if it was "concluded without love," and "the parents' right became a constraint on the children." In other words, the right of property encroached on an area that belonged to love. Jesus' mission was to replace the "law" and the right of property guaranteed by it with "love" (SS 11:289).

In Wagner's works, sexual love represents the opposite of ownership and objectification. Love rebels by nature and revolts against open oppression and its clandestine partner, moral "custom."[30] Time and again it opposes convention, even on those occasions when the wishes of the lovers happen to coincide with the aims of those who dispose over them, albeit in a sense other than the one intended by the latter. This is certainly the case with *Der fliegende Holländer* and—in keeping with the laws of comedy—*Die Meistersinger von Nürnberg*.

Seduced by the sight of the Dutchman's treasures, Daland has no hesitation in offering the stranger his daughter—the "greatest of my possessions"—as his wife. The only condition is that the Dutchman should like her. Whether Senta likes the Dutchman is a question that is not even asked. The exchange is agreed: "You'll give me jewels, pearls beyond price." In return, the proud father offers "the greatest jewel of all, a loyal wife—" Daland does not complete the sentence, but we can read his mind: "The exchange value of my daughter is greater than that of your treasures." But he would never say this aloud; his pride and greed are couched in genteel terminology as though he were discussing personal relationships, not objects. All innocence, he accepts his son-in-law not because of his wealth but because of his openhandedness, his "magnanimity" and "high ideals," which he claims to have noticed straightaway: "And even if you were not so wealthy, I'd still not choose another." But in an aside, he makes it clear that he has his eye on the Dutchman's visible wealth, not on his invisible virtues:

> Kann ein Eidam willkommener sein?
> Ein Thor, wenn das Glück ich versäume!
> Voll Entzücken schlage ich ein.
>
> (GS 1:264–65)

> [Can a son-in-law be more welcome?
> I'd be a fool to miss this chance!
> I'm delighted to agree to this deal.]

He does not stop to ask himself whether his daughter will be delighted with the deal. Her own happiness does not enter into it. By the end of the act, he openly admits to himself: "The aim of every father—a wealthy son-in-law, he's mine! To a man of property and high ideals I'd be happy to give my home and daughter" (GS 1:266). His home is evidently his overriding consideration, followed some distance behind by his daughter. What interests him is property, with "high ideals" a poor second.

In act 2 we discover that Senta has in fact had a suitor for some time in the person of the huntsman Erik. But Erik has few possessions and as a result believes that he has little chance of impressing Daland. "Your father, ah! he craves only treasures" (GS 1:275). We know from act 1 that Erik is right. But when Daland introduces the Dutchman to his daughter, he shows a certain sensitivity by apparently asking her to agree to something that he himself has long since decided on—an agreement that was not mentioned in act 1: "Give him your hand, for you're to call him your bridegroom; if you agree with your father, he'll be your husband tomorrow" (GS 1:278). These are convoluted lines: but Daland's injunction is clear, and Senta's agreement seems merely to affect the time of the marriage; Daland wants it to take place as soon as possible, and Senta's veto would at best postpone it.

In the event, such problems do not arise, as the potential son-in-law and daughter have long been obsessed with each other, although it takes a while for Daland to realize this. And because he assumes that the couple share his own views on ownership, he thinks it better to praise the treasures that are to be exchanged. "Admit it, she's a credit to her sex," he says to the Dutchman, and to Senta he shows some of the seafarer's jewels that he has already slipped into his pocket: "My dear child, surely you desire them? They're yours if you exchange rings." But Senta, according to the stage directions, "pays him no need, never for a moment averting her eyes from the Dutchman, just as the latter does not listen to Daland but remains lost in contemplation of the young woman" (GS 1:279).

Senta and the Dutchman have long since left behind them the prosaic world of ownership whose inhabitants covet possessions, who make provisions for their future, and who lead lives of habit and routine. Theirs is a nonmaterial world in which the only things that matter are the "longing for salvation," the "voice of deep compassion," and the "somber glow" of a love that is akin to death and transcends the bounds of quotidian reality.

The great double monologue for Senta and the Dutchman in act 2 prepares the ground for what became the central theme of *Tristan und Isolde*: the suspension of reality and the invalidation of the framework of values associated with existing society, both of which occur at the moment when the lovers experience the breakdown of the barriers between Eros and Thanatos. In *Tristan und Isolde*, too, the starting point of the action is the objectification of a woman, in this case Isolde. Her former fiancé, Morold, had gone to Cornwall to collect the tribute ostensibly owed by it to Ireland, but Tristan killed him in single combat and, in a gesture of contempt, sent his head back to Ireland. Kurwenal and the ship's crew mockingly remind Isolde of her shame: "His head, though, hangs in Ireland, paid as tribute by England" (GS 7:8). The inconceivable crudity of their comments shows in what low regard Isolde is held as a woman: even as the country's future queen she is no more than an object that acquires its value only through its owner.

Tristan is wounded in the course of slaying Morold and, as Tantris, travels to Ireland in order to be restored to health by Isolde, whose healing skills are legendary. She recognizes him from a fragment missing from his sword—the very fragment that she had found lodged in Morold's skull. She draws the sword, intending to kill Tristan with it, but she sees him gazing up at her, and suddenly her hatred turns to pity and thence to love.

Tristan's wounds heal and he returns home, only to turn up again in Ireland some time later in order to win Isolde as a wife for his uncle—to "sue for Ireland's crown for the tributary Cornish prince," as Isolde contemptuously puts it. The Irish have to endure this shame, as Morold is no longer alive to defend them. As a result, they have no choice but to sign a peace treaty with their powerful enemy and to send Isolde to Cornwall with Tristan as a token of this peace. There she has to marry the country's "tired kind" (GS 7:12). All this takes place against the wishes of Isolde, who takes leave of her father and mother in a state of profound embitterment; as she herself says, she "left her homeland cold and mute."

It is in this frame of mind that we first encounter her at the start of act 1 "wildly disturbed, numb, and wretched" (GS 7:3–4). In her heart of hearts, she is less appalled at the thought that she has been treated as a pledge in an "archfeud" (GS 7:21) and obliged to marry a tributary prince whom she despises than at the knowledge that it is Tristan, of all people, who has brought her back to Cornwall on another's behalf and treated her as a piece of booty; he is, after all, the murderer of her fiancé, a man, moreover, whose life she has twice saved, once when she failed to kill him and again when she cured him. And on each occasion she acted out of love, a love that has transformed her entire life.

From the moment that she allowed the sword to slip from her hand, she has known that the two were destined for each other—and there is little doubt that Tristan, too,

knows this on the very deepest level. What is so terrible for Isolde is that Tristan re-
presses this knowledge: "Mir erkoren,—mir verloren" [Chosen for me—lost to me]
(GS 7:4). With self-lacerating cynicism, she parodies the way in which Tristan, ex-
ulting in victory, praised her to his uncle as a valuable commodity.

> "das wär' ein Schatz,
>   mein Herr und Ohm;
> wie dünkt' euch die zur Eh'?
>   Die schmucke Irin
>   hol' ich her;
>   . . . .
>
> Isolde, die ist euer:
> mir lacht das Abenteuer!"
>
> (GS 7:13)

> ["She'd be a catch,
>   my lord and uncle;
> what do you think of her as a wife?
>   I'll bring
>   the Irish beauty here;
>   . . . .
>
> Isolde's already yours;
> the adventure smiles upon me!"]

Isolde feels that her dignity as a woman has been violated; she has been debased
to the level of an object, albeit a commodity of supreme value. When she over-
came her desire for revenge and was assailed by feelings of pity and love, allowing the sword to fall from her grasp, Tristan, she believes, was "measuring her up"
and "stealing" her "likeness" in an attempt to see whether she would "make a
suitable wife for Lord Marke" (GS 7:23–24).

How are we to explain Tristan's betrayal of Isolde? In the great love duet in act 2,
Tristan describes the burgeoning of his feelings for Isolde as the gradual awareness
of an "image" that he had not yet dared to look at, since night—the central symbol
of the work[31]—had not yet "hallowed his gaze" (GS 7:43). Prior to the transformation that the potion brings about, Tristan was completely committed to "day," which
symbolizes all the values that had ruled his life until then, values that night now reveals as "illusionary" (GS 7:39). These values include "honor," "fame," "glamour,"
and "morality," in short, the whole system of virtues associated with a life of
chivalry. Inevitably, he interpreted the mystery of love and the woman who revealed
that mystery to him in the light of ideas familiar from courtly society and its fixed
code of ethics. As a result, Isolde was placed on a pedestal, "where she resembled
the sun, in highest honor's gleam and light." How could she be his "in the flood of
bright day"? How could Tristan imagine that she was destined for him and that the
woman who was so perfect an embodiment of "the light of honor, the power of
fame" (GS 7:39), could belong to anyone other than the highest in the land? This is
why he praised her so fulsomely to Marke and revealed to all and sundry the image

conceived in the depths of his heart, "an image that my eyes did not dare to gaze on—lit by the light of day, it lay gleaming before me" (GS 7:40).

Tristan raises Isolde so high above him that he cannot think of himself as her lover, but by praising her and by insisting that she is worthy only of the king, he, too, objectifies her in a subtle manner by turning her into the object of the highest esteem. Isolde adds her own comment to this, using words that are supremely symbolic: "What falling night showed you, you had to hand over to the royal might of the star of day" (GS 7:43). In other words, Tristan conceived of a vision of love in the nighttime depths of his heart but has to entrust that image to the sun or king—the two are symbolically linked—and thus woo on another's behalf the woman destined for him alone. In this regard he is like Siegfried in *Götterdämmerung*. As Wagner himself observed in his "Epilogue to the *Ring*" (1871), "their intrinsic similarity stems from the fact that both Tristan and Siegfried, in thrall to an illusion that robs their actions of their freedom, woo on another's behalf the woman destined for them by primeval law and meet their end as a result of the misalliance that arises from it" (GS 6:268).

Only when he drinks what he believes to be poison are Tristan's eyes suddenly opened, and he no longer feels in thrall to deception. Only in the face of the night of death, before which all semblance vanishes and all considerations of the daylight world of courtly virtue fade into insignificance—only then is it possible for his love to express itself. Existing values are turned on their head, and day becomes the realm of deceit, night the womb of truth. "Fame and honor, power and profit" are now as meaningless for Tristan as Isolde's offended dignity. All these thoughts are consumed by their yearning for the "sacred night" of a love death in which "I" and "you" are no longer divided (GS 7:43–44).

THE BARTERED BRIDE IN THE *RING*

The most elaborate treatment of the theme of the bartered bride occurs in the *Ring*, where it may even be described as the cycle's overriding concern. We encounter an initial variation on it in *Das Rheingold*. According to the terms of the contract drawn up between Wotan and the giants, the latter are to receive Freia, the goddess of eternal youth, as their reward for building Valhalla. But each of the signatories has something different in mind here. There is no doubt that as the person who commissioned the work, Wotan does not seriously intend to comply with its terms but agrees to them only because he believes that when the time comes, Loge will help him out of his predicament.

And the two giants clearly had different ideas in mind when they demanded Freia as their reward. Every member of the audience must wonder how Fafner and Fasolt plan to divide their spoils. But Fafner has absolutely no interest in Freia as an object of lust, his only concern being to remove her from the company of the gods and thereby to strike at the very principle on which their lives are based. After all, she alone can tend the apples that the gods need to eat in order to remain immortal. In short, Fafner is concerned only with Freia's usefulness, and Fasolt with her beauty, a beauty that would bring light and warmth to his impoverished existence. He fails to understand why the gods, in their pursuit of power, fame, and possessions, pledge the goddess who embodies beauty and love. And he tells them so to their faces. By objectifying Freia in this way, the gods betray and destroy their own divinity.

> Die ihr durch Schönheit herrscht,
> schimmernd hehres Geschlecht,
> > wie thörig strebt ihr
> > nach Thürmen von Stein,
> setz't um Burg und Saal
> Weibes Wonne zum Pfand!
>
> (GS 5:220)
>
> [You who rule through beauty,
> you augustly glittering race,
> > how foolish to strive
> > after towers of stone,
> placing woman's delights in pawn
> for the sake of castle and hall!]

This is also the ironic subtext of Loge's Narration. Taking an amused delight in the gods' "consternation" and bad conscience, he describes at length how, in his search for a "substitute for Freia," he has scoured the world looking for a creature for whom "woman's delights and worth" are not of supreme importance.

> Nur einen sah ich,
> der sagte der Liebe ab:
> > um rothes Gold
> entrieth er des Weibes Gunst.
>
> (GS 5:225)
>
> [Only one man I saw
> who forswore love's delights:
> > for the sake of red gold
> he forwent women's favors.]

This, of course, is Alberich. With subtle contempt and without saying so openly—indeed, he even denies it—Loge places the gods on the same level as the Nibelung dwarf. One is reminded irresistibly of a puppeteer watching his marionettes dangling on the strings of his superior irony. After all, Alberich is not the only person who places possessions and material power above "woman's delights and worth"; Wotan, too, has placed the latter in pawn in an attempt to acquire the former. Loge's account of Alberich's acquisition of the ring by means of a "curse on love" fires Wotan's acquisitiveness: "The ring I must have" (GS 5:228). It is clear that in saying this he is not thinking of an alternative to Freia, whom he denies to the giants only a few moments later. The ring that Wotan steals and flaunts on his finger will subsequently come to signify the furthest stage in the gods' alienation from the self. And, as Alberich points out, the gods, by acting in this way, sin not only against themselves as individuals but against "all that was and is and shall be" (GS 5:253), thereby destroying the godlike nature of the world.

That Wotan's treaty with the giants was characterized by a Machiavellian escape clause was bad enough, but it would have been even worse if he had seriously intended to barter Freia, although he was prepared to sacrifice her when he became obsessed with the ring and, as a result, to depersonalize her by turning her into a reward equivalent to the giants' labors. It requires Erda's appearance and warning to persuade him to change his mind and dispose of the accursed ring.

Fafner, too, is immediately overcome by greed when he hears about the ring, and instead of the "eternal youth" promised by the goddess, he now hopes to use the gold to buy such youth, an idea that comes close to recalling the young Karl Marx's philosophy of money. What people cannot achieve through their own innate strengths, they can acquire through gold: "Everything which you are unable to do, your money can do for you: it can eat, drink, go dancing, go to the theatre." And, paraphrasing Fafner, one could add that it can buy "eternal youth." "It can buy everything; it is genuine *wealth*."[32] Fafner tells the besotted Fasolt:

> Glaub' mir, mehr als Freia
> frommt das gleißende Gold:
> auch ew'ge Jugend erjagt,
> wer durch Goldes Zauber sie zwingt.
>
> (GS 5:229)

> [Believe me, the glittering gold
> is worth far more than Freia:
> eternal youth may also be gained by him
> who obtains it by force through the gold's magic spell.]

Fasolt says nothing in reply to this, but he raises no objection to Fafner's suggestion that the gods use the gold to buy back Freia. He, too, has become corrupted and places material power above "woman's delights and worth."

It is not just possession of the ring that corrupts gods and giants alike; the mere news of its existence does so too. Although Wotan had sought to acquire power even before this (its corrupting influence is already clear from his behavior), the power that he coveted was to a certain extent still feudal in character—it was concerned with "honor," "fame," and their impressive symbol, the "resplendent" castle of the gods, with its towers and banqueting hall (GS 5:213–15). This feudal, personal rule is exercised through the visible paraphernalia of power, but with Alberich this now acquires a more objectified character, somewhat in the spirit of capitalism, and finds expression in the fetish of a nugget of gold that is treated as a mere abstract symbol in the form of the ring.

Bernard Shaw was by no means the first writer to interpret Wagner's myth as a reflection on the early capitalist world. (Shaw's book of 1898, *The Perfect Wagnerite*, was to prove hugely influential in terms of more recent stagings of the cycle.) Wagner himself compared Alberich's ring to a modern "stock-exchange portfolio" (GS 10:268). This comparison underlines the abstract power of an object that cannot be used in acts of physical violence, which explains why it can repeatedly be wrested from whoever happens to be wearing it. By contrast, feudal power is maintained and implemented in physical, concrete ways by means of well-fortified buildings (Valhalla with its towers, walls, and ramparts) and powerful weapons (spear and sword). As a material object, the sword Nothung allows the hero to commit acts of violence against his enemies, whereas the ring grants its wearer power over the world only because it is a symbol, albeit one grounded in myth and magic. As the abstract basis of the possibility of accumulating capital, the ring may be capable of allowing its wearer to win "the world's inheritance" and "measureless might" (GS 5:210–11), but it can be stolen from its wearer with a minimum of cunning and force, just as any artful dodger can steal money, checkbooks, documents, and credit cards from the most powerful capitalist in the world if the latter carries them around with him or her unprotected.

Wotan falls prey to the ring's corrupting influence the moment that he hears about its existence. Although his former rule had cast its dark shadows—as, indeed, all power, whether tyrannical or democratic, must do—it had basically served to sustain a moral order based on peace and regulated by treaties, the sort of order that creates the necessary transition from a state of nature to a *contrat social*. Alberich's power, by contrast, is fundamentally evil, evil in its aims and evil in the means that it employs to achieve its ends. And Wotan stumbles into this vicious circle of evil. By threatening to break the terms of his contract with the giants, he has already begun to undermine his own moral order based on loyalty, and by violating the principles of loyalty and faith, he enters the world of the ring, which embodies a principle diametrically opposed to the feudal principle of loyalty and faith that had determined his rule up to this point. One could call it the principle of demonized capitalism: all fellow feelings and social virtues, from sexual love to contractual loyalty, are now replaced by their egocentric and asocial opposites and by the evil of total individuation that seeks to turn the world into a mere object. The dialectic upheaval that accompanies the wholesale objectification of the world under the influence of the ring means, of course, that the person who owns it becomes an object in turn—in other words, the owner of the ring is both possessed of it and possessed by it: "The ring's lord as the ring's slave" (GS 5:255).

The ring guarantees power in place of love, which is not the same as sex. Alberich makes this plain: "If I cannot gain love by force, might I at least gain pleasure through cunning?" (GS 5:212). By buying Grimhilde's favors, he is able to father Hagen. Not even the goddesses are safe from Alberich's lust, as he contemptuously informs the outraged Wotan:

> Eure schmucken Frau'n—
> die mein Frei'n verschmäht—
> sie zwingt zur Lust sich der Zwerg,
> lacht Liebe ihm nicht.

> (GS 5:244)

[Your pretty women,
who spurned my wooing,
shall forcibly sate the lust of the dwarf,
though love smile upon him no longer.]

Love is denied him, and in its place comes the mere gratification of sensual desire; the lover's partner becomes a sex object that can be bought and used with the ring: "true love" becomes love as a commodity.[33]

The extent to which the world has been corrupted by the ring, allowing love to become a commodity and women an object of barter, is made clear by the scene in which Freia is redeemed. "Now it's bought back, may our youth return to us," Wotan announces quite openly (GS 5:263). Here the goddess's exchange value is assessed in a manner as graphic as it is painful for all concerned, with Freia's body used to measure the Nibelung gold (GS 5:257). Acutely aware of the demeaning nature of this exchange, the gods feel only shame and indignation. Fafner, concerned only with making a profit, coolly oversees the transaction, and Fasolt watches with real anguish as the embodiment of feminine beauty, which he had hoped would bring some poetry to his life, gradually disappears behind the gold that Fafner squeezes together "with brute force" (GS 5:257).

The last part of Freia to remain visible is her eye—the "glance" that always plays an important role in Wagner's works as a token of love (suffice it to recall Tristan's glance that causes Isolde to drop the sword).[34] And there is something profoundly significant about the fact that this gaze can be stopped only by the ring itself, the ring that represents the principle diametrically opposed to love and that signifies the loving glance that has been sold, thus turning on its head the original imagery surrounding the Rhinegold and its "eye" (GS 5:209); the Rhinedaughters hymn this in the cycle's opening scene in a striking example of the personification of natural phenomena that is typical of myth. Fasolt demands the ring to compensate for this loving glance and in doing so brings about his own death ("I got it for Freia's glance"; GS 5:264). Fafner seizes the ring and vents his cynical contempt on his murdered brother: "Now gaze your fill on Freia's glance: never again will you touch the ring!" (GS 5:264).

In *Das Rheingold* and, indeed, in the *Ring* in general, the myth of the curse of gold reflects our modern experience of what Karl Marx called the "perverting power" of money: "It tranforms loyalty into treason, love into hate, . . . servant into master, master into servant." This sentence, taken from Marx's *Economic and Philosophical Manuscripts*, was written in 1844, only four years before Wagner first conceived of the *Ring*, and, indeed, it could have been formulated with the *Ring* in mind, as could the following sentence: "Since money, as the existing and active concept of value, confounds and exchanges everything, it is the universal *confusion* and *exchange* of all things, an inverted world, the confusion and exchange of all natural and human qualities."[35] Through money, man can do "what he cannot do as a man." (In this way, Fafner believes that he can gain eternal youth through the gold.) "That which money can buy, that *am I*." The case of Alberich can be summed up in Marx's words: "I *am* ugly, but I can buy the *most beautiful* woman. Which means to say that I am not *ugly*, for the effect of *ugliness*, its repelling power, is destroyed by money." In short: "Does not money therefore transform all my incapacities into their opposite?"[36] This is certainly the reason for its fatal fascination, the curse of which is symbolized by the ring. Like Wagner, Marx drew a contrast between the fetishization of material possessions as determined by their monetary value and our human and personal relationship with ourselves, with nature, and with the entire objective world, something that could not be disposed of or exploited by the "sense of *having*."[37] This relationship found consummate expression in love.

If we assume *man* to be *man*, and his relation to the world to be a human one, then love can be exchanged only for love, trust for trust and so on. . . . Each of your relations to man—and to nature—must be a *particular expression* . . . of your *real individual* life. If you love unrequitedly, i.e. if your love as love does not call forth love in return, if through the *vital expression* of yourself as a loving person you fail to become a *loved person*, then your love is impotent, it is a misfortune.[38]

For both Marx and Wagner, the objectification of women was a classic example of the "inverting power" of money. Women are debased as objects of barter not only in *Das Rheingold* but also in *Die Walküre* and *Götterdämmerung*. Hunding is said to have "wooed a woman whom thieves, unasked, had given him as his wife" (GS 6:14). The woman in question—Sieglinde—is now liberated by her twin brother, Siegmund, their incestuous love bearing within it all the hallmarks of an erotic rebellion against ossified custom, constraint, and injustice.[39] Perpetually pursued, Siegmund protects those in trouble and fights all forms of oppression. His most recent feat of heroism was his unsuccessful attempt to protect a woman from being forced into marriage ("To meet that force, I flew to her aid"; GS 6:10). As a result, Hunding numbers Siegmund among the "unruly race" who are "hated" by all: "What others hold dear they deem unholy" (GS 6:11). Wotan has appointed him a revolutionary whose goal is to free the world from the curse on the ring and to do so, moreover, by means of the opposing principle of love. It is significant that like Walther von Stolzing in *Die Meistersinger*, Siegmund uses the image of spring to describe his unleashed passion—a spring that brings violent release from winter's rigid regime.

Wotan's plan to use Siegmund is doomed to failure from the outset, as the latter is incapable of acting in a way that is independent of the god's wishes, Wotan himself being prevented by his contracts from breaking the power of the ring. Only when we come to Siegfried do we find a hero whose actions are not guided by Wotan. In his loving union with Brünnhilde, Siegfried already anticipates a world beyond the alienating constraints of ownership and what Marx called the "category of having."[40] Significantly, the ring is no longer a symbol of "power-giving ownership" (GS 2:153) for either Siegfried or Brünnhilde but a pledge of their love (GS 6:204). As such, it symbolizes the opposite of the hatred that stemmed from Alberich's curse on love. As Brünnhilde tells Waltraute:

> Denn selig aus ihm
> leuchtet mir Siegfried's Liebe:
> Siegfried's Liebe
> —o ließ' sich die Wonne dir sagen!—
> sie—wahrt mir der Reif.
>
> (GS 6:205)

> [For Siegfried's love
> shines blissfully forth from it!
> Siegfried's love—
> if only my rapture could speak to you!—
> That love the ring embodies for me!]

In this way the ring is spiritually turned back into its original form as the Rhinegold, when it was not yet a dead object but a living, mythical being endowed with an "eye."

In *Götterdämmerung*, Siegfried is drawn into the fatal web of evil and, as the victim of a trick that destroys his memory and prevents him from recognizing Brünnhilde, humiliates the latter by treating her as a piece of booty for another man and as an object of barter for another woman, Gutrune. In turn Gutrune is reduced to the status of a commodity, an object that can be passed from hand to hand. In all of Wagner's output, no scene is more unsettling than the one in which Siegfried, in the guise of Gunther, bursts into the world of the Valkyries' Rock, which has been sanctified by love, and violently wrests the ring from Brünnhilde's hand, an act reminiscent of Wotan's assault on Alberich. The somber brutality of this scene, clearly suggesting rape, represents the profoundest humiliation that Wagner ever devised for a woman. Only when he lies dying does Siegfried recover his essential integrity. And when Brünnhilde restores the ring to the Rhinedaughters, she frees the world from the curse of objectification, and she does so, moreover, by acting in the name of a love both inalienable and unsalable.

EVA AS FIRST PRIZE IN THE SONG CONTEST

Die Meistersinger includes another example of the clash between objectification and love, even though the laws of comedy mean that the contrasts are not as pronounced and that ultimately they are reconciled. The goldsmith Veit Pogner offers his own daughter as the prize in the Mastersingers' traditional competition on Midsummer Day:

> Dem Singer, der im Kunst-Gesang
> vor allem Volk den Preis errang
>   am Sankt Johannistag,
>   sei er wer er auch mag,
>   dem geb' ich, ein Kunst-gewog'ner,

von Nürenberg Veit Pogner
mit all' meinem Gut, wie's geh' und steh',
Eva, mein einziges Kind, zur Eh'.

(GS 7:172)

[To the singer who, in the contest
before all the people wins the prize
    on Saint John's Day,
    be he who he may,
    to him I, a friend of art,
    Veit Pogner of Nuremberg, give
    with all my goods and chattels
    Eva, my only child, in marriage.]

In other words, Eva is lumped together with her father's household effects, even though he insists that he is not offering the winner a "lifeless gift"; Eva herself has the "casting vote" and can decide whether or not she accepts the winner as her husband (GS 7:173). Although this reservation means that Eva is less objectified, this objectification is sanctioned by a further provision.

Wem ihr Meister den Preis zusprecht,
die Maid kann dem verwehren,
doch nie einen And'ren begehren;
ein Meistersinger muß er sein:
nur wen ihr krönt, den soll sie frei'n.

(GS 7:174)

[The man to whom you Masters award the prize
the maid can refuse,
but she may never demand another;
he must be a Mastersinger;
she may woo only the man whom you crown.]

In short, Eva's casting vote is an irrelevance, and were it not for Sachs's intervention and his inspired ability to take charge of the lovers' fate, the action would take the same course as before, and Pogner's act of private sponsorship would end in disaster.

Eva is convinced that Walther is destined for her, and she refuses to marry anyone else: "You and no other" (GS 7:155). As with all of Wagner's female characters, her love is all-consuming, and she is not prepared to make concessions. In other words, she will not countenance a conventional marriage, still less will she renounce her love. When it emerges that Walther failed to pass the test and to become a Master and that he apparently, therefore, cannot be her husband, she immediately resolves to elope with him ("No time for reflection now!" GS 7:208). As we know, it is thanks to Sachs that this plan is foiled.

Eva's behavior confirms Wagner's views on sexual love and the family as expressed in *Opera and Drama*. Here, in a discussion of the Oedipus myth, he writes that because of its emotional spontaneity, love poses a threat to the family, which must be kept free from all "instinctiveness." Within the family—the "most natural but also the most restricted basis of society"—sexual love is reduced to the relations between husband and wife, as the family is held together not by spontaneity but by the "bonds of custom." Sexual love is "subversive," flouting custom in all its predictability (GS 4:56). In other words, love constitutes a potential revolt against the family and against the society that the family sustains.

This point is made abundantly plain by Eva's behavior once she has been struck by Cupid's dart. An obedient and caring daughter ("An obedient child speaks only when asked" and "Dear father, come!" GS 7:194–95), she feels only warmth and affection for her father, emotions typical of the sentimental family dramas of the late eighteenth century in which the children were generally motherless. But when her lover appears, she suddenly breaks free—"with a suppressed cry" (GS 7:205)—from the bonds of family domesticity. Her father no longer exists for her—and this applies as much to her spiritual father, Sachs, as to her physical father. Although she later acknowledges Sachs as the man who "awoke" her true feelings (GS 7:253), she refers to him simply as "the cobbler" (GS 7:209) when he thwarts her plans to elope—how appallingly heartless this expression seems on her lips. So dismissive is she of him that Walther brutally exclaims: "I'll put out his light" (GS 7:210).

Her ecstatic outpouring in act 3 in which she confesses her love for Sachs (and there is no other way of describing this passage) contains the following remarkable lines:

> Ich war doch auf der rechten Spur:
>> denn, hatte ich die Wahl,
>> nur dich erwählt' ich mir:
>> du warest mein Gemahl,
>> den Preis nur reicht' ich dir!—
>> Doch nun hat's mich gewählt
>> zu nie gekannter Qual:
>> und werd' ich heut' vermählt,
>> so war's ohn' alle Wahl!
>> Das war ein Müssen, war ein Zwang.

(GS 7:254)

> [But I was on the right path,
>> for, if I'd had the choice,
>> I'd have chosen none but you;
>> you would have been my husband,
>> to you alone I'd have given the prize!—
>> But now I have been singled out
>> for torments that I've never known before,
>> and if I am wed today,
>> then I had no choice!
> It was an obligation, a compulsion!]

It is impossible not to hear an echo of *Tristan und Isolde* in these lines.[41] Here the sense of being overwhelmed by the "torments" of love inevitably recalls the compulsive effect of the love potion. It is only logical, therefore, that this passage should be followed by a verbal and musical reminiscence of the "sad tale" of Tristan and Isolde (GS 7:254).

In *Tristan und Isolde*, the anarchic force of sexual love results in a radical reappraisal of existing values and the overthrow of moral and social order ("Where are honor and other sterling qualities now that Tristan, the fount of all honor, has lost them?" and now that "the truest of the true" [GS 7:52] is guilty of treachery and betrayal?) A similar upheaval threatens to take place against the background of the comedy in *Die Meistersinger*. There is no doubt that behind this idea of love as a compulsive force lies Schopenhauer's "Metaphysics of Sexual Love," an essay that caused Wagner much soul-searching. For Schopenhauer, the sex drive was the focus of the blind "will." It is sexual love that

> destroys the most valuable relationships, and breaks the strongest bonds. . . . Indeed, it robs of all conscience those who were previously honourable and upright, and makes traitors of those who have hithero been loyal and faithful. Accordingly, it appears on the whole as a malevolent demon, striving to pervert, to confuse, and to overthrow everything.[42]

Not only is love itself anarchic, so too is Walther's whole way of writing poetry and singing, a way that "fills the Masters with fear" (GS 7:198). His "sweet love song" (GS 7:182) is governed by no rules but only by what Wagner, in one of his favorite expressions, terms the "instinctive" nature of improvisatory inspiration. Inspired by love, it is cast in a form that suggests an analogy with sexual love.[43] Sachs makes it plain to the young knight that

> eu'r Lied, das hat ihnen bang' gemacht;
> und das mit Recht: denn wohl bedacht,
> mit solchem Dicht- und Liebesfeuer
> verführt man wohl Töchter zum Abenteuer.
>
> (GS 7:236)

> [your song made them uneasy;
> and for good reason: for when you think of it,
> it is with such fires of poetry and love
> that daughters are lured into adventure].

This, of course, is precisely what Walther had in mind. But as Sachs explains, "there are other words and tunes for the blissful state of wedlock" (GS 7:236). And it is these in which Sachs now proceeds to instruct the lovesick knight. The fires of poetry and love—which are one and the selfsame thing—point to chaos and unknown terrors.[44] Following the turbulent events of the previous night, which were ruled by the will and "the old *Wahn* [folly or illusion]" (GS 7:234), Sachs gives Walther a lesson in poetics that is entirely Schopenhauerian in spirit, aiming, as it does, to achieve an aesthetic catharsis of this Wahn, whether it finds expression in the aggressions and violence of the Midsummer Night riot, in lovesick passion, or in a poetic ardor that defies all rules. Art is intended to bring "peace to Wahn"—the allusion to Wahnfried, Wagner's home in Bayreuth, is by no means accidental.

The laws of comedy leave no choice in the matter, and so Sachs duly succeeds in reestablishing a state of precarious harmony between, on the one hand, the everyday world of family, society, and craftsmanship, with its grounding in well-established custom, and, on the other, the subversive force of love and an artistry that draws its strength from a new sort of inspiration. It is a state of harmony that remains under threat and that Walther, on the deepest level, is barely able to accept. Eva remains a part of Pogner's goods and chattels but is no longer a "bartered bride," having decided in favor of Walther as a free individual. As a symbol of his acceptance into the Masters' Guild, Walther receives a gold chain from Pogner, which as a subtly ironic sign of the gentleman's agreement between the avant-garde Junker and the conservative burghers, includes an image of King David (GS 7:269). Eva, we may recall, knew that she was bound by fate to Walther, as she had "long since seen" him in a "picture" of King David. Just as Tamino sees a portrait of Pamina in Mozart's *Zauberflöte*, Senta one of the Flying Dutchman, so Eva succumbs to the spell of a portrait, an ancient motif indicative of an erotic déjà vu experience or, to quote Ernst Bloch, a "kind of love-potion effect, conveyed by painted anticipation."[45] When Magdalene asks in a tone of mocking parody whether she means "the king with the harp and long beard in the Masters' sign," Eva emphatically rejects the idea; no, she means the radiant young hero who defeated Goliath (GS 7:155). But at the end of the opera, Walther does indeed acquire a long beard, and David junior is transformed into David senior. There is no doubt that Wagner is not being serious here. Rather, it is a deeply serious joke on the part of musical comedy as a genre, a genre in which conflicts and problems such as the objectification of women cannot be allowed to end tragically and do not even need to be resolved at all. Musical comedy needs only to mitigate them.

Nuremberg as an Aesthetic State

DIE MEISTERSINGER, *AN IMAGE AND COUNTERIMAGE OF HISTORY*

Now let's see how well Hans Sachs can control this folly.

—*Richard Wagner,* Die Meistersinger von Nürnberg

IN MANY respects *Die Meistersinger von Nürnberg* falls outside the Wagner canon—in other words, the works from *Der fliegende Holländer* to *Parsifal*—and in some ways it might even be thought of as marking a return to genres with which Wagner had experimented before he embarked on *Der fliegende Holländer*. In the first instance, it differs from Wagner's other music dramas in that it is a comedy like the early *Das Liebesverbot*. At the same time, it is a historical opera like *Rienzi*. Wagner had abandoned both of these genres. His reform of the musical theater presupposed a certain emotional intensity that is hard to square with the carefree nature of comedy, and historical opera belonged to the world of grand opera that Wagner claimed to have left behind him. Myth had gradually displaced history, and in those few cases in Wagner's Romantic operas where history still occurred, namely, in *Tannhäuser* and *Lohengrin*, it had been transformed into legend, with history clothing itself in the guise of the "wondrous." The "artwork of the future" had no further use for history, as any historical subject would inevitably have limited the work to the past, whereas myth, whether in the world of the *Ring*, with its lack of any tangible historical setting, or in the mythical Middle Ages of *Tristan und Isolde* and *Parsifal*, projects the future onto a dim and distant past. "All our wishes and burning instincts carry us forward into the future," Wagner wrote in 1851 in *A Communication to My Friends*, "and to these we seek to give recognizable form by means of images from the past and thus to invest them with a form that the modern present cannot provide." His music dramas are set "one day." As Thomas Mann noted in his essay *Leiden und Größe Richard Wagners* (Sufferings and greatness of Richard Wagner), the German word *einst* is ambiguous, as it can refer both to the remote past and to the distant future, or to quote Wagner himself in *Das Rheingold*, "how all things were" and "how all things shall be" (GS 5:261).[1]

A COMMUNITY WITHOUT A MUNICIPAL AUTHORITY

In short, *Die Meistersinger* seems to be an exception by dint of its concern with the past. Here history is no longer presented as legend but, divesting itself of its "wondrous" mantle, reverts to its secular form. In many respects, the past—the work is set in "Nuremberg around the middle of the sixteenth century" (GS 7:150)—is accurately reconstructed; we know, for example, that Wagner studied the original sources in an attempt to depict Meistergesang as authentically as possible and even introduced into his music pseudohistorical formal elements that were otherwise remote from his field of reference.[2] (It would be wrong to describe them as historical.) At first sight, even the work's contents seem curiously un-Wagnerian. Whereas the composer's heroes are normally anything but middle class, tending rather to transcend existing social norms and establish new ones in their place, *Die Meistersinger* culminates in a paean to the middle-class values of Renaissance Germany, values that the former knight Walther von Stolzing is finally forced to accept, for all his earlier attempts to shock.[3] In the very last sentence of the fourth of his *Unzeitgemäße Betrachtungen* (Untimely meditations), Nietzsche was clearly thinking of *Die Meistersinger* when he wrote that Wagner was "not the seer of a future, as he would perhaps like to appear to us, but the interpreter and transfigurer of a past."[4] Here Nietzsche intended this assessment entirely positively, but he was later to turn it against Wagner, seeing himself as the seer of the future who was resolved to shatter the ancient tablets of the law.

But the more we look at it, the more ambiguous becomes the world of the past that is conjured up in *Die Meistersinger*, a past whose remoteness from the storms of the present proves deceptive. Surprisingly, the community in which these events pursue their bourgeois course has positively anarchic features that result in a midsummer riot at the end of act 2, only to produce a new aesthetic harmony in the Festival Meadow at the end of the final act. Nuremberg is depicted as a home of the muses, but this city has no discernible political order. That it has a council emerges only in passing from a single reference, but otherwise we hear of no communal organizations or municipal authorities to whom the townsfolk might defer. And the fact that there is a German Reich at all emerges only in Hans Sachs's closing address, where it appears as largely irrelevant.

The Nurembergers live in a kind of aestheticized state of nature that regulates itself without any need for a social contract. In the riot at the end of act 2, a full-scale war threatens to break out, with every person for him- or herself—the very situation that according to early-European state theory makes the social contract indispensable and hence leads to the foundation of the state. Yet the participants in the Midsummer Eve riot can be restrained without the need for police intervention, simply by having cold water poured over them (GS 7:228). Even the night watchman—the only person to set foot onstage in an official capacity—appears only after the visitation has passed and the spectral shades have faded away, his solitary function being to call out the hour after the onset of darkness (during daylight hours the city appears to need no representatives of public order) and to appeal to the voice of reason in a religious, moral, and practical sense. This vaguely comical and moralizing town musician evidently has no powers of arrest. Just as the community in *Die Meistersinger* appears to manage without any municipal authorities, so the church seems to get by without the benefit of clergy. Although we hear and see the congregation singing a chorale at the afternoon service at Saint Catherine's Church, held annually as a prelude to the Midsummer Eve celebrations,[5] there is no sign of any vicar. Community and congregation are both apparently self-governing, with no need for any leadership.

Apart from the night watchman, there is only a single official figure in *Die Meistersinger*, the town clerk Sixtus Beckmesser, who, apart from the fact that he does not appear in any civic function, is portrayed not just as a comic character but as one who is positively farcical. The popular view of him is that he is stupid, and the townspeople have to remind themselves to take him seriously ("Shut up! Stop joking! He has a vote and a seat on the council!" GS 7:263). In turn, this suggests that the townspeople have little respect for their council, which is similarly kept offstage. This absence of either municipal authorities or a town council is all the more striking in that both play an important role as the epitome of middle-class order in Wagner's sources, including contemporary chronicles, sixteenth-century travelers' tales, and eighteenth- and nineteenth-century poems dealing with the municipal culture of the late Middle Ages and early Renaissance in Germany. This is clear from even the merest glance at the list of characters in Johann Ludwig Deinhardstein's "dramatic poem" *Hans Sachs* (1827) and the opera by Albert Lortzing that is based on it (1840, revised 1845). Both of these last-named works were familiar to Wagner.

The myth of Nuremberg that is universally thought of as culminating in Wagner's *Die Meistersinger* is by no means an invention of the Romantics but dates from the beginning of the sixteenth century. By this time in its history, the town numbered some thirty thousand inhabitants, making it the third largest city in the empire after Cologne and Augsburg. Prosperous and cultured, it was the favorite residence of Emperor Maximilian (the "last knight") and, with its castle, its magnificent spectacle of towers, churches, walls, and ramparts so memorably depicted in the famous woodcut in Hartmann Schedel's *Weltchronik* (World chronicle) of 1493, a brilliant centerpiece of the empire. It enjoyed trade relations with all of Europe and seems to have had a better reputation than other German towns and cities. In his letter to Willibald Pirckheimer of 25 October 1518, Ulrich von Hutten quotes a Venetian proverb to the effect that all the cities of Germany are blind but Nuremberg at least has one eye. A Latin epigram by Conrad Celtis reads: "Nestling at the heart of Germany amid Germany's fields, Nuremberg, mark this city well, gentle reader! No man on earth has seen its like: its soil could not be more pitiful, yet everything grows and proudly flourishes."[6] And Johann Cochläus included an enthusiastic chapter on Nuremberg in his *Kurze Beschreibung Deutschlands* (Brief description of Germany, 1512), praising its local government, which was said to be a model for all of Europe and the cause not only of the city's prosperity but of its political importance and extensive trade relations.

In his *Lobspruch der Stadt Nürnberg* (Encomium to the city of Nuremberg) of 1530, the historical Hans Sachs praises the town's magnificence and its "industrious populace" successfully engaged in "mercantile trade," "craftsmanship," and the "arts." "Who can rule such a populace and instill obedience?" he asks. And he answers his own question: "There is in this town a wise and solicitous council that rules solicitously and arranges things neatly."[7] In fact, the council was made up of only a narrow cross section of the old, established patriciate, which kept itself well apart from those families who were not entitled to sit on the council. Far from "arranging things neatly," it subjected them to the most spartan controls.

In the Festival Meadow scene, the entrance of the guilds is modeled on the traditional Sechseläuten festival, which was held every year in Zurich on the third Monday in April. Wagner saw it more than once during his years of political exile in Switzerland. But there was no such procession in Nuremberg, where the local craftsmen were not organized into guilds but remained under the strict supervision and legal control of the town council.[8] Sachs himself, in his *Lobspruch*, gives an indication of the extent to which life in Nuremberg was regulated by the municipal authorities: there were "officials without number," "a strict judiciary," and vigilant "police."[9] Indeed, he gives far more space to the maintenance of public order than to the cultivation of the arts, which he dismisses in only a handful of lines. Wagner's Midsummer Eve riot is unlikely to have taken place in sixteenth-century Nuremberg, and if it had done so, the town council would have responded with draconian measures. (In the Shrovetide plays from Nuremberg that were undoubtedly one of Wagner's sources, the slapstick action regularly culminates in some form of beating.)

The fact that in the case of Wagner's opera we need a fine-tooth comb to find the "countless officials" of whom the historical Hans Sachs writes is all the more remarkable in that Wagner clearly knew Sachs's poem "in praise of my fatherland," as he used its last two lines in his libretto, albeit with a significant shift of emphasis: "Auf daß sein [des Vaterlandes] Lob grün, blüh und wachs./Das wünschet von Nürnberg Hans Sachs" [So that its praise may flourish, bloom, and wax./This is the wish of Nuremberg's Hans Sachs].[10] Wagner uses words similar to these in Sachs's great address to the Masters in act 1, when he suggests that it should be the populace, rather than the Masters themselves, who judge the song contest on the Festival Meadow. There is no longer any mention of the historical Sachs's "fatherland," with its "harmony between community and council, and well-ordered burgher estates,"[11] but of a hoped-for alliance between folk and art: "Daß Volk und Kunst gleich blüh' und wachs',/bestellt ihr so, mein' ich, Hans Sachs" [That folk and art should bloom and wax,/you should now ordain, or so thinks Hans Sachs] (GS 7:175).

As far as Wagner's picture of Nuremberg is concerned, these sixteenth-century sources pale into insignificance beside the Romantic myth of Nuremberg as a town devoted to art.[12] Hugo von Hofmannsthal pointed this out as long ago as 1927 in a letter to Richard Strauss: "The great charm and great power of *Die Meistersinger* (taken purely as a poem), and its preeminence over all the other works by this unique man," lay in Wagner's incomparable evocation of the town as the background and, indeed, as the very soul of the work, a soul that unites within it all the strands of the action. As Hofmannsthal went on to point out, the myth of Nuremberg as promulgated by the German Romantics was merged here with Wagner's own account in *My Life* of the events that had befallen him in the town, an account retelling "in unforgettable detail" the scuffle that had taken place at night and the appearance of the night watchman who had restored order.

This town, in its entirety, still existed, completely unspoiled, in the 1830s, not merely reflecting the intellectual, emotional, and everyday world of the German burghers of 1500 but actually allowing us to picture that world. As such, it provided one of the great decisive experiences of all the Romantics, from Tieck and Wackenroder's *Herzensergießungen eines kunstliebenden Klosterbruders*, where we can sense the figure of Dürer in the background, to the Arnims, E.T.A. Hoffmann, and, finally, to Richard Wagner, in whom the Romantic age found its most perfect expression.[13]

The *Herzensergießungen eines kunstliebenden Klosterbruders* (The heartfelt effusions of an art-loving monk) was written jointly by Wilhelm Heinrich Wackenroder and Ludwig Tieck and contains a section in honor of Albrecht Dürer and Hans Sachs; here we find a tribute to old Nuremberg that contains few remaining signs of the profoundly prosaic reality of a strictly authoritarian town council but prepares the way, instead, for Wagner's outright aestheticization of the local community.

> Nuremberg! O town of erstwhile universal fame! How gladly I wandered through your narrow crooked streets; with what childlike love I observed your ancestral houses and churches, which bear the firm imprint of our fatherland's ancient art! What heartfelt love I feel for the creations of that age, creations that speak so vigorous, powerful, and true a language! How they draw me back to that gray century when you, Nuremberg, were the life-teeming school of our fatherland's art and when a truly fruitful and prodigal spirit flourished within your walls:—when Master Hans Sachs and Adam Kraft the sculptor and, above all, Albrecht Dürer and his friend Wilibaldus [*sic*] Pirckheimer and so many other highly praised men of honor were still alive! How often I longed to return to that age![14]

An echo of sentences such as these may be heard in Sachs's *Wahn* Monologue, in which he declares his love for "his" city of Nuremberg. In each case the city is transformed into the idyllic home of patriotic burghers with a keen understanding of art, a city that, however charming, is far more provincial and far less cosmopolitan than it was in the sixteenth century, when it was at the heart of a network of trade routes that extended across much of Europe.

HANS SACHS'S LITERARY METAMORPHOSES

Wagner's most important dramatic source—Deinhardstein's *Hans Sachs*—is strangely at odds with this Romantic myth of Nuremberg. At this stage in his career, Deinhardstein was a bon vivant in Vienna who wrote in his spare time, later earning his spurs as artistic director of the Burgtheater and as official censor of books, in which capacity he proved to be an assiduous supporter of Metternich's repressive regime. In 1828 the Berlin intendant Count Brühl arranged to perform *Hans Sachs* at the city's Königliches Schauspielhaus but took a dislike to Deinhardstein's prologue. As a result, he turned to no less a writer than Goethe with the request that he be allowed to preface the play with a performance of Goethe's 1776 *Hans Sachsens poetische Sendung.* (The full title of Goethe's poem is *Erklärung eines alten*

Holzschnittes, vorstellend Hans Sachsens poetische Sendung [Explanation of an old woodcut depicting Hans Sachs's poetic calling].) Goethe was touched to discover that someone still remembered his poem and agreed to Brühl's request, even offering to provide an introduction that would add to the audience's understanding and that would be spoken by a "mastersinger" in historical costume. In the event, the new prologue was more of an introduction to Goethe's poem—which was declaimed by Eduard Devrient—than to Deinhardstein's somewhat feeble play. In 1853, when preparing the piece for publication within the context of his collected works, Deinhardstein self-complacently included Goethe's prologue.[15]

In his foreword to this last-named volume, Deinhardstein adopts a markedly disdainful tone in dismissing the Romantic myth of Nuremberg, although in doing so he was merely reflecting the cultural situation in Vienna, where literary Romanticism had never really found a home for itself. Here Deinhardstein defends himself against the charge of critics who claimed that he had paid too little heed to Nuremberg's much-vaunted "middle-class grandeur," arguing that this grandeur was as overrated as the poetic significance of Meistergesang.

> As for poetry, it was not only not great in Nuremberg at the time at which the play is set, it was positively mediocre. The Mastersingers were unimaginative, formal, ridiculous individuals, and their whole approach to art did irreparable damage to German art at a time when it was still developing, as it sought to introduce formal rules and constraints where only the free stirring of a spiritual and intellectual nature can achieve its goal.

Deinhardstein's contempt for Meistergesang goes so far that he distorts Goethe's prologue by replacing the latter's mastersinger with a minnesinger. He even minimizes Sachs's importance by claiming that Sachs deserves "far less" admiration as a poet in general than as "the only poet" who maintained the claims of poetry at a time when it was being destroyed as a genre. This was also the subject of Deinhardstein's own prologue, which Brühl had declined to use for the production in Berlin.

Deinhardstein's view of Nuremberg and Sachs draws on two opposing traditions. On the one hand, he adopts the Enlightenment's dismissive attitude toward Meistergesang, and on the other he denounces Sachs's opponents as spiteful philistines. During his own lifetime and for several decades after his death, Sachs's works were widely read and his plays frequently performed, but by the Baroque age he had fallen into total neglect, a state of affairs due to the age's new poetological orientation, with its concern for Humanist learning and for the sort of romance models that Wagner was later to parody in Beckmesser's efforts at poetasterism. By now contemporaries no longer had any time for the worthy verse of a Nuremberg craftsman. Yet neglect was preferable to the contempt that the early Enlightenment reserved for Sachs and his allegedly limited view of art. Two eighteenth-century lines ridicule the *Knittelvers* of the rhymster-cobbler: "Hans Sachs war ein Schuh-/Macher und Poet dazu" [Hans Sachs was a shoe-/Maker and a poet, too]. That these oft-quoted lines were originally intended as a lampoon has now been largely forgotten, not least since Wagner placed them in Sachs's mouth at the end of the Cobbling Song in act 2: "Als Eva aus dem Paradies" (GS 7:211–12). In Lortzing's opera *Hans Sachs*, which is loosely based on Deinhardstein's "dramatic poem," Sachs's rival, the Augsburg city councillor Eoban Hesse (a figure who has little in common with his historical prototype), uses these lines in their originally contemptuous sense but applies them, "mockingly," to Sachs's apprentice Görg, who is also a poet: "Dann seid Ihr ja ein Schuh-/Macher und Poet dazu" [Then you're a shoe-/maker and a poet too]. Görg, for his part, adopts an "ironical" tone in his reply: "Ei, ei, ei, ei, das war sehr fein,/Zu brauchen auf 'nen Leichenstein" [Hey, hey, hey, hey, most kind of you! But please!/A tombstone is the place for lines like these].[16]

The poetry of the German Enlightenment had taken its cue from French Classicism, and it was not until this trend had passed and been replaced by the *Sturm und Drang* movement of the 1770s that the time was right for a new and more positive assessment of Sachs's work. It was Goethe who rediscovered Sachs in the course of his exploration of the world of the sixteenth century, a world in whose popular and powerful language he found an alternative to the anemic, late-courtly, and classicistic literature of his own day. With his slapstick plays and satirical comedies *Das Jahrmarktsfest zu Plundersweilern* (The annual fair at Plundersweilern), *Ein Fastnachtsspiel vom Pater Brey* (A Shrovetide play about Father Brey), and *Satyros*, Goethe picked up the tradition of Sachs's own plays and dedicated to his memory his poem *Hans Sachsens poetische Sendung*, traces of which can still be felt in Wagner's *Die Meistersinger*. When Sachs begins his final address ("Verachtet mir die Meister nicht/und ehrt mir ihre Kunst" [Do not despise the Masters/but honor their art for me; GS 270]),[17] he seems to be alluding to Goethe's grimly humorous assessment of all who were contemptuous of the Nuremberg Master: "In Froschpfuhl all das Volk verbannt,/Das seinen Meister je verkannt!" [Let all who have ever misjudged their master/Be banished forthwith to the frogs' pond!].[18]

Goethe's poem was first published in 1776 in Christoph Martin Wieland's periodical *Der Teutsche Merkur* to mark the bicentenary of Hans Sachs's death, with Wieland himself contributing a biographical sketch. Between them, Goethe and Wieland succeeded in rehabilitating the Nuremberg cobbler-poet whose doggerel verse, condemned at the start of the century as the nadir of German literature, was about to become the model for the opening scene of a work now widely regarded as the high point of German literature and arguably of modern literature in general: the hero's opening monologue in Goethe's *Faust*. It was Sachs's *Knittelvers*, Wagner told Cosima on 13 December 1878, that formed the basis of the "tremendous popular appeal" of the play. Six years earlier, in his essay *On Actors and Singers*, Wagner had argued that it was the combination of the naively popular and the sublime that made Goethe's play unique. The "miraculous structure that Goethe has raised on the foundations of this so-called *Knittelvers*," in which his own poetry was merged with that of the "rough-hewn art of our old folk poet Hans Sachs," seemed "never to abandon this basis of the most perfect popularity, while using it to soar aloft to the highest realm of classical meter" (GS 9:214–15).

As early as 1851, in *A Communication to My Friends*, Wagner had already described Hans Sachs as "the final manifestation of the artistically creative popular spirit" (GS 4:284–85), and it was because of this that he used the "rough-hewn art" of the Nuremberg Master as the material basis of his music drama. The historical

Sachs had written plays on the lives of Tristan and Siegfried (both of them were available to Wagner in his private library in Dresden), and now Sachs finally set foot onstage in person, referring to the "sad tale" of Tristan and Isolde (GS 7:254) and receiving the acclamation of the townsfolk with his own verses in the "Wach' auf" Chorus (GS 7:260). In the letter to Strauss from which I have already quoted, Hugo von Hofmannsthal stresses the extent to which this figure of Hans Sachs was created in the spirit of Goethe and especially of the latter's poem *Hans Sachsens poetische Sendung*:[19]

> The spiritual aura that surrounds Hans Sachs and, at the same time, the national, representative aspect of the character—these are aspects that Wagner owes to Goethe's wonderful interpretation of the figure of Sachs . . . ; also, the two allegorical female characters in the Prize Song are already prefigured here—the muse as the Humanist element and, in contrast with her, the simple domesticity and sensuality of the soul embodied in a woman.[20]

This last-named figure addresses Sachs in words that are repeated almost word for word in Sachs's *Wahn* Monologue:

> Ich hab' dich auserlesen
> Vor vielen in dem Weltwirr-Wesen,
> Daß du sollst haben klare Sinnen,
> Nichts Ungeschicklichs magst beginnen.
> Wenn andre durcheinander rennen,
> Sollst du's mit treuem Blick erkennen;
> . . . .
> Der Natur-Genius an der Hand
> Soll dich führen durch alle Land.
> Soll dir zeigen all das Leben,
> Der Menschen wunderliches Weben,
> Ihr Wirren, Suchen, Stoßen und Treiben,
> Schieben, Reißen, Drängen und Reiben,
> Wie kunterbunt die Wirtschaft tollert,
> Der Ameishauf durcheinander kollert!
> Mag dir aber bei allem geschehn,
> Als tätst's in ein'm Zauberkasten sehn.
> Schreib das dem Menschenvolk auf Erden,
> Ob's ihnen möcht' zur Witzung werden.[21]

> ["I have selected thee," she said,
> "From all who earth's wild mazes tread,
> That thou shouldst have clear-sighted sense,
> And nought that's wrong shouldst e'er commence.
> When others run in strange confusion,
> Thy gaze shall see through each illusion;
> . . . .
> Fair Nature's Genius by the hand

Shall lead thee on through every land,
Teach thee each different life to scan,
Show thee the wondrous ways of man,
His shifts, confusions, thrustings, and drubbings,
Pushings, tearings, pressings, and rubbings;
The varying madness of the crew,
The anthill's ravings bring to view;
But thou shalt see all this express'd,
As though 'twere in a magic chest.
Write these things down for folks on earth,
In hopes they may to wit give birth."

(Trans. Edgar Alfred Bowring)]

These lines clearly recall not only the turmoil of Midsummer Night in act 2 of *Die Meistersinger* but also the lesson that Sachs draws from it in his monologue at the start of act 3.

Mann, Weib, Gesell' und Kind,
fällt sich da an wie toll und blind:
    und will's der Wahn geseg'nen,
    nun muß es Prügel reg'nen,
    mit Hieben, Stöß' und Dreschen
    den Wuthesbrand zu löschen.—
. . . .
jetzt schau'n wir, wie Hans Sachs es macht,
daß er den Wahn fein lenken mag.

(GS 7:234–35)

[Man, woman, journeyman, and child
fall on each other as if crazed and blind;
    and if folly will bless it,
    then blows must rain down,
    with cuts, kicks, and thrashings
    to quench the fire of fury.—
. . . .
Now let's see how well
Hans Sachs can control this folly.]

In Wagner's opera, there is a fine-spun web of almost magical associations between the historical figure of Hans Sachs and the plays that he wrote, between his poetic interpretation by Goethe, the latter's poetic debt to the "rough-hewn art" of the Nuremberg Master, and, finally, Wagner's dramatization of the themes that Sachs himself once treated, including Wagner's setting of Sachs's historical lines. All of this results in a character in whom historical elements are inextricably linked with Goethean and Wagnerian elements.

HANS SACHS AS AN OUTSIDER: DEINHARDSTEIN AND LORTZING

All of this could hardly be further removed from Wagner's main source, Dein-hardstein's "dramatic poem." Here Sachs is depicted as a total outsider in a society of philistines, whom they loathe and deride as "Master Cleverclogs," someone who pays little heed to the "Leges Tabulaturae" and who "always wants to be dif-ferent" (to quote the baker Jakob), even though he is no more than a cobbler. "Is this your blessing, poesy? To be mocked and reviled?" Sachs asks himself. Even his lover, Kunigunde, cannot accept his lowly estate and blackmails him into "abandoning his vulgar trade," a trade that prevents her, as the daughter of a class-conscious goldsmith, from marrying him, quite apart from the fact that he is wealthy enough not to have to work. But the cobbler sticks to his last, and, even if it means losing the love of Kunigunde, he refuses to "seem more than I am." He finally leaves his ancestral town like some "latter-day Coriolanus."

It is purely by chance that he is persuaded to return to Nuremberg when, fleeing from the town, he encounters Emperor Maximilian and his retinue, who are on their way to Nuremberg with the express intention of meeting Sachs. By the time they arrive there, Kunigunde's father has been elected mayor and plans to marry her, against her will, to the Augsburg town councillor Eoban Hesse. In other words, the plot is motivated by class considerations and by the conceit that comes from political power, in which respect the work could hardly be more different from Wagner's *Die Meistersinger*. Sachs rejects this turn of events and is banished from the town. "The wolf who stole into our sheepfold, . . . Master Sachs is hounded from the town." But Emperor Maximilian, functioning as a deus ex machina, brings about a happy ending, and Sachs is paired off with his Kunigunde, who crowns him with the poet's laurel. The drama ends with a "joyful celebration" on the part of the townsfolk, who acclaim not Sachs, but the emperor: "Hail Em-peror Max! Hail Habsburg! Hail forever!" These are the final lines of the play and, as such, they use a popular encomiastic closing formula of a kind that ends even as distinguished a drama as Grillparzer's *König Ottokars Glück und Ende* (King Ottokar's happiness and downfall): "Hail! Hail! Three cheers for Austria! Habsburg forever!" The poet who is rejected by the burghers of his hometown finds support only with the highest power in the realm—an example of what Thomas Mann later termed "power-protected inwardness."[22]

The reader of Deinhardstein's *Hans Sachs* is bound to ask why a cobbler is so despised when other craftsmen such as the baker Jakob, the grocer Martin, and the locksmith Niklas are well-respected members of the community. It is true that as a craftsman the historical Sachs was prevented from taking part in local government, but he nonetheless enjoyed the respect of his fellow citizens, even if he often had problems with the censor and in 1527 was even banned from writing: "Solemn admonition from the council that he attend to his handiwork and shoemaking and refrain from issuing any books or rhymes in the future."[23] There is, then, a grain of historical truth in Deinhardstein's drama. But why is he treated as an outcast when he is so wealthy that he could hang up his boots and retire—something that the historical Sachs did indeed do near the end of his life? In Deinhardstein's Nuremberg, Sachs is virtually cast in the role of a Jew, rich and yet despised, feared or envied for his intellectual gifts, but nonetheless held in low esteem. He is a man of genius among small-minded, spiteful members of the petty bourgeoisie who drive him from their midst and would destroy him had he not gained the protection of the emperor like some court Jew.

For many years Deinhardstein's "dramatic poem" was a popular draw on German stages and was translated into several other languages. As such, it overshadowed Lortzing's comic opera of the same name, which was a setting of a libretto that Lortzing himself prepared in collaboration with Philipp Salomon Reger. Premiered in Leipzig in 1840, it failed to impress its early audiences, and so Lortzing revised the work, especially its ending. On this occasion his collaborator was Philipp Jakob Düringer. Unveiled in Mannheim in 1845, this new version proved no more successful than the old one, and it would be wrong, therefore, to claim that it was eclipsed by *Die Meistersinger*, the first prose draft of which also dates, coincidentally, from 1845, when Wagner was staying in Marienbad.

Lortzing's opera and Deinhardstein's play were the two principal sources of Wagner's opera, with Lortzing and his librettist Reger providing a number of important motifs, including the singing competition, the outdoor celebration, the theft and garbling of a love poem, and—more generally—the comic tone that the librettist and composer introduced into Deinhardstein's somber tragedy. But Wagner would not have needed to deny his source, as it was only in his hands that the new ideas found in Lortzing's opera were first made dramaturgically and psychologically compelling, allowing their tension and especially their humor to come into their own.

Arguably, Lortzing's most important innovation, however, and at the same time the most significant link between Deinhardstein and Wagner was his treatment of the townsfolk as an important participant in the action (in Deinhardstein's play they had had only a walk-on role), allowing him to revive the Romantic myth of Nuremberg and the popular image of Hans Sachs as interpreted by Goethe and Wackenroder, an aspect that Deinhardstein had suppressed. Even here, Sachs is hated by the establishment in the guise of the burghers and his fellow guild members (who in this case despise him not for his intellectual gifts but for his "simple-mindedness"), but the townsfolk love him, and, in his competition with Eoban Hesse at the start of act 2, they are very much on his side, supporting him in defiance of the self-interested verdict of the middle-class guildsmen. When Emperor Maximilian brings about the happy ending, he is merely carrying out the wishes of the populace.

Just as Sachs is the people's artist, so Maximilian I is the people's emperor. "Is he not father of his people?" Sachs asks in act 1. "Is there anyone in the empire who does not love the emperor?" Sachs's interlocutor is none other than the emperor himself, who has come to his workshop incognito. This idea of a people's king was inherited from the Romantics. "The true king will be a republic, the true republic a king," wrote Novalis in *Glauben und Liebe* (Faith and love),[24] and Achim von Arnim defined the "revolutionarily" minded ruler as the one in whose "own breast" the "voice of the people" rings forth.[25] And this is precisely what happens in Lortzing's *Hans Sachs*. Whereas Deinhardstein's Sachs was concerned only with poetry and love, Lortzing's Sachs asks: "What was it, then, that made you turn to poetry? Love's happiness, and our German fatherland." This package deal of love and fatherland is repeatedly hymned by Sachs, not least in his prize song at the start of act 2. When he decides to leave Nuremberg, he is consoled by the thought that "German land" may be found "elsewhere." Here there are already pre-echoes of German unification. Just as in 1848 the Frankfurt parliament elected the king of Prussia as emperor of Germany, so at the end of Lortzing's opera the townsfolk acclaim the emperor. The poetry may be worthless, but the sentiments are nonetheless genuine:

> Wir jauchzen laut aus voller Brust
> Heil Max Dir, Deutschlands Sonne!
> Du bist des Volkes Glück und Lust,
> Bist seine höchste Wonne.
> Drum jauchze, wer ein deutscher Mann:
> Heil lebe Maximilian!

> [We loudly cheer in full-toned voice
> Hail, Max, to you, the German sun!
> You are the people's joy and gladness,
> You are its highest pleasure!
> Let every German raise a cheer:
> Hail, long live Maximilian!]

WAGNER'S AESTHETIC UTOPIA

The Romantic notion of popular kingship played an important role in Wagner's thinking, too, especially at the time of his revolutionary activities in the late 1840s and again following his meeting with Ludwig II in 1864. Yet in spite of this enthusiasm, he cut the figure of Emperor Maximilian from his opera, preferring to replace him with Sachs himself, and Sachs in turn cedes his roles as lover and artist—two roles still associated with him in the versions by Deinhardstein and Lortzing—to a new couple in the persons of Eva and Walther von Stolzing. (To a certain extent, Walther may also be said to replace Maximilian in his role as the "last knight.") All of this leaves Sachs looking down on the action from a position of lofty superiority; at the same time it makes him seem a whole generation older and wiser. He has become a kind of people's tribune, in an aesthetic sense loved by the populace and respected by his fellow guildsmen, a burgher of patrician stamp whom no one wishes to deprive of his trade as a cobbler any longer. The cries of "Hail" at the end of the work are directed not at the Habsburgs' imperial power but at "Nuremberg's dear Sachs" (GS 7:271). It is now the poet, not the emperor, who draws together the various strands in the plot to produce a happy ending.

Wagner's Nuremberg, unlike that of his predecessors, is wholly depoliticized. Not only is the emperor missing (at the end of the work, there is even the possibility that the Holy Roman Empire might "dissolve in mist" [GS 7:271]), but, as we have seen, the town of Nuremberg lacks any municipal authority. And the mayor—a key figure in the works by both Deinhardstein and Lortzing—does not appear onstage at all, an absence particularly striking in the Festival Meadow scene. That such a key event in the civic life of the community should take place without the mayor and town councillors is utterly without precedent in the history of municipal culture. It is impossible to escape the conclusion that Nuremberg has been transformed into a kind of "aesthetic state" inspired by Schiller's series of letters *Über die ästhetische Erziehung des Menschen* (On the aesthetic education of man).[26] This state is in a transitional phase between a system of government based on privilege and a democracy, just as the old, normative poetics of the Mastersingers are being turned into a new and free type of artistry supported by the people and grounded in the creativity of the individual. As such, this change reflects Sachs's maxim in his lesson in poetics in act 3.[27] When Walther asks him, "How shall I begin according to the rules?" Sachs retorts, "You make your own rules, then follow them" (GS 7:239).

Following the fiasco of Walther's Trial Song in act 1, Sachs had tried to explain to the other Masters that his singing was not devoid of rules but merely that it obeyed other laws, even though Walther had not consciously grasped them.

> Des Ritters Lied und Weise,
> sie fand ich neu, doch nicht verwirrt;
> verließ er uns're G'leise,
> schritt er doch fest und unbeirrt.
> Wollt ihr nach Regeln messen,
> was nicht nach eurer Regeln Lauf,
> der eig'nen Spur vergessen,
> sucht davon erst die Regeln auf!
>
> (GS 7:185)

> [The knight's song and tune
> struck me as new, but not confused;
> if he left our well-trodden paths,
> he at least strode firmly and unwaveringly.
> If you want to judge by rules
> something that does not accord with your rules,
> forget your own ways
> and first seek out the rules.]

Here Sachs shows great astuteness in stressing the fact that all artistic rules are historically determined, whereas the Masters are carrying on as though their norms will last forever, ignoring their origins and historical development. Sachs clearly senses that in this way the art of the Mastersingers runs the risk of growing ossified and, by becoming academic, losing its popular basis. It needs a change of style and to be revived by the "popular spirit," hence his suggestion that once a year the townspeople should be the "judge" at the song contest (GS 7:174). It is a revolutionary idea. The Masters can decide on the rules only during a year-long parliamentary term, after which they must have themselves and the rules legitimized by the townsfolk.

Gesteht, ich kenn' die Regeln gut;
und daß die Zunft die Regeln bewahr',
bemüh' ich mich selbst schon manches Jahr.
Doch einmal im Jahre fänd' ich's weise,
daß man die Regeln selbst probir',
ob in der Gewohnheit trägem G'leise,
ihr' Kraft und Leben sich nicht verlier':
    und ob ihr der Natur
    noch seid auf rechter Spur,
    das sagt euch nur
    wer nichts weiß von der Tabulatur.

(GS 7:174–75)

[You'll admit that I know the rules well;
and I've busied myself this many a year
to see that the guild maintains the rules.
But once a year I think it wise
to test the rules themselves
and see whether in the dull course of habit
they have lost any of their strength and life;
    and whether you are still
    on the right track with nature
    is something you will be told only
    by someone who knows nothing of the *Tabulatur*.]

Meistergesang runs the risk of degenerating into an aristocratic art form remote from the people and hence of suffering the same fate as the other arts practiced by the nobility, all of which had died out. After all, that is why Walther sold his estates: "What drove me to Nuremberg was my love of art" (GS 7:166). Nuremberg's burghers feel a sense of pride at the knowledge that their art has replaced that of the aristocracy, and Pogner announces with a certain self-importance that "in the far-flung German empire we alone still cultivate art" (GS 7:172). This, of course, produces the paradoxical situation whereby the burghers are turning into aristocrats as a result of their ossifying art, whereas the aristocrat is joining the middle classes in order to revive art in the spirit of the people.

On Midsummer Day the Mastersingers exchange the hermetic and academic world of the *Singschule* (singing school) for the public arena of the popular festival, migrating from church chancel to open meadow. By appealing to "laymen's ears" (GS 7:171), they hope to demonstrate the popular basis of their art.

D'rum mocht's euch nie gereuen,
daß jährlich am Sankt Johannisfest,
statt daß das Volk man kommen läßt,
herab aus hoher Meister-Wolk'
ihr selbst euch wendet zu dem Volk'.

(GS 7:175)

[And so you should not regret it
if each year on Saint John's Day,
instead of making the people come to you,
you descend from your clouds
and appeal to the people in person.]

Thus Hans Sachs. But if the Masters really want to please the populace and if the festival is not to be a meaningless ceremony, as it appears to have become over time, then the townspeople should be allowed to have a say in judging the competition and not merely rubber-stamp the Masters' decision. This suggestion on Sachs's part is turned down, and he seems happy to accept this: "The girl's casting vote is enough for me" (GS 7:176), even though he had previously insisted that "a woman's opinion, completely untutored, seems to me just as valid as popular opinion" (GS 7:174).

By the end of the opera, however, Sachs has achieved precisely what he sought in vain to obtain in act 1. The new art that triumphs on the Festival Meadow in the person of Walther is no longer maintained by a privileged few but by the townspeople as a whole. When Walther ends his song, he is acclaimed by the populace: "Give him the laurel wreath. His be the prize!" (GS 7:269). Only now do the Masters—who in Wagner's imaginary Nuremberg replace the town councillors of history—rise to their feet and decide to confirm the townspeople's decision: "Yes, fair singer! Take the garland! Your song has won you the Masters' prize" (GS 7:269). In this way, the Masters put into practice the very reform that they had so emphatically turned down in act 1.

Art and artists alone set the tone in this totally aestheticized community, hence Hans Sachs's proclamation at the end of his closing address:

> Zerging' in Dunst
> das heil'ge röm'sche Reich,
> uns bliebe gleich
> die heil'ge deutsche Kunst.

(GS 7:271)

> [Though the Holy Roman Empire
> should dissolve in mist,
> we'd still be left
> with holy German art.]

These lines were evidently intended as a rebuttal of Heine's dictum of 1831: "The art of the present day must perish because its principle is still rooted in the superannuated *ancien régime*, in the Holy Roman Empire's past."[28] Wagner's counterthesis is that, even if the Holy Roman Empire *is* a thing of the past, its art is always with us. When the portals of art are thrown open in the future, it will be not to the "new art" prophesied by Heine, an art in "enthusiastic concord" with the "new age" and with the "politics of the day" and that "does not need to borrow its symbols from the insipid past,"[29] but to an art that is both old *and* new, an art divorced from politics and yet (or precisely because of that) in perfect accord with life. "Es klang so alt, und war doch so neu" [It sounded so old, and yet was so new], Sachs says of Walther's Trial Song (GS 7:198).

In his diary jottings of 1865, published in 1878 under the title "What Is German?" Wagner provided, as it were, a prose commentary on these lines from *Die Meistersinger*. He wrote: "Only with the loss of external political power, i.e., with the abandoned significance of the Holy Roman Empire, whose demise we lament today as the end of German majesty: only now is the essential German character really beginning to develop" (GS 10:39). Both this quotation and the lines from the end of *Die Meistersinger* cited earlier have a remarkable parallel in the Schiller's prose sketch of a poem that dates from 1797 and to which its first editor, Bernhard Suphan, gave the title "Deutsche Größe" (German greatness). "The Germans," wrote Schiller, "have established their own independent worth, which has nothing to do with any political worth that they may have, and even if the empire were to perish, German dignity would still be unassailable"; and "while the political empire totters, the spiritual empire has become increasingly secure and more perfect."[30] (Wagner, I should add, cannot have known these lines because they were not published until 1902.)

In his speech *Leiden und Größe Richard Wagners*, Thomas Mann referred to the lines from the end of the opera as a "key statement" expressing "a downright anarchic indifference to political structures, as long as German intellectual and spiritual values—'German art'—are preserved intact."[31] Politics becomes a democratized art, the German empire an aesthetic state with a constitution based on Schiller's series of letters *Über die ästhetische Erziehung des Menschen*: the "will of the whole" is consummated "through the nature of the individual," lending the latter a "social character" and thus "bringing harmony into society." "In the Aesthetic State everything—even the tool which serves—is a free citizen, having equal rights with the noblest." Here alone, argues Schiller, was the "ideal of equality" achieved.

> In the midst of the fearful kingdom of forces, and in the midst of the sacred kingdom of laws, the aesthetic impulse to form is at work, unnoticed, on the building of a third joyous kingdom of play and of semblance, in which man is relieved of the shackles of circumstance, and released from all that might be called constraint, alike in the physical and in the moral sphere.[32]

In the Nuremberg of *Die Meistersinger*, this aesthetico-political ideal becomes a reality, with the Festival Meadow providing a setting for what Schiller describes as the effect of taste, this being the constituent principle of the aesthetic state.

> From within the Mysteries of Science, taste leads knowledge out into the broad daylight of Common Sense, and transforms a monopoly of the Schools into the common possession of Human Society as a whole. In the kingdom of taste even the mightiest genius must divest itself of its majesty, and stoop in all humility to the mind of a little child.[33]

This is what constitutes Sachs's popularity, whereas Beckmesser, who zealously guards the "monopoly of the school," is ultimately exposed to shame and public ridicule.

This is not to say that there is not also an important difference between Wagner the cultural patriot and Schiller the Enlightenment cosmopolitan. Where Schiller speaks of human society, Wagner prefers to speak of the "folk," and where Schiller refers to "a sense of community," Wagner invokes the "spirit of the folk." Moreover, Wagner, unlike Schiller, had a covert political aim in mind when conjuring up his vision of a town transformed into an aesthetic state. On 24 July 1866, two years before the premiere of *Die Meistersinger*, he wrote to Ludwig, who was then toying with the idea of abdicating, and advised him to leave Munich, with its "popish intrigues" and the "terrible power enjoyed by its priests," and to settle in Nuremberg, with its "Enlightened, free-thinking population." There he could enjoy the "fresh Franconian air" and "breathe freely again." Wagner's hatred of the reactionary ultramontane spirit prevailing in a city that the king should abandon "to those to whom it already belongs on the strength of its name"[34] helps to explain the infamous lines about "foreign mists and foreign trumpery" in Sachs's closing address (GS 7:270). This is the historical background to these lines, with their implicit reference to the linguistic and cultural alienation of the empire from the folk following the death of Emperor Maximilian.[35] These lines sound far less chauvinistic when we not only know their historical context but are aware that Wagner was drawing a distinction between the reactionary city of Munich and the Enlightened and "free-thinking" Nuremberg.[36] It was doubly ironic that *Die Meistersinger* should receive its first performance in a city whose spirit it so opposed.

BECKMESSER: A JEW IN THE THORNBUSH?
EXCURSUS ON JEWS AND MUSIC IN *DIE MEISTERSINGER*

In exegesis be daring and bold!
If it makes no sense, add sense of your own!
—*Goethe*, Zahme Xenien

Sachs's closing address remains *the* major stumbling block in interpreting Wagner's music dramas, and in the context of what some writers have alleged to be the Jewish caricaturization of the outcast town clerk, it is also Exhibit A in the case against Wagner and his ostensibly pernicious ideology. This case claims that his national chauvinism and anti-Semitism are not confined to his philosophical writings but also infiltrate his music dramas, permeating their very substance. Is this really true of the character of the town clerk? In short, who exactly is Sixtus Beckmesser?

According to Eduard Hanslick, the answer is very simple. In his autobiography, the Viennese critic describes the Nuremberg town clerk and the Marker in the Mastersingers' guild as the composer's "most readily intelligible" figure.

> The town clerk Beckmesser in *Die Meistersinger* is a typical pedant, interested only in all that is petty and trivial, a philistine with no sense of beauty, an intellectually limited, narrow-minded word catcher who chalks up every note that deviates from the "rules"

as though it were a violation of art itself and, by totting up the individual mistakes, thinks he has destroyed the singer.

If, Hanslick went on, Wagnerians were to call him Beckmesser because of his criticism of Wagner, they would merely have "shown that they do not understand their Master and his most readily intelligible figure," as his own criticisms of Wagner were concerned not with "individual violations of the rules" but always with the "fundamental demands of music as an art."[37]

Hanslick seems to have been unaware of the fact that in his prose drafts of 1861, Wagner gave the Marker the name of Veit Hanslich, thereby directing his satire explicitly at his archenemy. Hanslick evidently felt that he was not the butt of Wagner's satire, in which regard his account differs from the one found in Wagner's autobiography, where the latter claims that when he declaimed the libretto at Josef Standhartner's home in Vienna in 1862, Hanslick, who was among the invited guests, had regarded the "entire poem as a pasquinade directed at him in person" and had felt correspondingly offended (ML 720). There is absolutely no reference to this in Hanslick's review of the Viennese premiere of *Die Meistersinger* on 27 February 1870. Quite the opposite, in fact; here Hanslick distances himself from Beckmesser's pedantic critique of Walther's melodies, which he describes as "felicitous rays of sunshine" in an otherwise wearisome first act. Consciously or otherwise, he gives no indication that Wagner may have had him in mind with the figure of Beckmesser.

Although Hanslick was critical of the poetic and musical conception of the opera, it was clear to him that the basic idea behind it was the "contrast between free poetry welling up from the inmost inspiration, and poetasterism of a mindlessly unimaginative kind," and he ended his review by conceding that a "freak" like *Die Meistersinger* was "nonetheless more interesting and more stimulating than a dozen run-of-the-mill operas by any of the countless opera composers currently active in Germany, whose works, though 'correct,' would still be accorded far more honor than they deserve if their composers were to be described as semi-talented."[38] In short, Hanslick regarded himself as very different from Beckmesser and raised no objections to the way in which the character was drawn.

In his autobiography, Hanslick insisted that his criticisms of Wagner were invariably directed at their underlying trend, a trend that could not be questioned merely by drawing up a list of individual infringements of individual rules. Yet, in his view, the Wagnerites always made the mistake of trying to prove that their hero was a genius by listing insignificant details, thus doing the very thing that Wagner ridiculed in Beckmesser. "Adulation, too, has its Beckmessers," Hanslick added laconically.[39]

There is really nothing that we can add to Hanslick's characterization of Beckmesser, which corresponds closely to Wagner's own interpretation of the figure as a typical—and typically German—pedant of a kind that he was to encounter some years later in the person of Ulrich von Wilamowitz-Möllendorf and the latter's polemical attack on Nietzsche's *Die Geburt der Tragödie* (The birth of tragedy). Every nation, he wrote in his open letter to Nietzsche of 12 June 1872, has within it "the seed of cretinism." In the case of the Germans, this found expression in their "envy and, related to it, their spitefulness, combined with an insincerity all the more pernicious in that it gives the impression of a worthiness inherited from former times" (GS 9:301). This could have been written with Beckmesser in mind, the most typical representative of all the Germans' most negative qualities.

In 1851, in *A Communication to My Friends*, Wagner had defined Beckmesser's role as follows: "I conceived of Hans Sachs as the final manifestation of the artistically creative spirit of the folk and in this sense contrasted him with the petty bourgeois Mastersingers, to whose unremittingly comical pedantry, with its insistence on the poetic rules of the *Tabulatur*, I gave concrete expression in the person of the 'Marker' " (GS 4:284–85). In a conversation with Cosima on 16 March 1873, Wagner adopted a more positive approach to this petty bourgeois German aspect of the work and its "unremitting comedy": taken together, the "popular poet" (Sachs), the "enthusiastic" amateur (Walther), and the "respectable pedantry" of the Mastersingers revealed "the German in his true character, in his best light."

"Pedantry" is the word that Wagner repeatedly uses to describe the figure of the Marker, and it certainly sums up Beckmesser's attributes as a comic character. From the Renaissance onward, the learned pedant was a popular object of satire for moralists (Montaigne devoted a whole essay to him), and he was also a traditional character in European comedy, most notably in the form of the *dottore* (doctor) in the commedia dell'arte tradition.[40]

It is this tradition, with its stock repertory of characters and motifs, that Wagner picks up, especially in act 2 of the opera.[41] Beckmesser is the aging lover from whose apparently safe grasp his bride is snatched by a younger man. As such, he is the sort of character who recurs in countless variants in improvised comedies and their literary successors. At the same time, Wagner has recourse in this act to the slapstick comedy of the Nuremberg Shrovetide plays, which always included a fight among their stock features. Beckmesser's nocturnal serenade, the women's disguises and mistaken identities, and the ensuing beating also look back to the motivic tradition of Spanish cloak-and-dagger comedies, a tradition on which Mozart drew in *Don Giovanni*; here the nighttime scene beneath Donna Elvira's balcony involves a related series of situations, with the men's disguise followed by a case of mistaken identity, Don Giovanni's serenade, and, finally, Leporello's beating.

This sort of comedy of intrigue and situation cannot be judged by the criteria of the theater of realism. Still less is it possible to adduce moral arguments here. To quote Schiller, the comedy of intrigue presupposes "absolute moral indifference,"[42] even involving a certain cruelty in terms of the spectator's malicious delight in human failings (suffice it to recall the notorious stuttering of the pedants who people these works), to say nothing of the delight in seeing the antihero and loser duped and exposed to ridicule: laughter at another's misfortune provides a sense of compensatory satisfaction, or so today's psychoanalysts would argue.

The extent to which we feel this malicious pleasure is proportional to the height from which the character falls from grace. Beckmesser is by no means predestined to play such a role. After all, he is a member of the most respected group of people in Nuremberg; unlike the historical Hans Sachs, he sits on the town council, and as town clerk he holds one of the most prestigious posts in the city. The Mastersingers, moreover, have appointed him their Marker, the supreme representative of their art. As such, he is far from being an outsider in a way that comic characters normally are but is one of the Nuremberg Masters, even a kind of first among equals. Not even Sachs himself has achieved this status, so that in act 2 Beckmesser can reproach his rival for being envious of his success: "It's the fact that he's not yet been elected Marker that torments this embittered cobbler." And he threatens to use all his influence with the other Masters to ensure that Sachs is prevented from being elected to the post: "You'll never be elected Marker!" (GS 7:216).

Yet, as we have already seen, the high regard in which he is held among the town's dignitaries does not prevent him from being mocked by the townsfolk, who describe him as "stupid" and laugh at his ungainly platform manner: "He's almost falling over!" (GS 7:263). Few scenes are more archetypally comic than that of the scholar who lives on a higher plane and falls to earth; among its earliest instances is a passage in Plato's *Theaetetus* where Socrates describes how the philosopher Thales fell into a well while looking at the stars and how he was laughed at by a Thracian servant girl.[43] This is exactly how the townspeople react when they see Beckmesser tottering on the singer's rostrum and finally falling to earth in a figurative sense. According to the stage direction, this academic pedant "disappears among the townspeople" following his disastrous attempt at the Prize Song (GS 7:265). Given his remoteness from the people, it is difficult not to regard this as a tragicomic paradox.

The high regard in which the burghers of Nuremberg hold Beckmesser and the contempt the common people feel for him are the result of his "erudition" (GS 7:187). The only Master who is not a craftsman by profession, he is also the only one to have a Latin forename, Sixtus. This in itself signifies a purely academic, scholastic training remote from the spirit of the people. In spite of his secret and reluctant admiration for Sachs, he shares the reservations of the Humanist and Enlightenment writers of the seventeenth and eighteenth centuries who adopted a deeply dismissive attitude toward the poetry of the historical Sachs. Time and again Beckmesser expresses his mistrust of Sachs's popularity. When Kothner insists that art should not "go chasing after the favors of the common herd," Beckmesser comments, with a sideways glance at Sachs: "This impudent fellow has already gone far in that direction, generally writing popular street songs" (GS 7:175). This is very much the sort of criticism that the writers of the Enlightenment leveled at Nuremberg's cobbler-poet.

Wagner, as we know, was intimately familiar with Goethe's *Faust*, and there is no doubt that, in part, he modeled Beckmesser on his namesake in Goethe's masterpiece; here Faust's assistant, Wagner, is likewise a caricature of a pedant who, remote from life, is completely absorbed by the rules of his Humanistic schooling, vaguely aware of his own sterility, and as a result keen to attach himself to a genuinely creative individual—in this case Faust, just as Beckmesser is "always by Sachs's side" (GS 7:170). In short, Beckmesser is a representative of the outdated rules of Humanist and Enlightenment poetry, rules that, generations earlier, had brought the historical Sachs into such disrepute. Now this poetry is itself the subject of mockery.

As Egon Voss has pointed out, Beckmesser inhabits yet another intellectual world, that of traditional opera[44] and, more generally, "absolute music," with its indifference to language and its specific patterns of phrasing and emphasis. In the figure of the Marker, Wagner has created an emblematic composer of conventional operas, a composer who manhandles the language in his attempt to do justice to musical rules. Beckmesser is not at all interested in providing his own words on the Festival Meadow; the text is essentially a matter of indifference to him as a composer, being as interchangeable as the linguistic structure of the libretto was among traditional opera composers. As he knows how popular Hans Sachs is as a poet and knows, moreover, to what extent the townspeople regard him with mockery and skepticism, he hopes to win their approval with a poem by Sachs. He avails himself of a song that he believes is the work of a rival who had played a mean trick on him the previous night. In the Marienbad prose draft of 1845, this is additionally motivated by the fact that it is not the guild but the townsfolk who award the prize at the public competition (SS 11:344–45).

Beckmesser's humiliation stems from the fact that unable to grasp the novelty of what he assumes to be Sachs's poem, he attempts to force it into the straitjacket of his own pedantic rules, so distorting it by its absurd tune that the result is sheer nonsense. Thus poetry takes its revenge when treated with such contempt. One cannot, of course, deny the psychological implausibility of this farcical turn of events. In his delight at the imbroglio and at the comedy of a situation in which, to quote Schiller, "the characters exist solely for the events that befall them,"[45] Wagner effortlessly ignored the demands of real-life plausibility. Or should we assume that Beckmesser garbles the Prize Song because, as a Humanist who writes in Latin, he has difficulty in deciphering Sachs's German handwriting?

In his *Geschichte der poetischen National-Literatur der Deutschen* (History of the poetic national literature of the Germans)—one of the most important sources of *Die Meistersinger*—Georg Gottfried Gervinus claimed that the historical Mastersingers were largely concerned with the novelty of their melodies, not their words, a claim that could have led Wagner to conclude that there was a fundamental imbalance between words and music similar to the one that he noted in modern opera.[46] In this way, Beckmesser becomes a caricature of the "absolute musician" who shows scant regard for the structure of his poetic source (here the poem that he assumes to be by his "librettist," Hans Sachs, but is in fact by Walther). Even in Beckmessser's Serenade in act 2, Sachs had already criticized the nonsensical word-setting and accentuation. "I think that tone and word should fit," he tells Beckmesser. In other words, musical and linguistic phrasing should be in agreement with each other (GS 7:220).

Sachs suggests an alternative way of accenting the opening lines of the serenade, an alternative that reflects the meaning of the words, but Beckmesser is so obsessed with his fixed musical rules and so determined to find a rhyme at all costs that he fails to heed the advice he is given. Sachs's lesson in poetics falls on stony ground, in marked contrast to the parallel situation with Walther in act 3. At the end of the opera, Beckmesser plays no part in the new aesthetic consensus that has arisen, and he remains the only person to learn nothing from Sachs's pedagogically inspired attempt to mediate between old and new.

In the opening act, David explains the rules of Meistergesang to Walther, stressing the interrelationship between singer, poet, and Master. The first two have no place in Walther's or Wagner's world of aesthetic ideas. For them, singer and poet are in the same relation to each other as absolute musician and librettist. The poet's task is to put together the words and rhymes in such a way that "they exactly fit a Master's tone." In other words, the words have to fit an existing musical formal pattern, a demand that is the exact opposite of Wagner's own poetical rules for the musical drama. Conversely, the Master, in David's words, is "the poet who, of his own endeavor, fashions a new melody out of notes to fit words and rhymes of his own invention." This is how the musical dramatist proceeds. Significantly, Walther replies:

> So bleibt mir nichts als der Meisterlohn!
>> Soll ich hier singen,
>> kann's nur gelingen,
> find' ich zum Vers auch den eig'nen Ton.

(GS 7:163–64)

> [Then the Master's reward alone shall be mine!
>> If I'm to sing here,
>> I can succeed only
> if I find the right tone for the verse.]

For Walther, only when acting together can singer and poet produce the means to sing and write poetry.

The Master, then, is the man who invents a "new tune" to go with words of his own composition. Beckmesser, by contrast, is not capable of writing a decent poem of his own or even of inventing a melody to fit the words of a plagiarized song. Twice he fails to produce an acceptable song. Faust's famous sideswipe at his assistant, Wagner, could just as well be applied to Beckmesser: "Well, well, keep at it! ply the shears and paste, / Concoct from feasts of other men your hashes, / And should the thing be wanting fire or taste, / Blow into flame your little heap of ashes!" (ll. 538–41; trans. Philip Wayne).

The pedant of the moralistic comedy tradition in his typically German guise as a blinkered academic; the aging lover who, in keeping with the rules of the commedia dell'arte, loses his bride to her much younger lover; the philistine with no understanding of original art—an art that is always changing and renewing itself, repeatedly overstepping traditional rules; and, finally, the absolute musician unable to appreciate poetic structures and ultimately, therefore, struck down by his comic nemesis: this is Beckmesser. How is it possible, in the face of all this evidence, to see in him a covert caricature of a Jew?

The libretto itself contains abolutely nothing to support this hypothesis—a hypothesis that has now more or less acquired the status of a proven fact in writings on Wagner. The mere fact that Beckmesser sits on the town council and enjoys considerable prestige both artistically and socially precludes any affinity with the social role of Jews in German history; certainly a Jew would never have enjoyed such prestige in sixteenth-century Nuremberg. Nor does Wagner himself offer any support for this theory elsewhere in his writings or letters or even in the confidences that he imparted to Cosima, who religiously recorded her husband's every anti-Semitic outburst. In short, it is impossible to answer this troublesome question by reference either to Wagner's letters and writings, where he may, of course, have felt the need to be diplomatic, or to any other instances where such a need did not arise. (The same is true of all the other characters in whom Wagner's critics have claimed to find Jewish features.)[47]

A trawl through the records documenting the reception history of the opera during the following decades likewise proves unrewarding; neither the *Bayreuther Blätter*, which would surely have been the first to receive and decode any secret signs from Wagner in this regard, nor the polemical writings of Wagner's enemies contain any supporting evidence. This is all the more remarkable in that in 1869, a year after the triumphant first performance of *Die Meistersinger* in Munich, Wagner republished *Jews in Music*, leading to violent Jewish protests against the first performance of the work in Vienna, with Hanslick mentioning the "famous Jewish pamphlet" in the very first line of his review, without, however, drawing any conclusions from it for the contents of the opera. Yet contemporaries would surely have had every reason to look for signs of anti-Semitism in an opera whose early performances had unfortunately coincided with the reappearance of the "famous Jewish pamphlet." Yet the Viennese reviewers rarely revealed any suspicions in this regard, the occasional protests being limited to the fact that local audiences were being regaled with a work by a notorious Jew hater.

Only a handful of contemporaries seem to have suspected that the work contains allusions to anti-Semitism. On 16 March 1870, for example, we find Cosima Wagner writing to Nietzsche: "Have you heard that a rumor is circulating in Vienna to the effect that Beckmesser's serenade is an old Jewish song in which W[agner] wanted to make fun of J[ewish] church music, with the result that the serenade was the signal for booing!"[48] For Cosima, the claim that Wagner had wanted to satirize synagogue music in Beckmesser's Serenade was no more than a mischievous invention of Wagner's enemies and, as such, was designed to ensure the work's failure. In spite of this, the same claim has been repeated in our own day. The English Wagnerian Barry Millington has sought to interpret the melodic line of Beckmesser's serenade as a parody of the "cantorial style" of the music sung in synagogues,[49] but his evidence is purely speculative. More recently, Hermann Danuser has systematically refuted this line of argument and at the same time exploded the popular myth that Beckmesser writes a "more advanced" style of music than Walther. Rather, Beckmesser's vocal line—significantly, it is supported by no orchestral melody—is an example of amateurish vocal music of an unvocal kind, short-breathed, mechanically made up of elements that quickly grind to a halt on a fermata, and, as such, very much unique unto itself. The meaningless melismas, with their chains of fourths reflecting the way in which the lute is tuned, are unrelated to synagogue chanting, with which Wagner was in any case unfamiliar, but are intended merely to represent the absurdity of a self-sufficient melodic line divorced from its source in the text.[50]

A second hypothesis, by contrast, deserves closer examination. This idea was first found decades after the first performance of *Die Meistersinger*, yet it has left an indelible mark on more recent writings on Wagner, having been repeated and even fine-tuned so often that it has virtually acquired the status of an authenticated fact. I am referring to Adorno's claim in his *Versuch über Wagner* (Essay on Wagner, 1952) that "all the rejects of Wagner's works are caricatures of Jews."[51] Danuser has described this claim as "logically untenable and factually revealing," inasmuch as it equates "negative characteristics in general with negative Jewish characteristics in particular," an equation that Danuser describes as simply unacceptable: "Negative characterization is limited to a specific work and obeys the laws of a universal type of reaction, not the particular exclusion mechanisms of Wagner's anti-Semitism."[52]

Adorno mentions three characters whom he regards as caricatures of Jews: the Nibelungs Alberich and Mime and the "impotent intellectual critic Hanslick-Beckmesser," whose model he believed he had found in one of the fairy tales of the Brothers Grimm that were familiar to Wagner: "Nothing is more apposite than the story of the Jew in the bramble bush." And he goes on to quote an extract from the tale: "Now as the Jew stood there caught in the bramble bush, the worthy lad was overcome by a mischievous idea: he took up his fiddle and began to play it. At once the Jew's feet started to twitch, and he began to leap about; and the more the lad played, the better the Jew danced." Wagner's music, Adorno concludes, is "a worthy lad that treats the villains in like manner."[53]

Again, Millington has sought to adduce detailed evidence to prove that Wagner identified Beckmesser with the Jew in the thornbush and invested the town clerk with correspondingly anti-Semitic features. Conversely, the American Germanist Hans Rudolf Vaget rejects the thesis advanced by Adorno, Millington, and all the other writers who have tried to posit a direct link between the fairy tale and the opera on the basis of internal evidence and allegorical speculation. At the same time, however, he concedes that there may be allusive references to the fairy tale, "The Jew in the Thornbush," at least on a subtextual level, thereby functioning as a "potentially anti-Semitic element" that would be picked up by those in the know and allow for an anti-Semitic interpretation to evolve in the work's subsequent reception history.[54] Yet it remains to be proved that *Die Meistersinger* has anything to do with the Grimms' fairy tale at all, whether on a textual or subtextual level.[55]

Even Adorno's claim that of all the fairy tales in the German tradition, none was closer to Wagner's heart than "The Jew in the Thornbush" is unproven. "The Jew in the Thornbush" was almost less well known in the nineteenth century than it is today, being included in virtually none of the selections of the Grimms' fairy tales. Whether Wagner had ever read such an obscure tale is extremely unlikely, and he could certainly not presuppose any knowledge of it on the part of his audiences. Still less would subtle allusions and the odd nod and wink to those in the know have been understood as such. Prior to Adorno, not a single writer had hit on the idea of drawing a parallel between Beckmesser and *Die Meistersinger* on the one hand and "The Jew in the Thornbush" on the other. If a substantive element in a work of art has gone undetected for almost a century, either the work is a failure or the element in question does not exist.

A detailed examination of the two texts ineluctably leads to the conclusion that the purported parallels between them rest simply on a series of misunderstandings. The contents of the fairy tale may be summarized as follows. Its main character is a typical fairy-tale hero for whom everything works out well in the end. One day he meets a "little man" on whom he takes pity and to whom he gives the three-pence that he has received from his last employer. In return, the man grants him three wishes. The lad asks for a fowling piece that will hit everything he fires at, for a fiddle that will make all who hear it dance as soon as he plays it, and, third, for people to be unable to refuse whatever he asks of them. The manikin grants him his wishes, and the lad goes on his way.

> It wasn't long before he met an old Jew with a long goatee beard. He was standing there, listening to the singing of a bird that was sitting high up in the topmost branches of a tree. "My goodness!" he exclaimed. "How can such a little creature have such a great big voice! If only it were mine!" . . . "If that's all," said the lad, "we'll have the bird down in no time." And with that he took aim and shot the bird, so that it fell to earth in a thornbush.

When the Jew crawls into the thornbush to fetch the dead bird, the lad picks up his fiddle. The Jew is compelled to dance and can rid himself of his compulsion only by persuading the lad to stop playing, which he does by giving him his purse of gold. But the Jew then runs off to the nearest judge and accuses the lad of stealing his money and beating him. The judge believes him and condemns the lad to be hanged for street robbery. The lad is already standing on the ladder, waiting to be executed, when he asks the judge for permission to play his fiddle one last time. His wish is granted, and the lad begins to play, with the result that everyone present starts to dance increasingly senselessly. Finally the judge agrees to spare the lad's life as long as he stops playing. Exhausted by dancing a second time, the Jew confesses that he had stolen the purse that he gave the lad, and he is led away to be hanged in place of the apprentice.[56]

As I have already noted, "The Jew in the Thornbush" played virtually no part in the reception history of the Grimms' fairy tales. As Vaget has demonstrated, only as a result of the experiences of the Third Reich was more attention paid to this particular tale, with Arnold Zweig, for example, describing it as "a true declaration on the part of the German folk soul in the matter of the Jews" and even claiming that the tale contains within it "everything that constitutes European anti-Semitism," including "the sadism of the concentration camps—the fairground atmosphere with its jokes and pranks at the pogrom."[57] However understandable this interpretation of the fairy tale may be against the background of the National Socialists' persecution of the Jews, it has to be said that "The Jew in the Thornbush" contains so many traditional fairy-tale motifs—the compulsive urge to dance at the sound of a magic instrument, the bird that when shot falls into a hedge, the dancing in the thornbush, the condemned man's last request and his saving himself by playing a magic instrument, and so on—that it is difficult to construe it as specifically anti-Jewish. Significantly, the story can be traced back to an older farce in which the role of the Jew is taken by a runaway monk; here, then, we have the popular

motif of anticlerical sentiment, whereas in the later version this becomes the
equally popular (or unpopular) motif of anti-Semitism. The stereotypes are interchangeable. This fact alone should discourage us from regarding the negatively
comic characterization of the Jew in the Grimms' fairy tale as a harbinger of
Auschwitz, even if, undeniably, the anti-Semitic stereotypes in the story as it appears in the third edition of the *Kinder- und Hausmärchen* (Grimms' fairy tales,
1837), from which I have just quoted, are markedly more pronounced than in the
first edition (1815).[58]

But what does "The Jew in the Thornbush" have in common with *Die
Meistersinger*? If we return it to its original context and free it from the ideas that
have been projected back onto it from a later ideological perspective, there is nothing to link the two texts apart from a handful of motivic coincidences. Writers who
incline to the view that "The Jew in the Thornbush" provides a key to understanding
Die Meistersinger refer in particular to Walther's "Meisterlied" in act 1. This song
is improvised by Walther from its enthusiastic opening (in which he picks up
Beckmesser's injunction to begin ["Fanget an"]) to its defiant ending. The subject
of his opening strophe, which is still dominated by Walther's sense of almost effusive exultation, is "the sweet song of spring" sung by the forest, which is contrasted
with the image of grudging winter (at this point we start to hear the sound of
Beckmesser's chalk scratching away censoriously inside his enclosed booth).

> In einer Dornenhecken,
> von Neid und Gram verzehrt,
> mußt' er sich da verstecken,
> der Winter, Grimm-bewehrt:
> von dürrem Laub umrauscht
> er lauert da und lauscht,
> wie er das frohe Singen
> zu Schaden könnte bringen.
>
> (GS 7:183)

> [In a hawthorn hedge,
> consumed by jealousy and grief,
> winter, grimly armed,
> had to hide away:
> with dry leaves rustling round him,
> he lies in wait and listens
> to see if he can spoil
> this joyful singing.]

We are clearly dealing with an allegory here: the spring song is Walther's own
song; winter is the envy-wracked Beckmesser; his booth is the hawthorn hedge;
and the dry leaves represent the condescending pedantry of the Marker, who is totally cut off from real life.[59]

Walther's song is then interrupted by scenes of confusion among the Masters,
leading him to stand on the chair on which the rules require him to remain seated

and to declaim the final strophe of his unmasterly Mastersong while the Masters continue to squabble around him.

> Aus finst'rer Dornenhecken
> die Eule rauscht' hervor,
> thät rings mit Kreischen wecken
> der Raben heis'ren Chor:
> in nächt'gem Heer zu Hauf,
> wie krächzen all' da auf,
> mit ihren Stimmen, den hohlen,
> die Elstern, Kräh'n und Dohlen!
>
> Auf da steigt
> mit gold'nem Flügelpaar
> ein Vogel wunderbar:
> sein strahlend hell Gefieder
> licht in den Lüften blinkt;
> schwebt selig hin und wieder,
> zu Flug und Flucht mir winkt.
> . . . .
>
> auf da steigt,
> ob Meister-Kräh'n ihm ungeneigt
> das stolze Minne-Lied.—
> Ade, ihr Meister, hienied'!

(GS 7:189)

> [From a dark hawthorn hedge
> the owl shot forth
> and with its screeching woke
> the hoarse chorus of ravens:
> in a vast nocturnal army
> they all begin to croak
> with their hollow voices,
> magpies, crows, and jackdaws!
>
> There rises up
> on a pair of golden wings
> a wonderful bird:
> its dazzling plumage
> glints brightly in the breezes;
> blissfully sweeping back and forth,
> it bids me fly and flee.
> . . . .
>
> upward it climbs,
> though Master-Crows disdain it,
> the proud love song.—
> Farewell, you Masters, below!]

In the earlier part of his song, the carping critic Beckmesser, crouching in his booth, was compared to winter lying in wait in a hawthorn hedge. Walther now expands on that allegory and turns it into a satire of the Masters in general. Beckmesser is now treated as an owl whose screeching sparks the Masters' squabbles, as they in turn are compared to a vast flock of cawing nocturnal birds whose discordant singing is heard inside the hedge, which has now become an allegory of lifeless, uncreative artistry. These night birds are contrasted with the magic bird with golden wings, which is a symbol of true art in the form of the genuine love song and soars aloft, fleeing from base pedantry and seeking the pure heights of creative freedom.

Is it really plausible that Walther's improvised allegory, closely reflecting each turn of events onstage, should conceal a reference to the Grimms' Jew in the thorn-bush merely because a bird and a thornbush are mentioned in the text? The motif of the thornbush has such a lengthy poetic tradition as an image of lifeless, desolate nature, with night birds as its typical attributes, that no unprejudiced reader would ever suspect a reminiscence of the thornbush in "The Jew in the Thornbush." There is absolutely no semantic connection between the bird and the thornbush in the Grimms' fairy tale on the one hand and those in Walther's Mastersong on the other; in the former they are merely requirements of the plot, and in the latter they have an allegorical and symbolic significance. Indeed, even their physical appearance is different in the two texts. In the fairy tale the bird is an ordinary natural phe-nomenon, whereas in Walther's song it is a magic creature with golden wings. In the fairy tale the thornbush has thorns that hurt, whereas in the song it contrasts with the living springtime forest and, as such, symbolizes the lifelessness of winter; there is a reference to its "dry leaves" but not to its thorns, and in consequence there is no question of anyone being injured by it. As a result, winter in its personified guise can hide in it.[60]

In the fairy tale, the Jew is portrayed as so acquisitive that he is prepared to suffer physical injury by crawling into the thornbush to retrieve the dead bird, whereas in the song winter is already ensconced in the bush from the outset, the barren na-ture of the bush being, as it were, its natural habitat. As a result, the song contains no reference to what, after all, is the central motif of the fairy tale: the dancing among the brambles. As for the bird, it does not fall dead into the bush but rises unhindered above the world of the "dark hawthorn hedge." In short, a comparison between the motifs of the bird and bush reveals only differences between the fairy tale and the song, neither of which overlaps with the other for even a moment in terms of its content or ideas. As there are no subsequent similarities between the text of the fairy tale and the later course of the action of Die Meistersinger, it may be taken as proven that "The Jew in the Thornbush" is of no relevance whatsoever to Die Meistersinger von Nürnberg.

The situation is so straightforward that Millington's assumption that there is a direct parallel between the fairy tale and the song is barely sustainable. Two partic-ularly egregious examples may serve to underline this point: first, Millington be-lieves that there is a parallel between Walther, who, in the final strophe of the song, stands on his chair and looks down on the Masters talking confusedly below him, and the apprentice of the fairy tale, who is depicted standing on the ladder leading up to the gallows; and, second, Millington argues that when Walther describes winter in the hedge as "Grimm-bewehrt," he is alluding to the Brothers Grimm and that "Grimm-bewehrt" (grimly armed) should be read as "Grimm-bewährt" (authenticated by Grimm). Are we really to believe that this negative allegorization of winter can appeal to the Brothers Grimm for its authentication? Even if Beckmesser has nothing to do with the Jew in the thornbush (and this should be clear by now), this still does not mean that he is not a Jew in either a literal or a figurative sense. Yet the allegory underlying Walther's song shows that Wagner cannot have intended to depict Beckmesser as a Jew. After all, Beckmesser is the most doctrinaire of the Masters, and, according to Sachs's closing address, the Masters embody all that is "German and genuine," in contrast to "foreign mists and foreign trumpery" (GS 7:270). If Beckmesser, either as winter in the thornbush or as an owl that wakens the "hoarse chorus" of the other nocturnal birds, is meant to be a Jew, then logically all the other Masters would have to be Jews too—for Beckmesser is nowhere stigmatized as an outsider. But Wagner cannot have had this in mind, otherwise the specifically German and the specifically Jewish would be identical. All attempts to interpret Beckmesser as a covert caricature of a Jew become so mired in contradictions with the text of the opera as to be ultimately untenable.

If this is so, how are we to interpret the fact that in the 1861 prose drafts of *Die Meistersinger* Wagner gave his Marker the name Hanslich—a name virtually indistinguishable from that of his archenemy Eduard Hanslick? This is the only proven fact that can lend any real credence to the claim that Wagner regarded Beckmesser as a Jew. Yet even this argument is easily refuted. At the time that Wagner prepared the first draft of *Die Meistersinger*, at Marienbad in 1845, he had yet to meet Hanslick, but soon he was on the best of terms with the critic, who was favorably impressed by *Tannhäuser* when he saw it in Dresden in September 1846. Hanslick published a detailed and positive review of it in the *Allgemeine Wiener Musikzeitung* and sent a copy of it to Wagner, who replied on 1 January 1847—a long letter that is one of the most important statements of his aesthetic outlook at this period. But in the 1845 prose draft, the figure of the as-yet-unnamed Marker is already a fully rounded character, with each of the comic situations in which he finds himself sketched out in detail. The reference to "Hanslich" was introduced in the 1861 drafts only after Wagner and Hanslick had fallen out, but no new features were added. As a result, it was only logical for Wagner to replace the name with that of Beckmesser when he started to prepare the libretto at the end of 1861. Wagner saw Beckmesser as the embodiment of an academic purist critic, which is also how he regarded Hanslick, with the result that Wagner's satirical barbs were undoubtedly directed at Hanslick, too. Also of relevance in this context is the fact that the Viennese critic was an out-and-out champion of "absolute music," a grotesquely distorted image of which is parodied in Wagner's description of Beckmesser's attempts at artistic production. By 1861 Wagner may have belatedly identified Beckmesser with Hanslick as a dogmatic critic and advocate of "absolute music," with its anachronistic fioriture and coloratura flourishes, but it is of no importance to Beckmesser's function in the opera whether or nor he is a Jew.

Millington disagrees. He believes that the nonsense verse that Beckmesser produces in the Festival Meadow illustrates the verbal and syntactical distortions of the German language that Wagner describes as typically Jewish in "Jews in Music" (GS 5:71). This comparison has already been convincingly refuted by Vaget, who argues that Beckmesser's garbling of what he thinks is Sachs's poem can be explained by reference to the "highly critical and embarrassing situation" in which he finds himself[61] and is typical of the "paradoxical, not to say oxymoronic role of the besotted pedant" in Humanist comedies.[62] If Beckmesser were a caricature of a Jew, he would have to speak in garbled sentences all the time, but this is by no means the case. He speaks a German that is barely distinguishable from that of the other Masters, in which respect he differs fundamentally from the pedants of Humanist comedy who are set apart from other characters by dint of their absurdly overlearned language, with its pseudo-Latin mannerisms designed to poke fun at their contempt for the language of the common herd.[63] If Wagner had wanted to portray Beckmesser even indirectly as a Jew, he could have used the convoluted speech patterns of the pedants found in earlier comedies, but he clearly had no such thought in mind. (The same is true of the character of Mime in the *Ring*. He, too, is said to be portrayed as a Jew. Yet he too speaks exactly the same alliterative language as the other characters in the cycle and is not, therefore, distinguished linguistically from them.)[64]

Wagner could have used a further stereotypical feature of the Renaissance pedant and, indeed, of "old men" in general as an indirect means of depicting Beckmesser as a Jew but which he failed to take advantage of: the characteristic of greed.[65] The elderly suitor of Renaissance comedy and its successors was invariably interested less in the young bride herself than in her fortune, a feature that survives even as late as *Der Rosenkavalier*. Surprisingly, Wagner ignored this traditional motif, even though it would have provided the only real link between Beckmesser and the Jew in the thornbush—further proof, if proof is needed, that it never occurred to him to make any connection between the typically German Marker and this or any other Jewish stereotype. Admittedly, Beckmesser accuses his rival of coveting Eva's sizable dowry: "Herr Sachs is after the goldsmith's rich legacy" (GS 7:243). It is, of course, a telltale suspicion, as people often accuse others of their own shortcomings, thereby exhibiting those faults as their own. But this is the only indirect reference in the text to any possible interest on Beckmesser's part in acquiring Pogner's fortune.

In short, the suggestion that in Beckmesser Wagner created a Jewish caricature is clearly contradicted by Beckmesser himself. The most recent writers on the subject—notably Jens Malte Fischer in his documentary monograph on "Jews in Music"—have suggested that although there may be no direct traces of Wagner's anti-Semitism in his music dramas, this anti-Semitism is nonetheless there, encoded, enciphered, and hidden away on what we would now describe as the level of a subtext.[66]

It is, of course, well known that literature and art in general, including even journalism, use coded messages to discuss subjects that are otherwise taboo. The existence of formal or informal censorship means that certain ideas are often treated subtextually; any direct statement is replaced by indirect signs and allusions that lie, as it were, beneath the surface of the text. As Ernst Jünger once said, censorship refines style. Authors count on this fact and may even play with it in order to ensure that their audiences can understand and decode their secret signals. Dolf Sternberger has drawn attention to a similarly covert style of writing that journalists are forced to use under dictatorships.[67] Nor is it only political and ideological considerations that oblige writers to resort to this type of coded language; sexual taboos are also sanctioned or circumvented in literature by being encoded. Whether of a political, ideological, aesthetic, or erotic nature, such encodings presuppose the existence of a taboo and a form of censorship that is imposed either by others or by the writer.

But what reason would Wagner have had to encode his anti-Semitism? Unfortunately, anti-Semitism was not a taboo subject at the time of *Die Meistersinger*, as is clear from the republication of "Jews in Music" shortly after the work's first performance. Why, then, would Wagner have encoded his anti-Semitism as a secret message in his opera while openly proclaiming it in his published articles and letters? The only conceivable motive would be the artistic quality of the work and the principle of aesthetic autonomy, in other words, the realization that art and ideological tendentiousness are mutually exclusive. If we accept this motivation, we must also concede that a work of art cannot be anti-Semitic. Be that as it may, subtextual signs of Wagner's anti-Semitism have yet to be identified in *Die Meistersinger*, and it is senseless to continue to look for them in the character of Beckmesser, as it is logically impossible for characters to contain concealed within them their exact opposite. In other words, a subtext cannot contradict the text itself. For how could "those in the know" decipher the secret signals and hints allegedly contained within the work?

Above all, however, it is clear from the fact that the world of Jewish culture is depicted in an entirely positive light in *Die Meistersinger* that these initiates could not, and cannot, respond to any anti-Semitic allusions in the work; after all, the main characters tend to have biblical names—behind Hans Sachs is John the Baptist, behind Eva is the first woman, and behind both David and Walther von Stolzing is the Jewish king David. Toward the beginning of the opera, Walther is likened to David, a young hero "with sword in his belt, the sling in his hand" (GS 7:155), and at the end—after a certain resistance—he is "adorned with King David's likeness" and accepted into the Masters' guild (GS 7:269), a development that hardly suggests rampant anti-Semitism. In particular, the songs contained in the work— the opening chorale, which is all about John the Baptist; Sachs's Cobbling Song ("Als Eva aus dem Paradies" [When Eva was driven from Paradise]); David's "Am Jordan Sankt Johannes stand" [Saint John stood by the river Jordan]; and, finally, Walther's Prize Song, with its twofold vision of "Eve in Paradise" and the "Muse of Parnassus"—produce an antithetical relationship between the worlds of biblical and modern middle-class characters. The only person in the whole work who sings a song without any biblical references is the "most learned town clerk" (GS 7:187), the only Humanist among the Masters who cannot quote from the

Bible. To describe him on these grounds as a Jew in a town clerk's clothing is eccentric in the extreme.

But how is it that a writer apparently as obsessed with an anti-Semitic ideology as Wagner has left no trace of this in his music dramas, so that in spite of all the speculative claims that these works are anti-Jewish in aim, it has still not been possible to find any indisputable evidence to support these allegations? In "Dostojewskij: Der Ideologe und Dichter," his essay on Dostoyevsky as an ideologist and poet, Horst-Jürgen Gerigk has shown how often the Russian poet contradicts the frequently fanatical ideologist. "In each case the master of the household is a different person; on each occasion, it is a different person who decides on the fittings and furnishings and on the roof over his head."[68] This is particularly true of Dostoyevsky's aversion to the Jews, an aversion scarcely less aggressive than Wagner's. Gerigk shows that "the poet Dostoyevsky thinks only along poetological lines" and that for him the "ethnic and religious categorization" of his characters is "random," being an interchangeable "marginal phenomenon" in terms of our poetical understanding of them.[69]

Hermann Danuser adopts a very similar approach to Wagner's musical dramas. Particular qualities, he argues, are always universalized, thereby ruling out all anti-Semitic tendentiousness. In arguing in this way, Danuser could have appealed to one of Wagner's own, later comments to his disciple Hans von Wolzogen: "R. tells him that we cannot represent special causes such as vegetarianism in our journal but must always stick to and show the ideal, leaving outsiders to fight for their special causes; as a result we can play no part in the agitation against the Jews" (CT, 24 February 1881). At this period in his life, then, Wagner's motto in terms of his cultural politics was the championship of ideals, not special causes, and the avoidance of any "agitation" that might result from the espousal of such ideals. And this is even more true of his work as a composer. Danuser concludes his case as follows:

> Anyone who, without compelling reasons for doing so, supports the theory that the negatively drawn characters in Wagner's music dramas are Jewish stereotypes is unnecessarily and in spite of his own attempts to combat anti-Semitism helping to sustain anti-Semitic readings of works of art and in this way not contributing to a reduction in anti-Semitism.[70]

This argument is debatable. What is uncontestable, however, is that Beckmesser has no Jewish characteristics on an overt or covert level; such features are found neither in the text nor in the paratext, neither in the surrounding context nor in any conceivable subtext.

The Myth of the Beginning and End of History

DER RING DES NIBELUNGEN

Die Nacht weicht;

nichts mehr gewahr' ich:

des Seiles Fäden

find' ich nicht mehr;

verflochten ist das Geflecht.

Ein wüstes Gesicht

wirrt mir wüthend den Sinn:—

das Rheingold

raubte Alberich einst:—

weißt du was aus ihm ward?

—*First Norn,* Götterdämmerung

[Night is waning;

I see no more:

the strands of the rope

I can find no longer;

the threads have become entangled.

A desolate vision

maddingly throws my mind into turmoil:—

Alberich once

stole the Rhinegold:—

do you know what became of him?]

IN 1945 THE AMERICAN WRITER John Steinbeck published his short story *The Pearl*. Based on an Indian folktale, it begins in the vicinity of the Mexican town of La Paz on the Gulf of California, where the pearl fisher Kino leads a limited but happy life with his wife, Juana, and their little son, Coyotito, until the day he finds a gigantic pearl. The priceless find plunges Kino into a world of covetous desire. One night he is attacked by strangers, and although he manages to kill one of them, they burn down his house and destroy his boat. Kino flees in order to sell the pearl in the capital. Possession of it has turned him into a completely different person, and the "Song of Evil" now drowns out the "Song of the Family" that had previously filled his thoughts. Fleeing across the mountains, he manages to kill his determined pursuers, but a bullet fired by one of them strikes down Coyotito. Kino and Juana return to the coast with their child's body.

> And when they came to the water's edge they stopped and stared out over the Gulf. And then Kino laid the rifle down, and he dug among his clothes, and then he held the great pearl in his hand. He looked into its surface and it was gray and ulcerous. Evil faces peered from it into his eyes, and he saw the light of burning. . . . And in the surface of the pearl he saw Coyotito lying in the little cave with the top of his head shot away. And the pearl was ugly; it was gray, like a malignant growth. And Kino heard the music of the pearl, distorted and insane. . . . And Kino drew back his arm and flung the pearl with all his might. Kino and Juana watched it go, winking and glimmering under the setting sun. . . . And the pearl settled into the lovely green water and dropped toward the bottom. . . . It settled down to the sand bottom among the fern-like plants. . . . A crab scampering over the bottom raised a little cloud of sand, and when it settled the pearl was gone. And the music of the pearl drifted to a whisper and disappeared.[1]

Steinbeck's short story is a sort of American Indian variant of Wagner's *Ring*, not least in terms of its author's symbolic use of musical leitmotifs in his narrative. The pearl that is forced from its shell is like the ring that is forged from the Rhinegold, a demon that lays waste to the harmonious state of nature and destroys the relationships between individuals. The cycle of evil ends only with the return of the ring or pearl to the bed of the Rhine or to the depths of the ocean from which it has been taken only to wreak havoc and destruction. In both cases the cursed object is restored to the elements from which it has come.[2]

MYTH AND MODERNITY IN THE *RING*

This comparison between the *Ring* and Steinbeck's short story affords yet further proof of the extent to which the cycle is grounded in ideas anchored in the mythical imagination of the earth's nations. This is one aspect of the *Ring*: its archaic side. But its other aspect is its modernity, a modernity that although clothed in mythical symbols is sometimes so insistent that there have even been attempts to deny the work's mythical character altogether. As Bernard Shaw wrote over a century ago on the very first page of *The Perfect Wagnerite*, "The Ring, with all its gods and giants and dwarfs, its water-maidens and Valkyries, its wishing-cap, magic ring, enchanted sword, and miraculous treasure, is a drama of today, and not of a remote and fabulous antiquity."[3] Shaw even permitted himself the conceit of transferring Valhalla, Nibelheim, and Riesenheim to London and of regarding Wagner's mythological society as a mirror of British society in his own day. How pleased he would have been to read an entry that Cosima noted down in her diary while she and her husband were visiting the London docks in 1877: "This is Alberich's dream come true, Nibelheim, world dominion, activity, work, every-where the oppressive feeling of steam and fog" (CT, 25 May 1877). And in his essay "Know Yourself," written two years before his death, Wagner himself interpreted the central symbol of the cycle—the ring—as a "stock-exchange portfolio" and, as such, a "terrible image" of the universal power of money (GS 10:268).

Wagner's myth, then, seems to be not self-referential but merely an allegorical account of modern society.[4] Moreover, is the *Ring* really a myth about the begin-ning and end of the world? Is this world not already corrupt before the very first note—the famous low E flat—rises mysteriously from the "mystic abyss" of the orchestra pit (GS 9:338)? Has not Wotan long since corrupted the world? Have not a whole series of events already taken place before the start of *Das Rheingold*, events that the director may be tempted to stage even before the conductor raises his or her baton for that first low E flat? And does the world not continue to exist even after the end of *Götterdämmerung*—a world no different from the one we have just seen destroyed—as Alberich appears to survive the disaster and will surely resume his struggle to regain the ring?

The concept of myth has become such an empty formula that as Günter Grass elegantly expressed it in his 1985 speech "Das Elend der Aufklärung" (The misery of enlightenment), every pile of excrement will soon be described as a myth.[5] To avoid sinking into the modish morass of mythomania, we need to stick to the terra firma of the scientific study of myth. "To know the myths," wrote Mircea Eliade, the Romanian writer on comparative religion, "is to learn the secret of the origin of things."[6] In his words, myths tells of "primordial events"[7] and relate to the creation or establishment of those events, thereby becoming an exemplary model of all fun-damental human activities in the form of an archetypal event that is constantly reactualized.

Wagner comes very close to this tenet of modern mythography in his 1850 pamphlet *The Wibelungs: World History from Legend*. Here he develops a theory of myth that may now strike us as curious but that he was inspired to advance by the writings of two scholars who were well known in their day, Carl Wilhelm Gött-ling's *Nibelungen und Gibelinen* (Rudolstadt, 1816) and Franz Joseph Mone's *Untersuchungen zur Geschichte der teutschen Heldensage* (Investigations in the history of German heroic legend) (Quedlinburg, 1836).[8] In Wagner's view, the Nibelungs were identical with the old Frankish dynasty of the Wibelungs, or Ghibellines. Basing his speculations on an idea of Göttling's that was based in turn on folk etymology, he argues that the name of the Nibelungs has been aligned with that of their historical enemies, the Welfs or Ghelphs, with the Guelphs/Welfs ranged against the Ghibellines/Wibelings, this last-mentioned name having been derived from that of the Nibelungs; hence Wagner's form Wibelungs (see GS 2:124).

It is easy to ridicule these etymological speculations, but a closer look at the matter suggests that Wagner was concerned less with any scientifically objective and linguistically unassailable justification of the link between the names than with a Romantically inspired connection between them and popular "belief." In other words, he was interested in an "alternative" historiography, with "folk history" replacing the traditional "history of lords and princes" (GS 2:124). (This is Wagner the revolutionary speaking.) At the same time, he was interested not in "dry chronicles" concerned with facts and the "pragmatic surface of events" (GS 2:125) but in history grounded in "the common people's insights into the nature of things" (GS 2:123).

And myth is the epitome of these insights. For Wagner, therefore, "the identification of the Frankish royal family with the Nibelungs of legend" (GS 2:120) may not be "genealogically" true, but it is true on the level of myth, a truth encapsulated in the identity of the two names as created "in the mouths of the people" (GS 2:124). In Wagner's view, the same idea of a mythological identity lies behind the Franks' claim to be descended from Troy: "The chronicler of history will smile pityingly at such a tasteless conceit, not one iota of which is true. But he whose purpose is to vindicate the deeds of men and races on the strength of their inmost views and impulses is concerned above all with what they believed or tried to make others believe about themselves" (GS 2:137). And Wagner offers a fascinating justification for this. Ancient Troy was the "first city" because, in the minds of the nations of the earth, it was "built by the most ancient races of men and surrounded by high (cyclopean) walls in order to preserve within it their holiest and most ancient relic" and to enclose "the wellspring of all patriarchism" (GS 2:138). According to Wagner, all the "greater nations in history . . . know such a holy city, built in imitation of the ancient city of the gods on earth; and they also know of its destruction at the hands of later generations" (GS 2:139). The nations of the earth have repeatedly "copied" this "first city," with the "sanctity" of that site transferred to the "new tribal seat" (GS 2:138). In the case of the Franks, this transfer was based on the conviction that their royal family was identical to the one that had once ruled in Troy: "When driven away from there, the king of immemorial right revived his ancient royal rights in them" (GS 2:140).

For Wagner, the example of this "first city" illustrates his belief that history is, as it were, made up of a repetition of mythical prototypes. This belief underpins the entirety of *The Wibelungs*, the subtitle of which makes this clear: *World History from Legend.* In his opening section, he discusses the idea of an "ancient kingship" that can appeal to a progenitor "sprung from the gods" and that Wagner, following in the wake of Joseph Görres's *Mythengeschichte der asiatischen Welt* (History of the myths of the Asiatic world) (Heidelberg, 1810), locates in Asia, the "original home of mankind" (GS 2:115–16). It is here, Wagner argues, that the history of the Frankish kings originates.

The way in which the power of the king is maintained within various nations, the tendency for this power to remain vested in a single family, the fidelity with which it was accorded solely to that family even in the latter's deepest degeneracy—all these things must have been deeply rooted in the consciousness of these nations: it rested on the memory of their original home in Asia, of the emergence of individual tribes within the family, and of the power of the head of that family in the person of the progenitor who was said to be "sprung from the gods." (GS 2:116)

These, then, are the foundations of Wagner's view of kingship, a view profoundly influenced by Romantic notions and one to which he remained true even during the revolution. For Wagner, the idea of an archetypal kingship was central to the Nibelung legend as "the tribal legend of the Frankish royal family" (GS 2:119). In turn, this idea became concentrated in the mythical figure of Siegfried, who is typically reembodied not only in all the German kings and emperors but also in the Nibelung hoard, which Wagner describes as "the embodiment of the ruler's power" (GS 2:120). In short, Wagner interprets history as a series of events based on recurring mythical patterns.[9]

Wagner's prototypes—protokingship, protoheroism, the first city, and so on—are exactly the same as the "numinous prototypes" defined by mythographers such as Kurt Hübner[10] and exemplified by the political and social lives of the Greeks, which likewise were structured around myth; here important political events were inaugurated with a specific appeal to an *arché*, a tale of the event's mythic origins that was not merely a folk memory but the exemplary model for present-day action, a paradigm of that later reenactment.

> The battle between the Greeks and the barbarians is still the battle between the Lapiths and the Centaurs; the battle between Athens and Mytilene over Sigeum is still the battle for Troy. Typical of this way of thinking are the introductory formulas of the prayers that frequently begin with the words "if ever," "as true as ever," and so on. In this way, the speaker recalls an earlier action by the god and hopes that it will now be repeated and be equally effective. Indeed, this earlier action, as an *arché*, guarantees that the eternal deity will prove to be the same.[11]

An arché, then, is an archetypal story in which a numinous being first performs a particular action that is later identically repeated. This is especially and most obviously true of natural occurrences that keep repeating themselves, the very occurrences that—as we shall see—gave Wagner his idea of myth. The return of spring is always the return of Persephone from Hades, and the onset of winter is her disappearance from the world aboveground. But the same cyclical view also characterizes the Greeks' perception of history. Just as the Platonic idea is a substantive entity that remains the same in everything that forms a part of it, so an arché is an "order of events of mythic substance,"[12] invariably recurring in the same form in each of the actions based on it.

In this context, etymological speculations on the fact that the name of a royal household is identical with that of its mythical prototype are significant. The extent to which names in myth are believed to reveal the truth is clear from the fact that the name of the progenitor of a family—a name generally traced back to a god or a hero—is retained through succeeding generations, thereby expressing the conviction that the substance of this mythical progenitor survives unchanged in his or her descendants.[13] The onomastic speculations of Wagner the theorist attest to his deep-rooted familiarity with the way in which mythical thinking operates, and this is particularly true when we consider the importance of names in his music dramas, whether it is their creation (Valhalla), their discovery (Siegmund), their concealment (Lohengrin), or their loss (Parsifal). As a system of primordial and reactualizable events and as a reliable way of interpreting reality, true myth is distinguished from fairy tales, whose unreliable fictions lack real substance. According to Schelling, the fairy tale is pure invention, whereas myth is "not invented but found"[14]—found as the archaic basis of our own experience of reality. As a result, the prelude to *Das Rheingold* cannot be equated with the fairy-tale formula "Once upon a time,"[15] as the opening pages of the score express the fundamental nature of myth in a way that is unique in the history of modern approaches to myth. Myth is concerned not with what happened "once upon a time" but with what happened once and continues to happen again and again.[16]

Let us recall these opening bars of *Das Rheingold*: the first thing that we hear is a sound more like an undifferentiated noise rising up from the depths, the famous low E flat on the double basses. On the basis of this passage—made up, in Reinhard Wiesend's words, of "a seemingly preexistent, amorphous primordial substance"— Wagner systematically develops all the musical parameters of the score.[17] This is the first note to be heard in the world, its low rumbling shortly joined by the fifth above it, after which eight horns enter in canon: the triad is born, and for the next 136 bars a musical universe is created consisting of nothing but the triad of E flat major. This key has always been associated with the mysterious, and as such it was used in *ombra* scenes in opera seria.[18] In *Das Rheingold* it is employed to express the mythical origin of things, the birth of the world.

No one has provided a more telling description than Thomas Mann of Wagner's attempt to return to the "first source and origin of all things." Just as Wagner was at pains to free the Siegfried legend from all "historical dross" and "later accretions" by going back beyond the courtly guise of the *Nibelungenlied* to the "foundations of the myth in the Edda," so he could not bring himself to "stop and begin at some point already burdened with a past and thus to start *in medias res*." Instead, he felt compelled to return "to the first source and origin of all things, the primeval cell, the first E flat of the prelude to the prelude," thereby constructing "a musical cosmogony, nay, a mythological cosmos," and creating "a poem for the musical stage that tells of the world's beginning and of its end."[19]

The static triad of the horn canon is now animated by means of arpeggiations in the cellos, creating a sense of flowing movement. The flowing water, the origin of life, becomes sound. The uppermost notes in the melodic line of this string figuration produce the first leitmotif of the *Ring*, a diatonically ascending line that illustrates and symbolizes the idea of becoming in nature. This now dominates all of this musical universe, striving ever upward through brighter and brighter registers, moving from darkness into light, from being to becoming, and from hearing to seeing, or, to put it at its most prosaic, from the orchestra pit to the stage.

The prelude moves melodically upward toward a climax at which, no longer content with merely listening, our ears demand that we should also see what we are hearing. The curtain opens, and we hear and see three elemental beings, water sprites, the daughters of the river Rhine, the first of whom launches into an obviously rocking melody: the wave movement of the Rhine transformed into a sequence of notes. Waves even form the roots of the Rhinedaughters' names: Woglinde (from *wogen* = to billow), Wellgunde (from *Welle* = wave), and Floßhilde (from *fließen* = to flow). And the words that they sing are onomatopoeic evocations of the element in which they swim, playfully punning on the words *Welle* (wave), *Woge* (billow), and *Wiege* (cradle). Just as their vocal line is born from purely instrumental sound, so their language is still half music, an approximation of speech in which words are not yet intelligible concepts but musical sounds from the dawn of time. Here not only do we see the origins of the world and all visible matter, we also witness the birth of language.

> Weia! Waga!
> Woge, du Welle,
> walle zur Wiege!
> Wagalaweia!
> Wallala weiala weia!

(GS 5:200)

> [Weia! Waga!
> Welter, you wave,
> swirl round the cradle!
> Wagalaweia!
> Wallala weiala weia!]

These alliterative lines set the tone for the mythical language that supports the vast poetic structure of the *Ring*. The etymological relationship between *Wiege* (cradle) and *Woge* (wave), with which Wagner plays in these opening lines of *Das Rheingold*, was particularly important to the composer, as the song of the waves was "like the world's lullaby," he told Cosima on 17 July 1869.

In the fourth of his *Unzeitgemäße Betrachtungen* (1876), Nietzsche argued that in his "mythological dramas" Wagner had "forced language back to a primordial state in which it hardly yet thinks in concepts and in which it is itself still poetry, image, and feeling." Wagner, Nietzsche went on, knew very well that mythological characters cannot speak a language whose "unsingable" compound words and complex sentences presuppose the abstract and prosaic modern world and that would "forcibly transport us to another, nonmythical world."[20] Wagner showed great boldness in choosing a kind of archetypal language for the *Ring* that reflects the archaic and archetypal structure of myth, yet his decision has earned him mockery and contempt ever since the text first appeared in print. His critics simply refused to accept his mythological conception of language, reserving their particular ridicule for the Rhinedaughters' "Wagalaweia." But the critics who make fun of this would logically also have to point the finger of ridicule at the

German mother who rocks her child to sleep with the words "eiapopeia." (The closest English equivalent of this word—"hush-a-bye"—lacks the onomatopoeic quality of the German.)

Wagner himself drew this comparison in his open letter to Nietzsche of 12 June 1872, in which he defended *Die Geburt der Tragödie*, his young friend's brilliant first book on philology, against the attacks of academic philologists. Here Wagner mentions the Rhinedaughters' song of the waves and claims that he was inspired by etymological research to create "a rootlike syllabic melody for my water maidens by analogy with the 'eiapopeia' of our nursery rhymes" (GS 9:300).[21] But for whom are the Rhinedaughters singing their lullaby? Whose "cradle" are they rocking? It is the "sleeping gold" that they are guarding; playfully they keep watch over the "slumberer's bed" (GS 5:201). In the depths of the Rhine, a golden age still reigns, an age symbolized, in keeping with its name, by the gold that has not yet been deprived of its mythical innocence and that expresses, in Mircea Eliade's words, "the fullness of the beginnings"—the crucial point in cosmogonic myth.[22]

The musical cosmogony of the prelude to *Das Rheingold* reenacts the moment at which the world was created. Here myth may be said to write and compose itself. Just as in cultures that still seek to justify themselves through myth, cosmogony is the exemplary model for every kind of higher activity, whether it is the founding of a city or the building of an architectural structure (all construction rites are reenactments of the cosmogonic act),[23] so cosmogony forms the paradigm of Wagner's *Ring* as a musical and dramatic work of art. This is especially true of its system of leitmotifs. The fabric of the relationships between the different leitmotifs is the musical garb of myth as a system of archetypal, primordial events, of tales about the origins of things that once took place at an indefinable point in time—in German, "*einst*"—and that are now cyclically repeated.[24]

No one has written more tellingly about this indefinable point in time as the setting for myth than Thomas Mann in his biblical trilogy *Joseph und seine Brüder* (Joseph and his brethren) and the various essays that relate to it, including his two major essays on Wagner. The word *einst*, he writes, has "two meanings, referring to both past and future, telling of the beginning and prophesying the end."[25] This idea recurs throughout his trilogy of novels. "*Einst* is a word that has no limitations, a word with two faces; it looks backwards, far backwards, into a solemnly twilit distance, and it looks ahead, far ahead into the distance, no less solemn through its inevitable coming than is the distant past through its having been." There is no doubt that Mann first became aware of the ambiguity of the word *einst* when he encountered Wagner's concept of myth, with its "knowledge of the world's beginning and end, knowledge conveyed through song and story." In *Leiden und Größe Richard Wagners*, Mann refers to "the language of *einst* in its twofold sense of 'how all things were' and 'how all things will be.'" And there follows a vague reference to the Norns' scene from *Götterdämmerung*, where the ambiguity of the term is articulated.[26]

The Three Norns represent three aspects of time: the First Norn tells of events that took place at the beginning of time, and the Third deals with matters bound up with the world's final destiny; the Second Norn covers the period between these extremes. Significantly, only the First and Third Norns use the term *einst* to describe what they know—the First refers to events long past, the Third to events in the future. "At the world-ash once [*einst*] I wove," says the First Norn as she tells of the mythical state of the world before Wotan cut his contractual spear from the ash tree's branches (GS 6:178). And the Third Norn announces the apocalyptic fire that will one day engulf the world: "The shattered spear's sharp-pointed splinters Wotan will one day [*einst*] bury deep in the fire-god's breast" (GS 6:181). According to Franz Joseph Mone, Wagner's authority on myth, "The Norns are the circle in which human life operates, Urthr and Skulld are the points at which it begins and ends, Werthandi is the vast distance between them."[27]

Wagner's network of leitmotifs is stretched between these two different meanings of *einst*. When they are first heard, they provide a basis on which to build, later recurring in constantly differing variants. Formally and conceptually, then, they resemble the archetypal figures and events that characterize the lives of nations that still derive their social norms from myth. The leitmotif is, as it were, their musical symbol. Take the Valhalla and Sword motifs; in both cases the "founding" nature of a numinous place or object is immediately obvious.

In classical antiquity, the majesty of a king, for example, was conceived of as a mythical entity invested in him by Zeus and continuing to exist in his family like an inheritance or genotype. It was also vested in the symbols of his rule such as his scepter, which was not simply an interchangeable symbol. As an example of this, Kurt Hübner considers the history of Agamemnon's scepter in the *Iliad*: Agamemnon inherited this scepter from his ancestors, one of whom had received it from Zeus. When oaths are sworn on a scepter, it has to be this particular scepter, which is part of the numinous substance of the dignity of kingship.[28] Here the reader will inevitably recall the role of the sword Nothung in Wagner's *Ring*; it, too, is a gift from the father of the gods, a mythological object that is passed down like an inheritance to which only its legitimate heir is entitled. This explains why only Siegfried can reforge it after it has been shattered by the god. This mythical substance is present even in the name of the sword and in the way in which it is apostrophized.[29] Siegfried's Forging Songs, which repeatedly invoke the name Nothung, are motivated by the word's mythological power.[30] In exactly the same way, Wotan's rune-engraved spear is a mythological entity whose negative counterpart is Alberich's ring, an object that perverts the mythological substantiality of the gold.

The gold in the Rhine is nature's most perfect gift. Its beauty promises to bring joy to our lives; it can bestow "radiant delight," proclaim the Rhinedaughters in a kind of dawn song addressed to the gold as it is woken to new life by the sun's rays. In short, the gold is not a piece of inanimate matter but a living mythological being whose "eye wakes and sleeps." It can smile and even laugh. The Rhinedaughters refer to it as a "friend" with whom they play and dance and sing (GS 5:209–10). But the gold conceals within it a demonic power. The man who curses the primeval cosmogonic power of life—the power through which the world came into being and by which it is maintained—can forge a ring from the gold, a ring that guarantees "measureless might" (GS 5:211) and even world dominion. It is Alberich who pronounces this curse on love. With it, evil enters the world and destroys its mythological integrity. This evil poisons the world, turning the beneficent mythological personality of the gold, symbolized by its eye, into a mere object that can be exploited, a reified force that destroys all human and moral ties. Possession of the ring means that objects now rule humankind, and the possessor becomes the possessed. "The lord of the ring as the slave of the ring," Alberich prophesies in the great speech in which he curses the ring (GS 5:255). But evil poisons love, too, destroying its oneness and giving sex an autonomy all of its own: "If I cannot gain love by force, might I at least gain pleasure through cunning?" Alberich asks immediately before stealing the gold from the Rhine (GS 5:212). (The product of this enforced love will be Hagen.)

It is worth reminding ourselves once again that Wagner compared the ring to a "stock-exchange portfolio" as owned by a modern capitalist. Does this not mean that he himself had already moved in the direction of a demythologized reading of the *Ring* such as the one brought into fashion by Shaw in his *Perfect Wagnerite*? The answer is: emphatically not. Wagner projected modern experiences onto myth, which in his view contained within it the archetypes of all essential historical developments. The curse of gold, for example, is also, but not exclusively, the curse of capital, for it also represents the recurrence of an archetypal mythical situation. After all, the motif is already found in the oldest mythological sources. (Suffice it to recall the obsession with gold on the part of King Midas of Phrygia.) Here Wagner based his account on the *Reginsmál* (The lay of Regin) from the Edda, where we already find the curse creating a constant succession of acts of cunning, deception, and murder, with the minds of the participants poisoned by the greed for gold. And Alberich's curse on the ring is modeled on an episode in the life of the dwarf Andvari, whose last remaining ring is stolen by Loki and who thereupon curses its future owners. (Admittedly, the curse on the gold is not central to the Eddaic poems but acquired this centrality only through Friedrich de la Motte Fouqué's dramatic 1808–10 trilogy, *Der Held des Nordens* (The hero of the north). This was a pioneering work in terms of the poetic reception of the Nibelung legend in the nineteenth century, and seems to have been the chief inspiration behind Wagner's version of events: here, as in virtually every other instance, Wagner learned his mythological sources through the intermediary of a modern adaptation.)[31]

For Wagner, then, myth was not an allegory of the social conditions that obtained in the modern world; rather, these conditions are reactualizations of the events prefigured in myth. In the section headed "The Descent into Hell," which opens *Joseph and His Brethren*, Thomas Mann argues that the essence of myth is "the repetition, the becoming present of something profoundly past," so that our forebears would, for example, "recognize the Flood each time that they were visited by a similar inundation." In myth, he went on, there was "no difference between being and meaning." The argument over "whether the Eucharist 'is' the body of the Sacrifice or whether it merely 'signifies' the body" is completely alien to it.[32] Myth, then, is not "allegorical" but "tautegorical," to use a terminological distinction proposed by Schelling in his *Philosophie der Mythologie*. In other words, myth speaks of itself, not of something else: "Everything in it is to be understood just as it expresses it, not as if something else were being thought and said." This is especially true of the gods who, in Schelling's words, "are not something different, do not signify something different, but signify only what they are."[33]

The arguments that Schelling uses to refute the "allegorical" interpretation of myth—especially the historical way of explaining events adopted by the Epicurean philosopher Euhemerus[34]—could well be applied to contemporary productions of the *Ring*, with their tendency to adopt a euhemeristic approach to the work.[35] According to Euhemerus,

> the gods are not superhuman beings belonging to some higher order but historical human beings who participate in real events—events in human and civic history. The gods are only heroes, kings, and lawgivers raised to godlike status. Nowadays, at a time when finance and trade are our main concern, they would be seafarers, discoverers of new trade routes, and the founders of overseas colonies.[36]

If legends about the gods are "euhemerized" and "related as human incidents,"[37] all that is ultimately left is a "moral philosophy dressed up as art."[38] Wagner's works have often suffered this fate in the contemporary theater, his myth watered down and robbed of its potency.

For Wagner, the experiences of modern history are not the result of a euhemeristic interpretation of myth but, as I have already noted, reactualizations of tales about our origins. When seen in this light, the linear temporality of history becomes the circular temporality of myth; the straight line of advancing time becomes the circle of recurring time,[39] and the unique historical event becomes a repeated phenomenon. The ring of myth encircles history. According to Wagner's main theoretical book, *Opera and Drama*, myth is "the beginning and end of history" (GS 4:91). Myth, in short, is the alpha and omega of history.

SIEGFRIED AND THE HEROIC MODEL

The iterative structure of myth is clear especially in natural phenomena that recur on a cyclical basis and form the starting point for Wagner's own theory of myth as put forward in his essay *The Wibelungs*.[40] According to Wagner, the first myth arises from our immediate observation of nature.

> Man receives his first impressions from surrounding nature, and none of nature's phenomena will have had such a powerful impact on him as the one that seemed to him to constitute the first cause of his existence or, at least, of his knowledge of everything contained in Creation: in other words, *light, day, the sun*. It was inevitable that we should first show our gratitude to this element and finally that we should worship it, the more so as its opposite, darkness and night, seemed joyless and therefore unfriendly and fearsome. Inasmuch as the light provided man with all that brought him joy and life, so he could also regard it as the very basis of his existence; it became the begetter, the father, the god; the emergence of day from night ultimately struck him as

the victory of light over darkness, of warmth over cold, and so on, and this idea may
have been the first to breed in man a moral consciousness and an awareness of what is
beneficial and harmful, friendly and hostile, good and evil.—This first impression of
nature must thus be regarded as the common basis of the religions of all nations. (GS
2:130–31)

These remarks on light, day, and the sun as archetypal mythical phenomena inevitably recall the hymn to light Brünnhilde sings when Siegfried wakes her from
her magic slumber: "Hail to you, sun! Hail to you, light! Hail to you, radiant
day!" (GS 6:166). And Wagner's reference to the "victory of light over darkness"
recalls Brünnhilde's paean to Siegfried as "conquering light" and "waker of life"
(GS 6:167). In Brünnhilde's eyes, Siegfried *is* the light. And we may well ask,
with the mythographer Jan de Vries, "Is the young hero who wakens the sleeping
Valkyrie from her enchanted slumber not the sun god who bids the earth to arise
from her long winter sleep in spring?"[41]

According to the "oldest interpretation of the myth," in other words, before this
myth was clothed in "the more human guise of early heroism," Wagner insists,
"Siegfried must be seen as the god of light or the sun god" (GS 2:119). In his original form, he is the "individualized light or sun god who triumphs over and kills
the monster of the night of primeval chaos:—this is the original meaning of
Siegfried's dragon fight, a fight such as the one fought by Apollo with the dragon
Python" (GS 2:131). Wagner recognized with great clarity a point that modern
mythographers have proved in detail, namely, that in heroic myth and in the
dragon fight that is central to it, cosmogonic myth—the original battle between
god the creator and the monster of chaos—is reactualized.

In this sense, the character of Siegfried in the *Ring* is likewise a "primordial
hero,"[42] and although he is no longer the light and sun god himself, it is he who re-
activates the latter's creation of the world. Those of us who hold Siegfried in such
high mythological regard inevitably find ourselves at odds with directors and critics who see in Siegfried no more than a bully, a protofascist, a puppet of Wotan's,
or a braggart who shamefully betrays the far superior figure of Brünnhilde.

Siegfried, no less than Parsifal, is a fool, yet his folly, while allowing him to become ensnared by evil, stems from his archaic naïveté, an innocence that cannot
handle the laws of polite society as embodied by the Gibichungs. As Jan de Vries
has pointed out, even the poet of the *Nibelungenlied*

condemned the world of appearances as represented by Worms around the year 1200
by introducing into it the figure of Siegfried from the remotest mythical past. There
can be no doubt that for the poet, Siegfried's world represented an ideal of inner
authenticity and strength. But the heroes of olden times are destroyed as soon as they
become caught up in the false appearance of courtly life.[43]

This is even more true of Wagner's Siegfried, whose godlike radiance is dimmed by
the somber machinations in which he is ensnared by the Gibichungs—admittedly
in the service of an oath of blood brotherhood, in other words, on the strength of
an archaic ethos involving loyalty.

In the victory of the dark world of civilization over the radiant mythological hero, light yields to darkness in the natural order of things, with the radiant figure of Siegfried superseded by the sinister Hagen, as Wagner himself explains in *The Wibelungs*.

> As day ultimately succumbs to night, as summer must in the end yield to winter, so Siegfried too is slain at last; in this way, the god became man, and as a mortal man he fills our thoughts with new and greater sympathy because, as the victim of an act that brings us joy, he stirs within us the moral motif of revenge, in other words, we long to avenge his death upon his murderer and thus repeat his action. In this way we ourselves take up and continue the age-old struggle, and its varying outcome is exactly the same as the constant alternation of day and night, summer and winter, and ultimately of the human race itself, which advances from life to death, from victory to defeat, from joy to sorrow, and thus, through a process of constant rejuvenation, makes us actively aware of the eternal nature of man and nature both in itself and through itself. (GS 2:131–32)

The mythological hero, whether Greek or Germanic, cannot be measured by the yardstick of modern intellectual or Humanist values. Goethe had already stressed this in *Dichtung und Wahrheit* (Poetry and truth), where he uses the example of Wieland's *Alceste* to criticize modern humanizing interpretations of mythological heroes, justifying his criticism by pointing out that the mythological hero's virtues "rest not on moral but on transfigured physical qualities."[44]

In Wagner's account of them, Siegfried's life and death conform exactly to what more recent students of myth such as Lord Raglan have termed the "hero-pattern." (Jan de Vries uses the term "Heldenschema" [hero pattern].) It is worth listing some of the elements that make up this pattern, at least to the extent that they are typical of Wagner's heroes. First, the hero's origins are in some way unusual, going beyond what we normally expect of human beings and involving either the extramarital begetting of the hero by a god (in Wagner's case, this act of procreation has been transferred back a generation, with Wotan as Siegfried's grandfather, not his father) or an incestuous relationship (in this case Siegmund and Sieglinde); second, the hero is born in secrecy; third, he is brought up by a semihuman mythological being (Mime); fourth, he soon gives proof of exceptional physical strength; fifth, his fight with a monster—usually a dragon—is an obligatory ritual initiation into the heroic world; sixth, as a result of this fight, the hero becomes invulnerable or acquires some incalculable treasure (in this case the Nibelung hoard); and, seventh, the dragon fight is generally followed by the hero's rescue and erotic conquest of a virgin (Brünnhilde), a conquest associated with the hero's overcoming of some exceptional danger (here Siegfried has to pass through the flames surrounding the Valkyries' Rock).

In myth, the dragon is a symbol of chaos. In the words of de Vries, the hero "must, as it were, go through this monster in order to be reborn as a new man. Chaos must first be restored before a new creation is possible."[45] But this creation finds expression in the act of sexual union, which is why there is always a direct connection in myth between the dragon fight and the hero's conquest in love. Wagner more or less equated these two events in the final act of *Siegfried*, when he twice uses the Dragon motif at Brünnhilde's words "As my gaze consumes you" and "As my arm holds you tight" (GS 6:174)[46]—yet another example of the mythological and hermeneutic power of Wagner's leitmotif technique.

There follows another element of the hero pattern: having enjoyed the rewards of his love, the hero is not allowed to rest on his laurels (in the poetry of the Middle Ages, this was construed as the sin of sloth) but must set out in search of new adventures (GS 6:182). And this is exactly what Siegfried does at the start of *Götterdämmerung*. Setting off does not mean that Siegfried fails to appreciate Brünnhilde or that he is keen to start other affairs, as recent writers have claimed. Brünnhilde herself urges Siegfried to leave in search of new adventures: "What would my love be worth if I did not let you go forth?" (GS 6:182). By exchanging gifts in the form of ring and horse, they will both be present in each other's thoughts even when they are separated.[47] For Brünnhilde, the ring *is* Siegfried, and for Siegfried, the horse *is* Brünnhilde, so that, like Tristan and Isolde, they exchange identities: "No longer do I think of myself as Siegfried," Siegfried tells Brünnhilde; "I am Brünnhilde's arm alone" (GS 6:185). Siegfried wants to be Brünnhilde, too, and Brünnhilde also wants to be Siegfried.

In bidding each other farewell, the lovers offer to bestow "Minne" on one another. By this, they mean not only love but also the promise to remember each other forever (GS 6:183). This idea of remembering is constantly repeated in Brünnhilde's parting words, and as Wagner knew very well—not least from Jacob Grimm's *Deutsche Mythologie*[48]—*Minne* was cognate with the Latin *memini* and *memoria* and with the English *mind*. When Siegfried later receives the drinking horn from Gutrune at the Gibichungs' court, he dedicates his first sip not to his hosts, as courtesy demands, but to Brünnhilde and to "true remembrance" (GS 6:194). (This is also the meaning of the Germanic custom of *Minnetrinken*.)[49]

Paradoxically and tragically, the horn contains a magic potion that has been given to Siegfried to make him lose his memory, so that if he suddenly forgets Brünnhilde and everything associated with her, no moral opprobrium attaches to him as a result. In spite of claims to the contrary, this potion does not symbolize some long-standing inner aversion to Brünnhilde;[50] it is merely an infamous instrument in Hagen's hands designed to brainwash Siegfried. In this way Siegfried becomes guilty while innocent. Otherwise, Brünnhilde's peroration makes no sense:

> Der Reinste war er,
> der mich verrieth!
> Die Gattin trügend
> —treu dem Freunde—
> vor der eig'nen Trauten
> —einzig ihm theuer—
> schied er sich durch sein Schwert.—
> Ächter als er
> schwur keiner Eide;
> treuer als er
> hielt keiner Verträge;
> laut'rer als er

liebte kein and'rer:
und doch alle Eide,
alle Verträge,
die treueste Liebe—
trog keiner wie er.

(GS 6:252)

[The purest of men it was
who betrayed me!
False to his wife
—true to his friend—
from her who was faithful
—she alone who was loyal—
he sundered himself with his sword.—
Never were oaths
more nobly sworn;
never were treaties
kept more truly;
never did any man
love more loyally:
and yet every oath,
every treaty,
the truest love—
no one betrayed as he did!]

It was out of loyalty, then, that Siegfried betrayed his love. This is the tragic paradox of his actions, the tragic nature of which has something truly classical about it: in keeping with the idea of hamartia set forth in the thirteenth chapter of Aristotle's *Poetics*, the hero's tragedy is based not on a moral flaw but on a failure of understanding.[51] In the specific case of Siegfried, this is the inability of a mythological individual to adapt to the laws of civilization. Hence the hero's early death brings the hero pattern full circle.

WOTAN'S CRIME AGAINST NATURE AND THE SOCIAL CONTRACT

The evil that destroys Siegfried stems from Alberich's rape of the Rhinegold. Of course, it is clear from the Norns' scene in *Götterdämmerung* that even before this Wotan had established his rule by cutting his spear from the world-ash, thereby violating nature. But, quite apart from the fact that in myth, with its cyclical structures, concepts such as "before" and "after" cannot be measured using the yardstick of linear historical time, this act of vandalism does nothing to lessen the enormity of Alberich's crime. The theft of the Rhinegold and Wotan's despoliation of the world-ash are related neither causally nor temporally but take place in two completely different worlds. There is absolutely no suggestion in the libretto that the theft of the Rhinegold could be a consequence of any initial guilt on the part of the father of the gods.

What exactly is Wotan's crime against nature? In the prologue to *Götterdäm-merung*, the First Norn sings of the world-ash and of the "Well of Wisdom" in the shadow of its branches. Wotan once came to this well, and, paying "one of his eyes" as a "toll for all time," he broke off a branch from the tree and carved his spear from it (GS 6:178). To appreciate the implications of this action and its mythic resonances, we need to cast an eye over the Edda. Here, in the *Völuspá* (The Sibyl's prophecy), the world-ash is called Yggdrasill.[52] Its branches extend over the whole world. Beneath one of its roots lies the Well of Mimir, in which wisdom and understanding are found. Odin (Wotan) drinks from this well in order to gain wisdom. In his revised edition of Friedrich Creuzer's *Symbolik und Mythologie der alten Völker* (Symbolism and mythology of the ancient nations, 1822), a text familiar to Wagner, Franz Joseph Mone points out that "just as life begins with water, so wisdom must be drunk."[53]

But in order to gain wisdom, Wotan has to pledge his eye, and this now remains in the well.[54] The perfect Wagnerite is, of course, puzzled by the fact that in *Das Rheingold*, Wotan seems to give a different reason for the loss of his eye when he tells Fricka:

> Um dich zum Weib zu gewinnen,
> mein eines Auge
> setzt' ich werbend daran.

(GS 5:216)

> [In order to win you as wife,
> my single eye
> I staked that I might woo you.]

Either this refers to Wotan's one remaining eye, which Wotan risked losing by wooing Fricka, or the loss of his eye at Mimir's Well and while wooing Fricka amounts to one and the same thing. After all, the sacrifice of his eye allowed Wotan to acquire wisdom, and this in turn permitted him to establish a new world order. The guardian of this world order is Fricka, with Wotan's marriage as a microcosm of it. She embodies the intelligence that Wotan has won through the loss of his eye. In conversation with Cosima on 23 June 1872, Wagner explained that the fact that Wotan has only one eye "expresses the belief that intellectual force precludes regular physical beauty." In cases where beauty is regular, "the brain is reduced in potency." In short, the loss of an eye and the resultant reduction in physical beauty means that for Wotan, conversely, his intellectual powers are immeasurably enhanced. And this is the precondition for his new order of things, an order that finds a mythological symbol in the spear that he cuts from the world-ash.

> Treu berath'ner
> Verträge Runen
> schnitt Wotan

> in des Speeres Schaft:
> den hielt er als Haft der Welt.

(GS 6:179)

> [The runes of trustily
> counseled treaties
> Wotan carved
> on the shaft of the spear:
> he held it as his grip on the world.]

Thus the Second Norn sings. In other words, Wotan concludes "treaties" (we already find this motif in the *Völuspá*), and these treaties are, as it were, enshrined in the runes on his spear. These treaties famously play an important role in the *Ring*, binding Wotan to the point where he is incapable of acting. "Keep your faith with contracts!" the giant Fasolt warns Wotan in *Das Rheingold*.

> Was du bist,
> bist du nur durch Verträge:
> bedungen ist,
> wohl bedacht deine Macht.

(GS 5:219)

> [What you are
> you are through contracts alone:
> your power, mark me well,
> is bound by sworn agreements.]

In the *Ring*, therefore, the gods are not all-powerful. Rather, their power is bound up with certain conditions. How is this possible? How is it that the gods, who by dint of their numinous power command the elements, creating thunder and lightning, building rainbow bridges, and ensuring their own immortality by eating magic apples, enjoy power—in the true sense of the word—only on the strength of treaties? There is no doubt that what Wagner means by this power is not the divine omnipotence that myth and religion ascribe to God and the gods but political power. And this can be gained only through treaties.

Udo Bermbach has recently examined the paradigmatic significance of the concept of the treaty in terms of the action of the *Ring*,[55] and he has done so, moreover, from a politological standpoint.[56] This concept has a long history in political theory; suffice it to recall the most influential eighteenth-century writer on the theory of contracts, Jean-Jacques Rousseau, whose political thinking was at least an indirect source of inspiration for Wagner. According to Rousseau, people originally— in other words, in their natural state—lived either in total independence of one another or in loose social groupings, before deciding—or being persuaded to do so—to establish a state on the basis of a *contrat social*, or social contract.

Wotan, too, has exchanged an independent state of nature for a political state based on a social contract. Nature is no longer the be-all and end-all but now has a rival that circumscribes what had previously been its sole right. By cutting his spear from the world-ash, Wotan not only violates his own natural integrity ("one of his eyes he paid as toll for all time"; GS 6:178) but also deals the tree and ambient nature a wound that makes it wither.

> In langer Zeiten Lauf
> zehrte die Wunde den Wald;
> falb fielen die Blätter,
> dürr darbte der Baum:
> > traurig versiegte
> > des Quelles Trank.

(GS 6:178–79)

> [In the span of many seasons
> the wound consumed the wood;
> fallow fell the leaves,
> barren, the tree grew rotten:
> > sadly the wellspring's
> > drink ran dry.]

In short, Wotan's new state already bears within it the stigma of a violation against nature. Every social contract presupposes a violation of the integrity of nature, but Wotan's social contract contains within it a further evil. Although his aim is to create a moral and legal order ("The runes of trustily counseled treaties Wotan carved on the shaft of the spear"; GS 6:179), his new state is not free from the egoism of power, as he himself confesses to Brünnhilde in act 2 of *Die Walküre*.

> Als junger Liebe
> Lust mir verblich,
> verlangte nach Macht mein Muth:
> > von jäher Wünsche
> > Wüthen gejagt,
> gewann ich mir die Welt.
> > Unwissend trugvoll
> > Untreue übt' ich,
> > band durch Verträge
> > was Unheil barg:
> listig verlockte mich Loge,
> der schweifend nun verschwand.

(GS 6:37)

> [When youthful love's
> delights had faded,
> I longed in my heart for power:
> > impelled by the rage
> > of impulsive desires,

> I won for myself the world.
>> Unwittingly false
>> I acted unfairly,
>> binding by treaties
>> what boded ill:
> cunningly Loge lured me on
> but vanished while roaming the world.]

Wagner's Loge is a composite figure, made up of elements of the Old Norse Loki as the personification of fire and of a trickster and rogue related to the Hermes of Greek mythology, a figure who maliciously undermines the pantheon of Germanic gods.[57] It is Wotan's "fading" love that allows his desire for power to take root within him without any need for him to renounce love in the way that Alberich did.

The desire for power means that from the outset these treaties are contaminated by the slow poison of "disloyalty," even if Wotan is unaware of this (he is "unwittingly false"). Like Faust, Wotan needs his Mephistopheles and finds him in the ingeniously cunning god of fire, Loge, who has more than one characteristic in common with Goethe's Devil.[58] "Lured" into wrongdoing by Loge, Wotan will not admit that the treaty he has signed with the giants involves a condition that he cannot meet: they are to build Valhalla as a power base and as a monument to his prestige, in return for which they are promised Freia, goddess of youth and beauty, as their wages. But without Freia's apples, the gods are doomed to perish, as Fafner—the evil-minded brother of the relatively good-natured Fasolt, who, in a manner reminiscent of King Kong, falls in love with Freia—is well aware. In order to find an alternative to Freia, Wotan finally agrees to steal the fateful ring from Alberich, an act in which he forfeits all vestiges of godlike dignity. And with that he enters the cycle of evil. Erda's warning persuades him to abandon the ring and, with it, the promise of world dominion, but this is not enough to eradicate evil from the world, as he has to pay off the giants with the ring and later is prevented from acting by his own nexus of treaties.

He describes this hopeless situation to Brünnhilde in act 2 of *Die Walküre*: "In my own fetters I find myself caught—I, least free of all things living!" (GS 6:36). Dominion turns to slavery, power to impotence: "I, lord of treaties, am now a slave to those treaties!" (GS 6:40). Only a free hero who is not bound by treaties could rescue the world from the vicious circle in which Wotan is caught and free it from the evil concentrated in the ring. Such a hero would have to act on his own initative, independently of the will of the god whose hands are tied by his treaties.

Wotan succumbs to the paradoxical illusion that the Volsung hero whom he has fathered is destined to perform this autonomous action, an act that will simultaneously put an end to Wotan's regime. In Siegmund and Sieglinde he attempts to provide the world with a new beginning in the spirit of the love that has been cursed and betrayed. But Fricka ruthlessly exposes his self-deception: Siegmund is not the free hero who acts independently but is an agent of Wotan's. "I cannot will a free man," he admits (GS 6:43), and in his despair and resignation he abandons the Volsungs. Total resignation ("My work I abandon"; GS 6:42) leads to a new paradox: only when abandoned can the Volsungs produce the free hero who is no longer guided by Wotan. This hero will be Siegfried.

THE PARADOX OF FREEDOM IN THE *RING*

No less paradoxical is the role Brünnhilde plays. Conceived as a means of implementing Wotan's plan to save the world, she carries out his true wishes only when she contravenes his express instructions and helps Siegmund in his encounter with Hunding after the Volsung has been abandoned by the father of the gods. This is the inspired paradox of the *Ring*: the Volsungs and the Valkyries were conceived by Wotan as the agents of his plan to save the world, but as such they are inevitably incapable of carrying out its underlying idea, namely, that of freeing the world from the curse on the ring, as they can perform this task only if they are free agents, acting independently of Wotan's instructions. In short, only when he cuts himself off from them do they break free from the vicious circle of Wotan's strategic scheme and can work toward the realization of the idea to which they owe their existence.

This is the crux of the action of the *Ring*. But it also means that Wotan's role as an active participant in world events comes to an end with the end of *Die Walküre*. That is why in *Siegfried* he becomes a mere observer of events, the "Wanderer" who can say to Alberich with total justification, "I came to watch and not to act" (GS 6:124). Wotan's inability to act is graphically illustrated by the shattering of his spear, which, rebelling against his inaction, he holds out to bar Siegfried's way. The ultimate dramaturgical consequence of this is Wotan's complete disappearance from the stage in *Götterdämmerung*.

In the midst of this world of corruption, Siegfried and Brünnhilde embody the integrity of the primordial state of nature, a state in which nature and love are all, and power and possessions do not yet exist. This also explains why Siegfried does not learn fear (GS 6:108). The ring as a token of power is a matter of total indifference to him. "Though the ring were to win me the world's inheritance," he tells the Rhinedaughters, "for the sake of love's favors I'd gladly forgo it" (GS 6:238). As a result, the curse has no power over him, as Alberich acknowledges:

> An dem furchtlosen Helden
> erlahmt selbst mein Fluch:
> denn nicht weiß er
> des Ringes Werth,
> zu nichts nützt er
> die neidliche Macht.

(GS 6:211)

> [Even my curse grows feeble
> in the face of the fearless hero:

for he does not know
what the ring is worth,
he makes no use
of its coveted power.]

For Siegfried and Brünnhilde, the ring is not a possession but a "love token" (GS 6:204).

The tragedy of Siegfried is that the fearless hero to whom power and possessions mean nothing is doomed to perish in a world ruled by cunning. "He whose senses have not been honed by fear will be swallowed up, blind and deaf, by the world," Mime tells his charge in lines that Wagner did not set to music in the opening act of *Siegfried* (SS 16:204). Siegfried's fearlessness makes him the victim of a fatal intrigue, leaving him vulnerable to Hagen's brainwashing and thereby robbing him of a part of his identity until the moment of his death: his love of Brünnhilde, so important for his mythological integrity, is lost; at the same time Brünnhilde's love is turned into a murderous hatred that likewise alienates her from her true nature until the moment when, on the eve of the world's destruction, the Rhinedaughters open her eyes.

It is to the Rhinedaughters—"the wise sisters of the watery depths," as she calls these elemental creatures (GS 6:253)[59]—that Brünnhilde owes not only her whole knowledge of the web of fatal intrigue into which she and Siegfried have stumbled but also the advice to return the ring to the Rhine and thus to free the world from the curse that lies on it. The Rhinedaughters have already given the same advice to Siegfried, but, "fool" that he is, he cannot understand them ("Runes he knows and cannot read them"; GS 6:239). And so they decide to tell Brünnhilde instead. As elemental beings embodying incorruptible nature,[60] they know more than the gods and heroes who knowingly or otherwise are enmeshed in a corrupt world—and they can share this knowledge only with the character who is closest to nature: the daughter of Erda, Brünnhilde. Like Gaia in Greek mythology, Erda is the primeval mother who maintains a sense of order in nature.[61] (Her motif is the opening motif of the *Ring*—the motif of nature and growth—transposed to C sharp minor.)

Since becoming enmeshed in the toils of the Gibichungs' cabal, Siegfried has lost the ability to understand not only the Rhinedaughters but also another voice of nature that could have warned him of a murderous attack on him—the second such warning that the Forest Bird would have issued. "It's long since I've heeded their warbling," he tells Hagen in reply to the latter's question whether he can "understand the language of birdsong" (GS 6:241). According to Peter Wapnewski, "this means that he has arbitrarily abandoned the protective and educative world of nature and entered the world of courtly convention."[62] The similarity between the Forest Bird's main melody and that of the Rhinedaughters indicates that its voice is that of indisposable, indestructible nature and not an instrument of Wotan's, as modern directors are fond of depicting it, in flagrant contradiction of both the words and the music.

Wagner even regarded the Forest Bird as a reincarnation of Siegfried's mother, referring to her toward the end of his life as "Sieglinde's maternal soul."[63]

Originally, he even intended to express this idea directly in words and music: in the 1851 prose draft, Siegfried says: "I think I hear my mother singing!"[64] In the first version of the libretto, this became: "I think my mother is singing to me!"[65] These lines were even set to music in the composition draft.[66] In the finished work, Siegfried merely says of the Forest Bird: "He must be telling me something—perhaps about my dear mother?" (GS 6:134) Whenever the Forest Bird sings, whether before or after the dragon fight, Siegfried's thoughts always revolve around his unknown mother. In a letter of 24 February 1869, Wagner told King Ludwig II of Bavaria that "when the Forest Bird warns Siegfried afresh about Mime's approach . . . we hear gently, oh so gently, his mother Sieglinde's loving concern for her son sound forth with tuneful tenderness—the son to whom, dying, she had given birth."[67] There is a remarkable reminiscence here of Wagner's earlier letter to his mother of 19 September 1846:

> Whenever I emerge from the smoke of the city and set foot in a beautiful leafy valley, stretch out on the moss, look up at the slender trunks of the trees, and listen to some dear forest bird until a tear that I would gladly have dried trickles down my cheeks, so great is my inner contentment,—at times like these I feel that I am stretching out my hand to you through a whole mass of strange things.[68]

At the same time, this sense of yearning desire to see his lost mother is unconsciously directed at his as-yet-unknown love, a "mortal woman" (GS 6:134) to whom the Forest Bird now directs him. The sight of her revives memories of his mother, whom he now invokes. Indeed, he even thinks that the awakened Brünnhilde is his mother, so that Brünnhilde has to explain to him: "You blithesome child, your mother won't come back to you" (GS 6:168). In short, the Forest Bird is part of the world of maternal nature and, as such, not subject to Wotan's jurisdiction. Indeed, it flees from Wotan and his ravens on the Valkyries' Rock when Wotan, in a final tragic and self-contradictory attempt to assert his power, bars Siegfried's way. (This self-contradiction stems in part from the fact that on the deepest level Wotan longs for a free hero who will shatter his power.) "The way that it showed you, you shall not go!" Wotan tells Siegfried, referring to the Forest Bird and adding that the man who awakens and wins "the sleeping maid" will make him "powerless forever" (GS 6:161).

And so Wotan is rendered "powerless forever" by Siegfried and Brünnhilde,[69] who are free from his contractual constraints. Siegfried rises above every form of dependence, whether of fate or of his own making. When the Rhinedaughters warn him of the curse that "night-spinning Norns wove into the rope of primeval law" and seek to strike terror into his heart,[70] he replies with antifatalistic defiance:

> Des Urgesetzes
> ewiges Seil,
> flochten sie wilde
> Flüche hinein,
> Nothung zerhaut es den Nornen!
> Wohl warnte mich einst

vor dem Fluch' ein Wurm,
doch das Fürchten lehrt' er mich nicht.

(GS 6:238)

[Primeval law's
eternal rope
—though they wove
wild curses into its strands—
Nothung will hew from the hands of the Norns!
A dragon once warned me
against the curse,
but it did not teach me fear.]

Freedom from fear is a sign of the individual's ability to rise above fate and to regard his or her own actions as not predetermined by destiny.

The image of the Norns' rope being sundered has already appeared in Brünnhilde's exultant declaration of her love at the end of *Siegfried*. In her ecstasy, she triumphs over the power of fate and the gods.

Leb' wohl, prangende
Götter-Pracht!
End' in Wonne,
du ewig Geschlecht!
Zerreißt, ihr Nornen,
das Runenseil!
Götter-Dämm'rung,
dunk'le herauf.

(GS 6:175–176)

[Farewell, resplendent
pomp of the gods!
End in rapture,
you endless race!
Rend, you Norns,
the rope of runes!
Dusk of the gods,
let your darkness arise!]

The following scene—the prologue of *Götterdämmerung*—shows us the rope of destiny breaking, long before Siegfried announces his intention of hewing it from the Norns' hands.

Yet, although the rope of destiny has frayed and the power of the gods been broken, a fatal power remains in the form of the world's treachery, the machinations of a civilization dominated by the evil that stems from Alberich's curse on love and from his lust for possessions and power and that now rests in Hagen's hands. Siegfried's failure to recognize this is the negative side of his fearlessness. The free individual cannot survive in this world of intrigue. On his very first step on the road to civilization, Siegfried falls into a fatal trap. Not until the gods have perished and the curse-laden ring has been returned to the Rhinedaughters does the existing state of the world come to an end, allowing the free individual to appear on the musical and dramatic horizon, an individual untrammeled by fate and capable of realizing an ideal love that we glimpse in an outburst of Utopian ecstasy in the closing moments of *Siegfried*.

THE FIRE THAT CONSUMES THE WORLD AND CREATES IT ANEW

In death, Siegfried and Brünnhilde rise above all sense of alienation and return to their state of mythological integrity, thus allowing us to hope for a better world of a kind suggested by the motif heard in the orchestra at the end of the work. The fire that Brünnhilde kindles will "cleanse the ring of the curse," she insists (GS 6:253). But this ekpyrosis is intended to purify not just the ring but the world as well.[71] Wotan's world order has sprung from a violation against nature, but with the end of this order and the return of the ring to the natural elements, the world is restored to its first, paradisiacal state. By ending, it begins anew.

The fire that consumes the world at the end of the *Ring* not only recalls the Ragnarök of Norse mythology but also harks back to a myth, widespread in the ancient world, of an eschatological fire that purifies the earth. And in each case the world is reborn through the force of the fire. According to Jacob Grimm, this universal conflagration is like the Flood in that "it is intended not to destroy the world forever but to purify it and bring with it a new and better world order."[72] This was clearly in Wagner's mind when he told Cosima on 25 November 1873 about "the idea in Scandinavian mythology of a new world to follow the downfall of the gods." Here Wagner must have been thinking of the *Völuspá*, where the end of the world is depicted in the following strophes:

> The sun turns black,   earth sinks in the sea,
> The hot stars down   from heaven are whirled;
> Fierce grows the steam   and the life-feeding flame,
> Till fire leaps high   about heaven itself.
>
> Now do I see   the earth anew
> Rise all green   from the waves again;
> The cataracts fall,   and the eagle flies,
> And fish he catches   beneath the cliffs.[73]

Remarkable though it may seem at first sight, the myth of the end of the world is also a foundation myth, for the final disaster is also conceived as a new creation, a point already made by Franz Joseph Mone in the context of the Germanic "twilight of the gods." This, he writes, is

the dawn of the newborn world. . . . The end of the world and the creation of the world have much in common and are in fact one and the same, the former being distinguished from the latter only by the increased activity of the forces that are active within it. The fire that destroys the world also marks the creation of the world, but one that is in every respect more powerful than the former, in other words, more spiritual, more beautiful, and better.[74]

The fact that the end of the world is identical to its creation is symbolized musically by the invertibility of the *Ring*'s opening motif: the diatonically rising line that illustrates the idea of growth becomes a descending line, the so-called Twilight of the Gods motif, first heard when Erda announces, "All things that are will end" (GS 5:262). In this rising and descending motif, the whole meaning of the tetralogy as a myth of the beginning and end of the world is held as though in a circle.

Such is the cyclical nature of myth that it cannot conceive of the idea that the world will end once and for all; for myth, the history of the world involves a perpetual cycle of destruction and renewal. In his theoretical writings such as *Opera and Drama*, Wagner appears to have thought that this cycle would one day come to an end, but there is no sign of this in the *Ring*, where the final motif opens the door on a new kind of world. It remains unclear whether Alberich will be represented in this new world—in the first version of *Siegfried's Tod*, he "sinks down" at the end "with a gesture of anguish" (GS 2:228), but no deeper conclusions can be drawn from this, as the principle of evil has been defeated with the return of the gold to the Rhinedaughters and the destruction of Hagen as Alberich's agent and heir.

The motif that is heard in the orchestra in the final bars of the *Ring* occurs only twice in the cycle, an economy designed to ensure that there is no doubt as to its meaning. It is the motif first stated by Sieglinde when Brünnhilde tells her that she will give birth to Siegfried. It is then taken up in Brünnhilde's peroration and entrusted to the violins in the final bars of *Götterdämmerung*, where it speaks a language clearer than Brünnhilde's closing words. Although normally described as the Redemption motif, it goes beyond any merely semantic definition, being, rather, the motif of birth and rebirth. It is significant that when Wagner completed the first draft of this passage on 10 April 1872, he wrote beneath it: "Thus it came about and was completed on the day that my Loldchen was born 7 years ago." In other words, Wagner related the final motif to the birth of his first daughter, Isolde, in 1865.

In the history of myth, birth has always been what Mircea Eliade has termed a "symbolic recapitulation of the cosmogony."[75] In this sense, Sieglinde's motif is the foundation motif, the cosmogonic motif par excellence, which is why the *Ring* comes full circle with it. Like a rainbow of hope, it rises at the end of *Götterdämmerung*, soaring radiantly over the Valhalla motif, which is consumed by Loge's semiquaver figurations denoting fire, and over the sinuous melody of the Rhinedaughters (the music of the natural elements), proclaiming that the world has been purified and undergone a *restitutio in integrum*. This in turn is strikingly illustrated by the way in which the musical argument moves beyond its troubled chromaticisms and returns to the pure sonorities of the intervals of the harmonic series. In this way the "fullness of the beginnings" (to quote Eliade) is restored, and the ring, in keeping with Brünnhilde's instructions,[76] is dissolved in the Rhine, allowing the star of hope to rise on a new world in place of the apoca-lyptic devastation that we have witnessed.[77]

In this way, the Nibelung myth extends from the paradisiacal primal state of nature as symbolized by the E flat major triad of the prelude and the wavelike melody of the Rhinedaughters to the reestablishment of a natural order pro-claimed by the final motif with its promise of a better future. Past and future meet in the single word *einst.* "Thus it comes about," says the narrator of Thomas Mann's epic novel *Joseph and His Brethren*, "when the twofold sense of the words 'one day' cast their magic spell, when the past is the future, when every-thing has long since taken place and must now take place again in the precise present!"[78]

Redemption and Apocatastasis

PARSIFAL *AND THE RELIGION OF THE LATE WAGNER*

The simplest and most moving of religious symbols, uniting

us in the common practice of our faith . . . , stems from the

knowledge of our need for redemption, knowledge that

preoccupies us in the most manifold forms. We already feel

that we partake of this redemption in that solemn hour when all

the world's phenomena dissolve as in a prophetic dream; . . .

only then will nature's lament, pure and yearning for peace, ring

forth for us, fearless, filled with hope, all-assuaging, world-

redeeming. As a result of this lament, the soul of all humankind

is purified and becomes conscious of its own high office in

redeeming all of like-suffering nature. It now soars above the

abyss of semblances, and the restless will, freed from the

terrible causality of birth and death, feels liberated from itself.

—Richard Wagner, "Religion and Art"

THE END IS THE BEGINNING, a *restitutio in integrum*, restoring all things and at the same time marking a new beginning. This is the message that we hear at the end of *Götterdämmerung*. The cyclical return to the original state of perfection: this is the classical idea of *apokatástasis pánton*, a term that is borrowed from the Acts of the Apostles 3:21, where it is translated as "the restitution of all things," and that was to be of importance for the entire Christian tradition.[1] It is often associated with the Heraclitean idea of ekpyrosis, the dissolution of the world into the primal element of fire from which it arose. (In this context, fire must be understood to mean *spérma*, the seed from which a new world will arise.)[2] This idea, too, is basic to Wagner's concept of the *Ring*, the ending of which marks a "restitution of all things" in the form of a return to the pure sonorities of the natural harmonic series unclouded by any chromaticisms.

THE RESTITUTION OF ALL THINGS

At the end of *Parsifal*, too, we find a restitutio in integrum, in this case symbolized by the reunion of two objects that had become separated, the spear, which has been returned to Monsalvat, and the Grail, which once again shines forth in all its purity.[3] Both objects are associated with Christ: the spear was thrust into his side as he hung on the cross, and the Grail is the vessel into which his blood flowed. In the final scene, Parsifal raises his eyes to the holy spear and tells Amfortas:

> Die deine Wunde durfte schließen,
> ihr seh' ich heil'ges Blut entfließen
> in Sehnsucht dem verwandten Quelle,
> der dort fließt in des Grales Welle!

(GS 10:375)

> [From the spear that was allowed to close your wound
> I see sacred blood flowing
> in its longing for its kindred source
> that flows and wells within the Grail!]

Here, then, the ending signifies the cyclical return to the beginning in an intensified form. Now the blood of the Redeemer, not that of the sinner, flows from the spear; spear and Grail become one through this sacred blood, and Amfortas's wound is healed when touched with the spear by which it had been dealt. The Grail community is restored, Klingsor's alternative world is exorcised, and nature returns to its state of paradisiacal innocence. Christianity is stripped of its historicity in *Parsifal* and restored to the iterative structures of myth. According to Kurt Hübner, "It is set in a mythological world and a mythological time, it is nowhere and never." At the same time the Redeemer appears not as a historical but as an archetypal figure. The only person to encounter him is Kundry, who, significantly, is "not localized in any period or any place."[4]

In short, the ending of Wagner's *Bühnenweihfestspiel* (literally, "a festival play with which to dedicate a stage") cannot be interpreted as part of a linear development that ends with the prospect of a wholly new world, a prospect suggested by many recent stagings of the work. When Parsifal, as the new Grail king, instructs the communicant knights in his final lines "No longer shall it be closed: reveal the Grail—open the shrine!" (GS 10:375), he does not mean that from then on the Grail will be displayed forever and that the hermetically sealed Grail community will be opened to the world.[5] Although Amfortas has long refused to display the Grail, this does not mean that once Parsifal has ordered the shrine to be opened, it must always remain open. It surely goes without saying that once the rite has been enacted, the Grail will be covered again and returned to its tabernacle—just as it was at the end of act 1, when Amfortas reluctantly allowed the sacred vessel to be uncovered. After he has blessed the knights with it, "the boys lock the vessel away in the shrine and cover the latter as before" (GS 10:343). This will happen in the future, too. The only thing that has changed is that the Grail is no longer locked away for good on Amfortas's instructions.

In exactly the same way, the final line of the work, "Redemption to the Redeemer!" (GS 10:375), presupposes a cyclical development to the action. There has been much speculation about this line in recent decades, and it has even been interpreted as the secret formula of a "new religion" with sinister implications,[6] even though neither the text nor the music provides any basis for such a speculative reading of it. Its meaning as *salvator salvandus*[7] is clear from the dramatic context. That the Redeemer in *Parsifal* is Christ himself, as present in the Grail, is clear from every line in the libretto in which this word appears, with one exception, to which I shall return in a moment. The only "redemption" here is Christ's redemptive act. This can mean only that Christ redeems himself. The circumstances in which this act of redemption takes place will become clear shortly.

The final line of the work expresses the idea that Parsifal has now fulfilled the request vouchsafed to him in his vision of the Redeemer following Kundry's kiss. When, in his horror, he tears himself from Kundry's arms and feels Amfortas's wound deep in his own heart, he is (according to the stage directions) "completely lost to the world" (GS 10:358). He sees the Grail before his mind's eye and hears the "Savior's cry."

> die Klage, ach! die Klage
> um das verrath'ne Heiligthum:—
> "erlöse, rette mich
> aus schuldbefleckten Händen!"

(GS 10:359)

> [Lamenting, ah! lamenting
> for the forsaken sanctuary:—
> "Redeem and rescue me
> from hands defiled by guilt!"]

The hands defiled by guilt are those of Amfortas, the "sinful guardian of the sanctuary," as Wagner called him in a program note dating from 1882 (SS 12:349). And this act of redemption takes place when Parsifal, having resisted Kundry's attempts to seduce him, brings back the sacred lance and replaces Amfortas as leader of the Grail community. Thus he brings "Redemption to the Redeemer."

But does this not mean that Parsifal, too, is a redeemer, greater, indeed, than Christ, who, it would seem, needs to be redeemed by Parsifal? In the finished libretto, Wagner painstakingly avoided depicting his hero initiating the act of redemption. In the 1877 draft, for example, Parsifal still tells Kundry: "Ich will dich lieben und erlösen" [I want to love you and redeem you],[8] but in the finished libretto this becomes "Lieb' und Erlösung soll dir lohnen" [Love and redemption shall reward you] (GS 10:362). In other words, Parsifal sees himself not as the instigator of redemption but as its agent. Not even in the earlier draft, of course, does he think that he can redeem Kundry by himself. In *Parsifal*, redemption is the work of the one true Redeemer, who uses the "pure" individual, purged by the knowledge of compassion, as his instrument. That Parsifal, entrusted with the task of redeeming Christ, who is immanent within the Grail, remains within the limitations imposed by his humanity is clear from his reaction to his Savior's lament. Overcome by remorse at his failure in the Grail Castle, he sinks to his knees: "Erlöser! Heiland! Herr der Huld! / Wie büß' ich Sünder solche Schuld?" [Redeemer! Savior! Lord of grace! / How can I, a sinner, atone for such a sin?] (GS 10:359).

Parsifal remains prey to human frailty, but from the time of his vision of the Savior onward, he knows that he has been appointed to act as an instrument of salvation and redemption. "Auch dir bin ich zum Heil gesandt" [For your salvation, too, I have been sent], he tells Kundry, leaving her (and us) in no doubt as to who is to be seen as "des einz'gen Heiles wahren Quell" [the fount from where true healing flows] (GS 10:361). It is the Savior with whose symbol—the "sign of the cross"—he exorcises the magic of Klingsor's world (GS 10:363). The Redeemer has to use a "pure fool" in order to redeem himself.[9] This is the meaning of the paradoxical final phrase, "Redemption to the Redeemer." It recalls the problem of Wotan's whole existence in the *Ring*: the god must leave it to a human hero "to perform the deed which, however needful to the gods, the god is forbidden to do" (GS 6:32).[10] This hero, of course, "lacking godly protection" (GS 6:32), must act entirely independently and on his own initiative, whereas Parsifal always acts with an eye to Christ's redemptive act. Christ himself is no longer able to act, as he has committed himself into the hands of humankind in the form of the Grail, finding expression as a holy relic that is handled by others but that does not act. As a result of this material passivity, Christ, immanent in the Grail, needs a human being to redeem him. This redemption amounts to a restitutio in integrum symbolized by the reunion of the spear and the Grail.

As Hans Küng has pointed out, the "major theme" of *Parsifal* is "our own participation in the process of redemption, with a clear emphasis on active involvement in that process, without God's earlier redemptive act in Christ thereby being negated or superseded." At no point in the work, Küng insists, does Parsifal regard himself as a "Christ substitute or divine figure."[11] Earlier, however, I mentioned an exception, a passage in the text where Parsifal is described unmistakably as Redeemer and, moreover, as Redeemer in his own capacity. Kundry addresses him thus in act 2:

> Bist du Erlöser,
> was bannt dich, Böser,
> nicht mir auch zum Heil dich zu einen?
> Seit Ewigkeiten—harre ich deiner,
> des Heiland's, ach! so spät,
> den einst ich kühn verschmäht.

(GS 10:360)

> [If you're the Redeemer,
> what prevents you, you evil man,

from uniting with me for my own salvation?
From time immemorial I have been waiting for you,
   my Savior, ah! so late,
   whom once I boldly reviled.]

For Kundry, Parsifal really does appear to become the Redeemer here, the Savior, a reincarnation of Christ, at whom she once laughed on his way to being crucified. But it must be remembered that it is Kundry the seductress who is speaking here: for her, redemption and salvation assume the guise of sexual congress with Parsifal. He must feel that he is her savior; indeed, she even promises him: "Mein volles Liebes-Umfangen/läßt dich dann Gottheit erlangen" [My loving embrace/will allow you to achieve godhood] (GS 10:361). Here Kundry speaks like the serpent in the Garden of Eden. Indeed, Wagner himself pointed out this parallel in his letter to Ludwig dated 7 September 1865: "You know, of course, the serpent of Paradise and its tempting promise 'Eritis sicut Deus, scientes bonum et malum.' "[12] The quotation is taken from Genesis 3:5: "Ye shall be as gods, knowing good and evil." Wagner had already used this phrase in his 1865 prose draft, where he has Kundry say: "Embrace me now in love, and you'll be God himself today" (SS 11:409).

What the serpent promised Eve, Kundry now promises Parsifal—just as Venus once promised Tannhäuser that he, too, would be "a god" (GS 2:6). But just as Tannhäuser retains an awareness that he is mortal and just as he yearns to suffer pain in the midst of pleasure, so Parsifal's fellow feeling for Amfortas's sufferings prevents him from being misled into thinking that he will achieve divinity through Kundry. In vain the temptress seeks to foist on him the roles of Redeemer, Savior, and Christ figure. Admittedly, Wagner drew an analogy between Christ and Parsifal in the aforementioned letter to Ludwig, at the same time pointing out parallels between Adam and Amfortas on the one hand and Eve and Kundry on the other. But such a parallel, he stressed, should be drawn only with "considerable caution,"[13] hence his later refusal to accept Hans von Wolzogen's interpretation of Parsifal as a reflection of the Redeemer. "I didn't think of the Savior at all," Wagner apparently told Cosima on 20 October 1878. In fact, Wolzogen later abandoned this view and saw Parsifal simply as an intermediary in Christ's continuing act of redemption.[14]

But who is it that is redeemed? In the first instance, it is the alienated Grail and hence Christ himself, inasmuch as the relic is now "freed from the care of sullied hands," to quote from the 1865 prose draft (SS 11:408). But it is also Amfortas, whose wound is healed and whose "yearning desire and unspeakable torments" (SS 11:408) are stilled. (His torments look backward to *Tristan und Isolde* but have now been reinterpreted as something negative in the light of Wagner's changing response to Schopenhauer.)[15] Finally, Kundry herself is redeemed, her baptism and death allowing her to find release from the torments of her eternal peregrinations. Both Amfortas and Kundry are redeemed through Christ's agency, by virtue of the spear from which his blood flows and by the sacrament that he initiated and gave to humankind as a token of our faith: "Die Taufe nimm/und glaub' an den Erlöser!" [Accept this baptism/and believe in the Redeemer!] (GS 10:371).

THE METAMORPHOSES OF KUNDRY

Who in fact is Kundry? I have already answered this question, at least in part, in my chapter on *Der fliegende Holländer*. Kundry is a reincarnation of the Herodias and Salome of the Bible, a figure who, according to a legend first recorded in the Middle Ages, was condemned, like Ahasuerus, to a restless, nomadic existence as a result of her murderous crime against John the Baptist. And according to writers such as Karl Simrock and Jacob Grimm, both of whom helped to codify Teutonic mythology, she led the Wild Hunt. Klingsor calls her an "arch-she-devil" (GS 10:345), a designation that points back to the early rabbinical tradition of Adam's first wife, Lilith,[16] the prototypically demonic and seductive woman who is also found in the Walpurgis Night scene in Goethe's *Faust* (ll. 4118–20).

But Kundry also appears to be related to a different cycle of legends: Klingsor, her master and—let us not mince words—pimp, recalls Simon Magus, a sorcerer from Samaria who figures in the Acts of the Apostles 8:9–24. Described as "the father of heresy" by such writers on church history as Irenaeus and Eusebius, he became the source of all manner of legends from the early Christian period onward. In the *Recognitiones*, which were once attributed to Pope Clement I, he is said to have studied in Egypt and to have been able to conjure up ghosts and raise the dead, to make himself invisible, to pass through walls and fire, and to be capable of other magic tricks that he used against Saint Paul the Apostle in a systematic attempt to subvert the early Christian Church, much as Klingsor attempts to undermine the Grail community. (Faust was later described as "second in magic" to the "First Magician," Simon Magus.)[17] Among his followers was a certain Helen, whom he had acquired from a brothel and who supported Simon's antiecclesiastical activities with the aid of her shameless harlotry. She, too, is found in the literary Faust tradition, where she figures as the idol in the "Hexenküche" (witches' kitchen) scene in part 1 of *Faust*. And she is probably one of Kundry's models. That Klingsor has power over her only because he has castrated himself and is therefore resistant to her charms is an original idea that Wagner has added to the character of Simon Magus. It too has an early Christian precedent in the figure of Origen, who mutilated himself in an attempt to escape from the lusts of the flesh, an act rejected by the church in much the same way that Klingsor's self-castration is derided by Titurel and the Grail community.[18]

Behind the figure of Kundry—and possibly also behind the tradition of Simon Magus—may lie a further figure from the esoteric Mosaic tradition. Just as Peter has an antagonist in Simon Magus, so Moses is contrasted with the pagan prophet Bileam, who acknowledges that the tribe of Israel is the chosen people but who becomes their enemy for precisely that reason. He too uses female decoys to tempt the Israelites into abandoning their God.[19]

But Kundry's clearest and most important prototype is the figure of Ahasuerus, the Wandering Jew. In the 1865 prose draft, Wagner writes that "the span of Kundry's life cannot be measured, for she lives under constantly changing rebirths in consequence of an age-old curse that condemns her, like the 'Wandering Jew,' to assume

different forms and bring men the suffering of love's seduction" (SS 11:104). She
has been cursed because she laughed at Christ on his way to being crucified, an
archetypal situation that invites us to feel pity. The failure to show pity in turn becomes a further archetypal situation, recurring in Parsifal's tragic failure in act 1,
when he neglects to show pity in the face of Amfortas's suffering.

Kundry not only fails to show pity but goes even further than Ahasuerus, who
refused to allow Christ to rest outside his house but drove him on his way. Instead,
she adopts the very opposite attitude, attempting, as it were, to invalidate pity by
means of a principle diametrically opposed to it: laughter. Christ's reaction to her
laughter is significant: "Da traf mich sein Blick" [His gaze then fell upon me] (GS
10:360). It is the inner gaze that fell on Peter when he thrice denied Jesus, causing
Peter to weep bitterly. But Kundry cannot weep until her curse has been lifted,
which happens at the moment of her baptism (GS 10:371–72). Her tears during
the Good Friday spell bring a permanent end to her convulsive laughter.[20]

In all her reincarnations, Kundry hopes to reencounter her Redeemer's "gaze,"
evidently wanting to experience the emotion that is always triggered by such a
gaze in Wagner's works: compassion and, hence, love. When Isolde is struck by
Tristan's gaze, she allows the sword to fall from her grasp: "I pitied him in his anguish." She cures him and sends him home, so that he may no longer "oppress me
with his gaze" (GS 7:11). And Gurnemanz seeks to rouse Parsifal to pity for the
swan that he has killed: "Lifeless his eye, do you see his gaze?" (GS 10:335).[21]
Parsifal now breaks his bow in his first involuntary, as yet "unknowing," act of
compassion. Kundry is unable to arouse such a sense of compassion.

> Nun such' ich ihn von Welt zu Welt,
>   ihm wieder zu begegnen:
>   in höchster Noth—
>   wähn' ich sein Auge schon nah',
>   den Blick schon auf mir ruh'n:—
> da kehrt mir das verfluchte Lachen wieder,—
>   ein Sünder sinkt mir in die Arme!
>   Da lach' ich—lache—,
>   kann nicht weinen.
>
>   (GS 10:360)

> [I seek him now from world to world,
>   hoping to meet him again:
>   in my greatest need—
> I think his eye is already close,
>   his gaze is already resting upon me:—
> then this accursed laughter returns,—
>   a sinner sinks into my arms!
>   Then I laugh—laugh—,
>   I cannot weep.]

Here the gaze does not produce what it normally produces—tears and pity—but
results in its opposing principle, laughter.

Kundry's "curse" "torments her endlessly through existence" and forces her to keep repeating this laughter: this is her original sin. And her laughter is associated in her mind with seduction. Indeed, the two are identical, as she herself admits: "Then this accursed laughter returns,—a sinner sinks into my arms" (GS 10:360). Such seduction goes beyond erotic enchantment and is tantamount to a loss of salvation and, as such, is the opposite of redemption. All who fall victim to Kundry's wiles forfeit any hope of salvation. Her laughter, like her seduction, is diabolical in the original sense of the term, a perversion of the divine order of things, a further example of original sin that is punished, as a result, by a curse that overrides the laws of nature, rescinding death (which came into the world as a consequence of Eve's original sin) and turning the primordial state of prelapsarian Paradise into a hellish curse in the form of the inability to die.

The origins of Kundry's laughter and its metaphysical implications have always been something of a puzzle for Wagnerian exegetes. Such laughter cannot be explained by traditional poetological theories of laughter, still less can it be interpreted in terms of the convulsive laughter of Adrian Leverkühn in Thomas Mann's *Doktor Faustus*, for all that Leverkühn's laughter is clearly related to Kundry's. (Mann himself repeatedly drew analogies between his novel and *Parsifal*.) It seems rather as though the laughter of both Kundry and Leverkühn has a common source in Baudelaire's 1855 essay *De l'essence du rire* (On the essence of laughter). Mann is known to have studied this essay in Max Bruns's German translation.[22] Whether Wagner had read it is not known, but in private conversations he invariably picked up far more ideas than he ever did from his reading, and we know from *My Life* (ML 620) that he was in regular contact with Baudelaire in Paris during the winter of 1860–61.

Klingsor's apostrophization of Kundry as "Ur-teufelin! Höllenrose!" [Arch-she-devil! Rose of hell!] (GS 10:345) recalls two separate works by Baudelaire, *Les fleurs du mal* (1857) and the aforementioned essay, *De l'essence du rire*. Here Baudelaire turns his back on the poetological tradition and defines comedy as "un des plus clairs signes sataniques de l'homme" [one of the clearest satanic signs of man], one of the pips of the "symbolic apple,"[23] by which he evidently meant both Persephone's pomegranate (by eating a pomegranate seed Persephone is tied to the underworld forever) and the apple in the Garden of Eden. Laughter is satanic. It was unknown in Eden, and Christ never laughed, although he often wept, a circumstance that for Baudelaire was enough to confirm the diabolical nature of laughter. There is no doubt that Baudelaire's definition inspired the laughter of Adrian Leverkühn, who enters into a pact with the Devil and whose oratorio on the subject of the apocalypse features the pandemonium of laughter. Yet Baudelaire's definition could equally well be applied to Kundry, who laughed at Christ, contemptuously denying his work as Redeemer and resisting him as a seductress and counter-redeemer—a reincarnation of the serpent of Genesis repeatedly urging us on to sin, a sin that here has sexual connotations.

On the strength of Kundry's similarity with the Wandering Jew Ahasuerus, it has been argued that she "represents everything that Wagner associated with Jewishness."[24] If this is so, Wagner must have been inordinately fond of Jews, as every listener with even a modicum of aesthetic sensitivity is bound to appreciate the potential for sympathy with which Wagner has invested the character of Kundry both musically and poetically. She was Jewish in, at most, one of her reincarnations, but she is also of Germanic extraction. "Herodias you were, and what else?" Klingsor asks her. She has been much else in the course of her reincarnations among the nations of the earth: "Gundryggia there, Kundry here" (GS 10:346). Gundryggia is believed to be the name of a Valkyrie that Wagner invented.[25]

The question of Kundry's racial or tribal origins in *Parsifal* is a nonstarter as a subject for serious discussion. Like Heine, Wagner similarly described the Flying Dutchman as a variant of the Wandering Jew, without thereby imputing to him Semitic origins. If, as Wagner says, Kundry is "like" the Wandering Jew, this means simply that she plays the same mythological role as Ahasuerus and that because she pitilessly mocked her Savior on his way to being crucified, she is condemned to a life of eternal wanderings.

In spite of this similarity with the mythological figure of Ahasuerus, Kundry is not Jewish but is depicted as a heathen. This is how the Esquires describe her: "Eine Heidin ist's, ein Zauberweib" [She's a heathen woman, a sorceress] (GS 10:329). Unlike the Wandering Jew, she does not always remain the same person, but on the strength of her eternal wanderings she is associated with the Buddhist belief in metempsychosis,[26] with its endless succession of rebirths, for which Wagner was later to find a counterpart in the Cabala.[27]

There are clearly affinities here with Wagner's abandoned plans to write an opera called *Die Sieger* (The victors) in 1856.[28] In this sketch the principal female figure is Prakriti, a member of the Chandala caste who falls in love with Ananda, a Buddha disciple who has taken a vow of chastity. In an "earlier birth," Prakriti was the daughter of a Brahman, and "in the spirit of the caste system," she had "proudly and arrogantly" rejected the passionate love of a son of the Chandala king, "scorning the unhappy boy. For this she had to atone and was reborn as a Chandala girl in order for her to feel the torments of unrequited love" (SS 11:325).

Although the two characters are in some respects the opposite of each other, the parallels between Kundry and Prakriti are impossible to ignore: in both cases a woman scorns an unhappy man and refuses to take pity on his sufferings (Schopenhauerian suffering is at the metaphysical and ethical heart of both *Parsifal* and *Die Sieger*), and in both cases she has to atone for this by suffering the torments of unrequited love in a later existence;[29] in *Die Sieger*, it is Prakriti's love of Ananda; in *Parsifal*, Kundry's for Parsifal. As Gurnemanz explains to the Esquires:

> Ja, eine Verwünschte mag sie sein:
> > hier lebt sie heut',—
> > vielleicht erneut',
> zu büßen Schuld aus früher'm Leben,
> die dorten ihr noch nicht vergeben.

(GS 10:330)

> [Yes, she may be accursed:
> > she's living here today,
> > perhaps reborn,

atoning for her guilt in an earlier life
that was not forgiven her then.]

Like Prakriti, she finds "redemption" through "renunciation" (SS 11:325). Renunciation, in the Schopenhauerian sense, is the extinction of all desire, in particular compulsive sexual desire, which is the focus of the blind will. Kundry finds
redemption in death, which for her, as for Ahasuerus and the Flying Dutchman,
means release from a seemingly endless existence; she is freed from the fatal
cycle of rebirths, allowing her to find "dissolution, total extinction" in nirvana (SS
11:404). Prakriti, by contrast, acquires "complete redemption by being accepted
into the Buddha's community," which, unlike that of the Grail, is open to the
opposite sex. With a "joyous yes," Prakriti takes a vow of chastity, which the
Buddha has made the only condition of her "union with Ananda." And "Ananda
greets her as a sister" (SS 11:325). The same idea occurs in *Parsifal*, where, following her baptism, Parsifal kisses Kundry "tenderly on the forehead" (GS
10:372). His brotherly kiss, devoid of all desire, is the opposite of the erotic kiss
that Kundry had implanted on his lips in act 2.

As we have seen, Wagner attempted to revise Schopenhauer's "Metaphysics of
Sexual Love" at the time that he was working on *Tristan und Isolde* (see SS 12:291),
but he appears to have abandoned this attempt when he came to write *Parsifal*. Indeed, there were already signs of this in *Die Meistersinger*, where the affirmative approach to love that we find at the end of *Tristan und Isolde* is already called into
question, at least in part: "Hans Sachs was wise and wanted none of King Marke's
fate" (GS 7:254). Renunciation is now seen as a wiser course than love. And this is
even more true of *Parsifal*. "Powerful is the magic of him who desires, but even more
powerful is that of him who renounces," Parsifal tells Amfortas at the end of the 1865
prose draft (SS 11:413).

Love as a powerful erotic force is contrasted with love as agape, "whose origin
and nature"—to quote Schopenhauer—"we know to be seeing through the *principium individuationis*." Just as erotic love is selfish, so agape is compassion,
grounded, as it is, in the teachings of the Veda: "Tat twam asi" [This art thou!].
"Whoever," writes Schopenhauer, "is able to declare this to himself with clear
knowledge and firm inward conviction about every creature with whom he comes
into contact, is certain of all virtue and bliss, and is on the direct path to salvation."[30] Such a person, I may add, using Wagner's own formulation in *Parsifal*, is
"made wise by pity." Paradoxically, Parsifal's experience of "Tat twam asi" comes
from Kundry's kiss, an instance of the selfishness of sexual desire that in Kundry's
expression makes him "Welt-hellsichtig" [able to see the world clearly] (GS 10:361).
With sudden insight he sees through the principium individuationis and acquires
an awareness of the metaphysical compassion that lies at the very heart of
Schopenhauer's system of ethics.

Erotic love is excluded from the world of the Grail, an exclusion heightened,
rather than relaxed, by Parsifal, thereby leading to the repudiation of women. In
this, the work differs from *Die Sieger*, where the Buddha integrates women into
the community. That this insistence on total chastity mirrors Schopenhauer's idea

of asceticism as a denial of the will to live is clear.[31] But such chastity is also the basic rule of all Christian religious communities in which the sexes are segregated. Like Wagner's Grail knights, the members of monastic orders lead lives of exemplary asceticism, although this cannot mean that sex—and with it, women—is driven from the world entirely or that the will to live is universally extinguished. (It is not, of course, the wish of all nunneries to drive all men from the world.) Only if the exclusivity and celibate lifestyle of the Grail knights is misunderstood as a universal form of human existence does a problem arise and sexuality appear to be demonized in *Parsifal* and women sidelined.[32]

In *Die Sieger*, as I have noted, Wagner experimented with the idea of a sexually integrated ascetic community.[33] At no point did he hanker after the ideals of the German *Männerbünde* (male societies), and in almost all his works he regarded women as more perceptive and intuitive than men. In this respect, *Parsifal* is an exception. And in this context it is worth recalling Wagner's interest in the teachings of Hebraic mysticism concerning the Trinity, set forth in August Friedrich Gfrörer's 1838 *Geschichte des Urchristentums* (History of early Christianity), where he argues that God the Father is complemented by the feminine principle of the Spirit, creating a union that in turn produces the androgynous Redeemer as an ideal prototype of humankind, but the first man—*adam kadmon*—forfeited his divine androgyny as a consequence of the Fall.[34]

On 6 January 1875 Wagner told Cosima that he found "this definition of the Trinity infinitely interesting," a definition which, he explained to her, was "made shortly before Christ's birth—God the Father, masculine; the Holy Ghost, feminine; the Redeemer as the world stemming from them." And he went on to interpret this in terms of Schopenhauerian philosophy: "Will, representation, and world, the world emerging from the division of the sexes." In other words, the division of the sexes results from the *status corruptionis* triggered by the Fall. If this idea found its way into *Parsifal*, it would confirm Kurt Hübner's theory that the reunification of spear and Grail as symbols of the male desire to dominate and of female conception represents a reconciliation between the sexes overriding the purely male principle of the Grail community.[35] (This is also the idea behind Wieland Wagner's "Parsifal Cross" and his 1951 Bayreuth production of the work.) In this way, the androgynous principle familiar to Wagner from Plato's *Symposium*—a work that he much admired—would be restored.[36] (In chapters 14–16 Aristophanes recounts the myth of the bisexual beings who originally peopled the earth and who were divided by Zeus, after which the male and female halves are consumed by desire for each other and by the longing to regain their original unity, this, in Plato's view, being the underlying aim of sexual love.)[37] Kundry's appearance at Parsifal's side in the Castle of the Grail (GS 10:375) would thereby signify the transcendence of this exclusively male principle that has obtained hitherto—and this in spite of her death, which is the only possible redemption for a "Wandering Jewess" following the endless cycle of her rebirths.

Just as Kundry's endless wanderings can be interpreted as an example of metempsychosis, so can they be seen to reflect the eternal cycle of nature. Kundry literally hibernates, waking up to new life each spring with nature.[38] At the start of act 3, Gurnemanz drags her out of an overgrown thornbush (like the bush in Walther's Spring Song in act 1 of *Die Meistersinger*, it is an image of the lifelessness of winter), and, by rubbing her limbs, he eases the numbness left by her winter's sleep. The Third Esquire derisively compares her to a "wild beast," prompting her profound and quick-witted reply: "Are the beasts not holy here?" (GS 10:329). In this way she uses the Grail knights' own injunction to reject the way in which she has been marginalized.

But Kundry is also the most beautiful of the "fleurs du mal," the tropical flowers in Klingsor's magic garden. Klingsor even calls her "Höllenrose" [rose of hell] (GS 10:345). She embodies pagan nature, nature that is not yet redeemed. As a result, her own redemption is symbolically associated with the redemption of nonhuman nature in the Good Friday scene, one of the most moving and inspired scenes in Wagner, drawing, as it does, on ancient motifs taken from Christian mysticism and legend.

The Good Friday spell begins to work its magic at the very moment when Kundry is baptized and her tears bedew the ground, thus washing away her accursed compulsion to laugh. Now woodland and meadow begin to grow brighter. Parsifal notices this "in gentle ecstasy," comparing their radiant beauty with the "morbid" charms of the "magic flowers" in Klingsor's garden. But, he asks Gurnemanz in dismay, should nature not join with the rest of humanity in grieving for the Redeemer's death on this "day of deepest anguish?" Gurnemanz replies:

> Du sieh'st, das ist nicht so.
> Des Sünders Reuethränen sind es,
> die heut' mit heil'gem Thau
> beträufet Flur und Au':
> der ließ sie so gedeihen.
> Nun freut' sich alle Kreatur
> auf des Erlösers holder Spur,
> will ihr Gebet ihm weihen.
> Ihn selbst am Kreuze kann sie nicht erschauen:
> da blickt sie zum erlös'ten Menschen auf;
> der fühlt sich frei von Sünden-Angst und Grauen,
> durch Gottes Liebesopfer rein und heil:
> das merkt nun Halm und Blume auf den Auen,
> daß heut' des Menschen Fuß sie nicht zertritt,
> doch wohl, wie Gott mit himmlischer Geduld
> sich sein' erbarmt und für ihn litt,
> der Mensch auch heut' in frommer Huld
> sie schont mit sanftem Schritt.
> Das dankt dann alle Kreatur,
> was all' da blüht und bald erstirbt,
> da die entsündigte Natur
> heut' ihren Unschulds-Tag erwirbt.

(GS 10:371–72)

[You see, that is not so.
It is the sinner's tears of true repentance
    that lave both field and meadow
    with their holy dew today:
    thus he made them flourish.
Now creatures all rejoice and,
    following in their Redeemer's gracious steps,
        they seek to dedicate their prayer to him.
They cannot see him on the cross
and so they look up to redeemed mankind,
who feels free from the fear and terror of sin,
made pure and whole through God's loving sacrifice:
grass and flowers in the meadow notice
that today they are not trampled underfoot by man
but that, as God with heavenly patience
    pitied him and suffered for him,
    so man, in devout grace, today
        spares them with his gentle tread.
Thus all creatures give thanks,
all that blooms and quickly fades,
now that nature, absolved from sin,
finds its day of innocence today.]

The symbolic relevance that this whole speech holds for Kundry—it is, after all, her tears of remorse that have conferred on nature its present radiance, she who is the redeemed figure to whom all those creatures in need of redemption now raise their eyes in turn—is clear from her reaction to it: "Kundry has slowly raised her head again and gazes up at Parsifal with tearful eyes filled with calm and earnest entreaty" (GS 10:372). Parsifal recognizes the mysterious correspondence between Kundry's redemption and the absolution accorded to nature, which, freed from sin, is restored to its erstwhile state of paradisiacal innocence: here, too, we find an example of *apokatástasis*, a restitutio in integrum. "Ich sah sie welken, die einst mir lachten" [I saw them wither, they who once laughed at me] (GS 10:372), Parsifal says, referring, of course, to the flowers in Klingsor's magic garden whose pagan spell he had broken by making the sign of the cross. "Ob heut' sie nach Erlösung schmachten?" [Are they pining for redemption today?]. And he turns to Kundry: "Auch deine Thräne ward zum Segensthaue: / du weinest—sieh! es lacht die Aue!" [Your tear, too, has become a bliss-bringing dew: you weep— behold! The meadow smiles!] (GS 10:372).

Significantly, it is in this scene that Kundry undergoes her final transformation, when she becomes a reembodiment of Mary Magdalene—the Mary Magdalene of both the New Testament and of Wagner's fragmentary *Jesus von Nazareth*, in which the composer adopts the traditional identification of the figure with the "sinner" in Saint Luke's Gospel (7:37–50). The erstwhile sinner washes Parsifal's feet, pouring over them oil from a vial and drying them with her hair (GS 10:370).[39]

According to Wolf-Daniel Hartwich, "Kundry's emotional history embraces the soteriological ages of paganism, Judaism, and Christianity in the figures of Herodias, Ahasuerus, and Mary Magdalene."[40]

The Good Friday spell represents a mystical realization of Saint Paul's teachings concerning the sigh uttered by all those creatures who suffer at the knowledge of their fatal destiny, a sigh heard in the "dull groaning" uttered by Kundry when concealed within the thorn thicket at the start of act 3 (GS 10:364). Wagner writes of "nature's lament" in his essay "Religion and Art" of 1880 (GS 10:249). According to chapter 8 of Paul's Epistle to the Romans, Adam's sin affected not only humankind but all of creation:

> For the earnest expectation of the creature waiteth for the manifestation of the sons of God. For the creature was made subject to vanity, not willingly, but by reason of him who hath subjected the same in hope, because the creature itself also shall be delivered from the bondage of corruption into the glorious liberty of the children of God. For we know that the whole creation groaneth and travaileth in pain together until now. (Romans 8:19–22)

This passage from Paul's Epistle to the Romans has always fascinated poets. Suffice it to recall Annette von Droste-Hülshoff's 1846 poem "Die ächzende Kreatur" (The groaning creature).

> Da ward ihr klar, wie nicht allein
> Der Gottesfluch im Menschenbild,
> Wie er in schwerer, dumpfer Pein
> Im bangen Wurm, im scheuen Wild,
> Im durst'gen Halme auf der Flur,
> Der mit vergilbten Blättern lechzt,
> In aller, aller Kreatur
> Gen Himmel um Erlösung lechzt.
>
> [She saw that she was not alone
> And that God's curse on humankind
> Afflicted with its dull-edged moan
> The timid worm and fearful hind,
> And that parched grass upon the lea
> Whose yellow leaves refreshment craved.
> In each and every beast she'd see
> Eyes raised in hope of being saved.]

The human race bears a guilt of which it is barely conscious, as the final strophe makes plain.

> Das ist die Schuld des Mordes an
> Der Erde Lieblichkeit und Huld,
> An des Getieres dumpfem Bann
> Ist es die tiefe, schwere Schuld,

Und an dem Grimm, der es beseelt,
Und an der List, die es befleckt,
Und an dem Schmerze, der es quält,
Und an dem Moder, der es deckt.

[This is the price we have to pay
For butchering earth's loveliness.
Beasts we subjected to our sway
And guilt must bear for their duress
And for the fury that they feel
And for the trick that taints them still
And for the pain that grips like steel
And for the mold that suits them ill.]

The guilt that is incurred for "butchering earth's loveliness" is expunged in the Good Friday meadow scene in the final act of *Parsifal*. People and nature celebrate their reconciliation beneath the sign of the cross. "Das merkt nun Halm und Blume auf den Auen, / daß heut' des Menschen Fuß sie nicht zertritt" [Grass and flowers in the meadow notice that today they are not trampled underfoot by man] (GS 10:372), Gurnemanz sings. Rather, man spares them by walking with a gentle tread. This image of man's reconciliation with nature is in symbolic contrast to Parsifal's entry in act 1, when his killing of the swan had shattered the sacred natural peace of the Grail's domains.

Du konntest morden? Hier im heil'gen Walde,
    deß' stiller Frieden dich umfing?
Des Haines Thiere nahten dich nicht zahm,
    grüßten dich freundlich und fromm?

(GS 10:335)

[So you could murder? Here in the sacred forest,
    whose restful peace enfolded you?
Did not the woodland creatures approach you tamely,
    greeting you gently and devoutly?]

WAR AND PEACE: WAGNER'S CONCEPT OF REGENERATION

In his essay "Religion and Art," written three years after the poem of *Parsifal*, Wagner described the violation of nature and the persecution of animals as typical of Western "militant civilization" (GS 10:239). Throughout the "regeneration essays" of these final years of his life, he adopted a pacifist stance that contrasts sharply with his militaristic attitude at the time of the Franco-Prussian War of 1870–71. "Let us recognize, with the Redeemer in our hearts, that it is not their actions but their sufferings that bring the men of the past closer to us, making them worthy of our remembrance, and that it is not the victor but the vanquished who deserves our sympathy" (GS 10:247). Wagner contrasts this message with the law of history, a history hitherto governed by the law of the jungle. This was true even of the Greek world, which was the inspiration behind the modern humanitarian ideal. The "rudest barbarian, no less than the artistically creative Greek," writes Wagner in "Religion and Art," regarded this law of the jungle as

> the only law that shaped the world: there is no blood guilt that even this nation, with its sense of formal beauty, did not bring down upon itself in rabid hatred of its neighbor, until one stronger than they fell upon them, that stronger nation falling in turn before a yet more powerful enemy, so that, as century gave way to century, ever fresh and more brutal forces have been brought into play, finally forcing us back, for our own protection, behind giant cannons and armored walls which, year by year, continue to grow in size. (GS 10:229–30)

Wagner contrasts this progressively embattled civilization with the picture of a culture imbued with the spirit of peace. "Violence can civilize, but culture must spring from the soil of peace, just as it derives its name from the cultivation of the actual soil. It is from this same soil that knowledge, science, and art have grown in every age" (GS 10:234). Wagner's regenerated world is in stark contrast to the civilization that is characterized by war, power, egotistical possessions, and the exploitation of both nature and the weaker sections of society—he speaks cynically of the "grain of humanity" threshed on the "threshing floor of war."[41] "Violence," he goes on, "is utterly excluded from such a course, as we need only to nurture the seeds of peace that have already taken root among us, albeit feebly and weakly" (GS 10:251–52).

Wagner's ideas about peace left their lasting mark on *Parsifal*, too.[42] When Gurnemanz makes it clear to Parsifal that he has violated the peace of nature, Parsifal breaks his bow and throws away his arrows. And when he regains the spear and sets off on his wanderings, he is resolved to suffer "wounds from every weapon" as long as he retains the sacred spear inviolate: "Denn nicht ihn selber / durft' ich führen im Streite" [This spear alone I could not wield in battle] (GS 10:367–68). This spear can no longer inflict wounds but exists only to heal them: it is now a symbol of peace. Was it not Amfortas who initiated the sequence of crimes when he used it as a weapon against his enemy, Klingsor?

Parsifal is a poem about peace, about the need for the human being to be at peace not only with her- or himself but also with nature. In his perceptive study of the work, Hans Küng has described its central idea as "the rejection, in favor of fellow feeling with man and nature, of our tendency to think in terms of power and self-assertiveness." This idea, in a world "whose power structures still function largely in a socio-Darwinian and Machiavellian way," is more than ever necessary today as a regulatory principle, reflecting, as it does, "the profoundest insights of Christian theology."[43] For Wagner, too, this principle was specifically Christian, as he made unambiguously plain. Even in his 1849 draft for a drama on the life of Jesus of Nazareth, Wagner had felt that what was genuinely revolutionary about Christ's act of redemption was the fact that it had overturned the law of history according to which violence could be defeated only by further acts of violence.

When Jesus was baptized by John, the people acknowledged him as the heir of David: but he went into the wilderness and took counsel with himself: should he assert his descent from David in the sense desired by the people? Were he to succeed in this, would he then be anything other than a confederate of those great men of the world who rely on the rich and heartless? (SS 11:285)

Would this not mean exchanging one form of violence for another, especially if, as the people expected, Jesus supported Roman tyranny? The outcome of his meditations in the wilderness was that

Jesus repudiated the line of David: through Adam he had come from God, and all men were his brothers; not through any earthly kingdom could he free them from their misery, but only by fulfilling that supreme divine vocation that he recognized as his, in which God became man in order that, through the one man who first recognized him in himself, he might bring himself to the consciousness of all mankind: the most wretched and most afflicted must be closest to him: through them knowledge must enter the world. (SS 11:285)[44]

By regarding his descent from David as secondary to his descent from Adam, Christ rejects any idea of a national and political mission in favor of a purely human one. According to Wagner, his assertion "My kingdom is not of this world" (John 18:36) represents his rejection of that "earthly hegemony" (SS 11:298 and 179).

Wagner was no doubt reminded of this dramatic fragment in 1874 and 1875 when, in preparing for *Parsifal*, he studied August Friedrich Gfrörer's work on the history of early Christianity. First published in 1838, Gfrörer's book is a highly ambitious work of critical exegesis, consisting in no small part of quotations from the Hebrew and Greek, but it provided Wagner with a broad introduction to the origins of Christianity and to the essentials of historicocritical biblical studies.[45] Given the anti-Jewish thrust of Wagner's regeneration essays, it is remarkable to find him appealing to Gfrörer as his authority on matters relating to the history of religion, as Gfrörer's book, which he much admired, is emphatically philo-Semitic in tone.[46] Here Gfrörer objects to discrimination against Jews and to the tendency to play off the New and Old Testaments against each other, although this is precisely what Wagner did. In particular, Wagner was fascinated by the figure of the early Christian heretic Marcion, who "wished to separate the New from the Old Testament" (CT, 23 January 1880). Like Marcion, Wagner drew a distinction between Christianity as a religion of love and compassion and the Old Testament Jewish religion,[47] which he saw as a religion of law and terror that had, he believed, fatally eclipsed the Christian religion of peace. "Wherever we have seen Christian armies set out in quest of pillage and bloodshed, even under the sign of the cross," Wagner writes in "Religion and Art," it is not the names of Jesus and the New Testament that have been invoked but those of Moses, Joshua, Gideon, and other Israelite generals. Only by appealing to the "old Judaic spirit" rather than to the religion of Christ was the church still able to impose its militant demands on the "civilized world" (GS 10:232–33).

That Wagner was able to follow Gfrörer in his positive view of Judaism stems from the fact that he was interested above all in the esoteric doctrines of early Judaism, including its mysticism and the historical origins of the Cabala, doctrines rejected by Orthodox Jews and by enlightened Jews of a later generation. Wolf-Daniel Hartwich has examined the impact of Jewish theosophy on the final libretto of *Parsifal*, comparing it with the 1865 prose draft and noting in particular the role Gfrörer played in influencing Wagner's ideas. In his detailed and groundbreaking article, he has paid particular attention not only to the sect of the Jewish Therapeutae, whose teachings, including vegetarianism and sexual asceticism, anticipate several aspects of life within the Grail community, but also to the theme of metempsychosis as it applies to Kundry, the idea of the *salvator salvandus*, and the enigmatic statement "Zum Raum wird hier die Zeit" [Here time becomes space] (GS 10:339). This influence would scarcely have been conceivable if Wagner had not been impressed by related ideas even before he began to study Gfrörer, ideas that place Wagner firmly within the tradition of the Christian—and especially Romantic—interest in the Cabala.[48] According to Hartwich, Wagner "thought and wrote along cabalistic lines even before he knew the Cabala."[49] Behind his official rejection of Jews, therefore, we find a secret sympathy for their theosophical traditions,[50] a sympathy that makes it impossible to interpret *Parsifal* as an anti-Semitic work, in spite of attempts to do so on the part of a number of Wagnerian scholars.

Gfrörer's main concern was to counteract the undermining of the Christian faith by modern biblical criticism, whose methodology he nonetheless uses, albeit in a wholly positive sense. His work culminates in an apologia for Saint John's Gospel, which he considers the only historically authenticated Gospel. On this point he had Wagner's enthusiastic support, and the picture of Christ's teachings that Gfrörer paints on the strength of this "most spiritual" of Gospels is one that Wagner took over in its entirety, not least because, on many points, it reflected ideas that he had held for decades. In conversation with Cosima on 3 September 1880, Wagner described Gfrörer as "the most sensitive of writers in his handling of religious matters." And Gfrörer offers an interpretation of Christ's "My kingdom is not of this world" that is very similar to the one that Wagner had given in 1849: "Purely spiritual is my kingdom—dominion, slavery, state institutions in general do not affect its inner core, its strength lies in what binds it to the eternal root of its existence, to God." This, according to Gfrörer, is the nub of Christ's message. And he concludes: "Without incurring the charge of presumptuousness, we may say, therefore, that the Lord spoke these words to *us* in particular."[51]

The unorthodox Christianity of Wagner's old age centers on Good Friday, not Easter Day. Christ's Resurrection has no role to play here, and, indeed, there is no place for it in this mythologically based religion. As Kurt Hübner has noted, "Everything bound up with myth is concerned only with the inner world and never breaks out into absolute transcendence."[52] There is no doubt that in this respect too Wagner was influenced by Gfrörer, who makes no secret of his misgivings about the Resurrection and Ascension. It was this, he claimed, that "bequeathed to Christianity those doctrines of a ruling Messiah, a thousand-year empire, Christ's second coming, the Last Judgment, and so on, all of them errors long since refuted by experience." These ideas, Gfrörer goes on, were nothing but a

> protective cover necessary to shield the pure kernel of Christianity from the decay of the Roman Empire and the tempests of the Middle Ages, and to commend it to that more modern Europe that is being urged in the direction of a more spiritual outlook by a thousand considerations over which we have no control.[53]

In other words, Gfrörer attempts to eliminate the Resurrection from Christianity, never actually denying it but arguing that it is immaterial to our understanding of Christ's act of redemption. "Only this much seems to me to be beyond dispute, that our Lord considered his mission complete when he died on the cross. What happened afterward was unexpected even by him and was not part of his plan."[54]

Like Gfrörer, Wagner looked forward to a time when Christianity would be restored to its original, purely spiritual form. To accompany it and help it on its way was, for the older Wagner, the task of art, as he explained in 1880 in the opening sentence of "Religion and Art." The mission of art was "to salvage the kernel of religion by recognizing the figurative value of the mythical symbols that religion would have us believe in their literal sense and by revealing their deep and hidden truth by means of an ideal presentation of them" (GS 10:211). This sentence has been interpreted in a Hegelian sense to mean that religion is subsumed by art,[55] but the considerable body of evidence in support of Wagner's positive attitude to Christianity toward the end of his life,[56] coupled with the train of thought found in the rest of this essay, makes it clear that he genuinely expected art and above all music—the "only art wholly in keeping with the Christian faith" (GS 10:221)—to bring about a rebirth of true Christianity, albeit, of course, Christianity of a mythical, cyclical nature, largely devoid of any transcendental elements. It is music that "with incomparable clarity reveals the most fundamental essence of the Christian religion" (GS 10:221–22). In this sense Wagner intended his Bühnenweihfestspiel as a "Christian" work that should not be desecrated by being performed in ordinary repertory theaters.[57]

Wagner's conversations toward the end of his life are characterized by a remarkable contradiction. On the one hand, he professed his belief in a purified Christianity "free from all denominational ties" (CT, 30 January 1880), and on the other he defended church rituals and the sacraments, including baptism and Communion. Following his marriage to Cosima in the Protestant Church in Lucerne, he repeatedly attended Holy Communion.[58] And he even played the missionary, notably when rebuking the freethinking Malwida von Meysenbug for not having her ward, Olga Herzen, baptized. "This wasn't right," he told Cosima,

> not everyone could fashion his religion for himself, children in particular need to have a sense of belonging; nor should one be left to choose; rather, it should be possible to say to a person, "You've been christened, through baptism you belong to Christ, now unite with him once again through Holy Communion." Baptism and Communion are indispensable, he said. No amount of knowledge can ever approach the impression left by the latter. People who ignore religion have a terrible shallowness about them. (CT, 9–13 December 1873)

Recalling his son's baptism, Wagner added: "Only in a common faith can people collect their thoughts in this way. Religion is a bond, you can't have a religion by yourself" (CT, 9–13 December 1873). This explains why, at the end of "Religion and Art," Wagner replies to the imaginary question whether he is trying to found a new religion with an emphatic no, rejecting such an exercise as hubristic (GS 10:251).

Wagner's idea of a "true religion" (GS 10:212) was of a pure form of Christianity sharing the ethical nucleus of Buddhism.[59] As such, it was pacifist in spirit, a spirit that he hoped would lead to the regeneration of humanity. In spite of his constitutional susceptibility to the pessimism of Schopenhauer and Gobineau, Wagner refused to abandon this hope. But his program of regeneration is ultimately the clearest expression of his mythical and cyclical thinking, which was determined by the idea of a restitutio in integrum.

Closely associated with this program was the idea that differences between the races might be overcome. "We cannot deny that the human race is made up of irremediably disparate races," Wagner wrote in 1881, in his essay "Heroism and Christianity," appealing in support of this statement to Gobineau's *Essai sur l'inégalité des races humaines* (Essay on the inequality of the human races, 1853–55).[60] Yet a "review of all the races makes it impossible to deny the oneness of the human *species*," the common factor being our "capacity for the highest moral development" (GS 10:276–77).

Wagner goes on to offer what he calls an "antidote" to racial inequality, arguing that by partaking of Holy Communion—"the only true sacrament of the Christian religion"—the "lowest races" may be raised to the level of the higher ones, and this sacrament consists of "the blood of Jesus" (GS 10:283):

> The blood of the Savior, flowing from his head, from his wounds on the cross— who might impiously ask whether it belongs to the white race or to any other? If we call it divine, so its source may be dimly approached in what we have termed the human species' unifying bond, namely, our capacity for conscious suffering. (GS 10:280–81)

This amounts to an indirect criticism of Gobineau. In February 1881, while he was reading Friedrich Pott's *Etymologische Forschungen* (Etymological studies), Wagner had come across a reference to Gobineau's as-yet-unread *Essai*, prompting him to comment that "what really matters is something different from racial strength" (CT, 14 February 1881). And in the entry for 23 April 1882, we read: "He [Wagner] reproaches Gob[ineau] for leaving out of the account the one thing that was given to mankind—a Savior, who suffered for them and allowed himself to be crucified!" In spite of his sympathy and admiration for Gobineau as a man, he repeatedly told Cosima about his misgivings concerning Gobineau's fatalistic ideas on race. "At lunch he literally explodes, arguing in favor of all that is Christian at the expense of the idea of race" (CT, 3 June 1881). Music in particular was to transcend the whole idea of race. Thus, in Wagner's eyes, *Tristan und Isolde* "is the music that removes all barriers, including those of race" (CT, 19 June 1881). Of course, even Wagner himself felt that there were elements of "Gobineau music" in his own works; on 17 October 1882, when discussing the end of *Siegfried*, for example, he told his wife, "That is race." He used exactly the same words on 19 June 1881 in connection with Beethoven's *Coriolan* Overture: "That is race, that is something for Gobineau." Here, as we have seen, Wagner was playing off *Tristan und Isolde* against "the music of race," interpreting the former as a way of transcending race. It is clear that in Wagner's view, his own type of music, which was intended to transcend all racial differences and make the human race aware of its essential oneness, was on a higher level than the "racial" music of Beethoven and even of his own music.

For Gobineau, racial differences were an accepted fact, whereas for Wagner, all human beings were one, a unity guaranteed by Christianity and consisting in suffering and fellow feeling—"godlike pity that flows through the entire human race as its fount and origin" (GS 10:281). In Wagner's view, the "Brahman religion" shared many of its moral concepts with Christianity, yet, unlike Christianity, it was "still a religion of race" (GS 10:281).[61] The Buddha rebelled against this "on behalf of humanity" (GS 10:282). Even as early as 1856, in his draft for *Die Sieger*, Wagner had expressly rejected the "caste mentality" (SS 11:325), interpreting Prakriti's rebirth as a Chandala as a punishment for her arrogance in thinking that she was a member of a superior caste.

The "blood of the Savior," Wagner wrote in "Heroism and Christianity," was a "divine sublimate" for "all of suffering humanity" and could not "flow in the interest of a single race, however favored, but is shed, rather, for the whole of the human race" (GS 10:282–83). Her mankind must be transformed in the spirit of Christ from a "natural" state characterized by racial antagonism to a "moral" state that achieves universal agreement among all members of the human race (GS 10:284–85).[62]

"One thing is certain," Wagner told Cosima on 17 December 1881: "the races are played out, and all that can now achieve anything—as I've ventured to express it—is the blood of Christ." Here, too, he was at odds with Gobineau's theory of race. The blood of Christ is partaken at Holy Communion, which also plays a central role in *Parsifal*. The transformation of the body and blood of Christ into bread and wine—in other words, into what Wagner regarded as a vegetarian meal—was the equivalent, in Wagner's view, of taking Christianity back to its original pacifist roots. In spite of the ill-tempered outbursts against the Jews that we find in his regeneration essays,[63] Wagner was opposed to racism,[64] with the result that these outbursts are difficult to square with the underlying idea of an irenic religion. This also explains why, in his letter to Angelo Neumann of 23 February 1881, Wagner emphatically distanced himself from "the present 'anti-Semitic' movement" by drawing his correspondent's attention to his essay "Heroism and Christianity." It goes without saying that he had no desire to make this movement the basis or subtext of his music dramas, least of all his Bühnenweihfestspiel. Had he so desired, the work would simply have been caught up in the racial antagonisms of what was then the current state of the world, rather than laying the foundations for the unification of the whole human race.[65] For this was the declared aim of his music, raising it in his eyes even above that of Beethoven: "music that removes all barriers, including those of race." He cited his own *Tristan und Isolde* in support of this claim (CT, 19 June 1881). As an opponent of every form of "racial religion" (GS 10:281), Wagner was bound to reject an ideology that perpetuated the differences between the races.

According to Wolf-Daniel Hartwich, the religion of the older Wagner "strives to achieve an aestheticoreligious reconciliation in the modern world, a world that in the nineteenth century was arming for battle between states, classes, and cultures."[66] As a result, the races had to be freed from their struggle to survive, the Christians from their bellicose spirit, the Jews from their Jewishness (as a "racial religion"), and the deity from dogmatic and institutional ossification. The aim was to achieve a sense of unity among the human race in general and a "universal moral consensus of a kind that true Christianity must seem to us to be called upon to develop" (GS 10:284–85).

"Religion and Art" culminates in a passage in which Wagner breathes new life into the myth of a paradisiacal harmony between ourselves and our neighbor on the one hand and between humankind and nature on the other. But Wagner does not leave his reader with this picture of peace, preferring to end instead with a vision of an apocalyptic disaster that humanity risks bringing down on itself by engaging in an increasingly dangerous arms race, a disaster that could be triggered by a mere "error." It must "give us cause for concern," Wagner begins this final section of his essay,

> that the advancing art of war is turning increasingly away from the guiding principles of moral forces and toward the development of mechanical forces. Here the most brutish powers of nature's lowly forces are involved in an elaborate game in which, despite all mathematics and arithmetic, the purblind will could one day interfere by breaking loose with elemental force. Even now, armored monitors,[67] against which the proud and glorious sailing ship cannot hold her own, offer a sight of spectral horror: mutely subservient men, no longer with the looks of men, operate these monsters and will not desert their posts, even though they are in the terrible stokehole; but, just as in nature everything has its destructive enemy, so art invents torpedoes for the sea, while elsewhere it devises dynamic cartouches and the like. It is altogether conceivable that not only this, but art and science, bravery and points of honor, life and property, could one day be blown sky-high as the result of some incalculable error. Once our peaceful prosperity has gone up in a puff of smoke, a time of general famine will surely follow, a time of dearth prepared for slowly yet with blind infallibility: and so we would once again find ourselves standing at the point from which world history first set out and might indeed receive the impression that "God had created the world in order for the Devil to take it," to use the expression that our great philosopher [Schopenhauer] found in Jewish-Christian dogma.—Then the will would reign in all its brutality. (GS 10:252–53)

Here Wagner casts himself in the role of the "plenipotentiary of doom," as he dubbed himself in 1880 (CT, 21 November 1880), describing a cataclysm that in contrast to the one that ends *Götterdämmerung* is merely destructive, offering no hope of redemption, no prospect of rebirth, no catharsis or apocatastasis. In moments of pessimism, when he looked around him at the "civilized world" whose states "are armed to the teeth as though for mutual extirpation, squandering their peaceful prosperity and methodically falling on each other's throats at the first sign from their general" (GS 10:232–33), Wagner may well have thought that this vision of terror was closer to the truth than his own hope of regeneration, with its return to the purity of humankind's origins. This vision of the end of the world offers no prospect of a new beginning, a vision in which the violins, far from intoning their motif of promise, lapse into a deathly silence.

An Encounter between Two Anomalies

KING LUDWIG II AND WAGNER

> We'll have to send Siegfried away; when he reaches manhood
> he'll have to mix with other people and get to know adversity,
> have fun, and misbehave; otherwise he'll become a dreamer,
> maybe a cretin like the king of Bavaria.
>
> —*CT, 5 November 1869*

> Serious and lighthearted discussion on Germany and the way
> it is organized, especially its princes: "I can't imagine myself
> bowing and scraping before such people," says R., "with the
> exception of the king of Bavaria; this is a wonderful
> relationship, he's my friend."
>
> —*CT, 26 July 1881*

SHAKEN BY the news of the mysterious death of "the only true king of this century," the French poet Paul Verlaine wrote the sonnet "A Louis II de Bavière" (To Ludwig II of Bavaria), the last six lines of which read:

> Vous fûtes un poète, un soldat, le seul Roi
> De ce siècle où les rois se font si peu de chose,
> Et le martyr de la Raison selon la Foi.
>
> Salut à votre très unique apothéose,
> Et que votre âme ait son fier cortège, or et fer,
> Sur un air magnifique et joyeux de Wagner.

[You were a poet, a soldier, the only king of this century in which kings make so little of themselves, and a martyr of reason in the name of faith. Hail to your wholly unique apotheosis, and may your soul have a proud funeral cortege, gold and iron, to the strains of a magnificent and joyful air by Wagner.]

Wagner's name is the final word in the poem, thus summing up the whole thrust of Ludwig's life—a life that seems in retrospect to have been obsessed with death from the outset. Wagner's name is the gold background of Ludwig's unique apotheosis. For Verlaine, his death was a voluntary, poetic act, a declaration of war on modern politics and on a run-down science that had destroyed all that was sacred and beautiful in the world.

In his letter to Wagner of 3 January 1872, Ludwig described the "ideal, monarchical, poetic heights and loneliness" of his life as his natural state.[1] Verlaine's lyrical epitaph would, one feels, have struck a chord with him. The fact that a king who had turned his back on public life and who was regarded by his contemporaries as a baffling anachronism had offered to help a composer who had turned his back on the culture industry of the nineteenth century had a certain symbolic rightness to it, as Cosima Wagner noted. "An anomaly, such as you are," she explained to her husband on 19 August 1879, "can be helped only by another anomaly, an additional cause of suffering for you." Such suffering was inevitable inasmuch as neither party could be reduced to a common denominator and because each of them wanted what the other was unable or unwilling to give.

"IN THE BEGINNING WAS THE DEED": WAGNER'S SUMMONS TO MUNICH

On 2 February 1861, three years after its local premiere in Munich, King Maximilian allowed his fifteen-year-old son to attend a performance of *Lohengrin* at the Court Theater. This was the first time that the prince had seen a performance of a Wagner opera, and it was to leave as lasting an impression as his first encounter with *Tannhäuser* at the end of the following year. Ludwig later regarded both events as causes for annual celebration. Thus we find him writing to Wagner on 10 February 1869: "At the end of December (the 22nd) it was seven years since I first heard *Tannhäuser*, and on 2 February it was eight since I first heard *Lohengrin*. These are days of celebration for me, days whose importance for me and my life is not equaled by even the leading feast days in the Christian calendar." In this way, Ludwig invested his first encounter with these two works with a mythical aura, regarding it as a seminal experience of almost cultic proportions, a private mystery inspired by the king's own understanding of his sacred role as monarch.

Ludwig was barely eighteen when he ascended the Bavarian throne on 10 March 1864. Within weeks he had instructed his acting cabinet secretary Franz von Pfistermeister to seek out Wagner and invite him to Munich. At this period, audiences in Munich were still largely hostile to the composer and his works.[2] In 1845 Wagner had sent the score of *Rienzi* to the then Munich intendant and received it back unopened. The first piece of his to be heard in the Bavarian capital was the overture to *Tannhäuser*, which Franz Lachner conducted at an All Saints' Day concert in 1852. The audience reacted in part with a baffled silence, in part with indignant hissing. Nonetheless, the new intendant of the Munich Court Theater, Franz von Dingelstedt, was resolved to include *Tannhäuser* in his program and even entered into negotiations with Wagner, who was then living in exile in Zurich. But his plans were greeted by protests on the part of both the government and the press: "The Orpheus who built barricades with his music during the Dresden May Uprising [in 1849] belongs in prison in Waldheim [where Wagner's friend, the revolutionary August Röckel, was currently serving a life sentence for his part in the uprising], not in the Munich opera house."[3]

It was above all the Bavarian foreign minister Ludwig von der Pfordten for whom Wagner was a thorn in the flesh. Pfordten had been a minister in the Saxon government at the time of the revolutions of 1848–49 and, because of the close links between the Saxon and Bavarian thrones, refused to take responsibility for a performance of an opera by an erstwhile insurgent. Following the first performance of *Lohengrin* in Munich in 1858, he told the actor Eduard Devrient of his "personal dislike of Wagner." The arrogance of which Wagner was guilty in his eyes was destroying all that was valuable about life and the state: "If the princes were to stick together as the democrats do, Wagner's music would never be performed."[4]

For the present, Dingelstedt had to abandon his plans, but two years later he was able to obtain the backing of King Maximilian, who was more receptive to Wagner's music than Pfordten and who was encouraged in his openness by Duke Max of Bavaria. (Duke Max, an ardent Wagnerian, later introduced the young crown prince Ludwig to Wagner's two essays, *The Artwork of the Future* and *"Zukunftsmusik"* [The music of the future].) "We have no wish to be more Saxon than the king of Saxony," Maximilian is reported to have remarked with reference to the fact that the Dresden Court Opera was again performing Wagner's works after a lengthy period of willful neglect.[5] *Tannhäuser* received its first performance in Munich on 12 August 1855 under the direction of Franz Lachner and proved singularly successful. The local premiere of *Lohengrin* followed on 28 February 1858, to rather less acclaim.

Wagner regarded his summons to Munich as little less than a miracle, and yet there was a logical inevitability to it: a year previously, he had published the poem of the *Ring*, prefacing it with a famous appeal to an unnamed German prince to provide a festival theater for a performance of the cycle. "Will this prince be found?" Wagner asked, ending with Faust's adaptation of the opening line of Saint John's Gospel: "In the beginning was the deed" (GS 6:281; see also *Faust* 1.1237). The sought-for prince was found. "The sentence that you quote in the preface of your poem of the *Ring*," Ludwig assured Wagner on 26 November 1864, "shall come true; I hereby exclaim: 'In the beginning may the deed be done!' " Ludwig had snatched Wagner back from the brink of disaster at a time when the composer was convinced that all was lost. "I feel I am on a knife-edge," he told Peter Cornelius on 8 April 1864; "some good and truly helpful miracle must now befall me, otherwise it will all be over!" Some sixth sense convinced him that "this delightful miracle is already on its way." Six days later Ludwig issued instructions for Wagner to be invited to Munich and for his emissary to present him with a portrait of the new king and a purse of money containing a ring.

Relying on memories passed down in her own family, the German novelist Annette Kolb reported these events—not unsurprisingly—as though they belonged in a world of fairy tale.

Thus and only thus did the handsome young king take the glittering ring from his hand and instruct his highest-ranking chamberlain to pursue Richard Wagner until he had found him and entrust the ring to him. "And bring him to me at once," he exclaimed, "for I wish to see him. To me, he is worth half my kingdom!" The king's highest-ranking chamberlain saw his master's impatience and knew that if he returned to Munich without Wagner, he would lose his golden key, all his emoluments, and his Order of the Eagle (Second Class). And so he set off without delay, searching high and low throughout the land in his attempt to find him. But each time that he thought he was getting close, the scent went cold, however quickly he tried to follow it. . . . But he finally ran him to ground at an inn in Stuttgart. Breathing a sigh of relief, he announced his visit, insisting on being received and refusing to be deterred. He then passed on the king's message and handed over the ring. At this, Richard Wagner, who had secretly been expecting a miracle, felt the beating as though of an eagle's wings. . . . He made no attempt to oppose the high chamberlain's demand that he should prepare to leave at once. Accompanied by the latter, Wagner traveled to Munich, responding to the summons of the king, who, radiant with happiness, received him with unparalleled delight. Everything would be done to ensure the success of his works. All his wishes would be met. When Wagner perceived the noble nature of the handsome young monarch, he too felt jubilant and sensed his youth return. Recalling his friends, he summoned them all to his side.[6]

Summon them he may have done, but it remains an open question whether Wagner's friends were suitable characters for a fairy tale. After all, they included two of his subversive comrades-in-arms from Dresden, the architect Gottfried Semper, who had helped build barricades in the city, and the musician and political writer August Röckel, who had been released from prison in Waldheim only two years earlier. Indeed, the fairy-tale atmosphere that Annette Kolb conjured up in her account of Wagner's summons to Munich is dismissed by Martin Gregor-Dellin in his biography of Wagner as "a farce with a first-class cast": Wagner's "friendship with Ludwig II has often been hymned as the fulfillment of a dream and the pinnacle of a career. In retrospect, this ostensibly magical, brilliant, and triumphant episode turns out to be an intermezzo of the most shameful and insidious kind."[7]

MYSTICISM AND DIPLOMACY: LUDWIG II AND COSIMA WAGNER

Gregor-Dellin's outrage is directed in particular at a letter that Cosima Wagner addressed to the king on 7 June 1866, humbly begging him to write an open letter in defense of her honor after the Munich *Volksbote* (folk messenger) had made suggestive remarks about her relationship with Wagner.[8] She had in fact already given birth to Isolde, Wagner's first daughter, and was expecting his second child, but in spite of this she played the innocent and insisted that although Wagner loved her deeply, their love was entirely platonic. Ludwig believed her, not least because it suited him to do so; he had, after all, conceived of the affair as positively metaphysical, with Wagner, Cosima, and himself involved in a sexless three-way relationship. On 14 November 1865, for example, he had written to the "most revered" Cosima, asking her to "unite with me and be to Him all that it is possible for a man to be to one who is worshiped as a saint."[9] "Oh, if only we three were already in the faraway land that spans the whole world, far from the sun, far from the days' parting lament," he wrote on 5 March 1866, paraphrasing *Tristan und Isolde*.[10] And so he did not hesitate to leap to Cosima's defense, upholding her honor in the form of an open letter to Hans von Bülow.

The discovery that he had been shamefully duped affected him deeply, yet he finally found it in him to forgive both Cosima and Wagner; he had been brought up, after all, to believe that honor was everything and that its integrity was synonymous with an unsullied reputation in society, quite apart from the fact that he must have been aware of the impossible situation in which the couple found themselves. And so we find him writing to Cosima on 15 March 1869 to assure her of his "loyal and heartfelt devotion, because, after our friend, you are the dearest creature on earth, the person most worthy of my trust."[11] Ludwig's love of Wagner was reflected in Cosima's love for Wagner, thereby presenting a striking parallel with Nietzsche's love of the Wagner household during the Tribschen period. Certainly, there were profound similarities. Both Ludwig and Cosima were convinced that only in their relationship with Wagner had they found true love. "I love no woman, I have no parents, no brother, no relations, no one whom I can love sincerely and with all my heart, apart from you! you whom I worship, you who are unique," Ludwig wrote to Wagner on 21 April 1866. Five years later, on 23 March 1871, Cosima confided in her diary that she "had neither father nor mother. R. has been everything to me, he alone has loved me."

It is clear from the voluminous correspondence between Ludwig and Cosima that he regarded her as a medium that often allowed him to draw closer to Wagner than any direct dealings would have done. Cosima, after all, could boast descent from the old French aristocracy, and from childhood onward she had been used to dissembling, to presenting a certain picture to the world, and to maintaining appearances, with the result that she was in a far better position to deal with the king than Wagner the *ingénu*, with his impulsive, unconventional behavior.

Wagner took advantage of this state of affairs, using Cosima as a kind of "cabinet secretary," to borrow a phrase Wagner's first grandson, Franz Wilhelm Beidler, used in his biography of his grandmother.[12] For both the king and Wagner, Cosima played an important role as a diplomatic mediator, repeatedly finding herself entrusted with information and confidences that the two men did not dare to communicate to each other directly. Cosima—well versed in the ways of French society—played this role brilliantly while always giving the impression that she was genuine and that everything was totally heartfelt. An attitude that to her was second nature was often deeply repugant to Wagner, as her diaries repeatedly make clear; in particular, he resented the fact that in his letters to Ludwig he had to adopt what for him was a totally unnatural style in which his true self was hidden behind the high-flown rhetoric. Time and again he found it impossible to maintain this style and relapsed into his normal tone, and on these occasions he wrote his most fascinating letters to the king. Cosima's letters, by contrast, maintain the same overwrought tone throughout, which Wagner would sometimes imitate; without her example, he would undoubtedly have been unable to strike this tone.

Entering Ludwig's emotional world, Cosima, in her letters to him, presents a picture of herself as a Catholic martyr who spends hours at a time on her knees before a crucifix or an image of the Virgin,[13] drawing her inner strength from Calderón's *autos sacramentales* and regarding the "Spanish idea of the monarchy" as a "divine revelation."[14] This explains her shock and dismay when, following Bavaria's defeat in its war with Prussia in 1866, Ludwig wrote to her—not Wagner—to announce his decision to abdicate in order to devote his life to Wagner as a "god in human form." She replied as follows: "In this godforsaken age, where faith is everywhere no more than a matter of horse trading, I truly believed in a monarchy by the grace of God, it was a religion for me, just like art; I believed in you above all or, rather, in you alone; as king you were to raise our art to new heights, my august liege." If he were to abdicate, "godless humanity would lead a pitiful existence, reduced, to a man, to the utmost vulgarity."[15]

Wagner's reaction, also dated 24 July 1866, could hardly have been more different. Casting himself in the role of Hans Sachs and knowing that the king was fond of identifying with Walther von Stolzing, he drew a humorous comparison between Ludwig's desire to abdicate and Walther's plans to flee and abduct Eva: "Aufgepaßt: das darf nicht sein!" [Beware: that may not be!] (GS 7:208). There is no word here of the divine right of kings. Instead, Wagner remains true to the idea of a people's monarchy that he had espoused during his revolutionary days. The king should leave monkish Munich, with its "popish intrigues" and the "terrible power enjoyed by its priests," and move to "the Nuremberg of *Die Meistersinger*, with its enlightened, freethinking population." There he could enjoy the "fresh Franconian air" and "breathe freely again."[16]

When read in parallel with Wagner's own correspondence with Ludwig, the letters exchanged by Cosima and Ludwig provide unique evidence of a premodern mentality in which an outdated, feudal, and aristocratic view of the world sees its only hope of salvation in a bourgeois aesthetic that could be raised above itself by means of its sacralization. Wagner was no longer to be a "subject" of the king, as the composer had occasionally signed himself in his letters to Ludwig, much to the latter's displeasure, but, to quote Ludwig's letter to Cosima of 20 October 1866, "a god who has descended from heaven in order to proclaim His new teachings and, by bringing joy to humanity, redeem the world! . . . How can a man like Him be the subject of another; this can never be." For Ludwig, Wagner was like a second Christ, and his art, for both Ludwig and Cosima, was a raised monstrance before which the godless modern age should fall prostrate in adoration.

THE FAILED FESTIVAL IN MUNICH

During Ludwig II's twenty-two years on the throne, Munich became a center for Wagner's operas, no fewer than four of which received their first performances there during the king's lifetime.[17] In 1864 Wagner himself conducted a production of *Der fliegende Holländer*, thereby rounding off the series of early "Romantic operas" that had begun with *Tannhäuser* in 1855. In 1865 the premiere of *Tristan und Isolde* brought to an end the six-year odyssey of a work suspected of being unsingable, and in 1868 *Die Meistersinger von Nürnberg* received its triumphant first performance in the city.

Uniquely in the history of opera, Ludwig sought in his theater the mysteries that confirmed his view of kingship, hence the unwavering determination with which he insisted on staging Wagner's works in the face of the composer's objections and of the claim that artistic standards were being compromised; both *Das Rheingold* (1869) and *Die Walküre* (1870) went ahead against Wagner's wishes. The history of opera is littered with examples of composers' desperate and tragically unsuccessful attempts to have their works staged. Rather less common is the case of a composer no less desperately concerned to prevent such a performance from taking place.

In a letter to Ludwig's court secretary Lorenz von Düfflipp (5 February 1868), Wagner suggested that

> it would not be impossible, should His Majesty the King so wish it, for the separate parts of the [*Ring*] cycle to be provisionally performed, perhaps at yearly intervals, so that a start could be made next year with *Das Rheingold*, continuing with *Die Walküre* the year after, and the whole work could eventually be produced in this way.

The fact that Wagner uses the word "provisionally" would seem to indicate that he had not lost sight of his ultimate ideal: staging all four works on four consecutive days. Indeed, this plan was initially to be realized in Munich. It was there that the festival theater of which he dreamed was to be built, a theater that had been an integral part of his *Ring* project from the very outset; in his view, the tetralogy could be properly staged only within the framework of a festival modeled on the Attic Dionysia. Such a festival would be as far removed as possible from the trivial concerns of the standard repertory theater, with all its commercial considerations and incidental concerns.[18] If relations between Wagner, Ludwig, and the Bavarian capital had taken a less unedifying turn and, beset by human foibles, not ended in scandal and disaster, there would probably have been no Bayreuth Festival. Yet there is little doubt that with its provincial ambience, the Bayreuth Festival came closer to Wagner's original idea than its Munich equivalent would have done in the sort of enormous theater that in keeping with Ludwig's plans would have dominated the city's skyline.

In the foreword to his 1863 edition of the poem of the *Ring*, the final appeal of which had been taken up with such enthusiasm by Ludwig, Wagner had stressed that in writing the *Ring* he was thinking of a "provisional" theater, "as simple as possible, perhaps only of timber" and "independent of the repertory system that obtains in our permanent theaters." He was anxious to avoid the sort of metropolitan audiences that sought only amusement in the opera house.

> For this I assumed one of the smaller towns in Germany, a town suitably situated and able to accommodate an exceptional influx of visitors, in other words, one where there would be no conflict of interests with a larger permanent theater nor with the sort of audience that is typical of our municipal theaters, with all their usual habits. (GS 6:273)

Wagner's description of the festival town that he envisaged was a vision of Bayreuth long before he had thought of using the small Franconian town as a suitable site for his festival.

Shortly after this preface had been published, at a time of the greatest material and emotional crisis in Wagner's life, Ludwig offered to build a festival theater in Munich for a production of the *Ring*. Such was his situation that it would have been madness for Wagner to turn down the king's offer. And yet he could not disguise the fact that his own idea for a festival had few points in common with the young king's grandiose scheme for a monumental stone theater, a theater of such imposing dimensions that it would have overshadowed every other theater in the whole history of stage architecture. It was inevitable that Wagner, who had just emerged from a period of black depression and profound material hardship, should be blinded by the brilliance of the limelight in which he suddenly found himself, and it is difficult to criticize him for briefly agreeing to Ludwig's plan and for suggesting Gottfried Semper as a suitable architect.

As designed by Semper, the festival theater would have been situated at the end of a long thoroughfare leading from the Brienner Straße to the Isar. In terms of the city's urban development, it was certainly an attractive proposition, but Wagner's lack of interest in such a monumental structure is clear from an entry in his Brown Book dated 9 September 1865: "How I hate this planned theater, indeed, how childish the king seems in insisting so passionately on this project: now I've got Semper and am supposed to see him and discuss this senseless project with him! I know of no greater torment than the one that faces me now."[19] On 29 January 1867, a little over a year later, we find him writing to August Röckel: "The last thing on my mind at present is a Wagner theater or even a Wagner street."

From the outset, Wagner had proposed an alternative in the form of a provisional theater in Munich's Glaspalast (Crystal Palace). For a long time, Semper worked on both plans simultaneously, even though neither he nor Ludwig had any real interest in the idea of a temporary theater, for all that this was far closer to Wagner's own concept of a festival. Indeed, Semper probably realized that Wagner was trying to obstruct his plans for a theater on the Isar—a theater that the architect saw as the culmination of his life's work. According to a letter that the painter Friedrich Pecht wrote to Semper on 17 March 1865, Wagner wanted only a "simple wooden shack." If the plans for a theater in Munich finally came to nothing, this was due not least to Wagner's diminishing interest in the project, and it is significant that following the abandonment of the project, he returned without further ado to his earlier idea of a temporary theater, an idea that was ultimately realized in Bayreuth.

Now it was the king's turn to evince a marked lack of interest in the idea of a theater in Bayreuth. The fact that after a lengthy resistance he finally gave his financial backing to the project, albeit in the form of a loan, is due to his sense of loyalty to Wagner rather than to any inner conviction. Essentially, he wanted Wagner for himself. The world premieres of *Das Rheingold* and *Die Walküre*, which embittered Wagner, and his insistence on a private performance of *Parsifal* in Munich show how little Ludwig understood Wagner's conception of the Bayreuth Festival. Even as late as 10 January 1883, in his last letter to the king, we find Wagner still attempting to dissuade Ludwig from insisting on a Munich production of "this work with which I bid farewell to the world." Not even Wagner's death, which in a sense turned this letter into his last will and testament, could persuade Ludwig to abandon his plans. Thus *Parsifal* received its unofficial first performance in Munich on 3 May 1884 as a performance held for Ludwig alone.

LUDWIG'S PRIVATE MYTH AND HIS EMPIRE OF DREAMS

The king's unwavering insistence on his right to stage Wagner's works was not simply the result of a monarch's whim that allowed him to ride roughshod over the composer's claim to artistic independence, nor, in the case of the *Ring*, was it merely his legitimate right to the work (a right contractually assigned to him by the author). Rather, it derived from his illusory belief that he needed to have his own private mystery, just as the faithful need to receive the sacrament. Here there was a conflict of interests between the world of the artist who was concerned only to see an adequate performance of his work and that of the royal hierophant who could no more live without a performance in the theater than priests and their congregations can live without the rituals laid down in the church calendar's cycle of feast days.

For the king, Wagner's operas were such stuff as dreams are made on, a drug that filled him with ecstasy and rapture. The nature of his dreams and the way in which he interpreted Wagner's musicalized myths find striking if dubious expression in the castles that he had built. Goethe's definition of architecture, in his *Maximen und Reflexionen* (Maxims and reflections), as "the art of music rendered mute" finds curious confirmation in these royal palaces, which represent the art of Wagner's music rendered mute—but Wagner's music as heard by Ludwig, as the musical background of a mystically transfigured Middle Ages that, brought back to life, transcended modern prosaic reality.

For Ludwig, Wagner's music inhabited the world of the Grail with its magical sonorities, its miraculous swan and dove, its sacred objects, hieratic gestures, anointed and unctuous rulers, poeticized history, the magic of nature, and a nocturnal religion of sound that leaves far behind it the bustle of our daily lives. Lohengrin, the Swan Knight who hails from a remote and mysterious land, legitimizing his existence through his charisma alone and refusing to answer questions about his name and background, was the figure with whom Ludwig identified from childhood, an identity beyond which he never really progressed.

Ludwig adapted legend and history alike to create a private myth that was distinctly autistic. The clearest signs of this are, on the one hand, the private performances that he organized and, on the other, the royal palaces he had built, palaces that far from being located in Munich, where they would have served to enhance his public prestige, were built in places remote from his capital: a secluded mountain valley (Linderhof), on top of a mountain (Neuschwanstein), and on an island in the middle of a lake (Herrenchiemsee). As such, they were intended for royal eyes alone. The common gaze was not allowed to profane them, with the result that Ludwig left instructions for them to be blown up after his death.

In place of a coherent historical tradition that would legitimize the institution of the monarchy and that could be displayed in acts of public ceremonial, we find a mysticized view of history that is no longer reenacted in the place where its events once took place or to which those events could be related. Rather, this world is transferred to an empire of dreams remote from the real world, its rituals enacted by a king who was ultimately a king for himself alone, just as he preferred to watch plays and operas in a darkened auditorium, with himself as the sole spectator.

Ludwig detested displays of public ceremonial, with the result that his own imaginary rule turned increasingly into a private performance. It now seems likely that this autistic retreat into the dream world of his own making was the result of hereditary schizophrenia, but it also stemmed from his legal position as king of Bavaria; he was effectively the prisoner of a modern constitutional state whose real power was vested in the hands of an elite ministerial bureaucracy.[20]

However much Ludwig I and his grandson Ludwig II may have resisted the idea, the Bavarian king was neither an absolute monarch nor a people's king but a ruler who was the puppet of his ministers, for all that they allowed him to realize his profligate dreams, at least to the extent that he could afford to do so within the framework of the civil list—the monarch's annual allowance from state funds. But he had no real power. Ludwig had ascended the throne with ambitious political ideas, and it took him a while to realize just how limited his power was and to see that his throne was essentially the poetic superstructure of a more prosaic reality in the form of a state run by ministers and bureaucrats, a state constructed by Maximilian von Monteglas in accordance with the rationalist, antitraditional principles of an enlightened bureaucracy.

This ministerial oligarchy played more or less the same role that the aristocracy played in Prussia. (In Bavaria the aristocracy was not an important factor in the country's power structures.) Ludwig I, who reigned from 1825 to 1848, had already tried to add a touch of regal romanticism to this prosaic reality, demonstrating a gift for government and a love of art that assumed a positively unworldly aspect under his grandson, leading to the latter's withdrawal into the role of the proverbial fairy-tale king, with the difference between the two men finding its most striking expression in their differing, if equally passionate, approaches to architecture. Whereas Ludwig I's building projects were intended, in Hermann Bauer's words, to be an "ornament to city and land,"[21] Ludwig II's castles were an attempt to cut himself off from both city and land.

Ludwig II's lack of interest in practical politics increasingly turned his office into what Franz Herre has termed an "iconostasis,"[22] a screen whose images of power and majesty were intended as a kind of "opium for the people," while behind these images a ministerial bureaucracy carried on the business of state. A monarch in name alone, Ludwig sought refuge in worlds increasingly remote from real life.

> Zum Spielzeug ist das Szepter dir geworden,
> Ein Zauberstab für eitle Phantasien,

Nur Wundermärchenbilder zu gestalten
Scheint dir die königliche Macht verliehn.

[The scepter has become a toy for you,
A magic wand for empty fantasies,
Your kingly might, it seems, can do no more
Than conjure up glib scenes from fairy tales.]

Thus Franz Pocci rebuked the king in a poem written in 1871.[23] But this did not worry the country's ministerial bureaucracy, as long as Ludwig's imagination remained within prudent financial bounds and he did not meddle in politics. They needed the monarchy to protect them, to gloss over political and social evils, and to secure their own dominant position.[24]

Forced to fill an ideological vacuum, the king created the semblance of an absolutist empire in his castles, especially at Herrenchiemsee, which was modeled on Versailles. Lohengrin and Louis XIV were in a sense the two role models between whom Ludwig found himself torn: on the one hand, the Swan Knight who needed no legitimation and, on the other, the absolute ruler who was above the law and whose court and palace at Versailles featured prominently in the works that Ludwig chose to have performed at his private theatricals.

But there was nothing that Wagner hated more than the absolutist French court of the seventeenth and eighteenth centuries. When, two weeks before his death, he heard of the decision to build a palace at Herrenchiemsee, he apparently told Cosima that he felt "ashamed at the whole relationship" with Ludwig and regretted "that Rothschild had not made him a gift of a million" (CT, 30 January 1883).[25] Such cynicism represents a radical departure from Wagner's lifelong ideals; after all, it had always been his aim to strip art of its commercial aspect, not least through his idea of a festival funded by means of a society of patrons. Are we to assume from this that Wagner-Wotan was now prepared to abandon the world to Alberich and to the power and curse of gold? No doubt his outburst was caused by a momentary fit of anger, but it is nonetheless significant.

Wagner's theater in Bayreuth was modeled on a Greek amphitheater, with a "democratic" auditorium that was in conscious contrast to the seating arrangements of traditional theaters, where the tiers and boxes reflected social hierarchies. At exactly the same time that Wagner was planning this theater, Ludwig was hoping to build a rococo theater in the grounds at Linderhof that would have been wholly in the very tradition—feudal and courtly in spirit—that was anathema to Wagner. Ludwig's theater, of course, was intended, in essence, for a single spectator, the king himself, who would have occupied a central box furnished with unparalleled extravagance.

Just as Ludwig attempted to create a new Versailles, so he transformed the fictional settings of Wagner's music dramas into scenes of everyday life, most notably in the form of life-size reconstructions at Linderhof of the Venus grotto, Hunding's hut, and Gurnemanz's cell and, above all, Neuschwanstein, which was to be a temple to Wagner, a summation of his operas, especially *Tannhäuser* and *Lohengrin*, which Ludwig always thought of as a single entity.

RELIGION AND ART: WAGNER CONTRA LUDWIG II

Hermann Bauer has spoken of Ludwig's mania for "verifying" his dream worlds.[26] Bound up with this mania was his insatiable desire to see *Parsifal* staged in Munich, drawing it into his immediate sway and, as it were, integrating it into the Holy Week liturgy. This desire could not have been further removed from Wagner's own aim, as expressed in "Religion and Art" (1880), where the composer argues that "the mythical symbols that religion would have us believe in their literal sense should be interpreted by art on a figurative level . . . whereas the priest is keen only that religious allegories should be regarded as actual truths." Wagner speaks of "allegories" when these images appear in a nonartistic context, but of "mythical symbols" when they are entrusted to the care of the "artist who openly and freely passes off his work as his own invention" (GS 10:211). Clearly, then, Wagner did not want *Parsifal* to be interpreted as a "sacred" work. As an autonomous piece, his Bühnenweihfestspiel cannot allow its contents to be dictated by an existing religious community. Rather, art must be independent of religion while freely availing itself of religious symbols.

"The path from religion to art is bad," Wagner told Cosima on 13 January 1880, "but the one from art to religion is good." Three months later, on 27 April 1880, he elaborated on this theme, arguing that art could use religious symbols, "but in a free spirit, not in the rigid forms imposed by the church"; since art is "a profound form of play," it frees these symbols from their dogmatic seriousness. It seems clear, therefore, that Cosima was merely reflecting Wagner's views when she wrote to Otto Eiser on 20 February 1878, rejecting Eiser's parallel between *Parsifal* and Calderón's autos sacramentales.

> With the help of his genius, Calderón dramatized church dogmas for the people, whereas *Parsifal* has nothing in common with any church or even with any dogma, for here the blood turns to bread and wine, whereas the opposite is the case in the Eucharist. *Parsifal* picks up the Gospel tradition, with its poet continuing to fashion and create, while ignoring all that already exists. The poet of the *autos* always set out from an existing belief and an existing doctrine, demonstrating it by means of allegorical figures and their actions, for all that these actions are undoubtedly wonderfully alive.

Here, too, Cosima uses the term "allegory" to describe characters that are not autonomous but defined by an existing system of dogma.

Wagner refused to regard his Bühnenweihfestspiel as a sacred work but ultimately dedicated it to the stage alone. In *Parsifal*, religion is dehistoricized; it is Christianity on which the purely iterative structures of myth have been superimposed, thus becoming an annual festival divorced from the church calendar. As a genre, the festival has a long history, among its earliest exponents being Goethe.[27] Grounded in the institution of the courtly masque, the festival soon broke free from these origins and became an autonomous work. Whereas the courtly festival remained geared to the uniqueness of a historical situation and a particular dynastic occasion, with the result that it could not, in principle, be repeated, the Wagnerian festival moved away not only from the nonaesthetic reason for its existence but from historical reality in general, including its specific dates and linear structures. In this way it entered the world of myth, with its cyclical structures. Just as the archetypal situations of myth keep recurring, so does the festival. In this respect, the festival is like the feast days of the church calendar, differing from them in that it no longer tells of soteriological events.

Ludwig, by contrast, clung to his belief that "a performance of *Parsifal* needs the poetry of spring, the spell of reawakening nature, in short, the temporal proximity to Good Friday," as the king's court secretary, Ludwig von Bürkel, wrote to Cosima on 20 January 1883.[28] For Ludwig, Bayreuth seemed an aberration. Whereas Wagner had sought to aestheticize religious symbols in *Parsifal*, Ludwig insisted on reversing that process and on restoring the composer's world of symbols to a sacred, not to say sacramentalized, sphere. To quote from "Religion and Art," he was keen for all mythical symbols "to be believed in their literal sense" (GS 10:211). This differing conception on Ludwig's part already emerges from his letter to Wagner of 30 August 1877, in which he describes the "Hermit's Cell" (that is, Gurnemanz's hut) at Linderhof.

> Everything about it reminds me of the solemnly serious Good Friday morning in your wonderful *Parcifal* [*sic*]. . . . There in this hallowed place I already hear a presentiment of the silver trombones from the Castle of the Grail; there in my mind's ear I hear the sacred chants wafting down from Monsalvat and its mountain fastness; there I feel so happy, at the source where Parcifal was blessed as the *true, authentic* king, becoming king through his humility and by destroying the evil within him, for it is in this that true power lies![29]

Ludwig then goes on to mention Kundry's baptism and redemption. Clearly he related the work to himself, to the solemnity of his own kingship and to the sacramental expiation that he always longed for, especially in regard to what he regarded as his sexual aberrations. For him, *Parsifal* held out the promise of salvation, and so it is entirely understandable that he should be eager to annex the "sacred" work and arrange private performances of it.

However much we may respect Ludwig for not abandoning Wagner in spite of all the disappointments that he suffered on a human level, we cannot ignore the fact that without Wagner his life would have lost its gravitational center. This explains why he idealized his relations with Wagner, avoiding any clash with sordid reality by keeping out of Wagner's way. (After 1868, the two men effectively met only twice, first during the 1876 Bayreuth Festival, and again in November 1880.) Ultimately the relationship worked only on a literary level, with the friendship between king and composer developing into a sort of epistolary novel in which the king was the author.[30]

With their garbled ideas on art and religion, Ludwig's letters to Wagner are almost entirely free of criticism and show no real attempt to grapple with serious issues. If lasting disagreements arose, he would withdraw into silence and the correspondence would grind to a halt, only for the old tone to be revived at a later date as though nothing had happened in the interim. By now Ludwig's life had long become the stuff of fiction as he withdrew behind the bulwark of poetic illusions. Clearly he thought that by picking up the effusive note of their earliest dealings he could forcibly restore the ideal unity between king and composer that he felt had typified their initial contacts.

In a conversation with Cosima on 1 November 1870, Wagner perceptively compared the king to Prince Oronaro in Goethe's dramatic satire *Der Triumph der Empfindsamkeit* (The triumph of sensibility), a figure who immures himself within a world of artistic appearances, cutting himself off from real life and preferring a doll to an actual lover. In much the same way Ludwig ultimately preferred an imaginary Wagner to his real-life equivalent, a figure who all too often left him feeling disillusioned. This was his only way of overlooking the human inadequacies of the mystagogue and thaumaturge whose works, he hoped, would afford him expiation and redemption.

In many respects, Ludwig's pseudosacralization of Wagner's works recalls their treatment at the hands of the National Socialists, who used them to adorn the altars of the Third Reich's political religion. For Hitler, these works seem to have performed a role similar to the one that they played in Ludwig's emotional life.[31] The National Socialists' addiction to myth and their "aestheticization of political life,"[32] including the political exploitation of religion and cultic ritual, were undoubtedly reinforced by Wagner's works, but there is little doubt that Wagner would have viewed this development with even more misgivings than their annexation by Ludwig II as part of a program of art as religion.

WAGNER AS A POLITICAL FIGURE

A vast gulf separated Ludwig's perception of himself and the view of a modern monarch promulgated by Wagner in the spoken and written word. In spite of his association with Ludwig, Wagner made no attempt to turn his back on the ideals that had motivated him as a revolutionary. Not even as a revolutionary had Wagner been hostile to the monarchy, as is clear from his 1848 speech to the Dresden Vaterlandsverein, "How Do Republican Aspirations Stand in Relation to the Monarchy?" His revolutionary ideal was that of a monarchical republic, a monarchy cast adrift from the aristocracy and directly united with the common people (SS 12:220–29). That he never abandoned this idea of a popular monarchy is clear from the series of articles that he published in 1867 under the title "German Art and German Politics." Thirteen installments appeared between 24 September and 19 December in the *Süddeutsche Presse*, the "great political journal" that Wagner summoned into existence with the support of Ludwig II.

These articles openly pick up ideas that Wagner had held during the revolutionary period of 1848–49, including his rejection of "German ultraconservatism" (GS 8:43) and of "reactionism" in general (GS 8:83), his condemnation of the Carlsbad Decrees (GS 8:40), and his belief in the need for the "arming of the people" (GS 8:52–53). Indeed, Wagner even hailed the murder of August Kotzebue by Karl Ludwig Sand as a triumph of progress over political and aesthetic reaction (GS 8:82). This proved too much for Ludwig, and publication of the articles was suspended.

When Wagner was invited to Munich in 1864, few believed that he had repudiated the revolutionary ideas that even as late as 1852 continued to find explicit expression in his writings. In 1865 the archconservative *Neuer Bayerischer Kurier* opined that

> the least evil that this stranger has brought to our country may be compared to the plagues of locusts that darken the sun for months on end and devour our fields. This terrible image of a national pestilence, this man who once manned the barricades and, at the head of a band of arsonists, tried to blow up the royal palace in Dresden, now intends to isolate the king and exploit him for the treasonable ideas of a party of subversives.

A glance at the violent arguments that raged for and against Wagner, filling whole columns of the daily press not just in Munich but in much of Bavaria throughout 1865, reveals that music played only a minor role here. Wagner, rather, was a political figure, a figure rebuked not just for his sybaritic lifestyle, his need for luxury, and his immoderate demands on the royal exchequer but more especially for his attempt to indoctrinate the king with his political ideas, playing the role of the Marquis of Posa to Ludwig's Don Carlos. Aesthetic fronts turned into political fronts as contemporaries continued to regard Wagner as an unreconstructed revolutionary.

Wagner's fiercest critics were, of course, the ultramontane and conservative newspapers, whereas liberal papers such as the *Münchner Neueste Nachrichten* stood up for him. Through August Röckel, he was able to maintain his links with the party of progress, which was tireless in its support of his former comrade-in-arms from the time of his appointment in Dresden. Writing in the *Augsburger Allgemeine Zeitung*—by far the most outspoken of the anti-Wagnerian newspapers—on 19 February 1865, Oskar von Redwitz complained, with some justification, that Wagner's supporters "honor the former revolutionary rather than the present composer." Generally, however, no distinction was drawn between the two.

On 29 November 1865 Wagner published an anonymous article in the *Münchner Neueste Nachrichten*, demanding a cabinet reshuffle with a more liberal majority. Ludwig, succumbing to pressure from his cabinet, the aristocracy, the royal family, and the church, was left with no choice but to ask Wagner to leave Munich. In turn this provoked the protests of the Bavarian party of progress and the liberal press that supported it, both of whom rejected the idea that "the king's high-born relatives, the members of the higher nobility, and the servants of the church and state who have provided him with evidence of the prevailing mood represent the mood of the people"—thus the *Augsburger Allgemeine Zeitung* of 11 December 1865. Driven from Munich, Wagner wrote to his political contact August Röckel on 12 December, entreating him not to abandon his hopes for a more liberal policy on the part of Ludwig II: "What matters to me above all else is not to undermine the liberals' faith in him." In short, the alliance between Wagner—a survivor of the Dresden May Uprising—and King Ludwig II was certainly not regarded by contemporaries, whether conservative or liberal, as the decision of a renegade.

The radical democrat Georg Herwegh, who was on first-name terms with both Marx and Wagner, wrote a furious satire of the people of Munich following

Wagner's dismissal, complaining that their "impenetrably thick skins" were impervious to beauty. "You tried in vain to make them see / Beyond the Munich Hofbräuhaus. / Like Lola Montez you must be / The terror of all decent folk" ("To Richard Wagner," January 1866). Lola Montez was the Irish adventuress Eliza Gilbert, who in 1846 had become the mistress of Ludwig's grandfather, Ludwig I, a liaison that had led indirectly to his downfall. In turn, Wagner was frequently pilloried in the local press as Lolus Montez. Even Franz Grillparzer mocked Wagner in this way in his epigram "Musikalisches" (Things musical). Curiously enough, in 1849 Wagner himself wrote a quatrain aimed at Lola Montez but oddly preemptive of his own situation in the mid-1860s: "Das Unbegreifliche / hier bleibt es Wunder, / das Ewig-Weibliche / bringt uns herunter" [Here the inscrutable's / Bound to bemuse us; / Woman will always / Be here to undo us] (SS 12:367).[33] Even Ludwig I saw the parallel (he did not die until 1868) and feared that his grandson would be overtaken by a catastrophe similar to the one that had befallen him twenty years earlier.

Following Wagner's banishment from Munich in December 1865, the Hoftheater dropped his works from its repertory for 1866. Bavaria's defeat in its war with Prussia cast a shadow over the political horizon, yet throughout all this Ludwig remained in touch with Wagner, who continued to do everything he could to exert his political influence, even succeeding in dissuading the king from abdicating. (After all, he had no use for a king without a country or money.) When Ludwig failed to inform his entourage and turned up unannounced at Tribschen on Wagner's birthday on 22 May 1866, spending two whole days with the bemused composer, he almost precipitated a national crisis. Ministers threatened to resign, Ludwig I read the riot act to his grandson, the press launched a series of violent attacks on the composer, and even the normally supportive *Münchner Neueste Nachrichten* distanced itself from him. Herwegh, by contrast, responded with his *Ballade vom verlorenen König* (Ballad of the lost king):

> Im Bayerland, im Bayerland,
> Da war der König durchgebrannt;
> Verschollen und verschwunden
> Seit einundzwanzig Stunden;
> Die Bayern sind sehr übel dran—
> Was fängt man ohne König an?
> . . . .
>
> Und Land und Ministerium
> Schimpft auf das Schwanenrittertum,
> Auf Wagner, Bülow, Venus,
> Aufs ein und andre Genus;
> Der König in der Republik
> Vertreibt die Zeit sich mit Musik.
>
> [Bavaria's king has run away:
> He's not been seen since yesterday.
> He's disappeared without a trace.
> What can have happened to His Grace?

The locals fume in mute distress.
Without a king they're in a mess.
. . . .
Both land and ministers of state
Heap curses on the Swan Knight's pate,
On Wagner, Bülow and their kind,
Regardless of their sex. You'll find
The monarch's busy musicking.
His land repines without a king.]

Yet a year that had begun so disastrously for Wagner ended on a note of triumph when the two ministers who had done most to drive him away—Franz Pfistermeister and Ludwig von der Pfordten (or "Pfi" and "Pfo," as Ludwig and Wagner dubbed their hated enemies)—were dismissed, and Chlodwig von Hohenlohe-Schillingsfürst, whom Wagner had repeatedly recommended for ministerial preferment, was appointed president of the council of ministers. I will have more to say in the next chapter on the political background of these developments and on Wagner's active role in them.

Ludwig and Wagner may have dreamed of a relationship similar to the one between the Duke of Ferrara and Tasso in Goethe's stage play. Here Tasso is not a court poet in the traditional sense of the term, producing his works for particular state occasions, but a writer who, relieved of material cares, is able to devote himself to the completion of his life's work. This is precisely what Ludwig intended for Wagner. Thus we find the latter writing to Mathilde Maier on 18 May 1864: "I have absolutely no obligations; I'm to have peace and quiet, with no cares to distract me and with the leisure to work—that's all."

The Antonios who begrudge the artist his honored status and finally drive him from court also dogged Wagner's life, and, like Goethe's Tasso, Wagner was partly to blame for his banishment thanks to his own arrogant behavior. In his letter to Cosima of 22 January 1866, Ludwig compared Wagner to Tasso on the strength of what he described as his persecution complex. Tasso, too, had "thought that he could see an elaborate network of hostile deceptions drawing together over his head. . . . He is tormenting himself by imagining all manner of cabals that are not (or not often) being hatched against him."[34] In this, however, Ludwig was almost certainly deceiving himself, for, unlike the Duke of Ferrara, he was not in control of the political situation. In her reply of 24 January 1866, Cosima proved remarkably self-contradictory, both confirming and denying Ludwig's comparison between Wagner and Tasso:

No doubt he *can* be compared to Tasso, who, as a poet in the single case that affected him, saw the whole wretchedness of the world, but Tasso is in the wrong, and when he is abandoned and on his own and yet stands there in all innocence, should we not abhor the world that condemns the genius to eccentricity?[35]

A further parallel between Tasso and Wagner was drawn by Gustav Freytag in the *Grenzboten*, following Wagner's expulsion from Munich.

On the whole, we shall recognize here an example of the sad old tale that invariably besets such relations between members of the aristocracy and their confidants in the world of art. For a time the patron is happy to abandon himself to the edifying impressions left by art on the souls of his fellow humans, he is inclined to ascribe to the artist the great and the beautiful that art has vouchsafed to him and to entrust to the said artist a part of his own judgment. But the artist, finding himself in a new situation and violently stirred by the brilliant colors that suddenly fill his life, now begins to make greater demands in his newfound love of power. He flouts the customs of the court, trampling on the habits and practices of his new surroundings, becoming irksome to many who, with or without entitlement, claim to have influence over the prince, while openly antagonizing others, with the result that many unite to resist him; he has revealed his weak points and he finally succumbs, the dream of his own importance evaporates, and both he and the prince lose much in the process, as both have to pay for their disenchantment with sacrifices of various kinds. Even before Tasso, this sort of thing had already befallen men stronger than Herr Wagner and princes who have had greater experience than the young king of Bavaria.[36]

Wagner and Bismarck

AN EPOCH-MAKING NONRELATIONSHIP

While, politically, Germany may perhaps be settling down to a

long period of hibernation under Prussian guardianship, *We*

shall no doubt be calmly and quietly preparing the noble hearth

at which the German sun shall one day be rekindled.

—Richard Wagner to Ludwig II, 24 July 1866

"THE GERMAN UNION must everywhere be able to show its teeth, even if it has nothing left to chew," Wagner wrote in one of his final essays, "What Use Is This Knowledge?" (1880). He followed this up with an embittered attack on Bismarck, whom he compared—as he had often done in the past—with Robespierre: "One imagines Robespierre presiding over his Committee of Public Safety when one conjures up a picture of the powerful leader locked away in isolation and ceaselessly searching for ways of increasing his power"—and hence of perpetuating war.

In 1870–71 Wagner had been an enthusiastic supporter of the war against France, but his mood had changed to one of pacifism, and there is no mistaking the note of irony when he writes that "we gladly believe in our leader's love of peace." But "true peace," he goes on, "can be achieved only by peaceful means." It should have occurred to this leader—whom Wagner obstinately refuses to name—that "the wantonly provoked and terrible war" would be better answered by "a different peace" from the one concluded in Versailles and Frankfurt am Main, which "merely invites us to prepare for war anew." The "recognition of the need and possibility of a true regeneration of the human race, which is now prey to a warlike mentality," should suggest the need for a treaty that "might prepare the way for world peace: then there would be no fortresses to capture, but only to demolish, no pledges to take that would safeguard us against a future war, but only pledges to safeguard our peace." And Wagner ends his reflections with the resigned observation that these "powerful leaders" can imagine world peace only "under the widely respected protection of an extraordinary number of cannons" (GS 10:254–55).

WAGNER, BISMARCK, AND THE IDEA OF A PRUSSIAN STATE

There were few men whom Wagner hated more than Bismarck in the final years of his life. Cosima Wagner's diaries contain countless violent outbursts against the Iron Chancellor, whom Wagner saw as the dragon of the apocalypse, driving humanity toward its destruction through a whole series of increasingly terrible wars. "I have lived to see the most miserable time that Germany has ever known, with this beastly agitator at its head," he fulminated on 18 March 1880. A year later, on 21 March 1881, he called Bismarck a "brutal barbarian." On 4 December 1881 he allowed himself to get worked up over the "constant 'I'" of Bismarck's Reichstag speeches, and on 24 November 1881 he even expressed his disgust at Bismarck's physical appearance: "'I can't stand bald pates,' R. exclaims drolly, 'Caesar has spoiled them for me.'" A glance at a newly discovered portrait of Napoleon encouraged him to remark, "How much more racial beauty, and expression, too, there is in this face than, for instance, in Bismarck's" (CT, 24 November 1881). And when, on 12 November 1880 Franz von Lenbach spoke respectfully about the chancellor, whom he had painted several times, Wagner "burst out in anger at this bulldog face that is always being painted." At this, Lenbach left in understandable indignation, even though Wagner had "tried to explain to him the reasons for his anger."

Wagner's hatred of Bismarck extended to all of Prussia. "Among the peoples of the earth," he complained on 21 January 1881, "it is always the stupidest tribes who are destined to rule over the others"; as an example he quoted "the Prussians among the Germans." According to the notes made by Daniela von Bülow following her stepfather's death in February 1883, one of Wagner's final outbursts was directed at Bismarck and his allegedly despotic behavior.

The relations between Wagner and Bismarck remain inadequately explored, with biographers of these two titans of the nineteenth century regularly overemphasizing or underplaying the importance of their relationship depending on their own political biases. The result has been either an unduly flattering portrait of the relationship or outright demonization. Carl Friedrich Glasenapp, whose life of Wagner represented the official view of the Bayreuth Circle, painted a picture of a relationship that was unproblematic and even cordial, and, following his example, countless later writers have helped to perpetuate the idea of a close intellectual affinity between the two men. "They are both laboring away at one and the same great work," wrote Moritz Wirth in 1883 in his *Bismarck, Wagner, Rodbertus: Drei deutsche Meister* (Three German masters). "Although they have sought to approach and solve the problems facing us from the opposite ends of our national field of labor, both had the same goal: the defense of the German character against foreign countries." Forty years later, August Püringer made the same point in an article published in the 1924 Bayreuth Festival program: "The spirit of Wagner and Bismarck! Only together can they bring salvation to us Germans!" According to Püringer, their names embody intellectual and military might, "just as the body's heart and lungs or heart and brain operate together."[1]

The idea of an affinity between Wagner and Bismarck was one of the myths that came into being while the Germans were forging their sense of national identity, a myth to which even Cosima contributed in her diary entry of 5 January 1873: "Bismarck created Germany, R. a German theater, and both started from scratch." And in 1888, in *The Case of Wagner*, Nietzsche noted that "there is something profoundly significant about the fact that Wagner's arrival coincided with that of the 'Reich.' "[2] Certainly, many contemporaries regarded Wagner as the official composer of the new German Reich. Karl Marx, for example, happened to pass through nearby Nuremberg in August 1876. The first Bayreuth Festival was then under way, encouraging Marx to describe the occasion in a letter to Friedrich Engels as "a fool's festival by Wagner the state musician," a description reinforced by the presence in Bayreuth of Emperor Wilhelm I.

There is no denying that even before the Reich had been founded, Wagner had already toyed with the idea of a link between his own festival and German unification. He needed "an emperor for the artwork of the future," he told Cosima on 12 December 1870. But he soon abandoned his illusory hope of a new Reich, and by 1872, when he laid the foundation stone for his new theater in Bayreuth, he rejected the idea of calling it a national theater—for "where is the 'nation' that would build this theater" (GS 9:328)? His rhetorical question was no doubt a reminiscence of the final section of Lessing's *Hamburgische Dramaturgie* (Hamburg dramaturgy), which is headed: "On the Well-Meaning Idea of Creating a National Theater for the Germans When We Germans Are Still Not a Nation!"[3]

Time and time again in conversation with friends and acquaintances, especially his friends from France, Wagner expressed his sense of shame at ever having pinned his hopes on the German Reich. And on 10 February 1878 we find him writing to Ludwig: "Few people, I imagine, thought that the barrenness of the Prussian idea of the state would be foisted upon us as quickly as this and passed off as the wisdom of the German Reich!"[4] In short, Wagner was anything but a composer in the pay of the German Reich, and whatever hopes he may initially have entertained, he had absolutely no influence on Bismarck's Germany. And yet, as Hannu Salmi has indicated, on two occasions there was the distinct possibility of a closer association between Wagner and Bismarck, first at the time of the war between Austria and Prussia in 1866 and, second, immediately after German unification.[5]

From 1864, Wagner had developed his plans for the reform of the theater of his day in close association with the young king of Bavaria. Art and politics were to feed off each other, with Wagner even imagining Bavaria as a model German state, but following Austria's heavy defeat in its war with Prussia in the summer of 1866, its ally Bavaria seemed to have lost the chance to play a leading intellectual and political role in the life of Germany. For this reason, if for no other, this turn of events deeply affected the relationship between Wagner and Ludwig; the dream of an alliance between king and composer faded visibly, and in Wagner's eyes Munich grew increasingly unattractive as the ideal venue for his art. The abandonment of Semper's plans to build a monumental festival theater on the banks of the Isar was merely the outward sign of this growing disenchantment.

Wagner's disillusionment with Bavaria is striking, given the pro-Bavarian nature of his political views before 1866. Until then, he had been unstinting in his scornful attacks on Prussia. In the diary jottings that he kept for Ludwig II between 14 and 27 September 1865 (subsequently edited and published under the title "What Is German?"), the Prussian statesman is depicted as notoriously hostile to the spirit of the people. Throughout its history, Wagner claimed, Berlin had always been at the center of an un-German civilization, and the kings of Prussia had routinely ignored the welfare of the German people. Wagner's most biting satire was reserved for Frederick the Great for identifying with the art and culture of the French Enlightenment.[6]

But Wagner's antipathy was also openly directed at the Prussian ruling house and its most powerful political representative, with the result that we find him commenting as follows on Bismarck and Wilhelm I in a letter to Ludwig.

> With what chilling frivolity sport is now being made with the fates of the noblest and greatest nation on earth: see how an ambitious Junker betrays his imbecile of a king in the most brazen manner imaginable, forcing him to play a dishonorable game that would appall the honest monarch if only he could see what was happening. (29 April 1866)

Wagner continued to strike this note in a letter of 20 June 1866, this time to his friend François Wille, who was also friendly with Bismarck; on this occasion we find him deriding the Iron Chancellor as "an inferior copy of the un-German character."

Wagner's dismissive attitude toward Prussia makes sense against the background of the political program that he drew up in early June 1866 and that reveals him as a champion of federalism rather than of the centralized form of government toward which Prussia was moving. But there was another reason for his rejection of Bismarck: he was dismayed that instead of princes, it was now diplomats who held the reins of political power. In his letter to Ludwig of 29 April 1866, he attacks the machinations of diplomats "who sit around, no longer able to tell the difference between what is honest and what is deceitful, since their sole concern is the game itself, a game that they assure their masters is fearfully difficult and requires both skill and experience if others are to be allowed to join in—be it for profit or loss!" The activities of these diplomats, Wagner prophesies, would finally result in "boundless confusion of a kind that no prince will be able to combat but to which will be added mass chaos—the chaos of a brutal mass in need of help."

According to Wagner, diplomats—in other words, professional politicians— could not be interested in the welfare of the people in the way that princes were. And they could not care less about the morality of political action. Wagner's concept of politics was still oriented toward the Romantic ideal of a republican monarchy which had influenced his actions at the time of the May Uprising in Dresden in 1849. But there was no longer any room for such an outlook within the modern political system that Prussia favored, a system in which state action assumed increasingly impersonal features.

By the summer of 1866 Prussia had finally established itself as the most powerful political force in Germany. The shock waves caused by the war between

Prussia on the one hand and Austria and Bavaria on the other affected even Wagner, persuading him to change direction.[7] Whereas he had previously attacked Bismarck and his political maneuvering with some vehemence, the war was not yet over when he wrote to August Röckel on 23 June 1866 to proclaim his new allegiance. "My friend," he implored his former comrade-in-arms from the days of the Dresden Uprising, "if you're resolved to continue to take an active role in politics, then stick to Bismarck and Prussia. So help me God, I know of no alternative."

WAGNER'S POLITICAL MISSION

Prior to Hannu Salmi's striking findings, few historians had paid much attention to the fact that in June 1866 Bismarck made secret contact with Wagner.[8] His aim was to ensure that Bavaria would side with Prussia in the war that was just beginning. Needless to say, he had been told about the remarkable composer to whom the young king of Bavaria was in thrall and attempted to use him as a political tool. Curious though it must seem to us today, in this period artists—itinerant virtuosos—saw far more of the world, and especially of the world's courts, than politicians, and thus were able to provide secret information for crowned heads or their leading diplomats and were often informally used as secret agents. Liszt's life affords more than one example of this.

Wagner maintained what for him was an unusual silence with regard to these politically explosive events: his letters to Ludwig and his other friends contain no mention of the feelers that Bismarck put out to him. Only his annals for June 1866 include the mysterious reference: "Dr Wille (Bismarck)." "Dr Wille" was the aforementioned François Wille, an old friend of Wagner's who had studied alongside Bismarck in Göttingen. At Bismarck's request, Wille called on Wagner and urged him to encourage Ludwig to mediate between Prussia and Austria. Wille's wife, Eliza, takes up the story in her reminiscences.

> The storm clouds were gathering in Germany at the start of that summer; war between Prussia and Austria was in the air, and, already afraid of war as such, people recoiled even more at the idea of a civil war that would lead to German unification. At the height of the summer Wille traveled to Lucerne, where Wagner was then staying and where Semper was currently submitting the ground plan of the theater that he was planning to build [in Munich]. Both men were present when Wille tried to persuade Wagner to use his influence to persuade the king of Bavaria to remain neutral and to offer to mediate between Austria and Prussia. Wagner felt only disgust at Bismarck and Prussia at this time, and so he refused, saying that where politics was concerned he had no influence on the king and that "whenever he (Wagner) raised the subject, the king would roll his eyes skyward and whistle"![9]

Writers on Wagner have ignored Eliza Wille's reminiscences in this context, no doubt because they failed to grasp the full significance of this incident.

But Wagner's decision to adopt a more positive attitude to Prussia must have been connected with Wille's mission, even if he initially refused to allow himself to be used as a political agent. This, at least, seems to be the conclusion to be drawn from his letter to Wille of 20 June 1866.

> The only way to make any impression on the young king of Bavaria is by firing his enthusiasm. I fail to understand how it would be possible for your most eloquent recommendation to inspire him with any interest in Herr von Bismarck's policies. . . . In no circumstances am I either able or willing to countenance the young king of Bavaria being advised to take an interest in these policies, and even if I *was* willing, this advice would be rejected, whatever form it might take, even if it came from a man who is an honest friend and to whom I am eternally indebted. In any case, you should not forget that my young friend's entourage is at present made up in such a way that I can communicate with him—even in writing—only if I show my hand: if you were to ask for an audience with the king, you would be prevented from seeing him by every conceivable means.[10]

In short, Wagner refused to act as a political intriguer, just as he had rejected a similar offer the previous year when approached by Maximilian von Thurn und Taxis. On that occasion, too, he had claimed to have no influence over the king: Ludwig's ministers made sure of that.[11] But Wille's approach evidently gave him food for thought, and the armed confrontation between Prussia and Austria clearly persuaded him to change his mind, as emerges from the letter that he wrote to Röckel only three days later, urging the latter to pin his political hopes on Prussia.

The pro-Austrian stance of the Bavarian cabinet under Ludwig von der Pfordten was of course known to the Prussians, and so Bismarck and Wille tried to use Wagner as a go-between in their attempts to smuggle a politician into the Bavarian government who would look on Prussia with a benevolent eye. Bismarck's favorite in Bavaria was Chlodwig von Hohenlohe-Schillingsfürst, who in 1874 became German ambassador in Paris and whom Wagner, too, saw as an ally. Whereas the composer's archenemy Ludwig von der Pfordten still regarded Wagner as an unregenerate revolutionary (he had been minister of culture in Saxony during Wagner's years in Dresden), Hohenlohe-Schillingsfürst might at least be more sympathetic to Wagner's art. When Wagner realized that all further opposition to Prussia was pointless, he fell in with Bismarck's plan and in a letter to Ludwig of 26 July 1866—at a time when the outcome of the war still hung in the balance—recommended that Hohenlohe-Schillingsfürst, who was well known for his Prussian sympathies, be appointed forthwith to head the Bavarian cabinet. "Appoint Prince Hohenlohe-Schillingsfürst at once,—discuss the matter with him in detail, and seek his advice." The next day Wagner wrote again, almost literally throwing himself at Ludwig's feet: "New people! New people! You are betrayed if you do not do this!—You can confidently regard everyone as your enemy who advises you against appointing Prince Hohenlohe. . . . The prince is distinguished, independent, well educated, liberal, at all events, a man who has an opinion. . . . I entreat you: receive the prince in person!" Even as late as the beginning of August, when the formation of a new Bavarian cabinet was being discussed, Ludwig was still not prepared to follow Wagner's advice. Although Wagner had claimed that his candidate was "independent" (a claim immediately cast in doubt by Wille's influence on Wagner), the black-and-white flag of the enemy could clearly be seen waving behind Hohenlohe, with the result that Ludwig still found it difficult to cut himself off from Pfordten. On 9 August Prince Paul von Thurn und Taxis informed Wagner of the king's decision: "Prince Hohenlohe did not win the confidence of His Exalted Majesty during recent cabinet meetings! His political affiliations are too clearly black and white in color."

At this point the peace treaty between Prussia and Bavaria had still to be signed, but once the terms had formally been agreed and ratified in Prague on 23 August, Ludwig no longer had any choice in the matter of who headed his cabinet. Prussia was anxious to win over the southern German states, and so Bavaria was allowed to retain its independence—in this regard it continued to enjoy the same status as Baden and Württemberg. And one of the main ways of achieving this aim was the election of civil servants who were sympathetic to Prussia, a policy that proved providentially farsighted when the Franco-Prussian War broke out in 1870. A secret agreement signed in the wake of the Treaty of Prague also ensured that in the event of war Bavarian troops would fight alongside their Prussian counterparts.

As early as 9 August, Prince Paul von Thurn und Taxis had assured Wagner that the cabinet secretary, Franz von Pfistermeister, and the prime minister, Ludwig von der Pfordten (the hated "Pfi" and "Pfo"), would soon be out of harm's way. Pfistermeister duly resigned on 5 October 1866, handing over his portfolio to Max von Neumayr, and it was not long before Pfordten followed suit. By 16 December, the king was able to write to Cosima: "I am now seriously thinking of appointing Prince Hohenlohe in Pfordten's place."

Pfordten thus had no alternative but to tender his resignation on 19 December, leaving Hohenlohe to take up his appointment on the 31st. Prussia had finally succeeded in placing one of its own politicians at the head of the Bavarian government—and one, moreover, who was acceptable to Wagner. That Wagner had played a decisive role in this appointment is undeniable. Indeed, Hohenlohe even had to defend himself against the reproach that he was prime minister by the grace of Wagner. Inevitably the composer was again likened to Lola Montez; just as she had once persuaded Ludwig I to reshuffle his cabinet, resulting in the "Lola Ministry," so history seemed to have repeated itself. Unsurprisingly, the new prime minister reacted with some acerbity to such suggestions.

AN AUDIENCE WITHOUT CONSEQUENCES:
WAGNER AND BISMARCK AFTER 1871

Wagner's second contact with Bismarck was ushered in by his poem *An das deutsche Heer vor Paris* [To the German army outside Paris] (GS 9:1–2), which he sent to the chancellor in January 1871. Bismarck's reply was laconic in the extreme, but Wagner regarded this as sufficient encouragement to insist on a meeting as soon as possible. Thanks to the good offices of Lothar Bucher and Marie von Schleinitz, he was granted an audience on 3 May 1871 during a visit to Berlin. According to Cosima's diary, the meeting passed off entirely to Wagner's satisfaction; Bismarck struck him as a man who was "great and simple by nature.... R. is utterly delighted by his genuine kindness. ... But, R. says, we can only observe each other, each in his own world; to have anything to do with him, to win him over, to ask him to support my cause, would never occur to me."

Bismarck later placed an entirely different gloss on this conversation, while describing its contents and lack of any practical outcome in almost identical terms. On 22 January 1893 he told the government adviser Heinrich von Poschinger:

> He hadn't brought a petition with him (money for Bayreuth). They sat us down together on a sofa, and he probably thought a duet would develop between the two of us, but that's not what happened. The master of musical sounds probably felt that he wasn't earning enough praise from me, and, having failed to blossom, he went away disappointed.[12]

Although writers on Wagner have often regarded the meeting between the composer and Bismarck as highly symbolic, its outcome was pitiful in the extreme. Bismarck made every effort to be polite—Cosima refers to "the most cordial communicativeness, arousing trust and sympathy"—but his words were diplomatic niceties. Wagner seems to have fallen victim to the error typical of every member of the middle classes, who, to quote Schiller, regards the "assurances of a generalized civility as tokens of personal fondness," and who, when finding himself deceived, accuses the other of "dissembling."[13]

The accounts of the meeting left by both Wagner and Bismarck agree that the question of any financial support for Wagner's festival was not raised. Bismarck appears to have taken Wagner in with his diplomatic politeness, leaving the latter with no opportunity to explain his actual concerns. At the same time, however, Wagner was so confident of his success with Bismarck that at the end of 1872 he even thought he could "coerce" the chancellor into offering Nietzsche a job in Berlin following the professional boycott imposed on the philosopher since the publication of *Die Geburt der Tragödie* (CT, 9 November 1872). In the event, Wagner did nothing, no doubt realizing that the plan was bound to fail. But on two subsequent occasions Wagner did appeal in writing to Bismarck. On 24 June 1873 he attempted to persuade the "great reviver of German hopes" to make good his earlier omission and support "the cultural idea that inspires me." And, heaping coals of fire on Bismarck's head, he reminded the latter how "aloof and indifferent" Frederick the Great had remained to the "rebirth of the German spirit through our great poets of the second half of the last century."

In spite of Wagner's attempt to ingratiate himself, Bismarck felt it unnecessary to acknowledge his letter with even so much as a line. Clearly, he was unimpressed by the fact that Wagner held him in higher esteem than he did Frederick the Great. In a diary entry of 9 October 1874, Cosima quotes a Hungarian admirer of Wagner: "If Bismarck were pursuing pan-German policies and not specifically Prussian ones, surely he would support the Wagner undertaking?" But Bismarck remained "specifically Prussian."

In spite of this, Wagner did not give up, and in December 1875 he made a further démarche in the direction of Berlin. On this occasion he received a brief reply from Bismarck bluntly refusing any kind of financial assistance, a bluntness all the more offensive for being in such stark contrast to the affability that he had shown at their private meeting. Wagner was invited to apply to the Reichstag instead of importuning a man as busy as Bismarck.

In the autumn of 1888, five years after Wagner's death, Cosima made a further attempt to gain state support for the Bayreuth Festival. On this occasion the emperor asked Bismarck to submit a report explaining why it was impossible to take the festival under the imperial wing. Bismarck duly responded by pointing out that such a move would cause difficulties in terms of domestic politics: "I believe therefore that to fulfill Frau Cosima Wagner's request would inevitably have financial implications for Your Majesty and that a protectorate located in Bayreuth would harm the internal politics of the German Reich in not inessential ways."[14]

In short, Bismarck's interest in Wagner clearly depended on the general political climate. The composer may have been of some use to him before 1871, but he lost all interest in Wagner once he had achieved his political aim of incorporating Bavaria into the German Reich. Wagner's music was a matter of the utmost indifference to Bismarck, and his cultural and political views interested him even less. Goethe's and Schiller's comment on the old empire could just as well be applied to its successor: where the intellectual and spiritual Germany began, the political Germany ceased to exist.[15] Bismarck was "not an ideologist," Wagner told Cosima on 7 December 1878. This was not a positive assessment but was intended, rather, to suggest that Bismarck's politics were innocent of any concept of culture.

"German unity," Wagner wrote in his essay "What Use Is This Knowledge?" "was won and contractually fixed, but what it might mean is hard to say." For Wagner, Bismarck's policies amounted to "Shall without Have, Will without Idea" (GS 10:254). In 1870 Wagner had hoped that Germany's victories would lead to a renewal of the German spirit, but by the end of his life he was convinced that "culture" could spring "from the soil of peace" alone, "just as it derives its name from the cultivation of the actual soil" (GS 10:234). As an alternative to the frenzy of a nation drunk on victory, Wagner held out an aesthetic message of compassion, arguing that "our sympathy belongs not to the victor but to the vanquished hero alone" (GS 10:247).

From Wagner's standpoint, Bismarck, with German unification, had created only a cultural vacuum, and although Wagner saw himself "nailed to the cross of the German ideal" (as he told his French friend Édouard Schuré on 4 September 1873), he clearly recognized that Bismarck had remained a specifically Prussian patriot. "What does such a Junker know about Germany?" he asked his wife on 16 December 1878, a rhetorical question that a member of Wagner's household subsequently sought to render indecipherable in the manuscript of Cosima's diaries. (A similar fate befell other onslaughts on Bismarck in the pages of her diary.) Bismarck may have brought about German unification, but in Wagner's eyes he had failed in the process to become what he believed everyone should want to become: a "German."

Two-Faced Passion

NIETZSCHE'S CRITIQUE OF WAGNER

In memory of Jörg Salaquarda (d. 8 June 1999)

You should now show people why philology exists and help
me to bring about the great "renaissance" in which Plato
embraces Homer, and Homer, filled with Plato's ideas, finally
becomes the very greatest Homer.

—*Richard Wagner to Friedrich Nietzsche, February 1870*

"I DO NOT KNOW how I could ever have enjoyed the *purest* of sunlit happiness
except through Wagner's music," Nietzsche wrote in the summer of 1875 in one
of his posthumously published jottings. "And this is true in spite of the fact that it
does not always speak of happiness but of the terrible and eerie subterranean
forces of human activity, of the suffering in all happiness and of the finite nature
of our happiness; the happiness that it exudes must lie, then, in the way in which
it speaks" (562).[1]

"Happiness": Nietzsche uses this word five times in the same sentence, a sentence written at a time when he had already started to drift away from Wagner in
many respects. More than a year previously he had written a series of unpublished
aphorisms in whose quiver we find nearly all the critical barbs that he was to shoot
at Wagner in later years. Following the "Master's" death, he never tired of passing
off his early Wagnerism as a form of self-deception. But there can be no denying the
very real happiness that Nietzsche derived from Wagner's music, a happiness placed
beyond doubt by countless remarks of his. This, wrote Thomas Mann in *Leiden und
Größe Richard Wagners*, was "the great love affair of Nietzsche's life."[2]

And, as he himself repeatedly admitted, Nietzsche loved Wagner, too, from the
bottom of his heart. On 27 April 1883, a little over two months after Wagner's
death, he looked back wistfully to the early years of their friendship in Tribschen
and, in a letter to Peter Gast, wrote: "At that date we loved each other and hoped
for everything *for each other*—it was a deep love, with no ulterior motives" (833).
This is an extraordinary confession from a man who saw it as one of his major
tasks in life to identify the sense of resentment behind apparently altruistic feelings,

revealing a psychologist's skill at laying bare the truth. "I loved him and no one else" (875). Shattering in its brevity, this astonishing statement dates from the spring of 1885, two whole years after Wagner's death.

Of course, happiness can end in unhappiness, and the most impassioned love can teach us the hitherto unknown feeling of hatred. But this does not alter the fact that happiness is happiness and that the love was once real. Nietzsche never denied this in the case of Wagner. Particularly during the final years of his lucid life, Wagner's name was synonymous with happiness for him. Until the end he continued to regard the Tribschen years, when he was a surrogate son for the Wagners, as the happiest of his life. Shortly before his final descent into madness, he wrote in *Ecce homo* ("Why I Am So Clever," section 5):

> Speaking of the recreations of my life, I must say a word to express my gratitude for what has been by far the most profound and heartfelt recreation of my life. Beyond a doubt, that was my more intimate relationship with Richard Wagner. The rest of my human relationships I hold cheap in comparison; but at no price would I wish to relinquish the days that I spent at Tribschen, days of mutual confidences, of cheerfulness, of sublime coincidences—and *profound* moments. . . . I don't know what experiences others have had with Wagner: *our* sky was never darkened by even a single cloud. (1100)

THE PRELUDE TO AN EPOCH-MAKING ENCOUNTER

For more than a century the relations between Nietzsche and Wagner have been smothered in a rank undergrowth of legends and rumors whose roots lie not least in the public silence that both men maintained over the reasons for their estrangement, a silence that naturally opened the way to boundless speculation.[3] To some extent, these speculations were scotched by the publication of Cosima Wagner's diaries in 1976–77 and above all by the appearance in print of Nietzsche's previously unpublished papers within the framework of the critical edition of his works (started in 1967 and still in progress), with the result that many of the more outrageous legends have now been rooted out.

Only with the publication of these previously unpublished jottings has it been possible to appreciate the paradigmatic importance of Wagner for Nietzsche. With their richly faceted analyses of the pros and cons of their relationship, they provide a counterweight to the exaggerations of Nietzsche's last two anti-Wagnerian tracts, *Der Fall Wagner* and *Nietzsche contra Wagner*. Against the background of his unpublished papers, Nietzsche's published statements on Wagner appear in a substantially different light.

It now becomes clear, for example, that Nietzsche's break with Wagner was by no means as radical as posterity, in its ignorance of the sources, long believed. The idea that he changed overnight from an unquestioning Wagnerian to an equally unquestioning anti-Wagnerian belongs to the past. Passion and criticism were as intimately linked in the mind of the early Nietzsche as polemics and passion were linked in his later statements on Wagner. This explains why Thomas Mann, in his *Leiden und Größe Richard Wagners*, was able to describe Nietzsche's published polemics against Wagner as "a panegyric in reverse, another form of eulogy."[4]

When Nietzsche first met Wagner in November 1868, he was only twenty-four, although his interest in Wagner's works and cultural program dates from the beginning of the decade. His earliest remarks attest to a deeply ambivalent attitude to the "music of the future," an ambivalence due to the fact that he had been brought up in a neoclassical aesthetic tradition, from which he was able to break free only gradually and with considerable scruples in the course of the 1860s. Only during the months leading up to his first meeting with Wagner at Heinrich Brockhaus's home in Leipzig on 8 November 1868 did he really start to appreciate Wagner. "I cannot bring myself to adopt an attitude of critical coolness toward this music," he wrote to Erwin Rohde on 27 October 1868 immediately after having heard the prelude to *Tristan und Isolde* and the overture to *Die Meistersinger von Nürnberg* at a concert in the city. "Every fiber, every nerve in me is twitching, and it's a long time since I had such a lasting sense of rapt otherworldliness as I did with this last-named overture" (308).

His letter to Rohde of 8 October 1868 is his first significant attempt to assess Wagner as a phenomenon. Here he confronts head-on the criticisms leveled at Wagner by his teacher in Bonn, the classical philologist and Mozart scholar Otto Jahn. Although he reproached Jahn for listening to Wagner's music "with his ears half shut," he agreed with his assessment of the composer as a "representative of a modern dilettantism that consumes and digests all artistic interests." Jahn was by no means the first to level this charge at Wagner. Nor was he the last. This charge continued to dog Wagner well into the twentieth century, as is clear from the example of both Mann and Adorno. Indeed, it was an important element in Wagner's own aesthetic diagnosis of himself as a modern experimental artist.[5]

But whereas Jahn had used the term "dilettantism" in a pejorative sense, Nietzsche immediately reinterpreted it to embrace a whole range of other allusions.

> But precisely from this standpoint it's hard not to be amazed at the extent to which each individual artistic disposition has developed in this man and at the way in which indestructible resolve is coupled with many-sided artistic talents, whereas "education," the more varied and all-embracing it becomes, normally appears with dulled eyes, weak knees, and enfeebled loins. (307)

In short, Wagner's dilettanism contains within it the highest potential for development in the face of a broken-backed cultural philistinism.

In the last of his *Unzeitgemäße Betrachtungen* ("Richard Wagner in Bayreuth"), Nietzsche argued that Wagner was "held in check by no traditional family involvement in any particular art form: he might as easily have adopted painting, poetry, acting or music as academic scholarship or an academic future; and a superficial view of him might suggest that he was a born dilettante." Nietzsche then goes on to use the phrase "perilous pleasure in the superficial tasting of one thing after another" (642), a critique that anticipates a basic idea of the *Essais de psychologie contemporaine* (Essays in contemporary psychology, 1883–86) by the French writer on *décadence* Paul Bourget, who was in turn to influence Nietzsche's later writings. (Bourget redefined dilettantism as a superficial savoring of heterogeneous forms of intellectual and practical life, with a tendency to feign the emotions associated with them.)

Nietzsche's letter to Rohde of 8 October 1868 includes not only a positive reappraisal of the concept of dilettantism but also a pre-echo of his later analysis of *décadence*, when he writes that "Wagner inhabits a world of emotion that is completely hidden from Jahn: Jahn remains a . . . healthy individual, for whom the legend of Tannhäuser and the atmosphere of Lohengrin are a closed world." And there follows the famous sentence that had a lifelong fascination for Mann, a sentence that for him summed up the whole nature of a writer who had not yet lost touch with himself as a result of his doctrine of the superman and the will to power: "What I like about Wagner is what I like about Schopenhauer—the ethical air, the Faustian aura, cross, death, grave, and so on" (307–8).

It was, of course, this ethical aura of the cross that Nietzsche was later—and paradoxically—to cite as the main reason for his estrangement from Wagner. But it is clear from the examples just quoted that before the two men had even met, Nietzsche's comments on Wagner already contained an echo of all the motifs that were to form the major themes of his analysis and critique of Wagner in the two decades that followed.

ALLIANCE WITH WAGNER

On Whit Monday 1869, shortly after his appointment as extraordinary professor of classical philology at the University of Basel, Nietzsche paid his first visit to Richard Wagner and Cosima von Bülow at their home at Tribschen on Lake Lucerne. Both Wagner and Cosima took to him at once, and during the weeks and months that followed, he became a vital link between Wagner and his son, Siegfried ("Fidi"). "Strictly speaking, you and my wife are the only real gain that life has brought me," Wagner wrote to Nietzsche on 25 June 1872, a month after the foundation stone of the Bayreuth Festspielhaus had been laid; "fortunately, of course, I now have Fidi, too; but I need a link between him and me, and only you can forge that link, much as the son is linked to the grandchild" (190). In short, Wagner was accepting Nietzsche in place of a son. King Marke and Tristan!

Quite apart from his intellectual contribution to the Tribschen ménage, Nietzsche was fully accepted into the family by both Wagner and Cosima. There can be few precedents for this relationship in the whole history of culture: here was one of the most pioneering thinkers of the modern age not only acting as an intellectual foil for one of its greatest artists but functioning as a general factotum, running errands, providing a link with the outside world, overseeing the publication of *My Life*, copying manuscripts such as *Siegfried's Tod* (Siegfried's death), supplying Cosima and the children with sweets, toys, and Brussels lace, and even helping to decorate the Christmas tree and to hide Easter eggs.[6]

Nietzsche increasingly sought to break free from Wagner's stranglehold, and even as early as 11 May 1871 Cosima thought that she had noted a "worrying streak, like an addiction to treachery, as though he were trying to avenge himself for some great impression." A later entry in her diary appears to throw some light on the nature of this "great impression": "It is as if he is trying to resist the overwhelming effect of Wagner's personality" (CT, 3 August 1871). Cosima was necessarily a biased observer, but her psychoanalytically compelling diagnosis of Nietzsche's behavior as a form of self-defense and revenge is certainly true of an essential aspect of his attempts to break free from Wagner, whose charismatic personality—described by many contemporaries—and refusal to be upstaged by others were bound to be felt as increasingly intolerable and inhibiting by Nietzsche, both privately and professionally. Defense reaction and suprapersonal opposition were inextricably linked here.

In his letter to Rohde of 28 January 1872, Nietzsche announced that he and Wagner had formed an "alliance" (357) that was based, naturally enough, on his first published book, *Die Geburt der Tragödie aus dem Geiste der Musik* (The birth of tragedy from the spirit of music), together with its preliminary studies. Nietzsche's interest in Greek tragedy is permeated with his passion for Wagner's music dramas, with each providing a surface in which the other is reflected. Typical of this whole approach are the final sentences of his lecture "Das griechische Musikdrama" (The Greek music drama) of 1870.

> Many arts operating to their fullest capacity and yet constituting a *single* work of art—that is the classical music drama. Anyone who, seeing this, is reminded of the ideal of the man who is at present reforming art will be bound to say that this artwork of the future is by no means a brilliant but deceptive mirage: all that we hope for in the future has already existed in the past, more than two thousand years ago. (601)

Here, then, Nietzsche draws no distinction between the "music drama" of classical antiquity and its modern successor. The "artwork of the future" is authenticated and legitimized by dint of the fact that it has already existed in the past.[7]

On this point Nietzsche seems to adopt a position even more extreme than Wagner's; after all, Wagner had stressed that whatever affinities there may have been between the two forms, Greek tragedy was not the same as modern music drama. Yet on another point Nietzsche had already moved away from Wagner even at this early date, albeit only in his unpublished jottings. In a note dating from the spring of 1871, we find him referring to the "tremendous aesthetic superstition" that consists in the belief that "in the fourth movement of his Ninth Symphony, Beethoven issued a solemn declaration concerning the boundaries of absolute music, indeed, that with it he had, as it were, unlocked the gates of a new art" (470). However cautiously this reservation may be expressed here, it was to have profound consequences for Nietzsche's later writings. Yet it was a central thesis of Wagner's whole aesthetic outlook that the final movement of the Ninth Symphony did indeed unlock the doors to a whole new world of music, a conviction symbolically documented by the symphony's performance to mark the laying of the foundation stone of the Bayreuth Festspielhaus on 22 May 1872, a performance that Nietzsche attended. Here the Ninth Symphony was the figurative foundation stone on which the musical drama was based.

It was Wagner himself who coined the term "absolute music." In the reform essays that he wrote in Zurich between 1849 and 1851, it had still been entirely negative in its connotations. But Nietzsche knew that a significant shift had taken place in Wagner's aesthetics since his reading of Schopenhauer in 1854.[8] In a fragment dating from 1874, he draws an explicit distinction between Wagner's "older doctrine," according to which music is the "means" and drama the "end" (a view advanced in *Opera and Drama*), and his "newer doctrine," whereby music and drama were in the same relationship as "the universal and the example" (497). In his 1887 polemical essay *Zur Genealogie der Moral* (On the genealogy of morals), Nietzsche adopted a markedly sarcastic tone in parodying what he saw as the "theoretical disjunction between his [that is, Wagner's] earlier and later aesthetic beliefs": in the footsteps of Schopenhauer, he now treated the musician as "a kind of mouthpiece of the thing-in-itself, a telephone from the beyond" (960–61).

If the "newer" Schopenhauerian doctrine was true, Nietzsche wrote in 1874, the "universal may not be dependent on the individual example, in other words, absolute music is in the right, and the music in the drama must also be absolute music" (497). Nietzsche was already convinced of this at the time of *Die Geburt der Tragödie*. In his unpublished jottings from 1870 and 1871, he insists that the value of an opera will be "all the higher, the more freely and unconditionally the music develops along increasingly Dionysian lines and the more it despises all the so-called demands of the drama."[9] From then on, Nietzsche generally used quotation marks round the term "dramatic music" in order to emphasize its illusory character and the vast gulf that separated it from music per se ("pure music").[10]

After "breaking free" from Wagner (873 and passim),[11] Nietzsche asked himself the skeptical question whether Wagner's "older doctrine" was more integral to his works than his "newer" one; in other words, he complained that in spite of his conversion to Schopenhauer, Wagner was still effectively writing music that was a means to the end of the drama. He was incapable of writing absolute music but was dependent on some stimulus from the stage. Throughout his published writings and unpublished jottings of the 1880s, including, for example, *Die fröhliche Wissenschaft* (The gay science) (aphorism 368),[12] Nietzsche argued that "from first to last," the "pose" was his real "aim" and the music was no more than a "means" to that end. It is clear from this that both as a Wagnerian and as an anti-Wagnerian, Nietzsche was an unreserved champion of absolute music.

NIETZSCHE AND WAGNER IN BAYREUTH

Nietzsche spent five days in Bayreuth between 18 and 23 May 1872, attending the foundation stone–laying ceremony of the new Festspielhaus. These were among the happiest days of his life, and in later years he repeatedly expressed the belief that they made up for the negative impression left by the first festival in 1876. At the end of May, Ulrich von Wilamowitz-Möllendorf's pamphlet *Zukunftsphilologie*

(Philology of the future) appeared, attacking *Die Geburt der Tragödie* and ridiculing Nietzsche's commitment to the "music of the future." Wagner's open letter in defense of Nietzsche was published in the *Norddeutsche Allgemeine Zeitung* on 23 June, but he was incapable, of course, of restoring Nietzsche's ruined reputation as a scholar. Even Friedrich Ritschl distanced himself from his former pupil, advising him in a letter: "You cannot possibly expect the 'Alexandrian' and scholar to condemn *knowledge* and to see in art *alone* a redemptive, liberating force that will change the world" (1306).

Whereas his visits to Tribschen had been a time of harmony, Nietzsche's visits to Bayreuth, where Wagner settled in April 1872, were marked by frequent differences of opinion, reflected in the critical aphorisms of 1874 that I have mentioned. These aphorisms are, as it were, preliminary studies for "Richard Wagner in Bayreuth," the fourth of Nietzsche's *Unzeitgemäße Betrachtungen*, which was not completed until 1876. The jottings of 1874 are an attempt to describe Wagner's character as an artist in all its contradictions, a critical analysis written against the background of the potential collapse of the Bayreuth enterprise as a result of what appeared to be the insurmountable problems connected with financing the project. For Nietzsche, the feared fiasco was an opportunity for him to launch an attack on Wagner that for the present he kept to himself—not least because shortly afterward the enterprise was rescued by a loan from King Ludwig. (The loan was paid off by Wagner's descendants.)

The aphorisms of 1874 already describe Wagner as a musical rhetorician and "misplaced actor" (482). There is further talk of his "dilettantism" (486) and the withering remark "None of our great musicians was still as bad a musician as Wagner was in his 28th year" (485). Virtually all the character defects that Nietzsche was later to list in his published writings are already adumbrated here, even if they are still seen in a conciliatory light: Wagner refuses to tolerate "any other individuals" such as Brahms (491); he reveals a "fondness for pomp and luxury" (517), has a "tyrant's sense of the *colossal*" (492), is "unrestrained and immoderate" in his day-to-day behavior (485), although this is at odds with his self-discipline as an artist (517); he "always wants to be in the right" (518), has dubious followers, and, last but not least, is hostile to Jews (491 and 493).

In "Richard Wagner in Bayreuth" these critical insights are conspicuous by their absence. The essay is epideictic, a genuine "festival address," as Nietzsche repeatedly describes it (1309). As often as possible he attempts to bring his own standpoint in line with Wagner's and to develop the latter's ideas a stage further. Among his central ideas is his characterization of Wagner as a "counter-Alexander" who reties the Gordian knot of culture and reunites its disparate tendencies through the "astringent power" of his art (654). This it could do by dint of the tendency of myth to condense and simplify, a tendency on which Wagner himself expatiates in the second part of *Opera and Drama*. Again he insists on his idea that Wagner is a kind of latter-day Aeschylus, and again he denies that there is a historical gulf between Greek tragedy and the modern music drama. Time is "merely a cloud," and the "pendulum of history" always returns "to the point from which it set out" (653).

"Richard Wagner in Bayreuth" was intended to glorify the first Bayreuth Festival, an occasion that Nietzsche later regarded as the turning point in his relations with Wagner. "*What had happened?*" Nietzsche asks in *Ecce homo*. "Wagner had been translated into German! The Wagnerite had become master of Wagner—German art! The *German* master! *German* beer!" But we should be skeptical about this later attempt to rewrite history, as there were other factors at work here, most notably Nietzsche's appalling ill health and crippling migraines, which prompted him to flee from Bayreuth and seek refuge in the spa town of Klingenbrunn (from where he did, however, return for the festival). From Klingenbrunn he wrote to his sister on 6 August: "It needs all my self-composure to bear the boundless disappointment of this summer. I'll not see my friends either; everything is now poison and loss for me" (435–36). His reference to "boundless disappointment" is, of course, ambiguous; behind his depression at his inability to sit through the long performances, is the suggestion that he felt a sense of disillusionment at the very form of the festival, which, with its social whirl, seemed to his migraine-clouded eyes to have moved away from the ideal so palpable at the foundation stone–laying ceremony only four years earlier. It was in this sense that he wrote to Mathilde Maier some two years later: "With regard to W[agner], I had envisaged something higher, his ideal—with *that* I had gone to B[ayreuth]—hence my disappointment" (letter of around 6 August 1878; 732).

ESTRANGEMENT AND BREACH

Although Nietzsche had broken intellectually with Wagner by 1878 at the latest, he still hoped to renew his former friendship with Bayreuth, still hoped that Wagner would have the greatness to respect the fact that his own course in life was radically different from his. This increasingly hopeless, not to say desperate, expectation finally assumed a positively eschatological aspect in his myth of a "friendship written in the stars," a friendship that would surmount the enforced estrangement and hostility between two such opposing men on earth (*Die fröhliche Wissenschaft*, aphorism 279).

On a purely superficial level, the breach between the two men dates from the arrival of the first part of *Menschliches, Allzumenschliches* (Human, all too human) in Bayreuth at the end of April 1878. Barely four months previously, Wagner had sent Nietzsche a copy of the privately printed poem of *Parsifal* with a dedication in which he described himself jokingly as "Oberkirchenrath" (Member of the high consistory, 296)—an allusion to the Christian contents of his final stage work. Nietzsche took this description very seriously. In his view, in writing *Parsifal*, Wagner had become one of the "priests" against whom Zarathustra's sermon is aimed in the second part of *Also sprach Zarathustra* (Thus spake Zarathustra).

In *Ecce homo* Nietzsche spoke of an ominous "crossing of the two books"—a "miracle of meaningful chance": "Was it not as though two *swords* had crossed?" Here, of course, Nietzsche is guilty of altering the facts to suit his case, as the poem of *Parsifal* had already been lying on his desk for more than four months when he sent Wagner two copies of *Menschliches, Allzumenschliches*. Moreover, it is clear from Cosima's diary that she and Nietzsche had read Wagner's detailed prose draft of *Parsifal* together as early as Christmas 1869, so that the work's underlying tendencies were already abundantly clear to him. And even as late as 10 October 1877, we find him writing to Cosima, "The glorious promise of Parcival [*sic*] may console us in all things where we need consolation" (294). All the more remarkable, then, is Nietzsche's change of attitude in early 1878, when he reveals far more reservations toward the poem. In a letter to Reinhart von Seidlitz of 4 January 1878, he records the "impression left by an initial reading": "more Liszt than Wagner, the spirit of the Counter-Reformation; for me, all too accustomed as I am to all that is Greek and to human universals, everything is too Christian, too limited to a particular time." Admittedly, the situations and their sequence were "of the highest poetry" and represented "the ultimate challenge to music" (728)— music of which Nietzsche can have had no idea at this date.

In spite of a handful of reservations, then, Nietzsche still had praise for certain aspects of *Parsifal* as a libretto. In total contrast, Wagner's verdict on *Menschliches, Allzumenschliches*, when he read it four months later, could not have been more annihilating. Nietzsche soon learned of Wagner's reaction from his publisher Ernst Schmeitzner and from various other individuals. On 31 May 1878, he told Peter Gast, not without justification, that "a sort of *excommunication*" had been issued against the book in Bayreuth (739). Wagner's essay "Public and Popularity" appeared in the August issue of the *Bayreuther Blätter*; its third section contains a veiled attack on the author of *Menschliches, Allzumenschliches*. Here Wagner pours scorn on the unnamed representatives of "science" who "look down on us artists, poets, and musicians as the late products of an obsolete method of viewing the world" and who attempt to replace "metaphysical vagaries" with the "knowledge" vouchsafed by natural science or history, until the "purely comprehending subject, pontificating ex cathedra, is left with the sole right to existence. A worthy close to the world tragedy!" (GS 10:79–85).

Menschliches, Allzumenschliches begins with a quotation from Descartes praising strictly methodical research as a source of pleasure, thereby setting the tone for the book as a whole; the "spirit of science"[13] is to replace the metaphysical and aesthetic speculations of Nietzsche's earlier writings. In this way, Nietzsche appropriates the standpoint taken by his teacher Friedrich Ritschl when criticizing *Die Geburt der Tragödie*: he had now moved away from his former position of condemning "insight" and seeing in art "only a redemptive, liberating force that will change the world," as Ritschl had once reproached him. Traditional metaphysics, morality, and aesthetics are subjected to a rigorous ideological critique. The new, higher culture that was already coming into existence is characterized by the principles of historical, psychological, and scientific thinking.

In the first book of *Menschliches, Allzumenschliches*, Wagner is not mentioned by name, but it is clear from the earlier quotation from "Public and Popularity" that in Nietzsche's eyes he was one of the main representatives of a culture that was drawing to an end. His 1876 essay "Richard Wagner in Bayreuth" had ended with the suggestion that Wagner was "not the seer of a future" but "the interpreter and transfigurer of a past" (719). Wagner had responded so positively to this essay that he must have felt deeply hurt when he realized the sort of role that Nietzsche now allotted to him in the development of culture, namely, that of explaining an outmoded culture to contemporaries and succeeding generations.

How could Wagner accept an understanding of culture in which he himself was left with only a retrospective role to play—he who had always projected his work of art onto the future and who, with predictable regularity, was mocked by his contemporaries as "the musician of the future"? He himself saw matters in a wholly different light: it was Nietzsche who had turned his back on all deeper culture and fallen victim to the sort of belief in progress that Wagner associated with philistines. (In "Public and Popularity" Wagner had maliciously lumped Nietzsche together with David Friedrich Strauß, whom Nietzsche had accused of being a cultural philistine in the first of his *Unzeitgemäße Betrachtungen*.) This diametrically different view of "culture" and of the role of art within it is the deeper reason for the breakdown of the relationship between Wagner and Nietzsche, a breach that goes beyond all purely personal considerations.

Nietzsche's unpublished jottings from these years also contain repeated references to his unease at Wagner's hatred of the Jews. In the person of Paul Rée, he had been introduced to a typically educated and assimilated Jew who, in spite of the subsequent breakdown of their friendship, was soon to become a model in his eyes of a free, cosmopolitan spirit and the harbinger of a metanational Europeanism. "Their cleverness prevents the Jews from becoming foolish in the way that *we* are foolish—in a national way, for example," we read in an unpublished jotting from July or August 1888. "They do not easily fall prey to our *rabies*, the *rabies nationalis*. They themselves are now an antidote to this ultimate illness of European reason."[14] For the Bayreuthians, by contrast, Nietzsche's friendship with Rée was yet one more example of the disastrous influence of the Jews, who had now cast their perfidious spell on Nietzsche, too.

In a jotting dating from the summer of 1878, Nietzsche ascribes Wagner's hatred of the Jews to potential self-hatred: "Could Wagner be a Semite? Now we understand his aversion to the Jews" (758). In another fragment from this period we read that the distinctive features of Wagner's art—its "terrible savagery, its sense of remorse and annihilation, its cry of joy, its suddenness"—are also "inherent to the Semite—I believe that Semitic races bring greater understanding to Wagner's art than the Aryan race does" (774). And finally: "What struck me about real Jew haters (like W[agner]) is their affinity with Jewishness rather than any dissimilarity" (789). This point is made repeatedly by Gustav Freytag and nineteenth-century caricaturists in general.

In a footnote to his postscript to *Der Fall Wagner*, Nietzsche finally asked:

Was Wagner a German at all? . . . It is difficult to find any German trait in him. Being a good learner, he learned to imitate much that was German—that's all. His own nature *contradicts* that which has hitherto been felt to be German—not to speak of a German musician.—His father was an actor by the name of Geyer. A Geyer [vulture] is practically an Adler [eagle]. (1086)

Adler is a common Jewish name, whereas Geyer is an old German family name, so that Nietzsche's envenomed barb would not strike home even if Wagner's step-father, who hailed from a family of pastors and choirmasters in Saxe-Anhalt, had in fact been his actual father.

This footnote turns the tables on Wagner; the composer's repeated insistence, from the time of "Jews in Music" onward, that Jews can only imitate the Germans is now applied to Wagner himself. In this context, Nietzsche's ideas on actors are supremely relevant. Aphorism 361 in *Die fröhliche Wissenschaft* is headed "On the Problem of the Actor." Here the Jews are described as "the nation with the greatest ability to adapt," suggesting that here we may see "a world-historical arrangement for training actors, a veritable breeding ground for actors. And it really is high time to ask: are there any good actors today who are not Jews?"[15] There seems little doubt that Nietzsche expects his reader to go on and ask the obvious question: is it not conceivable, then, that Wagner, as a "misplaced actor," was himself a Jew?

If Nietzsche came increasingly to hate Wagner, it was really because he saw him as the center of the Wagnerian movement. In his eyes, this was the great scandal of the phenomenon of Wagner: for him, Wagnerism was not an innocent byprod-uct of Wagner's activities but the result of his own character, which demanded a sycophantic following. This also explains why Nietzsche refused to allow himself to become the center of a following. "I avoid factions, I do not want any followers," he told Mathilde Maier on 15 July 1878 (731).

The 1882 world premiere of *Parsifal* in Bayreuth precipitated a further crisis in Nietzsche. Although his patron's certificate entitled him to a seat, he could not bring himself to use it but gave it to his sister and instead spent the time studying the vocal score of the work. His verdict on it was entirely negative. In his letter to Malwida von Meysenbug of 13 July 1882, he refers to "Hegelism in music" and "Cagliostricity" (742). This final reference reflects his reappraisal of Wagner's nature as an actor, with a new element of deceptiveness being added. Between now and his final anti-Wagnerian writings, Nietzsche was tireless in repeating the charge that Wagner was "the Cagliostro of the modern world" (*Der Fall Wagner*, section 5, 1068). Yet in a jotting from the summer of 1885, he qualifies this in a significant way: "I hope that I may be forgiven this by no means thoughtless idea, which is at least inspired not by hatred and aversion but by the spell that this incomparable man cast on me" (885).

When Nietzsche heard the prelude to *Parsifal* for the first time in Monte Carlo in January 1887, he completely revised his opinion of Wagner's final work, at least from a musical standpoint. In his jottings he speaks of

> the greatest favor that has been done to me for a long time. The power and austerity of the emotion indescribable, I know of nothing as profound as this in the whole of Chris-tianity, nothing that might inspire such fellow feeling. Completely uplifted and moved—no painter has painted such an indescribably sad and tender *look* as Wagner. (906)

Even more emphatic is his letter to Peter Gast of 21 January 1887: "Has Wagner ever done anything *better*?" And he follows this up with a panegyric of Wagner's late style, singling out for particular praise the very things that he had criticized elsewhere: the profound grasp of Christianity and especially the Christian and

Schopenhauerian virtue of fellow feeling (851). But in 1882 Nietzsche was still a long away from feeling this about the work.

NIETZSCHE AFTER WAGNER'S DEATH

Wagner's death on 13 February 1883 left another deep mark on Nietzsche's emotional world. He took to his bed when he heard the news, which reminded him not only of his deep sense of sadness at the irreplaceable human loss that he had felt at the time of his break with Wagner but—just as intensely—of his satisfaction at having finally broken free from Wagner and taken the decisive step toward self-autonomy. In his letter to Meysenbug of 21 February 1883, he writes:

> W[agner]'s death has affected me terribly; although I'm now out of bed, I still haven't got over it.—Even so, I believe that, in the long run, this event will be a source of relief for me. It was hard, very hard, to have to spend six years opposing someone whom one had revered and loved as much as I had loved W[agner]; and even as his opponent to have to force myself to remain silent—for the sake of the respect that the man *as a whole* deserves. (830)

The curious word "relief" occurs in three different letters from this period (830 and 832). Wagner's death no doubt brought Nietzsche a very real sense of relief because respect and love were now no longer a barrier to criticism. It is impossible to avoid the suspicion that Nietzsche's sense of relief consisted simply in his feeling that he was now rid of Wagner, a point that he makes in the postscript to *Der Fall Wagner*: "Redemption to the Redeemer" as "Redemption *from* the Redeemer" (1086–87).

Nietzsche even pulled himself together sufficiently to pen a letter of condolence to Cosima. Unfortunately, the letter has not survived, and we do not even know if Cosima read it. What we do know is that Nietzsche made three separate attempts to draft this letter—his final, desperately anguished attempt at a rapprochement with Wagner's widow. All three address her as "the most revered woman who exists in my heart" (298 and 300–301). There is no doubt that he understood the true nature of Cosima's relationship with Wagner, a relationship in which her love for her mortal husband was indistinguishable and inseparable from her devotion to the immortal "ideal" that he embodied. "You have lived for a single goal," he wrote, "and made every sacrifice for him; above and beyond him as a human being, you felt the ideal of this one goal and to this—which does not perish—you belong, your name belongs forever" (298).

But was it not this undying ideal—an ideal before which all the more dubious aspects of Wagner's personality pale into insignificance—with which Nietzsche, too, wanted to see his name linked? In a letter to Franz Overbeck of 27 October 1886, we find him expressing the hope that the more educated among "Wagner's followers" would see that he himself still believed "as much as ever in the ideal in which Wagner believed—what does it matter if I have had problems with the many human, all-too-human aspects that R[ichard] W[agner] himself placed in the way of his ideal?" (849).

For her part, Cosima was incapable of seeing that Nietzsche remained true to Wagner's "ideal" and that he still desperately hoped that this would recement their friendship. Nothing could have been further from her mind than to build bridges with Nietzsche, who had irreconcilably turned his back on Wagner in his recent remarks on the subject. In the years that followed, Nietzsche increasingly came to see Cosima as the fatal representative of the Wagnerism that had taken control of the real Wagner. And in a jotting from the winter of 1887–88, he reproaches her for "having *corrupted* Wagner." *Parsifal* was in part a "concession on W[agner]'s part to the Catholic instincts of his wife, Liszt's daughter," an expression of "that eternal *cowardice* that men feel in the face of the 'Eternal Feminine.'" In spite of all this, she remained "the only woman of real class whom I've ever known" (1018).

Although Nietzsche was left physically and emotionally shaken by Wagner's death, his letters from this period are nonetheless marked by their openly aggressive tone. I have already quoted from his letter to Meysenbug of 21 February 1883. (This letter came to light only in 1980, when it was discovered among Romain Rolland's unpublished papers.)

> W[agner] insulted me in a *fatal* way—I insist on telling you!—his slow retreat and—
> crawling to Christianity and to the church I felt as a personal slight: my whole youth
> and the direction that it had taken seemed to be defiled in that I had rendered homage
> to a mind that was capable of taking this step. (830–31)

The famous reference to a mortal insult, which is also found in the letter that Nietzsche wrote to Franz Overbeck the next day (a letter long familiar to scholars; 831),[16] must therefore be to Wagner's decision to reembrace Christianity, a decision that he felt amounted to a personal provocation. "Alas! You too sank down before the *cross*, / You too! You too—defeated like the rest!" we read in Nietzsche's poem *An Richard Wagner* (To Richard Wagner) of the autumn of 1884. "Before this spectacle I long have stood / And breathed the air of prisons, grief, and grave, / Between them clouds of incense, churchly whores" (870–71). But was this really such a novel experience for Nietzsche? After all, had he not written to Erwin Rohde on 8 October 1868—even before he had met Wagner in person—that what he liked most about Wagner's art was "the ethical air, the Faustian aura, cross, death and grave"?

In his letter to Peter Gast of 19 February 1883, Nietzsche again draws a distinction between "the elderly Wagner whom I had to resist" and the "real Wagner." As for the latter, Nietzsche was convinced that he would "in large measure be his *heir*." This is one of the most important formulations of Nietzsche's attitude to Wagner following the composer's death. For this reason, too, he was bound to feel "relief" that Wagner was no longer alive. "Last summer"—during the world-premiere performances of *Parsifal* in Bayreuth—"I felt that he had taken away from me all the people in Germany worth influencing" (830).

The king was dead, and Nietzsche now announced his successor while attempting to gain the backing of Wagner's leading followers. He placed his greatest hopes in the brilliant young scholar Heinrich von Stein, who respectfully sided with him, even though he had been a close confidant of Wagner and had played the very role that the Wagners had originally planned for Nietzsche himself, as private tutor to Siegfried Wagner.

The most bitter disappointment that Nietzsche suffered during these final years of lucidity was the sad realization that Stein had no real intention of switching camps but that, quite the opposite, he now tried to win over Nietzsche to the Wagnerian cause. "Even in death," Nietzsche told Meysenbug in his letter of late July 1888, "the seducer Wagner is taking away the handful of people on whom I could still have any influence" (973). At the end of the postscript to *Der Fall Wagner*, we find him complaining: "Ah, this old robber! He robs us of our young men, he even robs us of our women and drags them into his cave.—Ah, this old Minotaur! The price we have had to pay for him! Every year processions of the most beautiful maidens and youths are led into his labyrinth so that he can devour them" (1090). This is a curious variant of the Ariadne myth, which played so important a role in Nietzsche's life during these years. Perhaps it also contains an allusion to the premature death, in June 1887, of the thirty-year-old Stein, a death that left Nietzsche profoundly shaken.

After 1883, Nietzsche's polemical writings against Wagner veer markedly in tone between brusque rejection and anguished respect and love, especially when he recalls that Wagner was the only person in his life with whom he had been able to speak as an equal. "All in all," he wrote to Franz Overbeck on 14 July 1886, "R[ichard] W[agner] was the only person so far, or at least the first person, to feel what it is that makes me tick."

> Who else could sense that someone (like me) has lived between problems from his earliest youth *diu noctuque incubando* and that his difficulties and happiness stem from this one fact alone! As I say, it was Richard Wagner who did this: and that is why Triebschen [*sic*] was such a wonderful opportunity to relax and recover, whereas I don't know anywhere or anyone else any longer who would be of any use in helping me to recover. (847)

There is no doubt that Nietzsche was jealous of all who drew close to Wagner, whether in love or in hatred. He thought that he alone was entitled to feel these emotions—and that he alone had the right to criticize Wagner. Thus we read in a militant fragment from the spring of 1885:

> It goes without saying that I am unwilling to concede to anyone else the right to claim as his own this assessment of mine, and the disrespectful rabble that are like lice infesting the body of society today shall certainly not be allowed even so much as to utter a great name like that of R[ichard] W[agner], whether in praise or contradiction. (874)

Wagner's death had relieved Nietzsche of any obligation to spare the "Master." In the introductions to the new editions of his earlier works, he tends, therefore, to make good the enforced omission, and in his new works—*Jenseits von Gut und Böse* (Beyond good and evil, 1886), the fifth book of *Die fröhliche Wissenschaft* (1887), and *Zur Genealogie der Moral* (1887)—he adopts an openly critical attitude to Wagner, at the same time repeatedly praising him. Aphorism 256 of *Jenseits von Gut und Böse*, for example, ends with a lampoon of "the later Wagner" and his *Parsifal*, "Is This Still German?" (933–34); yet just before this, Wagner is held out as the precursor of a "united Europe" (931–33). This whole section is at odds with the ending of "Richard Wagner in Bayreuth," where Nietzsche had denied that Wagner was the "seer of a future" but defined him, rather, as the "interpreter and transfigurer of a past."

Prior to *Der Fall Wagner*, the most outspokenly anti-Wagnerian of Nietzsche's works does not in fact mention Wagner at all by name, and, indeed, it could not do so, as it is a prose poem peopled with fictional characters: *Also sprach Zarathustra* (1883–85). Such was his fondness for seeing symbolic links between events in his life that Nietzsche divined an ominous connection between Wagner's death and the ending of the first part of *Zarathustra*—and on this occasion the chronology supports him. "The final section was completed at precisely that sacred hour when Richard Wagner died in Venice," he explained in *Ecco homo* (1111).

Nietzsche treats Wagner's death as marking the end of the old culture from whose ashes the phoenix of the new culture would rise and the "higher man" would be born.[17] His death mirrors the death of the gods, which, according to Zarathustra's teachings, would produce the "superman." *Also sprach Zarathustra* represents an alternative to the world of the later Wagner—Nietzsche's *Anti-Parsifal*. In his chapter "Of the Priests" in part 2, he alludes directly to the closing line of *Parsifal*: "Redemption to the Redeemer." "I pity these priests," says Zarathustra to his disciples. "They seem to me prisoners and marked men. He whom they call Redeemer has cast them into bondage:—Into the bondage of false values and false scriptures! Ah, that someone would redeem them from their Redeemer!"[18] In *Parsifal*, it is the Grail that, mystically embodying the Savior but defiled by Amfortas's guilt, needs to be redeemed "from hands defiled by guilt" (GS 10:359)—thus the "Savior's Lament" that Parsifal hears in his mind's ear when kissed by Kundry in act 2. In this way the Grail is redeemed by Parsifal's act of salvation: "Redemption to the Redeemer."

In *Also sprach Zarathustra*, it is not the Redeemer who lies "in bondage." (There is an allusion here to Luther's hymn "Christ lag in Todesbanden" [Christ lay in the bonds of death].) Rather, it is the "priests" Amfortas and Parsifal whom the Savior and his otherworldly morality have subjected to the "bondage of false values." And it is a "priest" who is their creator: the "member of the high consistory" Richard Wagner himself. According to Zarathustra, anyone who lives in the proximity of priests "lives in the neighborhood of black pools, from out of which the toad, that prophet of evil, sings its song of sweet melancholy." Is this not the music of Wagner himself—in *Der Fall Wagner*, Nietzsche describes him as "our greatest melancholiac in music, . . . the master whose music sings of a heavyhearted, drowsy happiness" (1074)? "They would have to sing better songs to make me believe in their Redeemer," Zarathustra goes on; "his disciples would have to look more redeemed."[19]

It was above all the composer of *Parsifal* and his acolytes whom Nietzsche had in mind when, parodying the final line of Wagner's Bühnenweihfestspiel, he has Zarathustra exclaim: "Ah, that someone would redeem them from their Redeemer!"[20] That Nietzsche was thinking of Wagner here emerges from his postscript to *Der Fall Wagner*:

> It happened at Wagner's funeral: the first German Wagner Society, that of Munich, placed a wreath on his grave, with an inscription that immediately became famous: "Redemption to the Redeemer!" Everybody admired the lofty inspiration that had

dictated this inscription. . . . But many . . . made the same small correction: "Re-demption *from* the Redeemer!" One heaved a sigh of relief. (1086–87)

At what? At "breaking free" from Wagner (1086). Was not this the "relief" that Nietzsche had felt on Wagner's death? And had he not seen himself in the role of the Redeemer who wants to redeem others from their redemption?

The most important reminiscence of Wagner in *Also sprach Zarathustra* occurs in the chapter "The Sorcerer" in part 4 of the work.[21] Of course, this fictional fig-ure cannot be identified as Wagner without considerable reservations; *Also sprach Zarathustra* is not, after all, a roman à clef. But it is undeniable that Nietzsche repeatedly referred to Wagner as a sorcerer. Above and beyond any Wagnerian associations, the old sorcerer of *Also sprach Zarathustra* is also a symbol of late Romantic artists in general, artists who sought refuge in some metaphysical hin-terland and who "collapsed and sank down before the Christian cross" (932), to quote aphorism 256 from *Jenseits von Gut und Böse*.

Among Nietzsche's most important post-1883 insights into Wagner was his realization that the composer was one of the "French late Romantics" (931). Thus we read in an unpublished jotting from June or July 1885: "The proximity to mor-bid desires, the rutting heat of the raging senses over which the gaze is dangerously deceived by the mist and veil of the supersensory: where does this belong more than in the Romanticism of the French soul? Here a spell is at work that is bound to con-vert the Parisians to Wagner" (881). According to aphorism 254 of *Jenseits von Gut und Böse*, Nietzsche believed that this conversion had already taken place in music: "The more French music learns to adapt itself to fit the real needs of the modern soul, the more it will 'Wagnerize'—that much one can predict. It is already doing that enough even now" (930). The tremendous impact of Wagner's art on French music, literature, and art of the late nineteenth and early twentieth centuries fully vindicated Nietzsche's thesis that the Parisians would be "converted" to Wagner.

Although Nietzsche was in many ways critical of this affinity, he also saw it as a great sign of hope for the future in that it would put an end to the "pathological estrangement that the insane obsession with nationality has induced, and still induces, among the peoples of Europe." On a deeper level, he believed, these peoples wanted to be "one" (931). This viewpoint of Nietzsche's, which raises Wagner's art above all nationalistic (self-)appropriation and the provincialism of the Bayreuth Circle and places it before the background of a metanational culture, regarding the composer as a potential vehicle of European integration, is perhaps the most important and forward-looking of his insights within the context of his post-1883 engagement with Wagner and his works.

A DIAGNOSIS OF THE MODERN SOUL: WITH REFERENCE TO WAGNER

Described by Nietzsche as a "Turinese letter of May 1888," *Der Fall Wagner* was published at the end of September 1888. Far more important than the twelve chapters that it contains are its two postscripts and especially its epilogue, all three of which use Wagner's example as a means of analyzing the "modern soul" (1096) and, hence, the phenomenon of *décadence*. Ever since he had read Paul Bourget's *Essais* in the winter of 1883–84, Nietzsche had made this term his own. Originally it meant cultural decline, but since the time of Baudelaire and Théophile Gautier it had acquired a positive aspect that is also reflected in Nietzsche's view of *décadence*.[22]

Here the traditional, negative interpretation of *décadence* is combined in often puzzling ways with its Baudelairean reassessment, with the result that the same phenomenon can reveal both positive and negative facets. This is particularly true of Wagner, whom Nietzsche regards as the *décadent* artist par excellence and who is seen in a constantly shifting and, hence, disturbing play of light. For Nietzsche, *décadence* was a necessary stage through which life had to pass. In a letter to Carl Fuchs of mid-April 1886, he cites the example of Wagner in defining the *décadent* style as the breakdown of all sense of formal unity resulting from the predominance of individual stimuli and the principle of decomposition. (This definition is directly inspired by Bourget's essay on Baudelaire.) "This is *décadence*, a word that, it goes without saying between ourselves, is intended not to criticize but merely to describe." And he adds: "There are innumerable aspects of *décadence* that are uniquely attractive, valuable, novel, and worthy of our respect—our modern music, for example."[23]

One thing, at least, was certain for Nietzsche: anyone who wanted to transcend *décadence* must first experience it at firsthand, must first face up to it and see through it. "No less than Wagner, I am a child of the times," he writes in the preface to *Der Fall Wagner*. "That is to say: I am a *décadent*. But I understood this, I resisted it" (1056). In Nietzsche's eyes, Wagner was not capable of resisting *décadence* and thus of overcoming it, for Wagner was incapable of being true to himself. For the author of *Der Fall Wagner*, the real stumbling block was not Wagner's *décadence* but his "instinctual deceitfulness," as he wrote in the epilogue to the essay, a two-faced insincerity that allowed him to glorify the "master morality" of the *Ring* at the same time as the "gospel of the lowly" in *Parsifal*. This "*innocence among opposites*" is said to be typical of modern man. "Biologically speaking, modern man represents a *contradiction of values*, he sits between two stools, says yes and no in the selfsame breath" (1094–96). Although Nietzsche reproaches himself for a similar propensity for applying double standards, he nonetheless believes that he differs from Wagner by dint of his superior awareness and his willingness to engage in ruthless self-analysis, an analysis that must begin with "a resolute incision in this instinctive tendency to contradict" (1096).

This willingness to submit to rigorous self-diagnosis should not be confused with the abandonment of this instinctive contradictoriness or with a clear decision in favor of one or other system of values. For all that he might proclaim the values of "ascendant life" and the "will to power," Nietzsche remained on a purely instinctual level committed to the values of Christianity, to Wagner's art, and to the virtues and foibles of what he termed "declining life." In the notes that he prepared for a planned essay on mind and art between 1909 and 1912, it was this Nietzsche whom Thomas Mann preferred to call "*our* Nietzsche," in contrast to the writer who proclaimed the will to power and an amoral intensification of life: "From him we have inherited the psychological sensitivity, lyrical criticism, the experience of Wagner, the experience of Christianity, the experience of modernity—experiences from which we shall never fully divorce ourselves, any more than he himself ever fully divorced himself from them."[24]

Mann's assertion is confirmed by Nietzsche's remarkably impassioned renewal of interest in *Tristan und Isolde* in the days before he finally sank into madness. On 27 December 1888 he wrote to Carl Fuchs, attempting to encourage him to join forces with Peter Gast and publish an anti-Wagnerian essay, insisting that they should mention *Tristan und Isolde*: "It is the most *capital* work, with a fascination that is unprecedented not just in music but in all the arts" (1010). In his reply of 29 December, Gast expressed his doubts about this plan for an anti-Wagnerian essay, admitting that the second act of *Tristan und Isolde* was "a tremendous achievement" that put him in mind of a "*terra promessa*" (promised land). In turn, this prompted Nietzsche's response on 31 December: "You're right a thousand times over! Tell Fuchs. . . . In *Ecce homo* you'll find a tremendous page on *Tristan* and on my relationship with Wagner in general. W[agner]'s is the first name to appear in E[cce] h[omo]" (1012). The decision no longer to encourage the polemical essay by Fuchs and Gast also explains why on 2 January 1889 he refused permission for *Nietzsche contra Wagner* to be published as planned. Written the day before his paralytic collapse, this was the last letter that Nietzsche signed before he sank into the dark night of madness.

The "tremendous page on *Tristan*" in *Ecce homo* is the sixth paragraph of the section "Why I Am So Clever." It includes the following sentences:

> But even today I am still looking for a work as dangerously fascinating as *Tristan*, a work of such sweet and eerie infinity—and I seek it in vain in all the arts. All the strangenesses of Leonardo da Vinci lose their magic at the first note of *Tristan*. . . . I think I know better than anyone else the tremendous things that Wagner is capable of achieving—the fifty worlds of alien ecstasies for which none but he had wings; and as I am strong enough to turn even the most dubious and dangerous things to my advantage and in that way to become stronger still, I call Wagner the great benefactor of my life. The things in which we are related—namely, the fact that we have suffered more profoundly than other men of this century are capable of suffering, sufferings that we also caused each other—means that our names will always be linked; and as surely as Wagner remains misunderstood among Germans, just as certainly I too am misunderstood and always will be. (1101–2)

This sounds like a spiritual testament, and one can readily understand why Nietzsche was unwilling to revert to his old polemical tone and that he therefore withdrew *Nietzsche contra Wagner*. *Ecce homo* was to be his last word on the subject.

Wagner's is indeed the first name to be mentioned in *Ecce homo*. But not only Wagner himself; Cosima, too, is paid one final tribute there. In 1969 a document came to light from Gast's *Nachlaß* that Gast himself claimed to have copied from a manuscript that Nietzsche had sent from Turin to his publisher Constantin Georg Naumann in Leipzig at the end of December 1888. It contains a passage intended to replace the "existing third section" of the chapter "Why I Am So Wise" in *Ecce homo*, which was then with the printer. The original manuscript was destroyed by Nietzsche's mother and sister, together with other texts from the same period—an understandable act of vandalism, as this new section already bears signs of Nietzsche's impending breakdown, quite apart from the fact that it describes his family as "canaille" with whom it was "an insult to my divinity" to believe himself related. The same section contains the following passage:

> I have a sovereign feeling of disregard for everything that is nowadays called *noblesse*. . . . There is but a single case where I acknowledge my equal—I admit it with the deepest gratitude. Frau Cosima Wagner is by far the most distinguished of natures; and, in order not to say a word too little, I shall add that Richard Wagner was the man who was by far the most closely related to me. . . . The rest is silence. . . .[25]

This text has been known for only a little over thirty years. But there is more to it than this: as it stands at present, the second half of the penultimate sentence refers to Wagner, but in an earlier version of the text that Nietzsche's mother and sister evidently failed to destroy because they were unable to decipher it (this task was left to the Nietzsche scholar Mazzino Montinari), the same sentence reads: "Frau Cosima Wagner is by far the most distinguished of natures that exist and, in relation to me, I have always interpreted her marriage to Wagner as mere adultery . . . the case of Tristan."[26]

A few days later Nietzsche wrote a series of distracted notes to Cosima in which the medieval triangular relationship of Marke, Isolde, and Tristan is replaced by one from Greek myth: Theseus = Wagner; Ariadne = Cosima; and Dionysus = Nietzsche. In both cases Nietzsche appears to cast himself as the man who breaks up an existing relationship, whether erotic or marital. But a closer examination of the jotting from which I have just quoted suggests that the parallel with Tristan is as ambiguous as any picture puzzle. The reader will interpret it spontaneously as follows: Cosima is married to Wagner, just as Isolde is married to Marke, but the marriage is essentially adulterous, as Cosima is really intended for Nietzsche, just as Isolde was intended for Tristan. Marke and Wagner are in the same relationship to the younger men inasmuch as both are paternal friends, whereas the two women are much closer in age to their husbands' younger followers. The similarity in the relationships appears to suggest the equation of Wagner and Marke on the one hand and of Nietzsche and Tristan on the other. But the jotting can be interpreted in a different way, and this alternative reading is almost certainly correct: Nietzsche is the duped party, Cosima belongs to him, and her bourgeois marriage to Wagner is a violation of the real, mystical marriage with him, a marriage written in the stars. Wagner is thus a latter-day Tristan, thereby turning on its head the earlier relationship between the different generations. The result is a modern version of the triangular relationship familiar from the medieval legend; an unconventional love no longer breaks down the barriers of convention; rather, the middle-class Tristan is allowed to triumph over the man who broke the tablets of the law and proclaimed the reappraisal of all values—and yet he is condemned, like Marke, to a life of renunciation.

"But this time I am coming as the victorious Dionysus who will transform the earth into a festival," we read in one of the notes addressed to Cosima, "Princess

Ariadne, my lover" (3 January 1889). But even as victor, Nietzsche sees himself as Wagner in one of his "incarnations" (301–2). In the postscript to the very last letter that he ever wrote—to Jacob Burckhardt in Basel—we read: "The *rest* for Frau Cosima . . . Ariadne. . . . From time to time magic spells are cast" (1013). It is now no longer Wagner who is the "sorcerer" but Nietzsche himself. The records of the institution where Nietzsche was immured in Jena note: "He wants his compositions to be performed, has little understanding or recollection of ideas and passages from his works," and claims "my wife Cosima Wagner brought me here."[27] The literary role-playing with the characters of Ariadne, Theseus, and Dionysus that had been so important to him during the last ten years of his conscious life now assumed a frightening reality as he finally and fully identified with them.

I would not be going too far by claiming that Nietzsche's critical engagement with Wagner, from ardent affirmation to seething abnegation, was always central to the philosopher's thinking. In terms of his philosophy, Wagner was the paradigm of paradigms. This is the only way to explain how his assessment of Wagner continued, until the very end, to waver between extreme ardor and extreme coldness. The gulf between the unassailable "ideal" and the all-too-assailable reality made "the case of Wagner" a scandal for him. He was able to bridge this gulf only in rare moments of dreamlike happiness in both his life and his aesthetic experience—and also in his vision of a "friendship written in the stars," which constitutes aphorism 279 of *Die fröhliche Wissenschaft* and which is without doubt the most moving expression of his relationship with Wagner.

> We were friends and became estranged. But this is not a problem, so let us not conceal or obscure it from ourselves as though we had reason to be ashamed. . . . That we had to become estranged is the law *above* us: for precisely that reason we should also become more venerable in each other's eyes, and the memory of our former friendship should become more sacrosanct. There is probably a tremendous but invisible curve and stellar orbit in which our very different paths and goals may be included as brief sections of this orbit—let us rise to this thought! . . . And so let us believe in this friendship written in the stars, even though we had to be enemies on earth.[28]

Parallel Action

THOMAS MANN'S RESPONSE TO WAGNER

> With me, the accent should be placed on the conjunction
>
> of poet and musician, as a mere musician I'd not be of
>
> much significance.
>
> —*Richard Wagner, in CT, 16 August 1869*

In both art and literature my love of all things German begins at the precise point where all that is German acquires a European potential and validity and is capable of making a European impression and becomes accessible to every European. The three names that I have to cite when I consider the roots of my own intellectual and artistic development, names that form a bright constellation of eternally united minds, shedding their powerful light against the German sky—these names designate events that are not intimately German but that are European in importance: Schopenhauer, Nietzsche, and Wagner.[1]

THESE SENTENCES, taken from Thomas Mann's *Reflections of a Nonpolitical Man*, reflect the problematic role of all that is "German" within European and, indeed, world literature. For a long time, the German had no "European potential and validity," and not until the end of the eighteenth century did German literature acquire a status equal to that of other European literatures, occasionally even setting the tone. But by 1830 it had largely fallen silent again, at least in the ears of the majority of European listeners, with the result that the works of the great German writers of the later nineteenth century barely entered the general literary consciousness and never really became "world literature" in any comprehensible sense. This must seem paradoxical when we recall that it was Goethe who coined the term "world literature" to describe the cosmopolitan tendencies of literary activities in his own day, when translations were making works available to far wider audiences than ever before, a development that had started in Germany in the eighteenth century. "I am convinced that a world literature will be formed," he wrote to the Italian translator Karl Streckfuß on 27 January 1827, prophesying that "the German can and should contribute the most here; he will have a pleasing role to play in this development." In the event, Goethe's prediction was not to come true, at least as far as the impact of the German literature of the next few decades was concerned.

THOMAS MANN'S THREE GREAT WRITERS

Legion are the critics who have asked themselves why the great German epic writers of the nineteenth century from Stifter to Fontane continue to remain largely unknown to non-German-speaking audiences. Their answers generally run along the lines that the German novel lacks the universality and total overview of the tremendous political and social spectrum of the nineteenth century that we find in other literatures. Lacking, too, is said to be any boldness and decisiveness in the depiction of psychological tensions and passions.[2]

In the introduction to his *Reflections of a Nonpolitical Man*, Mann describes himself as "really a descendant—not, of course, a member—of the German middle-class narrative school of the nineteenth century," a school that "extends from Adalbert Stifter to the later Fontane" but which, in spite of its high standing, played no part in European developments.[3] Fifty pages later, however, Mann admits that his "love of all things German" began at the precise point where it became European, mentioning in this context the names of three figures who in his view were typical of the nineteenth century: Schopenhauer, Nietzsche, and Wagner. "These three are one."[4] Mann uses the term "Dreigestirn," literally, a triple star. This image may have been inspired by Nietzsche's aphorism in *Die fröhliche Wissenschaft*, quoted at the end of the previous chapter, in which Nietzsche, writing a year before Wagner's death, spoke of his closeness to, and estrangement from, his former friend. It was, he insisted, "a friendship written in the stars." For Thomas Mann, Schopenhauer, Wagner, and Nietzsche formed a single unity that left its mark on his own works, three stars whose constellation, attracting and repelling, complementing and balancing each other, influenced his whole intellectual and artistic world. It was not just to one of them that he devoted his life. Rather, each formed a counterweight to the others, maintaining a balance of power within Mann's mind.

It seems that for Mann there were two nineteenth centuries, one of which was "intimately German" and represented by the bourgeois epic, and the other German and European. The latter was not poetic or literary, however, but philosophical and musical. Certainly, the major contribution of the Germans to nineteenth-century culture, at least in the eyes of European observers in general, remains philosophy and music rather than literature.

As soon as Mann raises his sights from a national to a European level, the three figures of Schopenhauer, Wagner, and Nietzsche enter his field of vision, three figures who represent not literature but music and philosophy in a close reciprocal relationship: Schopenhauer and Nietzsche were outstanding musical philosophers, Wagner the outstanding philosophical musician. And yet all three were of great literary significance for Mann inasmuch as he felt that they embodied the one true German contribution to the world literature of the nineteenth century. For him, Schopenhauer and, especially, Nietzsche were eminent wordsmiths, and in his view the Wagnerian music drama was an essentially poetic construct, a status that it owed less to the word as such than to the music, which creates the characters and is itself a kind of language.

What could be more poetically beautiful or profound than Wotan's relationship with Siegfried, the paternally mocking and superior affection of the god for the boy who will destroy him, the loving abdication of the old regime in favor of the eternally youthful? The composer has the poet to thank for the wonderful sounds that he finds here. But then again, how much the poet has to thank the composer for, and how often the poet seems to understand himself only when he enlists the help of his second language to interpret and amplify, a language that for him hails from the realm of a subliminal knowledge unknown to the word in the world above.

Thus Mann's famous comment in his 1937 Zurich lecture on the *Ring*. "It has always seemed to me absurd to question Wagner's poetic gifts," he stresses here.[5] It is absurd to do so not least because no other German writer of the period had such a far-reaching impact on European literature, particularly on the French poetry of the late nineteenth and early twentieth centuries.

As both Nietzsche and Mann repeatedly stressed, the "literary" aspect of Wagner's works cannot be divorced from his music and his theatrical imagination. The music conditions the language just as the language conditions the music, which is why Wagner has always been a problem for those whose interest is purely literary, just as he is a problem for those whose interest is exclusively musical. And the same is true of their critical followers. But as Nietzsche writes in the fourth of his *Unzeitgemäße Betrachtungen*, only "the rarest of powers" can exercise control over two worlds as disparate as poetry and music, and here "censure of individual excesses and singularities, or of the more frequent obscurities of expression and thought, will always be no more than petty and unfruitful."[6] And Mann notes that with Wagner one invariably senses that language was not the supreme and unique medium, which is why it so often lacks "rigor and delicacy." From a "purely linguistic point of view," his works are always disturbing, with "an air of grandiose and overbearing ineptitude interspersed with passages of sheer genius, of a power, economy and elemental beauty that banish all doubt."[7]

Mann was not always so uncritical of the literary aspect of Wagner's music dramas. In the notes that he made for a planned essay, "Geist und Kunst" (Mind and art), between 1909 and 1912—the very time that he was undergoing a severe crisis with regard to Wagner's works—we read:

> He [Wagner] was a musician as a poet (musicians generally write appallingly badly, as they have no linguistic taste) and as a musician he was a poet. His texts are untenable as poems, as linguistic forms (they would not have made him very famous), his music is untenable as music. The texts are not possible without music, this music is literary.[8]

By the time of his great essays of the 1930s, Mann was able to see the musical aspect of Wagner's poetry and the poetic aspect of his music in a much more positive light, but here the same element appears as something entirely negative.

> No, one cannot respect Wagner! . . . His talent is admirable in its suspect modernity. But admiration and respect are one and the same only for *very* young people. . . . And what is it that he lacks? . . . It is the lack of the very thing that he praised as a virtue all his life and that the Germans also reckoned was a virtue on his part: a lack of literature.[9]

In these essayistic fragments, then, Mann's principal criticism of Wagner was his alleged "hostility to literature."[10] This may seem odd at first. How could Wagner, one of the most widely read and influential composers in the whole history of music, have been hostile to literature? Indeed, is Mann's claim not refuted by his own remark of a quarter of a century later: "It has always seemed to me absurd to question Wagner's poetic gifts"? The situation is more complex than this. Mann, no less than Wagner himself, drew a distinction between poetic gifts and literature. For Wagner, the term *literature* almost always has negative connotations. The "literary drama" (GS 4:4 and passim), in other words, drama without music, is a defective form for Wagner the writer on theatrical reform, a writer convinced that dramatic poetry needed to regain its grounding in music. As a result, he transferred the term *literature*, in a pejorative sense, to other art forms, at least to the extent that these forms were intended merely to be read and required no physical realization. Wagner was a self-declared opponent of modern written culture, and its dominant forms—notably the novel—lead a shadowy existence in his aesthetic system alongside the musical theater, which transcends mere literariness.

This was always a thorn in Mann's flesh, and even during periods when his attitude to Wagner was relatively positive—around 1900 and again in 1918 and 1933—he continued to reproach him for his ultimate lack of literary sophistication—and this in spite of Wagner's gifts as a poet and dramatist. At the same time, however, he always had a note of ironic contempt for Wagner's opponents among exclusively literary figures, an irony apparent even in a late essay (1943) such as *Schicksal und Aufgabe* (Fate and task).

> The German Goethean who knew his *Faust* by heart raised his voice in angry and scornful protest [at Wagner's alleged illiteracy], a respectable protest, to be sure, as it stemmed from a continuing link with the cultured world of German Classicism and Humanism from which this work had broken free. The educated middle-class German laughed at the "Wigalaweia" and all these alliterative excesses as though at some barbaric quirk. The tremendous—one can say, planetary—success that the bourgeois world, the international bourgeoisie, accorded this art on the strength of the sensual, nervous, and intellectual stimuli that it offered them is a paradox.[11]

Although Wagner's literary significance remains controversial even today, his impact on more than a century of world literature has been greater than that of any other German writer. As Bryan Magee has observed, "Wagner has had a greater influence than any other single artist on the culture of our age."[12] A list of the names of all the writers whose works reflect this influence would produce a representative conspectus of European literature between 1850 and 1930. "It was he more than any other artist," writes Raymond Furness, "who was able to fructify and enrich imaginative writing: it may safely be claimed that without Wagner the literature of at least a century would be immeasurably impoverished, as regards topics as well as structures."[13] In the whole history of culture, there is no other composer whose non-musical impact has been as extensive as Wagner's. Around the turn of the century he was above all else a literary figure, a role worth examining in outline in order for us to understand the background against which Thomas Mann came to Wagner.[14]

WAGNER AS A LITERARY PHENOMENON IN
THE EARLY MODERNIST MOVEMENT: A SUMMING UP

Significantly, it was in Paris—the capital of the nineteenth century—that Wagner's literary influence was first felt. As a movement, French *Wagnérisme* found literary expression in the *Revue wagnérienne* that Édouard Dujardin founded in 1884, but it can trace its origins to Baudelaire—more than two decades earlier. Other important French writers who played a part in the movement include Mallarmé and Verlaine, Villiers de l'Isle-Adam, Émile Zola, Maurice Barrès, Romain Rolland, Paul Claudel, Marcel Proust,[15] and, finally, Georges Duhamel, but it is clear from Kurt Jäckel's monumental monograph[16] that the vast majority of leading French writers of the late nineteenth and early twentieth centuries were influenced by Wagner to more or less lasting effect.[17] It has often been stressed that—to quote André Coeuroy—"France's Wagnerism was largely literary in character" (1933).[18] André Gide claimed that for Mallarmé and the *symbolistes*, Wagner was their "god" and that they "even sought literature in music."[19] Playing off Baudelaire against Berlioz, Paul Dukas noted that

> from the outset Wagner was much better understood by our poets than by our musicians, and in a far wider sense, far more in keeping with his true nature. They immediately recognized him as one of their own number and felt that he belonged to them almost as much as to composers. What the latter admired about Wagner was above all the creator of a new world of sound, the astonishing reformer of the older type of opera, the incomparable dramatic symphonist. Poets who judged him most profoundly went beyond all this and grasped the very real primacy of his poetic power.[20]

In English and especially Irish literature, Wagner's influence extends from Swinburne and Morris to Moore, Wilde, Shaw, Yeats, Beardsley, Joyce, Virginia Woolf, and D. H. Lawrence,[21] and in Italian literature his impact was felt by both Boito and D'Annunzio. Wagner himself was in personal contact with Boito as a translator and propagator of his works, and D'Annunzio proved to be his most impassioned prophet among the next generation of poets. Above all, the poetic movements of both Symbolism, whose poets appealed to the music drama and its attempt to render poetry more musical and more abstract, and *décadence*, which derived much of its stimulus from the eroticism and *sensibilité* of Wagner's music (it was with good reason that Erwin Koppen chose the title *Dekadenter Wagnerismus* for his authoritative book on fin-de-siècle European literature), repeatedly claimed that Wagner was the true source of their inspiration. And so, too, did the representatives of naturalism from Zola to Gerhart Hauptmann.

Wagner's legacy to modernism was above all a new understanding of myth, which was regarded no longer as "mythology," with all its antiquarian and didactic associations, but as a way of explaining reality—what Wagner, in *Opera and Drama*, called "the concentrated image of phenomena" (GS 4:31–32). Not least as a result of its impact on Nietzsche's *Die Geburt der Tragödie*, Wagner's rediscovery and redefinition of myth affected the central nervous system of the modernist movement, whether in the German literature of the turn of the century or, later, in the mythologically ori-ented novels of Thomas Mann and the dramatic poetry of Hugo von Hofmannsthal. As a librettist, Hofmannsthal came closest to the mythologically inspired music dra-mas of Wagner in his partnership with Richard Strauss and especially in his 1928 es-say on *Die ägyptische Helena* (The Egyptian Helen). Whatever criticisms he may have leveled at Wagner, there we find the clearest formal and thematic links with his aesthetic of "mythological opera."[22]

As a phenomenon, Wagnerism was in the main limited to Romance and En-glish literature of the turn of the century. Although many hundreds of works in German literature were based on Wagnerian themes, Wagner's influence was largely restricted, in Erwin Koppen's words, "to the very lowest echelons of literature."[23] Significantly, the few examples of literary Wagnerism of any importance within the German-speaking world are found in writers such as Nietzsche, Mann, and Hofmannsthal, who took their cue from French and Romance literature in general.[24]

If Wagner's influence on German literature was thinly spread, his impact on France and England affected literature at the very highest level. And he owed this unique literary resonance to the way in which he combined the roles of composer and librettist, raising the libretto above its purely functional role in a manner rem-iniscent of the Florentine Camerata, while never seeking to invest it with an ab-solute poetic significance divorced from the music. He never tired of emphasizing this point.[25] In spite of this, his music dramas were treated as literature, especially outside Germany, where they were read in much the same way that the librettos of Quinault and Metastasio had been read in their own day.

Through their choice of subject matter and the manner in which those subjects were treated, especially their combination of archaic myth and modern psychology, Wagner's music dramas caught the aesthetic mood of the times. The polarization and mirror imagery of eroticism and religiosity in *Tannhäuser* and *Parsifal*, the glorification of incest in *Die Walküre*, the apotheosis of free love that breaks down the barriers of convention, the identity of Eros and Thanatos in *Tristan und Isolde*, the curse of gold and the image of a society obsessed with the fetish of abstract possessions in the *Ring*, and the downfall of a dynasty and the corruption of a whole world in *Götterdämmerung*—these themes cast their spell on modernist writers in general, whether in France, England, Italy, Spain, or Germany. Three works were the most influential: *Tannhäuser*, *Tristan und Isolde*, and the *Ring*.

The way in which these themes were "orchestrated"—a way that, high-strung to the point of neurosis, Wagner's opponents condemned as a symptom of decline and of what Max Nordau termed "degeneration"[26]—together with the hypersensibility of his new poetic and musical language and his use of a symphony orchestra that—in Alfred Einstein's words—spoke with a hundred tongues,[27] set up a field of tension with the Germanic subject matter, the heroic facade, and the monu-mental attitudinizing that closely reflected the aesthetic mood of turn-of-the-cen-tury Europe.

Paradigmatic of the mood of this whole period—not just the fin de siècle—are the works of Thomas Mann.[28] From first to last, they follow in Wagner's wake, even if the direct allusions to his music dramas, so pronounced in his early works, are replaced in the novels and short stories of the second half of his life by a network of indirect allusions that is all the more dense in consequence and that culminates in his main work, *Joseph and His Brethren*, which, like the *Ring*, was conceived as a tetralogy. The most striking points of contact may be outlined in the order of the Wagnerian themes listed earlier, irrespective of the sequence in which Mann wrote the works in question; after all, the constancy with which certain Wagnerian motifs recur overrides all considerations of mere chronology. The polarity of eroticism and religion is the key theme of *Der Erwählte* (The holy sinner, 1951), and incest is central not only to "Wälsungenblut" (Blood of the Volsungs, 1905) but also to the Huij and Tuij episode in *Joseph in Ägypten* (Joseph in Egypt, 1936) and, once again, *Der Erwählte*.[29] The anarchic effect of sexual love is felt in *Der kleine Herr Friedemann* (Little Herr Friedemann, 1897), *Der Tod in Venedig* (Death in Venice, 1912), and the Mut-em-enet subplot in *Joseph in Ägypten*. The eroticism of death features prominently in the Hanno sections of *Buddenbrooks* (1901), in the short story "Tristan" (1903), and, again, in *Der Tod in Venedig*. The decline of a dynasty, finally, is integral to *Buddenbrooks*.

Mann's critical response to Wagner is inseparable from Nietzsche's critique of Wagner. One of Nietzsche's main theses was his belief that Wagner belonged with the "French late Romantics,"[30] with their predilection for erotic sensations, complex psychological states, and the aesthetic of the sublime. Also included under this heading was the "conversion" of their leading representatives; in their youth they had been rebels, whereas in old age they sank to their knees before the cross. Even before he discovered that Wagner and Baudelaire had been in personal contact, Nietzsche repeatedly called Baudelaire "a kind of Richard Wagner without music." (This particular quotation comes from a jotting of April–June 1885.)[31]

Nietzsche was the first to describe Wagner as a *décadent*. Originally intended as an insult, this term was reinterpreted by Baudelaire and Théophile Gautier in a more positive sense to describe an art of exquisite sensibility. The literature of *décadence* discovered the fascination of what Nietzsche had termed "life in decline," the magic of the world in the light of Baudelaire's "*soleil agonisant*" (dying sun), illness and death, biological decline offset by increasing spiritualization, a world of artifice, the sophisticated attractions of the big city, and an antibourgeois eroticism that denies its biological function.[32] According to Nietzsche, all this linked Wagner with the arts scene in Paris. "As an *artist* one has no home in Europe except in Paris," he wrote in *Ecce homo* in 1888; "the *délicatesse* in all five senses of art that Wagner's art presupposes, the fingers for nuances, the psychological morbidity, is to be found only in Paris."[33]

It was not only the thematic aspect of Wagner's music dramas that had such an important impact on the literature of early modernism but also their formal structure, the musicalization of poetry and the poeticization of music. As his own librettist, Wagner invested his music with a semantic weight that could be said to render it readable as poetry. This he achieved especially through the mnemonic system of leitmotifs that he developed in the *Ring* and that integrates all of the dramatic action and its characters in a densely structured complex of conceptual and symbolic relationships that operate on several layers of meaning. In this way,

Nietzsche wrote in *Der Fall Wagner*, Wagner had "immeasurably increased the linguistic ability of music."[34]

The motivic integration of characters and actions was epic in character, Mann repeatedly insisted in his essays on Wagner. And at the same time he showed to what extent the system of motifs links Wagner's art with the nineteenth-century novel, especially Zola and Tolstoy. But Mann could also have mentioned Theodor Fontane here, for Fontane's works also contain significant traces of Wagner's dramatic universe in spite of his lack of affinity with a phenomenon that he nonetheless reluctantly admired.[35] In his novel *Quitt* (Quits), one of the characters refers to the leitmotif as "le grand mot du grand Richard" (the great word of the great Richard),[36] and Fontane in turn repeatedly referred to the leitmotif in the context of his own novels. From the time of *L'Adultera* (The adulteress,1880), it increasingly formed a narrative structural element in them.

It is no accident that a number of the pioneering novelists of the twentieth century—Thomas Mann, Marcel Proust, James Joyce, and Virginia Woolf (who, like Mann, sought to come to terms with Wagner through the medium of the essay)—used the leitmotif as an integral part of their narrative technique. But there is no doubt that it was Mann who made the most decisive use of it in his narrative prose. According to his *Einführung in den Zauberberg* (Introduction to the magic mountain, 1939), he had used it in *Buddenbrooks* as a "purely naturalistic" and, "as it were, mechanistic" means of characterization (in other words, as a frequently comic way of labeling characters and situations), but from the time of *Der Tod in Venedig* it became a "symbolically allusive formula" that is used in a Wagnerian sense to embed the individually circumscribed situations and phenomena in a highly artificial network of associations—what Mann termed a "musical and conceptual complex of relationships."[37]

For Mann, the leitmotif was also an important means of grounding the narrative in myth, a technique first found in *Der Tod in Venedig* and *Der Zauberberg* (The magic mountain) and culminating in *Joseph and His Brethren*. In both theory and practice, Wagner had described myth as the true subject of the music drama, and Mann in turn integrated this theory into his poetics of the novel. At the same time, however, he emphatically denied Wagner's claim that myth was essentially related to drama inasmuch as myth and drama alone could offer a "concentrated image of phenomena," whereas the open form of the novel reflected the chaotic nature of modern civilization. But for Mann, myth, in keeping with its original meaning as "narrative," had a specifically narrative structure. Indeed, Mann believed that— Wagner's theorizing notwithstanding—narrative structures also asserted themselves in the *Ring*, which Mann repeatedly described as a "scenic epic."[38] For him, the great narrations and the role of the "all-knowing" orchestra, corresponding to that of the narrator in the novel, demonstrated that the tetralogy was essentially narrative in structure, not least as a result of its leitmotif technique. "It is epic on its innermost level, it is Homeric in origin," he wrote as early as 1908 in his *Versuch über das Theater* (Essay on the theater).[39] In this way, Mann turns Wagner's theory on its head: whereas in *Opera and Drama* Wagner had defined the mythological music drama as a symbolically concentrated novel, Mann defined the novel as a music drama restored to its epic origins.[40] As a result, he adapted Wagner's leitmotif technique in such a way that—especially in *Joseph and His Brethren*—it becomes the specific vehicle of myth. By repeating and varying the leitmotif, the different situations are all related to archetypal patterns and thus restored to a cyclical framework, with historical and linear time recast as the cyclical structure of myth.[41]

This is the underlying thrust of Mann's narrative style at least from the time of the *Joseph* novels. Here he took a decisive step, which he described in his 1936 essay *Freud und die Zukunft* (Freud and the future) as leading from the "bourgeois and individual to the mythically typical," exploring the "well-like depths of the ages, where myth is at home, providing a basis for the archetypal norms and forms of life."[42] But the very act of descending into the well-like depths of the ages meant that time, as a succession of archetypal situations, was suspended. Instead, those situations now took place simultaneously or, in Mann's own words, "successiveness must be drawn together as unity and as freely managed simultaneity."[43] The linear development of the traditional narrative is permeated by a simultaneity typical of the modern novel, a development influenced by the leitmotif technique of the mythologically grounded music drama.

Wagner's influence on the representatives of the early modernist movement was not limited to his advocacy of the integration of poetry and music. In his Zurich reform essays, he also demanded the restoration of the "original unity" of the "three purely human forms of art," namely, "dance, music, and poetry," all of which had been fully integrated in the *musiké* of ancient Greece (GS 3:67). In this way, he became one of the pioneers of a synesthetic art in which—to quote Baudelaire in *Les fleurs du mal*—"les parfums, les couleurs et les sons se répondent" [perfumes, colors, and sounds correspond]. As Harald Szeemann has indicated, this "hankering after a synthesis of the arts" is one of the salient features of modern art in general.[44]

As Mann had already pointed out in his *Versuch über das Theater*, Wagner's opposition to what he termed the "literary drama" made him one of the leading precursors of the theater reform movement of the turn of the century, from Mallarmé's *Richard Wagner: Rêverie d'un poëte français* (Richard Wagner : Reverie of a French poet) of 1885 to Appia's *Die Musik und die Inscenierung* (Music and staging) of 1899 and Meyerhold's "K postanovke 'Tristana i Izoldy' " (On staging "Tristan und Isolde") of 1909. The literary drama as a deficient form of drama, reduced to the written word and divorced from its physical presentation of stage, was to be replaced by a universal dramatic art that was to integrate aural and visual elements, thereby appealing to all our senses and investing the written form with a very real physicality.

As a result of the important part that theory played in his work, French writers of the second half of the nineteenth century—most notably Baudelaire in his essay *Richard Wagner et Tannhäuser à Paris* (1861)—came to regard Wagner as the epitome of the artist who combines art and criticism, a unity that, typical of modern art, was especially clear from Wagner's association with Nietzsche between 1869 and 1876.

Both for his contemporaries and for the generation that was active after his death, Wagner was a revolutionary who, for better or worse, overturned the established laws of music and opera, as well as those of poetry, and replaced the latter with the artificial archaisms of his dramatic poems, tearing down the boundaries of the craftsman's professional confinement to one particular discipline, and not only transcending the boundaries of any purely regional influence as implied by Germany's decentralized cultural life but also exerting a European influence that called into question the very concept of the national artist.

At the same time, Wagner's own life story flew in the face of all that was expected of German artists. Scandal upon scandal attended him on his peregrinations through Germany and Europe, and his affair with and marriage to Cosima von Bülow—the daughter of Liszt and the Comtesse Marie d'Agoult—granted him membership in a European family of artists of an aristocratic but distinctly bohemian stamp. Even before that, his friendship with King Ludwig II of Bavaria—himself surrounded by an aura of madness and hailed as a fantast by the aesthetes of Europe (Verlaine, as I have noted, apostrophized him in death as "le seul Roi de ce siècle" [the only king of this century])—had already ensured him special status.

And then there was Wagner's death in Venice in February 1883, an event immortalized in novels as different as D'Annunzio's *Il fuoco* (1900), Thomas Mann's *Der Tod in Venedig* (1912), and Franz Werfel's *Verdi* (1924), acquiring a mythical aura in the eyes of turn-of-the-century writers and, together with Venice itself, turning him into a symbol not only of *décadence* but of the erotic appeal of death and the aesthetic charm of decay.

Wagner himself, of course, had chosen Bayreuth, in the heart of the German provinces, as the center of his cult of the "artwork of the future," adapting to his own special needs a specifically German ideology with chauvinistic and anti-Semitic elements and even arrogating to himself the role of a German "Master," with his velvet beret as a symbol of his status. All these factors, together with the Christianity of his old age, had persuaded Nietzsche, when confronted by Wagner's urban and European impact, to speak of a histrionic mask, a ritualized denial of his cosmopolitan modernity.

In donning the mask of German nationalism, Wagner attempted to foist on the Jews the threatening aspects of modernity (including his own), and in his role as standard-bearer of a Utopian Christianity, he sought a system of values to which he could cling in a world that was heading toward nihilism. Significantly, however, the representatives of these various ideologies—German nationalism, Christianity, and anti-Semitism—were, as a rule, reluctant to claim him as one of their own, as they did not trust the authenticity of his attitude. Not until half a century later did Wagner, now appropriated by reactionaries, become a cult figure of National Socialist ideology. The gulf between the Wagnerism of a writer like Thomas Mann and that of Adolf Hitler serves as a paradigmatic reminder of the radically differing approaches to Wagner on the part of the modernists on the one hand and the reactionaries on the other.

In the German cultural scene of the second half of the nineteenth century, Wagner was an object of lasting scandal. He often violated expectations of the role of the artist, repeatedly provoking aggressive responses that found expression in what, for an artist, was an unprecedented flood of caricatures, polemics, lampoons, satires, and parodies that form the comic counterpart to literary Wagnerism. In *Der Fall Wagner*, Nietzsche undertook to "translate Wagner into reality, into the modern— let us be even crueler—into the bourgeois." This undertaking attracted countless later writers, some in a spirit of polemical criticism, others in a more playful vein, but in every case because they felt that this modernity was integral to the myths that Wagner had bestowed on the world in the form of his music dramas. "Would you believe it?" Nietzsche went on to ask rhetorically. "All Wagner's heroines, without exception, as soon as they are stripped of their heroic skin, become indistinguishable from Madame Bovary!"[45]

Even Bernard Shaw's fascination with the *Ring* took the form of parody in his book *The Perfect Wagnerite* (1898), in which he interpreted the work as an allegory of capitalist society. Parody, too, informs Thomas Mann's two Wagnerian short stories, "Tristan" and "Wälsungenblut," with the relationships between the characters in, respectively, *Tristan und Isolde* and *Die Walküre* projected onto a modern milieu. Here, of course, the parody is used, rather, as part of an ironic account of a particular stratum in society that is reflected in Wagner's mythological and musical universe. It does not constitute a critique of that universe, even if the irony inevitably reflects back on the work that is being parodied. Here we see clear signs of Nietzsche's legacy in the form of the philosopher's ironically impassioned judgment of the composer, a use of irony repeatedly pointed out by Mann, whose own relationship with Wagner, spanning more than half a century of critical engagement with the latter's work, Mann himself summed up in 1951 with the phrase "enthusiastic ambivalence that one could, at a pinch, call passion," which also characterized Nietzsche's view of Wagner. "Any expression will serve to describe a passion that has remained evergreen: the critically skeptical and the most exaltedly laudatory."[46]

WAGNER AS A SUPRA-GERMAN EXPERIENCE

"Nietzsche and Wagner—they were both great critics of all things German," Mann noted in his *Reflections of a Nonpolitical Man*. It was not least because of this, Mann went on, that Nietzsche was the only German whose critique of Wagner attained the same level of sophistication as the Wagner essays of writers like Baudelaire and Barrès. Wagner's own "Germanness" was "refracted and fragmented in a modern way, decorative, analytical, and intellectual"—as such, it was significant that he had so little recourse to actual German folk music in his music dramas— "hence his fascination, his innate ability to make a cosmopolitan, planetary impact."[47] And this was also true of the fascination that Mann felt for Wagner, for all that he believed that he was "not really a German" and certainly "not a German poet like Gerhart Hauptmann, for example." It was "almost obligatory for German Humanists to behave in an un-German and even anti-German manner." At all events, it could not be denied that it is believed by those whose opinion matters that a tendency toward cosmo-politanism—a tendency that undermines their sense of nationalism—is an indivisible part of the German national character; that people probably have to lose their Ger-manness in order to find it again; that no higher Germanness may be possible without an element of foreignness; and that exemplary Germans were Europeans who would have felt that it was barbaric to restrict themselves to nothing-but-Germans.[48]

And Mann follows this up with his reference to the three Germans whose names designate events that are not intimately German but European in importance: Schopenhauer, Wagner, and Nietzsche.[49]

Throughout his life, Mann regarded his experience of Wagner as "a spiritual experience of supra-German significance, an experience that I shared with Europe's intelligentsia." And he drew a link between Wagner and Ibsen, Zola, and the great social novels of the nineteenth century, novels with which Wagner's music dramas seemed to share the very thing that appeared to be missing from the post-Goethean literature of the nineteenth century: universality and bold psycho-logical insights.

> This German musician was no German musician in the old, cosy, and authentic sense. He was no doubt very German (can one be a musician without being German?). But what fascinated me about his art was not its German nationalism, its German poetry, or its German Romanticism—or at least only insofar as all this appeared intellectualized in the form of a decorative self-portrait; rather, it was the all-powerful European ap-peal that emanates from it, an appeal demonstrated by Wagner's current status, which is limited almost exclusively to non-German countries. No, I was not so German that I failed to see the profound psychological and artistic affinity between his own artistic devices and those of Zola and Ibsen, both of whom, like him, were preeminently masters of the symbol, the tyrannical formula, and of whom the French novelist in particular, a Naturalist and a Romantic like himself, appears as his true brother in his desire and capacity for intoxicating and overwhelming a mass audience. . . . The *Rougon-Macquart* cycle and the *Ring*: the "Wagnerian" does not lump them to-gether in his mind. Yet they do belong together—on the level of intuition, if not of love.[50]

In the case of Nietzsche, Mann shows that "regardless of the profound German-ness of his mind," he evinced a Europeanism grounded in his critical outlook and psychological insights[51]—and, of course, he mentions his own contribution to the Europeanization of the German prose narrative.[52] Adopting an ironic tone, he even accuses himself of "undermining all that is German" by dint of his "intellectual-ist" concerns.[53]

Mann comes to the conclusion that, paradoxically, it is the "supra-German" as-pect of Schopenhauer, Wagner, Nietzsche—and himself—that is typically Ger-man: "supra-German means German through and through."[54] Indeed, Mann even appeals for support to Bogumil Goltz, who had argued that the Germans do not have a limited national character like the French or English, but that they are a cosmopolitan nation—Mann calls them a "Weltvolk" (world nation).[55] This notion has a long tradition to it, deriving ultimately from the cosmopolitan notions of German Classicism and Idealism. Behind it lies the idea that the German "represents all of humanity," as Mann noted in his *Versuch über Schiller* (Essay on Schiller), which dates from only shortly before his death. The phrase occurs within the context of a discussion of Schiller's 1797 unfinished poem "Deutsche Größe" (German greatness). The claim that the Germans were cosmopolitan was also, of course, a form of nationalism, Mann conceded, albeit "sublimated and raised to its highest potential." (In this respect, Mann compares it to Dostoyevsky's Pushkin speech of 1880, in which the spirit of the Russian folk was credited with a like capacity for representing all of humanity.)[56] While expressing his skepticism concerning the sublimated nationalism of such a cosmopolitan ideology, Mann nonetheless used his Schiller speech to profess his belief in the idea of the supra-German as typical of the true and better kind of German. (Mann was speaking against a background of the way in which the nationalist idea had been hijacked by the Third Reich.)

In his essay *Leiden und Größe Richard Wagners* (1933), Mann borrowed whole passages from his *Reflections of a Nonpolitical Man* in order to reiterate his belief that Wagner owed the "universal impact" of his art to the "magnificent simultaneity and interaction of Germanness and cosmopolitanism."[57] Once again, he distinguished between two directions in German art and literature: one that in spite of its high standing belonged to a "secret Germany," denying itself "a European and universal potential," and another that although often inferior in quality was distinguished by its "universal applicability and enjoyability." For Mann, the most important example of this "universal applicability" was still Wagner. "Wagner's art is the most sensational self-portrait and self-critique of the German character that can be imagined; as such, it is capable of making all that is German interesting to even the most doltish of foreigners."[58]

Sentences such as these were not welcome in 1933. The authors of the unspeakable *Protest from Richard Wagner's Own City of Munich*, who forced Mann into exile, would have none of this "cosmopolitan and democratic outlook" on Wagner's part. Nor did they have time for the "insipid and patronizing praise accorded to Wagner's music for its 'universal applicability and universal enjoyability' or for its 'simultaneity of Germanness and modernity.'"[59] The authors failed to notice that Mann had taken over whole sections from his earlier *Reflections of a Nonpolitical Man* but they played off one text against the other, claiming that he had abandoned the maxims of the earlier essay. Thus they failed to realize that Mann's view of Wagner and his link between the German and the supra-German had not changed in the fifteen years that separated the two texts. The increasingly militant nationalism that refused to accept that the Germans' most salient feature was their self-transcendence from Germans to cosmopolitans, with nationalism transformed into supranationalism, merely served to confirm Mann's conviction that in the face of an aggressively inward-looking Germanism, this self-transcendence had become a necessity and that as a true German, he would have to leave Germany and live in self-imposed exile, emigrating in order to salvage his essentially supranational Germanness.

THOMAS MANN'S *JOSEPH* TETRALOGY AND ITS PARALLELS WITH THE *RING*

Mann took with him into exile his novel *Joseph and His Brethren*, the first two volumes of which had already appeared in Germany. His "mythological novel"[60] was written at a difficult time, when myth was being misused for murderous ends. Predictably, Mann had been accused by right-wing critics of violating the very essence of myth, and he had welcomed that criticism. But his affinity with myth was also held against him by left-wing colleagues,[61] with a writer such as Alfred Kurella complaining in *Internationale Literatur* that *Die Geschichten Jaakobs* (The tales of Jacob) was "in the spirit of the spirit of Germany's henchmen."[62] No wonder, then, that Mann responded all the more eagerly to positive comments by left-wing writers, including praise from his brother Heinrich in a letter of 25 December 1933: "rich poetry, probably your richest." Even more important in this context was Ernst Bloch's letter of 23 June 1940: "It is clear that your powerful *Joseph* is the clearest and most felicitious example of a refunctioning of myth." Although Mann will not have liked this term—in *Leiden an Deutschland* (Suffering for Germany) he speaks of the "humanization of myth"[63]—its very hideousness was welcome to him, as the "refunctioning" of myth was preferable to the suspicion that he was in any way associated with the functionalization of myth under the National Socialists.

As early as 1929, in his *Rede über Lessing* (Speech on Lessing), Mann had already declared war on the "maliciously life-threatening" misuse of myth and done all he could to "drive back into their matriarchal darkness the chthonic monsters that have already had too much grist to their mill."[64] Mann tried to solve the problem of justifying myth in the face of the rationality that was currently threatened by Fascism by forging a link between myth and Freudian psychology. Thus, on 18 February 1941 we find him writing to Karl Kerényi that "psychology is in fact the means by which to wrest myth from the hands of these shady Fascists and to 'refunctionalize' it by making it more humane. For me, this link represents the world of the future, a humanity blessed by the spirit above and 'by the depths that lie below.' "[65] This is the leitmotif that runs through *Joseph and His Brethren*,[66] forging together mind and soul, patriarchy and matriarchy, myth and logos, to form a single entity.[67]

In an earlier letter to Karl Kerényi, this one dated 24 March 1934, Mann had warmly welcomed the great mythographer's plan to write a treatise "on the return of the modern novel to myth" and to "treat this return as a true return *home*."[68] Kerényi himself had spoken of "a return of the European spirit to the highest mythic realities,"[69] and Mann certainly regarded this tendency as typical of the modern novel, refusing to allow himself to be misled by the Fascists' misuse of these mythical realities.

"It is no doubt a general rule," Mann noted in 1942 in his lecture on *Joseph and His Brethren*,

> that at certain times we lose our taste for all that is merely individual and specific, for the individual case, the "bourgeois" in its broadest sense. Into the foreground comes

the typical, ever-human, ever-recurrent, timeless, in a word: the mythical. For myth is the typical inasmuch as it is an archetypal norm and archetypal form of life, a timeless model and ever-present formula into which life enters by reproducing its features from the unconscious.[70]

This idea underpins *Joseph and His Brethren*, and it is one to which Mann returned again and again, often repeating it word for word, most notably in his 1936 lecture *Freud und die Zukunft*. "Our lives are grounded in myth," we read there,[71] hence Mann's determination in *Joseph and His Brethren* to return to "the beginnings, where everything existed for the first time."[72] Myth was synonymous with the "initial establishment of a spiritual form of life by means of what is living and individual," an "archetype, stamped by our forefathers, in which later life can be recognized and whose traces it follows." Thus we read in his *Rede über Lessing.*[73] In *Freud und die Zukunft*, Mann likewise defines the "epic idea" of *Joseph and His Brethren* as "following in the traces" of what has gone before, "life as *imitatio*," adopting prototypical patterns in the form of a "lived *vita*" (Mann borrowed this term from Freud's pupil Ernst Kris) as "lived myth."[74]

That this idea of "lived myth" has nothing in common with the mythomania of the National Socialists, and that there was a fundamental difference between aesthetic and political myth was as evident to Mann as it was unclear to his opponents. But how can the difference between these two interpretations be adequately defined?[75] In his chapter on the role of the Nibelung legend in the political symbolism of the twentieth century, Herfried Münkler has shown that myth can be used for political ends when concentrated in a specific image divorced from its narrative context and when its ending in particular is ignored. Although Münkler's comments are concerned mainly with the *Nibelungenlied* and only peripherally with the *Ring*, his remarks are nonetheless relevant here. "Political myths," he argues, with specific reference to Nazism, "almost always contain a critically destructive potential that may affect their instrumental use, but this potential is activated only when the narrative context of these evocative images is restored and the story, arbitrarily curtailed, is completed."[76]

This tendency to divorce isolated images from their mythological context and limit their meaning for propagandist ends is a fundamental feature of what Kurt Hübner has termed "political pseudomyths,"[77] whose most influential propagator was Georges Sorel. For Sorel, myth was the flywheel of an ideology that led to action. Its function was to create highly evocative images to express the "tendencies," "instincts," and "hopes" of a nation or party and thus to mobilize the nation's masses.[78] Political pseudomyths are not based on archetypes that have arisen spontaneously or been handed down through the ages but are fabricated,[79] even when they use and manipulate traditional myths in order to achieve their strategic ends.[80]

But such pseudomyths could not be used if their underlying structures did not answer a genuine need, a need made worse by the crisis of reason in the modern world. The exploitation and instrumentalization of this need by the National Socialists' mytho-ideologists and mytho-engineers does not constitute an indictment of myth. As Franz Fühmann has noted in his essay "Das mythische Element in der Literatur" (The mythical element in literature), it is unfortunately the case that

> myth can be misused very easily—more easily than many other human creations. This is not a value judgment. A seismograph is more liable to break down than a pile driver, and greater good or harm can be dispensed from a throne than from a tailor's cross-legged position on the floor. These essential characteristics say nothing for or against the people who embody them. One simply has to accept them.[81]

According to Fühmann, genuine myth is prevented from being misused by its contradictory structures. Whereas in fairy tales there is a clear-cut distinction between good and evil,[82] this polarity and others interpenetrate one another, rendering the myth readable on several levels. In myth, claims Fühmann, "there is always a contradiction."[83] This claim can be demonstrated by reference to countless examples from Wagner's myth-based dramas, where even the most virtuous and the most evil characters reveal ethical complexities that relativize their morality. Siegfried, the radiant hero, for example, is characterized by a profound moral contradiction that Brünnhilde sums up oxymoronically in her final peroration: "Der Reinste war er,/der mich verrieth!" she explains [The purest of men it was/who betrayed me!] (GS 6:252).

> ächter als er
> schwur keiner Eide;
> treuer als er
> hielt keiner Verträge;
> laut'rer als er
> liebte kein and'rer:
> und doch alle Eide,
> alle Verträge,
> die treueste Liebe—
> trog keiner wie er!

(GS 6:252)

> [Never were oaths
> more nobly sworn;
> never were treaties
> kept more truly;
> never did any man
> love more loyally:
> and yet every oath,
> every treaty,
> the truest love—
> no one betrayed as he did!]

Even Alberich, while appearing to rule over a world of radical evil, is not evil by nature but has become so only because of the suffering that he felt when his love was rejected and basely mocked. When Wotan and Loge tear the ring from him, it is the essential suffering of his criminal existence that he holds up to the gods, who become criminals without suffering such "shameful distress." For a moment, he becomes an object of the spectator's pity, encouraging us to sympathize with evil.

> Des Unseligen,
> Angstversehrten
> fluchfertige,
> furchtbare That,
> zu fürstlichem Tand
> soll sie fröhlich dir taugen?
>
> (GS 5:253)

> [Shall the curse-heavy,
> harrowing deed
> of the hapless,
> fear-stricken dwarf
> serve haply to gain you
> a princely toy?]

Indeed, Alberich even becomes something of a moralist when he points out that his own crime was more or less a private affair that does not affect the moral world order, whereas the crime that Wotan threatens to commit as the ruler of that order will turn the world upside down and affect all of existence.

> Frevelte ich,
> so frevelt' ich frei an mir:
> doch an allem, was war,
>   ist und wird,
> frevelst, Ewiger, du,
> entreißest du frech mir den Ring!
>
> (GS 5:253)

> [If ever I sinned,
> I sinned freely against myself:
> but you, you immortal, will sin
>   against all that was,
> is and shall be
> if you brazenly wrest the ring from me now!]

This lack of an unambiguous morality and the contradictory tensions within virtually all of Wagner's characters—and in myth in general—mean that they can be used as instruments of propaganda only at the cost of their artistic integrity. Mann's mythologically inspired works were protected against this kind of abuse from the outset because—unlike Wagner—Mann had before his eyes a living example of the way in which myth could be misused and he could "refunctionalize" it by humanizing it and turning it into the opposite of the forms that were being destroyed.

"Very deep is the well of the past."[84] Mann begins his *Joseph* tetralogy with this profound and cryptic sentence, an opening that significantly links his *opus summum* to Wagner's *Der Ring des Nibelungen*. This is not the place to examine the many parallels between his "mythological novel" and Wagner's principal work.[85] Essentially, both are grounded in myth, and both developed into tetralogies only while their authors were working on them, expanding the original scenario backward in time and descending ever more deeply into a mythical past. No less remarkable are the parallel geneses of the two works. Both were begun in Germany and continued in Switzerland, where their respective authors were living in exile. And in each case they were interrupted before their completion by what Joachim Kaiser has termed a "radiant intermezzo that deals with Germany on a historical and epic scale"; in Wagner's case, this work was *Die Meistersinger von Nürnberg*, and in Mann's it was *Lotte in Weimar*.[86]

Such are its manifold parallels with Wagner's *Ring* that Mann's novel is a classic example of his own idea of a "lived *vita*." As such, it is scarcely less important as a "lived myth" than his lifelong interest in Goethe. "The unexpected evolution that the story of Joseph had followed," Mann confessed in 1948 at the time of the novel's appearance in America within the covers of a single volume, "was somehow secretly determined by the recollection of Wagner's grandiose structure, it had moved in its footsteps."[87] It goes without saying, therefore, that his very first sentence forms an analogy with the beginning of the *Ring*, for *Das Rheingold*, too, begins deep down, its first "word" being the famous low E flat of the prelude to the prelude. In his two great Wagner essays of 1933 and 1937, *Leiden und Größe Richard Wagners* and *Richard Wagner und "Der Ring des Nibelungen"*—both of which were closely bound up with the publication of the first three volumes of *Joseph and His Brethren* in 1933, 1934, and 1936 respectively—Mann refers to this note as the "primeval cell" and "ultimate beginning of all things."[88]

"Back to the beginning, to the beginning of all things and their music!"[89] For Mann, this was the underlying thrust of the *Ring*:

> The depths of the Rhine, with their shimmering hoard of gold in which its daughters take so playful a pleasure—this was the world's original state of innocence, untouched as yet by greed or by any curse. At the same time it was also the *beginning of music*. And it was not just the music of myth that the poet-composer would give us, but the myth of music itself, a mythic philosophy and a musical poem on creation, including its development into a richly structured symbolic world that derives from the E flat major triad of the deeply flowing Rhine.[90]

Back to the beginning of all things: this is also the underlying theme of the *Joseph* novels and their "Prelude: Descent into Hell." But there is, of course, a significant difference. The prelude to the *Joseph* novels is a veritable descent into hell, a journey to "the mothers," as Mann described it in his 1942 lecture on the work.[91] The downward trajectory seems to be unending. The prelude to *Das Rheingold*, by contrast, starts out from the lowest possible point—the rumbling E flat pedal—

and depicts a musical ascent through the horn triads and the quaver and, later, semiquaver figurations in the cellos, producing the first diatonically ascending leitmotif of the cycle as the music strikes upward from the instruments' dark-toned registers to the brighter sonorities of their higher registers.

The sense of movement in Mann's "Descent into Hell" is completely different from this. "Very deep is the well of the past" reads the opening sentence of the prelude, but this is immediately followed by the question: "Should we not call it bottomless?" In other words, there is nothing to hold on to in the depths, as the narrator sinks ever more deeply into the "unsounded depths of the past."[92] Time and again he stumbles against places where he seems to gain a footing— "provisional origins," "first beginnings"[93]—but on each occasion "time coulisses"[94] are revealed whenever he looks behind them or beneath them; each coulisse reveals a new coulisse, until finally he reaches "the very last 'backward' "[95] in the Gnostic belief in the perfect first man, the *adam kadmon*, who is found at the point where the world was originally divided into the principles of matter, spirit, and the "archetypally human" soul that is held in a state of tension between them.[96]

Unlike the *Ring*, it is only at the end of the prelude that the beginning of all things is reached, a beginning beyond which there is no going back. And so it is no accident that on the very last page of the prelude Mann twice uses the German pronoun *Es* in a prominent position, its very sonorousness recalling its homonym "Es," which in the German system of nomenclature is the note E flat: "Denn es ist, ist immer, möge des Volkes Redeweise auch lauten: Es war" [For it is, always is, however much we may say "It was"].[97] But why does Mann reverse the directional flow of the prelude of *Das Rheingold*, using a technique of varied repetition borrowed from Wagner's music? Why do we seem to be descending, rather than rising? One thing is clear from this "Descent into Hell": Mann not only imitates Wagner, he also works against him, so that his cycle of novels is both an *imitatio* and a *contrafactum* of Wagner's four-part music drama. In the case of the prelude to the *Joseph* novels, creating a contrary structure is tantamount to the repeated calling into question of archetypal mythical certainties.

Wagner's tetralogy presents a self-contained mythological reality that is threatened in the course of the action and already overshadowed by a demythologized modern civilization, yet it still has the first and last word, encompassing the whole dramatic action between its first and last notes. It begins with the triadic world of E flat major and what Wagner himself called "the world's lullaby" (CT, 17 July 1869). This is sung by the mythological incarnations of the primeval element of water and initiates a drama that moves increasingly away from the paradisiacal integrity of its beginnings, before returning by a circular route to that state of innocence at the end of the cycle.

The *Joseph* novels no longer lay claim to the same mythical unity. Mythical narratives tend to return to the point at which they set out, a tendency that Mann transcends in his *Joseph* novels by asking after the origins of myth as such. Hence his repeated ability to go back beyond what seems to be the farthest horizon of myth and to relate each primordial event to another primordial event that lies even farther back in time, finally reaching an ultimate metaphysical apriority that both legitimizes and relativizes the first certainties of myth, justifying both their inevitability and the impossibility of transcending them.

This impossibility is also the subject of the chapter "How Abraham Found God" in *Der junge Joseph* (Young Joseph), where Abraham's "work on the divine"[98] is described as a process of continuous transcendence of mythical certainties, a return, link by link and cause by cause, through the chain of existence, until he finds not just the first link but what holds the whole chain together. The God of Abraham is no longer an immanent godhead manifest in many mythological gods but the one and only transcendent deity, "a powerful Thou, saying 'I,' independent of Abraham and independent of the world. He was in the fire but was not the fire—wherefore it would have been very wrong to worship fire. . . . He must be much greater than all his works, and just as necessarily outside of his works."[99]

In the *Joseph* novels, then, unlike the *Ring*, myth is not circumscribed but is transcended by the metaphysical. The idea underlying "Descent into Hell" and the Abraham chapter was already adumbrated in 1929 in Mann's *Rede über Lessing*, where he writes: "World events are like scene shifting, with beginnings in place of sets, luring us backward to increasingly early beginnings in the infinite, and—in keeping with our silent supposition—the first beginnings of all things do not lie in time but are transcendent."[100]

But myth is indifferent to transcendence; it operates entirely within time, within circular time, which, unlike historical and linear time, has neither an absolute beginning nor an absolute end, being neither unique nor irreversible. In *The Tales of Jacob*, Mann distinguishes between these two temporal structures, describing one as a "rolling sphere," the other as a "line": "And there is no beginning to the rolling sphere."[101]

FESTIVAL

Like the *Ring*, the *Joseph* novels constitute a festival. "The festival in the sense of a mythical ceremony and a serenely serious repeat of some archetypal event is really the basic motif of my novel," Mann told Karl Kerényi on 16 February 1939.[102] Play, festival, cheerful serenity (Mann uses the term *heiter*, which has a much wider semantic field than any English equivalent, ranging from the serene to the cheerful and even the comic): it was in their spirit that myth was to be salvaged, they alone that could prevent myth from being "functionalized" and associated with some manipulable political reality. In 1967, in his essay "Ist die Kunst heiter?" (Is art jovial?) Adorno argued that in the light of the recent past, namely, Auschwitz, "serenely cheerful art is no longer conceivable."[103] Mann, by contrast, regarded "the sovereign serenity of art" as "the best means of dealing with the hatred and stupidity" of Fascism.[104] Even after the collapse of the Third Reich, Mann was still able to write to Agnes E. Meyer on 10 October 1947, referring to *Der Erwählte* and *Felix Krull*.

> Comedy, laughter, and humor seem to me more and more a cure for the soul; I thirst after them after the barely enlivened horrors of *Faustus*, and I take it upon myself to

devise the most comical thing I can find now that the world situation is so bleak. Anyone who could write *Joseph* at the time of Hitler's victories will not allow the future to get him down.[105]

Here we find epic humor as a form of aesthetic resistance to Nazism, cheerful serenity as a metaphysical and humane alternative to a world overshadowed by hatred and terror, by fanaticism and fatalism.[106] Cheerful serenity in the sense understood by Goethe was to be the keynote of myth, guarding it against all the dangers of misuse. In this spirit Mann sought to preserve Wagnerian myth in his *Joseph* novels, thus restoring it to its true nature after a period when its impact had been cruelly and fatally compromised.

The Disinherited Heir to the Throne

FRANZ WILHELM BEIDLER, WAGNER'S

"LOST GRANDSON"—A POSTLUDE

For Dagny R. Beidler

Wehvolles Erbe, dem ich verfallen

[Woeful inheritance to which I'm condemned]

—Richard Wagner, Parsifal

EVEN AMONG WAGNERIANS, it is not widely known that in addition to his four grandchildren from the marriage of Siegfried and Winifred Wagner, the composer had a fifth grandchild, by the name of Franz Wilhelm Beidler (1901–81), who until the birth of Wieland in 1917 was the "Master's" only grandson. Yet Beidler is almost completely forgotten today, his name virtually erased from the family's turbulent history. In a letter to Ernest Newman dated October 1937, Beidler described himself, not without reason, as Wagner's "lost grandson" (364).[1]

THE CAREER OF THE DISINHERITED HEIR TO THE THRONE

Beidler was the son of Isolde von Bülow and the Swiss conductor Franz Beidler, whom she married in 1900. Although legally Isolde was the daughter of Hans von Bülow, it was no secret that she was in fact Wagner's first daughter by Cosima; Wagner called her Loldchen as a term of special affection (369). Even Carl Friedrich Glasenapp, Wahnfried's court historiographer, was aware of the relationship (370). But a row erupted between Beidler senior and Cosima at the 1906 Bayreuth Festival, and Isolde, loyally standing by her husband, found herself drawn into it. Until then it had been accepted in Wahnfried that Isolde was Wagner's daughter and that her son, Franz Wilhelm, was the heir to the throne, but now attempts were made to exclude both of them from the succession.

The result was a spectacular court case that Isolde brought against her mother in 1913. Tried before the Civil Division of the Bayreuth District Court, the case was doomed from the outset. Isolde refused to accept that she had been "robbed of her father," as the contemporary papers put it. In June 1914 Thomas Theodor

Heine's satirical paper *Simplicissimus* published a caricature of Isolde, parodistically captioned: "Wagner darf ich nicht heißen;/Bülow möcht' ich nicht sein:/doch Beidler muß ich mich nennen!" [Wagner I may not call myself;/Bülow I don't want to be:/but I have to be known as Beidler!] (362 and 370–71). The court rejected her complaint on the grounds that "pater est, quem nuptiae demonstrant" (he is the father whom marriage proves to be the father).[2]

The Beidler case preoccupied the world's press on the eve of the First World War, the final scandal of a world that was on the point of disappearing forever. It provoked vehemently polemical criticism of the whole "spirit of Bayreuth" and what Maximilian Harden waspishly described as the deceitful mask of the "genteel inhabitants of a consecrationally festive Wahnfried" with their "dynastic pretensions" (375). Nine days after the court had handed down its decision, the heir to the Austrian throne was assassinated in Sarajevo, and the world turned to other concerns.

Isolde was already suffering from tuberculosis, and the court's decision proved to be her deathblow. She died on 7 February 1919 and was quietly buried in Munich's Waldfriedhof. For ten years, the news of her daughter's death was kept from Cosima Wagner. Whenever she asked after her, she was told that her lost daughter was still at Davos, in the "magic mountain." Cosima had no inkling that the thunderbolt of war had brought the unreal world of sanatoriums to an end—for Thomas Mann an embodiment of the crisis and collapse of a predemocratic upper-class society. This was the end of the tragedy of Isolde Wagner, the "child of love and enthusiasm," as Cosima had once described her (363).

But, in the best tradition, the tragedy was to be followed by a satyr play. While his wife lay dying, Beidler had started an affair with the singer Emmy Zimmermann, the unholy fruit of which was a daughter who came into the world on Wagner's birthday—the exact year is uncertain, but it was some time during the First World War—and who was given the name Eva Senta Elisabeth. She later married the Communist actor and Brechtian Ernst Busch and became a successful cabaret artiste. Not until 1990 did she reveal her father's identity in an interview, a revelation confirmed in her autobiography, *Und trotzdem* (And yet), which was published the following year.[3]

Meanwhile, Beidler had also been conducting an affair with one of his servants, Walburga Rass from Upper Bavaria, who was the mother of two of his children, Franz Walter and Elsa. Following the death of his mother, Franz W. Beidler urged his father to legitimize this relationship. Beidler senior died in the same year as Cosima and Siegfried Wagner (1930), whereas his second wife, Walburga, lived until 1975. Their daughter, Elsa, married the writer Hans Breiteneichner from Söcking on Lake Starnberg. In 1966 the Beidlers' grave in the Munich Waldfriedhof was deconsecrated, and, as no one in the Wagner family felt any responsibility for the mortal remains of Wagner's first daughter, Isolde, the daughter of her former servant declared her willingness to have the coffin moved to the Breiteneichner vault in the cemetery at Söcking. Not until some years later did the name Isolde Beidler appear on the gravestone beneath a cross surmounted by a shingle roof, but the inscription gave no indication of any Wagnerian connection.

Following his mother's death, Franz W. Beidler repudiated his father, whom he blamed for his mother's misfortunes, and as a result was thrown back on his own resources. In the wake of Siegfried's marriage and the birth of his first son, Wieland, in 1917, he forfeited what he described jokingly in a letter to Klaus Mann (12 November 1933) as his "unique claim to the Bayreuth throne" (363). Shortly after his birth in 1901, his grandmother Cosima had described him as "a little Bayreuthian who will, I hope, be true, hardworking, and capable of both indignation and enthusiasm" (363). Beidler certainly grew up to be hardworking and capable of both indignation and enthusiasm, but he was never a "true" Bayreuthian.

Even his education was uncharacteristic: of all Wagner's grandchildren, he was the only one to choose an academic career, studying jurisprudence and political science before taking his doctorate in 1927 with the constitutional historian Fritz Hartung. Its subject was the history of German parliamentarianism. On receiving his doctorate, Beidler worked for the Prussian Ministry of Science, Art, and Education, where his colleagues included the Jewish music teacher and cultural reformer Leo Kestenberg. Throughout his life Kestenberg sought to forge a bond between art and socialism, and this became Beidler's ideal, too, an ideal that also colored his response to the works of his grandfather, whom he always regarded as a revolutionary of 1848–49. On Hitler's seizure of power, he was dismissed from his post at the Prussian Ministry of Culture; not only had he made no secret of his rejection of National Socialism, but he was married to a daughter of the Jewish medical scientist Sigmund Gottschalk.

His decision to emigrate was made easier by the fact that he had retained his Swiss citizenship. In a letter of June 1933, we find him describing himself as "unreliable as a nationalist, poisoned by Marxism, and related in marriage to a Jew, as I am now and as I shall, of course, always remain, and so I find nothing more to detain me in my beloved homeland" (386). He and his wife went first to Paris and then, following in his grandfather's footsteps, moved to Switzerland in August 1934. He demonstratively adopted the name of Beidler-Wagner and wrote to his beloved half-aunt Blandine von Gravina née von Bülow: "I feel a commitment to history to show that there is at least one of Wagner's descendants who has not taken the shameful course that has led from the falsification of all Wagner's ideas in Bayreuth to the 'philosophy' represented by Herr Hitler" (387).

BEIDLER AND THOMAS MANN

In Zurich, Beidler's lost homeland gave way to the welcoming household of Thomas Mann. Mann already knew Beidler from Munich and Berlin, as he tells us in *Die Entstehung des Doktor Faustus* (The genesis of Doctor Faustus), where he describes Beidler as "Wagner's grandson and eerily similar to him in appearance."[4] Mann's Zurich diaries make it clear that Beidler and his wife were frequent—and never unwelcome—visitors. Beidler had never really had a father and had lost his gravely ill and embittered mother at an early age, so that only in Zurich did he finally feel a sense of peace and security in the bosom of a family.

Another frequent visitor to the Mann household was the writer's father-in-law, Alfred Pringsheim, with whom Beidler likewise struck up a cordial friendship. He had been friendly with Pringsheim's son Klaus during his time in Berlin. Both men had written for the German Social Democrat newspaper *Vorwärts*, and Klaus Pringsheim was also a committed comrade-in-arms in the battle to implement Kestenberg's aesthetical-socialist reforms. It was at Alfred Pringsheim's home in Munich that Beidler first met Thomas Mann.

At the funeral service for Alfred Pringsheim in Zurich on 27 June 1941, Beidler spoke in memory of the dead man. Beidler had been eager to meet Pringsheim, whom he regarded as "the first patron of the Bayreuth enterprise" and to whom Wagner himself had once written a letter of thanks. Beidler recalled this in his address, which revolved entirely around what, for him, was the central problem of the change of direction that Wagnerism had taken in recent years: "In the Pringsheim family, on both the father's and the mother's side, the authentic tradition of early Wagnerism has been preserved, a tradition that must be strenuously distinguished from later and more dubious manifestations of this curiously mutable phenomenon" (294).

Alfred Pringsheim, argued Beidler, was the typical representative of a middle class that had increasingly abandoned its original political aspirations and turned into a cultured middle class no longer aware of the extent to which the authoritarian state, under whose wings it had crept, had taken the ground from under its feet. "Blamelessly guilty, Alfred Pringsheim witnessed the total collapse of the world in which he worked and in which he was at home. The embodiment of German culture, spiritually and personally linked to it in a way that few others were, he was obliged to see himself driven out as one who was 'foreign to the species' " (296).

In Alfred Pringsheim's son Klaus and above all in his son-in-law Thomas Mann, Beidler saw a return of the middle class's original role in which culture was in harmony not only with politics but also with the republicanism of such early Wagnerians as Pringsheim's own parents; his mother, Hedwig Dohm, was a daughter of the great pioneer of women's emancipation in the nineteenth century, and her father, Ernst, had been one of Wagner's first literary champions. For Beidler, the history of the Pringsheim family was thus the history of the rise, fall, and rebirth of authentic Wagnerianism.

Mann took a lively interest in Beidler's published writings. In the main these dealt with the literary and ideological impact of Wagner and the *Ring*, which Beidler was already interpreting from a sociocritical and Utopian standpoint even as early as the 1930s. Yet there is an important difference between Mann's writings on Wagner and Beidler's. For Mann, Wagner's works were inspired by myth, but myth illumined by the light of psychoanalysis, their interpretation looking backward to Schopenhauer and forward to Freud, whereas Beidler saw Wagner first and foremost as a social revolutionary. At the risk of overexaggeration, one could say that Mann interpreted Wagner—and especially the *Ring*—in what he believed was the spirit of Freud, Beidler in that of Bernard Shaw. In his essay "Richard Wagner in England," published in the *Neue Zürcher Zeitung* on 14/15 May 1939, Beidler described Shaw's *The Perfect Wagnerite* as a socio-Utopian alternative to the erotic mysticism of another Irish Wagnerian, George Moore. It was presumably Beidler's article that alerted Mann to the existence of Shaw's essay: his diary contains repeated references to it from 27 June 1939 onward.

Of some significance in this context is Mann's reaction to Beidler's essay "Wagner als Idee" (Wagner as idea), which appeared in *Melos* in February 1933 to mark the fiftieth anniversary of Wagner's death. Here Beidler interpreted the *Ring* as

a work that is, as it were, distilled from an extract of the century. Here a new Dante formulates his powerful indictment of the principle that had transformed the world of his own day, creating the artistic and prophetic counterpart of the political activities of men like Mikhail Bakunin and of Marx's scientific critique. With brilliant symbolic force, he reduces all the tensions, relationships, and conflicts of the new social order to their lowest common denominator, and the hidden meaning of contemporary events is laid bare in an artistic vision. The complex system of mines and the iron and steelworks of the Ruhrgebiet [Ruhr Basin] are turned into the workshops of Nibelheim, the anonymity of capital and the insecurity of the shareholder are revealed in the Tarnhelm's disguise. The demonic power of the ring—in other words, of the capitalist striving for power and profit—permeates all the relationships in the work, dissolving all the old links and undermining law and custom. The powers that have ruled since the dawn of time—here they are called gods—become caught up in the capitalist jungle, and the world awaits the coming of man, man who, renouncing possessions and profits, finds the strength to perform the liberating act and supersede gods and dwarfs. (277)

But the "revolutionary arc" strives to break free from the "arc of resignation"— these being the "two great arcs of the nineteenth century"—resulting in the "flight from the world and the longing for death in *Tristan und Isolde*" and the philosophy of "folly" in *Die Meistersinger von Nürnberg* (287).

Having read Beidler's essay, Mann wrote to him on 23 December 1933, complimenting him on it and conceding that it "touched" at certain points on his own lecture, *Leiden und Größe Richard Wagners*, which he had delivered in February of that year. But he then went on to admit that Wilhelm Danckert's essay "Wagner als Tiefenpsychologe" (Wagner as a depth psychologist), which had appeared immediately after Beidler's in the same issue of *Melos*, "contained perhaps even more powerful echoes of certain observations in my own essay" (317). After all, psychoanalysis was more important in Mann's eyes than any socialist Utopia, even though in his lecture he had emphasized that "throughout his life" Wagner had been "something of a socialist and cultural Utopian in the sense of advocating a classless society based on love and free from luxury and the curse of gold," a society "such as he dreamed of as constituting the ideal audience for his art."[5] For Beidler, too, this idea of society remains basic to the *Ring*, even if ultimately tinged with a sense of resignation.

In May 1934 an essay of Beidler's appeared in the Manchester *Guardian*. It dealt with the way in which Wagner's beliefs and ideals had been falsified in Hitler's Germany and especially with the way in which the underlying idea of the *Ring* had been "ideologically reinterpreted" and finally eliminated altogether by the National

Socialists' cult of Wagner (283–87). In his article "Kunst und Leben: Zur Genesis der Ring-Tetralogie" (Art and life: On the genesis of the *Ring* tetralogy), which appeared in the *Neue Zürcher Zeitung* on 29 May 1938, he described Wagner's major work as a powerful artistic synthesis of "the ideas and postulates of revolutionary social criticism during the first half of the century," illustrating his argument by referring to various details of the plot, such as Mime's comparison of the Nibelungs' activities as smiths before and after Alberich's theft of the gold: "What is this if not an analytical contrast, reduced to the simplest artistic formula, between the economic thinking of two generations, the guild craftsman's meeting of individual needs and the industrialist's and capitalist's pursuit of financial profit?" (291).

THE BIOGRAPHER OF COSIMA WAGNER

There is little doubt that Beidler's sociocritical and Utopian analyses of the *Ring* were of less interest to Mann than Beidler's principal work, his ongoing biography of Cosima Wagner, which he subtitled "The Road to the Wagner Myth" and from which he read to Mann on several occasions. The book was intended as "a sociological study in the guise of a biography" (395), a scrupulously annotated investigation of the subject from the twin standpoints of cultural sociology and social psychology. In the completed sections of the work, Beidler succeeded in realizing this aim to compelling effect, at the same time combining critical analysis with narrative brilliance. Mann was so inspired by one of his early conversations with Beidler on the subject that according to his diary entry of 1 September 1933, he himself thought of

> writing a novel centered on the world of Wagner, Liszt, Cosima, and Nietzsche, a supremely interesting subject, the most complex, most multilayered European-German topic. The antipathy between Liszt and his son-in-law (very pronounced [as Mann had discovered from Beidler]). Liszt's European mentality contrasted with Wagner's emergence from Germany's petty bourgeoisie. Liszt's daughter, intellectually mundane and non-German (not to say "un-German") by birth. . . . Also Nietzsche, brought up in a vicarage, in a spirit of Humanism and academe, brilliantly transformed by debilitating illness into a European hostile to all things German.[6]

Mann was not the only one to be enthusiastic about Beidler's methodologically and conceptually novel biography; so too was Ernest Newman, to whom Beidler sent a copy in 1937, so much so, indeed, that Newman recommended it to his own (and Mann's) American publisher, Alfred A. Knopf. Beidler even signed a contract with Knopf, but his work on the biography gradually ground to a halt. Beidler found more and more of his time taken up with his work as secretary of the Association of Swiss Writers, and his status as an émigré prevented him from consulting the Bayreuth archives.

Beidler had intended to adopt a critical approach to his sources, but as long as he was denied access to those sources, his book remained an impossibility. Once the war was over, he resumed work on the book, but, self-critical to a fault, he felt that he lacked the energy to bring together so many disparate strands. As a result, his work remained unfinished, although a series of accompanying essays fortunately means that the gaps in the biography can be filled, at least in part. One of these essays was an analysis of the relationship between Nietzsche and Cosima in the light of the Ariadne myth (265–74); it presciently anticipates the findings of later Nietzsche scholars.

Beidler's life of his grandmother is a portrait of a Franco-German society that is particularly fascinating for its colorful mixture of aristocratic and middle-class culture in Cosima's upbringing and personality, a mixture that explains why she was later able to play the part of "mistress of Bayreuth" in a manner that was as incomparable as it was questionable. In a letter to the historian Michael Karbaum of 14 October 1974, Beidler spoke of the "institutionalization of the festival after Wagner's death," seeing in it "an especially egregious example of the cultural and sociopolitical amalgam of feudal aristocracy, the new aristocracy of financiers, and members of the upper classes that became the upper stratum of the new Reich and later Wilhelminianism as a result of *commercium et connubium* [commerce and intermarriage]" (417). Cosima Wagner was admirably suited to playing this role by dint of her background.

Beidler's biography of Cosima was based in essence on the belief that it was she herself who was responsible for a shift in emphasis that meant that Wagner's works and their impact were now considered ultraconservative.

> Through the allure of this *grande dame* par excellence, the paradox became a reality, and works that had been created, if not as a slap in the face for the upper crust of society, at least not as a pat on their backs, now became the focus around which this very class foregathered at precisely measured intervals. . . . Although this may suggest the triumph of Wagner's art, what it actually indicated is that an art that had sprung from the democratic movement of the first half of the nineteenth century had now become the mirror, plaything, and even means of transfiguring fin-de-siècle upper-class society. (398–99)

The Second Dethronement: Beidler and the New Bayreuth

Once the Second World War was over and the reopening of the Bayreuth Festival came up for discussion, Franz W. Beidler, the "lost grandson," suddenly found himself in demand again. As early as 1946, Bayreuth's mayor Oskar Meyer approached him with the request that he reorganize the festival; after all, his opposition to National Socialism was the "safest guarantee that the intellectual and artistic derailment that the Bayreuth tradition has suffered under Winifred's leadership and that has had a particularly disastrous effect on the Wagnerian cause will remain a thing of the past" (408). Unsurprisingly, Beidler was "moved, even shaken," when he received this appeal, and he wrote to assure Meyer of his "total willingess to help" (408).

Before the year was over, he had already drawn up a set of "guidelines for the reorganization of the Bayreuth Festival," central to which was the transfer of the estate of Richard and Cosima Wagner to an "autonomous foundation." The honorary president of the council would be Thomas Mann, whom Beidler described as "the internationally leading representative of that 'other Germany,' which in spite of painful experiences to the contrary we still consider to be the true one. . . . He must now be rightfully described as the foremost and profoundest of all Wagnerians in the positive sense of this term" (409).

In *Die Entstehung des Doktor Faustus*, Mann reports on the sense of excitement and agitation occasioned in him by Beidler's proposal. This later account of his response gives the impression that after a brief, albeit intense, period of uncertainty, he rejected the idea of becoming honorary president of the festival foundation. In fact, contemporary sources tell a rather different story. At the time, he showed far greater commitment to Beidler's plan than he was later prepared to admit, losing interest in it only when it turned out that the joint will of Siegfried and Winifred Wagner made it impossible to turn the Wagners' private fortune into a foundation against the express wishes of the Wagner family.[7]

When the Bayreuth Festival finally reopened in 1951 without Beidler's involvement, he registered his misgivings in "Bedenken gegen Bayreuth" (Misgivings about Bayreuth), an essay that was published by the Deutsche Akademie für Sprache und Dichtung (German Academy for Language and Poetry) and that enraged dyed-in-the-wool Wagnerians by continuing to stress Bayreuth's partial responsibility for National Socialism. "All that happened in 1933 is that the seeds of discord that had been sown there for decades finally began to germinate. If National Socialism can be said to have any ideology or any views at all, they are— to a frighteningly large degree—the views of Bayreuth" (301). Beidler could never bring himself to attend the festival, which was run by his cousins, however much he may have respected their work, which represented a radical departure from traditional, well-worn paths. "I am one of the very few people who have decided *not* to forget," he wrote in 1960 (413).

Like his efforts on behalf of Bayreuth, his decades of commitment to the Association of Swiss Writers ended acrimoniously in 1971, when the Gruppe Olten (Olten Group), including a number of Switzerland's leading writers, from Peter Bichsel and Friedrich Dürrenmatt to Max Frisch and Adolf Muschg, decided to leave the association, which had safeguarded the livelihoods of many exiled writers during the Third Reich. The secessionists argued for a political understanding of literature and for the goal of a "democratic, socialist society" (392). However sympathetic Beidler may have been to their aims on the basis of his own experiences in life—shortly before his death he described himself as a "left-wing socialist" (415)—the brusque and publicity-conscious manner of their defection alienated him. His maternal ancestry meant that his socialism was still tinged with an aristocrat's sensitivity to matters of form and good manners.

By the end of his life, Beidler found himself in what he described as "the famous, but not necessarily enviable, position of being caught between two stools. . . . It is no wonder that the older I get, the more I become convinced that contradiction is the true, central task of the 'mind,' if I may express myself in this way" (416). This had also become clear to him as a subscriber to *Neue deutsche Literatur*, a prominent literary journal published in the German Democratic Republic. In 1959 he wrote to invite the editors to show "greater independence and to be more critical of the cultural policies of the Soviet Union," a request that prompted the following reply from Christa Wolf on behalf of the editorial board: "What you demand of us you will not find here even in the future. Why should we write against our own convictions? You will surely not expect this of us?" (416).

In 1977 Beidler was knocked down while waiting at a tram stop and lost a leg, condemning him to four years of suffering before death finally released him on 3 August 1981, only a few months short of his eightieth birthday. In many ways his life had reflected the German history of the twentieth century: as a child he had sat on Cosima Wagner's lap, and in old age he had corresponded with Christa Wolf. It is hard to imagine a greater contrast. As a free socialist who felt committed to Wagner's revolutionary legacy; as an émigré who resisted Wagner's annexation by the National Socialists; as someone who, by marrying a Jewish woman, could not be accused of Wagner's idiosyncratic attitude to the Jews; as an intellectual aristocrat with no time for Wagner's egomania and plebeianism; and as an idealist who avoided and scorned the intrigues of the Bayreuthians, Franz Wilhelm Beidler— this "disinherited heir to the throne" and "lost grandson"—revealed the face of the other, better, truer Wagner, the Wagner whom we can dimly discern behind all his dubious masks. And, with it, we may also glimpse the "ideal" that was so often obscured by his adherents and successors, an ideal that lies behind the human, all-too-human aspects of his troubling personality.[8]

PREFACE

1. Thomas Mann, *Im Schatten Wagners: Thomas Mann über Richard Wagner. Texte und Zeugnisse, 1895–1955,* ed. Hans Rudolf Vaget (Frankfurt am Main, 1999), 38.

2. Ibid., 76.

3. Joachim Kaiser, *Leben mit Richard Wagner* (Munich, 1990), 39.

4. Bernd Zegowitz, *Richard Wagners unvertonte Opern,* Heidelberger Beiträge zur deutschen Literatur, ed. Dieter Borchmeyer, vol. 8 (Frankfurt am Main, 2000).

5. Dieter Borchmeyer and Jörg Salaquarda, eds., *Nietzsche und Wagner: Stationen einer epochalen Begegnung* (Frankfurt am Main and Leipzig, 1994), 509.

6. Ibid., 510.

7. In the introduction to his wide-ranging book *Wagner and Literature* (Manchester, 1982), the Irish Germanist and comparatist Raymond Furness writes: "That a musician should have had such an overwhelming effect on literature is even more remarkable, but the age was ready for a shift towards music in the arts, and it was Wagner who provided a unique and almost mystical stimulus. It . . . may safely be claimed that without Wagner the literature of at least a century would be immeasurably impoverished, as regards topics as well as structures" (p. x).

8. Peter Wapnewski, *Der traurige Gott: Richard Wagner in seinen Helden,* 2d ed. (Berlin, 2001), 23–24.

9. See my "Wagner-Literatur: Eine deutsche Misere. Neue Ansichten zum 'Fall Wagner,' " in *Internationales Archiv für Sozialgeschichte der Literatur* (Tübingen, 1993), 1–62; trans. by Stewart Spencer as "Wagner Literature: A German Embarrassment. New Light on the Case of Wagner," *Wagner* 12 (1991): 51–74 and 116–37.

10. Only in the case of Beckmesser have I included a critical survey of recent books and articles on Wagner, as the claim that Beckmesser is a caricature of a Jew is a classic example of what I mean when I refer to tendentious writings lacking any factual basis.

11. What we need more than anything in Wagner studies is a critical edition of the composer's theoretical writings, few of which are currently available. Among the few recommendable editions in print are Klaus Kropfinger's edition of *Oper und Drama* (Stuttgart, 1984) and Egon Voss's *Späte Schriften zur Dramaturgie der Oper* (Stuttgart, 1996).

12. For the most part, the relevant books and articles are cited in the notes.

CHAPTER ONE. LOVE'S MADNESS, FAIRY-TALE ENCHANTMENT, AND A SICILIAN CARNIVAL: *DIE HOCHZEIT, DIE FEEN,* AND *DAS LIEBESVERBOT*

1. I have purposefully ignored Wagner's first work for the stage, his tragedy *Leubald* (WWV 1), as this was clearly not an opera but a play with music that would have been modeled on Beethoven's incidental music for Goethe's *Egmont.*

2. Wagner probably decided against destroying the music because it had been praised by his composition teacher, the Leipzig Thomaskantor Theodor Weinlig. Wagner later donated the score to the Würzburg Music Society, although he seems to have retained a certain fondness for the work. In 1879 the manuscript score was offered for sale at what Wagner considered an excessive price, with the result that he began legal proceedings in an attempt to regain possession of it. The case dragged on and on, until Wagner finally lost it in February 1881; see WWV, p. 105.

3. See *Richard Wagner: Sämtliche Werke,* ed. Carl Dahlhaus and Egon Voss (Mainz, 1970–), 15:xvii.

4. Quoted in *Die deutsche Literatur: Texte und Zeugnisse. Mittelalter,* ed. Helmut de Boor, vol. 1, bk. 2 (Munich, 1965), 1428–33.

5. Johann Gustav Gottlieb Büsching, *Ritterzeit und Ritterwesen* (Leipzig, 1823), 2:59–60.

6. The motif of a knight fighting in a simple shirt is found elsewhere in medieval literature, notably in the French fabliau *Les trois chevaliers et del chaine* (The three knights and the chain), in which a knight, eager to demonstrate his love, submits to the same trial, sending his lady his blood-soaked shirt, which she provocatively wears at a banquet in the presence of her husband. Büsching retells the plot of this fabliau in some detail in *Ritterzeit und Ritterwesen* (2:164–6), but without referring to *Frauentreue,* which he recounts without mentioning the motif at all. Remarkably, we find a later parodic reminiscence of this motif in the context of Nietzsche's first meeting with Wagner. In his letter to Erwin Rohde dated 9 November 1868, Nietzsche reports the events leading up to the meeting and describes how he had ordered a tailcoat to be made for the occasion. When the tailor's messenger arrived and demanded to be paid at once, Nietzsche refused, and a fight broke out with the man, with the two combatants battling over the tailcoat: "Scene—I'm fighting in my shirttails, as I'm trying to put on the new trousers."

7. For an account of the relationship between *Frauentreue,* Büsching's *Ritterzeit und Ritterwesen,* and Wagner's *Die Hochzeit,* see Bernd Zegowitz, *Richard Wagners unvertonte Opern,* 25–26.

8. Büsching, *Ritterzeit und Ritterwesen,* 2:85–86.

9. On this and the following section, see Kurt Ruh, "Zur Motivik und Interpretation der *Frauentreue,*" in *Festschrift für Ingeborg Schröbler zum 65. Geburtstag,* ed. Dietrich Schmidtke and Helga Schüppert (Tübingen, 1973), 258–72, esp. 261.

10. Ibid., 272.

11. Zegowitz, *Richard Wagners unvertonte Opern,* 37.

12. Ibid., 30.

13. Egon Voss, *"Wagner und kein Ende": Betrachtungen und Studien* (Zurich and Mainz, 1996), 18.

14. See Udo Bermbach, *Der Wahn des Gesamtkunstwerks: Richard Wagners politisch-ästhetische Utopie* (Frankfurt am Main, 1994), 290–97.

15. Voss, *"Wagner und kein Ende,"* 15.

16. Ibid., 26–27.

17. Ibid., 29.

18. E.T.A. Hoffmann, *Werke* (Frankfurt am Main, 1967), 2:254–55 and 257.

19. See Dieter Borchmeyer, *Das Theater Richard Wagners* (Stuttgart, 1982), 402 n. 198.

20. On this and the following sections, see *Richard Wagner: Die Feen,* ed. Michael von Soden and Andreas Loesch (Frankfurt am Main, 1983).

21. Karl Schumann, "Das Delirium der romantischen Zauberoper: Richard Wagners Jugendwerk *Die Feen* im Münchner Theater am Gärtnerplatz," *Süddeutsche Zeitung,* 11 July 1989.

22. Paul Bekker, *Richard Wagner: Das Leben im Werke* (Stuttgart, 1924), 89; trans. by M. M. Bozman as *Richard Wagner: His Life in His Work* (New York, 1931), 79.

23. Werner Breig, "Wagners kompositorisches Werk," in *Richard-Wagner-Handbuch,* ed. Ulrich Müller and Peter Wapnewski (Stuttgart, 1986), 363; trans. by Paul Knight and Horst Loeschmann as "The Musical Works," in *Wagner Handbook,* ed. John Deathridge (Cambridge, Mass., 1992), 405.

24. See Ulrich Müller and Oswald Panagl, " 'Ein Blick sagt mehr als eine Rede': Motiv und Bedeutung des Blicks in den Musikdramen Richard Wagners," in *Bayreuther Festspiele: Das Festspielbuch 2001*, ed. Peter Emmerich (Bayreuth, 2001), 109–121.

25. Jean Starobinski, "Racine et la poétique du regard," in *L'œil vivant* (Paris, 1961), 71–89.

26. See the documentation in *Richard Wagner: Die Feen*, ed. Soden and Loesch, 137–56.

27. The following section is based on the chapter "Revolution der Lust: Richard Wagners *Liebesverbot*," in *Die Götter tanzen Cancan: Richard Wagners Liebesrevolten*, by Dieter Borchmeyer (Heidelberg, 1992), 25–44.

28. See Voss, "*Wagner und kein Ende*," 48.

29. Quoted in *Richard Wagner: Die Feen*, ed. Soden and Loesch, 214–15.

30. For a discussion of the performance history of *Die Feen*, see Oswald Georg Bauer, *Richard Wagner: Die Bühnenwerke von der Uraufführung bis heute* (Frankfurt am Main, Berlin, and Vienna, 1982), 11–15; trans. by Stewart Spencer as *Richard Wagner: The Stage Designs and Productions from the Premières to the Present* (New York, 1983), 13–17.

31. Schumann, "Das Delirium der romantischen Zauberoper."

32. Dieter Rexroth, "Richard Wagners Jugendoper *Das Liebesverbot*," program for the new production at the Bavarian State Opera on 13 February 1983, 5–10.

33. Friedrich Nietzsche, "Warum ich so klug bin," in *Ecce home*, in *Sämtliche Werke: Kritische Studienausgabe in 15 Bänden*, ed. Giorgio Colli and Mazzino Montinari (Munich, 1980), 6:288–89, § 5; trans. by Walter Kaufmann as *Ecce homo*, in *Basic Writings of Nietzsche* (New York, 1968), 703–4.

34. On the score of *Das Liebesverbot* in comparison with that of *Die Feen*, see especially Ludwig Finscher, "Wagner als Opernkomponist: Von den *Feen* zum *Rienzi*," in *Richard Wagner: Von der Oper zum Musikdrama*, ed. Stefan Kunze (Bern, 1978), 25–46; see also Friedrich Lippmann, "*Die Feen* und *Das Liebesverbot*, oder Die Wagnerisierung diverser Vorbilder," in *Wagnerliteratur—Wagnerforschung*, ed. Carl Dahlhaus and Egon Voss (Mainz, 1985), 14–46; and Egon Voss, "Wagners *Jugendsünde?* Zur großen komischen Oper *Das Liebesverbot oder Die Novize von Palermo*," in "*Wagner und kein Ende*," 44–58. By far the most outspoken defense of Wagner's early works, including *Rienzi*, is that of Joachim Kaiser, "Das verfemte Frühwerk," in *Leben mit Wagner* (Munich, 1990), 39–84. Kaiser draws particular attention to the thematic links between these early operas and Wagner's mature music dramas.

35. See Walter Pache, "Shakespeares *Measure for Measure* und Richard Wagners Jugendwerk *Das Liebesverbot*," *arcadia: Zeitschrift für vergleichende Literaturwissenschaft* 12 (1977): 1–16. That Wagner's "free sensuality" falls somewhat short of the claims that he makes for it in his autobiographical writings, ultimately culminating in marriage, is a point well made by Egon Voss in "*Wagner und kein Ende*," 54.

36. Voss, in "*Wagner und kein Ende*," 53.

37. Quoted by Rexroth, "Richard Wagners Jugendoper," 6.

38. Nietzsche, *Zur Genealogie der Moral*, pt. 3, ch. 2 of *Sämtliche Werke*, 5:340; English trans. Kaufmann, *Basic Writings of Nietzsche*, 98.

39. WWV, p. 138.

40. Voss, "*Wagner und kein Ende*," 49.

41. *Johann Wolfgang von Goethes Werke: Hamburger Ausgabe* (Munich, 1981), 10:485 and 514–15; trans. by Robert R. Heitner as "Italian Journey," in *Goethe: The Collected Works* (Princeton, 1994), 6:390–91, 413, and 414.

42. Gerhart von Graevenitz sees a link between Wagner's idea of a popular king and the German Romantics' theory of the state. "The true king will be a republic, the true republic

a king," Novalis wrote in *Glaube und Liebe*, and Achim von Arnim reminds the "revolutionarily minded" ruler that "the voice of the nation" resounds "in his own breast"; see Graevenitz, *Zur Geschichte einer Denkwohnheit* (Stuttgart, 1987), 269.

CHAPTER TWO. ON THE USES AND DISADVANTAGES OF HISTORY FOR THE MUSIC DRAMA—GRAND OPERA: *DIE HOHE BRAUT, RIENZI,* AND THEIR CONSEQUENCES

1. Richard Wagner, *Sämtliche Werke*, ed. Carl Dahlhaus and Egon Voss (Mainz, 1970–), vol. 31 (in preparation).

2. Isolde Vetter, " 'Leubald. Ein Trauerspiel.' Richard Wagners erstes (erhaltenes) Werk," in *Die Programmhefte der Bayreuther Festspiele 1988* 7 (*Die Meistersinger von Nürnberg*), 1–19 and 95–208.

3. Johann Wolfgang von Goethe, *Dramen, 1765–1775*, ed. Peter Huber and Dieter Borchmeyer (Frankfurt am Main, 1985), 281.

4. The following section is based on the chapter "Die Franzosen vor Nizza oder Revolution aus Liebe," in *Die Götter tanzen Cancan: Richard Wagners Liebesrevolten*, by Dieter Borchmeyer (Heidelberg, 1992), 45–90.

5. See WWV, p. 149. For a detailed description of the source, together with an account of the genesis of the opera and its subsequent fate, see Isolde Vetter, "Wagnerforschung— literarisch. Richard Wagner als Librettist von Johann Friedrich Kittls Oper *Bianca und Giuseppe, oder: Die Franzosen vor Nizza* (1848)," in *Wagnerliteratur—Wagnerforschung*, ed. Carl Dahlhaus and Egon Voss (Mainz, 1985), 163–80; trans. by Stewart Spencer as "Wagner and Kittl," *Wagner* 5 (1984): 20–30.

6. See Wagner's letter to August Lewald of 12 November 1838, Richard Wagner, *Sämtliche Briefe*, ed. Gertrud Strobel and others (Leipzig, 1967–2000, and Wiesbaden, 1999–), 1:352–53.

7. Wagner, *Sämtliche Briefe*, 1:323–27.

8. WWV, p. 147. The 1840 sketch was first published in *Wagner* 4 (1983): 13–26; the 1838 draft appeared in *Wagner* 10 (1989): 50–65.

9. See the section on grand opera in Gerhart von Graevenitz, *Mythos: Zur Geschichte einer Denkgewohnheit* (Stuttgart, 1987), 262–66, esp. 265–66.

10. Heinrich Heine, *Sämtliche Werke*, ed. Werner Vordtriede (Munich, 1972), 3:125.

11. See also Udo Bermbach, *Der Wahn des Gesamtkunstwerks: Richard Wagners politisch-ästhetische Utopie* (Frankfurt am Main, 1994), 33–36.

12. See Ludwig Finscher, "Auber's *La muette de Portici* und die Anfänge der Grand-opéra," in *Festschrift Heinz Becker*, ed. Jürgen Schläder (Laaber, 1982), 87–105.

13. See Dietmar Rieger, "*La muette de Portici* von Auber/Scribe: Eine Revolutionsoper mit antirevolutionärem Libretto," *Romanistische Zeitschrift für Literaturgeschichte* 10 (1986), 349–59; Albert Gier, "Jakobiner-Austreibung: Das Volk in den Grands Opéras von Eugène Scribe," in *"Weine, weine du armes Volk": Das verführte und betrogene Volk auf der Bühne*, ed. Peter Csobadi and others (Anif/Salzburg, 1995), 233–42; and Herbert Schneider and Nicole Wild, *La muette de Portici: Kritische Ausgabe des Librettos und Dokumentation der ersten Inszenierung* (Tübingen, 1993). Schneider has examined the different versions of the libretto in some detail and believes that it was only in the course of their work on the original three-act opera that Scribe and Auber invested the libretto with features that can be interpreted as antirevolutionary, a development due not least to their regard for the censor. In spite of this, contemporary audiences had no difficulty reading between the lines and discerning revolutionary tendencies in the work. The revolutionary vocabulary is far more explicit in the original version of the libretto and the oppression of

the populace far more graphically illustrated. This version begins with an account of the fishermen's imminent uprising, which initially appears in a wholly positive light. At this stage, Masaniello joins in the uprising for purely political reasons and not in order to avenge the wrong done to Fenella, who in this version is still his daughter. Later in this version, Masaniello begins to distance himself from the fanaticism of the mob and from the lack of scruples shown by its demagogic ringleaders, here embodied in the figure of Pietro. Here, too, the populace's lack of character and inability to make up its mind is far more implacably condemned than in the final version of the libretto. Goethe's remark to Eckermann in a conversation on 14 March 1831 to the effect that the "whole opera is basically a satire of the common people" is certainly true of this original version. At the end, the old oppressors are acclaimed by the people and the rebellion ends in total failure, with the result that the ending is so depressing and even cynical that the opera could never have succeeded onstage in this form, a point that the *jury de lecture* duly noted in its report.

14. On the dramaturgy of grand opera, see Anselm Gerhard, *Die Verstädterung der Oper: Paris und das Musiktheater des 19. Jahrhunderts* (Stuttgart and Weimar, 1992); trans. by Mary Whittall as *The Urbanization of Opera* (Chicago, 1998).

15. Finscher, "Auber's *La muette de Portici*," 99.

16. See Henning Krauß, ed., *Literatur der Französischen Revolution: Eine Einführung* (Stuttgart, 1988), esp. 36–50 (revolutionary audiences), 51–93 (the theater), 94–113 (revolutionary songs), and 168–91 (rhetoric).

17. See Finscher, "Auber's *La muette de Portici*," 99.

18. Graevenitz, *Mythos*, 266.

19. Ibid., 263.

20. Christhard Frese, *Dramaturgie der großen Oper Giacomo Meyerbeers* (Berlin-Lichterfelde, 1970), 19.

21. Ibid., 204.

22. See Vetter, "Wagnerforschung—literarisch," 173.

23. Bernd Zegowitz, *Richard Wagners unvertonte Opern* (Frankfurt am Main, 2000), 51–57. Here Zegowitz takes issue with my standpoint (Borchmeyer, *Die Götter tanzen Cancan*), arguing that the depoliticization of Kittl's libretto reflects a conscious change of attitude on Wagner's part between the German and French drafts of 1838 and 1840. But the French draft is so brief, not least as a result of the suppression of all the passages in dialogue form, that it is difficult to decide whether any given motif has been omitted for political reasons or merely with the intention of shortening the draft.

24. Georg Wilhelm Friedrich Hegel, *Vorlesungen über die Philosophie der Geschichte*, ed. Theodor Litt (Stuttgart, 1961), 593.

25. See Dieter Borchmeyer, " 'Altes Recht' und Revolution: Schillers *Wilhelm Tell*," in *Friedrich Schiller: Kunst, Humanität und Politik in der späten Aufklärung*, ed. Wolfgang Witkowski (Tübingen, 1982), 69–113.

26. See Isolde Vetter's line of reasoning in "Wagnerforschung—literarisch," 173.

27. Quoted by Finscher, "Auber's *La muette de Portici*," 99.

28. Wagner, *Sämtliche Briefe*, 2:586–87.

29. Here Wagner is thinking of the February Revolution that broke out in Paris in 1848, although he may also be alluding to the July Revolution of 1830. It seems unlikely, however, that he is referring to the Revolution of 1789, which he generally described only in negative terms, thus making it all the more astonishing that he invests this event with such positive features in *Die hohe Braut*. In *My Life* he recalls correcting the proofs of Karl Friedrich Becker's *Weltgeschichte* in 1830.

I remember being absolutely horrified by the heroes of the French Revolution as described here; knowing nothing of France's earlier history, I found that my tender human sympathies were outraged by the atrocities of the revolutionaries, and my feelings were dominated by these purely human emotions for so long that even in later years it cost me a real struggle to devote my attention to the purely political significance of those tremendous events.

It was while Wagner was working on these proofs for his brother-in-law that the July Revolution broke out in Paris: "The world of history came alive for me from that day on; and naturally I supported the revolution, which assumed the form of a courageous and victorious popular struggle untainted by the terrible excesses of the first French Revolution" (ML 46–47). In *Die hohe Braut*, Wagner projected this positive image of the July Revolution on the French Revolution of 1789. Only in this way could he celebrate the event in the theater.

30. Wagner, *Sämtliche Briefe*, 2:590.

31. Ibid., 2:587.

32. Ibid.

33. In his book *Wagners unvertonte Opern* (86–100), Bernd Zegowitz presents a convincing case for interpreting *Die glückliche Bärenfamilie* as a "German *Spieloper* with Biedermeier elements" in the manner of Lortzing, Flotow, and Nicolai.

34. Egon Voss, " 'Mit Abscheu ließ ich die Arbeit liegen': Zu den wiederaufgetauchten Manuskripten von Wagners komischer Oper *Männerlist größer als Frauenlist oder Die glückliche Bärenfamilie*," in *Richard Wagners unvollendete Jugendoper "Männerlist größer als Frauenlist oder Die glückliche Bärenfamilie." Komische Oper in zwei Akten nach Tausendundeiner Nacht*, ed. Richard-Wagner-Museum mit Nationalarchiv und Forschungsstätte der Richard-Wagner-Stiftung Bayreuth (Berlin, 1996), 23–29.

35. See WWV, pp. 164–92; John Deathridge's definitive book on the opera's genesis, *Wagner's* Rienzi: *A Reappraisal Based on a Study of the Sketches and Drafts* (Oxford, 1977); and Egon Voss's afterword to his edition of the libretto, *Rienzi: Vollständiges Textbuch. Nach der Originalpartitur herausgegeben von Egon Voss* (Stuttgart, 1983), 67–80. Equally indispensable is Reinhard Strohm's Dokumentenband (volume of documentary sources), *Richard Wagner: Sämtliche Werke*, vol. 23 (Mainz, 1976).

36. Quoted from Voss's *Rienzi*, 11.

37. Here and later, my account is based on Konrad Burdach's classic book *Rienzo und die geistige Wandlung seiner Zeit* (Berlin, 1928). On the theme of the returning phoenix, see 61–94. See also Walther Rehm, *Europäische Romdichtung*, 2d ed. (Munich, 1960), 77–79.

38. On the historical background and the sources of Wagner's Rienzi, as well as an examination of other versions of the story, see Helmut Kirchmeyer's comprehensive and gripping account, *Das zeitgenössische Wagner-Bild*. Vol. 1: *Wagner in Dresden* (Regensburg, 1972); see also Elisabeth Frenzel, *Stoffe der Weltliteratur* (Stuttgart, 1981), 641–43.

39. Wagner changed this line when setting the text to music; see Voss, *Rienzi*, 21. In GS 1:48 it reads "Der ganzen Welt gehöre Rom" [May Rome belong to the whole world].

40. In the full score, this line reads "die ihr verloren" [the men you've lost]; see Voss, *Rienzi*, 49.

41. Burdach, *Rienzo und die geistige Wandlung seiner Zeit*, 117.

42. On this point, see ibid., 25–27.

43. Friedrich Engels, *Cola di Rienzi: Ein unbekannter dramatischer Entwurf*, ed. Michael Knieriem (Wuppertal, 1974).

44. Ibid., 27.

45. Ibid., 42.

46. Ibid.

47. Ibid., 16.

48. *Sämmtliche Werke von Julius Mosen* (Oldenburg, 1863), 3:380.

49. Ibid., 389–90.

50. See Burdach, *Rienzo und die geistige Wandlung seiner Zeit*, 41–61.

51. Quoted ibid., 49–50.

52. See Voss, *Rienzi*, 66.

53. August Kubizek, *Adolf Hitler: Mein Jugendfreund* (Graz and Göttingen, 1953), 142 and 343; trans. as *Young Hitler: The Story of Our Friendship* (Maidstone, 1973), 65–66.

54. Albert Speer, *Spandauer Tagebücher* (Frankfurt am Main, 1975), 136; trans. by Richard Winston and Clara Winston as *Spandau: The Secret Diaries* (London, 2000), 88.

55. Speer, *Spandauer Tagebücher*, 136, and *Spandau*, trans. Winston and Winston, 88.

56. This point needs to be stressed in order to refute the claims that Theodor W. Adorno advanced in his *Versuch über Wagner* (Frankfurt am Main, 1974), 10–11; trans. by Rodney Livingstone as *In Search of Wagner* (London, 1981), 13–14; see also Ernst Hanisch, "Ein Wagnerianer namens Adolf Hitler," in *Richard Wagner, 1883–1983: Die Rezeption im 19. und 20. Jahrhundert* (Stuttgart, 1984), 65–75. Even as levelheaded and meticulous a scholar as Egon Voss has claimed in his edition of the libretto that "the affinity between, on the one hand, the subject matter, its presentation, and, above all, the eponymous hero and, on the other, Fascism, National Socialism, and the Third Reich, with its associations of *Volk* and Führer, is impossible to overlook." Voss draws attention to what he sees as the parallels between the lives of Rienzi and Hitler, concluding that although there is no "direct causality" between Rienzi and Hitler, "it would be tantamount to a dangerous suppression of the truth to continue to deny a link between them"; see Voss, *Rienzi*, 67–68; see also Voss, *"Wagner und kein Ende": Betrachtungen und Studien* (Zurich and Mainz, 1996), 59–60. But Voss is guilty of putting the cart before the horse here.

57. Bermbach, *Der Wahn des Gesamtkunstwerks,* 37–54, esp. 47.

58. Graevenitz, *Mythos*, 261 and 263.

59. See the afterword to Voss's, *Rienzi*, 76, and *"Wagner und kein Ende,"* 68. Voss argues that neither *La muette de Portici* nor *Robert le diable* was an important influence on *Rienzi*. Dramaturgically speaking, he believes that Spontini's *Fernand Cortez* was of far greater importance, and the work's musical models are to be sought in Italian operas, especially Bellini.

60. See Wagner, *Sämtliche Briefe*, 10:261–65.

61. Gotthold Ephraim Lessing, *Briefe 1753* (letters 22 and 23).

62. On the monopolization of force and the emotional control associated with modern centralized politics as practiced by absolutist courts, see the groundbreaking book by Norbert Elias, *Über den Prozeß der Zivilisation*, 2d ed. (Bern and Munich, 1969).

63. *Sämmtliche Werke von Julius Mosen*, 3:23.

64. Graevenitz mistakenly attempts to claim as his own the standpoint adopted by Rienzi's fellow conspirators; see his *Mythos*, 263. In general, he paints an extremely distorted picture of Rienzi, even describing him as a "perverse Brutus who puts private love before patriotic duty and who, in his concern to show mercy to the few, neglects to protect the many" (264). It is difficult to imagine a more comprehensive misreading of Wagner's opera.

65. In Mozart's case, Metastasio's libretto was substantially altered by Caterino Mazzolà. Here the ruler's *clementia* is humanized and depoliticized in the spirit of the Age of Sensibility; see Dieter Borchmeyer, "Herrschergüte versus Staatsraison: Politik und Empfindsamkeit in Mozarts 'La clemenza di Tito,'" in *Bürgersinn und Kritik: Festschrift für Udo Bermbach zum 60. Geburtstag*, ed. Michael Th. Greven, Herfried Münkler, and Rainer Schmalz-Bruns (Baden-Baden, 1998), 345–66.

66. According to Graevenitz, "In the figure of Masaniello, *La muette de Portici* established a type of hero who is characteristic of the whole genre, a man who, however well meaning, hesitates and is led astray"; see his *Mythos*, 262. If this is true, then Rienzi is the very antithesis of the typical grand operatic hero.

67. For a detailed analysis of *Die Sarazenin* and its structural affinities with grand opera, see Zegowitz, *Richard Wagners unvertonte Opern*, 103–41.

68. Wagner, *Sämtliche Briefe*, 4:274.

69. See Petra-Hildegard Wilberg, *Richard Wagners mythische Welt: Versuche wider den Historismus* (Freiburg im Breisgau, 1996), esp. 77–184. Wilberg's book is the most important and detailed account of Wagner's theory of myth. Thanks not least to its close reading of *The Wibelungs*, it succeeds in demonstrating how closely Wagner's view of history is bound up retrospectively with myth.

70. Graevenitz, *Mythos*, 270.

71. WWV, pp. 329–30.

72. See Dieter Borchmeyer, "Die 'Erlösung' des Romans im musikalischen Drama," in *Das Theater Richard Wagners* (Stuttgart, 1982), 125–51; trans. by Stewart Spencer as "The 'Redemption' of the Romance in the Musical Drama," in *Richard Wagner: Theory and Theatre* (Oxford, 1991), 128–59; and Dieter Borchmeyer, "Thomas Mann und Richard Wagners Anti-Poetik des Romans," in *Poetik und Geschichte: Viktor Žmegač zum 60. Geburtstag*, ed. Dieter Borchmeyer (Tübingen, 1989), 390–411.

73. Quoted by Auguste Ehrard, "L'Opéra sous la direction Véron (1831–35)," *Revue musicale de Lyon* 5 (1907/8): 81.

74. Quoted by Danièle Piston, "L'Opéra de Paris au siècle romantique," *Revue internationale de musique française* 4 (1981): 8.

75. Friedrich Nietzsche, *Sämtliche Werke: Kritische Studienausgabe in 15 Bänden*, ed. Giorgio Colli and Mazzino Montinari (Munich, 1980), 6:34; trans. by Walter Kaufmann as "The Case of Wagner," in *Basic Writings of Nietzsche* (New York, 1968), 632.

76. See Graevenitz, *Mythos*, 269. Graevenitz is, of course, guilty of exaggeration when he claims that "Shaw's much lauded political allegory of the *Ring* is no more than an extension of Heine's allegory of *Robert le diable*, a similarity that extends even to the ironic style. In short, it, too, is a hermeneutic mirror image of the literary procedure adopted in the grand operas of Scribe and Wagner" (269). Since Graevenitz sees Wagner merely as a follower of Scribe, Shaw's interpretation of Wagner is bound to seem a pale imitation of Heine's interpretation of Scribe.

77. Jane Fulcher, "Meyerbeer and the Music of Society," *The Musical Quarterly* 67 (1981): 214: "Meyerbeer's style, then, was social for many critics in nineteenth-century France, who saw it as suited to a theatre that depicted collective groups and grand moral ideals."

CHAPTER THREE. THE TRANSFORMATIONS OF AHASUERUS:
THE FLYING DUTCHMAN AND HIS METAMORPHOSES

1. Robert W. Gutman, *Richard Wagner: The Man, His Mind, and His Music* (London, 1968), 89.

2. See Hans-Jürgen Schrader's detailed chapter "Schnabelewopskis und Wagners *Fliegender Holländer*," which examines all the known sources of the work, in *Heinrich Heine und die Romantik*, ed. Markus Winkler (Tübingen, 1997), 191–224.

3. Ulrich Weisstein, "Wagner loben ist nicht schwer, Wagner lesen um so mehr: Produktion, Reproduktion und Rezeption in Sentas Ballade im zweiten Akt des *Fliegenden Holländers*," *Jahrbuch Deutsch als Fremdsprache 1987*, 42–64, esp. 50.

4. Richard Wagner, *Sämtliche Briefe*, ed. Gertrud Strobel and others (Leipzig, 1967–2000, and Wiesbaden 1999–), 2:314.

5. See Dieter Borchmeyer, "Heinrich Heine und sein abtrünniger Adept: Richard Wagner," in *Literatur im Wandel: Festschrift für Viktor Žmegač zum 70. Geburtstag*, ed. Marijan Bobinač (Zagreb, 1999), 53–72, esp. 62–63.

6. Quoted from Richard Wagner, *Ausgewählte Schriften*, ed. Dietrich Mack (Frankfurt am Main, 1974), 110 (Mack reproduces the text of the first edition). On Wagner's later revisions, see Karl Richter, "Absage und Verleugnung: Die Verdrängung Heinrich Heines aus Werk und Bewußtsein Richard Wagners," in *Musikkonzepte 5: Wie antisemitisch darf ein Künstler sein?* ed. Heinz-Klaus Metzger and Rainer Riehn (Munich, 1978), 5–15, esp. 8–9. See also Isolde Vetter, *"Der fliegende Holländer" von Richard Wagner: Entstehung, Bearbeitung, Überlieferung* (diss., Technische Universität, Berlin, 1982).

7. Quoted by Peter Bloom, "The Fortunes of the Flying Dutchman in France," *Wagner* 8 (1987): 42–66; for a detailed examination of the relationship between Dietsch's *Le vaisseau fantôme* and Wagner's opera, see Barry Millington, "The Sources and Genesis of the Text," in *Richard Wagner: "Der fliegende Holländer,"* ed. Thomas Grey (Cambridge, 2000), 25–35.

8. See Elisabeth Frenzel, *Stoffe der Weltliteratur* (Stuttgart, 1981), 330–31.

9. On the origins and history of this myth, see Monika Körte and Robert Stockhammer, eds., *Ahasvers Spur: Dichtungen und Dokumente vom "Ewigen Juden"* (Leipzig, 1995).

10. Frenzel, *Stoffe der Weltliteratur*, 15–21.

11. Quoted by Friedrich Sengle, *Biedermeierzeit* (Stuttgart, 1971), 1:2. For many of the ideas in this section, I am indebted to Sengle's definitive book on the age of Weltschmerz, esp. 1:1–33.

12. Johann Nestroy, *Komödien*, ed. Franz H. Mauthner (Frankfurt am Main, 1979), 3:16. (This quotation is taken from act 1, scene 4.)

13. Heinrich Heine, *Sämtliche Werke*, ed. Werner Vordtriede (Munich, 1969), 2:579.

14. Adelbert von Chamisso, *Sämtliche Werke*, ed. Volker Hoffmann (Munich, 1975), 1:611–13.

15. See Sengle, *Biedermeierzeit*, 1:8.

16. Georg Büchner, *Werke und Briefe*, ed. Werner R. Lehmann (Munich, 1988), 119. The "song" referred to earlier is Christian Friedrich Daniel Schubart's poem *Der ewige Jude*.

17. Ibid., 124.

18. Ibid., 391.

19. Ibid., 69. On the theme of love and death in Büchner and its affinities with Wagner, see Walter Hinderer, "Liebessemantik als Provokation," in *Codierungen von Liebe in der Kunstperiode*, ed. Walter Hinderer (Würzburg, 1997), 311–38, esp. 335–37.

20. Gerhart von Graevenitz, *Mythos: Geschichte einer Denkgewohnheit* (Stuttgart, 1987), 273.

21. WWV, p. 225.

22. Quoted in Graevenitz, *Mythos,* 272.

23. Wilhelm Hauff, *Hauffs Werke*, ed. Max Drescher (Leipzig, n.d.), 2:76.

24. Ibid., 81.

25. Quoted by Sengle, *Biedermeierzeit*, 1:5.

26. Charlotte Stieglitz, *Gedichte und Briefe*, ed. Franz Josef Görtz (Frankfurt am Main, 1987), and Sengle, *Biedermeierzeit,* 1:6.

27. According to Karl Simrock, "the legend of the Wandering Jew derives from that of the Wild Huntsman"; see *Deutsche Mythologie*, 6th ed. (Berlin, 1887), 206. A copy of the 1869 edition of Simrock's book was in Wagner's library in Wahnfried.

28. See Wolfram von Eschenbach, *Parzival und Titurel*, ed. Karl Simrock (Stuttgart, 1862), 2:535. Wagner owed his knowledge of Wolfram's *Parzival* in part to Simrock's edition. Like Grimm (see later in the text), Simrock posited a link between Herodias—who, as so often at this period, was identified with her daughter Salome—and the Wild Hunt: "It is said that Herodias was consumed by love for John the Baptist, a love that he did not return; when his head was brought to her on a salver and she tried to cover it with tears and kisses, it recoiled and began to blow furiously, so that the hapless woman was blown away into space." Since then she has been "at the head of the Wild Hunt." See Wolf-Daniel Hartwich, *"Deutsche Mythologie": Die Erfindung einer nationalen Kunstreligion* (Berlin and Vienna, 2000), 192–93.

29. Frenzel, *Stoffe der Weltliteratur,* 365–67.

30. See Peter Szondi, *Das Lyrische Drama des Fin de siècle* (Frankfurt am Main, 1975), 40–42.

31. Heine, *Sämtliche Werke*, 1:383–84.

32. Jacob Grimm, *Deutsche Mythologie*, 2d ed. (Göttingen, 1844), 260–62.

33. See Secundus Reimarus, *Geschichte der Salome von Cato bis Oscar Wilde* (Leipzig, 1907/8), reissued in 1913 as *Stoffgeschichte der Salome-Dichtung*. Suffice it to mention Flaubert's "Hérodias" from his *Trois contes* (1877). Like Wilde, Flaubert draws a distinction between Salome and Herodias but, unlike Wilde, provides no erotic motive for the killing of John the Baptist. (Jules Laforgue's parody is aimed in part at Flaubert's version of the tale.)

34. See Erwin Koppen, *Dekadenter Wagnerismus: Studien zur europäischen Literatur des Fin de siècle* (Berlin and New York, 1973).

35. Quoted in Szondi, *Das Lyrische Drama*, 48.

36. Quoted in *Ahasvers Spur*, ed. Körte and Stockhammer, 189–91; trans. E.F.J. Payne as *Parerga and Paralipomena* (Oxford, 1974), 2:261.

37. Friedrich Nietzsche, *Sämtliche Werke: Kritische Studienausgabe in 15 Bänden*, ed. Giorgio Colli and Mazzino Montinari (Munich, 1980), 6:18; trans. by Walter Kaufmann as "The Case of Wagner," in *Basic Writings of Nietzsche* (New York, 1968), 617.

38. Wagner, *Sämtliche Briefe*, 9:137.

39. See Susanne Vill, ed., *"Das Weib der Zukunft": Frauengestalten und Frauenstimmen bei Richard Wagner* (Stuttgart, 2000); see also Dieter Borchmeyer, " 'Über das Weibliche im Menschlichen' in Richard Wagners Musikdramen," in *"Das Weib der Zukunft,"* ed. Vill, 34–43.

40. Ernst Bloch, *Das Prinzip Hoffnung* (Frankfurt am Main, 1959), 1628; trans. by Neville Plaice, Stephen Plaice, and Paul Knight as *The Principle of Hope* (Oxford, 1986), 1376.

41. Hans Mayer, *Richard Wagner*, ed. Wolfgang Hofer (Frankfurt am Main, 1998), 76; see also Dieter Borchmeyer, *Das Theater Richard Wagners* (Stuttgart, 1982), 185–87 (the chapter containing these pages was not taken over into the English translation of 1991).

42. See Borchmeyer, *Das Theater Richard Wagners*, 187–89.

43. See the detailed book by Andrea Schneider, *Die parodierten Musikdramen Richard Wagners: Geschichte und Dokumentation Wagnerscher Opernparodien im deutschsprachigen Raum von der Mitte des 19. Jahrhunderts bis zum Ende des Ersten Weltkrieges* (Anif/Salzburg, 1996).

44. Nietzsche, *Sämtliche Werke,* 6:34, and *Basic Writings of Nietzsche*, trans. Kaufmann, 631–32.

45. See Borchmeyer, *Das Theater Richard Wagners*, 358–59; and Dieter Borchmeyer and Stephan Kohler, eds., *Wagner Parodien* (Frankfurt am Main, 1983), 282–315.

46. See Vetter, *"Der fliegende Holländer,"* 19.

47. See Schneider, *Die parodierten Musikdramen*, 39–44.

48. Quoted in *Wagner Parodien*, ed. Borchmeyer and Kohler, 170.

49. Ibid., 153.

50. Ibid., 154.

51. Ibid., 169.

52. Ibid., 192.

53. Ibid., 174.

54. Ibid., 196–97.

55. Ibid., 141.

56. Ibid., 143.

57. Ibid., 147.

58. Ibid., 141.

59. Ibid., 144.

60. Ibid., 146–47.

61. See Dieter Borchmeyer, "Richard Wagner und der Antisemitismus," in *Wagner-Handbuch*, ed. Ulrich Müller and Peter Wapnewski (Stuttgart, 1986), 137–61, esp. 149–50; trans. by Stewart Spencer as "The Question of Anti-Semitism," in *Wagner Handbook*, ed. John Deathridge (Cambridge, Mass., 1992), 166–85.

CHAPTER FOUR. VENUS IN EXILE: *TANNHÄUSER* BETWEEN
ROMANTICISM AND YOUNG GERMANY

1. See Volker Mertens, "Richard Wagner und das Mittelalter," in *Richard-Wagner-Handbuch*, ed. Ulrich Müller and Peter Wapnewski (Stuttgart, 1986), 19–59; trans. by Stewart Spencer as "Wagner's Middle Ages," in *Wagner Handbook*, ed. John Deathridge (Cambridge, Mass., 1992), 236–68. A fuller version of this article appeared under the same title in *Richard Wagner und sein Mittelalter*, ed. Ursula Müller and Ulrich Müller (Anif/Salzburg 1989), 9–84, esp. 14–23. This volume of essays also included an earlier version of the present chapter, "Venus im Exil: Antike und Moderne im Mittelalter. Eine Studie über Wagners *Tannhäuser*," 103–34.

2. Thomas Mann, *Gesammelte Werke* (Frankfurt am Main, 1974), 12:76–77.

3. Heine, *Sämtliche Werke*, ed. Werner Vordtriede (Munich, 1972), 3:565.

4. Ludwig Tieck, *Erzählungen des Phantasus* (Nuremberg, 1946), 42–43.

5. Ibid., 70.

6. Heine, *Sämtliche Werke*, 2:707.

7. Charles Baudelaire, "Richard Wagner et *Tannhäuser* à Paris," in *Œuvres complètes*, ed. Claude Pichois (Paris, 1976), 2:794; trans. by Jonathan Mayne as "Richard Wagner and *Tannhäuser* in Paris," in *The Painter of Modern Life and Other Essays* (London, 1995), 125.

8. Baudelaire, "Richard Wagner et *Tannhäuser* à Paris," 2:790, and "Richard Wagner and *Tannhäuser* in Paris," trans. Mayne, 122.

9. See Dolf Sternberger, "Ein geheimer Sängerkrieg zwischen Richard Wagner und Heinrich Heine," in *Die Programmhefte der Bayreuther Festspiele 1973* 2 (*Tannhäuser*), 69–80, reprinted in *Richard Wagner: Tannhäuser. Texte, Materialien, Kommentare*, ed. Attila Csampai and Dietmar Holland (Reinbek, 1986), 256–71; see also Stewart Spencer, "*Tannhäuser*: Mediävistische Handlung in drei Aufzügen," *Wagner 1976* (London, 1976), 40–53. On the question of Wagner's sources, see Mertens, "Wagner und das Mittelalter," 21–26; English trans. "Wagner's Middle Ages," trans. Spencer, 238–41; Mary A. Cicora, *From History to Myth: Wagner's Tannhäuser and Its Literary Sources* (Berlin, 1992); and

the articles by Volker Mertens (15–31) and Ulrich Müller (32–46) in *Richard Wagner: ". . . der Welt noch den Tannhäuser schuldig,"* ed. Irene Erfen (Regensburg, 1999).

10. Heine, *Sämtliche Werke*, 3:569.

11. Ibid., 575.

12. E.T.A. Hoffmann, *Poetische Werke* (Berlin, 1957), 6:57.

13. C.T.L. Lucas, *Ueber den Krieg von Wartburg* (Königsberg, 1838), 270.

14. Ibid., 43.

15. Reproduced in the original, together with English and French translations, in *Die Programmhefte der Bayreuther Festspiele 1985* 1 (*Tannhäuser*), 1–14.

16. Hoffmann, *Poetische Werke*, 6:39–40.

17. See Dieter Borchmeyer, *Das Theater Richard Wagners* (Stuttgart, 1982), 194–95 (this passage was not taken over into the 1991 English translation).

18. For a comparison between Wagner's and Mangold's operas, see Heleen Mendl-Schrama, "The other *Tanhäuser*," *Wagner* 7 (1986): 83–94; see also Elisabeth Frenzel, *Stoffe der Weltliteratur* (Stuttgart, 1976), 731–33.

19. Tieck, *Erzählungen des Phantasus*, 61.

20. See Frenzel, *Stoffe der Weltliteratur*, 713–16.

21. Heine, *Sämtliche Werke*, 3:560–61.

22. Ibid., 2:612.

23. Richard Wagner, *Sämtliche Briefe*, ed. Gertrud Strobel and others (Leipzig, 1967–2000, and Wiesbaden, 1999–), 2:153.

24. On the importance of representations of the Madonna in Wagner's works, see Peter Wapnewski, *Der traurige Gott: Richard Wagner in seinen Helden* (Munich, 1978), 89–113; Borchmeyer, *Das Theater Richard Wagners*, 282–86; trans. by Stewart Spencer as *Richard Wagner: Theory and Theatre* (Oxford, 1991), 362–65.

25. Heine, *Sämtliche Werke*, 2:616.

26. Ibid., 787.

27. Ibid., 1:694–96.

28. Ibid., 3:270.

29. See Olaf Briese, "Venus—Madonna—Maria: Über Heines Marienverständnis," in *Aufklärung und Skepsis: Internationaler Heine-Kongreß 1997 zum 200. Geburtstag*, ed. Joseph A. Kruse, Bernd Witte, and Karin Füllner (Stuttgart and Weimar, 1998), 436–49.

30. Gabriele Brandstetter, *Erotik und Religiosität: Zur Lyrik Clemens Brentanos* (Munich, 1986), 26–28.

31. Edgar Wind, *Pagan Mysteries in the Renaissance* (London, 1958), 75–77.

32. Ibid., 77.

33. Brandstetter, *Erotik und Religiosität*, 29.

34. See Heide Eilert, "Madonna—Verderberin und Venus," in *Das Kunstzitat in der erzählenden Dichtung: Studien zur Literatur um 1900* (Stuttgart, 1991), 125–36.

35. Rudolf Kassner, *Englische Dichter* (Leipzig, 1920), 139.

36. Mann, *Gesammelte Werke*, 8:202.

37. Quoted in Joseph von Eichendorffs *Das Marmorbild: Erläuterungen und Dokumente*, ed. Hanna H. Marks (Stuttgart, 1984), 86–88.

38. Joseph von Eichendorff, *Joseph Freiherrn von Eichendorffs Werke*, ed. Gustav Karpeles (Leipzig, n.d.), 2:100.

39. Tieck, *Erzählungen des Phantasus*, 72.

40. Eichendorff, *Eichendorffs Werke*, 2:105–6.

41. Dietz-Rüdiger Moser, *Die Tannhäuser-Legende: Eine Studie über Intentionalität und Rezeption katechetischer Volkserzählungen zum Buß-Sakrament* (Berlin and New York, 1977).

42. Burghart Wachinger has proposed an alternative explanation of the origins of the Tannhäuser Ballad, suggesting that it is a variant of the folktale in which a mortal marries a woman from another world; he stays with her in her own world (sometimes depicted as a mountain) before returning to the world of humans and, in some cases, ultimately reentering the fairy kingdom. (This pattern provides one of the main themes of German Romantic operas, including *Die Feen* and *Tannhäuser*.) Wachinger draws attention to two early-fifteenth-century narratives associated with the Monti Sibillini near Norcia in the Umbrian mountains. Here too a knight undertakes a pilgrimage to Rome and in the presence of the pope confesses to having stayed in the Monti Sibillini; see Burghart Wachinger, "Tannhäuser-Ballade," in *Die deutsche Literatur des Mittelalters: Verfasserlexikon* (Berlin, 1995), 9:611–16; see also the same author's article "Von Tannhäuser zur Tannhäuser-Ballade," *Zeitschrift für deutsches Altertum* 125 (1996): 125–41.

43. WWV, p. 287.

44. See Jacob and Wilhelm Grimm, *Deutsches Wörterbuch*, vol. 12, pt. 1 (Leipzig, 1956), 48–49.

45. Ludwig Achim von Arnim and Clemens Brentano, *Des Knaben Wunderhorn* (Heidelberg, 1819), 1:86–87.

46. Ibid., 90.

47. Ibid., 89.

48. The term *hôhe minne* describes the unconsummated love for a woman whom the poet places above himself in social standing. It is often—incorrectly, in the present translator's opinion—rendered into English as "courtly love," a term coined by the French scholar Gaston Paris in the late nineteenth century. The expression *nidere minne* (modern German "niedere Minne") describes a sexual relationship with a woman of lower social standing. For more on this and on the historical Tannhäuser, see Stewart Spencer, "Tannhäuser und der Tanhusaere," in *Opern und Opernfiguren: Festschrift für Joachim Herz*, ed. Ursula Müller and Ulrich Müller (Anif/Salzburg, 1989), 241–48.

49. See Wind, "Sacred and Profane Love," in *Pagan Mysteries*, 141–51, especially the section on the "fountain of love" on pp. 145–48.

50. See Hans Mayer, "Tannhäuser und die künstlichen Paradiese," in *Richard Wagner: Mitwelt und Nachwelt* (Stuttgart and Zurich, 1978), 191–200; reprinted in Hans Mayer's *Richard Wagner*, ed. Wolfgang Hofer (Frankfurt am Main, 1998), 82–92.

51. Features of the Persephone myth were transferred to her as early as Botticelli's *Primavera*, which depicts the garden of Venus. Here Venus is portrayed as the flower-strewing Flora, who assumes one of the guises of Persephone as the bringer of spring; see Wind, *Pagan Mysteries*, 115–17.

52. Søren Kierkegaard, *Either/Or*, ed. and trans. Howard V. Hong and Edna H. Hong (Princeton, 1987), 1:61–64.

53. Ibid., 1:89–90.

54. Baudelaire, "Richard Wagner et *Tannhäuser* à Paris," 2:794, and *The Painter of Modern Life*, trans. Mayne, 125.

55. Kierkegaard, *Either/Or*, 1:64–65.

56. On Kierkegaard's concept of Classicism, see his *Either/Or*, 1:49–58.

57. Baudelaire, "Richard Wagner et *Tannhäuser* à Paris," 2:796, and *The Painter of Modern Life*, trans. Mayne, 127.

58. There is a certain affinity here with Renaissance Platonism, which similarly rebelled against the tendency to confuse virtue with stoic frigidity. In *De voluptate*, Lorenzo

Valla's dialogue of 1431, the Christian, in his spiritual fervor, and the Epicurean, with his "sensuous fantasy," believe that it is possible to find common ground, whereas neither is able to tolerate stoic impassivity; see Wind, *Pagan Mysteries*, 141.

59. Tieck, *Erzählungen des Phantasus*, 72.

60. Heine, *Sämtliche Werke*, 3:570.

61. I thank Dolf Sternberger for pointing this out; on the "secret song contest between Wagner and Heine," see also Sternberger's major book on Heine, *Heinrich Heine und die Abschaffung der Sünde* (Hamburg and Düsseldorf, 1972).

62. Given the complex genesis of the work, it is unduly simplistic to speak of the Dresden version; see Reinhard Strohm, "Zur Werkgeschichte des 'Tannhäuser,'" *Die Programmhefte der Bayreuther Festspiele 1978* 3 (*Tannhäuser*), 12–13 and 64–76; see also WWV, pp. 287–95, where four stages in the work's genesis are identified and described, and Egon Voss's postscript to Richard Wagner, *Tannhäuser und der Sängerkrieg auf Wartburg: Textbuch der letzten Fassung mit Varianten der Partitur und der vorangehenden Fassungen* (Stuttgart, 2001), 81–99; on the Paris version, see Carolyn Abbate's definitive study, "The 'Parisian' Tannhäuser" (diss., Princeton University, 1984).

63. Kierkegaard, *Either/Or*, 1:90.

64. On the following, see Dieter Borchmeyer, "Die Götter tanzen Cancan: Richard Wagners und Heinrich Heines Venusberg-Phantasmagorien," in *Die Götter tanzen Cancan: Richard Wagners Liebesrevolten* (Heidelberg, 1992), 91–144.

65. Wind, *Pagan Mysteries*, 114.

66. Ibid., 119–20. For the way the Graces' dance in Botticelli's *Primavera* influenced the history of modern dance (especially Isadora Duncan), see the fascinating book by Gabriele Brandstetter, *Tanz-Lektüren: Körperbilder und Raumfiguren der Avantgarde* (Frankfurt am Main, 1995), 149–58.

67. Heine, *Sämtliche Werke*, 2:731.

68. Ibid.

69. Werner Vordtriede, in his edition of Heine's *Sämtliche Werke,* shares this view (2:952).

70. This is proved by Heine's letter to Michael Schloß dated 10 June 1854, in which he points out an error on the part of his correspondent: "As for Wagner, you have misunderstood me; I have not written any essays about him but only a poem that forms part of a cycle to be included in the first volume of my *Vermischte Schriften*"; quoted in *Dichter über ihre Dichtungen: Heinrich Heine*, ed. Norbert Altenhofer (Munich, 1971), 2:263. As Altenhofer points out, this poem can only be "Jung-Katerverein für Poesie-Musik."

71. Heine, *Sämtliche Werke*, 2:676.

72. Ibid.

73. Ibid., 677.

74. Kierkegaard, *Either/Or*, 1:90: "Don Juan, then, is the expression for the demonic qualified as the sensuous; Faust is the expression for the demonic qualified as the spiritual that the Christian spirit excludes."

75. Heine, *Sämtliche Werke*, 2:693.

76. Ibid., 1:381–82.

77. Ibid., 2:732–33.

78. Ibid., 733.

79. Ibid., 733–35.

80. Ibid., 737–39.

81. See G. Desrat, *Dictionnaire de la danse historique, théorique, pratique et bibliographique depuis l'origine de la danse jusqu'à nos jours* (Paris, 1895; reprint, Hildesheim and New York, 1977), 72: "Cancan or *chahut*: This name has been given to a kind of epileptic

dance or delirium tremens, which is to actual dance what slang is to the French tongue; as Delveau [the author's correct name is Alfred Delvau] would say, it is the slang of choreography. . . . Modern in origin, the cancan dates from 1830, the year in which public balls were almost completely transformed and no longer the exclusive preserve of the petty bourgeoisie."

82. Ibid., 72.

83. Heine, *Sämtliche Werke*, 2:693.

84. Ibid., 709–13.

85. Ibid., 759–60.

86. See Desrat, *Dictionnaire de la danse*, 72.

87. Heine, *Sämtliche Werke*, 2:639; this quotation lies behind the title of Max Niehaus's popular book *Himmel, Hölle und Trikot: Heinrich Heine und das Ballett* (Munich, 1959).

88. Pier Angelo Fiorentino, quoted by Ivor Guest, *The Ballet of the Second Empire, 1858–70* (London, 1953), 42; see also Sibylle Dahms, "Der Einfluß von Wagners Werk und Kunsttheorie auf Tanz und Ballett," in *Richard Wagner, 1883–1983: Die Rezeption im 19. und 20. Jahrhundert*, ed. Ursula Müller (Stuttgart, 1984), 145–62, esp. 153.

89. The link between Heine and Isadora Duncan's *Der Tanz der Zukunft* (1903) was first suggested by Benno von Wiese, the author of a particularly penetrating study on Heine's aesthetics as it relates to dance. See Benno von Wiese, "Das tanzende Universum," in *Signaturen: Zu Heinrich Heine und seinem Werk* (Berlin, 1976), 67–133, esp. 129–30: "Is Isadora Duncan not far closer to him than the famous families of dancers of his own day?"

90. Heine, *Sämtliche Werke*, 2:639–40.

91. Ibid., 640.

92. Ibid., 1:498–99.

93. See Gabriele Brandstetter and Brygida Maria Ochaim, *Loïe Fuller: Tanz, Licht-Spiel, Art Nouveau* (Freiburg, 1989), 96–98, esp. 96: "Loïe Fuller was the first of the countless well-known and less well known dancers who appeared as Salome around the turn of the century (suffice it to mention Maud Allan, Adorée Villany, Ruth St. Denis, and Ida Rubinstein) and who gave rise to a veritable Salome fashion, or 'Salomania.'"

94. Heine, *Sämtliche Werke*, 1:384–85.

95. Ibid., 2:639.

96. Ibid., 640.

97. Ibid., 655–56.

98. Ibid., 656–57.

99. Ibid., 640 (l.13).

100. See Gabriele Brandstetter, "Psychologie des Ausdrucks und Ausdruckstanz: Aspekte der Wechselwirkung am Beispiel der 'Traumtänzerin Magdeleine G.,'" in *Ausdruckstanz: Eine mitteleuropäische Bewegung der ersten Hälfte des 20. Jahhunderts*, ed. Gunhild Oberzaucher-Schüller (Wilhelmshaven, 1992), 199–211.

101. Heine, *Sämtliche Werke*, 2:647.

102. Desrat, *Dictionnaire de la danse*, 72.

103. Heine, *Sämtliche Werke*, 3:532–33.

104. Ibid., 4:283.

105. Jacob Grimm, *Deutsche Mythologie*, 2d ed. (Göttingen, 1844), 461.

106. For Kierkegaard, this view did not arise: for him to have imagined Don Juan—the embodiment of sensuality—as a dancer could not have been more absurd.

107. Heine, *Sämtliche Werke*, 4:284.

108. Ibid., 284–86.

109. Heinrich Heine, *Werke*, ed. Stuart Atkins (Munich, 1978), 2:1214; these lines were unpublished during Heine's lifetime and survived only in manuscript form.

110. Heine, *Sämtliche Werke*, 4:286.

111. Ibid., 282. A more idiomatic but less literal translation of this phrase—"We are playing with fire" or "We are living on the edge"—loses the idea of dancing.

112. Heine, *Sämtliche Werke*, 2:287. In his essay "Die Februarrevolution," Heine even compares the French Revolution to a Bacchanal, which he repeatedly associates with the frenzy of the cancan. (His model, as before, is a classical bas-relief, with all its mythological details.) See Wiese, "Das tanzende Universum," 96–97.

113. Heine, *Sämtliche Werke*, 4:287.

114. Oswald Georg Bauer, "Das *Tannhäuser*-Bacchanal," in *Wagnerliteratur— Wagnerforschung*, ed. Carl Dahlhaus and Egon Voss (Mainz, 1985), 215–21, esp. 218.

115. In addition to the aforementioned works by Dahms (note 88) and Bauer (note 114), see Theresa Cameron, "The Bayreuth Productions of the *Tannhäuser*-Bacchanale, 1904–1967," in *Ausdruckstanz*, ed. Oberzaucher-Schüller.

116. Isadora Duncan, *Der Tanz der Zukunft* (Leipzig, 1903), 34.

117. See Dahms, "Der Einfluß von Wagners Werk," 154–55.

118. Isadora Duncan, *My Life* (New York, 1927), 144.

119. See *Mallarmé—Debussy—Nijinskij—de Meyer: Nachmittag eines Fauns. Dokumentation einer legendären Choreographie* (Munich, 1989).

120. See the detailed account by Cameron, "The Bayreuth Productions of the *Tannhäuser*-Bacchanale."

121. Quoted from the prose draft published for the first time in *Die Programmhefte der Bayreuther Festspiele 1985* 1 (*Tannhäuser*), 1–14, esp. 4.

122. Ibid., 6–7.

123. See Hans Mayer, "Tannhäuser als Außenseiter," in *Richard Wagner*, ed. Wolfgang Hofer (Frankfurt am Main, 1998), 93–103.

124. Wagner, *Sämtliche Briefe*, 4:377.

125. Ibid., 8:152.

CHAPTER FIVE. *LOHENGRIN*: THE MYTHICAL PALIMPSEST OF
WAGNER'S LAST ROMANTIC OPERA

1. Wolfgang Schadewaldt, "Richard Wagner und die Griechen," in *Richard Wagner und das neue Bayreuth*, ed. Wieland Wagner (Munich, 1962), 167.

2. Thomas Mann, *Gesammelte Werke*, 2d ed. (Frankfurt am Main, 1974), 9:929.

3. Friedrich Schiller, *Schillers Werke* (Weimar, 1957), 5:130.

4. Ibid., 121.

5. Ibid., 134.

6. Charles Baudelaire, "Richard Wagner et *Tannhäuser* à Paris," in *Œuvres complètes*, ed. Claude Pichois (Paris, 1976), 2:799; trans. by Jonathan Mayne as "Richard Wagner and *Tannhäuser* in Paris," in *The Painter of Modern Life and Other Essays,* by Charles Baudelaire (London, 1995), 130.

7. Schiller, *Schillers Werke,* 5:128.

8. Mann, *Gesammelte Werke*, 9:930 (the quotation is taken from act 2, scene 5 of Kleist's *Amphitryon*).

9. Heinrich von Kleist, *Sämtliche Werke*, ed. Curt Grützmacher (Munich, 1967), 456–58 (the quotations are taken from act 2, scene 5); trans. by Charles E. Passage as *Amphitryon: The Legend and Three Plays* (Chapel Hill, N.C., 1974), 255–56.

10. Schiller, *Schillers Werke*, 5:129.

11. Ibid., 133.

12. Johann Wolfgang von Goethe, *Goethes Gespräche*, ed. Wolfgang Herwig (Zurich, 1969), 2:242.

13. See Wolf-Daniel Hartwich, *"Deutsche Mythologie": Die Erfindung einer nationalen Kunstreligion* (Berlin and Vienna, 2000), 97–113, esp. 112; see also Ulrike Kienzle, "Der vertriebene Gott: Über Glaube und Zweifel in Wagners *Lohengrin*," in *Bayreuther Festspiele: Das Festspielbuch 2001*, ed. Peter Emmerich (Bayreuth, 2001), 82–108.

14. Hartwich, *"Deutsche Mythologie,"* 112.

15. Richard Wagner, *Sämtliche Briefe*, ed. Gertrud Strobel and others (Leipzig, 1967–2000, and Wiesbaden, 1999–), 4:273–74.

16. See Dieter Borchmeyer, "Renaissance und Instrumentalisierung des Mythos: Richard Wagner und die Folgen," in *Richard Wagner im Dritten Reich*, ed. Saul Friedländer and Jörn Rüsen (Munich, 2000), 66–91, esp. 79–81.

17. See Dieter Borchmeyer, "Mozarts rasende Weiber," in *Mozarts Opernfiguren: Große Herren—rasende Weiber—gefährliche Liebschaften*, ed. Dieter Borchmeyer (Bern, 1992), 167–212.

18. On the distinction between "magic" and the "miracle" or "wonder," as defined by Jacob Grimm, see Hartwich, *"Deutsche Mythologie,"* 107.

19. See ibid., 100; see also Udo Bermbach, "Der Fürst als Republikaner: Zu Richard Wagners *Lohengrin*," in *Wo Macht ganz auf Verbrechen ruht: Politik und Gesellschaft in der Oper* (Hamburg, 1997), 218–37.

20. See Dieter Borchmeyer, *Das Theater Richard Wagners* (Stuttgart, 1982), 260; trans. by Stewart Spencer as *Richard Wagner: Theory and Theatre* (Oxford, 1991), 339–40.

CHAPTER SIX. LOVE AND OBJECTIFICATION IN THE MUSIC DRAMA:
TRISTAN'S ISOLDE AND HER SISTERS

1. See Dieter Borchmeyer, *Das Theater Richard Wagners* (Stuttgart, 1982), 286–87; trans. by Stewart Spencer as *Richard Wagner: Theory and Theatre* (Oxford, 1991), 366–67.

2. See Borchmeyer, *Das Theater Richard Wagners*, 259–60, and *Richard Wagner*, trans. Spencer, 338.

3. For a detailed book on *Tristan und Isolde* and its production history, see Brigitte Heldt, *Richard Wagner: Tristan und Isolde. Das Werk und seine Inszenierung* (Laaber, 1994).

4. I was in the audience on this occasion and recall the performance having to be curtailed at this point.

5. See Erwin Koppen's definitive book, *Dekadenter Wagnerismus: Studien zur europäischen Literatur des Fin de siècle* (Berlin and New York, 1973).

6. See the volume that was published to accompany the Berlin Philharmonic's performances of the work, *"O sink hernieder, Nacht der Liebe": Tristan und Isolde—Der Mythos von Liebe und Tod*, ed. Sabine Borris and Christiane Krautscheid (Berlin, 1998).

7. See Edgar Wind, "Amor as a God of Death," in *Pagan Mysteries in the Renaissance* (London, 1958), 152–70.

8. Ibid., 154.

9. Ibid.

10. See Borchmeyer, *Das Theater Richard Wagners*, 270, and *Richard Wagner*, trans. Spencer, 341.

11. Johann Wolfgang von Goethe, *Goethes Werke: Hamburger Ausgabe* (Munich, 1981), 4:176.

12. Ibid., 186–87.

13. See Borchmeyer, *Das Theater Richard Wagners*, 282–84, and *Richard Wagner*, trans. Spencer, 362–63.

14. Morten Bartnaes adopts a more critical approach to the "mystical" aspect of *Tristan und Isolde*—and also to my views on the subject—in his book *Richard Wagners "Tristan und Isolde": Literarische Alleinswerdung als literaturwissenschaftliches Problem* (Hanover, 2001).

15. See Borchmeyer, *Das Theater Richard Wagners*, 281; and *Richard Wagner*, trans. Spencer, 361.

16. Friedrich Nietzsche, *Sämtliche Werke: Kritische Studienausgabe in 15 Bänden*, ed. Giorgio Colli and Mazzino Montinari (Munich, 1980), 8:191.

17. See Hartmut Reinhardt, "Richard Wagner und Schopenhauer," in *Richard-Wagner-Handbuch*, ed. Ulrich Müller and Peter Wapnewski (Stuttgart, 1986), 101–13, esp. 105–17; trans. by Erika Swales and Martin Swales as "Wagner and Schopenhauer," in *Wagner Handbook*, ed. John Deathridge (Cambridge, Mass., 1992), 287–96.

18. See Borchmeyer, *Das Theater Richard Wagners*, 284–85, and *Richard Wagner*, trans. Spencer, 365–66.

19. Wolfgang Golther, ed., *Richard Wagner an Mathilde Wesendonk: Tagebuchblätter und Briefe, 1853–1871* (Leipzig, 1914), 130–31; English trans. from *Selected Letters of Richard Wagner*, ed. Stewart Spencer and Barry Millington (London, 1987), 432.

20. This is contested by Morten Bartnaes in *Wagners "Tristan und Isolde,"* 133–34. Bartnaes even suggests that Wagner did not send this letter to Schopenhauer because he ultimately realized that the ideas expressed in it were already to be found in Schopenhauer's own writings, but Bartnaes offers little evidence in support of this claim.

21. Arthur Schopenhauer, *Sämtliche Werke*, ed. Arthur Hübscher (Wiesbaden, 1972), 3:582–83; trans. by E.F.J. Payne as *The World as Will and Representation* (New York, 1966), 2:508.

22. Schopenhauer, *Sämtliche Werke*, 2:389 and 444, and *The World as Will and Representation*, trans. Payne, 1:329 and 376.

23. See Peter Wapnewski's penetrating book on *Tristan und Isolde*, including his comments on the work's genesis and repercussions, in the revised and enlarged edition of his 1981 monograph *Tristan der Held Richard Wagners* (Berlin, 2001).

24. Schopenhauer, *Sämtliche Werke*, 2:444, and *The World as Will and Representation*, trans. Payne, 1:376.

25. Schopenhauer, *Sämtliche Werke*, 3:582, and *The World as Will and Representation*, trans. Payne, 2:507.

26. See Claudia Maurer Zenck, "Komponierte Weiblichkeit—Rollenprofil der Isolde oder: Als Frau Isolde zu hören," in *"Das Weib der Zukunft": Frauengestalten und Frauenstimmen bei Richard Wagner*, ed. Susanne Vill (Stuttgart, 2000), 95–123.

27. In his very last essay, "On the Womanly in the Human," on which he was still working at the time of his death, Wagner was evidently thinking of *Die Walküre* when he wrote about the fatal consequence of "conventional marriages based on property and possessions" (SS 12:343). Such marriages, he believed, betrayed the specifically human element in marriage and in the fidelity grounded in individual love; see Dieter Borchmeyer, *"Über das Weibliche im Menschlichen* in Wagners Musikdramen," in *"Das Weib der Zukunft,"* ed. Vill, 34–43.

28. This section is a revised and shortened version of the chapter "Richard Wagners *Verkaufte Braut*: Verdinglichung und Liebe im Musikdrama," in *Die Götter tanzen Cancan: Richard Wagners Liebesrevolten,* by Dieter Borchmeyer (Heidelberg, 1992), 145–82.

29. See the stimulating, if speculative, book by Klaus Kirschbaum, *Die "verkaufte" Braut: Zur Vorgeschichte einer Auslobung* (Bonn, 1990). Kirschbaum's theory that it was Eva herself who, even before she knew Walther von Stolzing, persuaded her father to marry her off in order to obtain Sachs as her husband (in which case she would not be a "bartered" bride) is an interesting one, even though there is no evidence for it in the text.

30. On the Wagnerian category of moral "custom," see Borchmeyer, *Das Theater Richard Wagners*, 244–45, and *Richard Wagner,* trans. Spencer, 308–10.

31. On the myth of night in *Tristan und Isolde* and the significance of this myth against the background of European poetry about the night, especially the Romantics' cult of night, see Borchmeyer, *Das Theater Richard Wagners*, 261–69, and *Richard Wagner*, trans. Spencer, 326–38.

32. Karl Marx, *Die Frühschriften*, ed. Siegfried Landshut (Stuttgart, 1964), 258; trans. by Rodney Livingstone and Gregor Benton as *Early Writings* (London, 1992), 361.

33. The "Commodity of Love" was the title that Brecht originally intended for *Der gute Mensch von Sezuan*; see Jan Knopf, *Brecht-Handbuch: Theater* (Stuttgart, 1980), 201.

34. See Ursula Link-Heer, "Der 'androgyne Wagner' und die Dramaturgie des Blicks," in *"Das Weib der Zukunft,"* ed. Vill, 84–95, esp. 89–91; see also Ulrich Müller and Oswald Panagl, " 'Der Blick sagt mehr als eine Rede': Motiv und Bedeutung des Blicks in den Musikdramen Richard Wagners," *Bayreuther Festspiele: Das Festspielbuch 2001* (Bayreuth, 2001), 109–21.

35. Marx, *Die Frühschriften*, 301, and *Early Writings*, trans. Livingstone and Benton, 378–79.

36. Marx, *Die Frühschriften*, 298–99, and *Early Writings*, trans. Livingstone and Benton, 377.

37. Marx, *Die Frühschriften*, 240, and *Early Writings*, trans. Livingstone and Benton, 352.

38. Marx, *Die Frühschriften*, 301, and *Early Writings*, trans. Livingstone and Benton, 379.

39. See Borchmeyer, *Das Theater Richard Wagners*, 244–50, and *Richard Wagner*, trans. Spencer, 308–20. Among the many recent and detailed studies on the incest motif, see especially Udo Bermbach, *Der Wahn des Gesamtkunstwerks: Richard Wagners politisch-ästhetische Utopie* (Frankfurt am Main, 1994), 290–97; Nike Wagner, *Wagner Theater* (Frankfurt am Main and Leipzig, 1998), 89–107; trans. by Ewald Osers and Michael Downes as *The Wagners* (London, 2000), 57–71; and especially Christine Emig, *Arbeit am Inzest: Richard Wagner und Thomas Mann* (Frankfurt am Main, 1998).

40. Marx, *Die Frühschriften*, 240, and *Early Writings*, trans. Livingstone and Benton, 352.

41. See Egon Voss, *"Die Meistersinger von Nürnberg* als Oper des deutschen Bürger- tums," in *"Wagner und kein Ende": Betrachtungen und Studien* (Zurich and Mainz, 1996), 118–44, esp. 120; trans. by Stewart Spencer as "Wagner's 'Meistersinger' as an Opera for the German bourgeoisie," *Wagner* 11 (1990): 39–62, esp. 40–41.

42. Schopenhauer, *Sämtliche Werke*, 3:610–11, and *The World as Will and Representation*, trans. Payne, 2:533–34.

43. See Borchmeyer, "Improvisation und Metier: Die Poetik der Meistersinger," in *Das Theater Richard Wagners*, 206–30; English trans. "Improvisation and Vocational Skill: The Poetics of *Die Meistersinger,"* in *Richard Wagner*, trans. Spencer, 250–86.

44. Voss, *"Die Meistersinger von Nürnberg* als Oper des deutschen Bürgertums," 121, and "Wagner's 'Meistersinger' as an opera for the German bourgeoisie," trans. Spencer, 41. The word "Wahn" used here has no simple equivalent in English. It is often translated as "illusion" or "self-delusion," but, as used by Wagner, it also resonates with ideas of madness, folly, fancy, and the artist's inspirational *furor.*

45. Ernst Bloch, *Das Prinzip Hoffnung* (Frankfurt am Main, 1959), 370; trans. by Neville Plaice, Stephen Plaice, and Paul Knight as *The Principle of Hope* (Oxford, 1986), 318.

CHAPTER SEVEN. NUREMBERG AS AN AESTHETIC STATE: *DIE MEISTERSINGER*, AN IMAGE AND COUNTERIMAGE OF HISTORY

1. Thomas Mann, *Gesammelte Werke*, 2d ed. (Frankfurt am Main, 1974), 9:372. This chapter is based on my article "Nürnberg als Reich des schönen Scheins: Metamorphosen eines Künstlerdramas," first published in *Deutsche Meister—böse Geister? Nationale Selbstfindung in der Musik*, ed. Hermann Danuser and Herfried Münkler (Schliengen, 2001), 286–302.

2. See Egon Voss, " 'Es klang so alt,—und war doch so neu,'—Oder ist es umgekehrt? Zur Rolle des Überlieferten in den *Meistersingern von Nürnberg*," in *"Wagner und kein Ende": Betrachtungen und Studien* (Zurich and Mainz, 1996), 145–54. Voss shows that although Wagner, in his search for historical authenticity, borrowed certain words and phrases from Johann Christoph Wagenseil's 1697 *Buch von der Meister-Singer Holdseligen Kunst*, he made little use of Wagenseil's music examples, as their tonality and rhythms could not be integrated into his own musical language. As a result, he replaced the historically authentic music of the Mastersingers with pseudo-Baroque figurations and contrapuntal procedures that were easier to integrate into his score and that were designed to suggest an "antiquated, formalized art that was no longer really alive" (149). "On the level of the text, Wagner's approach to tradition shows a pronounced tendency toward historical accuracy aimed at the greatest possible authenticity, alongside a poetic freedom that approaches tradition within the spirit of that freedom. On the level of the music, by contrast, there is no question of this kind of historical accuracy" (154).

3. See Voss's penetrating chapter "*Die Meistersinger von Nürnberg* als Oper des deutschen Bürgertums," in *"Wagner und kein Ende*," 118–44; trans. by Stewart Spencer as "Wagner's 'Meistersinger' as an opera for the German bourgeoisie," *Wagner* 11 (1990): 39–62.

4. Dieter Borchmeyer and Jörg Salaquarda, eds. *Nietzsche und Wagner: Stationen einer epochalen Begegnung* (Frankfurt am Main and Leipzig, 1994), 719.

5. A curiosity that would be scarcely conceivable in the German-speaking world today is the reappearance of the chorale from the opening scene of *Die Meistersinger*, albeit to new words, by Percy Dearmer (1867–1936) as no. 290 in the New English Hymnal of 1994 (p. 476): "Holy God, we show forth here / Jesus' death our sins to clear."

6. Steffen Radlmaier, ed., *Das Nürnberg-Lesebuch* (Cadolzburg, 1994), 19.

7. Ibid., 29–30.

8. On the political and social structure of historical Nuremberg, see Udo Bermbach, "Die Utopie der Selbstregierung: Zu Richard Wagners *Die Meistersinger von Nürnberg*," in *Wo Macht ganz auf Verbrechen ruht: Politik und Gesellschaft in der Oper* (Hamburg, 1997), 240–42, and "Die Meistersinger von Nürnberg: Politische Gehalte einer Künstleroper," in *Deutsche Meister—böse Geister?* ed. Danuser and Münkler, 274–85.

9. Radlmaier, *Das Nürnberg-Lesebuch*, 30–31.

10. Ibid., 32.

11. Ibid., 31.

12. See Peter Uwe Hohendahl, "Reworking History: Wagner's German Myth of Nuremberg," in *Re-Reading Wagner*, ed. Reinhold Grimm and Jost Hermand (Madison, Wis., 1993), 39–60.

13. Willi Schuh, ed., *Richard Strauss–Hugo von Hofmannsthal: Briefwechsel*, 3d ed. (Zurich, 1964), 576–78.

14. Radlmaier, *Das Nürnberg-Lesebuch*, 60–61.

15. The following quotations in the text are taken from Franz Zademack's edition of Deinhardstein's drama in *Die Meistersinger von Nürnberg: Richard Wagners Dichtung und ihre Quellen* (Berlin, 1921), 7–114.

16. All quotations from Lortzing's opera are taken from the 1840 edition of the libretto, which unfortunately is not included in Zademack's collection of source material.

17. On the rhetorical structure of Sachs's closing address, see Peter-Philipp Riedl, "Demosthenes auf der Festwiese: Öffentliche Rede in Richard Wagners *Die Meistersinger von Nürnberg*," in *Resonanzen: Festschrift für Hans Joachim Kreutzer*, ed. Sabine Doering and others (Würzburg, 2000), 391–403.

18. Johann Wolfgang von Goethe, *Goethes Werke* (Hamburger Ausgabe), ed. Erich Trunz (Hamburg, 1948), 1:139.

19. See Peter Wapnewski's detailed demonstration in *Richard Wagner: Die Szene und ihr Meister* (Munich, 1978), 74–80.

20. Schuh, *Strauss–Hofmannsthal*, 577.

21. Goethe, *Goethes Werke*, 1:136.

22. Mann, *Leiden und Größe Richard Wagners,* in *Gesammelte Werke*, 9:419.

23. Radlmaier, *Das Nürnberg-Lesebuch*, 298.

24. Novalis, *Schriften*, ed. Paul Kluckhohn and Richard Samuel, 3d ed. (Darmstadt, 1977–), 2:488.

25. Achim von Arnim, *Erzählungen in einem Band*, ed. Walter Migge (Munich, 1971), 655.

26. This thesis is disputed by Udo Bermbach, whose interpretation of *Die Meistersinger* otherwise coincides closely with the one advanced in this chapter and in particular with the idea that Wagner's imaginary Nuremberg is unpolitical; see his *Wo Macht ganz auf Verbrechen ruht*, 238–70 and 309. Although Bermbach denies that Schiller influenced Wagner's aesthetic concept in this regard, his influence is easily demonstrated, not least by Wagner's own reference to Schiller's *Über die ästhetische Erziehung des Menschen* in his essay "Shall We Hope?" (GS 10:121); see also Dieter Borchmeyer, *Das Theater Richard Wagners* (Stuttgart, 1982), 24–26, 64–65, 116–17, 139–40, 236–37, and 245; trans. by Stewart Spencer as *Richard Wagner: Theory and Theatre* (Oxford, 1991), 9, 60, 144, 295, and 311. Bermbach's rejection of the term "aesthetic state" to describe Wagner's Nuremberg stems from his view that Schiller intended it to refer to a form of organization with political connotations, but this is emphatically not the case with the aesthetic state.

27. See Borchmeyer, *Das Theater Richard Wagners*, 207–30, and *Richard Wagner*, trans. Spencer, 250–86.

28. For a more detailed demonstration of this point, see Borchmeyer, *Das Theater Richard Wagners*, 209–11, and *Richard Wagner*, trans. Spencer, 253–55.

29. Heinrich Heine, "Gemäldeausstellung in Paris 1831," in *Die deutsche Literatur: Bd. IV—19. Jahrhundert*, ed. Benno von Wiese (Munich, 1965), 27–28.

30. Friedrich von Schiller, *Sämtliche Werke*, ed. Gerhard Fricke and Herbert G. Göpfert (Munich, 1962), 1:473–77.

31. Mann, *Gesammelte Werke*, 9:418.

32. Schiller, *Sämtliche Werke*, 5:667–69; trans. by Elizabeth M. Wilkinson and L. A. Willoughby as *On the Aesthetic Education of Man* (Oxford, 1967), 215–19.

33. Schiller, *Sämtliche Werke*, 5:668, and *On the Aesthetic Education of Man*, trans. Wilkinson and Willoughby, 217.

34. Otto Strobel, ed., *König Ludwig II. und Richard Wagner: Briefwechsel* (Karlsruhe, 1936), 2:79.

35. See Herfried Münkler, "Kunst und Kultur als Stifter politischer Identität: Webers *Freischütz* und Wagners *Meistersinger*," in *Deutsche Meister*, ed. Danuser and Münkler, 45–60. Münkler sees a connection between Sachs's reference to the "false foreign majesty" of "foreign mists and foreign trumpery" and rulers such as Charles V, who, knowing little German, surrounded themselves with Spanish and Italian advisers. Of such rulers, it might be said that "no prince will soon understand his people" (GS 7:270). The German word *wälsch/welsch* means "Romance," specifically French and Italian, but it soon came to be used dismissively of foreigners in general. For Herder, the election of Charles V as emperor of Germany was the final nail in the coffin of the German empire, whose last credible representative was Maximilian: "Until the days of Maximilian, the German nation was a revered nation, honest in its manner of thinking and its way of acting. Ever since foreign nations have ruled it with their customs and languages, in other words, from the time of Charles V onward, it has gone downhill"; quoted on p. 56.

36. In this context it is worth mentioning the "Wach' auf" Chorus, which is often quoted in connection with chauvinistic readings of *Die Meistersinger*. As we know, the words of this chorus are adapted from lines by the historical Hans Sachs, but, as Egon Voss has pointed out, the "Wacht auf" of the original has been changed to "Wach' auf," thereby privatizing the emotions. Sachs's line, in the plural, is addressed to all "lovers of the evangelical truth," whereas Wagner's line is addressed to a single individual. In Sachs's original, the following lines take as their starting point the intimate setting of the traditional dawn song, presupposing a nocturnal tryst between lovers that is brought to an end either by the dawn chorus of birds or by a third party who, keeping vigil for the lovers, announces the onset of dawn. (A similar situation occurs in act 2 of *Tristan und Isolde*.) Sachs then uses these lines as the basis of a theological metaphor. Wagner takes over only the first eight lines, removing them from their metaphorical context and restoring them to the intimate setting from which they had started out, thereby interpreting the song not as an appeal to a group of believers but as words spoken by one lover to another. "Of course," writes Voss, "this subtle transformation of the original has not prevented the chorus from being described as the 'Wacht auf' Chorus and from being interpreted as such. The National Socialists in particular were none too fastidious on this point and used the chorus for their own propagandist ends, interpreting it as Wagner's appeal to the Germans in the sense of a nationalist ideology"; see Voss's "*Wagner und kein Ende*," 154.

37. Eduard Hanslick, *Aus meinem Leben*, ed. Peter Wapnewski (Kassel and Basel, 1987), 357.

38. Eduard Hanslick, *Vom Musikalisch-Schönen: Aufsätze und Musikkritiken*, ed. Klaus Mehner (Leipzig, 1982), 284–98, esp. 287, 292, and 298.

39. Hanslick, *Aus meinem Leben*, 358.

40. On the "apparently omnipresent figure of the 'pedante' " in European comedy of the early modern period, see the detailed chapter by Ulrich Schulz-Buschhaus, "Kommunikationsverlust und erotische 'Idiotie': Zur Gestalt des Pedanten in der italienischen Renaissance-Komödie," in *Literaturhistorische Begegnungen: Festschrift für Bernhard König* (Tübingen, 1993), 339–56.

41. See M. Owen Lee, "Some Metaphors in the Text of *Die Meistersinger*," in *Wagner in Restrospect: A Centennial Reappraisal*, ed. Leroy R. Shaw, Nancy R. Cirillo, and Marion S. Miller (Amsterdam, 1987), 63–69.

42. Schiller, *Sämtliche Werke*, 5:845.

43. See Peter L. Berger, *Erlösendes Lachen: Das Komische in der menschlichen Erfahrung* (Berlin, 1998), 19.

44. Voss, "*Die Meistersinger von Nürnberg* als Oper des deutschen Bürgertums," 138–39, and "Wagner's 'Meistersinger' as an Opera for the German Middle Classes," trans. Spencer, 57.

45. Schiller, *Sämtliche Werke*, 5:846.

46. See Borchmeyer, *Das Theater Richard Wagners*, 221–23, and *Richard Wagner*, trans. Spencer, 274–76.

47. "The texts of Wagner's works contain not a single character who is openly defined as Jewish. Nor did Wagner himself ever draw explicit attention to such a layer in his works either in their indirect paratexts or, more particularly, in his poetological writings and commentaries on them" (Hermann Danuser, "Universalität oder Partikularität? Zur Frage 'jüdischer' Charakterzeichnung in Wagners Werk," in *Richard Wagner und die Juden*, ed. Dieter Borchmeyer, Aami Mayaani, and Susanne Vill [Stuttgart, 2000], 79–100, esp. 79–80).

48. Borchmeyer and Salaquarda, *Nietzsche und Wagner,* 67–68. Cosima expresses a similar sentiment in her diary entry of 14 March 1870. Thomas S. Grey points out that Cosima's comments are supported by Ludwig Nohl's report on the Vienna production, published in the *Neue Zeitschrift für Musik* on 11 March 1870. Nohl, who was an early Wagnerian, refers to "an erroneous report to the effect that Beckmesser's song is based on a Jewish melody and that it was chosen by the composer to make fun of the Jews and their music." This inaccurate information, Nohl continues, provoked "intense and persistent hissing" on the part of Wagner's opponents during Beckmesser's Serenade. In short, a Wagnerian such as Nohl did not believe that there was any truth in the rumor that Beckmesser's Serenade was a satire of Jewish music; see Thomas S. Grey, "Selbstbehauptung oder Fremdmißbrauch? Zur Rezeptionsgeschichte von Wagners *Meistersingern*," in *Deutsche Meister*, ed. Danuser and Münkler, 303–25.

49. Barry Millington, "Nuremberg Trial: Is There Anti-Semitism in *Die Meistersinger?*" *Cambridge Opera Journal* 3 (1991): 247–60; see also Barry Millington, ed., *The Wagner Compendium* (London, 1992), 304.

50. Danuser, "Universalität oder Partikularität?" 97.

51. Theodor W. Adorno, *Versuch über Wagner* (Frankfurt, 1981), 19; trans. by Rodney Livingstone as *In Search of Wagner* (London, 1981), 23.

52. Danuser, "Universalität oder Partikularität?" 86.

53. Adorno, *Versuch über Wagner*, 21, and, *In Search of Wagner*, trans. Livingstone, 25. Adorno's belief that Beckmesser is a caricature of a Jew has been taken up by a number of English and American writers in recent years, including not only Barry Millington but also Paul Lawrence Rose. See Rose's *Richard Wagner: Race and Revolution* (New Haven and London, 1992), 11–12; Marc Weiner, *Richard Wagner and the Anti-Semitic Imagination* (Lincoln, Neb., and London, 1995), 103–94, esp. 103–35; and David J. Levin, "Reading a Staging / Staging a Reading," *Cambridge Opera Journal* 9 (1997): 47–72.

54. Hans Rudolf Vaget, "*Der Jude im Dorn* oder: Wie antisemitisch sind *Die Meistersinger von Nürnberg?*" *Deutsche Vierteljahrsschrift für Literaturwissenschaft und Geistesgeschichte* 69 (1995): 271–99, esp. 297; see also Vaget's article "Sixtus Beckmesser: A 'Jew in the Brambles'?" *The Opera Quarterly* 12 (1995): 34–45.

55. See Dieter Borchmeyer, "Beckmesser: Der Jude im Dorn?" *Bayreuther Festspiele: Das Festspielbuch 1996*, ed. Peter Emmerich (Bayreuth, 1996), 89–99.

56. Quoted from Jacob and Wilhelm Grimm's *Kinder- und Hausmärchen gesammelt durch die Brüder Grimm: Vollständige Ausgabe auf der Grundlage der dritten Auflage (1837)*, ed. Heinz Rölleke (Frankfurt am Main, 1985), 466–70.

57. Arnold Zweig, "Der Jude im Dorn," *Die neue Weltbühne* 32 (1936): 717–21 and 744–47, esp. 718 and 721.

58. See Vaget, *"Der Jude im Dorn,"* 282–83.

59. Wolf-Daniel Hartwich sees a link between the contrastive pairing of spring and winter on the one hand and a mythological framework inspired by Karl Simrock's *Deutsche Mythologie* on the other, a framework that also includes *Parsifal* and its seasonal symbolism. One could also add the related themes of spring, love, and incest in act 1 of *Die Walküre* ("Winterstürme wichen dem Wonnemond"; GS 6:16–17); see Wolf-Daniel Hartwich, " 'Johannisnacht!' Richard Wagners *Meistersinger von Nürnberg* als mythologische Komödie," in *"Deutsche Mythologie": Die Erfindung einer nationalen Kunstreligion* (Berlin and Vienna, 2000), 120–38 and 197.

60. A glance at the Grimms' dictionary shows that the rhyme "dornenhecken/verstecken" was very popular in an earlier period; see Jacob and Wilhelm Grimm, *Deutsches Wörterbuch* (Leipzig, 1860), 2:1295.

61. Vaget, *"Der Jude im Dorn,"* 289–90.

62. Schulz-Buschhaus, "Kommunikationsverlust und erotische 'Idiotie,' " 348.

63. Ibid., 349–51.

64. According to Hermann Danuser, if Wagner had wanted to depict Beckmesser and other characters as Jews, "he needed only to abandon alliterative verse for their speeches in order to exclude them from the communicative cosmos of his world of art"; see Danuser, "Universalität oder Partikularität?" 89.

65. See Schulz-Buschhaus, "Kommunikationsverlust und erotische 'Idiotie,' " 342–44.

66. Jens Malte Fischer, *"Das Judentum in der Musik": Eine kritische Dokumentation als Beitrag zur Geschichte des Antisemitismus* (Frankfurt am Main, 2000), 15.

67. Dolf Sternberger, *Figuren der Fabel: Essays* (Frankfurt am Main, 1950), 211.

68. *Jahrbuch der Dostojewskij-Gesellschaft* 1 (1992): 90–103, esp. 91.

69. Ibid., 99.

70. Danuser, "Universalität oder Partikularität?" 100.

CHAPTER EIGHT. THE MYTH OF THE BEGINNING AND END OF HISTORY:
DER RING DES NIBELUNGEN

1. John Steinbeck, *The Pearl* (London, 2000), 89–91.

2. This chapter represents a summation of a number of earlier works, most of which are listed in the following notes. In terms of its structure, it is based most closely on my chapter "Wagners Mythos vom Anfang und Ende der Welt," in *Der Ring des Nibelungen: Ansichten des Mythos*, ed. Udo Bermbach and Dieter Borchmeyer (Stuttgart, 1995), 1–26. Within the framework of this chapter, it is not possible to consider even the most important of the countless recent interpretations of the *Ring*, although three of them at least deserve to be mentioned here: Peter Wapnewski, *Weißt du wie das wird . . . ? Richard Wagner: Der Ring des Nibelungen* (Munich and Zurich, 1995); Udo Bermbach, ed., *"Alles ist nach seiner Art": Figuren in Richard Wagners Der Ring des Nibelungen* (Stuttgart and Weimar, 2001), which contains an excellent account of interpretations of the *Ring* during the last ten years (1–26); Dieter Borchmeyer, "Wagner-Literatur: Eine deutsche Misere. Neue Ansichten zum 'Fall Wagner,' " in *Internationales Archiv für Sozialgeschichte der Literatur* (Tübingen, 1993), 1–62, esp. 29–37, which contains interpretations from the previous decade.

3. Bernard Shaw, *The Perfect Wagnerite* (London, 1898), 1.

4. This view has been espoused in particular by the director Joachim Herz; on this and on the problematic nature of the concept of allegory and its applicability to the world of mythical images in the *Ring*, see Dieter Borchmeyer, "Vom Anfang und Ende der Geschichte: Richard Wagners mythisches Drama. Idee und Inszenierung," in *Macht des*

Mythos—Ohnmacht der Vernunft? ed. Peter Kemper (Frankfurt am Main, 1989), 176–200; see also Dieter Borchmeyer, "*Faust* und *Der Ring des Nibelungen*: Der Mythos des 19. Jahrhunderts in zwiefacher Gestalt," in *Wege des Mythos in der Moderne: Richard Wagner, Der Ring des Nibelungen. Eine Münchner Ringvorlesung*, ed. Dieter Borchmeyer (Munich, 1987), 133–58.

5. See Dieter Borchmeyer, "Mythos," in *Moderne Literatur in Grundbegriffen*, ed. Dieter Borchmeyer and Viktor Žmegač, 2d ed. (Tübingen, 1994), 292–306, esp. 306.

6. Mircea Eliade, *Myth and Reality* (London, 1964), 13–14.

7. Ibid., 11.

8. See Edward R. Haymes, "Richard Wagner and the 'Altgermanisten': *Die Wibelungen* and Franz Mone," in *Re-Reading Wagner*, ed. Reinhold Grimm and Jost Hermand (Madison, Wis., 1993), 23–38. It was Göttling who was entrusted with the task of editing the sixty-volume *Ausgabe letzter Hand* of Goethe's works.

9. The way in which Wagner's view of history was tied up with myth was examined for the first time by Petra-Hildegard Wilberg in her impressive book *Richard Wagners mythische Welt: Versuche wider den Historismus* (Freiburg im Breisgau, 1996), esp. 77–184, where the author analyzes *The Wibelungs* in detail.

10. Kurt Hübner, *Die Wahrheit des Mythos* (Munich, 1985), 136–37.

11. Ibid., 137.

12. Ibid., 137–38.

13. Ibid., 178.

14. Friedrich Wilhelm Joseph von Schelling, *Philosophie der Mythologie* (Darmstadt, 1966), 1:16. In making this claim, Schelling was distancing himself from the view, commonly held by writers on German aesthetics in the years around 1800, that myth was a product of poetry. According to Schelling, original mythologies reveal a wholly unpoetical character (18). Myth, he argues, was clearly "meant as truth . . . for the most insignificant element in our concept of the gods is that they are feared as beings, whereas only real beings are feared, or beings who we think are real" (68).

15. In Nikolaus Lehnhoff's Munich production of the *Ring* in 1987, the character of Loge wrote this fairy-tale formula on a blue stage cloth during the prelude.

16. See Gerhard Schmidt-Henkel, *Mythos und Dichtung: Zur Begriffs- und Stilgeschichte der deutschen Literatur im 19. und 20. Jahrhundert* (Bad Homburg, Berlin, and Zurich, 1967), 250.

17. Reinhard Wiesend, "Die Entstehung des Rheingold-Vorspiels und ihr Mythos," *Archiv für Musikwissenschaft* 49 (1992): 122–45, esp. 127. Wiesend has shown, on the basis of the first complete draft of 1853–54 and the first fair copy of the full score of 1854, that the prelude achieved its definitive form only after the rest of the work had been conceived in outline; in other words, Wagner's autobiographical account of the genesis of the prelude occurring during a "vision" in La Spezia is yet another myth that he invented in a spirit of mythopoeic fantasy.

18. See Ludwig Finscher, "Mythos und musikalische Struktur," in *Der Ring des Nibelungen*, ed. Bermbach and Borchmeyer, 27–38, esp. 29.

19. Thomas Mann, "Richard Wagner und 'Der Ring des Nibelungen,' " in *Wagner und unsere Zeit*, ed. Erika Mann (Frankfurt am Main, 1963), 136–37.

20. Dieter Borchmeyer and Jörg Salaquarda, eds. *Nietzsche und Wagner: Stationen einer epochalen Begegnung* (Frankfurt am Main, 1994), 694–95.

21. Ibid., 182.

22. Eliade, *Myth and Reality*, 46.

23. Mircea Eliade, *The Myth of the Eternal Return, or Cosmos and History*, trans. Willard R. Trask (Princeton, 1974), 30.

24. Kurt Hübner has already described this in his chapter on Wagner in his ground-breaking book *Die Wahrheit des Mythos*, 399–401. Hübner's findings have been confirmed musicologically by Ludwig Finscher, "Mythos und musikalische Struktur," 27–37.

25. Thomas Mann, *Gesammelte Werke*, 2d ed. (Frankfurt am Main, 1974), 4:40.

26. Ibid., 9:372.

27. Friedrich Creuzer and Franz Joseph Mone, *Symbolik und Mythologie der alten Völker*, vol. 5, pt. 1 (Leipzig and Darmstadt, 1822), 353. In the *Völuspá* the three Norns are called Urðr, Verðandi, and Sculd, all three names being derived from forms of the verb "to be": *urðum* = became; *verðandi* = becoming; and *skulu* = shall. As such, their names point to the past, present, and future. See Rudolf Simek, *Dictionary of Northern Mythology*, trans. Angela Hall (Cambridge, 1993), 237. The fact that Wagner has his three Norns spinning—an occupation not associated with them in Norse mythology—shows that he was keen to draw a parallel with the three Fates of Roman mythology (and the Moirai of Greek myth).

28. Hübner, *Die Wahrheit des Mythos,* 118–19.

29. On the mythological life of the sword in general, see Jacob Grimm, *Deutsche Mythologie* (Göttingen, 1844), 839. See also the enlightening chapter by Ute Schwab, "Lebendige Schwerter und lateinische Schlachtvögel," in *Verborum Amor: Festschrift für Stefan Sonderegger*, ed. Harald Burger and others (Berlin and New York, 1992), 3–33.

30. Even this archaic property has modern implications, at least according to Lutz Köpnick, who argues that, far from being archaic, Siegfried's method of reforging the broken sword presupposes the practice of modern steel production; see Lutz Köpnick, *Nothungs Modernität: Wagners* Ring *und die Poesie der Macht* (Munich, 1994).

31. See the detailed evidence adduced by Elizabeth Magee, *Richard Wagner and the Nibelungs* (Oxford 1990).

32. Mann, *Gesammelte Werke*, 4:31–32.

33. Schelling, *Philosophie der Mythologie,* 195–96; see also Hübner, *Die Wahrheit des Mythos,* 21, 63, and 397.

34. Schelling draws a distinction between the Epicurean, historical interpretation of myth and the Stoic interpretation based on natural history. The latter interpretation appears to have influenced Wagner's view of myth in no small way; see Schelling, *Philosophie der Mythologie,* 67.

35. An exemplary exception to this rule was Alfred Kirchner's Bayreuth production of the *Ring* (1994–98), a production that revealed an ingenious combination of the archaic and the modern, not least as a result of Rosalie's designs. "One of the most important aims of our production," stressed Alfred Kirchner and Rosalie,

was to take seriously the mythological structure of the *Ring*, in which respect it differs from the typical productions of the tetralogy of the last twenty years. It is curious that myth has enjoyed a veritable revival in the humanities in recent decades, and at the same time an aggressively demythologizing approach has been adopted onstage toward one of the greatest mythological creations of the modern age. To take myth seriously does not, of course, mean relapsing into the past. After all, recent research into myth has taught us that it depicts archetypal events that are constantly repeated in our lives and thus ever present. In this way, Wagner was able to use myth to express the experiences of his own age, and we too can recognize ourselves in this myth, a myth that deals with us ourselves and tells our own story. . . . This is an attempt to encapsulate myth in its remoteness (from us) and in its closeness (to us). In our production, remoteness is the same as archaizing, and closeness is synonymous with modernization.

For Kirchner and Rosalie, modernization means "recourse to the artistic resources of the avant-garde in the form of quotations, collage, and montage. It is our aim to conjure up myth using the artistic means of our own day. . . . If the essence of myth is the reactualization of archaic events, then our production is indeed 'mythological,' not actualizing, but reactualizing"; see Alfred Kirchner and Rosalie, "Mythos als Szene: Anmerkungen zur Neuinszenierung von *Der Ring des Nibelungen,*" in *Der Ring des Nibelungen,* ed. Bermbach and Borchmeyer, 189–95, esp. 189–91.

36. Schelling, *Philosophie der Mythologie,* 26–27.

37. Ibid., 86.

38. Ibid., 28.

39. See Wolf-Daniel Hartwich's book on Karl Simrock's *Deutsche Mythologie* and his "mythological concept of time," *"Deutsche Mythologie": Die Erfindung einer nationalen Kunstreligion* (Berlin and Vienna, 2000), 65–76.

40. See Dieter Borchmeyer, "Siegfried," in *"Alles ist nach seiner Art,"* ed. Bermbach, 68–80.

41. Jan de Vries, *Heldenlied und Heldensage* (Bern, 1961), 266.

42. Eliade, *Myth of the Eternal Return,* 37.

43. Vries, *Heldenlied und Heldensage,* 91.

44. Goethe, *Werke,* ed. Dieter Borchmeyer (Munich, 1992), 5:587.

45. Vries, *Heldenlied und Heldensage,* 297.

46. See Dieter Borchmeyer, *Das Theater Richard Wagners* (Stuttgart, 1982), 348 (this section was not included in the 1991 English translation).

47. On the mythological significance of the horse as the animal closest to humans, see Grimm, *Deutsche Mythologie,* 621–30. The horse Grane is one of the mythological characters in the *Ring.* In his Brussels production of the cycle (first staged in the Belgian capital in 1991 and revived in Frankfurt in 1994), Herbert Wernicke took this aspect of the work so seriously that the horse was played by an actor. As a "person," Grane can represent Brünnhilde in Siegfried's thoughts, just as the ring is intended to represent Siegfried in Brünnhilde's eyes; in the ring, the original mythological personality of the gold seems to spring to life again for the lovers, thereby reversing the process of depersonalization that had begun with Alberich's curse on love, but this proves to be an act of fatal self-deception on the lovers' part, as we discover at the end of act 1 of *Götterdämmerung,* when Siegfried, in the guise of Gunther, brutally reappropriates the ring.

48. Grimm, *Deutsche Mythologie,* 52–56.

49. See the compelling account by Blanka Horacek, "Wesenszüge der Liebe in mittelhochdeutscher Dichtung und in Musikdramen Richard Wagners," in *Geist und Zeit: Wirkungen des Mittelalters in Literatur und Sprache. Festschrift für Roswitha Wisniewski zu ihrem 65. Geburtstag* (Frankfurt am Main, 1991), 355–76, esp. 355–59.

50. Although difficult to justify in terms of either the words or the music, Peter Wapnewski has advanced this view in a number of different publications. In the *Wagner Handbook,* for example, he writes:

There is more to this scene than meets the eye. What it involves is not simply a drug-induced personality change; rather, the potion brings Siegfried's true character to light. He wants to be free in his own way—that is, to revoke the past and to shed both the burden of memory and a duty imposed by a too-constraining bond. . . . His seduction takes place because he wants to be seduced. He desires Gutrune almost as soon as he sees her; the potion is merely the catalyst of his wishes and lusts.

See Peter Wapnewski, "The Operas as Literary Works," in *Wagner Handbook*, ed. Ulrich Müller, Peter Wapnewski, and John Deathridge (Cambridge, Mass., 1992), 57–58. In a later book (*Liebestod und Götternot: Zum "Tristan" und zum "Ring des Nibelungen"* [Berlin, 1988], 43), Wapnewski even claims that Siegfried is "totally obsessed by the principle of disloyalty" and thinks that stage directors would be "well advised to show Siegfried already fascinated by Gutrune even before he drinks his first drink to fidelity in love" (22). It is difficult to imagine a director less well advised by Wagner's words and music. See also the revised edition of Wapnewski's *Der traurige Gott: Richard Wagner in seinen Helden* (Berlin, 2001), 219–21.

51. See Manfred Fuhrmann's definition of *hamartía* as "an error: the erroneous assessment of a situation caused by a failure of *diánoia* and based, therefore, on a lack of insight"; Aristotle, *Poetik*, ed. Manfred Fuhrmann (Munich, 1976), 67.

52. On the mythology of the world-ash, see Grimm, *Deutsche Mythologie*, 756–60.

53. Creuzer and Mone, *Symbolik und Mythologie der alten Völker*, vol. 5, pt. 1, 360–61.

54. For more on this motif, see Grimm, *Deutsche Mythologie*, 553.

55. Udo Bermbach, *Der Wahn des Gesamtkunstwerks: Richard Wagners politisch-ästhetische Utopie* (Frankfurt am Main, 1994), 281–90; see also Bermbach's chapter "Politik und Anti-Politik im Kunst-Mythos," in *Der Ring des Nibelungen,* ed. Bermbach and Borchmeyer, 39–58; trans. by Stewart Spencer as "Politics and Anti-Politics in Artistic Myth," *Wagner* 17 (1996), 3–24.

56. See Borchmeyer, *Das Theater Richard Wagners*, 245–46, and *Richard Wagner*, trans. Spencer, 308–10.

57. Wagner may have been alerted to the "identity of Logi and Loki" by the relevant passage in Jacob Grimm's *Deutsche Mythologie* (220–25). On the figure of the trickster, see Paul Radin, Karl Kerényi, and C. G. Jung, *Der göttliche Schelm*, 2d ed. (Hildesheim, 1979); and Klaus-Peter Koepping, "Trickster, Schelm, Pikaro," *Kölner Zeitschrift für Soziologie und Sozialpsychologie* 26 (1984): 195–215, esp. 202–4.

58. See Wolfgang Mohr's still informative article "Mephistopheles und Loki," *Deutsche Vierteljahrsschrift für Literaturwissenschaft und Geistesgeschichte* 18 (1940): 173–200; see also Dieter Borchmeyer, "*Faust:* Goethes verkappte Komödie," in *Die großen Komödien Europas*, ed. Franz Norbert Mennemeier (Tübingen, 2000), 199–226; here Mephistopheles is compared in detail to the mythological trickster figure of Hermes/Loki/Loge.

59. Their teasing behavior may not immediately qualify the Rhinedaughters as "wise," but they inhabit a state of nature, and so their wisdom remains naive, their attractiveness consisting in the interplay of childlike high spirits and profundity. The depth of their insights is clear from the end of *Das Rheingold*: "Traulich und treu/ ist's nur in der Tiefe:/ falsch und feig'/ ist, was dort oben sich freut" [Trusty and true/ it is here in the depths alone:/ false and fey/ is all that rejoices above!] (GS 5:268). According to Cosima's diary entry of 12 February 1883, Wagner read Fouqué's *Undine* on the eve of his death and began to play "the Rhinedaughters' song of lament" on the piano, adding: "I'm well disposed to them, these subservient creatures of the deep, these creatures of yearning." Comments such as these should discourage directors from portraying the Rhinedaughters as tarts, a trend that came into fashion with Patrice Chéreau's Bayreuth production of 1976.

60. When Fricka accuses the "watery brood" of seducing men with their "lewd bathing" (GS 5:229), she is speaking as a typical representative of a morality divorced from nature. It

is also worth noting the circumstances in which she makes this dismissive accusation—at the very time that Loge is discussing the return of the ring, a move that neither Wotan nor Fricka, for her own selfish reasons, supports. When Loge suggests descending to Nibelheim via the Rhine, Wotan rejects the idea: "Not through the Rhine" (GS 5:233). There he would be obliged to listen to the voice of his own guilty conscience in the form of the Rhinedaughters' singing. The Rhinedaughters are the voice of nature, once unspoiled but now violated by the desire for power and possessions. There is no doubt that they behave cruelly toward Alberich, just as nymphs traditionally behave cruelly toward lustful satyrs in pastoral poetry; and they later attempt to beguile Siegfried into returning the ring to them, yet they are essentially unapproachable, standoffish creatures who play with erotic love without ever actually engaging in it.

61. See Grimm, *Deutsche Mythologie*, 229.

62. Peter Wapnewski, "Siegfried singt sein letztes Lied: Zur zweiten Szene des dritten Aufzugs der *Götterdämmerung*," in *Erzählungen in Erzählungen: Phänomene der Narration in Mittelalter und Früher Neuzeit*, ed. Harald Haferland and Michael Mecklenburg (Munich, 1997), 445–54, esp. 447.

63. Quoted by Curt von Westernhagen, *Die Entstehung des "Ring"* (Zurich, 1973), 187; trans. by Arnold Whittall and Mary Whittall as *The Forging of the "Ring"* (Cambridge, 1976), 156. The same idea is also expressed by Judith Gautier in *Richard Wagner and His Poetical Work* (Boston, 1883), 120.

64. Otto Strobel, *Skizzen und Entwürfe zur Ring-Dichtung* (Munich, 1930), 84.

65. Ibid., 156.

66. See a detailed demonstration of this thesis in Wolfgang Osthoff's article "Richard Wagners Buddha-Projekt *Die Sieger*: Seine ideellen und strukturellen Spuren in *Ring* und *Parsifal*," *Archiv für Musikwissenschaft* 40 (1983): 189–211, esp. 204–6.

67. Otto Strobel, ed., *König Ludwig II. und Richard Wagner: Briefwechsel* (Karlsruhe, 1936), 2:258.

68. Richard Wagner, *Sämtliche Briefe*, ed. Gertrud Strobel and others (Leipzig, 1967–2000, and Wiesbaden 1999–), 2:521–22.

69. See the compelling analysis by Ulrike Kienzle, "Brünnhilde: Das Wotanskind," in *"Alles ist nach seiner Art*," ed. Bermbach, 81–103.

70. See Borchmeyer, *Das Theater Richard Wagners*, 239–40, and *Richard Wagner*, trans. Spencer, 300.

71. Wagner was undoubtedly introduced to the idea of ekpyrosis by Jacob Grimm's *Deutsche Mythologie* (775–77).

72. Ibid., 777.

73. *The Poetic Edda*, trans. Henry Adams Bellows (New York, 1957), 57.

74. Creuzer and Mone, *Symbolik und Mythologie*, vol. 5, pt. 1, 464–66.

75. Eliade, *Myth and Reality*, 33.

76. Brünnhilde invites the Rhinedaughters "ihr in der Fluth / löset ihn auf" [in the floodwaters / let it dissolve] (GS 6:253).

77. In *Der Wahn des Gesamtkunstwerks*, Udo Bermbach argues that "although the ring is returned to the Rhinedaughters, they do not turn it back into pure gold, with the result that it remains in its processed state, a state produced by the illusory desire for power and rule" (306). If this were true, it would mean that the "wise daughters of the watery depths" had inherited Brünnhilde's property but failed to carry out her final request: "Das Feuer, das mich verbrennt, / rein'ge vom Fluche den Ring: / ihr in der Fluth/löset ihn auf, / und lauter bewahrt / das lichte Gold, / der euch zum Unheil geraubt" [Let the fire that consumes me / cleanse the ring of its curse: / in the floodwaters / let it dissolve, / and safely guard / the shining gold / that was

stolen to your undoing] (GS 6:253). Bermbach believes that the *Ring* ends on an entirely negative note, a belief that is difficult to square with the words and music. He speaks of the "hopelessness of this ending," of a "doubtful situation," and of "total annihilation" (305–6). Only with *Parsifal*—the "fifth part of the *Ring*"—does the cycle come to an end on a note of "nonresignation" and "with the hope of a better world" (311). As such, this ending of *Götterdämmerung* could hardly be further removed from the one I outlined. In his production of the *Ring* for the 2000 Bayreuth Festival, Jürgen Flimm introduced the youthful figure of Parsifal at the end of *Götterdämmerung* as a symbol of hope for the future; see Udo Bermbach and Hermann Schreiber, eds., *Götterdämmerung: Der neue Bayreuther Ring* (Berlin and Munich, 2000), 29–30 and 240–41. But by 2001 this ending had been replaced by another, in which the element of hope was seen as an integral part of the action of the *Ring* itself and, as such, was at odds with Bermbach's own interpretation of the ending.

78. Mann, *Gesammelte Werke*, 4:828.

CHAPTER NINE. REDEMPTION AND APOCATASTASIS:
PARSIFAL AND THE RELIGION OF THE LATE WAGNER

1. This idea has recently led to violent debates among writers on Goethe's *Faust*. Among those who believe that the idea of apocatastasis—in the sense understood by Origen—is crucial to our understanding of the final scene are Arthur Henkel and Albrecht Schöne; see Arthur Henkel, "Das Ärgernis Faust," in *Goethe-Erfahrungen: Studien und Vorträge* (Stuttgart, 1982), 163–79; and Albrecht Schöne, *Fausts Himmelfahrt: Zur letzten Szene der Tragödie* (Munich, 1994) and also Schöne's commentary on *Faust* in the Frankfurt edition of Goethe's works (Frankfurt am Main, 1985–), vol. 7, pt. 2. The opposing view is advanced by Rolf Christian Zimmermann, "Goethes *Faust* und die Wiederbringung aller Dinge," *Goethe-Jahrbuch* 111 (1994): 172–85. This chapter takes no account of the specifically Origenistic variant of the idea of apocatastasis, with its supersession of evil at the end of the world. Although the principle of evil, as represented by Alberich and Hagen on the one hand and by Klingsor and Kundry on the other, is eliminated at the end of both *Götterdämmerung* and *Parsifal*, it would be pure speculation to claim that Origen's influence plays any part in this.

2. See Johannes Hoffmeister, *Wörterbuch der philosophischen Begriffe*, 2d ed. (Hamburg, 1955), 194 ("Ekpyrosis") and 67 ("Apocatastasis").

3. This chapter is a much revised and expanded version of an earlier chapter that appeared under the same title. See "Erlösung und Apokatastasis: 'Parsifal' und die Religion des späten Wagner," in *Richard Wagner: Mittler zwischen Zeiten*, ed. Gerhard Heldt (Anif/Salzburg, 1990), 127–57. On the religious aspects of *Parsifal*, see also Dieter Borchmeyer, "Parsifal's Religion," in *The Enigma of Parsifal: A Collection of Essays*, ed. Brian Coghlan and Ralph Middenway (Adelaide, 2001).

4. Kurt Hübner, "Meditationen zu Richard Wagners Schrift 'Religion und Kunst,'" in *Der Ring des Nibelungen: Ansichten des Mythos*, ed. Udo Bermbach and Dieter Borchmeyer (Stuttgart and Weimar, 1995), 129–42, esp. 141.

5. See, for example, Hans Mayer, "Richard Wagner und die Jugend," *Die Programmhefte der Bayreuther Festspiele 1982* 1 (*Parsifal*), 39–48, esp. 47; and *Richard Wagner*, ed. Wolfgang Hoder (Frankfurt am Main, 1998), 204.

6. See Hartmut Zelinsky, "Die 'feuerkur' des Richard Wagner oder die 'neue religion' der 'Erlösung' durch 'Vernichtung,'" in *Wie antisemitisch darf ein Künstler sein?* ed. Heinz-Klaus Metzger and Rainer Riehn (Munich, 1978), 98–102. According to Zelinsky, Wagner's "new religion" was based on an ideology of annihilation aimed at the physical

liquidation of the Jews of a kind later realized in the concentration camps of the National Socialists: *Erlösung* as *Endlösung*, or redemption as final solution. Zelinsky has repeated what is essentially the same tendentious view in numerous other publications, most recently in his chapter "Verfall, Vernichtung, Weltentrückung: Richard Wagners antisemitische Werk-Idee als Kunstreligion und Zivilisationskritik und ihre Verbreitung bis 1933," in *Richard Wagner im Dritten Reich*, ed. Saul Friedländer and Jörn Rüsen (Munich, 2000), 309–41. This view has found a number of adepts, including Paul Lawrence Rose (*Wagner: Race and Revolution* [London, 1992]) and Joachim Köhler (*Wagners Hitler: Der Prophet und sein Vollstrecker* [Munich, 1997]; trans. by Ronald Taylor as *Wagner's Hitler: The Prophet and His Disciple* [Cambridge, 2000]). Conversely, in her analysis of responses to *Parsifal* in the *Bayreuther Blätter*, Mary Cicora came to the conclusion in 1987 that not even the most orthodox Wagnerites hit on the idea of interpreting *Parsifal* as an anti-Semitic work. Indeed, the last of the articles that she examines, dating from 1930, appears to distance itself from National Socialist thinking; see Mary A. Cicora, *Parsifal Reception in the Bayreuther Blätter* (New York, 1987).

7. See Wolf-Daniel Hartwich, "Jüdische Theosophie in Richard Wagners *Parsifal*: Vom christlichen Antisemitismus zur ästhetischen Kabbala," in *Richard Wagner und die Juden*, ed. Dieter Borchmeyer, Ami Maayani, and Susanne Vill (Stuttgart and Weimar, 2000), 103–122, esp. 117–18. In this important chapter, Hartwich seeks to demonstrate the impact of esoteric Jewish teachings on Wagner's later works and to trace the idea of a God in need of redemption in esoteric Jewish writings, an idea that was to return, with far-reaching consequences, in the writings of the Gnostics. At least on an outward level, the phrase "Redemption to the Redeemer" recalls the redemption model of the Gnostics, and, indeed, Wagner's expression has even been used by writers on Gnosticism to explain this model. (I owe this information to a personal communication from the Heidelberg theologian and expert on Gnosticism Klaus Berger.) But the theme of redemption in *Parsifal* differs in significant ways from Gnostic theology, whose Christ figure seeks to free the "Sophia" enmeshed in the toils of the world from her state of self-alienation and restore her to her former unity with the origin of all things. In *Parsifal*, by contrast, the Redeemer assumes the form of the Grail and places himself in the hands of humankind, but he does not alienate himself in this way. Although humanity proves unworthy of him, he does not become caught up in the toils of the world, so that his sanctity remains inviolate. The Redeemer, therefore, needs not a Super-Redeemer in the Gnostic sense but only the restoration of the integrity of his chosen community. Strictly speaking, this restitutio in integrum affects not the Grail but only its guardians. This separates *Parsifal* from Gnosticism, even if Wagner may have been inspired to produce the line "Redemption to the Redeemer" by the Gnostic tradition.

8. Richard Wagner, *Sämtliche Werke*, vol. 30, *Dokumente zur Entstehung und ersten Aufführung des Bühnenweihfestspiels "Parsifal,"* ed. Martin Geck and Egon Voss (Mainz, 1970), 84.

9. The idea of folly as a state of mind that annuls the laws that govern intelligence in the secular world and to a certain extent accepts its judgment has a long Christian tradition, going back to Erasmus's *The Praise of Folly*. It is also found in the First Epistle of Paul the Apostle to the Corinthians 4:10: "We are fools for Christ's sake." A similar sentiment occurs in 1 Corinthians 1:27: "But God hath chosen the foolish things of the world to confound the wise."

10. See Hartwich, "Jüdische Theosophie in Richard Wagners *Parsifal*," 117–18: the "idea of a God in need of redemption who chooses a human to free him" is found in both *Götterdämmerung* and *Parsifal* and is also the basic idea behind *Jesus of Nazareth*: "Wagner's Christology is aimed at freeing God from his own law." By this, Hartwich is referring less to Judaic law than to the laws of society in general, laws that guarantee

power, dominion, and possessions. Once Jesus' religion of love has annulled the law, it will also put an end to "God's sufferings" by reuniting him with his original nature.

11. Hans Küng, "Sehnsucht nach Erlösung," *Die Programmhefte der Bayreuther Festspiele 1982* 1 (*Parsifal*), 1–38, esp. 33–34.

12. Otto Strobel, ed., *König Ludwig II. und Richard Wagner: Briefwechsel* (Karlsruhe, 1936), 1:174.

13. Ibid., 174.

14. Hans von Wolzogen, "Parsifal-Nachklänge: 'Erlösung dem Erlöser,' " *Bayreuther Blätter* 13 (1890): 341–45. For Wolzogen, it is clear beyond doubt that the phrase "Redemption to the Redeemer" relates to Christ within the Grail, an interpretation based on the Savior's Lament that Parsifal hears in his inner ear after he has been kissed by Kundry. At no point in the work is Parsifal described as the Redeemer either by himself or by anyone else, whether directly or indirectly, the only exception being Kundry, who, as Wolzogen states, is "prey to a delusion" (341). It is merely the "means" by which "the divine Redeemer is himself freed from the hand of sin that has desecrated his sacred symbol since Amfortas's fall from grace" (344). Whatever we may think of Wolzogen generally, it is impossible to contradict him on this point.

15. In his letter to Mathilde Wesendonck of 30 May 1859, Wagner famously described Amfortas as "my third-act Tristan inconceivably intensified"; Wolfgang Golther, ed., *Richard Wagner an Mathilde Wesendonk: Tagebuchblätter und Briefe, 1853–1871* (Berlin, 1904), 144.

16. See Hartwich, "Jüdische Theosophie in Richard Wagners *Parsifal*," 120.

17. See Günther Mahal, *Faust: Die Spuren eines geheimnisvollen Lebens* (Reinbek bei Hamburg, 1995), 310–11.

18. "It was an important feature of the Christian Church that only perfectly healthy and strong individuals were allowed to take the vow of total renunciation of the world, whereas every physical infirmity and especially every mutilation rendered them unfit"; Richard Wagner, "Heroism and Christianity," GS 10:279.

19. Wolf-Daniel Hartwich argues, with some plausibility, that Wagner was familiar with this tradition; see Hartwich, "Jüdische Theosophie in Richard Wagners *Parsifal*," 114–15.

20. See Dieter Borchmeyer, "Kundrys Lachen, Weinen und Erlösung: Eine Betrachtung zu Richard Wagners *Parsifal*," *Internationale katholische Zeitschrift "Communio"* 20 (1991): 447–51.

21. The scene with the dead swan is based on a Buddhist legend. Here it is the young Buddha who rebukes his cousin Devadatta for killing a swan. Mathilde Wesendonck wrote a poem on the subject after Wagner's death which clearly shows the influence of *Parsifal*. Here the Buddha's reproach includes the words: "You did this and feel no remorse? / . . . Just look at this, just look in his eye, a world of pain and anguish stares at you from his gaze"; quoted by Wolfgang Osthoff, "Richard Wagners Buddha-Projekt *Die Sieger*: Seine ideellen und strukturellen Spuren in *Ring* und *Parsifal*," *Archiv für Musikwissenschaft* 40 (1983): 200–201.

22. See Rosemarie Puschmann, *Magisches Quadrat und Melancholie in Thomas Manns "Doktor Faustus"* (Bielefeld, 1983), 171–73. Puschmann draws a parallel here between *Doktor Faustus* and *Parsifal*, without, however, taking into account Wagner's knowledge of Baudelaire.

23. Charles Baudelaire, *Œuvres complètes* (Paris, 1961), 1:980.

24. Hartmut Zelinsky, "Rettung ins Ungenaue: Zu Martin Gregor-Dellins Wagner-Biographie," in *Richard Wagner: Parsifal*, ed. Heinz-Klaus Metzler and Rainer Riehn (Munich, 1982), 102. This idea has been repeated by numerous later writers, including Ulrich Drüner in his commentary on *Parsifal* (Munich, 1990), 73–75, and Marc A. Weiner, *Richard Wagner and the Anti-Semitic Imagination* (Lincoln, Neb., 1995), where Kundry is described as Wagner's "only female anti-Semitic figure" (239). These speculations have

been rendered otiose by Wolf-Daniel Hartwich's chapter "Jüdische Theosophie in Richard Wagners *Parsifal*," 118–21.

25. See Ulrike Kienzle, "Komponierte Weiblichkeit im *Parsifal*: Kundry," in *"Das Weib der Zukunft": Frauengestalten und Frauenstimmen bei Richard Wagner*, ed. Susanne Vill (Stuttgart and Weimar, 2000), 153–90, esp. 158.

26. See the chapter on the role of metempsychosis in Schopenhauer's and Wagner's thinking in Ulrike Kienzle, *Das Weltüberwindungswerk: Wagners Parsifal—ein szenisch-musikalisches Gleichnis der Philosophie Arthur Schopenhauers* (Laaber, 1992), 154–59.

27. This is demonstrated by Wolf-Daniel Hartwich in "Jüdische Theosophie in Richard Wagners *Parsifal*," 119–20.

28. See Wolfgang Osthoff's detailed examination of the sources, "Richard Wagners Buddha-Projekt," 189–211; see also Bernd Zegowitz, *Richard Wagners unvertonte Opern* (Frankfurt am Main, 2000), 247–72; on the idea of reincarnation, see esp. 260–62.

29. Hartwich draws a distinction between the Indian and the cabalistic doctrine of metempsychosis, pointing out that Buddhism does not ascribe our rebirth to a particular act but justifies it by reference to our karma, which he defines as an "abstract summation of good and bad deeds that decides the question of our rebirth." According to the cabalistic teaching of "Gilgul," by contrast, our sufferings in this life are a punishment for a particular failing in a previous existence. Wagner was familiar with this cabalistic interpretation from the writings of August Friedrich Gfrörer. Hartwich believes that Wagner's characterization of Kundry was ultimately influenced more by the cabalistic interpretation of metempsychosis than by its Buddhist counterpart. One may raise the objection that in his draft for *Die Sieger*—in other words, long before he came into contact with the Cabala—Wagner had already ascribed Prakriti's rebirth as a Chandala to a particular wrong that she had committed in an earlier life; in other words, her karma played no part in this.

30. Arthur Schopenhauer, *Sämtliche Werke*, ed. Arthur Hübscher (Wiesbaden, 1972), 2:442; trans. by E.F.J. Payne as *The World as Will and Representation* (New York, 1966), 1:374.

31. See Kienzle, *Das Weltüberwindungswerk*, 116–18.

32. See the section " 'Verteufelung' der Sexualität und Ausgrenzung der Frau," ibid., 118–20.

33. See also Wagner's remarks on the "Shaker sects in America," whose male and female members, "after the solemn affirmation of their heartfelt vow of abstinence, join in singing and dancing within the temple"; "Religion and Art," GS 10:250.

34. Hartwich, "Jüdische Theosophie in Richard Wagners *Parsifal*," 113.

35. Hübner, "Meditationen zu Wagners Schrift 'Religion und Kunst,'" 140–41; for a more detailed examination of this point, see Kurt Hübner, *Die Wahrheit des Mythos* (Munich, 1985), 390–92.

36. On Wagner's repeated rereading of the *Symposium*, see CT, 8 April 1870 and passim.

37. On the role of androgyny in Wagner, see Jean-Jacques Nattiez, *Wagner Androgyne*, trans. Stewart Spencer (Princeton, 1993); and Ursula Link-Heer, "Der 'androgyne Wagner' und die Dramaturgie des Blicks," in *"Das Weib der Zukunft,"* 84–94.

38. See Wolf-Daniel Hartwich, *"Deutsche Mythologie": Die Erfindung einer nationalen Kunstreligion* (Berlin and Vienna, 2000), 189–98, esp. 196–97: "The resuscitation of the heathen woman is associated with the mythologically personified struggle between spring and winter, with the text using the same imagery as in Walther's Spring Song in *Die Meistersinger von Nürnberg*."

39. In *Jesus von Nazareth*, we read: "Mary takes a precious flask from her bosom, . . .

pours it on his head, washes his feet, then dries and anoints them while sobbing and weeping"; SS 11:279–80.

40. Hartwich, "Jüdische Theosophie in Richard Wagners *Parsifal*," 120.

41. This is not the place to examine the individual aims of these late essays, some of which must be reckoned among the most harebrained eccentricities of Wagner's whole career. Suffice it to mention his scheme for a "true and inner union" between Socialists, "vegetarians, animal protection societies, and temperance societies" (GS 10:240) and his idea for a "mass migration" to southern climes, where the world's population would rediscover a "lost Paradise" in the form of a state of universal peace among people and harmony with nature (GS 10:238 and 242). Only the rich, Wagner went on, would suffer from such an arrangement, but if these "grabbing, grasping moneybags of civilization, fattened on the sweat of our brow, were to raise a hue and cry, we should lay them on their backs like pigs and reduce them to a stunned silence at the surprising sight of the sky, which they have never seen before" (GS 10:243).

42. See, for example, the chapter "Utopie des ewigen Friedens" in Kienzle's *Das Weltüberwindungswerk*, 122–30.

43. Küng, "Sehnsucht nach Erlösung," 36.

44. See Richard Wagner, *Dichtungen und Schriften*, ed Dieter Borchmeyer (Frankfurt am Main, 1983), 10:246–48, for a note on the religious and philosophical background to this passage and its links with Hegelian dialectics.

45. Among the other works on theology and religion that Wagner studied in the context of *Parsifal* are Ernest Renan's book on the life of Christ and (with considerable displeasure) Franz Overbeck's essay *Über die Christlichkeit unserer heutigen Theologie* (CT, 9 November 1874). Particularly surprising is the admiration that Wagner felt for the first volume of Gfrörer's *Geschichte des Urchristentums* (Stuttgart, 1838), which describes Jewish theology and popular education at the time of Christ and deals in detail with the subject of mysticism and the Cabala.

46. See Hartwich, "Jüdische Theosophie in Richard Wagners *Parsifal*," 119–21.

47. On 27 January 1881, Wagner told Cosima that he "recognizes no other religion except compassion."

48. Writing in the Bayreuth Festival program for *Parsifal* in 1982, the Israeli composer Josef Thal described Wagner's "exploration of sonority above and beyond the strict teachings of functional harmony" as a "quasi-cabalistic approach to the world of sound"; *Die Programmhefte der Bayreuther Festspiele 1982* 1 (*Parsifal*), 68; see also Hartwich, "Jüdische Theosophie in Richard Wagners *Parsifal*," 121–22.

49. Hartwich, "Jüdische Theosophie in Richard Wagners *Parsifal*," 108.

50. This may also explain why, at the end of his life, Wagner again showed sympathy for Halévy's *La juive*, in which he saw "the finest expression of the Jewish character" (CT, 27 June 1882); see also Hartwich, "Jüdische Theosophie in Richard Wagners *Parsifal*," 104–5.

51. Gfrörer, *Geschichte des Urchristentums*, 3:104–6.

52. Hübner, "Meditationen zu Wagners Schrift 'Religion und Kunst,' " 135.

53. Gfrörer, *Geschichte des Urchristentums*, 3:250–51.

54. Ibid., 254.

55. Udo Bermbach adopts this line in *Der Wahn des Gesamtkunstwerks: Richard Wagners politisch-ästhetische Utopie* (Frankfurt am Main, 1994), 317: "Religion—as Hegel would say—is subsumed by art." Bermbach ends his book with a purely speculative interpretation of *Parsifal* that strips Wagner's *Bühnenweihfestspiel* of all its Christian aspects and reduces it to the level of the composer's revolutionary writings, summing this up in the formula "The Aes-

theticization of the Revolution" (307–12). The work's moral core—"compassion"—is derived from eighteenth-century moral philosophy, thereby largely bypassing Schopenhauer, and is defined as a "social concept that allows us to establish a link with Wagner's political and revolutionary hopes during his years in Dresden and Zurich" (318). The Grail is seen as a symbol of "art itself," and the closing line of the work, "Redemption to the Redeemer," is said to encapsulate the "self-referentiality of art" (328). It will be clear that Bermbach's interpretation of *Parsifal* is diametrically opposed to my own in terms of its methodology and ideas.

56. These are irrelevant for Bermbach. Even Ulrike Kienzle, who, unlike Bermbach, interprets *Parsifal* as a "parable of the philosophy of Arthur Schopenhauer" (the subtitle of her book), describes the older Wagner's worldview as "religious atheism"; see Kienzle, *Das Weltüberwindungswerk*, 54–56, on which point she has Bermbach's explicit support (360 n. 144). See, by contrast, Hübner, "Meditationen zu Wagners Schrift 'Religion und Kunst,'" 129–41. Hübner stresses the fact that Wagner's view of Christianity does not stand up to theological scrutiny, but he notes that it has affinities with Christianity on important metaphysical and ethical points—just as Wagner felt close to Christianity in its pure and original form. It goes without saying that Wagner was not an atheist, either openly or in secret: those people "who do not believe in God and who think that such figures as Jesus of N. or a great creative genius move according to the ordinary processes of nature" were little more than "donkeys," he told Cosima on 11 June 1878. Of course, he repeatedly had difficulty imagining God as a personal being (see his comment to Cosima of 20 September 1879: "I do not believe in God, but only in the divine, which is revealed in a Jesus without sin," in other words in a "divine" human being), as he was constantly put off by the idea of a "Jewish Jehovah" (CT, 10 February 1880). It seems that Wagner could conceive of divine personality only in human form—in the figure of Christ.

57. See Wagner's letter to Ludwig II dated 28 September 1880: "How, indeed, might it be possible or permissible for a drama in which the most sublime mysteries of the Christian faith are openly presented onstage to be performed in theaters such as ours, side by side with an operatic repertory and before an audience such as ours?" Strobel, *Ludwig II. und Richard Wagner*, 3:182.

58. For the relevant documentation, see Dieter Borchmeyer, *Das Theater Richard Wagners* (Stuttgart, 1982), 393 n. 297; trans. by Stewart Spencer as *Richard Wagner: Theory and Theatre* (Oxford, 1991), 387.

59. See Küng, "Sehnsucht nach Erlösung," 8 and 21–23. Küng stresses that Wagner was well aware of the difference between "true" religion and a substitute religion, hence Wagner's rejection, at the end of "Religion and Art," of the suggestion that he was attempting to establish a new religion. Küng also supports Wagner's idea of a convergence between Christian and Buddhist ethics (24–25), seeing in him the forerunner of an ecumenical world religion.

60. Two years before his death, Wagner was inspired by his reading of Gobineau's *Essai* to propose a racial interpretation of the *Ring*: "the gods white; the dwarfs yellow (Mongols); the blacks the Ethiopians; Loge the half-caste" (CT, 17 November 1882). Clearly, then, it did not occur to Wagner to interpret the Nibelungs Mime and Alberich as Jews.

61. In "Know Yourself," Wagner describes Judaism as "the most astonishing example of racial consistency that world history has ever seen" (GS 10:271). In his eyes, it represented a pagan religion that was not, therefore, a true religion (GS 10:271–72).

62. The best account of this is Wolf-Daniel Hartwich's "Religion und Kunst beim späten Wagner: Zum Verhältnis von Ästhetik, Theologie und Anthropologie in den 'Regenerationsschriften,'" *Jahrbuch der deutschen Schillergesellschaft* 40 (1996): 297–323.

63. Remarkable though it must seem, Wagner was an anti-Semite but an opponent of

racism, whereas Gobineau was a racist but not an anti-Semite. Indeed, Gobineau even considered Judaism a particularly privileged branch of the human race—a "chosen race"; see Hartwich, "Religion und Kunst beim späten Wagner," 307.

64. On Wagner's critique of Gobineau and the latter's theory of race in general, see ibid., 305–7 and 314–16.

65. For Wagner, polemics, including anti-Jewish polemics, belonged under the heading of journalism, not art, which he regarded as rising above all "special causes," grounded, as it was, in the universal world of the "ideal" (see CT, 24 February 1881).

66. Hartwich, "Jüdische Theosophie in Richard Wagners Parsifal," 104.

67. Monitors were armored warships used for reconnaissance. Wagner no doubt read newspaper reports about the frequent fatalities in the stokeholds of these and other steamships.

CHAPTER TEN. AN ENCOUNTER BETWEEN TWO ANOMALIES:
KING LUDWIG II AND WAGNER

1. All quotations from the correspondence between Ludwig and Wagner are taken from Otto Strobel, ed., *König Ludwig II. und Richard Wagner: Briefwechsel*, 5 vols. (Karlsruhe, 1936–39), and are referred to by their date alone.

2. On the performance history of Wagner's works in Munich, see Dieter Borchmeyer, " 'Barrikadenmann und Zukunftsmusikus': Richard Wagner erobert das königliche Hof- und Nationaltheater," in *Nationaltheater: Die Bayerische Staatsoper*, ed. Hans Zehetmair and Jürgen Schläder (Munich, 1992), 48–73.

3. Quoted in Sebastian Röckl, *Ludwig II. und Richard Wagner* (Munich, 1913–20), 1:3.

4. Ibid., 16.

5. Ibid., 4.

6. Annette Kolb, *König Ludwig II. von Bayern und Richard Wagner*, 2d ed. (Munich, 1963), 12–13.

7. Martin Gregor-Dellin, *Richard Wagner: Sein Leben, sein Werk, sein Jahrhundert* (Munich and Zurich, 1980), 523; trans. by J. Maxwell Brownjohn as *Richard Wagner: His Life, His Work, His Century* (London, 1983), 335.

8. Martha Schad, ed., *Cosima Wagner und Ludwig II. von Bayern: Briefe. Eine erstaunliche Korrespondenz* (Bergisch Gladbach, 1996), 232–34.

9. Ibid., 55.

10. Ibid., 186.

11. Ibid., 516.

12. Franz Wilhelm Beidler, *Cosima Wagner-Liszt: Der Weg zum Wagner-Mythos*, ed. Dieter Borchmeyer (Bielefeld, 1997), 208–10.

13. Schad, *Cosima Wagner und Ludwig II. von Bayern*, 82.

14. Ibid., 88.

15. Ibid., 241–42.

16. Strobel, *König Ludwig II. und Richard Wagner*, 2:76–81.

17. The majority of the sources cited here are taken from the monumental book by Detta Petzet and Michael Petzet, *Die Richard Wagner-Bühne König Ludwigs II.* (Munich, 1970); also Röckl, *Ludwig II. und Richard Wagner*; Eduard Stemplinger, *Richard Wagner in München, 1864–1870: Legende und Wirklichkeit* (Munich, 1933); and Borchmeyer, " 'Barrikadenmann und Zukunftsmusikus.' "

18. See Dieter Borchmeyer, *Das Theater Richard Wagners* (Stuttgart, 1982), 19–28 and 35–37; trans. by Stewart Spencer as *Richard Wagner: Theory and Theatre* (Oxford, 1991), 3–13 and 22–24.

19. Richard Wagner, *Das Braune Buch: Tagebuchaufzeichnungen 1865 bis 1882*, ed. Joachim Bergfeld (Zurich, 1975), 83; trans. by George Bird as *The Diary of Richard Wagner* (London, 1980), 71.

20. Here I rely in particular on the argumentation put forward by Franz Herre, *Ludwig II. von Bayern: Sein Leben, sein Land, seine Zeit* (Stuttgart, 1986), esp. 22–58 and 77–93.

21. Hermann Bauer, "Wagner, der Mythos und die Schlösser Ludwigs II.," in *Wege des Mythos in der Moderne: Richard Wagner, Der Ring des Nibelungen*, ed. Dieter Borchmeyer (Munich, 1987), 169–81, esp. 173.

22. Herre, *Ludwig II. von Bayern*, 346.

23. Quoted ibid., 345.

24. See ibid., 247–48.

25. This passage was inked over in the manuscript of Cosima's diaries in an attempt to render it illegible, but the editors were able to decipher it.

26. Bauer, "Wagner, der Mythos und die Schlösser Ludwigs II.," 62 and passim.

27. See Dieter Borchmeyer, *Goethe: Der Zeitbürger* (Munich, 1999), 138–48, and "Die Festspielidee zwischen Hofkultur und Kunstreligion: Goethe und Richard Wagner," in *Theodramatik und Theatralität*, ed. Volker Kapp, Helmuth Kiesel, and Klaus Lubbers (Berlin, 2000), 167–86.

28. In this, he could of course have appealed to Wagner himself: in his letter to Ludwig dated 14 April 1865, Wagner famously claimed that he had been inspired to write *Parsifal* by the magical spring weather on Good Friday 1857, a claim later repeated in *My Life* in a dubious attempt to adapt the truth to suit the king's imagination. In conversation with Cosima, Wagner revealed that this account of the work's genesis was in fact made up: it was "all as far-fetched as my love affairs, it was not a Good Friday at all, just a pleasant mood in nature that made me think 'This is how a Good Friday should be.' "

29. Strobel, *König Ludwig II. und Richard Wagner*, 3:110.

30. Oswald Georg Bauer, "Richard Wagner und König Ludwig II. oder Die verlorenen Illusionen," *Die Programmhefte der Bayreuther Festspiele 1986* 1 (*Tristan und Isolde*), 1–31, esp. 6–7.

31. See Dieter Borchmeyer, "Renaissance und Instrumentalisierung des Mythos: Richard Wagner und die Folgen," in *Richard Wagner im Dritten Reich*, ed. Saul Friedländer and Jörn Rüsen (Munich, 2000), 66–91.

32. Rolf Schnell, *Dichtung in finsteren Zeiten: Deutsche Literatur und Faschismus* (Reinbek bei Hamburg, 1998), 39–57.

33. It may be added that Wagner got to know Lola Montez in the company of Franz Liszt; see CT, 20 November 1878.

34. Schad, *Cosima Wagner und Ludwig II. von Bayern*, 127–28.

35. Ibid., 129.

36. Quoted by Gregor-Dellin, *Richard Wagner*, 878–79; this passage was not included in the 1983 English translation.

CHAPTER ELEVEN. WAGNER AND BISMARCK:
AN EPOCH-MAKING NONRELATIONSHIP

1. The foregoing quotations are taken from Hannu Salmi's "*Die Herrlichkeit des deutschen Namens . . .:*" *Die schriftstellerische und politische Tätigkeit Richard Wagners als Gestalter nationaler Identität während der staatlichen Vereinigung Deutschlands* (Turku, 1993), 235–36. Karl Johann Rodbertus (1805–75) was an eminent German socialist.

2. Friedrich Nietzsche, *Sämtliche Werke: Kritische Studienausgabe in 15 Bänden*, ed. Giorgio Colli and Mazzino Montinari (Munich, 1980), 6:39.

3. Georg Witkowski, ed., *Lessings Werke* (Leipzig and Vienna, n.d.), 5:378.

4. Otto Strobel, ed., *König Ludwig II. und Richard Wagner: Briefwechsel*, 5 vols. (Karlsruhe, 1936–39), 3:116.

5. Salmi, "*Die Herrlichkeit des deutschen Namens*," 193–207 and 235–43.

6. Ibid., 171–73.

7. This has been convincingly demonstrated by Salmi in "*Die Herrlichkeit des deutschen Namens*," 193–207.

8. Ibid., 197–99.

9. Eliza Wille, *Erinnerungen an Richard Wagner* (Zurich, 1982), 95.

10. Richard Wagner, *Briefe, 1830–1883*, ed. Werner Otto (Berlin, 1986), 298–99.

11. See Salmi, "*Die Herrlichkeit des deutschen Namens*," 198–99. The following account is likewise based closely on Salmi's line of argument.

12. Quoted by Salmi, "*Die Herrlichkeit des deutschen Namens*," 239.

13. Friedrich Schiller, *Sämtliche Werke*, ed. Gerhard Fricke and Herbert G. Göpfert, 3d ed. (Munich, 1962), 5:660.

14. See Salmi, "*Die Herrlichkeit des deutschen Namens*," 243.

15. "Deutschland? Aber wo liegt es? Ich weiß das Land nicht zu finden, / Wo das gelehrte beginnt, hört das politische auf" [Germany? But where does it lie? I know not where to find this land: / where the learned Germany begins, the political one ends] (*Xenien 95: Das deutsche Reich*).

CHAPTER TWELVE. TWO-FACED PASSION: NIETZSCHE'S CRITIQUE OF WAGNER

1. All the page numbers added in parentheses after the quotations in this chapter refer to Dieter Borchmeyer and Jörg Salaquarda, eds., *Nietzsche und Wagner: Stationen einer epochalen Begegnung* (Frankfurt am Main and Leipzig, 1994).

2. Thomas Mann, *Gesammelte Werke*, 2d ed. (Frankfurt am Main, 1984), 9:373.

3. This chapter summarizes the contents of a number of articles I wrote on Wagner and Nietzsche. Of these, the most important are "Nietzsches Wagner-Kritik und die Dialektik der Décadence," in *Richard Wagner, 1883–1983: Die Rezeption im 19. und 20. Jahrhundert. Gesammelte Beiträge des Salzburger Symposions* (Stuttgart, 1984), 207–28; "Richard Wagner und Nietzsche," in *Richard-Wagner-Handbuch*, ed. Ulrich Müller and Peter Wapnewski (Stuttgart, 1986), 114–36; trans. by Michael Tanner as "Wagner and Nietzsche," *Wagner Handbook*, ed. John Deathridge (Cambridge, Mass., 1992), 327–42; " 'Ich habe ihn geliebt und Niemanden sonst': Nietzsches Wagner-Kritik zwischen Passion und Polemik," in *Nietzsche und die Musik*, ed. Günther Pöltner and Helmuth Vetter (Frankfurt am Main, 1997), 93–114; and the postword to Borchmeyer and Salaquarda, *Nietzsche und Wagner*, 1271–1386 (see also the bibliography on pp. 1265–70 of this documentary study). This postword was intended to do equal justice to both Wagner and Nietzsche in as unprejudiced a manner as possible. The authors nurtured the naive hope that in this way they would settle the argument once and for all. A recent denunciatory book by a fundamentalist Wagnerian makes it clear that this was illusory; see Manfred Eger, *Nietzsches Bayreuther Passion* (Freiburg im Breisgau, 2001).

4. Mann, *Gesammelte Werke*, 9:373.

5. See the detailed evidence in the postword to Borchmeyer and Salaquarda, *Nietzsche und Wagner*, 1282–84.

6. See CT, 31 March 1872, and Nietzsche's letter to his mother and sister of mid-April 1872 (362).

7. See the detailed summary of the evidence in *Das Theater Richard Wagners*, by Dieter Borchmeyer (Stuttgart, 1982), 151–76; trans. by Stewart Spencer as *Richard Wagner: Theory and Theatre* (Oxford, 1991), 160–77.

8. See Borchmeyer, *Das Theater Richard Wagners*, 102–24, and, *Richard Wagner,* trans. Spencer, 107–27.

9. Friedrich Nietzsche, *Sämtliche Werke: Kritische Studienausgabe in 15 Bänden*, ed. Giorgio Colli and Mazzino Montinari (Munich, 1980), 7:187.

10. Ibid., 188.

11. On this concept of Nietzsche's, see ibid., 2:15–17 (*Menschliches, Allzumenschliches*, foreword, section 3).

12. Ibid., 3:617.

13. Ibid., 2:27.

14. Ibid., 13:532.

15. Ibid., 3:609.

16. The crude speculations associated with this expression can no longer be sustained in the light of Nietzsche's letter to Malwida von Meysenbug, in which its meaning is demonstrably clear. Curt von Westernhagen was the first writer to draw attention to a possible connection between this "mortal insult" and Wagner's October 1877 letter to Nietzsche's doctor, Otto Eiser. In this letter, the contents of which were later divulged to Nietzsche through Eiser's professional indiscretion, Wagner, genuinely concerned for the welfare of his young friend and repeating a well-known medical fallacy of the time, had expressed the belief that Nietzsche's illness was "the result of onanism"; see Dieter Borchmeyer, "Wagner-Literatur: Eine deutsche Misere. Neue Ansichten zum 'Fall Wagner,' " in *Internationales Archiv für Sozialgeschichte der deutschen Literatur* (Tübingen, 1993), 1–62, esp. 22–24; trans. by Stewart Spencer as "Wagner Literature: A German Embarrassment," *Wagner* 12 (1991): 51–74 and 116–37, esp. 69–71; see also Borchmeyer and Salaquarda, *Nietzsche und Wagner*, 1346–48.

17. Nietzsche, *Sämtliche Werke*, 4:356–58.

18. Ibid., 117.

19. Ibid., 117–18.

20. Ibid., 117.

21. Ibid., 313–15.

22. See Dieter Borchmeyer, "Décadence," in *Moderne Literatur in Grundbegriffen*, ed. Dieter Borchmeyer and Viktor Žmegač (Tübingen, 1994), 69–76.

23. Friedrich Nietzsche, *Sämtliche Briefe: Kritische Studienausgabe in 8 Bänden*, ed. Giorgio Colli and Mazzino Montinari (Munich, 1986), 7:176–77.

24. Quoted by Hans Wysling, "Geist und Kunst: Thomas Manns Notizen zu einem Literatur-Essay," in *Quellenkritische Studien zum Werk Thomas Manns* (Bern and Munich, 1967), 208.

25. Nietzsche, *Sämtliche Werke*, 6:268. The final two sets of ellipsis points are present in the original and do not indicate an editorial omission.

26. Ibid., 14:473. The ellipsis points are present in the original.

27. See Werner Ross, *Der ängstliche Adler: Friedrich Nietzsches Leben* (Munich, 1984), 780.

28. Nietzsche, *Sämtliche Werke*, 3:523–24.

CHAPTER THIRTEEN. PARALLEL ACTION: THOMAS MANN'S RESPONSE TO WAGNER

1. Thomas Mann, *Gesammelte Werke*, 2d ed. (Frankfurt, 1974), 12:71–72.

2. This is the line taken, above all, by Roy Pascal, *The German Novel* (Manchester, 1956), esp. 297–99.

3. Mann, *Gesammelte Werke*, 12:21.

4. Ibid., 79.

5. Thomas Mann, *Wagner und unsere Zeit: Aufsätze, Betrachtungen, Briefe*, ed. Erika Mann (Frankfurt am Main, 1963), 147.

6. Friedrich Nietzsche, *Sämtliche Werke: Kritische Studienausgabe in 15 Bänden*, ed. Giorgio Colli and Mazzino Montinari (Munich, 1980), 1:487–88.

7. Mann, *Wagner und unsere Zeit*, 76.

8. Quoted in *Im Schatten Wagners: Thomas Mann über Richard Wagner. Texte und Zeugnisse, 1895–1955*, ed. Hans Rudolf Vaget (Frankfurt am Main, 1999), 33.

9. Ibid., 35.

10. Ibid., 29.

11. Ibid., 189.

12. Bryan Magee, *Aspects of Wagner* (London, 1968), 86.

13. Raymond Furness, *Wagner and Literature* (Manchester, 1986).

14. The following section is based on my chapter "Richard Wagner als literarisches Ereignis der europäischen Frühmoderne: Versuch einer Bilanz," in *Die Wirklichkeit der Kunst und das Abenteuer der Interpretation. Festschrift für Horst-Jürgen Gerigk*, ed. Klaus Manger (Heidelberg, 1999), 37–52.

15. The relationship between Wagner and Proust has been examined in detail by a number of recent writers, including Émile Bedriomo (*Proust, Wagner et la coincidence des arts* [Tübingen and Paris, 1984]), who throws light on some of the structural and stylistic parallels between Proust's and Wagner's main works, as well as on the cyclical nature of these works and the significance of the leitmotif. See also John E. Jackson, "Proust and Wagner," in *Bayreuther Festspiele: Das Festspielbuch 1999*, ed. Peter Emmerich (Bayreuth, 1999), 88–113. The most outstanding work on the subject is by Ronald Perlwitz, "Wagner-Rezeption in *À la recherche du temps perdu*. Ein deutscher Komponist in einem französischen Roman: Okkultierung und Evidenz," in *Die Macht der Differenzen: Beiträge zur Hermeneutik der Kultur*, ed. Reinhard Düssel and others (Heidelberg, 2001), 327–68.

16. Kurt Jäckel, *Richard Wagner in der französischen Literatur* (Breslau, 1931–32).

17. See ibid., and Danielle Buschinger, "Die Wagner-Rezeption in der französischen Literatur des 20. Jahrhunderts," in *Richard Wagner, 1883–1983: Die Rezeption im 19. und 20. Jahrhundert. Gesammelte Beiträge des Salzburger Symposions*, [ed. Ursula Müller] (Stuttgart, 1984), 351–410; see also Martine Kahane and Nicole Wild, *Wagner et la France* (Paris, 1983).

18. Quoted in *Richard Wagner: Das Betroffensein der Nachwelt. Beiträge zur Wirkungsgeschichte*, ed. Dietrich Mack (Darmstadt, 1984), 131.

19. Quoted by Roger Bauer, "Paul Claudel und Richard Wagner," in *Richard Wagner und das neue Bayreuth*, ed. Wieland Wagner (Munich, 1962), 53.

20. Paul Dukas, "L'Influence Wagnérienne," *Wagner et la France: Numéro Spécial de la Revue Musicale* (1 October 1923): 4–5.

21. See Stoddard Martin, *Wagner to "The Waste Land": A Study of the Relationship of Wagner to English Literature* (London, 1982); see also Raymond Furness's summary in "Richard Wagner und Irland," in *Richard Wagner*, [ed. Müller], 277–90.

22. See Dieter Borchmeyer, "Der Mythos als Oper: Hofmannsthal und Richard Wagner," *Hofmannsthal-Forschungen* 7 (1983): 19–66.

23. Erwin Koppen, *Dekadenter Wagnerismus: Studien zur europäischen Literatur des Fin de siècle* (Berlin and New York, 1973), 82.

24. Wagner's influence on the German literature of the turn of the century has been impressively charted by Heide Eilert, who has produced a number of new findings in her book *Das Kunstzitat in der erzählenden Dichtung: Studien zur Literatur um 1900* (Stuttgart, 1991).

25. See Dieter Borchmeyer, *Das Theater Richard Wagners* (Stuttgart, 1982), 11–13 and 254–56; trans. by Stewart Spencer as *Richard Wagner: Theory and Theatre* (Oxford, 1991), ix–xi (the second passage was not included in the English translation).

26. Max Nordau, *Entartung*, 2 vols. (Berlin, 1892–93); trans. anonymously as *Degeneration* (New York, 1895).

27. Alfred Einstein, "Verdi und Wagner," *Melos* 18 (1951): 41.

28. See Borchmeyer, *Das Theater Richard Wagners*, 316–34, for a detailed analysis of Mann's early Wagnerian short stories. This chapter was not taken over into the 1991 English translation.

29. See the two brilliant works by Christine Emig, *Arbeit am Inzest: Richard Wagner und Thomas Mann* (Frankfurt am Main, 1998); and "Wagner in verjüngten Proportionen: *Wälsungenblut* als epische Wagner-Transskription," *Thomas-Mann-Jahrbuch* 7 (1994): 169–85.

30. Dieter Borchmeyer and Jörg Salaquarda, eds., *Nietzsche und Wagner: Stationen einer epochalen Begegnung* (Frankfurt am Main and Leipzig, 1994), 931–33.

31. Ibid., 873.

32. See Dieter Borchmeyer, "Décadence," in *Moderne Literatur in Grundbegriffen*, ed. Dieter Borchmeyer and Viktor Žmegač (Tübingen, 1994), 69–76.

33. Borchmeyer and Salaquarda, *Nietzsche und Wagner*, 1100–1101.

34. Ibid., 1075.

35. See Borchmeyer, *Das Theater Richard Wagners*, 316–23 (this section was not included in the 1991 English translation); see also Dieter Borchmeyer, "Fontane, Thomas Mann und das 'Dreigestirn' Schopenhauer-Wagner-Nietzsche," in *Theodor Fontane und Thomas Mann: Die Vorträge des internationalen Kolloquiums in Lübeck 1997*, ed. Eckhard Heftrich and others (Frankfurt am Main, 1998), 217–48.

36. Theodor Fontane, *Sämtliche Werke*, ed. Walter Keitel (Darmstadt, 1962), 1:378.

37. Mann, *Gesammelte Werke*, 11:611.

38. Ibid., 9:375.

39. Ibid., 10:27.

40. See Dieter Borchmeyer, "Thomas Mann und Richard Wagners Anti-Poetik des Romans," in *Poetik und Geschichte: Viktor Žmegač zum 60. Geburtstag*, ed. Dieter Borchmeyer (Tübingen, 1989), 390–411.

41. Dieter Borchmeyer, "Mythos," in *Moderne Literatur in Grundbegriffen*, ed. Borchmeyer and Žmegač, 292–308.

42. Mann, *Gesammelte Werke*, 9:493.

43. Ibid., 4:828.

44. Harald Szeemann ed., *Der Hang zum Gesamtkunstwerk: Europäische Utopien seit 1800* (Aarau and Frankfurt am Main, 1983).

45. Borchmeyer and Salaquarda, *Nietzsche und Wagner*, 1079.

46. Vaget, *Im Schatten Wagners*, 217; see also Sven Friedrich, "Ambivalenz der Leidenschaft: Thomas Mann und Richard Wagner," in *Bayreuther Festspiele: Das Festspielbuch 2000*, ed. Peter Emmerich (Bayreuth, 2000), 134–58.

47. Mann, *Gesammelte Werke*, 12:76–77.

48. Ibid., 71.

49. See Dieter Borchmeyer, " 'Ein Dreigestirn ewig verbundener Geister': Wagner, Nietzsche, Thomas Mann und das Konzept einer übernationalen Kultur," in *Wagner—Nietzsche—Thomas Mann: Festschrift für Eckhard Heftrich*, ed. Heinz Gockel, Michael Neumann, and Ruprecht Wimmer (Frankfurt am Main, 1993), 1–15.

50. Mann, *Gesammelte Werke*, 12:81–82.

51. Ibid., 86.

52. Ibid., 88.

53. Ibid., 101.

54. Ibid., 119.

55. Ibid., 242–43.

56. Ibid., 9:923–24.

57. Mann, *Wagner und unsere Zeit*, 113.

58. Ibid., 116–18.

59. Quoted from the documentation assembled by Dieter Borchmeyer, "Thomas Mann und der 'Protest der Richard-Wagner-Stadt München' im Jahre 1933," *Jahrbuch der Bayerischen Staatsoper* 6 (1983): 51–103, esp. 51.

60. Mann, *Gesammelte Werke*, 11:658.

61. See Friedrich Dieckmann, "Thomas Mann nach Hitlers Machtantritt: Die Tagebücher, 1933/34," in *Hilfsmittel wider die alternde Zeit: Essays* (Leipzig and Weimar, 1990), 53–134, esp. 102–4; see also Hermann Kurzke, *Mondwanderungen: Wegweiser durch Thomas Manns Joseph-Roman* (Frankfurt am Main, 1993), 168–70.

62. Dieckmann, "Thomas Mann nach Hitlers Machtantritt"; and Kurzke, *Mondwanderungen*, 170–71.

63. Mann, *Gesammelte Werke*, 12:732.

64. Ibid., 9:244–45.

65. Ibid., 11:651.

66. Ibid., 4:54.

67. On this section, see Dieter Borchmeyer, "Mythos und Romanstruktur: Thomas Manns Joseph und seine ästhetischen Brüder," in *Mythos im Text: Zur Literatur des 20. Jahrhunderts*, ed. Rolf Grimminger and Iris Hermann (Bielefeld, 1998), 195–216, and " 'Zurück zum Anfang aller Dinge': Mythos und Religion in Thomas Manns *Josephs-Romanen*," *Thomas Mann Jahrbuch* 11 (1998): 9–29.

68. Mann, *Gesammelte Werke*, 11:634.

69. Ibid., 631.

70. Ibid., 656.

71. Ibid., 9:493.

72. Ibid., 11:665.

73. Ibid., 9:229.

74. Ibid., 492–93.

75. On the following section, see Dieter Borchmeyer, "Renaissance und Instrumentalisierung des Mythos: Richard Wagner und die Folgen," in *Richard Wagner im Dritten Reich*, ed. Saul Friedländer and Jörn Rüsen (Munich, 2000), 66–91.

76. Herfried Münkler, "Mythischer Sinn: Der Nibelungen-Mythos in der politischen Symbolik des 20. Jahrhunderts," in *In den Trümmern der eignen Welt: Richard Wagners "Der Ring des Nibelungen,"* ed. Udo Bermbach (Berlin and Hamburg, 1989), 255.

77. Kurt Hübner, *Die Wahrheit des Mythos* (Munich, 1985), 357–65.

78. Ibid., 364.

79. See Kurt Lenk, "Politische Mythen im Nationalsozialismus," in *Die Bedrohung der Demokratie von rechts: Wiederkehr der Vergangenheit?* ed. Manfred Sicking and Alexander Lohe (Cologne, 1993), 54–66, esp. 55:

Myth is the politics of "as if," a politics that pragmatically and cynically replaces fictions in order to ensure that social reality fits a particular myth. What distinguishes modern political myths from classical myths is their planned creation and deliberate use in the political struggle. . . . The criterion that must be applied is not whether the myth is true or false; what is significant, rather, is the mobilizing power of the myths for the imagination of the masses. What is at stake here is the planned and conscious pressing into service of emotional powers for political ends.

80. Jean F. Neurohr writes of a "mobilization of the past." See *Der Mythos vom dritten Reich: Zur Geistesgeschichte des Nationalsozialismus* (Stuttgart, 1957), 18.

81. Franz Fühmann, *Essays, Gespräche, Aufsätze, 1964–1981* (Rostock, 1981), 83–140, esp. 129.

82. Ibid., 94.

83. Ibid., 105.

84. Mann, *Gesammelte Werke*, 4:9.

85. The fullest account may be found in Eckhard Heftrich's monograph *Geträumte Taten: Joseph und seine Brüder. Über Thomas Mann*, vol. 3 (Frankfurt am Main, 1993).

86. Joachim Kaiser, "Thomas Mann und der *Ring des Nibelungen*," in *Leben mit Wagner* (Munich, 1990), 180–200, esp. 181–82.

87. Mann, *Gesammelte Werke*, 11:677.

88. Ibid., 9:375 and 512.

89. Ibid., 522.

90. Ibid., 522.

91. Ibid., 659.

92. Ibid., 4:53.

93. Ibid., 9.

94. Ibid., 22.

95. Ibid., 42.

96. Ibid., 39–40.

97. Ibid., 54.

98. Ibid., 388.

99. Ibid., 431–32.

100. Ibid., 9:229.

101. Ibid., 4:189–90.

102. Ibid., 11:648.

103. See the documentation in Petra Kiedaisch, *Lyrik nach Auschwitz? Adorno und die Dichter* (Stuttgart, 1995); the Adorno quotation appears on p. 68.

104. Thomas Mann, *Briefe, 1948–1955*, ed. Erika Mann (Frankfurt am Main, 1979), 314.

105. Mann, *Gesammelte Werke*, 3:348.

106. See Dieter Borchmeyer, "Heiterkeit contra Faschismus: Eine Betrachtung über Thomas Manns Josephsromane," in *Heiterkeit: Konzepte in Literatur und Geistesgeschichte*, ed. Petra Kiedaisch and Jochen A. Bär (Munich, 1997), 203–18.

CHAPTER FOURTEEN. THE DISINHERITED HEIR TO THE THRONE:
FRANZ WILHELM BEIDLER, WAGNER'S "LOST GRANDSON" — A POSTLUDE

1. The numbers in parentheses refer to Franz Wilhelm Beidler's *Cosima Wagner-Liszt: Der Weg zum Wagner-Mythos. Ausgewählte Schriften des ersten Wagner-Enkels und sein unveröffentlichter Briefwechsel mit Thomas Mann*, ed. Dieter Borchmeyer (Bielefeld, 1997).

2. On the course and legal outcome of the case, see ibid., 367–84.

3. Eva Busch, *Und trotzdem: Eine Autobiographie* (Munich, 1991).

4. Thomas Mann, *Wagner und unsere Zeit: Aufsätze, Betrachtungen, Briefe*, ed. Erika Mann (Frankfurt am Main, 1963), 165.

5. Ibid., 114.

6. Thomas Mann, *Tagebücher, 1933–1934*, ed. Peter de Mendelssohn (Frankfurt am Main, 1977), 165–66.

7. See the detailed documentation in Beidler, *Cosima Wagner-Liszt*, 409–11.

8. See Nietzsche's letter to Franz Overbeck dated 27 October 1886, quoted in *Nietzsche und Wagner: Stationen einer epochalen Begegnung*, ed. Dieter Borchmeyer and Jörg Salaquarda (Frankfurt am Main and Leipzig, 1994), 849.